Engaging Questions

A Guide to Writing

Third Edition

Carolyn E. Channell, *Southern Methodist University*

Timothy W. Crusius, *Southern Methodist University*

Mc Graw Hill

ENGAGING QUESTIONS: A GUIDE TO WRITING, THIRD EDITION

Published by McGraw-Hill Education, 2 Penn Plaza, New York, NY 10121.

Some ancillaries, including electronic and print components, may not be available to customers outside the United States.

This book is printed on acid-free paper.

1 2 3 4 5 6 7 8 9 LCR 25 24 23 22 21 20

ISBN 978-1-260-25606-2 (bound edition)
MHID 1-260-25606-5 (bound edition)
ISBN 978-1-260-70802-8 (loose-leaf edition)
MHID 1-260-70802-0 (loose-leaf edition)

Portfolio Manager: *Erin Cosyn*
Lead Product Developer: *Mary Ellen Curley*
Marketing Manager: *Byron Kanoti*
Content Project Managers: *Rick Hecker and Katie Reuter*
Buyer: *Susan K. Culbertson*
Design: *Jessica Cuevas*
Content Licensing Specialist: *Brianna Kirschbaum*
Cover Image: *Vdant85/Shutterstock*
Compositor: *Aptara®, Inc.*

Library of Congress Cataloging-in-Publication Data

Names: Channell, Carolyn E., author. | Crusius, Timothy W., 1950- author.
Title: Engaging questions: a guide to writing/Carolyn E. Channell and Timothy W. Crusius.
Description: Third edition. | Dubuque, IA: McGraw-Hill Education, [2019]
Identifiers: LCCN 2019020109 | ISBN 9781260256062 (hard cover: alk. paper) | ISBN 1260256065 (hard cover: alk. paper)
Subjects: LCSH: English language–Rhetoric–Handbooks, manuals, etc. | English language–Grammar–Handbooks, manuals, etc. | Report writing–Handbooks, manuals, etc.
Classification: LCC PE1408 .C3963 2019 | DDC 808/.042071–dc23
LC record available at https://lccn.loc.gov/2019020109

mheducation.com/highered

DEDICATION

For James L. Kinneavy

ABOUT THE AUTHORS

Carolyn E. Channell taught high school and community college students before joining the faculty at Southern Methodist University, where she served as a senior lecturer and specialist in first-year writing courses. For many years, she was also a writing program administrator and coordinator of computer-assisted instruction. Her research interests involve literacy in the digital age. She resides in Richardson, Texas, with her husband David.

Timothy W. Crusius is Professor Emeritus of English at Southern Methodist University, where he taught beginning and advanced composition. He is the author of books on discourse theory, philosophical hermeneutics, argumentation, and Kenneth Burke. His long-standing interest in the relation between dialogue and rhetoric has led in recent years to a fascination with the art of questioning, his current research focus. He resides in Tijeras, New Mexico, with his family.

BRIEF CONTENTS

Comprehensive digital handbook is available in McGraw Hill connect

CONTENTS

PART II
Writing in the Aims 49

PART IV
Writing in the Genres 457

CONNECT CHAPTERS—AVAILABLE IN THE EBOOK AND SMARTBOOK® 2.0

McGraw Hill connect

WHY *ENGAGING QUESTIONS?*

The Spirit of Writing as Discovery

Engaging Questions is dedicated to the spirit of writing as discovery, encouraging students to interact—with the texts they read and write, as well as with peers, professors, and others involved in a writing project. By emphasizing interaction and critical thinking, *Engaging Questions* transforms passive learners into active learners empowered to ask their own questions and pursue those questions wherever they lead:

> ***Judge a person by their questions, rather than their answers.*** VOLTAIRE

- **In reading and thinking before writing,** to interpret texts and assignments and to evaluate the credibility of sources.
- **In planning and organizing,** to investigate the writing situation, to find a topic, and to formulate a coherent thesis.
- **In drafting,** to consider choices of style, voice, and genre and question the effectiveness of the choices made.
- **In revising and editing,** to anticipate readers' experience with the text and see where changes could make the text more readable and effective.

BEST PRACTICES Sources of Information for Profiles

1. Besides interviewing the person you are profiling, talk to people who know your subject as well as or better than you do, such as friends, associates, family members, and other relatives.
2. Find out if your person has written anything that you might gain access to: articles, books, texts for speeches, diaries, journals, blogs, even e-mail exchanges she or he might be willing to share.
3. Ask if you may look at scrapbooks or photo albums your subject might have.
4. Look for information via Google, news stories you can find via your local paper's index or your library's databases (see pages 364–66), Who's Who publications, résumés, bios written by your subject or by someone else, and so on. Ask your subject for help in accessing such information.
5. Arrange to attend meetings or other gatherings of people in which your subject plays a prominent role.

CONCEPT CLOSE-UP Visualizing the Structure of a Case

A case has the following structure:

The claim answers the question, **What are you asserting?**
Reasons answer the question, **Why do you make this claim?**
Evidence answers the question, **What information confirms your reasoning?**

Engaging Questions works equally well as a print text in a traditional classroom or as an ebook in courses of all kinds. No matter the setting or format of your course, and regardless of the kinds of writing you teach, everything comes together in the art of questioning, in writing as discovery.

An Inquiry-Based Approach

With *Engaging Questions*, students will learn to see writing as essential to thinking, discussing, and reading, all of which develop around the questions they pose and pursue. These key questions are built into each assignment chapter, guiding students through a process that is both creative and critical, inviting genuine engagement, and preparing them to become skilled thinkers and confident writers.

Part I of *Engaging Questions* assists students in developing a set of highly transferable skills that they will return to again and again whenever critical thinking, reading, and writing are in play. Students will learn to ask fundamental questions about their own writing, as well as that of others, such as:

- What is the rhetorical situation?
- What is critical reading?
- What could I write about?

Parts II, III, and IV introduce students to the specific questions that apply to each kind of writing and to such related activities as doing research, making an argument, avoiding plagiarism, and speaking to groups. For example:

- How do writers make a case?
- How do I write a visual analysis?
- How do I decide if a source is reliable?
- How do I deliver an oral presentation?

In the third edition of *Engaging Questions*, each chapter will open with a list of such questions, establishing the framework of that chapter as well as the learning objectives covered therein. The result is an innovative, comprehensive, and coherent approach to writing instruction.

ENGAGING QUESTIONS

In this chapter, you will engage with the following questions:

- What does it mean to edit a piece of writing?
- Why do writers edit their work?
- How do writers evaluate their work for coherence and flow?
- What key points can writers keep in mind when editing their work?

THE ART OF QUESTIONING **What Really Persuades Us?**

Many people say they are persuaded only by reasons and evidence. That is, *logos* matters most. Aristotle thought that *ethos* might be more powerful: If we think that a writer is intelligent, well informed, and trustworthy and has genuine concern for our needs, we will tend to believe most of what that person says. Look at advertising and you will probably conclude that *pathos* is the prime persuader. Nearly all ads appeal to emotions and attitudes most of all.

What do you think? Consider the last important decision you made. How did you persuade yourself to do one thing rather than another? If someone tried to persuade you, what kinds of appeal did the person use? Which of these appeals had the most impact on the decision you made?

Highlights of the Third Edition

The third edition of *Engaging Questions* continues to use critical thinking, reading, and writing as its framework for instruction. The new edition also features the following significant updates:

- The table of contents has been redesigned to foreground the instruction and assignment types that are critical to the first-year writing course and makes this coverage accessible in the print edition as well as in the ebook. Two new chapters feature coverage of literary analysis–including a new student sample paper–and writing résumés and letters of application.
- Learning objectives tied to each main section of chapter coverage align across print and digital editions, as well as in instructor support materials. Within the text, these objectives are presented as sets of questions for students to consider at the start of each chapter. Instructors will find the same content, posed as conventional objectives with Bloom's levels and verbiage, within the Instructor's Manual.
- Annotated reading selections, including formatted student papers, are now accessible within the ebook and conform to WCAG design requirements.

Here is a quick look at some of the other changes you will find within the chapters:

Chapter 1: Critical Thinking and the Art of Questioning

- New op-ed example addresses the dangers of "alternative facts."

Chapter 2: Reading Critically and the Art of Questioning

- New A-head section instructs students on "dealing with the difficulties of scholarly texts."

Chapter 4: Narrating Experiences

- New professional reading by Brent Staples, "Just Walk on By: A Black Man Ponders His Power to Alter Public Space," exemplifies narration in relation to the author's own experience with everyday racism.

Chapter 5: Describing People and Places

- Coverage of profiles has been expanded to cover "describing people and places," including a new professional reading selection profiling New Jersey's Meadowlands.

Chapter 6: Presenting Information

- New professional informative reading presents data on the educational and professional opportunities available to young people today.
- Throughout, refreshed examples demonstrate how to evaluate research effectively.

Chapter 7: Exploring a Concept

- New professional example of concept exploration, written by sociologist Allan Johnson, asks the question "What Is a 'System of Privilege'?"; a second example features Mark Twain's classic "Corn-pone Opinions," an exploration of the concept of conformity.

Chapter 8: Comparing Perspectives

- Features a revised student paper that compares perspectives on the ethics of eating meat.

Chapter 10: Making an Argument

- Previously titled "Making a Case," this chapter teaches students how to develop their own opinions on controversial topics into a well-supported case, or argument.
- Features a new professional example by teacher and blogger José Vilson who makes the case for more teachers of color.

Chapter 11: Arguing to Persuade

- Previously titled "Appealing for Action," this chapter now emphasizes instruction on persuasion and features two new professional examples of persuasive writing that make appeals for action–an op-ed from the *LA Times* on the banning of plastic bags and an article on the practice of forest bathing.

Chapter 12: Writing an Evaluation

- Presents two new examples of evaluation, including a review of a smartphone and a professional report evaluating "the promises and pitfalls" of online education platforms.

Chapter 13: Choosing Modes of Development

- Now available in the print edition of *Engaging Questions*, this chapter includes updated coverage of the various modes writers use to develop their work, as well as guidance on how these modes can be applied across assignment types.
- New textual and visual examples throughout demonstrate modes of conceptual description, scientific description, and comparison and contrast.
- New professional reading selection examines and calls out specific examples of the range of modes covered within the chapter.

Chapter 14: Editing Fundamentals

- New professional examples demonstrate the moves a writer makes when editing for paragraph sequence and transitions.

Chapter 17: Evaluating Sources

- Updated discussion and examples of evaluating sources for credibility and reliability.
- Entirely new section addresses the question "How do I recognize false information?"

Chapter 18: Incorporating Source Materials

- New professional reading by a specialist in information technology includes annotations that demonstrate effective note-taking on a source.

Chapter 20: Documenting Your Sources: MLA

- Includes new instruction for citing online sources, including a new example citation for a video on YouTube.

Chapter 21: Documenting Your Sources: APA

- Fully updated to reflect the latest guidelines put forth by the *Publication Manual of the American Psychological Association*, 7th edition.

New! Chapter 25: Writing a Literary Analysis

- Entirely new coverage of literary analysis now includes instruction on how to interpret both poetry and short stories.
- New coverage of poetry analysis walks students through Robert Frost's "Stopping by Woods on a Snowy Evening."
- Chapter features full text of Kate Chopin's "Désirée's Baby" accompanied by a new student paper that analyzes the story's themes for a contemporary audience.
- New examples throughout demonstrate how to ask questions about the features of a story; how to find an angle for a literary analysis; how to think as a writer and claim voice; and how to handle topic sentences and conclusions, including first drafts, revisions, and edited versions from one student's paper.

Chapter 32: Designing Documents and Using Graphics

- Now available in the print edition, this coverage includes updated examples of graphics and document types throughout.
- Chapter now puts special focus on models for business documents created on the job; an entirely new chapter (Chapter 39) addresses writing résumés and letters of application.

Chapter 34: Writing Portfolios

- Features updated coverage of preparing electronic portfolios and puts emphasis on the importance of backing up all work.

Chapter 35: Mastering Essay Exams

- Updated examples of essay exam topics and questions.

Chapter 37: Writing a Review

- Features new professional review of a restaurant.

New! Chapter 39: Writing Résumés and Job Letters

- Entirely new chapter instructs students on writing to gain employment, including how to write résumés and letters of application.

CONNECT COMPOSITION FOR YOUR COURSE

Connect Composition helps instructors use class time to focus on the highest course expectations by offering their students meaningful, independent, and personalized learning, and an easy, efficient way to track and document student performance and engagement.

The following tools are available within *Connect Composition*.

Feature	Description	Instructional Value
Power of Process	Assignments for *Before, During*, and *After Reading* are created for each reading selection in every chapter, including student examples. Additionally, instructors can select from a bank of more than 80 professional reading selections.	Guides students through performance-based assessment activities using the pedagogy of strategies instruction. Students use strategies to read and respond to the text, and instructors can assess students' depth of engagement with the text. Instructors may also choose from pre-built templates for guiding students through Literal and Critical Reading as well as Research and Writing.
Writing Assignments	Students can engage in peer review through the writing tool, while instructors can create rubrics and assess student writing around specific learning outcomes.	Students draft responses to writing prompts and receive feedback from instructors. Grammar checkers and originality detection alerts them to issues before they hand their work in. An available rubric provides assessment transparency to students, and allows them to see why they got their grade and how to improve. Instructors may also customize this rubric, or create their own.
Adaptive Assessment	A module is aligned to each chapter. Additional grammar-focused modules are aligned to each section in the Grammar and Style Handbook.	Provides students with adaptive practice and additional learning resources for important topics, either before or after class, or in a support course.
SmartBook® 2.0	SmartBook 2.0 highlights key concepts and creates a personalized study plan.	SmartBook 2.0 is an adaptive study resource that transforms class time from dull definitions to dynamic debates. Find out more about the powerful personalized learning experience available in SmartBook 2.0 at www.mheducation.com/highered/connect/smartbook

For more information on any of these features, please email a member of the McGraw-Hill English team at english@mheducation.com.

Co-requisite Course Support

Engaging Questions also comes with a pre-built Connect course that provides customizable assignments for instructors to choose from, including support for co-requisite models. Within the pre-built course, suggested assignment combinations provide students with plenty of practice in critical reading and writing, as well as choosing correct style, grammar, and punctuation.

In addition, co-requisite course support is now available in the *Engaging Questions* Instructor's Manual. Within this resource, pacing guides for each chapter of the text offer co-requisite class support activities, as well as a chart to help instructors align co-requisite instruction with the goals of the composition course. Please contact your sales representative, or a member of the McGraw-Hill English team, at english@mheducation.com, for more information.

Learning for Everyone

McGraw-Hill works directly with Accessibility Services Departments and faculty to meet the learning needs of all students. Please contact your Accessibility Services office and ask them to email accessibility@mheducation.com, or visit www.mheducation.com/about/accessibility for more information.

ACKNOWLEDGMENTS

A book like this could never be brought to completion without the work of a host of people, far too many to be recognized in the space we have.

We would like to call special attention to our developmental team on the first edition. Thank you to Cara Labell, whose ideas and expertise greatly affected the book's focus, visual design, reading selections, and overall readiness for use in the classroom. Dawn Groundwater, with her energy, honesty, and vision, also deserves special mention. We also wish to acknowledge the work of an outstanding research librarian at SMU, Rebecca Graff, who went far beyond professional duty in helping us.

The meticulous work and generous help of Elizabeth Murphy, Mary Ellen Curley, Erin Cosyn, and Kelly Villella made possible this third edition of *Engaging Questions*, which includes an enhanced SmartBook. A special thanks to Rick Hecker and Debra Kubiak for managing the details of the book's production and design and to Byron Kanoti and Dani Bennett for working tirelessly to introduce *Engaging Questions* to students and instructors across the country. We owe more to the people at McGraw-Hill Education than we can adequately express.

Finally our appreciation goes out to our colleagues who provided feedback on our evolving plans for the project, drafts of manuscript, and our digital vision. Thank you.

Angelina College
Diana Throckmorton

Arizona State University
Angela Clark-Oates

Baylor University
Jesse Airaudi

Brigham Young University
Brett McInelly

Cedar Valley College
Andrew Anderson
Elsie Burnett (Board of Advisors)
Suzanne Disheroon
Beth Gulley
Rebekah Rios-Harris
Marilyn Senter

Central Michigan University
Jennifer Jeremiah

Central New Mexico Community College Main
Jonathan Briggs

Claflin University
Linda Hill (Board of Advisors)
Peggy Ratliff (Board of Advisors)
Mitali Wong

Clayton State University
Mary Lamb

Coastal Bend College
Kathleen Cuyler
Christi Morgan

College of Coastal Georgia
Anna Crowe Dewart
Meribeth Huebner Fell

Community College of Aurora
Susan Achziger

Community College of Baltimore
Annmarie Chiarini

Delaware Technical Community College
Preston Becker
Lauren Canady

Del Mar College
Erica Berteros

Des Moines Area Community College
Lynn LaGrone
Will Zhang

Dutchess Community College
Angela Batchelor

Eastern Washington University
Polly Buckingham
Justin Young

El Centro College
Carrie Sanford

Finger Lakes Community College
Jacqueline Tiermini

Front Range Community College
Amy Holly

Georgia Southwestern State University
Paul Dahlgren

Georgia State University, Perimeter College
Emory Abbott
Kirk Swenson

Great Basin College, Elko
Joshua Webster

Hampton University
Shonda Buchanan
Bryan Herek (Board of Advisors)
DaRelle Rollins (Board of Advisors)
Christina Pinkston Streets

Highpoint University
William Carpenter

Indiana University-Purdue University, Fort Wayne
Steven Amidon (Board of Advisors)
Karol Dehr
Jennifer Stewart (Board of Advisors)

Indiana University-Purdue University, Indianapolis
Scott Weeden
Mel Winniger

Ivy Tech Community College, Indianapolis
Judith LaFourest
Olga Ivanovic

Ivy Tech Community College, Terre Haute
Phyllis Cox
Lucinda Ligget
Leslie Stultz

Johnson County Community College
Sayanti Ganguly-Puckett
James McWard
Ted Rollins (Board of Advisors)
Matthew Schmeer (Board of Advisors)

Joliet Junior College
James Baskin

JS Reynolds Community College
Beth Bersen-Barber
Marti Leighty

Kansas City Kansas Community College
Jim Krajewski

Kapiolani Community College
Georgeanne Nordstrom

Macomb Community College
Linda Brender

Madison Area Technical College
Cherif Correa

Milwaukee Area Technical College
John Allen

Moberly Area Community College
Renee Field
Tarasa Gardner
Sherry Todd

Murray State College
Jeana West

North Central Texas College
William Franklin (Board of Advisors)
Rochelle Gregory (Board of Advisors)

North Dakota State University
Amy Rupiper-Taggart
Joshua Webster

North Lake College
Brett Bodily

Northwest Arkansas Community College
Audley Hall (Board of Advisors)
Curtis Harrell (Board of Advisors)
Timothy McGinn

Northwest Vista College
Britt Benshetler
Crystal Manboard

Oakland Community College
Subashini Subbarao

Oklahoma State University
Joseph Myers

Pima Community College
Kristina Beckman-Brito

Pittsburg State University
Lyle Morgan

Purdue University North Central
Jesse Cohn
Bob Mellin
Jane Rose

Queens University of Charlotte
Marion Bruner (Board of Advisors)
Helen Hull (Board of Advisors)

Quinnipiac University
Glenda Pritchett

Richland College
Regina Favors

Rowan-Cabarrus Community College
Donna Johnson Ginn
Shelly Palmer

Sacramento Community College
Jeff Knorr

Saginaw Valley State University
Kim Lacey

Salt Lake Community College
Ron Christiansen (Board of Advisors)
Brittany Stephenson (Board of Advisors)

San Jacinto College
Ann Pearson

Santa Fe College
Rhonda Morris

Savanna State University
Emma Conyers
April Gentry (Board of Advisors)
Gwendolyn Hale

Seminole State College
Ruth Reis-Palatiere

Sheridan College
Keri DeFeo

Sinclair Community College
Susan Callender
Kate Geiselman

Southeast Missouri State University
Trishina Nieveen Phegley (Board of Advisors)

Southern Illinois University, Carbondale
Ronda Dively

Southern Illinois University, Edwardsville
Anushiya Sivanarayanan

Spokane Community College
Angela Rasmussen

Tidewater Community College, Chesapeake
Joseph Antinarella (Board of Advisors)

Truckee Meadows Community College
Robert Lively

Truman State University
Monica Barron
Christine Harker

Tulsa Community College
Joseph Myers

University of California, Irvine
Lynda Haas

University of Idaho
Jodie Nicotra (Board of Advisors)
Karen Thompson (Board of Advisors)

University of Rhode Island
Kim Hensley Owens

University of Utah
Jay Jordan
Susan Miller

University of South Alabama
Larry Beason
Allison Morrow
Patrick Shaw

University of Wisconsin, Stout
Andrea Deacon

Utah State University, Logan
Whitney Olsen

Vance Granville Community College
Maureen Walters

Virginia State University
Michael McClure

Waubonsee Community College
Mary Edith Butler
Gary Clark
Billy Clem
Ellen Lindeen
Jeanne McDonald (Board of Advisors)
Daniel Portincaso
Sarah Quirk

Wentworth Institute of Technology
Joan Holt

Western Michigan University
Jonathan Bush (Board of Advisors)

Westmoreland County Community College
Michael Hricik

Wichita State University Tech
Tina Sorenson
Danita White

Wright State University
Sarah McGinley

PART I

Exploring Writing and Reading

CHAPTER 1

Critical Thinking and the Art of Questioning

ENGAGING QUESTIONS

In this chapter, you will engage with the following questions:

- What is the relationship between questioning and critical thinking, reading, and writing?
- What is the relationship between thinking critically and stating opinions?
- Why is it important to question meaning in language?
- Why is it important to question the accuracy of statements?
- How do writers think critically about statements based on values and beliefs?
- What are the benefits of critical thinking?

MOST PEOPLE EQUATE INTELLIGENCE AND EDUCATION WITH KNOWLEDGE—that is, having a large store of information in one's head. Of course, knowledge is important. A college education is partly about acquiring more knowledge by taking a wide range of courses. However, what you can do with what you know matters more. You can look up information you lack. You cannot look up the ability to think critically, interpret information, evaluate it, and put it to new uses.

By **thinking critically** we mean *the ability to examine anything you or someone else has done, said, or written to discover how sound or useful it is.* Critical thinking depends on **the art of questioning,** which means *finding, asking, and pursuing the questions that enable you to examine what you or someone else has done, said, or written.* Thinking critically and questioning go hand in hand. Together, they promote genuine engagement with writing and the other language activities essential to success in college, career, and life.

Why Is Questioning Important?

Questioning helps you become engaged when performing any of the following language activities:

- **Thinking** Thinking underlies everything we do. Without it, any other activity–including discussion, reading, and writing–is meaningless. Critical thinking first begins with questioning what we think, read, observe, or hear. Through critical thinking, we examine and revise our beliefs and opinions.

- **Discussing** Talking with other people, which means listening to them and asking them questions, not just holding the floor ourselves, has enormous value. It is central not only to forming friendships but also to learning from and collaborating with classmates, colleagues, and others. Discussion allows us to try out and refine first thoughts in response to the thoughts and reactions of other people. Thought nurtures discussion; discussion nurtures thought.
- **Reading** Reading is central to both college and career. It fuels our thinking and discussions. Whether the text is a magazine or a book, an e-mail or a report, reading it effectively means not just passing the eyes over the page but going beyond the surface to understand and question what the text says. Like thinking critically, reading critically requires thoughtful engagement.

To learn more about reading critically, see pages 13–31.

- **Writing** Because writing requires us to express our ideas completely and precisely, it is central to both college and career. Lab reports, essay exams, and research papers are common tools used to measure whether students have absorbed facts, mastered concepts, and become engaged enough to think critically and creatively about what they have learned. Writing does not end with graduation. In our knowledge-based economy, people spend up to 50 percent of their time at work composing e-mails, reports, proposals, letters, and so on.[1] Even in community and personal activities, from writing letters to the editor to updating a Facebook page, writing is how we represent ourselves. Most importantly, writing our thoughts down helps us examine them; writing is a tool for questioning what we think and read and discuss.

Thinking, discussing, reading, and writing are too deeply intertwined to describe fully; **Figure 1.1** will help you envision how intertwined they are.

BEST PRACTICES The Importance of Informal Writing

Throughout *Engaging Questions,* we will invite you to write in various informal ways. Each Writer's Notebook provides valuable informal writing practice, but the activities can take many different forms, such as online journals, files on your computer, or even old-fashioned notebooks.

Informal writing supports all of the language activities described above. While thinking, people make outlines, flowcharts, lists, and notes. During class discussions and meetings, people write notes to hold onto interesting ideas. While reading, people annotate the margins of books or ebooks with informal notes to themselves. And writing itself usually begins with informal writing, sometimes called freewriting, intended to get early thoughts out where they can be examined. The more you write informally, the easier it will be for you to write in more formal ways.

1. Deborah Brandt. *The Rise of Writing: Redefining Mass Literacy.* Cambridge UP, 2015.

FIGURE **1.1**

The Circle of Language Activities

What is the common thread in the activities that these people are engaging in?

Top: © Flying Colours Ltd/Getty Images, RF; right: © Radius Images/Getty Images; bottom: © Laura Doss/Getty Images; left: © Ingram Publishing/Getty Images, RF

Thinking, discussing, reading, and especially writing all start with asking questions. The sections that follow demonstrate how focusing on a few crucial questions—such as *What do I really think? What does that word mean? Is that statement accurate?* and *Is that statement true?*—can help us become more critical thinkers, readers, writers, and discussion participants. These and other questions will appear throughout this book. We hope you will keep them with you and use them to dig deeper and discover what is important to you and to your readers.

ACTIVITY 1.1 *Collaborative Activity*

Exploring the Connection between Writing and Discussing

Spend five minutes freewriting (writing nonstop) about a question that interests you, such as a course to take as an elective or the qualities that make a good friend. Then, discuss these questions in groups of three or four. Add to your freewriting any further thoughts that occurred as a result of discussion. Finally, write a paragraph about this process: Did your freewriting stimulate thought about your topic? Why or why not? To what extent did discussion help refine your ideas? ■

What Do I Really Think?

"What do I really think?" is a serious and challenging question. It is serious because critical thinking must be honest, and it is challenging because being honest is not easy. Sometimes students are taught to keep their opinions out of their writing, yet critical thinking cannot begin without opinions. Frequently, we know what we are supposed to think because other people tell us what the "right" opinions are. To get beyond what "everybody thinks," however, we must consider what we really think, as student Tony Lee does in the following blog post.

Steroids for Your Brain

Coffee. Red Bull. Adderall.

Set for another study session, I am enhancing my focus and ability to stay awake so that I can do better in my classes. The truth of the matter is that with the drugs and energy supplements I can push myself to study longer and work more than someone not taking the supplements can. Basically, I'm taking steroids for my brain to help me achieve a goal. Unlike steroids, however, there are no long-lasting side effects, and my reward is knowledge.

Is using these drugs a form of cheating? Is using them similar to an athlete taking steroids? The thing with steroids is that they don't themselves build muscle; you have to be willing to put time in to lift weights. In the same way, although Adderall or Ritalin helps you stay awake and focus on what you study, you actually have to open a book and learn the material. So is it any different from physical enhancers?

Lee knows what he thinks and has expressed his opinion clearly. The problem is that too often thinking *stops* with stating an opinion, whereas critical thinking *begins* with an opinion. Now we have something to examine, to explore with questions. What questions can we ask?

What Does That Word Mean?

The meaning of even the most ordinary word needs examination. What prevents us from asking, "What does that word mean?" is the assumption that "everybody knows" what it means, and therefore we do not need to ask. The assumption is usually wrong.

For example, what does *enhancement* mean? It means *anything* people can do to improve their ability to perform a task better. Certainly Adderall, a drug used to treat attention deficit disorder (ADD), can increase concentration and therefore enhance Lee's ability to study. However, if Lee takes Adderall on a doctor's prescription to treat ADD, what he is doing may qualify not as enhancement, but only as restoring the normal ability to concentrate.

What does *cheating* mean? It means *violating the rules that all participants in an activity are supposed to observe.* Steroid use is dangerous and unwise for people who train with weights, but it is cheating in professional baseball because the rules governing the game prohibit it.

So what can we say about Lee's question, "Is using these drugs a form of cheating?" The answer is: It depends. It would be cheating if the honor code at Lee's university prohibited the use of brain-enhancing drugs. Otherwise, it cannot be called cheating.

Just by examining what the words *enhancement* and *cheating* mean, we can answer Lee's question and therefore advance the thinking begun in his blog post.

To learn more about exploring a concept, see pages 161–91.

ACTIVITY 1.2 *Writer's Notebook*

Reflecting on Key Terms

Return to the question you freewrote about in Activity 1.1 on page 4. In one or two paragraphs, explore the meaning of a key term, such as *elective* or *friend.* ■

Is That Statement Accurate?

What other questions might help us examine Lee's blog post? Just as we can fail to examine the meaning of words because we think "everybody knows" what they mean, we can fail to examine statements because "everybody knows" that they are accurate.

Consider Lee's statement that drugs like Adderall have "no long-lasting side effects." Is this accurate? The answer to the question is a matter of fact. To answer it, we must locate authoritative information. Perhaps Lee is right, perhaps he is wrong, or perhaps the long-term effects depend on the individual, how much the person takes, and for how long. Whatever the case may be, the question needs to be asked and answered, or else we may assume that a statement is accurate when it is not. Letting inaccurate statements slide by is another common way critical thinking can go wrong; it is just as common as not thinking about what words mean.

To learn how to conduct an effective Internet search, see Chapter 16, pages 366–69.

ACTIVITY 1.3 *In Your Own Work*

Checking the Accuracy of Statements

Freewrite for five minutes on an opinion you hold, explaining why you believe that opinion is correct. Then look over what you wrote. Did you make any statements that you are not positive are totally accurate? Did you make any statements that you think are accurate but that someone else might challenge? Do an Internet search to check the accuracy of any factual statements you made. Then revise your statements to eliminate inaccuracies and to incorporate information that improves what you wrote. ■

Is That Statement True?

There are many other questions we could ask about Lee's blog post. A short list of such questions follows on pages 8-9. First, let's consider a general point: If we are truly dedicated to critical thinking, then nobody should get a free pass. We have been considering a student's blog post, but the same process can be applied to the work of others, no matter who they are. Let's consider the passage below, excerpted from a book by Michael Walzer, a distinguished philosopher:

> My subject is toleration—or, perhaps better, the peaceful coexistence of groups of people with different histories, cultures, and identities, which is what toleration makes possible. I begin with the proposition that peaceful coexistence (of a certain sort: I am not writing here about the coexistence of masters and slaves) is always a good thing.
>
> —MICHAEL WALZER, *ON TOLERATION*

We value "toleration" and "peaceful coexistence," so we are likely to agree with Walzer's proposition without thinking it through. Nevertheless, we should resist this temptation and ask, "Is peaceful coexistence *always* a good thing?"

Note that we are asking a question that is different from the one we asked about Adderall's long-term side effects. That one—"Is it accurate to say that Adderall has no long-term side effects?"—is a question of fact. This one—"Is peaceful coexistence always a good thing?"—is a question of value. Data, or facts, can answer the first question, but no amount of data can answer the second, because questions about what is good or desirable are questions of *belief* and not of accuracy. The answers to questions of belief must be based on our knowledge and experience.

How, then, can we think critically about Walzer's statement that peaceful coexistence is always a good thing? The sentence in parentheses—"I am not writing here about the coexistence of masters and slaves"—offers one way to think about what he says. Clearly, Walzer does not believe that *everything* should be tolerated. He excludes masters and slaves because he considers slavery intolerable. What other conditions might also be intolerable?

ACTIVITY 1.4 *Collaborative Activity*

Thinking through What Walzer Says

In groups of two or three, discuss the limits of toleration. What behavior can we peacefully coexist with and what behavior must we oppose by persuasion, law, or force? For instance, can we tolerate organizations in the United States that promote terrorism and other forms of violent protest? How long can we peacefully coexist with Iran when its government seeks the destruction of Israel? Then write one or two paragraphs in which you explore your beliefs about this topic. ■

What Do You Gain from Thinking Critically?

You gain a number of things by devoting time and effort to thinking through a statement like the one Walzer made about toleration and peaceful coexistence:

1. Instead of letting what he says slide by, your mind is engaged with what you are reading.

When you think critically and respond thoughtfully, you take part in the conversation—a key goal of education.

© Stockbyte/PunchStock/Getty Images, RF

2. You have something to look for as you read and to talk about. If you go on to read the book that contains Walzer's passage, you will read in part to see if the author deals with the relation between tolerance and peaceful coexistence in a way that answers your questions and resolves your doubts.
3. You become interested in words and the relation of words to reality. You are not only thinking but also *thinking as a writer thinks,* as a person who works with words and their meanings. If you write about tolerance and peaceful coexistence yourself, you are much better prepared to do so because you thought critically about what Walzer said. Indeed, *the very ability to say something of your own depends on asking questions.* Otherwise you can do little more than repeat what someone else has said.
4. You claim power by asking and pursuing questions. Usually people defer to authority figures like Walzer and let him ask the questions. Asking one yourself can help you claim authority. All it takes is finding a good question, being willing to ask it, and then pursuing it wherever it leads.
5. You take part in the conversation–a key goal of education–by thinking and responding thoughtfully. When you ask a question, you show that you are listening carefully enough to think of a question worth asking.

In sum, from practicing the art of questioning you gain the ability to think critically, to determine what you really think, to challenge what "everybody knows," and to decide for yourself what is really true and why. We invite you to turn the world upside down. Instead of being satisfied with obvious answers, learn to value questions. For only when you pose questions, especially those that challenge the obvious answers, can real thinking begin.

THE ART OF QUESTIONING Common Critical Thinking Questions

In this chapter we have seen the value of asking four critical thinking questions:

1. **What do I really think?**
2. **What does that word mean?**
3. **Is that statement accurate?**
4. **Is that statement true?**

There are many more such questions. Indeed, *any question that helps you explore what you or someone else has said is a good question.* Here are a few more commonly asked critical thinking questions.

5. What does "x" assume?

Almost every statement is based on assumptions. Asking questions can help us determine whether we should accept or challenge assumptions. For example, consider this statement: "Jane is smart; her IQ is 130." It assumes that the tests purporting to measure intelligence are reliable. Because the reliability of these tests is frequently disputed, we can challenge this assumption.

6. What does "x" imply?

Asking questions about what follows from a statement can help us determine whether we should accept it. For example, if someone says, "Internet privacy should be protected no matter what," then you can ask, "Are you willing to give up free Internet access to protect your privacy?" "Are you willing to protect the privacy of terrorists?" You can ask these questions because the statement implies them.

7. Is "x" a good analogy?

Frequently statements are based on analogies or comparisons. The claim that animals have rights, for example, is based on an analogy, a comparison with people's rights, such as the right to vote or the right to a trial by jury. Obviously animals do not have the *same* rights as human beings, so what rights should they have and why?

8. How many kinds of "x" can we distinguish?

Often a single word or concept has many meanings. *Love* can mean the feelings of a parent for a child or a lover for the beloved. The biblical command to "love thy neighbor as thyself" has nothing to do with emotions. Here *love* means treating others with courtesy and respect. Many concepts are like "love"; they are used to refer to numerous situations or behaviors. We often need to distinguish among the meanings of a word.

9. What is a good example of "x"?

Thinking of concrete examples can often help us understand and think critically about abstract ideas. For example, *peaceful coexistence* may initially seem a wonderful thing. However, when we think about a concrete example of peaceful coexistence, such as Britain and France peacefully coexisting with Nazi Germany in the 1930s, we realize that it may come at a high price.

10. What are the likely consequences of "x"?

With any proposal for action, we should consider what is likely to happen. If someone says, "We should withdraw our troops from Afghanistan as soon as we can," we should ask questions like the following: "If we pull out, will Afghanistan again fall under Taliban control?" "Will the Taliban allow al-Qaeda to reestablish a base of operations there?" "What will happen to women and girls there?"

READING 1.1

Alternative Facts: Bad for Society and Business

VIRGIL SCUDDER

CEO of a public relations firm and author of World Class Communication *(2012), Virgil Scudder wrote this op-ed in November 2017 for the* South Florida Sun Sentinel. *Arguing that a democratic society cannot function well without truth and trust, Scudder joins a chorus of voices warning us that the decrease in "honest and ethical behavior" since the 2016 election must be taken seriously. Nothing less than the health of society depends on truth and trust.*

Truth and trust, two cornerstones of a smooth-functioning democratic society, are having a bad year—in fact, several bad years. 1

In a recent study, the highly regarded Edelman Trust Barometer for 2017 showed the largest-ever drop in trust across institutions of government, business, media and non-government organizations. 2

Among other things, it indicated that an average person posting a statement online is generally more likely to be believed and trusted than a science expert or business or government leader. 3

Edelman senior vice president Kety Esquivel said, "The cycle of distrust is magnified by a media echo chamber that reinforces personal beliefs while shutting out opposing points of view." 4

The foundation of trust is truth—the ability to believe that what we are told is factual and presented in context. But truth can be hard to discern these days. Enter the era of "alternative facts." 5

The late Senator Daniel Patrick Moynihan was fond of saying, "Everybody is entitled to his own opinion, but not his own facts." Too many people, especially in politics and in business today, haven't read their Moynihan. What they say and do fly in the face of honest and ethical behavior. 6

Hasn't that always been the case? Yes, but seemingly to a much lesser degree. 7

A global auto company fakes emission tests to put cars on the road that can increase deaths and illness from excessive air pollution. A major bank creates false accounts for customers and charges them fees for services they never signed up for. Politicians put out numbers on such issues as taxation and climate change that are pure fabrications. Actions like these are almost invariably accompanied by lies, evasions or deceptions. 8

Tom Hudson, vice president of news at WLRN [TV, Miami, Florida] said, "The current environment, especially fake news charges and attacks on media, is corrosive to our civil conversation, erodes our sense of community, and unmoors our society from being able to have civil debates and conversations about some of our biggest problems." 9

Florida International University journalism professor Fred Blevens, PhD, agrees, saying our society needs more news literacy and critical thinking, two things that he stresses in his classes. 10

Unethical behavior, including putting out information that is false or misleading, not only confuses the public but can take a great toll on a business, including fines, loss of reputation and alienated customers, according to Travis Winslow, vice president of ethics and compliance at Carnival Corporation. Winslow believes every company needs a strong ethics program that is enforced. Winslow notes, "The purpose of having ethical standards is protection of the bottom line. Without trust, customers won't come back." 11

Alfred Sanchez, president and CEO of the Greater Miami Chamber of Commerce, sees the building of trust through ethical behavior as essential to the continued growth and prosperity of the entire region. He puts it this way: "In large part, the South Florida business community is a close network of companies that rely on each other for consistent growth. Operating under unethical business practices will not only undermine a company's reputation but can also impact other companies' growth potential." 12

A good reputation based on ethical behavior is also an important factor in an individual's career success. Many people have lost high positions at the peak of their careers when unethical behavior in their early days suddenly comes to light. 13

For the good of our country, our institutions and all of us as individuals, the era of deception, blind acceptance of "alternative facts" and listening only to people who reinforce our views must end. Holding our leaders and institutions to truth-telling and ethical behavior will bring back the trust our society so desperately needs. 14

Writer's Notebook

Asking Critical Questions

Analyze the reading selection by asking one or more of the ten critical questions listed on pages 8–9 and write a paragraph answering your question or questions. Exchange paragraphs with other students and then, in class discussion, address all the concerns and issues your class found worth discussing. ■

CREDITS

page 5: Tony Lee. "Steroids for Your Brain." *Another View, Blogspot*, 26 Oct. 2008. **page 7:** Michael Walzer. *On Toleration*. Yale University Press, 1997. **page 11:** Scudder, Virgil. (2017). "Alternative Facts: Bad for Society and Business." *South Florida Sun Sentinel*. Reprinted by permission of Virgil Scudder.

CHAPTER 2

Reading Critically and the Art of Questioning

ENGAGING QUESTIONS

In this chapter, you will engage with the following questions:

- What does it mean to read critically?
- What kinds of information do readers use to make inferences?
- How do writers use questions to interact with a text?
- How do writers interact with difficult scholarly texts?
- How do writers use questions to find suitable topics for a response essay?
- How do the elements of the rhetorical situation apply to the writing process for a personal response essay?

WHY INCLUDE A CHAPTER ON READING IN A BOOK ABOUT WRITING? Reading is complementary to writing. It provides the raw material for having something to say. It also increases vocabulary, making it easier to think and express ideas. And it develops the art of questioning and critical thinking described in Chapter 1. The habit of questioning when you read carries over to the habit of questioning when you write, allowing writers to see where their writing needs rethinking and revising.

There are many ways to read, depending on your purpose. Skimming may be appropriate when you are looking for bits of information. Slower, repeated reading is needed when your goal is to understand and retain the specialized information in textbooks. When the goal deepens from just gathering information to following an author's train of thought in order to respond to his or her ideas and opinions, then critical reading is necessary. Most of the reading you do in college—and in business—requires this kind of critical engagement.

What Is Critical Reading?

Critical reading is *active and involved interaction with a text, not just reading to find out what it says, but reading to respond to it by asking and answering questions.* Reading critically is like engaging in a silent dialogue with the text and its author. When we read, we seldom think about our dialogue with the text, but we are often unconsciously asking and answering questions like the following:

What does this word mean, based on the words around it?

What is likely to come next?

Is the author being ironic?

Why do I find this part of the text confusing?

Is this a convincing argument?

What do I think about this new idea?

Through questions like these, we not only monitor our comprehension but construct our own ideas about the meaning of a text.

The following passage provides an example of a reader's dialogue with a text. In this excerpt from an *Atlantic Monthly* article, the writer is concerned that his use of the Internet is undermining his ability to read deeply.

Is Google Making Us Stupid?

NICHOLAS CARR

The main source?

Prediction: He's going to talk about McLuhan. "The medium is the message."

For me, as for others, the Net is becoming a universal medium, the conduit for most of the information that flows through my eyes and ears and into my mind. The advantages of having immediate access to such an incredibly rich store of information are many, and they've been widely described and duly applauded. "The perfect recall of silicon memory," *Wired*'s Clive Thompson has written, "can be an enormous boon to thinking." But that boon comes at a price. As the media theorist Marshall McLuhan pointed out in the 1960s, media are not just passive channels of information. They supply the stuff of thought, but they also shape the process of thought. And what the Net seems to be doing is chipping away my capacity for concentration and contemplation. My mind now expects to take in information the way the Net distributes it: in a swiftly moving stream of particles. Once I was a scuba diver in the sea of words. Now I zip along the surface like a guy on a Jet Ski.

Here comes his point.

Digital files. Artificial intelligence an aid to human intelligence.

Clever metaphor to illustrate the point.

A simile describes how he now reads.

Questions for Discussion

1. Do you agree with Carr that using the Internet reduces your ability to concentrate when reading? How would you describe the difference between your experience of reading online and reading a printed book? Are there some kinds of texts for which you prefer one medium over the other?
2. Marshall McLuhan is famous for saying, "The medium is the message." Discuss what this means. Do you think the medium (printed versus online, for example) of your communication affects the message? For example, consider how e-mail messages differ from text messages or posts on Twitter or Facebook.

How Does Critical Reading Work?

What distinguishes critical reading from reading to get the gist is the ability to find underlying meanings, to "read between the lines." Reading between the lines means following complex lines of thought, understanding what is implied but not stated explicitly, and noting how the parts add up to construct the big picture. An important skill for reading between the lines is the ability to draw inferences from evidence in the text.

CONCEPT CLOSE-UP Drawing Inferences

Inferences are educated guesses about what we do not know, based on facts we do know. In a windowless classroom, for example, we may not know whether it has started to rain, but by observing students entering with wet hair and soaked jackets, we would be able to infer that it is raining.

Readers infer meanings of unfamiliar words by looking for synonyms or, better yet, patterns of synonyms in a text. Consider the sentences below from the reading selection on page 13:

Unfamiliar word

Context clue

Synonym for

> For me, as for others, the Net is becoming a universal medium, the conduit for most of the information that flows through my eyes and ears and into my mind. . . . As the media theorist Marshall McLuhan pointed out in the 1960s, media are not just passive channels of information.

If the word *conduit* is unfamiliar, you can infer its meaning because you know that liquids usually "flow" and that "channels" (like the English Channel) are waterways. Putting these pieces of information together, you realize that *conduit* must mean a pipeline or waterway.

Readers also infer meaning by bringing outside knowledge to a text. When Clive Thompson, quoted in the passage on page 13, talks about the "perfect recall of silicon memory," the reader infers that he is talking about information stored on computers. This inference is based on knowledge that computers store data on silicon chips.

ACTIVITY 2.1 *Writer's Notebook*

Drawing Inferences from a Cartoon

Visual texts also require readers to draw inferences. This is especially true of cartoons. Readers have to use prior knowledge to draw inferences about meaning.

The following cartoon by Adam Zyglis appeared in *The Buffalo News.*

To infer the point of the cartoon, you have to connect outside knowledge with observations of the text. In your Writer's Notebook, answer the following questions.

- What is the purpose of a school science fair?
- How is the science experiment of the girl on the right similar to those of the other two children? How is it different from theirs?

- What current events problem is Adam Zyglis calling our attention to? How do the sign above the girl and the words on her tee shirt show the seriousness of this problem?
- Cartoons often make us laugh by taking something we usually see in one context and showing it to us in another unlikely context. How does this cartoon persuade readers to laugh at parents who choose not to vaccinate their children?

Readers must draw inferences from visual texts such as cartoons, which require knowledge of current events. ■

ACTIVITY 2.2 *Collaborative Activity*

Interpreting a Visual

Working with a partner, find another cartoon. Bring copies to class or arrange to project the image. In a brief oral presentation, explain what observations you used to draw inferences about the cartoonist's comment on the topic. How would you state the cartoonist's point in your own words? ■

What Questions Guide Critical Reading?

Because critical reading is interacting with a text, you need to be able to focus your attention on it. Begin by finding a place where your friends are unlikely to seek you out, and turn off your smartphone. Like any serious task or skill, critical reading is more successful if you work methodically by doing the following:

- *Preview the text.*
- *Read* the text slowly to discover the key ideas and the author's angle on the topic.
- *Reread* the text to deepen your comprehension and to evaluate the author's reasoning.

Previewing the Text

Find out what you are getting into before you plunge into reading a text. Besides gauging how long it will take you to read it, you should also ask the following questions about the text and its rhetorical situation. The **rhetorical situation** means *the variables in any writing situation:* the author and his or her purpose for writing, the audience to whom the text is addressed, and the decisions the author makes in constructing the text to suit purpose and audience. Chapter 3, Writing and the Art of Questioning, explains rhetorical situation in more detail. (See Figure 3.1 on page 40.) Questions to ask include:

- **What is this text about?** From the title, what can you infer about the *topic* and the author's *angle,* or point of view, on the topic? Skim the subheadings if the text has them; if not, look at the opening of each paragraph. Skim the introduction and the conclusion. Based on your preview, try to predict what questions this text will answer. Make a list of questions about the topic that you expect to find answered in the reading. Looking for answers to these questions will make your reading more purposeful.
- **What do I already know about the topic? What opinions do I have about it?** Before reading, take a moment to recall what you may already know about the topic of the text. Refreshing your memory about relevant facts and issues readies you for thinking about what the text will offer. Reflect as well on your own bias, if you have one, and what the origins of that bias might be.
- **Who wrote this text? When and where was it published?** What can you find out about the author or authors? Biographical details about an author (such as date of birth and level of education) and the author's political or philosophical positions and other writings offer many clues for comprehending the text. The Internet is a good resource for this step.
- **Who is the audience for this text?** The author had a readership in mind while composing. Your comprehension will be better if you consider who this readership was and why the author wrote to those readers. How do you match or differ from the intended readers?
- **What special features does the text contain that might aid comprehension?** Aspects of layout and visual presentation such as photographs and other images, charts or graphs, boxes or sidebars, and subheadings can all aid understanding. Subheadings are especially helpful when sampling a text to predict what it will say.
- **Epigraphs** (from the Greek, meaning "to write on" or inscribe) are another common feature. Epigraphs are usually *brief quotations from some other text, set above and apart, followed by the author's name and sometimes the title of the source.* They set up the theme of a reading. Take a moment to look up the source and author of an epigraph; this information will help you draw inferences about the relevance of the passage.

We will work with a reading titled "Notes of an Alien Son: Immigration Paradoxes" to illustrate the stages of critical reading. Skim the reading on pages 17–19. Then look at our answers below to the questions for previewing a text.

- **What is this text about?** Skimming Codrescu's essay through to the end, we see that he is describing his mother's experience as a Romanian immigrant. It will show the contradictions between her expectations for a better life in America and what she actually found–and why immigrating might have been a "good deal after all."

- **What do I know about the topic? What opinions do I have about it?** From the title, you might infer that the author is an immigrant, the son of immigrants. Skimming it, you notice that he is describing his mother's difficulties in adjusting to life in America. What do you know about some of the problems people have when coming to the United States from other cultures? What opinions do you have about American customs and culture and why adjusting to it is sometimes difficult?
- **Who wrote this text? When and where was it published?** The author is Andrei Codrescu, a well-known writer of essays, novels, and poetry. He is the MacCurdy Distinguished Professor of English at Louisiana State University and a regular columnist on National Public Radio. Codrescu was born in Romania and lived there with his family while the country was under communist rule, which ended in a revolution in 1989. The family left in 1966 when Codrescu was twenty. This essay was published originally in 1994 in *The Nation* magazine.
- **Who is the audience for this text?** Readers of *The Nation* are the well-educated public, people concerned with political and social issues. This essay has been reprinted in numerous anthologies or collections of essays on the immigrant experience.
- **What special features does the text contain that might aid comprehension?** This is a brief text, without a need for subheadings. However, a closer look reveals that Codrescu uses signal words, like *first* and *second,* to clue the reader to the moves he makes in writing the essay. He speaks of "one" paradox, the two stages of his mother's sense of loss, and the two things she learned. He also uses chronological signal words, such as *at this point,* to help readers see the evolving process of her understanding.

READING **2.1**

Notes of an Alien Son: Immigration Paradoxes

ANDREI CODRESCU

My mother, ever a practical woman, started investing in furniture when she came to America. Not just any furniture. Sears furniture. Furniture that she kept the plastic on for fifteen years before she had to conclude, sadly, that Sears wasn't such a great investment. In Romania, she would have been the richest woman on the block. 1

2 Which brings us to at least one paradox of immigration. Most people come here because they are sick of being poor. They want to eat and they want to show something

for their industry. But soon enough it becomes evident to them that these things aren't enough. They have eaten and they are full, but they have eaten alone and there was no one with whom to make toasts and sing songs. They have new furniture with plastic on it but the neighbors aren't coming over to ooh and aah. If American neighbors or less recent immigrants do come over, they smile condescendingly at the poor taste and the pathetic greed. And so, the greenhorns find themselves poor once more: This time they are lacking something more elusive than salami and furniture. They are bereft of a social and cultural milieu.

My mother, who was middle class by Romanian standards, found herself 3
immensely impoverished after her first flush of material well-being. It wasn't just the disappearance of her milieu—that was obvious—but the feeling that she had, somehow, been had. The American supermarket tomatoes didn't taste at all like the rare genuine item back in Romania. American chicken was tasteless. Mass-produced furniture was built to fall apart. Her car, the crowning glory of her achievements in the eyes of folks back home, was only three years old and was already beginning to wheeze and groan. It began to dawn on my mother that she had perhaps made a bad deal: She had traded in her friends and relatives for ersatz tomatoes, fake chicken, phony furniture.

Leaving behind your kin, your friends, your language, your smells, your childhood, is 4
traumatic. It is a kind of death. You're dead for the home folk and they are dead to you. When you first arrive on these shores you are in mourning. The only consolations are these products, which had been imbued with religious significance back at home. But when these things turn out not to be the real things, you begin to experience a second death, brought about by betrayal. You begin to suspect that the religious significance you had attached to them was only possible back home, where these things did not exist. Here, where they are plentiful, they have no significance whatsoever. They are inanimate fetishes, somebody else's fetishes, no help to you at all. When this realization dawned on my mother, she began to rage against her new country. She deplored its rudeness, its insensitivity, its outright meanness, its indifference, the chase after the almighty buck, the social isolation of most Americans, their inability to partake in warm, genuine fellowship and, above all, their deplorable lack of awe before what they had made.

This was the second stage of grief for her old self. The first, leaving her country, 5
was sharp and immediate, almost toxic in its violence. The second was more prolonged, more damaging, because no hope was attached to it. Certainly not the hope of return.

And here, thinking of return, she began to reflect that perhaps there had been 6
more to this deal than she'd first thought. True, she had left behind a lot that was good, but she had also left behind a vast range of daily humiliations. If she was ordered to move out of town she had to comply. If a party member took a dislike to her she had to go to extraordinary lengths to placate him because she was considered petit-bourgeois and could easily have lost her small photo shop. She lived in fear of being denounced for something she had said. And worst of all, she was a Jew,

which meant that she was structurally incapable of obtaining any justice in her native land. She had lived by the grace of an immensely complicated web of human relations, kept in place by a thousand small concessions, betrayals, indignities, bribes, little and big lies.

At this point, the ersatz tomatoes and the faux chicken did not appear all that important. An imponderable had made its appearance, a bracing, heady feeling of liberty. If she took that ersatz tomato and flung it at the head of the Agriculture Secretary of the United States, she would be making a statement about the disastrous effects of pesticides and mechanized farming. Flinging that faux chicken at Barbara Mandrell would be equally dramatic and perhaps even media-worthy. And she'd probably serve only a suspended sentence. What's more, she didn't have to eat those things, because she could buy organic tomatoes and free-range chicken. Of course, it would cost more, but that was one of the paradoxes of America: To eat as well as people in a Third World country eat (when they eat) costs more. 7

My mother was beginning to learn two things: one, that she had gotten a good deal after all, because in addition to food and furniture they had thrown in freedom; and two, America is a place of paradoxes; one proceeds from paradox to paradox like a chicken from the pot into the fire. 8

Writer's Notebook

Practicing Previewing

Choose a different reading and preview it on your own. This might be a reading your instructor assigns, or one of the readings in Chapters 4 through 12. Write answers to the questions that appear on page 16. ■

Reading the Text

After you have skimmed a text and answered the previewing questions, you are ready to settle in and read the text slowly, straight through. Try to keep moving forward. You can go back over difficult passages, but do not stop reading just because you do not fully understand them. Finishing the text will give you insights that will make the difficult passages more accessible when you go back to them. Have a pen or pencil ready to mark up the reading as described below.

As you read, mark the text with **annotations**–that is, *notes in the margins.* Annotating is essential to reading critically. If you do not want to mark up a book, photocopy the reading or use sticky notes. The important thing is to use a pen or pencil, not a highlighter. You want to preserve your thoughts as you read; you cannot do this with a highlighter.

Annotating helps you preserve your thoughts as you read. This is essential to reading critically.

© Gary Conner/ PhotoEdit

THE ART OF QUESTIONING Some Questions for Annotations

How should you annotate? Here are some questions your annotations might answer:

- **What words do I not know?** You can look them up now and write the definition in an annotation or circle them and look them up later. Why is it important not just to skip them? In the short run, the more you skip, the less you comprehend. In the long run, looking up the words will help build your vocabulary and enable you to infer the meaning of words in future readings, allowing you more time to engage with the ideas as you read.
- **What are the main points as opposed to subordinate passages?** Mark the main ideas in the margin so you can easily find them later. Use brackets to show which paragraphs go together to develop each main idea.
- **What words signal turns in the author's train of thought?** Words like *however* and *but* show that the author will contradict something just stated. Expressions like *for example* suggest that the author will elaborate on an idea. Circle or underline these words, and note how the author's train of thought shifts.
- **Where does the author introduce viewpoints other than his or her own?** Authors often introduce other people who agree or disagree with their ideas. They may present others' viewpoints as direct quotations but often use paraphrases.

- **How well am I connecting with this reading?** If you find some parts of a text difficult to comprehend, put a question mark in the margin to tell yourself what you need to return to later. If you can connect any prior knowledge, observation, or personal opinion to something in the text, note it in the margin.

We have reprinted the first two paragraphs of the reading by Codrescu to demonstrate the kinds of annotations a critical reader could make.

My mother, ever a practical woman, started investing in furniture when she came to America. Not just any furniture. Sears furniture. Furniture that she kept the plastic on for fifteen years before she had to conclude, sadly, that Sears wasn't such a great investment. In Romania, she would have been the richest woman on the block.

In other words, cheap furniture. Tone is humorous, ironic.

Signals the first major point.

Which brings us to at least one paradox of immigration. Most people come here because they are sick of being poor. They want to eat and they want to show something for their industry. But soon enough it becomes evident to them that these things aren't enough. They have eaten and they are full, but they have eaten alone and there was no one with whom to make toasts and sing songs. They have new furniture with plastic on it but the neighbors aren't coming over to ooh and aah. If American neighbors or less recent immigrants do come over, they smile condescendingly at the poor taste and the pathetic greed. And so, the greenhorns find themselves poor once more: This time they are lacking something more elusive than salami and furniture. They are bereft of a social and cultural milieu.

Here is the point, the paradox: They have plenty but they are still poor.

Shifts to the neighbors' point of view.

An inexperienced person.

Hard to find.

ACTIVITY 2.3 *Collaborative Activity*

Comparing Annotations

Write annotations to the remainder of Codrescu's essay. In small groups, compare your annotations. Did you agree on the main points? Did you have similar questions about any part of the reading? ■

ACTIVITY 2.4 *Writer's Notebook*

Adding to Your Vocabulary

In your reading journal, make a list of words that you had to look up or for which you had to use context clues to infer the meaning. Write the definition next to each. You might also "flex" your knowledge of a word by writing some other words with the same root:

indignities—indignity—dignity

Then, for each vocabulary word, write an original sentence using the word in a way that demonstrates your understanding of its meaning. Using the word a few times will help you establish it in your working vocabulary. ■

Rereading the Text

When you are preparing to discuss a reading in class or to use it in your own writing, you will want to reread it or at least portions of it. Go back to passages that you marked as difficult. You will understand them better once you have finished the entire reading. Activities 2.5–2.10 help you get the most out of rereading.

Recognizing Shifts in Point of View and Voice

Writers shift point of view more often than you might expect. Attentive readers note where the author is speaking for himself or herself, and where he or she has slipped into someone else's perspective and voice. For example, an author might present an opposing view without signaling the shift with quotation marks or a transitional expression. If you have been paying attention to the point of view established by the author, you can infer where the point of view shifts.

We noted in Codrescu's essay that he briefly shifts in paragraph 2 to the perspective of the American neighbors who might view new immigrants as having "poor taste" and "pathetic greed." You know that this is not Codrescu's own point of view, not his voice, because he sympathizes with his mother and other immigrants who, as he says in paragraph 4, seek out material objects as "consolations."

ACTIVITY 2.5 *Collaborative Activity*

Identifying Voice

In pairs or small groups, reread the paragraph below and decide in which sentences Codrescu shifts from his own point of view and voice to the point of view of his mother.

> My mother, who was middle class by Romanian standards, found herself immensely impoverished after her first flush of material well-being. It wasn't just the disappearance of her milieu—that was obvious—but the feeling that she

had, somehow, been had. The American supermarket tomatoes didn't taste at all like the rare genuine item back in Romania. American chicken was tasteless. Mass-produced furniture was built to fall apart. Her car, the crowning glory of her achievements in the eyes of folks back home, was only three years old and was already beginning to wheeze and groan. It began to dawn on my mother that she had perhaps made a bad deal: She had traded in her friends and relatives for ersatz tomatoes, fake chicken, phony furniture. ■

Analyzing Figurative Language

Figurative language (or figures of speech) is *language used in a nonliteral way to convey meaning in a vivid and powerful way.* Two common figures of speech are metaphors and similes. **Metaphors** make *an implicit (or not-on-the-surface) comparison between two things that are not apparently very much alike at all:* "The news story went viral" implicitly compares the spread of news with the spread of a virus. A **simile** also *makes a comparison between two unlike things, but it does so explicitly,* using words such as *like* or *as:* "The news spread like a virus." Other common figures of speech include analogy (an extended metaphor or simile), personification (attributing human qualities to animals, ideas, or objects), and hyperbole (exaggeration for emphasis).

We already noted on page 13 that Nicholas Carr used a metaphor to describe his former reading style ("Once I was a scuba diver in the sea of words") and a simile to describe what has happened to his reading ("Now I zip along the surface like a guy on a Jet Ski"). Figurative language adds voice and angle to writing. The metaphor of the scuba diver suggests depth and silence, while the "guy on a Jet Ski" suggests superficiality and noise.

ACTIVITY 2.6 *Writer's Notebook*

Interpreting Figurative Language

Reread paragraph 4 in Codrescu's essay on page 18. In your Writer's Notebook, discuss the effect of Codrescu's use of death as a simile for the loss experienced by new immigrants. Codrescu also uses the word *religion* metaphorically in this paragraph, but he is not referring to an actual religion such as Judaism or Christianity. How would you interpret the meaning of "religion" in the context of this paragraph? Writers often extend an idea through a series of related metaphors, as Codrescu does here. Highlight or underline all of the references to religion in paragraph 4. How do these assembled religious metaphors contribute to the point Codrescu is making about material objects in the lives of immigrants who are experiencing "a kind of death"? Be ready to discuss your answers to these questions in class. ■

Paraphrasing Difficult Passages

To learn more about paraphrasing, see Chapter 18, pages 387–89.

The reading you do in college is sometimes difficult. Paraphrasing can help you make sense of challenging passages. A **paraphrase** is a *restatement in your own words and sentences.* Paraphrasing is like translating the passage into language you can better understand–using shorter, more direct sentences and more familiar vocabulary. It ought to substitute your own language for the author's voice, sentence patterns, and word choices. A paraphrase should be in your own voice, which usually means trading more literal language for any metaphors or similes, unless you put them in quotation marks.

Below is a passage from Codrescu's reading in which he explains the immigrant's disillusionment with American material goods. Note that the paraphrase, on the right, is approximately as long as the original. A paraphrase is not a summary, and it should contain all of the points in the original passage. As the color coding indicates, all the points in the original appear in the paraphrase.

Original Passage	**Paraphrase**
When you first arrive on these shores, you are in mourning. The only consolations are these products, which had been imbued with religious significance back at home. But when these things turn out not to be the real things, you begin to experience a second death, brought about by betrayal. You begin to suspect that the religious significance you had attached to them was only possible back home, where these things did not exist. Here, where they are plentiful, they have no significance whatsoever. They are inanimate fetishes, somebody else's fetishes, no help to you at all.	New immigrants to America feel the loss of their friends, family, and culture. Codrescu compares this sense of loss to mourning a death. To console themselves, they turn to material objects such as cars and furniture, things that they could not buy in the old country but could only dream of possessing. They believed in the power of these objects to give meaning to life. But the immigrant discovers, sadly, that the products are cheap and shoddily made. This discovery is a second loss, as the immigrant mourns the loss of hope. Paradoxically, the products had meaning only in the old country, when they were out of reach. Here, they are nothing but junk, and the buyer finds that they are useless in providing any sort of consolation.

ACTIVITY 2.7 *Writer's Notebook*

Practicing Paraphrase

Using the advice and the example paraphrase, write a paraphrase of another passage. More help with writing paraphrase is available in Chapter 18; see pages 387–89. For a passage to paraphrase, you might look at the alternative reading you may have already previewed and annotated, or you may use the passage below, from Codrescu's essay. You will need to go back to see where the passage fits into the text so that you can write a good paraphrase that clarifies what point in time Codrescu refers to here.

> At this point, the ersatz tomatoes and the faux chicken did not appear all that important. An imponderable had made its appearance, a bracing, heady feeling of liberty. ■

Finding the Writer's Moves in a Text

One way of seeing the big picture of any text you are reading is to go behind the scenes and think about how the text was constructed. **What moves did the writer make in creating it?** Groups of paragraphs often work together to perform a function, such as providing an introduction, background information, an opposing view, or an illustration.

Recognizing these universally available moves and distinguishing them from their specific content is a way to analyze any text. A good strategy is to make a descriptive outline showing the major subdivisions. For each subdivision of the reading, a descriptive outline answers two questions:

- What is the move or function of this section? In other words, what is it doing?
- What is the main point or content of this section? In other words, what is it saying?

Writing a descriptive outline requires two skills: analyzing the function of each section and paraphrasing the most important point or points in each section. Following is an example showing the subdivisions of this short reading by Codrescu.

Subdivisions of "Notes of an Alien Son: Immigration Paradoxes"

Paragraphs 1–2

Does: Gives an example of one problem, or paradox.

Says: When Andrei Codrescu's mother emigrated from Romania, she found a better life materially, but she had to accept the loss of her home, friends, and family—her supportive social and cultural environment.

Paragraphs 3–4

Does: Gives an example of another problem, or paradox.

Says: American products turned out to be cheaply made junk that did not last. They had been more powerful as dream than as reality. Realizing their dreams were built on false expectations is an even greater loss for the immigrants than leaving home and family.

Paragraph 5

Does: Sums up the two main points of the essay so far.

Says: His mother suffered two losses: first, the loss of her cultural and social environment, and second, the loss of her belief in products as a consolation for the first loss.

Paragraphs 6–7

Does: Puts the problems into a larger context or perspective.

Says: She realized that going back to Romania would be worse. In Romania, her life was bound by a bureaucracy run by favors and bribes. In America, she had freedom, an amazing discovery.

Paragraph 8

Does: Sums up the main point of the whole essay.

Says: His mother learned that the benefits of emigrating were worth the costs and also that life in America was more complicated than she had envisioned.

ACTIVITY 2.8 *Thinking as a Writer*

Finding a Writer's Moves in a Different Reading

Analyze the reading selection you previewed, read, and annotated (as instructed on pages 19–21). Note the major subdivisions and the main point of each subdivision. Make an outline to show (1) how each subdivision functions (the role it performs) and (2) what it says (the point it makes). Use the example outline above as a model. ■

Summarizing the Text

To learn more about summarizing, see Chapter 18, pages 389–91.

Writing a summary of a reading helps you see the text as a whole, not a series of parts. It is often necessary to sum up the entire content of a reading, such as when you want to explain someone else's argument in a paper of your own or when writing an annotated bibliography to let others know the content of your sources.

To write a summary, you must first sort out the main ideas from the supporting details and then put the main ideas into your own words—that is, paraphrase them. Writing a descriptive outline, as explained above, is an excellent strategy for drafting a summary. Once you have found the major subdivisions of a reading and paraphrased their key points, you have material to work with for a summary.

Simply splicing the paraphrases together, however, may not result in a smooth summary. The biggest challenge is to unite these paraphrases into a coherent piece of writing that reflects the train of thought in the original passage. You will need to add transitions and possibly some additional information from the original text. You may use brief quotations. Bear in mind, however, that a summary should be no more than one-third the length of the original.

An example summary of "Notes of an Alien Son: Immigration Paradoxes" follows. The original complete text is on pages 17–19.

Summary of "Notes of an Alien Son: Immigration Paradoxes"

When Andrei Codrescu's mother emigrated from Romania she had to accept the loss of her home, friends and family, her social and cultural support. In exchange, she dreamed of a better lifestyle materially, with new furniture and a car. However, she was disappointed by the reality: mass-produced food with no flavor and cheaply made cars and furniture that fell apart. She felt that she had "been had." In her anger, she saw only the bad side of America—the greed, the selfish individualism, people's blasé lack of appreciation for what they have. Realizing that her dreams were built on false expectations was an even greater loss than leaving home and family, because now she had no hope for any kind of consolation.

Covers paragraphs 1 and 2

Covers paragraphs 3 and 4

Covers paragraph 5

But then she realized that going back would be worse. In Romania, she had had no rights. Even where she lived could be dictated to her. As a Jew, she had no legal standing. Her life was bound by a bureaucracy run by favors and bribes. In contrast, the freedom in America gave her a "heady feeling of liberty." She could protest, she could even throw things and be confident that the penalties would be light.

Covers paragraphs 6 and 7

Codrescu's mother realized that even if America was a "place of paradoxes" where a good tomato costs more than it would in a Third World country, freedom made emigrating "a good deal after all."

Covers paragraph 8

ACTIVITY 2.9 *Writer's Notebook*

Summarizing a Reading

After having worked through the critical reading stages for an alternative reading, write a summary of it using the advice on page 26 and the model above. You should also consult Chapter 18 for more advice on how to write summaries; see pages 389–91. ■

Responding to a Reading

During and after rereading, you should have more extensive responses to a stimulating text, with more thoughts than can fit in a marginal note. That is why serious readers and researchers keep reading response journals for recording thoughts, reactions, and opinions that are more extensive than brief annotations.

You could simply write your thoughts in a spiral notebook or in a file you keep on your computer, or you could follow the suggestion of many reading experts and use a double-entry journal, a notebook, or online document divided into two columns with quotations or paraphrases of the text in one column and your reactions on the right. Following is an example of a double-entry reading journal:

What the text says:	**What I say back to the text:**
Par. 2: Codrescu shows how isolated immigrants can be: "there was no one with whom to make toasts and sing songs."	This passage explains why many new immigrants want to live in neighborhoods with others who share their customs and language. I think as they assimilate, they lose this dependency, but that is sad too because their children often forget about their roots.
Par. 3: "She had traded in her friends and relatives for ersatz tomatoes, fake chicken, phony furniture."	His mother expected American products to be a good part, and they weren't. Why not? Possibly because Americans are more interested in saving money on necessities like food and furniture so they can spend it on other more status-symbol things.
Par. 4: "She deplored its rudeness, its insensitivity, its outright meanness, its indifference, the chase after the almighty buck, the social isolation of most Americans, their inability to partake in warm, genuine fellowship and, above all, their deplorable lack of awe before what they had made."	This is a pretty harsh description of Americans. It shows how an outsider notices the downside of our fast-paced, materialistic lifestyle–things that we might acknowledge if pointed out to us, but that we just accept as how it is. It would be interesting to get other opinions about this, such as from exchange students.

Par. 6: ". . . she had left behind a vast range of daily humiliations."	Romania has changed now that it is a democracy and part of the European Union. She may not even want to leave if she lived there today, but the point of the essay is still relevant because it describes a universal experience for the many who still want to escape to America for freedom and a better life.
Par. 8: "America is a place of paradoxes. . . ."	What does he mean here? What other examples can I think of? An example would be American middle-class women who can choose to eat a healthy diet but are forced by fashion images to eat the calorie intake of someone in a developing country. They are free and yet they are controlled by media messages. That's a paradox.

The advantage of the double-entry journal is that it shows the connection between what you read and what you thought about what you read. The double-entry journal is useful for stimulating your own thinking in response to the text. You can also consult it for citing the passages in the text when writing in response to a reading.

ACTIVITY 2.10 *Writer's Notebook*

Double-Entry Journal

Use a double-entry template to make your own notes and responses to Codrescu's text. Is there any connection among the comments you made in the right-hand column? Write two or three paragraphs describing these connections. ■

How Do I Deal with the Difficulties of Scholarly Texts?

The reading you do in college often includes scholarly texts—that is, books and articles written by professors for people who have a high level of knowledge on the topic, such as other professors and advanced students in the field. You will encounter scholarly texts in many of your courses and when doing research on your own for various writing projects. (See page 368 in Chapter 16 for more about different types of scholarly articles.) In this chapter, we give you some tips for reading these especially challenging texts. Follow this advice *after* you have skimmed potential sources for your project and chosen one to drill down on because it looks useful for your project.

Our example text was written by a professor in the history of political thought. It is not just about history, but about how political ideas are presented and sold to gain public support. This is an important topic because throughout history and up into the present day, people are constantly persuaded to favor one position over others. In this case, the professor is interested in how a single symbol, a bolt of lightning, was used to persuade the people of France to rally around the cause of the French Revolution, to topple the monarchy and install a democratic government.

The text appears on pp. 32–35. Before reading it, preview it using the Questions for Previewing, which we have reprinted below.

What is this text about? The title tells you it is about revolution, and the illustration shows that it is about the French Revolution in particular. Skimming the first sentences of many paragraphs, you may notice the frequency of words relating to science. You deduce that the author is going to talk about the role of science in the political thought of the eighteenth century.

What do I already know about the topic? What opinions do I have about it? Many topics encountered in college will be new to you. Test your knowledge on this one by jotting down what you may already know. If you find your storehouse is empty, do something to stock it with some basic information. Many students find it worthwhile to begin by first reading *down*—that is, by reading a less specialized text such as an encyclopedia entry or textbook pages covering the topic. For the French Revolution, you might try the History Channel website.

Who wrote this text? When and where was it published? Read the head note to Kevin Duong's article to find out something about the author and his interests. You might be surprised to see the term "flash mob" in the title of a scholarly article. Remember that scholars are people too, and they should write with voice and angle. You see that Duong is having a little fun with his topic and appealing to his audience with a humorous pun on lightning. The French Revolution, however, was a serious and bloody business. You are probably familiar with the role played by the guillotine in the overthrow of King Louis XVI and his wife, Marie Antoinette. One year of the Revolution, 1793–1794, was known as the Reign of Terror, with more than 1,400 people killed by the Revolutionaries. As you read this article, look for the author's voice and angle on the Revolution.

Who is the audience for this text? By the first sentence of the second paragraph, you can see that Duong is off and running with lots of names of historical figures he expects his audience is already familiar with. He is, after all, writing primarily to other professors of history, history of ideas, art history, or the history of science and technology. We have provided marginal comments on some of the names Duong drops to save you time in using our example, but you will have to look up many names and vocabulary words when doing research on your own. It's part of the process of learning. But having said that, be careful not to let all the unfamiliar names distract you from the content: what is the main argument of the text? Getting the big ideas in any article is much more important than dwelling on details.

What special features does the text contain that might aid comprehension? Many scholarly articles follow a standard pattern of organization with subdivisions such as an *abstract* summarizing the whole, an introduction including a *review of literature* already out there on a topic, the *claim or thesis* to be proven, an *argument* with reasons and evidence to support the claim, a *conclusion*, and a list of *references* or end notes. Or the article may have *subheadings* to guide readers through the text.

Most scholarly articles are organized as exposition, not narration, like Codrescu's story about his mother's experience in America. Expository writing has a logical structure based on generalizations and specifics that develop them.

Consider this brief passage from Duong's article:

Revolutionary scientists designed a variety of strategies to make the will of the people discernable. They ranged from the statistical to the legalistic. However, one particular approach stood out, both for its intrinsic peculiarity and for its frequency: attempts to analogize the will of the people to lightning strikes.

Most general statement. | More specific. | Most specific.

Being able to pick out the main ideas, the most general points, from the more specific ones, such as facts and examples, will help you navigate scholarly articles. And nearly all scholarly articles make an argument; the generalizations offer thesis and reasons, while the specifics offer evidence in support. Duong argues to show how the lightening bolt worked as persuasion for the political idea of democracy.

ACTIVITY 2.11 *Collaborative Activity*

Reading Visuals

This article contains many historical images that are in the public domain, or free to use, because of their age. (All of the images can be viewed on the *Public Domain Review* website.) In the first image, Lady Liberty holds two symbols of the Revolution, lightning bolts and the red cap, which itself has a long political history. The second image depicts Benjamin Franklin performing a famous experiment in which he attached a metal key to a kite string during a thunderstorm to prove that lightning and electricity were one and the same.

In small groups of two or three, interpret the meaning of these two images. What persuasive similarities do you notice between the two images reprinted here? What inferences can you draw about Kevin Duong's angle on his topic, based on details from the pictures? ■

READING 2.2

Flash Mob: Revolution, Lightning, and the People's Will

KEVIN DUONG

Kevin Duong is an Assistant Professor in Political Studies at Bard College. His interests include the history of political thought, revolution and violence, modern social theory, and feminism and gender studies. This reading is excerpted from an essay of the same name that appeared in the Public Domain Review *in November 2017. Duong's essay uses illustrations that belong to the public domain, meaning they are creative works that no one holds copyright or trademark on, usually because the copyright has expired.*

We have already begun annotating the essay with information about historical figures. As you read, add annotations of your own based on the five questions in the "Art of Questioning" box on *page 20.*

It is often observed that the French Revolution was a revolution of scientists. 1

Nourished by airy abstractions and heartfelt cries to Jean-Jacques Rousseau, its leaders sought a society grounded, not in God or tradition, but in what Edmund Burke decried as "the conquering empire of light and reason". To be sure, if we tallied the professional affiliations of the members of the first National Assembly, we would find it overwhelmingly populated by lawyers. But the revolution's symbols and motifs were not derived from legal practices and traditions, and it was not as men of law that Maximilien Robespierre and Jean-Paul Marat called for the death of their king and the creation of a democratic republic. Rather, they did so as scientists—middle class intellectuals who saw in government a field ripe for experimentation, innovation, and improvement. 2

Nowhere was this as clear as in their approach to "the will of the people." Of the many puzzles to which revolutionaries applied themselves as scientists, few seemed so pressing and so intractable. It is obvious what a king's will looks like, or so we like to think. Kings 3

Detail from *La Liberté Triomphante* (1792), showing Liberty brandishing a thunderbolt in one hand and a Phrygian cap on a stick in the other.

Source: Bibliothèque nationale de France, département Estampes et photographie, Reserve QB-370 (26)-FT 4 [De Vinck, 4461].

Rousseau (1712–1798) was a philosopher of the French Enlightenment, best known for his belief that in a state of nature, humans are essentially good but are corrupted by social forces that develop within civilizations.

Edmund Burke (1729–1797) was an Anglo-Irish Conservative politician who feared mob rule—and thus opposed the French Revolution.

The governing revolutionary body in France from June 17th to July 9th in 1789.

Robespierre (1758–1794) was a leader of the French Revolution.

Marat (1743–1793) was a radical leader of the Reign of Terror after the Revolution, when many people were put to death if they were suspected of opposing the Revolution.

King Louis XVI and his wife, Marie Antoinette, were put to death at the guillotine.

Liberty Triumphant

A Phrygian cap is a cone-shaped red hat that came to symbolize liberty and freedom.

are individuals, they have bodies, and they can tell us what to do. However they choose to communicate their will—through voice, a gesture, a written pronouncement—it is relatively clear when such acts belong to them. But "the people" enjoy no such obvious body and no evident means of self-expression. What does the will of the people actually look like? And how do we hear their voice if they don't have a mouth with which to speak? As French revolutionaries enthroned the will of the people, they stepped into uncharted terrain. Democratic revolution, it turned out, required men capable of visualizing the invisible and making appear what escaped our immediate senses. Indeed, it seemed to require the labor of scientific inquiry applied to the people themselves. Like the invisible composition of air, the secret patterns of a magnetic field, or the stratifications of the earth's soil, democratic politics was governed by a hidden law that the scientist-statesman had to uncover.

Revolutionary scientists designed a variety of strategies to make the will of the people discernable. They ranged from the statistical to the legalistic. However, one particular approach stood out, both for its intrinsic peculiarity and for its frequency: attempts to analogize the will of the people to lightning strikes. The historian Mary Ashburn Miller has documented the long history of symbolizing sovereignty as lightning.[1] In the absolutist imagination, lightning symbolized royal power and its Jupiterian pretensions. The frontispiece to Thomas Hobbes' 1651 *Leviathan* features a thunderbolt alongside a crown, cannon, and other items in absolutism's symbolic ensemble. 4

> Absolutism is the belief in a single authority, such as an absolute monarch, or king.

> Hobbes (1588–1679) was an English political philosopher best known for his book *Leviathan*, in which he argued for a strong central, autocratic, government during England's Civil War.

With the Revolution, French intellectuals seized this lightning and redirected it against their king. In 1792, as the Revolution radicalized into a democratic revolution, members of the National Convention found themselves debating what to do with Louis XVI. On December 3, 1792, Robespierre answered that the king should be summarily executed rather than tried for treason, because "a people does not judge as does a court of law. It does not hand down sentences, it hurls down thunderbolts."[2] Louis XVI was struck down by the guillotine in the Place de la Révolution on January 21, 1793. 5

> A large square in Paris now known as the Place de la Concorde.

The trope was ubiquitous, not only in texts and speeches, but also in the visual culture of the Revolution. An allegorical print from 1792 features "Liberty," the figurehead and personification of the people. She is depicted striking down the remnants of monarchy with a fist full of lightning. Behind her, powerful bands of light (and enlightenment) repel the dark clouds that allude to the obscurity of monarchical superstition. 6

> A trope is the metaphorical use of a word or image—in this case, lightning.

. . .

It was no accident that lightning was chosen as a model for the will of the people. The language of science and the language of politics were melding together in the crucible of democratic revolution, and not only in France. A fascination with 7

---

1. Mary Ashburn Miller, *A Natural History of Revolution: Violence and Nature in the French Revolutionary Imagination, 1789–1794* (Ithaca and London: Cornell University Press, 2011).
2. Maximilien Robespierre, "Speech to the Convention, 3 December 1792", in *Regicide and Revolution: Speeches at the Trial of Louis XVI*, ed. Michael Walzer, trans. Marian Rothstein (New York: Columbia University Press, 2010), 133.

> The Jacobins were a political club made up of the most radical revolutionaries. The Jacobins were responsible for the Reign of Terror, a year of mass executions of anyone suspected of not supporting the Revolution.

electricity connected scientists of all stripes across the Atlantic, and tugging on those threads reveals a web of radicalism in late eighteenth-century scientific culture. Take two of the leading Jacobins: Marat and Robespierre. Marat was one of the heroes (or demons) of the Revolution. But before 1789, he was a scientist: in 1782, he had published a prominent study of electricity entitled *Recherches physiques sur l'électricité*. The next year in 1783, in the village of St Omer, a Monsieur de Vissery equipped his home with a lightning rod. Villagers believed the rod actively summoned lightning to their homes, and so they petitioned for the rod's removal. The case eventually reached the Conseil d'Artois, where a young Robespierre took up the case to defend Vissery in the name of scientific progress. Robespierre won the case, and it made his reputation as a progressive lawyer. In his enthusiasm, he wrote to Benjamin Franklin. In the letter dated 1 October 1783, he thanked the American for the "sublime discovery" of lightning conduction.[3]

Franklin was well known for having tamed lightning by conducting it from the 8
sky in his "kite experiment" of 1752. Revolutionaries like Robespierre were more than a little obsessed with this fact. In his person, Franklin seemed to offer a paragon of scientific statesmanship. After all, besides taming lightning, Franklin served as ambassador to France from 1776-85. Yet he was not the only scientist of electricity to enthrall the French. On August 26, 1792, the National Convention set aside time from their busy schedule of waging revolution to confer honorary citizenship to the English scientist Joseph Priestley. ... Priestley was a friend of Franklin and known for discovering oxygen and founding Unitarianism. But Priestley was also a scientist of lightning. Throughout the 1770s, he authored and edited several editions of the *History of Electricity*, which was eventually translated into other languages. In 1774, he delivered a paper on lightning storms to the Royal Academy and exchanged

Benjamin Franklin Drawing Electricity from the Sky (ca. 1816), by Benjamin West.
Source: Philadelphia Museum of Art, Gift of Mr. and Mrs. Wharton Sinkler, 1958-132-1.

3. Maximilien Robespierre, "Letter to Benjamin Franklin, 1 October 1783", in *The Papers of Benjamin Franklin*, Vol 41, ed. Ellen R. Cohn (New Haven, CT: Yale University Press, 2014), 61.

letters with Jeremy Bentham concerning atmospheric lightning. In 1775, he wrote to the American scientist Andrew Oliver about the origins of electricity. And in 1778, he sat on an English Board of Ordinance tasked with optimizing the shape of lightning conductors.[4]

French revolutionaries idolized Priestley and Franklin because they sincerely believed 9
that science was intimately connected with the struggle for freedom. For these men, the cause of science was the cause of democracy. The sentiment traveled both ways. When Priestley was not investigating electricity and air, he preoccupied himself with championing the French Revolution in England. His combination of revolutionary fervor and scientific fame made him a target for Burke in *Reflections on the Revolution in France* (1790). Evidently, Priestley's neighbors agreed that he was a threat to social order. In 1791, they burned down his Birmingham home and laboratory, forcing Priestley to flee to America in 1794 where he was welcomed by yet another revolutionary scientist and French Revolution enthusiast: Thomas Jefferson (himself an occasional diplomat to France).

These men shared an enthusiasm for democracy and electricity which, oddly 10
enough, informed one another. Yet it shouldn't be surprising. When faced with new political questions about democracy, these men applied themselves as they were wont to do, namely as scientists. The outcome was a transatlantic circuit of research, discovery, evidence—and radical politics.

---

4. Robert E. Schofield, *The Enlightened Joseph Priestley: A Study of His Life and Work from 1773 to 1804* (University Park, PA: The Pennsylvania State University Press, 2004), 121–4.

Questions for Discussion

1. Images of light and darkness run as a pattern throughout this essay. Find some of the references to light. What are some of the things light is associated with? Where are images of darkness found, and what are they associated with? How do these images reinforce what you see as Duong's angle on his topic?
2. A revolution means the overthrowing of one power by another, in this case, the French monarchy by the French people. Duong names some figures associated with the side of the monarchy. Who were these people, and what values did they adhere to?
3. How does Duong use style in his writing to liven up this article? Find some passages where you can "hear" his voice and personality. Do these passages make the article more difficult or less difficult to read?
4. Can you think of any other political movements where abstract concepts were given concrete symbolism for the sake of persuading people to embrace the cause?

The Assignment

Just as writing a summary of a reading helps you to see the whole text coherently, writing a personal response essay helps you assess your own thinking in response to a reading. Writing your response helps you examine, revise, and possibly gain new insights into the text. On his blog, the best-selling writer Steven Johnson explains how writing a book review helps him appreciate the book more deeply: ". . . [A]ctually sitting down to write out a response to something makes you see it in a new way, often with greater complexity." For this assignment, write a short essay explaining your response to a text that you choose or that your instructor assigns. Begin by reading the text critically using the process and strategies described in this chapter.

What Could I Write About?

To stimulate your thinking, ask yourself questions like the following:

- What is the central issue raised in the reading? What are the author's views on this issue? Did you have views on the issue before reading? If so, how would you compare your prior thinking with the author's?
- Do your observations and experiences confirm, illustrate, or contradict what the text says?
- Did the reading present any new ideas that had not occurred to you before? Did the reading raise some new questions you had never considered? Did it question some assumption or belief you had been holding?
- If you could ask the author one question, what would it be? Why would this question matter to the line of thought or argument in the text?
- What other writers' views have you read on this topic? How do their views compare with the views expressed in this reading?
- Even if you did not accept all of the views and ideas in this reading, what can you take away from it to add to your knowledge about the topic?

When writing your response, tie your own thoughts to specific passages in the text.

What Is My Rhetorical Situation?

When previewing a reading, readers should ask questions about the rhetorical situation, as explained on pages 16–17. Likewise, when preparing to write, writers should consider the rhetorical situation for their own texts. Consider the rhetorical situation for an essay responding to a reading.

Writer: What Is My Purpose?

The purpose of a response essay is to express the writer's ideas about the text. A response can be an evaluation of the reading or it could simply discuss the ideas that the writer found important and worth further thought. See the list of moves in the section below titled Text: What Moves Can I Make?

Reader: Who Is My Audience?

The response essay shares the results of your critical reading with other readers of the same text.

Text: What Moves Can I Make?

Response essays can do some or all of the following:

- **Draw connections between the world of the text and your own world,** things you have experienced, prior knowledge you bring to the text.
- **Offer insights into the meaning of the text,** as revealed by relationships between parts of the text, analysis of the language, style, arrangement, and voice of the author.
- **Evaluate the thinking;** tell why the writing is convincing to you or not.
- **Reflect on the significance of the text,** explaining the degree to which reading it contributed to your understanding of the topic.
- **Make specific and accurate references** to passages in the text while making any of the moves listed here.

CREDITS

page 13: Nicholas Carr. "Is Google Making Us Stupid?" *Atlantic Monthly,* 1 July 2008. **page 17:** Andrei Codrescu. "Notes of an Alien Son: Immigrant Voices." *Review of Contemporary Fiction,* 1 Apr. 2010. Used by permission of the author. All rights reserved. **page 35:** Duong, Kevin. (2017, Nov. 9). "Flash Mob: Revolution, Lightning, and the People's Will." *Public Domain Review.* https://publicdomainreview.org/2017/11/09/revolution-lightning-and-the-peoples-will/ . Used with permission. **page 36:** Steven Johnson. "More on the Shallows." *StevenBerlinJohnson.com,* 2010, www.stevenberlinjohnson.com/2010/06/more-on-the-shallows.html.

CHAPTER 3

Writing and the Art of Questioning

ENGAGING QUESTIONS

In this chapter, you will engage with the following questions:

- What does it mean to communicate effectively?
- What are the elements that make up a rhetorical situation?
- Why is it important to consider the rhetorical situation in relation to a writing assignment?
- How do writers choose the appropriate voice for specific rhetorical situations?
- Why does voice matter in writing?
- What does it mean to "have an angle" on a topic?
- How do writers identify appropriate topics for composing literacy narratives?
- How do the elements of the rhetorical situation apply to the composing process for a literacy narrative?

THE KEY POINT IN CHAPTER 1 IS THAT THINKING BEGINS WHEN YOU ASK QUESTIONS. In this chapter we consider the kinds of questions that writing requires. A good way to begin is to think about the act of writing. What are you doing when you write?

What Is Good Writing?

Writing well is not simply writing correctly. It is **communicating effectively.** Good writing, whether a letter, a memo, a report, or a paper in school, sends a message from a writer to a reader. For example:

- We send a text or write an e-mail to a professor to set up a meeting.
- We write letters to customers to explain a new service.
- We write a letter to the editor to tell the community our views on a proposed law or policy.
- We write a paper in a class on popular culture to share our research on how popular music shapes group identity.

Short or long, formal or informal, in school, at work, or in another setting, writing is always communication, and good communication responds appropriately to its *rhetorical situation.*

What Is the Rhetorical Situation?

The relationship among the **writer,** the **reader,** and the **text** forms the **rhetorical situation;** *these are the variables always present when we think about a writing task.*[1] (See Figure 3.1.)

The effectiveness of any piece of writing depends on how well the author has thought about these three basic elements of communication and how they relate to each other. See Figure 3.1 for some questions to consider.

Notice that the categories overlap and interrelate: The context for a piece of writing determines what is appropriate to include in the message. Facebook, for example, is a more public context than a personal e-mail or text message. Audience also influences the text, as writers choose what to put in or leave out depending on how much the audience already knows about a topic.

Why Ask about the Rhetorical Situation?

Without a sense of audience and purpose, no one can write well. Inattention to the rhetorical situation results in disorganized memos that employees ignore or misunderstand, public speeches that last too long and make an audience drowsy or restless, and lectures that leave students confused.

When we ask about angle, we are looking for something of our own to say, a key point we will elaborate on shortly. If we find something we want to say, we are more likely to care about saying it well. If we have something to say, we also think about readers we want to reach. Connecting with them suddenly matters to us, so we care about how we sound. That is, we care about *voice.*

What Is Voice?

Voice refers to the writer's presence in a text, *how the writer "sounds."* When we read carefully, we can "hear" a person–a personality–in the words. Once again, the rhetorical situation determines how you want to sound. In informal social writing such as comments on a Facebook page, there is almost no such thing as too much personality. In other rhetorical situations, such as when writing a letter to a customer, the voice will sound more formal and reserved: Impatience, anger, and even humor in excess can be offensive in workplace communications. In some science writing an objective tone is appropriate. Voice varies according to the situation, but in all cases we should hear a person saying something that matters in a way that holds the reader's attention and is appropriate to the context and the genre of the text.

1. In this book **rhetoric** means *the art of writing well.* We learn this art by doing it and by developing knowledge about how to do it better, the purpose of this book and all writing courses.

FIGURE **3.1**

The Rhetorical Situation

Top: © Image Source/Getty Images, RF; bottom right: © FocusTechnology/Alamy; bottom left: © Digital Vision/Getty Images, RF

About the Writer

- Why am I writing this text? What is my **purpose** (to inform, to persuade, to entertain, to express my feelings, and so on)?
- What is my **angle,** or **point of view,** on the topic?
- Why do I have my angle? That is, what did I hear, read, or experience that led me to my point of view?
- What does my angle imply about my **voice,** how I want to sound to my readers?

About the Reader

- For whom am I writing this text? That is, who are my **readers,** people I most want to reach?
- Will my readers find my topic and my angle useful, interesting, something they can relate to?
- What **prior knowledge** of my topic do my readers have or what background do they need?
- In what **context** (academic, business, public, personal) will my audience read and talk about this text?

About the Text

- What kind, or **genre,** of text is this, and what **conventions** govern it?
- What **expectations** do readers have for texts of this genre?
- In what **medium** (print or digital, spoken or read) is this genre typically available?
- What **design** features are associated with this genre?

Read to hear the voice in each of the following two passages on the same topic, paleontology. The first is from a museum website at the University of California. The author is not identified. The second is from an essay published originally in the literary magazine *Harper's*. The author, David Quammen, writes with a concern for the environment.

READING 3.1

What Is Paleontology?

UNIVERSITY OF CALIFORNIA MUSEUM OF PALEONTOLOGY

. . . [P]aleontology is the study of what fossils tell us about the ecologies of the past, about evolution, and about our place, as humans, in the world. Paleontology incorporates knowledge from biology, geology, ecology, anthropology, archaeology, and even computer science to understand the processes that have led to the origination and eventual destruction of the different types of organisms since life arose.

READING 3.2

Planet of Weeds

DAVID QUAMMEN

Hope is a duty from which paleontologists are exempt. Their job is to take the long view, the cold and stony view, of triumphs and catastrophes in the history of life. They study the fossil record, that erratic selection of petrified shells, carapaces, bones, teeth, tree trunks, leaves, pollen, and other biological relics, and from it they attempt to discern the lost secrets of time, the big patterns of stasis and change, the trends of innovation and adaptation and refinement and decline that have blown like sea winds among ancient creatures in ancient ecosystems.

Writer's Notebook

Analyzing the Rhetorical Situation

Write one or two paragraphs answering the following questions about the pair of reading selections on paleontology. (Readings 3.1 and 3.2).

1. How do the contexts for each piece of writing determine the authors' choices of what material to include? What information is similar in the two? What is different?

2. How would you describe the difference in purpose for each passage?
3. How would you describe the writer's angle on paleontology in each passage?
4. How would you describe the writer's voice in each passage? How do the elements of purpose, context, audience, and angle affect the writer's decisions about voice? ■

Why Does Voice Matter?

Learning to control the voice in your writing can increase your satisfaction with a writing project and improve your grade. A former student at the University of Hawaii, Monique Fournier, describes her discovery of the difference voice can make:

> Six years ago, I dropped out of college after completing my sophomore year. I assumed that it was because college wasn't for me, that I just wasn't meant for the classroom. It turns out that I wasn't ready for college writing. I now believe that once a writer finds her voice, she can easily apply it to any college-level writing assignment. Writing those first two years was difficult for me because I was simply plugging chains of words into every paper without any "me" glue to hold them together. Realizing I had a voice, and taking steps to uncover it, has helped me (and my grade point average) immensely.
>
> —Monique Fournier, "Bees and Fears: Why I Write"

Fournier realized that she had a voice and took "steps to uncover it." That sounds easy, but what steps did she take? Where does voice come from?

To write with voice, we need the following:

- An angle, a point of view toward whatever we are writing about
- The courage to assert it

Writers adjust their voice to suit their purpose, topic, audience, and genre, but the essential question at the heart of writing with voice is, **What stake do I have in my topic?**

What Is an Angle?

What is this "me" that Fournier calls the glue that holds her words together? It comes from personal engagement, having a stake, in your topic. Writers often refer to this as "having an angle." For example, consider the two passages on page 41 on paleontology. On the museum website, the writer's angle is the broad range of knowledge included in the modern study of paleontology. This angle promotes paleontology; it suggests that the reader might want to visit the museum or even take a course.

The other passage shows a darker angle on paleontology as the study of nature's indifference toward the plants and animals that have become extinct. Listing the specific objects that paleontologists study, the author shows his view of paleontology as a study of ancient mysteries. Not everyone would see it that way, but Quammen's angle fits his purpose, which is to interpret what the science means to him. In each case, the author has a point of view that gives voice to the writing.

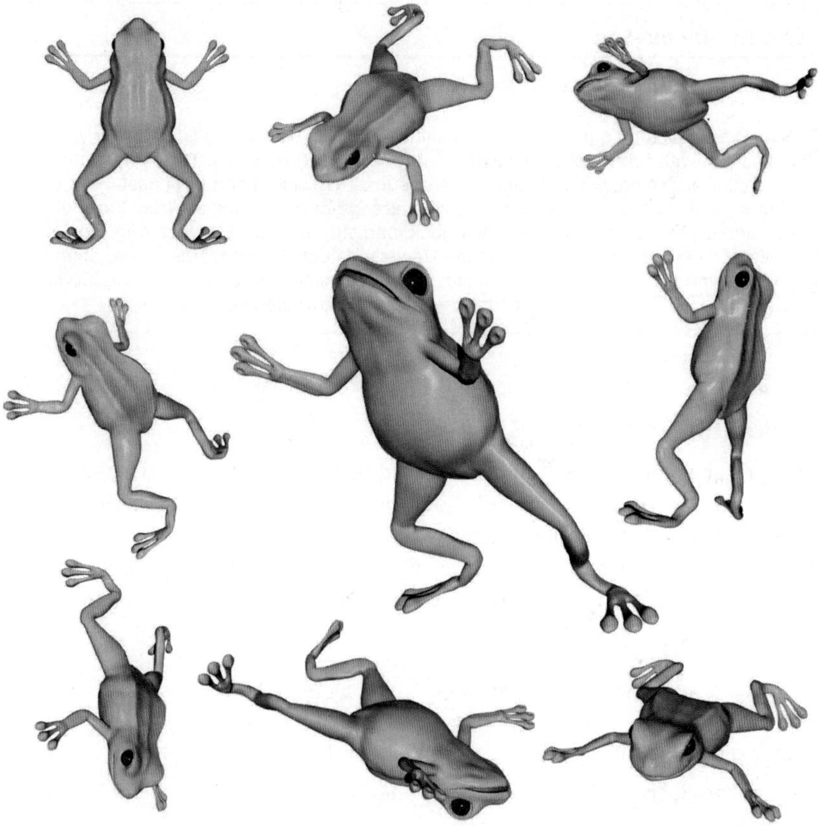

FIGURE 3.2

A Writer's Angle Shows Point of View

A writer's angle is similar to a photographer's angle on a subject. The angle reflects the creator's point of view.

A good way to think about angle is to compare writing with taking a photograph. Through your camera lens, you decide how to frame a scene or a person. You may try out different angles, with different amounts of background, foreground, and contrast between light and dark. All of these decisions affect how you want to present your subject. Pictures show the photographer's angle on the subject (see Figure 3.2).

Engaging with Topics: How Can I Find an Angle?

Whether you are writing about a social problem like bullying or a scientific topic like climate change, reflecting on your experiences and prior knowledge will help you find an angle. On any topic (represented here by "x"), questions that help to find an angle include the following:

- How does "x" affect me? Why does "x" matter?
- What is my opinion of "x"? What does it mean to me?
- What is the most interesting thing about "x"?
- How is "x" relevant to anything else I have observed or experienced?
- How is "x" relevant to anything else I have read about or studied?
- If I had to put "x" into a larger picture or category, what would that be?

FIGURE **3.3**

A Writer's Angle Is Influenced by the Rhetorical Situation

How would you describe the rhetorical situation as related to this promotional material?

Erewhon-by-the-Sea

Convention and Visitor's Bureau

Located on a picturesque stretch of coastline, Erewhon-by-the-Sea is a popular vacation destination, with both rocky coastline and powder-sand beaches. The Erewhon marina offers charter fishing, whale watching, and sunset cruising along the coast. If you like seafood, Erewhon is the place for you, with a range of dining options from local lobster, crab, and clams, to cod, mackerel, haddock, and striped bass. Erewhon offers golfers a choice of five courses, some with ocean views and tidal water hazards. These amenities make Erewhon not only a vacation destination but a mecca for retirement living. Come for a visit and you'll want to stay because there is truly nowhere like Erewhon.

Angle and Rhetorical Situation

A writer's angle on a topic is also influenced by the rhetorical situation, such as the audience, the purpose, and the genre or kind of text that he or she needs to write. Figure 3.3 shows a promotional description of a coastal town.

Because the audience for this description is people interested in finding a place to relax and recreate, this description of the town plays up its vacation amenities.

ACTIVITY 3.1 *Writer's Notebook*

Changing the Angle

Revise the description of "Erewhon-by-the-Sea" based on one of the following angles:

- The viewpoint of a resident *interested in honoring and preserving the city's colonial history.*
- The viewpoint of an artist seeking to attract other artists *interested in painting scenic landscapes.*
- The viewpoint of an adventure-seeker *looking for places to hike and bike.*

Be sure to consider how the voice, message, and purpose of this writing would change with the angle. ■

ACTIVITY 3.2 *In Your Own Work*

Describing Your Hometown

Write a one- or two-paragraph description of your hometown from an angle that interests you. Who would be an appropriate audience for a paragraph written from this angle? To share your description with classmates, post it on an online discussion board or on a blog. ■

The Assignment

The start of a college writing class is a good time to take stock as a writer. What strengths or abilities do you have, and in what areas do you hope to improve? Looking at the learning goals for your course or writing program will help you assess your skills.

For this assignment, you will focus on some aspect of your writing that matters to you. Maybe there is something about writing that you particularly enjoy, or something that challenges you, such as a problem you would like to overcome. Maybe it is an experience you had with writing–in your childhood, in high school, or maybe outside school–that influenced your development. This will be a brief essay, so focus on a specific topic connected with your writing. What might you benefit from thinking more about? How might readers benefit from knowing about your experiences with writing?

What Could I Write About?

Some ideas for topics include:

- A teacher, relative, or other role model of a writer
- Some advice or instruction that helped or did not help
- A book, reading, or author that inspired you or influenced you
- A particular assignment or some writing that you did outside the classroom

What Is My Rhetorical Situation?

As we discussed earlier, the rhetorical situation is a combination of a writer with something to say, a reader the writer wishes to reach, and a kind (or genre) of text appropriate to the writing task.

Writer: What Are My Purpose and Angle, and How Will They Be Reflected in My Voice?

Your purpose is to reflect on some aspect or experience that has influenced you as a writer.

We have been talking about angle because it is what makes your writing matter to you and matter to your readers. If you do not have something you want to say, your writing will be empty. What do you really think about your development as a writer? What point would be worth sharing with your teacher and your classmates? Why would your point matter to them?

All of the elements discussed influence how you sound in your essay. Envision your audience as the real people they are, and speak to them in the same voice you would use in a conversation or class discussion about writing. Your voice and angle grow out of your life, so do not discount the specific details of your experience, such as teachers' comments, books you have read, papers you have written.

Reader: Who Is My Audience?

Your instructor and your classmates are a natural audience for your essay. In your class, you are part of a community focused on developing as writers. Your instructor is your guide, so sharing some experience or reflecting on some aspect of your writing will help him or her get to know you. You and your classmates will share work and helpful critiques. Getting to know each other as writers will make everyone more comfortable exchanging writing and advice.

Text: What Moves Can I Make?

The genre (kind of writing) for this writing project is the **essay.** An essay is *a short composition in which the author expresses his or her personal views on a topic.* The word itself comes from the French *essai,* meaning "to attempt" or "to try or test out." The writing shows the thought processes of the writer. Essays are more polished than journal entries. A main point or central idea gives the essay coherence, and transitions signal the writer's train of thought.

The following short essay was written by a student in response to the activity outlined above. Read through it once just to see what she has to say, and then go back to note her attention to elements of the rhetorical situation discussed in this chapter.

Griffin 1

Allison Griffin

Professor Channell

English 1301

September 10, 2015

Where My Writing Came from, and Where It Went

As a child, I loved to write. I wanted to be a writer. I wrote about anything 1
and everything. I created fictional stories to release my imagination and poems to express my emotions. I wrote down prayers and kept journals that preserved my deepest worries, fears, and moments of happiness, and kept track of my changing

aspirations. I remember getting lost in my writing time. I would jot down my thoughts and watch them develop into something interesting, to me at least.

I had special places I put pen to paper. My most inspirational times were when 2
I was surrounded by nature; the solitude I found crouched under a tree liberated my thoughts. I also remember turning my closet into a writing sanctuary equipped with pens, paper, and pillows. My mom sometimes worried when I disappeared into my closet for hours, but she also looked forward to my reappearance with a new creation for her to read. I had this pure gratification from writing, the desire to write for its own sake, but also competed successfully in writing contests, which fed my dream to be a writer. I could transform my voice for creative writing prompts, poetry and stories that other people liked.

Notice I've been writing in the past tense. I wish it weren't true, but long ago I 3
betrayed my longing to create with words. When did my attitude change, and why? I am studious, and in middle school devoted all my writing time to school assignments. I didn't realize it then, but the formulas and guidelines caused me to lose my appetite for simply expressing myself. Sentences with huge SAT words dominated my writing. I got caught up in writing the ideal essay to please my teachers. Each year a new teacher would offer a "better" formula for the "perfect" paper.

Of course, there were occasional essays in high school that I felt good 4
about—and I couldn't wait to share them. Somehow they were different from the rest, but my teachers always seemed to find the parts that broke the rules, diminishing my pride and satisfaction. Gradually I learned to strangle my voice because the more "me" I put in a paper the more I was criticized.

My mom has wondered about what happened to that part of me that loved to 5
write. Maybe it was all the formulas and rules that caused me to lose my voice, or maybe during adolescence I became too afraid to reveal myself. After not using my voice for so long, I found this paper hard to write and harder to share with others. But maybe I did find my voice again, or perhaps it was always there, hidden beneath all the rules and formulas for a while. Whatever happened, I realize what I have lost and want to recover my passion for writing.

Questions for Discussion

In small groups or as a class, discuss the following questions:

1. What is Griffin's **purpose** for writing?
2. For whom is she writing—that is, what **readers** does she have in mind and how does she make it interesting for them?
3. What is her **angle** or point of view on her past writing experience?
4. How would you describe her **voice,** the way she sounds to you? Point out specific places in the text where you can "hear" Griffin's voice. Is it appropriate for her **purpose,** her **audience,** and her **angle** on the topic?

CREDITS

PART II

Writing in the Aims

CHAPTER 4

Narrating Experiences

ENGAGING QUESTIONS

In this chapter, you will engage with the following questions:

- What is the relationship between an experience and a narrative?
- Which thinking and writing skills can be gained by writing about personal experiences?
- What features of storytelling can be applied to personal experience essays?
- How do writers identify appropriate topics for personal experience essays?
- How do the elements of the rhetorical situation apply to the writing process for a personal experience essay?
- How do writers apply the steps of the writing process to personal experience essays?

WE LEARNED TO LOVE STORIES AS CHILDREN, AND WE CONTINUE TO LOVE THEM AS WE GROW. This chapter is about one kind of story, the **personal narrative,** *an account of something that has happened to us.* It answers two key questions: What happened? Why does it matter? Answering the first question draws readers into your story simply because people are interested in what happens to other people. Answering the second makes what happened an experience, something meaningful, worth remembering.

Experiences are not always major events. The *New York Times* has a weekly feature called "Metropolitan Diary," in which readers share their experiences of city life. Online, an array of travel blogs share the experiences of travelers who enjoy seeing different cultures. The diary entries and blogs like those published by Lonely Planet are effective because they have **angles,** *distinctive points of view or interpretations that make you think.*

What Is Interpreting Experience?

An **experience** is something that stands out in memory, *a departure from the routine.* When we have a memorable experience, we share it with others and talk about how we might understand it. As writers we create **narratives,** *stories based on memorable experiences.* We offer these stories to readers for enjoyment and contemplation, and we interpret them to explore what they mean.

CONCEPT CLOSE-UP Angle in Personal Narrative

All good writing depends on the writer having an angle on his or her topic. In personal narratives, the angle shows that the writer has thought about the experience and developed a point of view on it. The angle does the following:

- Helps the writer decide what details are relevant to include in the story
- Helps the reader see how the story is relevant to people other than the writer

ACTIVITY 4.1 *Writer's Notebook*

Interpreting Experience

Has a "little" experience struck you as surprising, funny, or thought provoking? It could be a conversational exchange or some other interaction between people; an observation about animal behavior; something you noticed on the freeway, at the mall, in a restaurant. Describe the experience for your readers, making it as vivid as you can. How would you describe your angle on the experience? ■

Why Write to Interpret Experience?

Narratives are among the most common kinds of writing we encounter. People write and read them because human beings enjoy sharing experiences and exploring what they mean. Personal narratives also develop thinking and writing skills applicable to all kinds of writing, among them the following:

- Sharing the meaning of an experience enables you to gain and hold reader attention. The key question is, **"How can you connect your experience with the lives, interests, and concerns of other people?"**
- In narrative genres such as memoirs, travel writing, and blogs, sharing experience provides the opportunity to assert your attitudes, ideas, and opinions. In other genres, such as political speeches or newspaper editorials, narratives can provide evidence and make emotional appeals.
- Interpreting experiences allows you to develop your **voice,** *how you sound to your readers.* Depending upon the purpose of your story, you may sound, for example, serious and sincere or warm and funny.
- Sharing stories about specific events helps you move beyond **stock responses**–*the standard things people say about something that happens.* We all know the typical reaction to a friend's betrayal of trust, but we can get beyond this stock response by posing questions such as the following: Was this person really a friend in whom I should have placed my trust? What role did I play in setting myself up to be betrayed? Critical thinking, which involves asking such questions, matters in all significant writing.

How Do Writers Interpret Experiences?

Narrative essays share five characteristics with fiction. That is, they work as all stories work by pulling together voice, plot, conflict, concrete and relevant details, and shared insight (see Figure 4.1).

Voice

Stories are told by a **narrator,** *the person telling the story.* You are the "I" who is writing about something that happened to you, and therefore your presence contributes to the story's meaning, mainly as point of view. For example, if you are writing about an event that occurred when you were younger and more limited in your understanding, you might tell the story from your more mature viewpoint but include scenes that show the viewpoint of your younger self.

Plot and Conflict

Every story has a **plot,** another word for *plan* or *story line.* Most plots begin by setting the scene and providing background information. Then, as the action of the story builds, the plot develops. The story's action depends on **conflict,** a *problem or source of tension,* which comes from lack of harmony in desires, ideas, or behavior. It can exist within a person, between people, or between a person and the circumstances. In most plots, there is a high point where the action or tension reaches a climax. In an autobiographical narrative, the plot usually ends by showing the narrator's personal growth or increased understanding.

FIGURE **4.1**

The Five Features of Storytelling

There are five important elements to successful storytelling: voice, plot, conflict, concrete and relevant details, and shared insight.

Concrete and Relevant Details

Stories contain sensory details: sights, sounds (including dialogue and people's voices), scents, and the way things feel to the touch or on the skin. Details make experiences vivid. In choosing what to include or leave out, favor details that contribute to bringing out the point of the story.

Shared Insight

Whether stated or implied by the action, personal narratives reveal the significance of an experience. This significance amounts to *shared insight* because readers come to see how your story relates to their lives and how it might help them interpret similar experiences.

READING **4.1**

Just Walk on By: A Black Man Ponders His Power to Alter Public Space

BRENT STAPLES

Born in 1951 and educated at Widener University and the University of Chicago, Brent Staples is a journalist and the author of Parallel Time: Growing Up in Black and White. *First published in 1986, "Just Walk on By" is a modern classic, a potent reflection on one of the subtler forms of racism African Americans struggle with almost daily.*

The opening sentence suggests that the narrator is about to commit a crime, but by the second paragraph it is clear that the voice is ironic. Instead of being angry about the woman's fear of him, he shows that he has developed a somewhat humorous perspective on such daily experiences.

1 My first victim was a woman—white, well dressed, probably in her early twenties. I came upon her late one evening on a deserted street in Hyde Park, a relatively affluent neighborhood in an otherwise mean, impoverished section of Chicago. As I swung onto the avenue behind her, there seemed to be a discreet, uninflammatory distance between us. Not so. She cast back a worried glance. To her, the youngish black man—a broad six feet two inches with a beard and billowing hair, both hands shoved into the pockets of a bulky military jacket—seemed menacingly close. After a few more quick glimpses, she picked up her pace and was soon running in earnest. Within seconds she disappeared into a cross street.

Note how Staples establishes his ethos, or good character, by mentioning his status as a graduate student at the University of Chicago. He has now made two moves to put readers on his side in the conflict between who he is and how others see him.

Personal narratives are often structured around a central conflict. In this case, the main conflict is between how others, such as the frightened white woman, see the narrator and his true nature as a nonviolent "softy."

2 That was more than a decade ago. I was 22 years old, a graduate student newly arrived at the University of Chicago. It was in the echo of that terrified woman's footfalls that I first began to know the unwieldy inheritance I'd come into—the ability to alter public space in ugly ways. It was clear that she thought herself the quarry of a mugger, rapist, or worse. Suffering a bout of insomnia, however, I was stalking sleep, not defenseless wayfarers. As a softy who is scarcely able to take a knife to a raw chicken—let alone hold it to a person's throat—I was surprised, embarrassed, and dismayed all at once.

Her flight made me feel like an accomplice in tyranny. It also made it clear that I was indistinguishable from the muggers who occasionally seeped into the area from the surrounding ghetto. That first encounter, and those that followed, signified that a vast, unnerving gulf lay between nighttime pedestrians—particularly women—and me. And I soon gathered that being perceived as dangerous is a hazard in itself. I only needed to turn a corner into a dicey situation, or crowd some frightened, armed person in a foyer somewhere, or make an errant move after being pulled over by a policeman. Where fear and weapons meet—and they often do in urban America—there is always the possibility of death.

> Good stories result in insights—that is, a better understanding of reality. In recent years, the news has included many black men shot by police officers. The underlying cause may be revealed here.

3 In that first year, my first away from my hometown, I was to become thoroughly familiar with the language of fear. At dark, shadowy intersections in Chicago, I could cross in front of a car stopped at a traffic light and elicit the *thunk, thunk, thunk, thunk* of the driver—black, white, male, or female—hammering down the door locks. On less traveled streets after dark, I grew accustomed to but never comfortable with people who crossed to the other side of the street rather than pass me. Then there were the standard unpleasantries with police, doormen, bouncers, cab drivers, and others whose business it is to screen out troublesome individuals *before* there is any nastiness.

> Staples is describing not one but many experiences. Some he simply sketches, as in this paragraph, but note the specifics of sounds and scenes, and the examples of people who have seen him as trouble.

4 I moved to New York nearly two years ago and I have remained an avid night walker. In central Manhattan, the near-constant crowd cover minimizes tense one-on-one street encounters. Elsewhere—visiting friends in SoHo, where sidewalks are narrow and tightly spaced buildings shut out the sky—things can get very taut indeed.

> Note the jump in time, but the smooth continuity of the theme of fears his presence causes when he is out walking at night.

5 Black men have a firm place in New York mugging literature. Norman Podhoretz in his famed (or infamous) 1963 essay, "My Negro Problem—and Ours," recalls growing up in terror of black males; they "were tougher than we were, more ruthless," he writes—and as an adult on the Upper West Side of Manhattan, he continues, he cannot constrain his nervousness when he meets black men on certain streets. Similarly, a decade later, the essayist and novelist Edward Hoagland extols New York where once "Negro bitterness bore down mainly on other Negroes." Where some see mere panhandlers, Hoagland sees "a mugger who is clearly screwing up his nerve to do more than just *ask* for money." But Hoagland has "the New Yorker's quick-hunch posture for broken-field maneuvering," and the bad guy swerves away.

> Historical background shows that fear of black men is nothing new, making what Staples is claiming more persuasive.

6 I often witness that "hunch posture," from women after dark on the warrenlike streets of Brooklyn where I live. They seem to set their faces on neutral and, with their purse straps strung across their chests bandolier style, they forge ahead as though bracing themselves against being tackled. I understand, of course, that the danger they perceive is not a hallucination. Women are particularly vulnerable to street violence, and young black males are drastically overrepresented among the perpetrators of that violence. Yet these truths are no solace against the kind of alienation that comes of being ever the suspect, against being set apart, a fearsome entity with whom pedestrians avoid making eye contact.

> Takes away reader resistance by conceding that urban violence perpetrated by black males occurs often enough to justify women being fearful of it. Still, the anxiety is exaggerated and makes every black man on the street a potential threat.

Staples provides background that helps to explain his own experience. Every experience has a background story, and Staples has woven in his childhood experiences that help to explain the stance, or attitude, he learned to take when confronted with the possibility of violence.

7 It is not altogether clear to me how I reached the ripe old age of 22 without being conscious of the lethality nighttime pedestrians attributed to me. Perhaps it was because in Chester, Pennsylvania, the small, angry industrial town where I came of age in the 1960s, I was scarcely noticeable against a backdrop of gang warfare, street knifings, and murders. I grew up one of the good boys, had perhaps a half-dozen fist fights. In retrospect, my shyness of combat has clear sources.

This reflection on "manliness" and his opting for being "timid, but a survivor" is Staples' angle in this essay—that is, the point of view that unifies the entire narrative. Note that his rejection of one kind of manliness, the kind that stresses intimidation, is not a matter of race but rather of gender: how we construct masculinity.

8 Many things go into the making of a young thug. One of those things is the consummation of the male romance with the power to intimidate. An infant discovers that random flailings send the baby bottle flying out of the crib and crashing to the floor. Delighted, the joyful babe repeats those motions again and again, seeking to duplicate the feat. Just so, I recall the points at which some of my boyhood friends were finally seduced by the perception of themselves as tough guys. When a mark cowered and surrendered his money without resistance, myth and reality merged—and paid off. It is, after all, only manly to embrace the power to frighten and intimidate. We, as men, are not supposed to give an inch of our lane on the highway; we are to seize the fighter's edge in work and in play and even in love; we are to be valiant in the face of hostile forces.

This paragraph helps to establish Staples' ethos, or character. His family's experiences explain his decision to be timid where many men might choose to be aggressive.

9 Unfortunately, poor and powerless young men seem to take all this nonsense literally. As a boy, I saw countless tough guys locked away; I have since buried several, too. They were babies, really—a teenage cousin, a brother of 22, a childhood friend in his mid-twenties—all gone down in episodes of bravado played out in the streets. I came to doubt the virtues of intimidation early on. I chose, perhaps even unconsciously, to remain a shadow—timid, but a survivor.

Staples returns to a point made earlier—that fear of black men makes life more risky for them. In paragraphs 10 and 11, he offers several examples of the real dangers black men face in situations that usually would not imperil white men at all. He weaves in more specific experiences to show how common these experiences are for black men.

10 The fearsomeness mistakenly attributed to me in public places often has a perilous flavor. The most frightening of these confusions occurred in the late 1970s and early 1980s when I worked as a journalist in Chicago. One day, rushing into the office of a magazine I was writing for with a deadline story in hand, I was mistaken for a burglar. The office manager called security and, with an ad hoc posse, pursued me through the labyrinthine halls, nearly to my editor's door. I had no way of proving who I was. I could only move briskly toward the company of someone who knew me.

11 Another time I was on assignment for a local paper and killing time before an interview. I entered a jewelry store on the city's affluent Near North Side. The proprietor excused herself and returned with an enormous red Doberman pinscher straining at the end of a leash. She stood, the dog extended toward me, silent to my questions, her eyes bulging nearly out of her head. I took a cursory look around, nodded, and bade her good night. Relatively speaking, however, I never fared as badly as another black male journalist. He went to nearby Waukegan, Illinois, a couple of summers ago to work on a story about a murderer who was born there. Mistaking the reporter for the killer, police hauled him from his car at gunpoint and but for his press credentials would probably have tried to book him. Such episodes are not uncommon. Black men trade tales like this all the time.

> The only place in the essay where Staples admits the rage he's had to suppress for being perceived as a criminal in public places. His resentment of white writers like Podhoretz also emerges here: They see the paranoia in blacks their own racism helps to create but are often blind to their own paranoia.

In "My Negro Problem—and Ours," Podhoretz writes that the hatred he feels for blacks makes itself known to him through a variety of avenues—one being his discomfort with that "special brand of paranoid touchiness" to which he says blacks are prone. No doubt he is speaking here of black men. In time, I learned to smother the rage I felt at so often being taken for a criminal. Not to do so would surely have led to madness—via that special "paranoid touchiness" that so annoyed Podhoretz at the time he wrote the essay. 12

I began to take precautions to make myself less threatening. I move about with care, particularly late in the evening. I give a wide berth to nervous people on subway platforms during the wee hours, particularly when I have exchanged business clothes for jeans. If I happen to be entering a building behind some people who appear skittish, I may walk by, letting them clear the lobby before I return, so as not to seem to be following them. I have been calm and extremely congenial on those rare occasions when I've been pulled over by the police. 13

> Martin Luther King Jr. said that black people live on tiptoe, always uncertain and under stress, never quite at ease. Here we see concretely what living on tiptoe means. A powerful conclusion to this personal narrative.

And on late-evening constitutionals along streets less traveled by, I employ what has proved to be an excellent tension-reducing measure: I whistle melodies from Beethoven and Vivaldi and the more popular classical composers. Even steely New Yorkers hunching toward nighttime destinations seem to relax, and occasionally they even join in the tune. Virtually everybody seems to sense that a mugger wouldn't be warbling bright, sunny selections from Vivaldi's *Four Seasons*. It is my equivalent of the cowbell that hikers wear when they know they are in bear country. 14

Questions for Discussion

1. "Where fear and weapons meet—and they often do in urban America—there is always the possibility of death" (paragraph 2). Because Staples, as a black man, is telling his own story, his emphasis is on the tension between black and white citizens. But urban violence, the meeting of fear and weapons, has many other sources of tension, some of which are not racial at all. What other sources of tension come to mind? Compared to race, how important are they?
2. Find examples of concrete sensory details, appeals to sight, sound, touch, and so on. How is each example relevant to the interpretation of the experience?
3. Reread paragraph 14. What is the impact of this last paragraph? Why did Staples end "Just Walk on By" this way?

Thinking as a Writer

What Is the Rhetorical Situation?

1. What is Staples' *purpose* in writing this essay? What is his *angle* on the topic? How would you describe his *voice*?
2. Who is Staples' intended *audience*? Many of his readers have no experience with racial prejudice as it existed when he was growing up or now. How does the writer help such people understand and connect with his story?
3. Personal narratives offer shared insight into life. What did you learn about the past and present from Staples' narrative? ■

READING 4.2

Driving Away

KATHERINE KRUEGER-LAND

The following narrative, written by a student in a first-year composition course at Southern Methodist University, tells a common story—the struggle with substance abuse—in a compelling way. Note especially how well the author handles dialogue.

The first car I ever owned was a fifteen-year-old, lipstick-red, '91 Ford Thunderbird. 1991: The car was too recent to be cool, but too old to be reliable. Still, I loved it. My parents bought it for me when I got out of rehab and moved down to La Grange, Texas, to live with my Aunt Priscilla and Uncle Kelley. 1

I was lucky that they would take me; I had nowhere else to go. I was considered a serious gamble: no one wanted a relapsed Katherine on their hands. Yet they took me in, helped me get a job waiting tables, and treated me like an adult. I consider them my second family. 2

Apart from having had relatively few options, there was one other enticing reason to choose Texas: Nick Nolan. Although I intended to stay sober and made him swear never to tempt me, it still seemed a good idea to have an old friend around just in case I changed my mind. 3

Nick and I had been running buddies since high school. During our freshman year in college, I spent fall and spring breaks down at A&M partying with him. We had a platonic relationship built entirely around getting as stupidly high as possible and sustaining it until we dropped. 4

Nick Nolan was fun: quick to laugh, quick to anger, cruel and uproarious, dishonest, manipulative and narcissistic, and at times disarmingly self-effacing. He was a violent drunk, an adventurous stoner, and a suicidal, self-harming depressive with the impulsivity of a toddler. In short: perfect. 5

Perfect, that is, if you want to grab an 8-ball and a shotgun and trespass on an airfield to shoot off rounds at your own pants hanging in a tree, drive to the coast but miss the sunrise just to pass out stoned watching cartoons in a motel room, and wake up in time to crash your Houston dealer's family dinner—"watch out for the dogs and don't wake the baby"—where your nose bleeds all over the new couch. 6

But that was before I got sober. 7

I had been in La Grange for two months when I finally heard from Nick. I was working at the Marburger Antique Fair helping out a family friend, Becky Barnsdall, at her stall in Tent D. During my lunch hour I would wander around the nearby fairgrounds and comb through the junk. I was admiring a display of decapitated dolls' heads when he called me. 8

"Hey Nick what's up?" 9

"Dude, I had a freakin' heart attack yesterday!" *A heart attack?* 10

"Wait, what?" 11

"I know, right?" 12

"Are you ok?" 13

14 "Tommy just picked me up from the hospital with a fifth."

15 "Should you be drinking?" I whispered, self-conscious in front of the dolls.

16 "Probably not," he said.

17 With my cell phone still pinned to my ear, I started tracking across the hay-strewn grounds toward my car, past armless mannequins, old Coca-Cola bottles, wooden toy-wagons, and buckets full of colorful glass beads. On the other end of the line Nick told me his story: the chest pains, the gasping, the ambulance, the hospital stay.

18 "So now that I'm better you have to come celebrate."

19 "I'm working."

20 "Quit."

21 "I need the money. Besides, you're drinking; it won't be any fun for me."

22 "Then you'll just have to drink with us."

23 "You know I can't do that, Nick."

24 He sighed, "I know, I know," and paused. "Krueger, man, I'm not going to make you do anything you don't want to do."

25 "I know," I answered. And I believed it.

* * *

26 I was at his house on the Tuesday afternoon three months later when Nick was again rushed to the hospital. We were sitting on the couch inside watching South Park with the dog, JD. Named for James Dean, he was half Dalmatian, half pit bull, and the sweetest dog you ever met. He liked to sit on top of the sofa back like a giant cat and lean his sweet warm face on your shoulder.

27 Nick had gone into the other room to get his guitar; he generally could not watch TV without doing something else at the same time. Several minutes elapsed before I heard the knocking. I called but he did not answer. All I heard were two more muffled knocks.

28 I got up from the sofa and peered around the doorframe into the bedroom and there he was, lying on his back, his face turning red, his right hand clutching his left side. As he struggled to breathe he looked up at me, his eyes wide and pleading. The sight momentarily shocked me: I'd never known him to be afraid of anything. I bent over him to see if he was hurt, but I already knew what was happening. I reached for my phone.

29 "911, what is your emergency?"

30 "I think my friend is having a heart attack."

31 "Is he breathing?"

32 "Yes."

33 "Is he awake?"

34 "Yes."

35 "Is he able to tell you what's wrong?"

36 "No, he's gasping, he can't talk."

37 "What is your location, ma'am?" I didn't know the address.

38 "I'm on McCommas, past Winding, uhh, hold on—"

39 "Are you in a house?"

40 "Yes. Hold on—" I rifled through the papers on his desk, but couldn't find any letters addressed to him.

41 "And what is the address of the house, ma'am?"

"It's his house, I don't know the address, just hold on—" I gave Nick an exasperated 42
look and dashed out of the room, climbing over the dog to keep him from getting out the front door, and ran to the mailbox. "2389 Alhambra. That's 2-3-8-9 A-l-h-a-m-b-r-a."

In a rush of nylon jackets and plastic gloves, the paramedics came and with cool 43
efficiency swept him off the floor, onto a gurney, into the ambulance, and off to the hospital. I followed them, and found Nick in a bed divided by curtains from three other patients in a small holding area. He sat up when he saw me.

"The doctor said I need to quit doing drugs," he smiled weakly. 44

"How do you feel?" He looked small to me. He's tall and strong, but lying down and 45
wearing a hospital gown, he looked frail.

"Bad." 46

"You look like it," I said. He chuckled, and then coughed. 47

"They told me I'd die if I don't quit," Nick said. 48

"So will you?" 49

"Yeah, maybe." 50

I left Nick in the hospital hooked up to an IV watching television and drove home. 51
Being in the hospital had made me claustrophobic. After all, I'd only just checked myself out of a hospital a few months before. Perversely, I felt a little nostalgic for the insanity of living life in self-destruct mode. But I didn't want to go back. I didn't want to wear shoes without laces and have my blood pressure taken at 5:00 a.m. everyday and sit in a group talking about feeling worthless. *Still,* I thought, *it wasn't all bad.*

* * *

The last time I saw Nick, I was just stopping by on my way up from La Grange to 52
Dallas, where I was soon to move. I was sitting out on his back porch on the sofa we had once lit on fire (quite by accident) listening to him tell stories, which he's good at, and make plans, which he's even better at, although he never follows through on anything. After a few minutes he paused, dug around in the dirty seat cushions for a lighter, and lit a cigarette for himself, and one for me. He smoked Camel Turkish Golds, the ones with the pretty blue borders. I smoked Pall Malls, in a soft-pack, back then.

"I need to quit smoking," he said. He meant pot, I was sure. 53

"Yeah, maybe." 54

"I need to quit with the coke, too." 55

"You look thin," I told him. 56

"I'm down to 130 now. I was 175 a couple months ago." 57

Jeez, I thought. *At 6´3˝, 130 pounds isn't much.* 58

"You look really thin," I repeated. And he looked tired, too. And not in a didn't-sleep- 59
last-night way, but in a haven't-really-slept-in-weeks way.

"I don't eat much." 60

"That's the coke." 61

"And the pot." 62

"You look tired." 63

"I know. I haven't been sleeping." 64

"Maybe you should quit." 65

"Yeah, maybe." 66

I was surprised to see him so reflective. Maybe he really would quit, maybe he was 67
finally ready. I got up to leave, sliding open the glass back door—JD bouncing cheerfully into the house behind me. I grabbed my purse, slipped on my shoes, and was just trying to open the front door without letting the dog out when I looked up and saw Nick standing by the back door.

"Hey, wait, if I'm going to quit, then you need to smoke with me one last time." 68

"I can't, Nick, you know that." 69

"Sure you can. I'll even let you roll it, old school." 70

"No, Nick." *But I could.* 71

"Come on." 72

"No, Nick." *But I want to.* 73

"Just one more time, and then we'll both quit together." 74

"I already quit. I quit a year ago." 75

"Exactly, it'll be no big deal." 76

"It *is* a big deal," I said, angrily. He had promised not to pressure me. 77

"No, it's not." *You pathetic fool,* I thought. *You have no idea what I went through. You* 78
have no idea how hard it was to leave everything behind.

"You just don't get it, Nick. You can't stick with anything, and you don't understand 79
how anyone else can either. That's why you'll never get sober. That's why the stuff is going to kill you."

And with that, I climbed over the dog and squeezed out the front door. I was shaking 80
with anger and fear as I paced down the driveway, and started to climb into my old red T-Bird. I was tempted to turn back, to apologize and have one more good time with my old running buddy, but I was already in motion, the decision already made. *No, I won't do it. I want to, but I won't.* I had passed the test.

I glanced back and saw him standing there, one hand holding open the front door, the 81
other firmly grasping JD's collar as he wriggled wildly, desperate to run after the passing cars.

We looked at each other, and it seemed to me he was a lot farther away. He was 82
miles away, years away. Already he was part of another time, another life, one I could not go back to. There was a gulf between us and a long narrow bridge: I had driven across, and he had not, and that's all there was to it.

"Have a good drive," he called. 83

"Thanks." 84

"Come back soon." 85

"I will," I lied, and drove away. 86

Questions for Discussion

1. Note especially in paragraphs 8, 17, and 26 the use of effective descriptive detail. How do the details contribute to the themes of the story?
2. Conflict is essential to a good narrative. What are the sources of conflict in "Driving Away"? How does the author develop them?
3. Review two instances of conversation in the story. What are the exchanges like? How and why is the writer's use of dialogue effective?

Thinking as a Writer

What Is the Rhetorical Situation?

1. What is Krueger-Land's *purpose* in writing this essay? What is her *angle* on the topic? How would you describe her voice?
2. Who is the writer's intended *audience*? If you have never struggled with addiction yourself, how did the writer help you to understand and sympathize with people who do struggle with it?
3. The story gives us insight into friends, people we love and need but whose impact on us can be negative as well as positive. How would you describe this insight? How does the insight apply to your friendships? ■

The Assignment

Write a narrative sharing a personal experience and offering insight into its meaning. The goal is to tell an interesting story that leaves your readers with insight they can relate to their own lives.

What Can I Write About?

Stories that hold the reader's interest involve conflict or tension. Consider experiences that did one or more of the following:

- Resulted in intellectual or moral growth, an increase in maturity.
- Challenged your beliefs, attitudes, or values.
- Allowed you to see your behavior from someone else's perspective.
- Disappointed or surprised you about your own character or the character of someone you thought you knew.
- Led you to see some past event in a new context or category that transformed its meaning.
- Called conventional wisdom about right and wrong into question.
- Created a dilemma, a choice between two paths of action, neither of which is entirely satisfactory.

Remember that the significance of an event is *not in the event itself but in what you make of it,* the angle or point of view you bring to it or discover in thinking or writing about it. Nevertheless, finding the right topic for you does matter. If you are having trouble locating yours, consider the following possibilities:

- **Distinctive people, places, and objects.** Staples focused on just one dimension of racial prejudice: the fear many people have of black men; Krueger-Land focused on one part of her experience with drugs, the temptation to go back to them. Stories about places include journeys to wilderness or foreign places and revisiting places from our past.

- **A troubling memory.** Perhaps you liked a person that others did not like, perhaps even someone you should not have liked. Or you did something unethical, but you would do it again. Or you visited a place meant to stimulate a certain reaction, but you actually responded "inappropriately."
- **Class readings.** The readings in this chapter may remind you of an experience you should write about. Perhaps a concept you encountered in one of your courses gives you a new angle for understanding a past event.
- **Your own or other people's blogs.** Look over your blog for promising topics, such as reunions with friends from high school, something that happened at work or at home with your family, and decisions you have made since starting college.
- **Work or community experience.** Consider times of conflict or tension where you work or the insights you have gained from internships, volunteer work, church activities, attending social events, and the like.

How Do I Interpret Experience? Questioning the Rhetorical Situation

Begin by picturing a **rhetorical situation** for your writing project, a real-world context for communicating. You should consider the *key variables in any act of communication:*

- A writer with something to say
- A reader the writer wishes to reach
- A kind of text appropriate to the writing task

These three variables will affect many decisions in the composing process.

Writer: What Is My Purpose, and What Impression Should Readers Have of Me?

Autobiographical narratives share an interesting and meaningful experience with an appropriate readership. Because the experience comes from your life, your purpose is self-expression. You are revealing a part of yourself. Because you are sharing a part of yourself with others, you want them to enjoy reading the story and gain from it insight that they will remember.

Your purpose implies your role as a writer for this assignment. Both Staples and Krueger-Land assume the role of the experienced person, someone who is "in the know" from having experienced being a feared minority in predominantly white neighborhoods or being a recovered addict. Your role in writing your story will be much like theirs: No one else knows your life better than you do; no one else is in a better position to say what it means.

Being experienced does not mean that you know everything or have all the answers. You can freely admit to gaps in your knowledge, even to being puzzled about your own motives or the motives of someone else in your story. Just be honest about what happened to you and how well you understand it.

Audience: Who Is My Reader?

Because almost anyone can read and enjoy an interesting story, it is tempting to think of your readers as everyone. However, stories are always told *to someone,* and actual readerships are never everyone. The key question is: Who might gain most from reading about your experience? They should be your readership.

Why is it important to have a definite readership in mind? First, you have to assume a certain level of existing knowledge. Staples, for example, does not explain who Beethoven and Vivaldi are, or what the latter's *Four Seasons* sound like. He has to assume a certain amount of knowledge about music and trust our imagination to conceive how a black man whistling classical tunes would be perceived by others in a public place. Otherwise he would have to explain too much. Likewise, you will not want to clutter your narrative with too much explanation. Second, the readership you choose helps you to decide what to include and what to emphasize in your story. Krueger-Land was writing primarily for people who may not fully understand how hard it is to escape addiction, which is why she emphasized her entanglement with a person from her earlier, drug-dominated life.

Text: What Moves Can I Make?

Readings 4.1 and 4.2 in this chapter and the student example at the end of this chapter make all or some of the following basic moves:

- Establish the time and place of your experience.
- Provide vivid details in descriptions, selecting from everything you could describe only those details that connect with what your story means.
- Share what you said and thought, using some dialogue or conversational exchange when appropriate.
- Zoom in for "close-ups" of important moments in your experience.
- Supply transitional paragraphs to help your readers move from one part of your experience to another.
- Structure your story around a central conflict.
- Imply or state directly what your story means.

How Do I Interpret Experience? Engaging the Writing Process

No two people compose in exactly the same way, and even the same person may go through the writing process in different ways with different assignments. Nevertheless, because no one can attend to everything at once, there are phases in handling any significant writing task. You begin by preparing to write, generating content and finding your angle.

The next phase is planning and drafting your paper, getting a version, however rough it may be, on paper or screen so that you have something to work with during the next two stages. The first stage is revision, where your attention should be on content, arrangement, and style. The second is editing to take care of problems at the paragraph and sentence level, such as loss of focus and coherence, awkward or unclear sentences, and errors of grammar, spelling, and punctuation.

Preparing to Write

When you have decided what story to tell, explore it by writing informally to generate ideas and material for drafting.

ACTIVITY 4.2 *Writer's Notebook*

Asking Questions about the Elements of Your Narrative

Using lists, diagrams, and/or a series of notes to yourself, jot down your responses to the following questions:

- **Characters:** Besides you, what other people played a role in this experience? Of these, who were the most important? Why?
- **Setting:** Picture a scene from the experience. What sensory details have stuck in your memory? What do you recall seeing, tasting, hearing, smelling, or touching? Ask *why* you recall those details: Perhaps you can discover a pattern in what you remember that will lead to an insight or imply what the story means.
- **Plot:** What conflict or tension makes this experience interesting for you and for your readers? What was the moment of greatest tension? How was the tension resolved? If it was not fully resolved, what problems or issues remain?
- **Angle:** Explore possible meanings or interpretations of the experience. What was your point of view when you were living it? As you look back on it, has your interpretation of it changed? What central insight or insights can you offer? ■

ACTIVITY 4.3 *Writer's Notebook*

Discussing Your Topic Idea

Post your best ideas for your narrative on your class's discussion board. When everyone has posted, read through the posts and send replies to at least three classmates. In your reply, ask questions to stimulate thought about the event's significance, the conflict or tension that could drive a good plot, and the relevance of the experience to others. ■

Asking Questions: Framing the Plot

Choosing where to begin your story is one of the more important choices you will make. For instance, how much background do you need to provide so your readers will understand the story?

Some narratives open with background material, some with the action itself. Either way, draw your readers in with something specific, such as Krueger-Land's new living situation after rehab or Staples' reference to his "first victim."

Once you have decided how to open the story, plot out the key scenes. Think of your essay as if it were a video with action, setting, characters, and dialogue. Often one of these elements dominates a particular scene. For example, Krueger-Land's memory of the fun she once had with Nick dominates the early scenes in her narrative.

ACTIVITY 4.4 *Writer's Notebook*

Listing Key Scenes

Depict your experience in a series of scenes. If you were making a film, which moments would you show in action, and which would a narrator summarize? In Staples' story, there are two kinds of key scenes:

- Ones that depict the fear he causes just by being a large black man
- Ones that reveal the peril to his own life and safety simply because he inspires fear by walking in public places

List two or three key scenes in your experience. How can each contribute to building the tension, and which one will you use to resolve it? ■

Borrowing a Film Technique: The Storyboard

Some writers of fiction and nonfiction borrow the storyboard technique used in filmmaking (see Figure 4.2 on page 66). Carolyn Coman–author of many acclaimed novels for young people, including *What Jamie Saw*–got the idea of storyboarding from reading comic books with her young daughter. Coman draws a blank square for each main scene in a story and, using stick figures, draws the central action of the scene. Sketching the scene is a kind of visual drafting. As with a rough draft, when you reread it, you discover surprises, clues to meaning. As Coman says, "The size of the stick figures, the amount of white space around them, the kinds of marks you make . . . all of these have things to tell you about tone, distance, point of view."[1]

It also helps you organize around a main idea. If you write a sentence or two beneath each drawing, the storyboard will help you find connections between scenes and identify the angle or main idea of your narrative. Even a single sentence about the emotion or tension each scene conveys will help you organize and sort the material.

1. Carolyn Coman, "Seeing the Whole Story: Storyboarding," *Highlights Foundation*, www.highlightsfoundation.org.

A storyboard made of individual diagram cards offers several advantages. You can do the following:

- Add, delete, or rearrange scenes
- Sketch visually or verbally a scene's setting and characters
- Create dialogue
- Indicate what you will be telling the reader

An alternative is to make a series of boxes on sheets of plain paper, in the style of a comic book, and draw your scenes in sequence.

Student Example: Molly Tilton's Storyboard for a Personal Narrative

Figure 4.2 shows an example of how one student used the storyboard technique to get her story started and focused. Molly Tilton wrote about an experience she had while working as a waitress in a diner. A regular customer, Frank, was waiting for his daughter to join him for breakfast; as the event unfolded, Tilton gained some insight about her own life. Sketching scenes for her story helped Tilton order the events, including the use of a flashback, and decide which moments to focus on in her narrative.

FIGURE **4.2**

An Example of a Simple Storyboard

Storyboards don't need to be elaborate to be helpful in piecing your story together. Grab a pencil and some paper and try sketching out simple "scenes" that capture critical moments of your personal story.

Courtesy of Molly Tilton

ACTIVITY 4.5 *In Your Own Work*

Visualizing Your Story

Using storyboard sketches on index cards, work out a plan for your story. Think about how you might open the essay, how you might work in background information, and how the essay should end. ■

Drafting Your Paper

What should be most on your mind as you are writing your first draft of the narrative? Focus on your voice and on development and organization.

What Voice Is Appropriate in Personal Narratives?

When we say that writing has voice, we mean that readers can sense the human presence in the words. The author's personal interest and angle on the topic are evident in the writing. *Well-chosen details convey your lived experience best* and connect with readers more effectively than general statements.

Consider these sentences from Staples' "Just Walk on By."

> I often witness that hunch-posture, from women after dark on the warrenlike streets of Brooklyn where I live. They seem to set their faces on neutral and, with their purses strung across their chests bandolier style, they forge ahead as though bracing themselves against being tackled.

Staples expresses well the terror of people, especially white women, in walking alone at night in our cities. His description implies what his "victims" are feeling and thinking without having to say what they are.

ACTIVITY 4.6 *Thinking as a Writer*

Developing and Organizing Your Personal Narrative

You have many options in writing your story. It can start at the beginning, at the end, or in the middle. You can omit events that do not contribute to your point and zoom in on details that do. You can use flashbacks and flash-forwards.

Begin by writing a central episode or scene. Structure the other scenes around it. Then concentrate on background, transitions, and opening and concluding strategies. ■

ACTIVITY 4.7 *Writer's Notebook*

Composing Your Scenes

Concentrate on details of setting, character, and action. Consider posting your scenes on a blog or discussion board or sharing them with other students in some other way to receive feedback. ■

Revising Your Draft

In revising, concentrate especially on the following:

- **Interpretation** Consider what writing about the experience has revealed to you. Perhaps the meaning of it has changed and therefore needs reformulating.
- **Focus** Look for opportunities to add relevant details that come to mind as you revise.
- **Shape** Craft your story into a well-paced narrative. Get to the action as quickly as possible. Keep the story moving. Make statements of your thoughts and emotions short and simple.

Write a brief assessment of your draft. Exchange your draft and assessment with at least one other student and use the revision questions in the Art of Questioning box to help each other decide what needs to improve.

THE ART OF QUESTIONING Revision Checklist for Interpreting Experiences

1. Make a list of the best images in the draft. Do these words and phrases present concrete, sensory details of the place?
2. What do these images have in common? Do they imply a theme or central idea? If you cannot find a theme or idea emerging *through the details,* review the draft again to locate its best scene. What theme for the whole story might be developed from it?
3. What conflict does the narrator face? Do you encounter the conflict early in the story? How does it build and come to a crisis or point of maximum tension? How is it resolved?
4. What parts of the essay do not contribute to the theme or the conflict? Consider cutting them.
5. Can you make any suggestions for improving the organization? Should events be presented in a different order? Should the story open or end more quickly?
6. Are there any places in the story where the author spends too much time talking about emotions, how he or she feels? Replace with details that convey emotion without having to say what it is.
7. Either to clear up confusion or to satisfy curiosity, what might your reader like to know more about? Consider developing parts of the essay to answer questions your reader might have.

Student Example: Excerpts from Tilton's Draft

The most common revision problem when interpreting experience is underdevelopment, not supplying enough detail for the reader to understand the story. Here is a paragraph from Molly Tilton's first draft of "The Monday Omelette," a story about fathers and daughters, the revised version of which appears on pages 71–73:

> He would ask a lot of questions per usual and tell me how much he missed me that day. I would apologize and say that I would see him tomorrow morning and that we could go to lunch, knowing that the plan would most likely fall through. Then he would drag himself upstairs to bed, without the smile on his face.

Here is the revised version:

> He would ask a lot of questions per usual and tell me how much he missed me that day. He would always assure me it was OK. I would apologize and tell him that I would try to see him the next day. That promise always sounded empty. After the divorce, I couldn't guarantee when I would see him. Alternating between my mother's and father's houses was sometimes too complicated. And then I had my friends. I was busy. I was sorry. After I hung up the phone, I would imagine him turning off the TV and dragging himself upstairs to bed. I pictured the let-down expression on his face. He had been ditched, stood up by his own daughter.

The revised paragraph is not just longer, but better. Note the improvements:

- "After the divorce" adds important information: It explains why father and daughter have to make plans to see each other.
- The details about her own life make standing up her father understandable, even if she is using them as an excuse.
- Because she cannot know for sure how her father reacted when she did not show up, it is better to say "I would imagine" what his response was.
- Taken together, the details she adds give greater support to her feelings of guilt, which readers will then understand and relate to more easily.

Examine your own essay for opportunities to add detail. The key question is: **What do my readers need?** Tilton saw that they needed to know more about the father-daughter situation and why she feels guilty. She added only what she needed to include, and the result was a stronger story.

Editing Your Revised Draft

An important concern in editing is cohesion, whether sentences connect smoothly. People sometimes use the word *flow* to describe cohesion. When writing has cohesion, each sentence picks up on something in the one before it, and readers' expectations about what comes next are rewarded. When writing lacks cohesion, it sounds choppy. Below are some examples to show how editing can improve cohesion. In this passage, student Molly Tilton describes the man in the diner waiting for his daughter:

Before Editing

Frank waited for another forty minutes. With a smile, he told me, "My daughter will be here soon, but I am just going to order anyway."

This point interrupts the point about the phone call.

Then his cell phone rang. He was sitting in the beat-up gray booth, and I felt the room go dark. Something had come up. She would not be able to meet him.

This sentence too abruptly shifts the topic from Frank's daughter to the narrator.

I was a daughter. I had done this. I had broken similar news to my own father before.

After Editing

This point now helps to set up the scene for the call.

Forty minutes later, he was still sitting alone in the beat-up gray booth, waiting. With a smile he told me, "My daughter will be here soon, but I'm just going to order anyway."

Then his cell phone rang . . . I felt the room go dark. Something had come up. She would not be able to meet him.

Adding a transitional sentence helps the reader see the connection that the writer left unstated.

Suddenly, the scene felt familiar to me. I was a daughter. I had done this. I had broken similar news to my own father.

The following two passages follow a flashback scene in which the narrator recalls having "stood up" her father after she had told him she would visit him.

Before Editing

This sentence offers a great image, but it would work better as a transition from the flashback to the present time.

I went into the kitchen to bring out Frank's meal. I was sweating from guilt of being a daughter. When I delivered Frank his omelette, he lifted his face, fake-smiled, and said "Ahh, Miss Molly. Thank you so much!"

After Editing

The image now works as a transition from Tilton's thoughts about her own father to her experience with the other father in the diner.

Sweating from the guilt of being a daughter, I went back into the kitchen to bring out Frank's meal. When I delivered his omelette, he lifted his face, fake-smiled, and said "Ahh, Miss Molly. Thank you so much!"

ACTIVITY 4.8 *In Your Own Work*

Editing Your Revised Draft

Every writer has editing problems. Keep a checklist of your editing problems. For instance, list words that you misspelled. If you did not punctuate a sentence correctly, write down the sentence and circle or underline the correct punctuation mark. If you need examples to remember other types of problems—such as editing for flow—take one from your paper. Check your revised draft for your most common problems.

When editing at the sentence-level, try reading your revised draft aloud. Repetitions and wordy passages are easier to hear than to see. Study your instructor's marks and comments on every paper. Add new editing problems to your list as needed. *Always check your next paper for the problems you have listed.* In this way you can reduce your characteristic editing problems. ■

REVISED STUDENT EXAMPLE

Tilton 1

Molly Tilton

Professor Channell

English 1301

May 6, 2016

The Monday Omelette

"Hi! My name is Molly and I will be taking care of you today. Coffee, anyone?" 1
These were the words I spoke daily when working as a waitress at Bacarri's Diner on Cape Cod this past summer.

> Establishes the setting for the story, both time and place.

The weekend people were sometimes tough customers: the grumpy old man 2
whose orange juice was not cold enough, the woman whose bacon was too burnt, and the screaming three-year-old girl who threw her pancakes on the ground. A mother complained about the coffee spills from my hands shaking from nervousness. I apologized, grabbed five napkins, and blamed it on the wobbly tables.

Serving breakfast on Monday morning always seemed so simple. After a 3
weekend of impatient customers, I was delighted to wait on regulars, who were kind and respectful.

> Good contrast between hectic weekends and weekday customers.

The diner was an old-fashioned, low-key place. The light blue walls were hung 4
with Marilyn Monroe photos, and Elvis was almost always playing on the jukebox. The paint was chipped and the white tile floor, although clean, looked dingy. These details only augmented the retro feeling. The older folks said they felt like they were back in the sixties.

> Details chosen to imply the generation of people who like the diner—her parents' generation.

All the regulars sat at the off-white countertop. Frank came in everyday, usually 5
twice. He smiled like a child, but his white hair gave away his age. He would wear a collared shirt and khaki pants every morning. In the afternoons, he was more relaxed, usually wearing his beat-up jean shorts. His lunch order never varied: a hot dog and a cup of beans. I never really got to know Frank that well. He did not talk much, but called me "Miss Molly" and said I reminded him of his daughter.

> Introduces key character and establishes relation in her mind between Frank and her own father.

Tilton 2

6 The weekends were special for Frank. His daughter met him for breakfast, and they would sit in one of the booths, chatting about Hailey's busy life. She was in her third year of law school. Hailey had Frank's smile and his delicate face. Her long brown hair perfectly draped over her sundress. She usually ordered French toast or a grilled muffin. When Hailey was there, Frank upgraded his breakfast order to the egg-white, sausage-and-peppers omelette.

Details indicate the ties between father and daughter in appearance and show how special seeing his daughter is to Frank.

7 On this Monday morning, Frank arrived around 8:30 and took a seat in one of the booths instead of his weekday perch at the counter. I poured him a cup of coffee, and he told me he was not going to order at the moment because he was waiting for his daughter to meet him for breakfast. His face was glowing when he told me. I could feel his excitement. He sat there for ten minutes and, still smiling, asked for more coffee.

8 Forty minutes later he was still sitting alone in the beat-up gray booth, waiting. With a smile he told me, "My daughter will be here soon but I'm just going to order anyway."

9 Then his cell phone rang. He answered. "Hi, where are you? Oh, that's OK. I know about Mondays. No, it's OK. We'll do it another day." I felt the room go dark. Something had come up. She would not be able to meet him.

The narrative tension builds with each reference to the passing of time.

10 Suddenly, the scene felt familiar to me. I was a daughter. I had done this. I had broken similar news to my own father.

11 I pictured my dad, sitting on the brown leather couch on a Friday night watching the news—anticipating my arrival. He was drifting off to sleep. Then his phone rang.

12 "Hi, Dad. It's me. I'm sorry, but I'm going to stay at Courtney's tonight. I'll call you in the morning, OK?"

Putting Frank's experience into the context of her own life gives Tilton an angle for interpreting her experience.

13 He would ask a lot of questions per usual and tell me how much he missed me that day. He would always assure me it was OK. I would apologize and tell him that I would try to see him the next day. That promise always sounded empty. After the divorce, I couldn't guarantee when I would see him. Alternating between my mother's and father's houses was sometimes too complicated. And then I had my friends. I was busy. I was sorry. After I hung up the phone, I would imagine him

Tilton 3

Effective understated ending, with no explicit statement of the lesson inherent in the story.

turning off the TV and dragging himself upstairs to bed. I pictured the let-down expression on his face. He had been ditched, stood up by his own daughter.

Sweating from the guilt of being a daughter, I went back into the kitchen to bring out Frank's meal. When I delivered his omelette, he lifted his face, fake-smiled, and said "Ahh, Miss Molly. Thank you so much!" 14

CREDITS

page 56: Staples, Brent. (1986). "Just Walk On By: Black Men and Public Space." *Ms. Magazine*. Used with permission. All rights reserved. **page 57:** Courtesy of Katherine Krueger-Land **page 71:** Courtesy of Molly Tilton

CHAPTER 5

Describing People and Places

ENGAGING QUESTIONS

In this chapter, you will engage with the following questions:

- What are the distinguishing characteristics of a profile?
- What are the purposes of profile writing?
- What modes apply to the specific tasks of profile writing?
- How do writers identify appropriate topics for profiles?
- How do the components of the rhetorical situation apply to the writing process for a profile?
- How do writers apply the steps of the writing process when composing a profile?

MOST PEOPLE FIND NOTHING MORE INTERESTING THAN OTHER PEOPLE. That is why we gossip, tell stories about ourselves and others at parties, watch television shows about famous people, enjoy Facebook, and Instagram, and read biographies. The important questions are: Who is this person? What is she doing now? Why does this person and his activities matter? The **profile** answers these questions by *depicting people who matter to us so that our readers will know about them too.*

What Is a Profile?

A **profile** *describes a subject of interest to the writer, such as a person, organization, place, event, or situation.* While some profiles can be purely informative–facts about a corporation or a prominent figure in business–the profile essay, which is the assignment in this chapter, is more subjective. A **profile essay** expresses the *writer's interpretation of the subject; the writer chooses what to include and omit based on the impression of the subject he or she wants readers to have.* This impression comes from the writer's *angle* or point of view, which gives the paper focus and purpose. A profile should show why the subject matters to the writer and should matter to readers as well.

CONCEPT CLOSE-UP More about Profiles

Profiles depict a person, place, organization, event, or situation. They do the following:

- Provide *snapshots,* not a complete or even necessarily balanced view.
- Seek to create a *memorable impression.*

- *Convey information but not in a detached or objective way:* The interpretation is yours, the writer's, and therefore implies what matters to you.
- Are often *ethical and moral,* concerned with right and wrong, good and bad, the desirable and the undesirable.
- Strive for *lifelike immediacy.*

Mark Zuckerberg, creator of the social networking site Facebook, has been profiled countless times in recent years. Though celebrity profiles can be very satisfying for us to read, might a profile of the ordinary be more enriching and meaningful to our lives?

Why Write Profiles?

We encounter profiles in many places: in human interest pieces written for magazines, newspapers, and television shows; online in blog posts and on websites; in speeches that pay tribute to important people. Profiles are also often part of larger pieces of writing; for example, a profile of Abraham Lincoln may be included in a book about the Civil War.

In a world of more than 7 billion people who inhabit nearly all places on our planet and who come together in an almost infinite number of organizations, events, situations, and online social networks, why single out this person, or that place, organization, and so on, for attention?

In our media-saturated world, one answer is obvious: because someone or something is famous, and people therefore want to know more. It explains profiles of a person like Bill Gates, a place like the White House, an organization like Habitat for Humanity, an event like a basketball team losing a game 100 to 0, and a situation like the unending conflict between Israel and Palestine.

THE ART OF QUESTIONING What Matters?

Profiles involve ethics; that is, they always imply questions such as the following:

- What counts most in life?
- How should I treat other people?
- What's the right thing to do?
- How can I maintain integrity amid all the pressures to do what others want me to do or what the immediate situation seems to require?

Writers select subjects for profiles based on their values; how they depict their subjects implies what matters to them. Consequently, the most important question when you read or write a profile is this: **Why does this matter?** Put another way: **Why do you care?**

However, some of the best profiles are about the little known, even the seemingly insignificant. How do we explain these? Such profiles reveal a motive more profound than satisfying media-generated curiosity. They are protests against obscurity, a struggle for attention and memory. "This person," they say or imply, "no matter how unknown otherwise, matters." "This place, organization, event, or situation you have never heard of is more important than you think." Such profiles enlarge reader awareness and reveal the value of someone or something that may never make the evening news or even turn up in a Google search.

The questions, "Why does this matter? Why do I care?" are important in writing profiles. Hold them in mind as you read the profiles by Joel Achenbach, Elizabeth Murphy, and Molly Tilton in this chapter. **What do they value? Do you value the same things? Why or why not?** Keep them in mind also as you move into the assignment. The questions have everything to do with the subject you select and how you treat it.

How Do Writers Compose Profiles?

Profiles strive for lifelike immediacy, ways to connect readers intimately to the subject. Some of the strategies writers use to compose successful profiles include:

- Vivid description.
- Interesting details from available background information.
- Quotations of what people say and what others say about them.
- Use of dialogue to report conversational exchanges.
- Use of photographs and other visual means of transmitting information, such as maps and drawings.

In the readings that follow you will see how all of these tools work in detail.

READING 5.1

Writing with the Master

JOEL ACHENBACH

Joel Achenbach is the author of seven books and a distinguished journalist for the Washington Post. *His profile of John McPhee, a legendary writer and teacher of writing and a major contributor to the development of literary nonfiction, pays tribute to a mentor, not only for Achenbach but also for several generations of McPhee's students. As you read, pay special attention to what counts as good writing as McPhee practiced and taught it. The virtues he embodied are the virtues of good writing generally, not just in journalism.*

This profile appeared in the Princeton Alumni Weekly *(November 12, 2014), which explains why the year of graduation from Princeton appears along with the names of people mentioned in the article.*

1 John McPhee '53 has many moves as a writer, one of which he calls a "gossip ladder"—nothing more than a stack of quotations, each its own paragraph, unencumbered by attribution or context. You are eavesdropping in a crowd. You take these scraps of conversation and put them in a pile. Like this:

> Attention-getting and interesting opening, a collection of memorable statements from McPhee.

2 *"A piece of writing needs to start somewhere, go somewhere, and sit down when it gets there."*

3 *"Taking things from one source is plagiarism; taking things from several sources is research."*

4 *"A thousand details add up to one impression."*

5 *"You cannot interview the dead."*

6 *"Readers are not supposed to see structure. It should be as invisible as living bones. It shouldn't be imposed; structure arises within the story."*

7 *"Don't start off with the most intense, scary part, or it will all be anticlimactic from there."*

8 *"You can get away with things in fact that would be tacky in fiction—and stuck on TV at 3 o'clock in the morning. Sometimes the scene is carried by the binding force of fact."*

> After piquing our interest, this paragraph supplies the information we need to know: whom the profile is about and the context of the author's experience with McPhee.

9 The speaker in every instance is John McPhee. I assembled this particular ladder from the class notes of Amanda Wood Kingsley '84, an illustrator and writer who, like me, took McPhee's nonfiction writing class, "The Literature of Fact," in the spring of 1982. In February [of 2015], McPhee will mark 40 years as a Princeton professor, which he has pulled off in the midst of an extraordinarily productive career as a staff writer for *The New Yorker* and the author of more than two dozen books.

10 When the editor of this magazine asked me to write something about McPhee's class, I knew it would be the easiest assignment ever, though a little nerve-wracking. It was because most of McPhee's former students have saved their class notes and marked-up papers (Marc Fisher '80: "I've never lived anywhere without knowing where my notes from his class are").

> Note the humor in the word choice: "forensically," as if they were examining the body of a murdered person. Also note the humor in McPhee's noose comment.

11 When I meet Rick Klein '98 at a coffee shop down the block, we examined forensically Rick's class papers and the McPhee marginalia, the admonitions and praise from a teacher who keeps his pencils sharp. McPhee never overlooked a typo, and when Rick (now the hotshot political director at ABC News) wrote "fowl" instead of "foul," the professor's pencil produced a devastating noose.

McPhee's greatest passion was for structure, and he required that students explain, in a few sentences at the end of every assignment, how they structured the piece. (McPhee noted on a piece Rick wrote about his father: "This is a perfect structure—simple, like a small office building, as you suggest. The relationship of time to paragraphing is an example of what building a piece of writing is all about.") 12

Rick reminds me that the class was pass/fail. 13

"You were competing not for a grade, but for his approval. You were so scared to turn in a piece of writing that John McPhee would realize was dirt. We were just trying to impress a legend," he says. 14

Note Achenbach's voice here. He is still speaking as the student anxious about winning McPhee's approval.

Which is the nerve-wracking part, *still*. He is likely to read this article and will notice the infelicities, the stray words, the unnecessary punctuation, the galumphing syntax, the desperate metaphors, and the sentences that wander into the woods. "They're paying you by the comma?" McPhee might write in the margin after reading the foregoing sentence. My own student work tended toward the self-conscious, the cute, and the undisciplined, and McPhee sometimes would simply write: "Sober up." 15

He favors simplicity in general, and believes a metaphor needs room to breathe. "Don't slather one verbal flourish on top of another lest you smother them all," he'd tell his students. On one of Amanda's papers, he numbered the images, metaphors, and similes from 1 to 11, and then declared, "They all work well, to a greater or lesser degree. In 1,300 words, however, there may be too many of them—as in a fruitcake that is mostly fruit." 16

When Amanda produced a verbose, mushy description of the "Oval with Points" sculpture on campus, McPhee drew brackets around one passage and wrote, "Pea soup." 17

That one was a famously difficult assignment: You had to describe a piece of abstract art on campus. It was an invitation to overwriting. As McPhee put it, "Most writers do a wild skid, leave the road, and plunge into the dirty river." Novice writers believe they will improve a piece of writing by adding things to it; mature writers know they will improve it by taking things out. 18

Note how Achenbach transitions in paragraphs 19 and 20 from one section of his profile, on typical assignments McPhee gave, to another section, on McPhee's character as a teacher.

Another standard McPhee assignment came on Day One of the class: Pair up and interview each other, then write a profile. It was both an early test of our nonfiction writing skills and a clever way for McPhee to get to know his students at the beginning of the semester. 19

McPhee's dedication to his students was, and is, remarkable, given the other demands on his time. One never got the sense that he wished he could be off writing a magazine story for *The New Yorker* rather than annotating, and discussing face-to-face, a clumsy, ill-conceived, syntactically mangled piece of writing by a 20-year-old. 20

In this paragraph Achenbach explores the unselfish depth of McPhee's involvement with his students and his concern for writing well regardless of the circumstances.

He met with each of his 16 students for half an hour every other week. Many of his students became professional writers, and he lined up their books on his office shelf, but McPhee never has suggested that the point of writing is to make money, or that the merit 21 of your writing is determined by its market value. A great paragraph is a great paragraph wherever it resides, he'd say. It could be in your diary.

"I think he loves it when students run off and become field biologists in Africa or elementary school teachers," Jenny Price '85 tells me. She's now a writer, artist, and visiting Princeton professor. 22

McPhee taught us to revere language, to care about every word, and to abjure the loose synonym. He told us that words have subtle and distinct meanings, textures, implications, intonations, flavors. (McPhee might say: "Nuances" alone could have done the trick there.) Use a dictionary, he implored. He proselytized on behalf of the gigantic, unabridged *Webster's Second Edition*, a tank of a dictionary that not only would give a definition, but also would explore the possible synonyms and describe how each is slightly different in meaning. If you treat these words interchangeably, it's like taping together adjacent keys on a piano, he said. 23

Achenbach develops his profile with specific teaching techniques used by McPhee.

Robert Wright '79, an acclaimed author and these days a frequent cycling companion of McPhee, tells me by email, "I'd be surprised if there have been many or even any Ferris professors who care about words as much as John—I don't mean their proper use so much as their creative, deft use, sometimes in a way that exploits their multiple meanings; he also pays attention to the rhythm of words. All this explains why some of his prose reads kind of like poetry." 24

Just to write a simple description clearly can take you days, he taught us (once again I'm citing Amanda's class notes): "If you do it right, it'll slide by unnoticed. If you blow it, it's obvious." 25

We had to learn to read. One of his assignments is called "greening." You pretend you are in the composing room slinging hot type and need to remove a certain amount of the text block to get it to fit into an available space. You must search the text for words that can be removed surgically. 26

"It's as if you were removing freight cars here and there in order to shorten a train—or pruning bits and pieces of a plant for aesthetic and pathological reasons, not to mention length," McPhee commanded. "Do not do violence to the author's tone, manner, style, nature, thumbprint." 27

He made us green a couple of lines from the famously lean Gettysburg Address, an assignment bordering on sadism. A favorite paragraph designated for greening was the one in Joseph Conrad's *Heart of Darkness* that begins, "Going up that river was like traveling back to the earliest beginnings of the world, when vegetation rioted on the earth and the big trees were kings. An empty stream, a great silence, an impenetrable forest. The air was warm, thick, heavy, sluggish. There was no joy in the brilliance of sunshine." (McPhee, in assigning this, wrote: "Caution: You are approaching what may be my favorite paragraph in a lifetime of sporadic reading.") 28

One time the young Bob Wright used the word "minced" in an assignment. In their bi-weekly office conference, McPhee challenged Bob to justify the word. Bob offered his reasoning. McPhee looked up "minced" in the hulking *Webster*'s. "You found the perfect word," McPhee declared. 29

McPhee's career coincided with the rise of "New Journalism," but he never was really part of that movement and the liberties it took with the material. A college student often feels that rules are suffocating, that old-school verities need to be obliterated, and so some of us were tempted, naturally, to enhance our nonfiction—to add details from the imagination and produce a work of literature that's better than "true" and existed on a more exalted plane of meaning. We'd make things up. McPhee wouldn't stand for it. 30

Amanda remembers being called into his office one day: "I could tell something was wrong because he wasn't his usual smiling self. He had me sit down and glared at me a moment. Then he asked me very sternly whether I had made up the character I had allegedly interviewed for my paper that week about animal traps and snares—I'd talked to an elderly African American friend of my grandparents, whose snare-building skills helped him survive the Depression. Once I convinced him that Oscar was a real person, McPhee sat quietly a moment, then smiled and said it was one of the best papers he had received. Those were some of the finest words I'll ever hear." 31

Perhaps there are writers out there who make it look easy, but that is not the example set by McPhee. He is of the school of thought that says a writer is someone for whom writing is more difficult than for other people. Some people joke about lashing themselves to the chair to get a piece of writing done, but McPhee actually has done it, with the belt of his bathrobe. 32

Note Achenbach's use of testimonials from other former students in paragraphs 31, 33, and 34 to develop his profile with additional specifics.

Here's David Remnick '81, the McPhee student who is now McPhee's editor at The *New Yorker*: "You were working with a practicing creative artist, a writer of 'primary texts,' as the scholars say, but one who was eloquent, detailed, unfancy, and clear in the way he talked about essential things: description, reporting, structure, sentences, punctuation, rhythm, to say nothing of the emotional aspects of writing—anxiety, lostness, frustration. He didn't sugarcoat the difficulty of writing well. If anything, he highlighted the bitter-tasting terrors, he cherished them, rolled them around on his tongue. But behind all that was an immensely revealing, and rewarding, glimpse of the writing life. Not the glamour or the readings or the reviews. No, he allowed you to glimpse the process, what it meant to write alone in a room." 33

Marc Fisher, my *Washington Post* colleague, points out that part of McPhee's magic was getting students to slow down. "He catches adolescents at exactly the moment when we've been racing to get somewhere in life, and he corrals our ambition and raw skills and somehow persuades us that the wisdom, the power, and the mystery of telling people's stories comes in good part from pressing down on the brakes, taking it all in, and putting it down on paper—yes, paper—in a way that is true to the people we meet and the lives they lead." 34

I doubt many of us ever took a class that resonated so profoundly over the years. Part of it was that McPhee felt invested in our later success, regardless of our vocations. You could knock on his door years later and confer with him about your writing, your personal issues, your hopes and dreams. How many teachers are willing to be Professor For Life? 35

The profile concludes with a specific experience that relates to Achenbach's angle on his subject.

These are tough times in my business, which the people in suits now refer to as "content creation." Revolutionary changes in how we consume information have created challenges for anyone who is committed to serious, time-consuming writing, the kind that involves revision and the search for that perfect word. 36

But I don't think anyone can obliterate the beauty of a deftly constructed piece of writing. This is particularly the case if you've written it yourself. It's like hitting a great golf shot; you forget the shanks and slices and remember the one exquisite 3-iron. 37

One day in McPhee's class, he praised a sentence I'd written about the Louise Nevelson sculpture "Atmosphere and Environment X," near Firestone Library. He had me read it aloud. The hook was set. I don't always think about it consciously, but that's pretty much what I've been trying to do for more than three decades—write another sentence that might win the approval of John McPhee. 38

Questions for Discussion

1. Note the stress on "putting it down on paper" in paragraph 34. When would such an approach be appropriate for writing something? Do you always compose on a computer screen? If not, when do you use paper and pencil or some other nonelectronic tool for writing?
2. Learning anything that requires a high level of skill and judgment involves mentors, whether they are teachers in schools or not. What mentors have you had? What difference did they make in what you were learning to do?
3. The article singles out for attention what McPhee cared about most in teaching his students to write well. List his emphases. What do you consider most important? What do you consider least important? Why?

Thinking as a Writer

What Is the Rhetorical Situation?

1. What is Achenbach's *purpose* in writing this essay? What is his *angle* on the topic? How would you describe his *voice*?
2. Achenbach's intended audience is obviously Princeton alumni. How might other people respond to his essay?
3. Using Concept Close-Up: More about Profiles (page 74) as a guide, answer the following question: How does Achenbach use the *conventions* for creating a subjective profile? Specifically, how does he use background information about John McPhee? How does he include McPhee's voice, the sort of things he said, and the manner he used in saying them? How does he use detail to give his subject fuller humanity, a view of McPhee from more than one side? ■

READING **5.2**

Perpetual Meadowlands: Among the Reedbeds of the Hackensack

ELIZABETH MURPHY AND JAMES WRONA

A poet and editor, Elizabeth Murphy directs Grid Books and cofounded the interdisciplinary journal The Straddler. A collection of her poems appeared in 2018.

James Wrona is a portrait, travel, and landscape photographer based in New York City.

"Perpetual Meadowlands" is a profile of something we encounter in and around almost every city in the United States and all over the world: "green" areas gravely damaged by human activity. We want such places as an escape from urban life, yet we know they are not what they seem to be. What attitude, then, should we take toward them? This is the provocative question the article raises.

1 Viewable from the New Jersey Turnpike, from New Jersey Transit en route to Secaucus, from the parking lot of the Meadowlands Sports Complex in Bergen County, from the air approaching or departing Newark Airport, or up close, from one of its many trails, parks, or conservation sites, the more than 8,400 acres of largely undeveloped marshland along the Hackensack and Passaic rivers, which includes portions of thirteen New Jersey municipalities, is difficult to define.

2 Perpetual meadow is the agricultural term for an expanse of grassy land that is neither wetland nor pasture and where the presence of water restricts the growth of woody plants and trees. Here tall grasses called phragmites (common reeds) thrive, as do asphodel, the stalky, green-white flowers that are sometimes the subject of poetry, but are more often regarded as weeds.

3 Daily, hundreds of commuters take in views of the Meadowlands. The scenes outside their windows are hardly picturesque: endless rows of power lines; withered tree stumps in brown-gray swamps; mile after mile of tall, obstinate reeds; a gloomy tour of the skylines of northeast New Jersey's industrial cities. From the window of a passing train or car, it is easy to look out and see emptiness—a wasteland where perhaps a meadow once was.

© James Wrona

4 The PJP Landfill is one of the oldest in the Meadowlands. It collected trash from the time of horse-drawn wagons until, in the late 1960s and early '70s, it was leased and used for the dumping and burying of hazardous waste. Not long after, the drums of waste started leaking. Chemical fires and spontaneous combustions began occurring underground

and continued for more than thirty years, emitting volatile gaseous contaminants all the while.[1]

Though the fires have since been extinguished, and many of the 5,000 drums removed, and the landfill capped and seeded in an attempt to restore the land, the hills remain equipped with a system of PVC piping, a means of continuous gas ventilation, and are surrounded by gravel-lined ditches designed to stop the spread of toxic runoff, or leachate, into groundwater. Tall fences prevent trespassers—James and me on this day—from exploring the alien surfaces. 5

Still, these hills that once burned, as one PJP employee put it, "like Dante's inferno,"[2] appear greener and lusher than the fields of phragmites along the marsh. From a distance, it almost seems that these rolling green hills had always existed for the sole purpose of cultivating grass, not unlike a meadow. Closer up, they are more pathetic than off-putting.[3] 6

Industrial Meadows

The Meadowlands are a place of contradictions. Decades of dredging and dumping have altered the Jersey marshland's ecology, ridding it of forests and species of animal and plant; changing the courses of bodies of water. Today the Meadowlands are home to several active landfills as well as experiments in conserving those, like PJP, that have been closed. The Meadowlands are a sanctuary for migratory birds and a Superfund site. The New Jersey Meadowlands Commission has designated areas of the wetland for educational and recreational purposes, like hiking, canoeing, and kayaking. Despite talk of lingering contaminants, including dioxin (a compound used in many pesticides and herbicides, including—in the case of the Newark factory responsible for its leakage here—Agent Orange),[4] some locals treat undeveloped portions of the Meadowlands like parks. They hike, swim, go fishing. 7

The trail behind Gunnel Oval Park is an old railroad track. On either side, weeds, overgrown brush, and trees suggest a nature hike far from the city and the industrial sights of lower Manhattan. When I look beyond the brush, I am reminded of recent walks along the High Line in Manhattan's Meatpacking District, where grasses and wildflowers are never far removed from the sounds and sights of city life and construction. To our left, just beyond the trees, Kearny Marsh, 400 acres of waterbird habitat, spreads out toward the Hackensack and the New Jersey and Manhattan skylines. Closer to where we stand, the marsh is dotted with debris—jettisoned shopping carts, old tires. Further on, an active landfill crawls with construction vehicles pushing garbage up the sides of slowly growing brown hills. On the other side of our path, just beyond the brush, high fencing protects a lot where gravel is dumped and sorted. The sound of gravel spilling on gravel seems natural, surprisingly familiar; the sound of hard rain hitting water. 8

---

1. Robert Sullivan, *The Meadowlands: Wilderness Adventures on the Edge of a City* (New York: Doubleday, 1998), 146–147.
2. Sullivan, 151.
3. A retail commercial and residential development project has recently been proposed for the landfill site. Jared Kofsky. "Retail project planned for former Jersey City landfill site." *Jersey Digs*, 27 March 2018. https://jerseydigs.com/retail-project-planned-former-landfill-site-routes-1-and-9-jersey-city/
4. "Dioxin Is Only New Jersey's Latest Environmental Problem." *New York Times*, 19 June 1983.

© James Wrona

For many who have written about or documented the Meadowlands, it is these contradictions that inspire fascination. And we all seem to be searching for some sort of resolution, as if uncluttering our perceptions might unclutter the landscape as well. In his book, *The Meadowlands: Wilderness Adventures on the Edge of a City*, Robert Sullivan documents much of the disarray, but also lands on some satisfying resolutions. In order to describe the mostly "uninterrupted panorama" of the landscape, for example, he must also uncover an explanation for its tallest structures, the radio towers. He relates a conversation with a man who works the control station at the base of one these towers. The salt in the marsh, the engineer informs him, acts as a conductor for radio signals.[5] 9

Radio towers represent an altogether different type of industrial landscape than, say, the factories along the New Jersey Turnpike, or the Turnpike itself. Like the stalky reeds that grow at their base, the towers are suited to their environment. Though there have been complaints by nearby residents, who have come to resent the towers as eye-sores, there is something congruous about their relationship with the land that supports their function—as if their being there is only natural. 10

The Mediterranean Problem

Kearny Marsh reminds James of a trip he took many years ago to the South of France. For a photographer, the Meadowlands present what he describes as "the Mediterranean problem." On one side we have the Alps (in our case, mountainous landfills, industrial landscape), and on the other, the Mediterranean (Kearny Marsh, the Hackensack). The challenge, then, was to compose a series of photographs that conveys both: river and skyline, habitats and trash piles, reedbeds and radio towers. ... It was not merely the train tracks or trees that complicated our view. The distinct and yet inseparable sights of nature and industry that characterize a place like the Meadowlands are difficult to reconcile, and so also to capture. Just as the natural landscape has evolved to accommodate its industrial neighbors, industry has, in certain ways, been absorbed by the nature of the marsh. Our task was not to set one view against another, but to continually adjust our focus to see *beyond* one *to* the other, to illustrate the seemingly opposing aspects which nevertheless grow from, and thrive in, the same landscape. 11

Perhaps as a result of all these contradictions, the Meadowlands can easily inspire expressions of mixed intention—as can be seen in both our use of the land and in the ways we represent it. Buried in the landfills and marshes are layers of our history, 12

5. Sullivan, 61.

archaeologies of lives, and in some cases, mere leftovers. Rubble shipped from London during the Second World War mingles with tossed oyster shells from Manhattan dinner tables, remnants of the old Penn Station, and, purportedly, the bodies of victims not meant to be discovered. Today the Manhattan and Jersey City skylines stand in subtle contrast to the glassy rivers and grassy beds. The flat marsh attracting migratory birds is neighbor to an active landfill where seagulls come to feed. Near the corner of Ridge Road and Disposal Road, a labyrinthine dock snakes through the reeds, a park where visitors can observe the ecosystems below and above them, while just across the street service roads cut through overgrown fields, an abandoned ball park, and unmarked construction sites.

From Kearny Marsh we move on to Richard W. DeKorte Park, where we are at last 13
within reach of the waters of the Hackensack. As I contemplate the potential hazards of touching the water with my hand or foot, James crouches down to shoot close-ups of the reeds. Later I would see the photos and note the towers mimicking the reeds; the reeds mimicking the towers; the water mirroring nature and industry without discrimination. Sitting now on the rocks that line the walkway by the river's edge, I watch him as he gets closer to the ground, and more comfortable even, lying on his side among the reeds and asphodel, camera in hands, with nothing to support him but a bed of dried plant life.

Questions for Discussion

1. Profiles of places almost demand photographs. How do the two photos we have included in the article help you understand the Meadowlands? What emotional impact do they have?
2. Perhaps the key sentences in the selection are these: "Just as the natural landscape has evolved to accommodate its industrial neighbors, industry has, in certain ways, been absorbed by the nature of the marsh. Our task was not to set one view against another, but to continually adjust our focus to see *beyond* one *to* the other, to illustrate the seemingly opposing aspects which nevertheless grow from, and thrive in, the same landscape." Explain in your own words what the author is saying. Why is it *not* our task "to set one view against another"?
3. Most people enjoy visiting national parks or forests, apparently wild places unspoiled by industry and at least minimally exploited for profit. How does our view of such places differ from "green" places like the Meadowlands or city parks in the middle of cities? Is our view of wild places also conflicted or fraught with contradiction? If so, how would you characterize the conflicts or contradictions?

Thinking as a Writer

What Is the Rhetorical Situation?

1. What is Murphy's *purpose* in writing this essay? What is her *angle* on the topic? How would you describe her *voice*?
2. Who is Murphy's intended *audience*? Is there anything in the article you can cite that implies her target readership?

3. Using Concept Close-Up: More about Profiles (page 74) as a guide, answer this question: How does Murphy use the *conventions* for creating a profile? Specifically, how does she use background information and detailed description to create a vivid impression of the Meadowlands and our complex relationship to attractive places that pollution has damaged? ■

The Assignment

Write a profile about a person, organization, place, event, or situation. We recommend writing a single-person profile because it is easier to research and control. We also recommend that you at least be acquainted with the person you choose to profile. Extending and deepening a relationship you already have usually works better than establishing a new one from scratch.

What Can I Write About?

The most important criterion for making your selection is that the subject matters to you. Genuine interest in and involvement with your subject cannot be faked. Here are some possible topics:

- An older family member, a family friend, a mentor (such as a coach or teacher), someone in the community you interact with often, someone you work for or with, or a close, personal friend.
- Profiles in newspapers and magazines are about at least locally well-known people, such as artists, musicians, entertainers, sports figures, politicians, business leaders, and so on. If you happen to know a "high-profile" subject, as journalists call such people, she or he can be a good choice.
- Situations you, your family, or your local community face, such as entering the military, taking your first job, raising children, taking care of older relatives, or coping with illness or injury.
- Places you have lived or visited often, such as a foreign country; places you go to visit family, conduct business, or take vacations; the neighborhood where you grew up or live now.
- Significant happenings or gatherings of people, such as a concert or sporting event; something you witnessed that made the news and/or was a topic of conversation on your campus or in your local community.

How Do I Write a Profile? Questioning the Rhetorical Situation

Begin by picturing a **rhetorical situation** for your writing project, a real-world context for communicating. You should consider the key variables in any act of communication: a writer with something to say, a reader the writer wishes to reach, and a kind of text appropriate to the writing task. These three variables will affect many decisions in the composing process.

Writer: What Is My Purpose, and What Impression Should Readers Have of Me?

The purpose of a profile is to depict a person, place, organization, or some other suitable subject that you care about, that matters to you. You are informing, telling readers what they need to know to understand your subject. Using your own point of view, your angle, you are also communicating an interpretation of your subject, what it means, the value it has—in short, why it should matter to your readers. Your readers should perceive you as knowledgeable about your subject, consistent in your point of view, and interested in depicting your subject in a memorable way.

Audience: Who Is My Reader?

Profiles often communicate with a broad audience because human beings are social animals and enjoy reading about other people. However, skillful profiles have *particular readerships* in mind. Given the subject you have chosen and the angle you have on it, ask yourself this question: **What group of people will gain the most from reading it?** What do they need to know to understand your subject? What could you tell them that they will find interesting, intriguing, or challenging? How can you get them involved in the ethical issues your subject raises—that is, questions of right and wrong, good and bad?

Text: What Moves Can I Make?

To create a meaningful and memorable impression of the person you are writing about, you can do some or all of the following:

- Include conversational exchanges that you have had with your subject or that were reported to you by someone you interviewed.
- Quote a favorite saying of your subject that reveals his or her character or wisdom.
- Depict an action that shows what matters to your subject.
- Discuss events that you and your subject were part of, especially events that allow you to discuss your subject's values and characteristic commitments.
- Describe your subject's physical makeup and what you have seen him or her wearing if such details are relevant to the central impression you want your readers to have.
- Describe places where you and your subject have interacted, such as your subject's home or work environment.

People working to accomplish something, such as installing a community garden in your neighborhood, make good profile subjects.

© Tony Anderson/Digital Vision/Getty Images, RF

- Connect your subject to some enterprise that plays a major role in your subject's life, such as what he or she does for a living; the causes he or she supports; games, hobbies, sports, or leisure activities that indicate long-term interests or facets of personality.
- Give background about your subject's life history, such as where the subject was born and went to school and whom he or she married, especially when such information helps to explain why your subject became what he or she now is.
- Discuss the impact your subject has had on your life and the kind of relationship you have had with him or her (friend, mentor, business associate, and so on).
- Include a photo of your subject performing some action and comment on its significance.

Remember that these are moves you *can* make, not moves you must make, and that there are many other moves not listed here you could make. What you do depends on your angle, the information you have or can acquire, what you can do to make your subject interesting, and the central impression you want your readers to have.

How Do I Write a Profile? Engaging the Writing Process

No two people compose in exactly the same way, and even the same person may go through the writing process in different ways with different assignments. Nevertheless, because no one can attend to everything at once, there are phases in handling any significant writing task. You prepare to write by generating content and finding your angle.

The next phase is planning and drafting your paper, getting a version, however rough it may be, on paper or screen so that you have something to work with during the following two stages: revising your draft by making changes to the content, arrangement, and style of your writing; and editing your draft to take care of problems at the paragraph and sentence level, such as lack of focus and coherence; awkward or unclear sentences; and errors of grammar, spelling, and punctuation.

Exploring Your Topic

Most profiles draw on both what the writer knows already about the person profiled–that is, experience with that person–and additional information gathered from research. Start by investigating your experience.

Mining for Details about a Person

It is remarkable what we know about relatives, friends, acquaintances, and colleagues yet do not fully realize that we know. The following questions should help you recover some of what you know about the person you have chosen to profile.

In your writer's notebook or in an electronic file, write down everything that occurs to you in response to each of the following questions:

1. What does the person look like?
2. How does the person dress?
3. What is it like to talk to this person? Are there characteristic facial expressions, qualities of voice, mannerisms, gestures, accent, and so on that you recall?
4. How would you describe the person's character? For instance, how does she or he handle problems and setbacks?
5. What achievements and activities is the person proudest of?
6. How self-aware is the person? Does the person's self-conception match your view of him or her?
7. What does the person most like to talk about? What topics does she or he avoid or say nothing about when others raise them?
8. Where have you talked with the person? What did you notice about the home, office, or other place where the two of you talked?
9. What sort of people does your person have as friends or associates? If you have met some of them, what were your impressions? What did they say about your person?
10. If you were talking with someone else who does not know the person as well as you do, what story or stories would you tell? What stories about your person do you recall others telling you?

ACTIVITY 5.1 *Writer's Notebook*

Assessing Your Materials

After you finish brainstorming your topic using the ten questions on page 89, step back and begin looking for *patterns and convergences* in the material. Do you see a dominant theme in your person's life, something that she or he is always concerned with or pursuing? Do you detect fundamental loyalties or commitments, a basic philosophy, outlook, or set of controlling attitudes or values?

Profiles create memorable impressions, and therefore you need to be seeking the impression you want to create for yours. You may not know yet what it will be, but probably somewhere in your first exploration there are clues or intuitions. Write them down, even if you have doubts, even if some of the details do not fit. You are not committing yourself to anything yet, but you need some first ideas for further thought and to help guide the research you will probably need to do. ■

Preparing to Write

You can see from the example profiles at the beginning of this chapter that the amount of research required varies considerably. Achenbach's profile drew extensively on the files of McPhee's students; Murphy drew on her extensive experience with the Meadowlands and what was written about them by others. How much you need depends on how long you have known and how well you know the person you have chosen and on your instructor's assignment requirements.

Interviewing is the most common form of research in doing profiles, and we will devote special attention to it shortly. What other ways of acquiring information might be available to you?

See Chapter 16, Finding Sources, and Chapter 17, Evaluating Sources, for more on using print and online materials.

BEST PRACTICES Sources of Information for Profiles

1. Besides interviewing the person you are profiling, talk to people who know your subject as well as or better than you do, such as friends, associates, family members, and other relatives.
2. Find out if your person has written anything that you might gain access to: articles, books, texts for speeches, diaries, journals, blogs, even e-mail exchanges she or he might be willing to share.
3. Ask if you may look at scrapbooks or photo albums your subject might have.
4. Look for information via Google, news stories you can find via your local paper's index or your library's databases (see pages 364–66), Who's Who publications, résumés, bios written by your subject or by someone else, and so on. Ask your subject for help in accessing such information.
5. Arrange to attend meetings or other gatherings of people in which your subject plays a prominent role.

Conducting Interviews

Interviews are *guided conversations,* and they are guided largely by the questions you ask. On the one hand, you want as natural and free-flowing a conversation as possible, something close to what would happen if you were sitting next to someone on an airplane and just happened to strike up a conversation. On the other hand, there is information you need and questions you have thought of in advance to elicit it, and you do not want the interview to end with too few of those questions asked and answered. Interviews are, therefore, a challenge, a push-pull between *let it flow* and *steer it toward what you need to know.* Following are important considerations when conducting interviews (also see Figure 5.1):

1. **The medium matters.** We recommend face-to-face interviews over telephone interviews, and telephone interviews over online chats or e-mail exchanges. Of course, you conduct interviews any way you can, but as you move down the line in methods of communication, you lose more and more information. Face-to-face interviews give you the full experience of good talk, including gestures, facial expressions, changes in posture, and information from the surroundings. Over the telephone, you have only the interviewee's voice in addition to what is said; with online communication you have only the written text to work with.
2. **Bring a camera with you.** Photographs of your subject and places associated with him or her can help supplement descriptions and confirm the impression you want to create. Many profiles include photographs.
3. **Plan to bring an audio recorder.** Ask your interviewee before the conversation begins whether or not you can use the recorder. Have a notebook with you as well for making quick notes between questions, during a response, and immediately after the interview when your memory is freshest. However, do not allow note-taking to intrude into the conversation—fast jottings are all you will have time for during the interview itself.
4. **Bring with you a set of questions** that are printed out or written on your notepad and rank ordered from the most to the least important. The questions should address holes in your knowledge detected after recalling what you know already about your person and after pursuing some of the suggestions in Best Practices (page 90) for gaining additional information. They should also fill out what you have learned that you and your readers are likely to find most interesting.

   Often your questions will either not lead to anything interesting or will turn up much more than you anticipated. In the first case, be ready to pose another question as soon as you can; in the second case, let the person talk until you sense the well is going dry, even if it means you do not get to ask a few of your less important questions.
5. Finally, as your interview draws to a close, ask if you may arrange another meeting later and/or pose follow-up questions over the telephone or via e-mail. Also ask about additional sources of information listed on page 90 that you can obtain only if the interviewee is able and willing to supply them—texts of speeches, for instance.

Face-to-face interviewing is an art well worth learning how to do. Start practicing it now, on this assignment, because you will need it for information-gathering on the job or for community-based leadership positions.

FIGURE **5.1**

Things to Remember for an Interview

When conducting an interview, there are a few important things to remember to help you get the most out of it: (1) speak to your subject face-to-face, (2) take the person's picture, (3) record the interview, and (4) have good questions prepared.

Selecting Details Based on Your Angle

Profiles are always based on far more information than the writer can actually use in the profile itself. If you feel somewhat overwhelmed by all the information you have gathered, that is normal. Here is how to gain a measure of control over it sufficient to write a first draft.

First, remember that profiles are always *partial depictions of your person, and the source of the partiality is your angle or point of view.* Put another way, you need to create a memorable impression, and it can only come from your point of view. It is time to decide on your point of view and commit yourself to it–at least until you see how well it works in a first draft.

Remember also that your point of view is what it is, and so it cannot be wrong. Have confidence in it and suspend judgment until you get the first draft completed. Only then can you assess your point of view according to the only criterion that matters: Did it work? Were you able to write an engaging profile? If not, adjusting your point of view may be one of the keys to revising it.

For Joel Achenbach, John McPhee is the role model for a master writing teacher. For Murphy, the Meadowlands represent the complicated landscapes cities tend to create and that most people must learn to cope with somehow.

In formulating your point of view, then, ask two questions:

- Why does my subject matter to me?
- How can I connect what matters to me with my readers' concerns and interests?

Answer these questions and you have what you need to select information from all the data you have gathered. If an item relates *directly* to depicting what matters to you and your readers, include it in your plan for the first draft; if not, leave it out.

Drafting Your Paper

As you write your draft, focus on the following concerns.

What Voice Is Appropriate for a Profile?

Profiles are informative, not primarily expressive; thus the focus is on the subject profiled, not on the writer. Nevertheless, your voice matters, as it always does in writing. Sound like a well-informed insider with an intimate knowledge of your subject. That is how you project authority. Beyond that, voice depends largely on point of view, how you understand your subject.

For example, listen to these paragraphs from Achenbach's profile of John McPhee:

> McPhee's dedication to his students was, and is, remarkable, given the other demands on his time. One never got the sense that he wished he could be off writing a magazine story for *The New Yorker* rather than annotating, and discussing face-to-face, a clumsy, ill-conceived, syntactically mangled piece of writing by a 20-year-old.
>
> He met with each of his 16 students for half an hour every other week. Many of his students became professional writers, and he lined up their books on his office shelf, but McPhee never has suggested that the point of writing is to make money, or that the merit of your writing is determined by its market value. A great paragraph is a great paragraph wherever it resides, he'd say. It could be in your diary.
>
> "I think he loves it when students run off and become field biologists in Africa or elementary school teachers," Jenny Price '85 tells me. She's now a writer, artist, and visiting Princeton professor.

Much of the profile depicts McPhee as a daunting, indeed, intimidating task master; in these paragraphs we see his dedication to his students and how he cared so much about them–the human touch, without which his methods of teaching writing might only have driven students away. Because of these paragraphs we can see why McPhee's students remained so attached to him long after the course they took with him was over. The admiring voice of the author seems entirely justified.

Developing and Organizing Your Profile

The following organizational principles apply to arranging your materials:

- Start with something memorable, an attention-getting opener that indicates what your profile is about and why it matters to you and your reader.
- Provide most of your background information next, after you have your reader's attention and interest.
- Structure the remaining material by looking for a sequence that makes sense. For instance, you may need to describe a situation before you cite what your subject said or did. Or perhaps one story or memory may provide a good lead-in to or context for another.
- Save something especially memorable for the conclusion. You want to end as strongly as you began.

Commonly writers set out to follow a plan and then depart from it as they draft. The plan they thought would work has to be modified or even abandoned as they write. If that is what happens to you, do not be concerned. As long as the final version of your profile has a structure that readers can understand and follow, you have solved whatever organizational problems you may encounter.

Revising Your Draft

Writing is revising. A first draft is a start, but most need significant rewriting–for instance, parts taken out, new parts added, and parts rearranged. The strongest revisions begin with your own assessment. It is a good idea to put your draft aside for a while, preferably a day or two. Then, when you have some distance from it, go back and read what you wrote.

Try to see it as your readers will see it. The questions in The Art of Questioning will help you find ways to improve the draft.

THE ART OF QUESTIONING Revision Checklist for Writing a Profile

1. **Does the draft create a memorable impression?** What word or words best state your angle, or interpretation, of your subject?
2. **Is there anything in the profile that does not contribute to the impression?** If so, it should be background information. Cut anything else.
3. **Does your draft capture your subject's full humanity?** If yours seems "flat," one-dimensional, revise by adding anecdotes, descriptions, comments from other people, and so on to reveal more sides or aspects of your subject. Here is a major opportunity for improving your paper by developing it better.
4. **Does your profile have immediacy and intimacy?** Isolate the places in your paper where you have described your subject, so that the reader can see and hear what you experienced. Go back to the notes you took during exploration and research. **What details might be added?** Sight and sound usually dominate descriptions, but touch, smell, and taste can sometimes contribute as

well. Developing your descriptions is another way to make your profile more effective.

5. **Have you quoted your person and/or cited snippets of revealing conversation?** *Your reader needs to hear your subject talking.* What was said and in what way, with what gestures, facial expressions, tone of voice, and so on?
6. **Have you made your relationship with your subject clear?** Read through your paper again, concentrating entirely on voice and self-presentation. **What is your attitude toward your subject?** Where does it emerge most clearly and forcefully? **How do you sound to your reader?** Do you think how you sound is appropriate given your relationship to the person?
7. Does your profile at least imply questions like: **What matters in life? How should we live? How ought we to deal with other people?** Find the places in your essay where ethical questions like these are relevant. Can you develop them better without turning your profile into a sermon or moralistic lesson?

ACTIVITY 5.2 *Collaborative Activity*

Getting a Second Opinion

Either before you attempt a revision or at some point during the revising process, it always helps to have someone else, such as a classmate, a tutor, your instructor, a willing friend, look at your draft. Be sure that the person understands the assignment and what you are trying to do to create the memorable impression profiles make.

Share the questions listed in the previous section with the person reviewing your draft. Show the person what you have done or plan to do to improve the draft. Then ask for the person's honest and full assessment and any suggestions for improvement. ■

ACTIVITY 5.3 *In Your Own Work*

Revising Your Draft

After assessing the draft yourself and getting a second opinion, formulate a revision strategy—that is, an approach to carrying out the revision. Here are some suggestions:

- First, decide what you think the useful criticism and suggestions are. Not all the feedback will be equally helpful, and some of it will not help at all. Reassess your own self-criticisms—do you still see the same problems?
- Second, being as specific as you can, make a list of items you intend to work on. "The first anecdote on page 3 needs more descriptive detail" is an example of what we mean by specific.

- Third, divide your list into two categories: revisions that will change all or much of the paper—called global revisions—versus spot revisions that require only altering a paragraph or two in one place.
- Fourth, do the global revising first. Ponder the best order for doing them. For instance, if you decide to rearrange sections in your profile, do that first before working on transitions or other flow problems.
- Fifth, after completing the global revisions, deal with the spot revisions by beginning with those most likely to improve your draft the most.

Remember that revisions cannot be done all at once, in one step. Focus your attention on solving one problem at a time. *Remember also that carrying out your plan will often result in unplanned insights.* You might discover, for instance, that in developing one anecdote you now see connections with another. Adjust your plans to take full advantage of revision surprises. ■

Student Example: Excerpts from Molly Tilton's Draft

Molly Tilton's profile, "Mr. Santa Claus," appears on pages 99–102. Let's look at some excerpts from her first draft so you can see some of the significant improvements revision can make.

Excerpt 1: Opening Paragraph

In the back corner of an office in United Liquors' headquarters in Braintree, Massachusetts, the phone rang. Terri, the director of The Ray Tye Medical Aid Foundation, answered; she yelled, "Mr. Tye, Senator Ted Kennedy is on the phone, and has a prospective patient for the foundation." Mr. Tye took the call and then came into Terri's office to explain to her a young child's life-threatening situation.

In her revised opening, Tilton gets to the point faster:

In a back corner of United Liquors' headquarters in Braintree, Massachusetts, lives are being saved. Mr. A. Raymond Tye, a prominent businessman and philanthropist, strides into his place of work one morning with his cane and a mission. "Terri," he cries, "Come into my office to discuss some prospective patients for the foundation, twin boys conjoined at the head. They need our help." From that point the real work begins.

Excerpt 2: Paragraph 6 about Terri

Terri, the director of the foundation, is faced with tough decisions every day. She, along with Mr. Tye, decides on the patients the foundation will support. Doctors and politicians call The Ray Tye Medical Aid Foundation asking for financial help for someone they know. Patients and their family members fill out online applications asking for medical assistance. It is Terri's responsibility to contact hospitals to find out more about the patient's condition, as well as keeping in touch with ill patients. The majority of applications come from Haiti, Iraq, China, and Massachusetts; the foundation does not pay for travel costs but usually sets

> up patients with another foundation who can assist them. The foundation reviews all patient applications but only helps those who are facing life-threatening ailments and do not have health insurance.

In her revision of this paragraph, Tilton uses **specific details** to bring more life-like immediacy to Terri, allowing readers to see her as a real person:

> Terri Carlson, the director of the foundation, has worked for the foundation for two years. Prior to this, she worked for United Liquors as credit manager. In recent years, Terri, a devoted wife and mother of two, has worked long hours while juggling her responsibilities at home. She wears business attire every day to work, showing her serious attitude, but her bright red hair exemplifies her bubbly spirit. Even though Terri is in her 40s, she has the high-pitched voice of a child and gets excited over the littlest accomplishments. Her lovable personality makes it easier for people all over the world to connect with her, even over the phone. As the director, Terri has the responsibility to read through the applications, contact hospitals about patients' conditions and medical histories, find the hospitals with the most expert specialists, keep in touch with current patients, and establish lasting relationships with recovered ones. She is able to accomplish all of this with only the aid of a computer, a telephone, and a calculator.

ACTIVITY 5.4 *In Your Own Work*

Revising for Focus and Development

Exchange your draft with another student and help each other find ways to improve focus and development. Look especially for lack of sufficient detail in description. Also remember other options for development in profiles, such as quotations and reported conversations. ■

ACTIVITY 5.5 *In Your Own Work*

Using Visual Supplementation

A picture may not be worth a thousand words, but having some can help your reader visualize your subject and places associated with the information gathered through interviews and conversations. They can also confirm what you say about your subject. Consider using photos if you have not included them; if you have included them, consider how to acquire better ones if you are not entirely happy with them. Also consider order and placement. If there is more than one, which should come first, second, and so on? Where in the paper should you place a photograph? Usually placing it close to the paragraph it is most relevant to works best. ■

Editing Your Revised Draft

Excessive repetition is a common editing problem. When the same word is used too frequently, readers notice. Writers seldom detect unintentional repetitions by silent reading; read your draft aloud so you hear them.

Because Molly Tilton's angle on the founder and the foundation itself was so respectful, and because Mr. Tye was so much her elder, Molly chose to refer to him throughout the essay as Mr. Tye rather than by his full name on first mention and from then on by his last name only, as is customary. This decision created some passages where editing for repetition would have streamlined the writing, such as the excerpt below from paragraph 5.

Original Version

Mr. Tye has provided hope to thousands of people all over the world with his selfless acts and has constantly encouraged others to share what they can for those in dire need. The impact Mr. Tye has had on others shows tangibly in the hundreds of thank you notes and hugs he has received since 2002, the year of the foundation's establishment. Mr. Tye's office is decorated with wooden sculptures from Africa and steel plaques from organizations that have honored Mr. Tye for his remarkable work. In May 2009, Catholic Charities honored Mr. Tye for his philanthropic efforts throughout the city of Boston; making him the first Jewish man to receive a Catholic Charities award.

There are several options for ways to refer to people:

1. Use a pronoun
2. Use a synonym or substitute word
3. Use a different version of the person's name

Using these options, Molly created the edited version below:

Revised Version

A. Raymond Tye has provided hope to thousands of people all over the world with his selfless acts and has constantly encouraged others to share what they can for those in dire need. The impact his generosity has had on others shows tangibly in the hundreds of thank you notes and hugs he has received since 2002, the year of the foundation's establishment. Mr. Tye's office is decorated with wooden sculptures from Africa and steel plaques from organizations that have honored him for his remarkable work. In May 2009, Catholic Charities honored him for his philanthropic efforts throughout the city of Boston, making Mr. Tye the first Jewish man to receive a Catholic Charities award.

ACTIVITY 5.6 *In Your Own Work*

Editing for Other Repeated Words

When you notice the same word appearing in sentences in sequence, there are two ways to reduce the repetition:

1. Think of a different word but one that still sounds natural—not as if you found it in the thesaurus.
2. Combine two of the sentences into one.

In the sixth paragraph of Molly's essay, the word *work* appears several times, as a verb and as a noun. Practice reducing repetitions by editing the passage below. Compare your edited version with those of others in your class.

> Terri Carlson, the director of the foundation, has worked for the foundation for two years. Prior to this, she worked for United Liquors as credit manager. In recent years, Terri, a devoted wife and mother of two, has worked long hours while juggling her responsibilities at home. She wears business attire every day to work, showing her serious attitude, but her bright red hair exemplifies her bubbly spirit. . . . ■

ACTIVITY 5.7 *In Your Own Work*

Detecting and Editing Repetitions

Read through your revised draft with special attention to the problem of repeated words. You might ask someone else to read the paper and circle or underline repetitions if you have trouble detecting them. Use the suggestions in the student examples to add more variety or conciseness as you reduce the repetitions. ■

REVISED STUDENT EXAMPLE

Tilton 1

Molly Tilton

Professor Channell

Writing 205

April 4, 2015

Mr. Santa Claus

In a back corner of United Liquors' headquarters in Braintree, Massachusetts, lives are being saved. Mr. A. Raymond Tye, a prominent businessman and philanthropist, strides into his place of work one morning with his cane and a mission. "Terri," he cries, "Come into my office to discuss some prospective patients for the foundation, twin boys conjoined at the head. They need our help." From that point the real work begins. 1

Short introductory paragraph gets to the point and the action quickly. Gains reader interest and attention.

Tilton 2

At the end of Campanelli Drive sits a gray warehouse. The mirrored glass walls on the sides of this building contribute a faintly contemporary architectural style, but the building is of little significance to the town of Braintree otherwise. The only cars that travel down the road are large supply trucks and employee vehicles. When you walk into the building's lobby, Sheila, the Braintree division's secretary, greets you with a smile and asks how she might assist you. On the first floor, over sixty United Liquors employees work diligently in cubicles. Up the stairs, in a recently renovated part of the building, you reach a common meeting room and a door to the right with a sign reading, "The Ray Tye Medical Aid Foundation." Inside are three cubicles, and in the back left corner is Mr. Tye's personal office. Terri Carlson is the only employee of the foundation. Her cubicle has one large desk, one computer, a chair, two file cabinets, a printer, and three cabinets full of office supplies, all she needs to operate this foundation. 2

This and following paragraphs supply needed background knowledge.

The Ray Tye Medical Aid Foundation was started to offer financial assistance to people around the world who suffer life-threatening illness and need in-hospital medical care to save their lives. In honor of Tye's 80th birthday, his wife, friends and family collected two million dollars in order to establish The Ray Tye Medical Aid Foundation. This small foundation has helped to save or prolong 183 lives. Patients have been helped no matter what their location, race, sex, or religious affiliation. The patients that the foundation has helped are from all over the world, including the U.S. This past year, I had the privilege of being the first volunteer to work at this foundation; it was in this capacity that I became closely acquainted with Terri and Mr. Tye. 3

Establishes writer's connection with her subject and, therefore, her authority.

Mr. Tye is a first-generation entrepreneur who started his own company, United Liquors, which went on to become one of the largest liquor distributors in Massachusetts. Living a colorful life, he attended Tufts University, fought in World War II, and fathered five children. Now in his 80's, he has dedicated his life to helping others, and received countless accolades for his philanthropic efforts. He always dresses in professional attire, making him a serious business man, which most find intimidating, until he lets out his vibrant smile. His appearance speaks to his kind spirit, from his white bushy eyebrows to his portly belly. In fact, Terri often tells the story of one patient, a cancer survivor, who referred to Tye as "Mr. Santa Claus." 4

Needed background material, but includes personal details about Tye that make him human, engaging.

Tilton 3

Mr. Tye has provided hope to thousands of people all over the world with his 5
selfless acts and has constantly encouraged others to share what they can for those in dire need. The impact his generosity has had on others shows tangibly in the hundreds of thank you notes and hugs he has received since 2002, the year of the foundation's establishment. Mr. Tye's office is decorated with wooden sculptures from Africa and steel plaques from organizations that have honored him for his remarkable work. In May 2009, Catholic Charities honored him for his philanthropic efforts throughout the city of Boston, making Mr. Tye the first Jewish man to receive a Catholic Charities award. He states on the foundation's website:

Use of memorable detail to confirm Tye's achievements.

> It is a strong belief of my own that giving should really be called receiving because the elemental act of giving returns many pleasant rewards to the giver. In fact, it might be said that there is not a more self-serving act than a liberal manifestation of generosity. . . . Seeing the happiness generosity creates in the recipients is another positive reinforcement—a big return for a small investment.

Good use of material gathered from her subject's own writing.

Accordingly, the motto of The Ray Tye Medical Aid Foundation is simply "We will never stop caring."

Terri Carlson, the director of the foundation, has worked for the foundation 6
for two years. Prior to this, she worked for United Liquors as credit manager. In recent years, Terri, a devoted wife and mother of two, has worked long hours while juggling her responsibilities at home. She wears business attire every day to work, showing her serious attitude, but her bright red hair exemplifies her bubbly spirit. Even though Terri is in her 40s, she has the high-pitched voice of a child and gets excited over the littlest accomplishments. Her lovable personality makes it easier for people all over the world to connect with her, even over the phone. As the director, Terri has the responsibility to read through the applications, contact hospitals about patients' conditions and medical histories, find the hospitals with the most expert specialists, keep in touch with current patients, and establish lasting relationships with recovered ones. She is able to accomplish all of this with only the aid of a computer, a telephone, and a calculator.

Tilton 4

Each week, the foundation receives four or more lengthy applications from people around the world seeking help. All prospective patients must fill out an online application. Terri and Mr. Tye review all patients' applications but help only those who face life-threatening conditions and do not have health insurance. 7

Use of specific, extended example to illustrate the help Tye's foundation provides.

Recently, media in the United States told the story of twin Egyptian boys whose heads were conjoined. These boys, Mohamed and Ahmed Ibrahim, are patients that Tye discovered himself. On a Sunday morning in August 2002, he read an article about them in *The Boston Globe* and decided to help them. Their operation was estimated to cost two million dollars; the Ray Tye Medical Aid Foundation donated $100,000, making it one of the leading donors. The thirty-four hour operation was successful in October 2003, and the boys have been making steady progress since then. After their extensive surgery and therapy, the boys learned how to walk on their own and learned how to speak English. 8

Short, to-the-point concluding paragraph wraps up the profile in a memorable way.

Mohamed and Ahmed live happy and healthy lives with their family, thanks to Mr. Tye and Terri's tireless efforts to make a difference in their lives. They were able to see for themselves the progress the twin boys had made when they visited Braintree, Massachusetts, in September 2009. At the time of the twins' visit, Mr. Tye stated to a Boston news reporter: "If you can do something to save a life there is an inner feeling of satisfaction that you can derive from nothing else." 9

CREDITS

CHAPTER 6

Presenting Information

ENGAGING QUESTIONS

In this chapter, you will engage with the following questions:

- What is the relationship among data, information, and knowledge?
- What are the purposes of informative writing?
- What are the common features of informative writing?
- How do writers identify appropriate topics for informative writing?
- How do the elements of the rhetorical situation apply to the writing process for an informative writing assignment?
- How do writers apply the steps of the writing process to an informative assignment?

WITH MORE THAN 2.5 QUINTILLION BYTES OF DIGITAL CONTENT CREATED EACH DAY, no one can doubt that we live in the information age. With all this information at hand, and browsers like Google to help us find it, we can answer one key question about information rather easily: What is known about "x"? with "x" representing almost any topic. However, two other questions matter more when we write to communicate information:

- **What do my readers need or want to know?**
- **How can I help them understand what the information means?**

These questions are so important that no other purpose for writing has so many genres devoted to answering them: maps, brochures, newspaper and magazine articles, dictionaries, encyclopedias, journals for people in specialized areas of study, documentary films, websites, and owner's manuals, among many others. The list is so long and includes every communication medium because modern, open societies depend on access to information. Every context for writing—college, business, community, government, even personal communication—generates enormous amounts of informative writing. Presenting information well, then, is an important skill.

Sixteenth-century philosopher Sir Francis Bacon said, "Knowledge is power." But knowledge only has power when it is communicated well.

What Is Presenting Information?

Information is **data,** *what we commonly call "the facts," interpreted and organized to make it useful to others.* By interpreting and presenting the information we are exposed to, we construct **knowledge,** *our understanding of any subject.* "Knowledge is power," as the philosopher Francis Bacon said: It enables us to do things we otherwise could not do. For most of history we had no idea that microscopic organisms existed, much less that some cause disease. The science we call microbiology put all the information together and interpreted it, so that now we know this virus or that bacterium causes a particular disease. Because of such knowledge we have gained the power to both prevent and cure many diseases.

The Concept Close-Up box shows the relation of data to information and knowledge.

CONCEPT CLOSE-UP Assessing Data

Data (the facts) are *statements about a topic that are not in dispute.* From all the facts gathered about a topic, writers select **information,** *data a particular readership needs or wants to know.* **Knowledge** results from *the interpretation the writer gives the information*—what the writer takes it to mean. The following triangle depicts the relation between data, information, and knowledge:

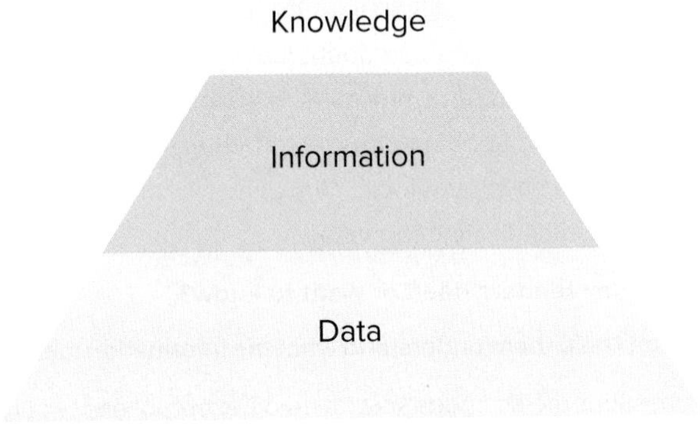

Because data are the base of the triangle, what we assume to be true beyond question, it is especially important to be critical of "the facts." Data must be all of the following:

Accurate	We can be misled by sources who thought they were telling the truth (misinformation); we can be misled by people who knew they were telling lies (disinformation).
Current	Data can be out of date: once true, but false now.
Sufficient for the need at hand	Data can be too little or too much: If too little, we do not have enough to go on; if too much, we are confused or overwhelmed.
Communicated in a way the intended readership can understand	Much technical data is accurate, current, and sufficient but useless to us because we do not understand the words and numbers that express it.

Why Present Information?

Knowledge is always power—the power to help others, to correct misinformation, to increase our understanding of ourselves and the world.

Communicating information is so important that it dominates writing in all areas of our society. In the academic world, textbooks, handouts, lectures, and course websites are all primarily informative. In the business world, e-mails, memos, reports, performance assessments, and quarterly earnings are primarily informative. In community life, local magazines, community newsletters, signs posted along streets announcing meetings, and most presentations done in schools and other civic gathering places are primarily informative. Indeed, our society moves by and through a sea of information that keeps everything afloat and at the same time threatens to drown us in too much of a good thing. For this reason we all have a high stake in managing information so that it does not overwhelm us. The next question, therefore, is especially important.

How Do Writers Present Information?

The key idea in informative writing is the *reader's need or desire to know something.* We lose sight of this sometimes when we go to a standard reference work, like a dictionary. What we find seems "just there," off by itself in a book or on a web page without relation to anything else. Yet we would not be checking up on a word if we felt no need to know what it means or how to use it correctly. All information is motivated by need or desire, and therefore, for a writer, *sizing up a reader's need or desire and satisfying it* define the challenge of presenting information.

Consequently, the most common features of informative writing are meant to catch readers' attention and keep them reading. These include:

- **Anecdotes,** *short narratives* that help readers connect with the topic and relate it to their lives.
- **"Up-front" statements that indicate why the information matters,** or how readers can profit from knowing it.
- **Headings that indicate where the writer will answer the reader's key questions,** such as why something happens, how the reader can avoid bad consequences or act to make good ones more likely, and so on.
- **Statements that create a realistic context for readers,** such as how to buy or sell something wisely, solve practical problems, or understand a widely discussed issue better.

The simple truth is that we have abundant information and a shortage of reader attention. Informative writers, therefore, compete with each other to gain and hold readers. Remember this and you will understand how to compose effective informative writing.

Beyond reaching readers, what matters most is **genre,** *the specific kind of informative writing you are doing.* We are about to examine two of many informative genres: a magazine article and a research report. As all genres do, each of these conforms to certain **conventional expectations**—that is, *what people expect to find in a specific genre.* As you read the following selections, consider how each meets your expectations for the kind of writing usually found in a magazine article and a research report.

READING **6.1**

Tomorrow, I Love Ya!

ERIC HOOVER

A senior writer for the Chronicle of Higher Education, *Eric Hoover specializes in college admission and enrollment issues. In this selection his subject is the extensive research done on procrastination, a problem for most people, including college students.*

1 Joseph R. Ferrari has a name for people who dillydally all the time. Sometimes, he spits out the term as if it were stale gum or a polysyllabic cuss word. When he dubs you a "chronic procrastinator," however, he does not mean to insult you. He is just using the psychological definition for someone who habitually puts things off until tomorrow, or next week, or whenever. The afflicted need not feel lonely: Research suggests that the planet is crawling with dawdlers.

2 Procrastinators vex Mr. Ferrari, a psychology professor at DePaul University, yet he owes much to the dilatorily inclined. Without them he could not have helped blaze a trail of inquiry into procrastination (the word comes from the Latin verb *procrastinare*—"to defer until morning"). The professor is as prompt as the sports car that shares his name, but he sees the symptoms of compulsive stalling everywhere.

Central point of piece: the complexity of procrastination.

3 Mr. Ferrari and other scholars from around the world are finding that procrastination is more complex—and pervasive—than armchair analysts might assume. And helping people climb out of their pits of postponement is not as simple as giving them a pill or a pep talk.

4 The task is particularly challenging in the hothouses of procrastination known as college campuses. Free time, long-term deadlines, and extracurricular diversions conspire against academic efficiency. Students are infamous for not tackling their assignments until the jaws of deadlines are closing.

Calls attention to the extent of the problem, especially among college students.

5 Professors may call such students slackers or sloths; psychologists define them as "academic procrastinators." According to recent studies, about 70 percent of college students say they typically procrastinate on starting or finishing their assignments (an estimated 20 percent of American adults are chronic procrastinators).

6 Choosing to do one task while temporarily putting another on hold is simply setting priorities, which allows people to cross things off their to-do lists one at a time. Procrastination is when one keeps reorganizing that list so that little or nothing on it gets done.

Emphasizes the seriousness of the problem by pointing to consequences.

7 For some students, that inertia has costs. Researchers say academic procrastination raises students' anxiety and sinks their self-esteem. The behavior also correlates with some of higher education's thorniest problems, including depression, cheating, and plagiarism among students.

8 Dozens of colleges have created counseling sessions or workshops for procrastinators. Yet Mr. Ferrari and other researchers say many institutions treat the problem superficially instead of helping students analyze their own thought processes and behavioral patterns in order to change them. Give a hard-core procrastinator nothing more than time-management tips, they warn, and you might as well hand him a page of hieroglyphics.

"Telling a chronic academic procrastinator to 'just do it' is not going to work," Mr. Ferrari says. "It's like telling a clinically depressed person to cheer up." 9

Learning about Loafers

Laggards have always been tough cases. Even God could not inspire St. Augustine of Hippo, the fourth-century philosopher and theologian, to act right away. As he slowly came to accept Christianity, Augustine wrote in *Confessions,* the future bishop wavered. Clinging to temporal pleasures, Augustine famously asked of God: "Give me chastity and continency—but not yet." 10

Late in his life, Leonardo da Vinci, the genius who missed deadlines, lamented his unfinished projects. Shakespeare's Hamlet pondered—and pondered—killing his uncle Claudius before sticking him in the final act. Grady Tripp, the English professor in Michael Chabon's novel *Wonder Boys,* couldn't finish his second book because he refused to stop writing it. 11

Introduces key term: Discounting.

In a world of unmade beds and unwritten essays, the postponement of chores is commonplace. Now and again, humans put aside tasks with long-term rewards to savor immediate pleasures, like ice cream and movies, through a process called "discounting." For chronic procrastinators, however, discounting is a way of life. 12

The scientific study of procrastination was (appropriately enough) a late-blooming development relative to the examinations of other psychological problems. Only in the 1980s did researchers start unlocking the heads of inveterate loafers, who suffer from more than mere laziness. 13

Mr. Ferrari, a co-editor of *Procrastination and Task Avoidance: Theory, Research, and Treatment* (Plenum Publications, 1995), has helped clarify the distinction between delaying as an act and as a lifestyle. Not every student who ignores assignments until the last minute is an across-the-board offender, known to psychologists as a "trait procrastinator." Many students who drag their feet on term papers might never delay other tasks, such as meeting friends for dinner, showing up for work, or going to the dentist. 14

As Mr. Ferrari explains in *Counseling the Procrastinator in Academic Settings* (American Psychological Association, 2004), a book he edited with three other scholars, there is no typical profile of an academic procrastinator (though family dynamics may influence the behavior). Studies have found no significant relationship between procrastination and intelligence or particular Myers-Briggs personality types. 15

Characteristics of academic procrastinators.

Research does show that academic procrastinators tend to lack self-confidence, measure low on psychologists' tests of "conscientiousness," get lost in wishful thoughts, and lie low during group assignments. 16

In one study, Mr. Ferrari found that students at highly selective colleges reported higher rates of academic procrastination than students from less selective institutions. In another, the motives for academic procrastination among students at an elite college differed from students' motives at a nonselective one (the former put off assignments because they found them unpleasant, while the latter did so because they feared failure or social disapproval). 17

Two types of procrastinators.

Mr. Ferrari identifies two kinds of habitual lollygaggers. "Arousal procrastinators" believe they work best under pressure and tend to delay tasks for the thrill. "Avoidant procrastinators" are self-doubters who tend to postpone tasks because they worry about performing inadequately, or because they fear their success may raise others' expectations of them. 18

Other findings complicate fear-of-failure theories. Some researchers say an inability to control impulses explains procrastinators best. And a recent study by Mr. Ferrari and Steven J. Scher, an associate professor of psychology at Eastern Illinois University, suggests that people who are typically negative avoid assignments that do not challenge them creatively or intellectually, whereas people who are typically positive more easily tackle less-stimulating tasks. 19

Science is not likely to resolve the mysteries of procrastination anytime soon. After all, among researchers a debate still rages over the very definition of procrastination. Mr. Scher suspects there are different types of the behavior, especially if one defines it as not doing what one thinks one should do. 20

"A common thing that many people put off is doing the dishes," Mr. Scher says. "But there are also times when those same people will all of a sudden find that doing the dishes is the most important thing they have to do—thereby putting off some other type of task." 21

Homework-Eating Dogs

Psychologists do agree on one thing: Procrastination is responsible for most of the world's homework-eating dogs. Where procrastinators go, excuses follow. 22

Links procrastination with lying to excuse it.

Students who engaged in academic procrastination said more than 70 percent of the excuses they gave instructors for not completing an assignment were fraudulent (the lies were most prevalent in large lecture classes taught by women who were "lenient"), Mr. Ferrari found in one study. In another, procrastinating students generally said they experienced a positive feeling when they fibbed; although they did feel bad when they recalled the lie, such remorse did not seem to prevent them from using phony excuses in the future. 23

Mr. Ferrari has also experimented with giving bonus points for early work. In a study published in the journal *Teaching of Psychology,* he found that such incentives prompted 80 percent of students to fulfill a course requirement to participate in six psychological experiments by a midpoint date. On average, only 50 percent had done so before he offered the inducement. 24

Major criticism of current approach of many professors to procrastination: students encouraged not to meet deadlines.

Mr. Ferrari believes that academe sends mixed messages about procrastination. Most professors talk about the importance of deadlines, but some are quick to bend them, particularly those who put a premium on being liked by their students. In one of Mr. Ferrari's studies, 90 percent of instructors said they did not require the substantiation of excuses for late work. 25

"We're not teaching responsibility anymore," Mr. Ferrari says. "I'm not saying we need to be stringent, strict, and inflexible, but we shouldn't be spineless. When we are overly flexible, it just teaches them that they can ignore the deadlines of life." 26

Ambivalence about deadlines pervades American culture. People demand high-speed results, whether they are at work or in restaurants. Yet this is also a land in which department stores encourage holiday shoppers to postpone their shopping until Christmas Eve, when they receive huge discounts. And each year on April 15, television news reporters from coast to coast descend upon post offices to interview (and celebrate) people who wait until the final hours to mail their tax returns. 27

"As a society," Mr. Ferrari says, "we tend to excuse the person who says 'I'm a procrastinator,' even though we don't like procrastinators." 28

But do all people who ignore assignments until the 11th hour necessarily suffer or do themselves harm? 29

One of Mr. Ferrari's former students, Mariya Zaturenskaya, a psychology major who graduated from DePaul last spring, says some last-minute workers are motivated, well organized, and happy to write a paper in one sitting. Although students who cram for tests tend to retain less knowledge than other students, research has yet to reveal a significant correlation between students' procrastination and grades. 30

A finding contrary to what many people think.

"Some students just need that deadline, that push," Ms. Zaturenskaya says. "Some people really are more efficient when they have less time." 31

Treating the Problem

Before Jill Gamble went to college, she had little time to waste. As a high-school student, she had earned a 3.75 grade-point average while playing three sports. Each night she went to practice, ate dinner, did her homework, and went to bed. 32

After matriculating at Ohio State University, however, her life lost its structure. At first, all she had to do was go to classes. Most days she napped, spent hours using Instant Messenger, and stayed up late talking to her suite mates. 33

As unread books piled up on her desk, she told herself her professors were too demanding. The night before her Sociology 101 final, she stayed up drinking Mountain Dew, frantically reading the seven chapters she had ignored for weeks. "My procrastination had created a lot of anxiety," Ms. Gamble recalls. "I was angry with myself that I let it get to that point." 34

Extended example of common college student procrastinator and efforts to remedy the problem.

She got a C-minus in the class and a 2.7 in her first quarter. When her grades improved only slightly in the second quarter, Ms. Gamble knew she needed help. So she enrolled in a course called "Strategies for College Success." 35

The five-year-old course uses psychological strategies, such as the taking of reasonable risks, to jolt students out of their bad study habits. Twice a week students spend class time in a computer lab, where they get short lectures on study skills. Students must then practice each skill on the computer by using a special software program. 36

Instructors use weekly quizzes to cut procrastination time from weeks to days and to limit last-minute cramming. The frequent tests mean one or two low scores will not doom a student's final grade, ideally reducing study-related stress. 37

Students complete assignments at their own pace, allowing faster ones to stay engaged and slower ones to keep up, yet there are immovable dates by which students must finish each set of exercises. Enrollees learn how to write and follow to-do lists that 38 reduce large tasks, such as writing an essay, into bite-size goals (like sitting down to outline a single chapter of a text instead of reading the whole book).

Each student must also examine his or her use of rationalizations for procrastinating. 39
The course's creator, Bruce W. Tuckman, a professor of education at Ohio State, says he also teaches students to recognize the underlying cause of procrastination, which he describes as self-handicapping.

Another explanation for procrastination: provides ready excuse for not doing well.

"It's like running a full race with a knapsack full of bricks on your back," Mr. Tuckman 40
says. "When you don't win, you can say it's not that you're not a good runner, it's just that you had this sack of bricks on your back. When students realize that, it can be easier for them to change."

Many of the worst procrastinators end up earning the highest grades in the class, 41
Mr. Tuckman says. And among similar types of students with the same prior cumulative grade-point averages, those who took the class have consistently outperformed those who did not take it.

Treatment for procrastination can work: The problem has solutions.

After completing the course, Ms. Gamble says, she stopped procrastinating and 42
went on to earn a 3.8 the next semester. Since then, she has made the dean's list regularly, and now helps counsel her procrastinating peers at Ohio State's learning center.

"In workshops, we'll say, 'How many of you identify yourselves as procrastinators?' 43
and they will throw their hands in the air and giggle, even though procrastination is a very negative thing," Ms. Gamble says. "Why do we do this so willingly? The answer is that we let ourselves procrastinate. If someone was doing it to us, we wouldn't be so willing to raise our hands."

A Universal Problem

Psychologists generally agree that the behavior is learned and that students choose 44
to procrastinate, even though they may feel helpless to stop. Mr. Ferrari, the DePaul professor, describes the behavior as a self-constructed mental trap that people can escape the same way smokers can kick the habit.

Mr. Tuckman qualifies his optimism by saying one cannot hope to cure procrastination 45
so much as reduce it.

"It's very hard to go from being a hard-core procrastinator to a nonprocrastinator," 46
says Mr. Tuckman, one of many researchers who has developed a scale that measures levels of procrastination. "You're just so used to doing it, there's something about it that reinforces it for you."

Scholars are learning that procrastination knows no borders. At a conference of 47
international procrastination researchers this summer at Roehampton University, in England, Mr. Ferrari and several other scholars presented a paper that compared the prevalence rates of chronic procrastination among adults in Australia, England, Peru, Spain, the United States, and Venezuela. They found that arousal and avoidant procrastinators were equally prevalent in all of the nations, with men and women reporting similar rates of each behavior.

Interesting cultural variation in attitudes toward procrastination.

That is not to say all cultures share the same view of procrastination. Karem Diaz, a pro- 48
fessor of psychology at the Pontifical Catholic University of Peru, has studied the behavior among Peruvians, whose expectations of timeliness tend to differ from those of Americans.

"In Peru we talk about the 'Peruvian time,'" Ms. Diaz writes in an e-mail message. "If we are invited to a party at 7 p.m., it is rude to show on time. . . . It is even socially punished. Therefore, not presenting a paper on time is expected and forgiven." 49

Few Peruvians are familiar with the Spanish word "*procrastinacion*," which complicates discussions of the subject. "Some people think it is some sexual behavior when they hear the word," Ms. Diaz says. Yet the professor has been intrigued to find that some Peruvians identify themselves as procrastinators, and experience the negative consequences of the behavior even though social norms encourage it. 50

Strategies for helping people bridge the gap between their actions and intentions vary. A handful of colleges in Belgium, Canada, and the Netherlands have just begun to develop counseling programs that draw on cognitive and behavioral research. The early findings: Helping students understand why they dawdle and teaching them self-efficacy tends to lessen their procrastination—or at least make it more manageable. 51

Timothy A. Pychyl, an associate professor of psychology at Carleton University, in Ottawa, Ontario, says group meetings are a promising approach, particularly those in which students make highly specific goals and help each other resist temptations to slack off. "For many people, it's an issue of priming the pump . . . as simple as making a deal with oneself to spend 10 minutes on a task," Mr. Pychyl says. "At least the next day they can see themselves as having made an effort as opposed to doing nothing at all." 52

Clarry H. Lay, a retired psychology professor at York University, in Toronto, who continues to counsel student procrastinators, uses personality feedback to promote better "self-regulation" among students. In group sessions, he discusses the importance of studying even when one is not in the "right mood" and of setting aside a regular place to work. Some participants become more confident and efficient. Others see improvements, only to experience relapses. 53

Clever and memorable ending.

Each semester one in five students miss the first session. Some sign up early but never show, while others arrive late or attend sporadically. But Mr. Lay understands. The counselor is a chronic procrastinator himself. 54

Questions for Discussion

1. Hoover and the experts he cites do not mention the impact of technology on procrastination. How big a role does time spent on social networking or other online activities (watching videos, playing games) play in your tendency to put off tasks? How big a role does it play in accomplishing such tasks?

2. Ferrari, one of the scholars Hoover cites, distinguishes "arousal procrastinators" from "avoidance procrastinators." State the difference in your own words. Do you think it is possible to sometimes be one, sometimes the other, depending on the task? Can arousal and avoidance be combined, working together to cause procrastination?
3. How did Hoover attempt to gain your attention at the beginning of the article? If you wanted to keep on reading, what did he say that piqued your interest?

Thinking as a Writer

What Is the Rhetorical Situation?

1. What is Hoover's *purpose* in writing this essay? What is his *angle* on the topic? How would you describe his *voice*?
2. Who is Hoover's intended *audience*? Is he writing for instructors, for college students who procrastinate, for all college students, for lawyers, or for some other more general readership? Is there anything in the article you can cite that implies his target readership?
3. Using the Concept Close-Up: Assessing Data (page 104) as a guide, answer the following questions: What data does Hoover draw on? How did the article inform you—that is, what does it say that is news to you? What do you know about procrastination as a result of the information he presented and how he led you to understand it? ■

Collaborative Activity

Organizing Headings

As a class or in small groups, analyze the structure of the four subheadings in Hoover's article. How does he divide each heading into parts, points, or kinds of information? Does his organization of the headings seem logical to you and easy to follow? Why or why not? ■

For more on using and documenting sources, see Chapters 19, 20, and 21.

Collaborative Activity

Integrating Sources

Hoover handles source material well by integrating it into his prose; identifying the names and qualifications of his sources; and mixing summary, paraphrasing, and quoting. As a class, work through all or part of his article, studying what he does with each use of source material and listing the various techniques employed. ■

READING 6.2

On Their Way? A Portrait of Young Adults

MARTHA ROSS AND NICOLE BATEMAN

A Washington, D.C., think tank with branches in Qatar and India, the Brookings Institute's mission is to "provide innovative and practical recommendations that advance three broad goals: strengthen American democracy; foster the economic and social welfare, security and opportunity of all Americans; and secure a more open, safe, prosperous, and cooperative international system."

Martha Ross and Nicole Bateman do research for the Metropolitan Policy division at Brookings. Ross is a Fellow there and Batemen is a Senior Research Assistant.

A good job providing entry into the middle class increasingly requires a college education, but large numbers of young people in the United States may not reach this level of economic refuge. About 40 percent of all 18 to 24 year-olds are not in school and do not have a college degree, placing them at risk of unemployment or unsteady, low-wage work as they approach adulthood. 1

Understanding who makes up that 40 percent, and where they live, are important steps toward helping more young people connect to educational and economic opportunity. 2

Educational Attainment—a Sobering Picture

Labor market sorting by education starts young. Nearly 80 percent of 23–24-year-olds with a Bachelor's degree have a job, compared to 60 percent of those with a high school diploma or less. Recent labor market projections show that the importance of education in the labor market may only accelerate: jobs requiring a graduate degree are expected to grow twice as fast as those requiring only a high school diploma or less. 3

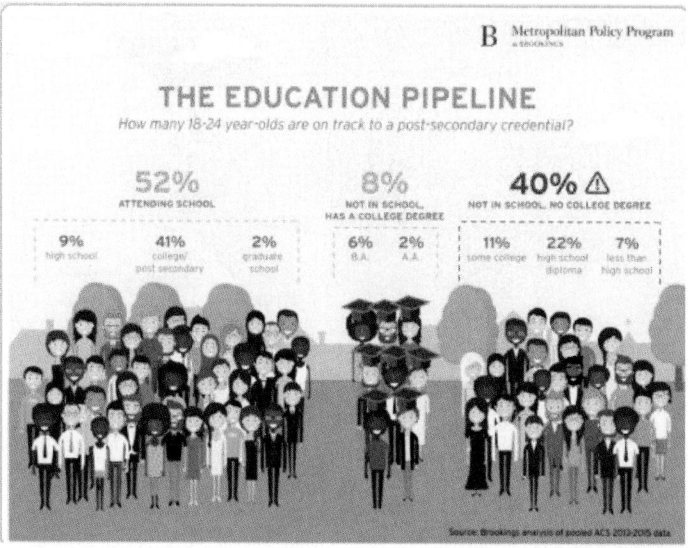

© Brookings Institute

Among all young people in the U.S. ages 18 to 24, seven percent did not complete high school, 22 percent have a high school diploma but no other credential, and 11 percent have completed some college but did not earn a degree. This "some college" group is a mixed one; some of these young people are probably in good shape having 4 completed occupational-related programs in fields such as IT, healthcare, and auto mechanics. On the other hand, the group also includes individuals who took one or more courses not necessarily focused on particular skills or industries, left school without a credential, and may have incurred student debt along the way. Unfortunately, evidence suggests that the majority of those with some college experience and no degree have not obtained an alternative credential such as an educational certificate, professional certification, or license.

Significant Variation Locally

Places with low levels of education are not well-positioned to compete in an economy 5
shifting towards technology and professional services. As economist Enrico Moretti described, "A handful of cities with the 'right' industries and a solid base of human capital keep attracting good employers and offering high wages, while those at the other extreme, cities with the 'wrong' industries and a limited human capital base, are stuck with dead-end jobs and low average wages." The educational attainment of local young people is thus an important indicator of how a city is positioned for future growth and prosperity.

In this respect, some places are on much more solid footing than others. Educational 6
attainment among 18 to 24 year-olds varies widely at the local level, reflecting demographics, the strength of regional economies, and dominant sectors in those economies. Among large

Young adults ages 18-24 who are not in school and have a high school diploma or less, as a share of all young adults

U.S. cities and countries with populations over 500,000 people

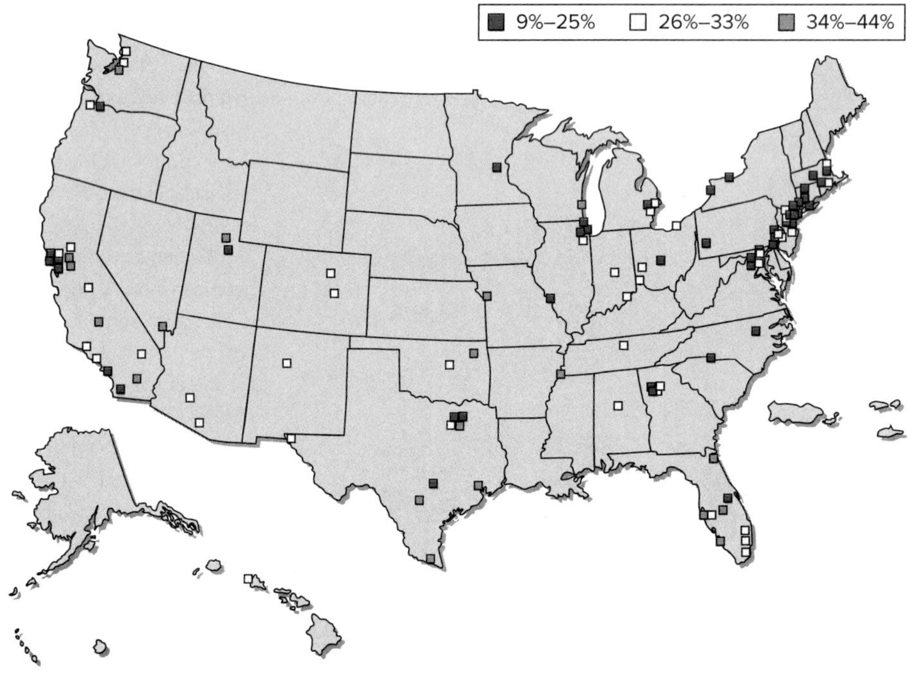

Source: Brookings analysis of pooled ACS 2013–2015 data.

cities and counties, the share of young adults who are not in school and have no more than a high school diploma ranges from 40 percent and above (Detroit, Polk County, Fla., Phoenix, Kern County, Calif., and Clark County and Las Vegas in Nevada), to 10 percent and below (Boston and San Francisco). Employment in the tourism and agricultural industries (as in Las Vegas and Clark, Polk, and Kern counties) does not typically require high levels of education. The presence of relatively large Latino populations (Phoenix, Las Vegas, and Clark and Kern counties) also plays a role, since Latinos overall—and young Latino immigrants in particular—have lower educational levels than other groups. Boston and San Francisco, meanwhile, are technology hubs that attract and draw from well-educated labor pools.

Thus, we face two major, inter-related challenges: 1) Too many young people face bleak employment prospects based on their educational levels and skills; and 2) These young people are concentrated in regions that are themselves struggling economically—part of the nation's economic divergence in which a fortunate few metro superstars dramatically outpace the others on wages, job growth, and productivity. 7

Workforce Development, Meet Regional Economic Development

It is not an original idea that an educated workforce supports economic growth. Historically, however, economic development has sought to attract workers from other regions more than supporting efforts to develop homegrown talent. 8

Our Metro colleagues have argued that should change, and that business leaders and economic development groups should invest in and cultivate long-term economic assets—including the skills of local residents—in order to promote more inclusive growth and create better outcomes for people, firms, and communities. Meanwhile, some of the most successful workforce development strategies are the result of close collaboration between educators, community groups, and employers. 9

To increase economic opportunity for young people and prepare the future labor force, we should adhere to the following principles, and support active partnerships across sectors (education, business, community groups, government) to make it happen: 10

1. **Continue to increase access to post-secondary school or training,** but set our goals around completion. Enrollment is only a first step; too many students leave without earning certificates or degrees. 11
2. **Recognize that a Bachelor's degree is not the only game in town.** A four-year investment in time and money is not feasible or desirable for all, but apprenticeships, associate degrees, and short-term training programs represent real learning experiences and can generate significant payoffs in the labor market. 12
3. **Hire based on skills rather than degrees,** which are not always an accurate measure of what a person knows and can do. Evaluate the skills required for particular job openings, and assess job seekers accordingly in order to find the right match. This creates a hiring pool more attuned to employer needs, and opens up positions to a wider range of job seekers previously locked out by an AA or BA requirement. 13
4. **Lastly, ensure that employers are not passive recipients of talent.** Through active partnerships with educators and training organizations—for example, providing input on curriculum and offering internships—employers can strengthen the talent pool from which they draw and help their own bottom line. 14

These ideas point to solutions that are entirely within the realm of the 15
possible, and in fact, they are already being implemented—but at nowhere near the scale required. The country is doing itself no favors by consigning millions of young people to the margins of the labor market and economic mainstream, even as many employers say they can't find the workers they need. In forthcoming research, we will look more closely at 18-to-24-year-olds who are out of work and identify local strategies to help young adults increase their skills and find pathways into the work world. We need to think and act more boldly if we want to ensure that economic growth and prosperity are shared more widely across both people and places.

The authors thank Natalie Holmes for much of the data analysis supporting this post.

Questions for Discussion

1. All informing is motivated by some need or desire to know something. What need or desire does this article satisfy? How does it attempt to catch and hold reader attention?
2. Information often corrects misinformation or disinformation, which in turn leads to misunderstanding. How might this article correct some misunderstanding?
3. Information varies in the degree of importance it has for individual people. How important is the information in this article for you? How could you use it for a paper in a college course?

Thinking as a Writer

What Is the Rhetorical Situation?

1. What is the writer's *purpose* in this article? What is the authors' *angle* on the topic? How would you describe the piece's *voice*?
2. Who is this article's intended *audience*? Is it written for people who are experts about the economic status of young adults, for people who are curious to learn more about them, for people with some degree of bias against them, for young adults themselves, or for some combination of these groups? Is there anything in the article you can cite that implies its target readership?
3. Using the Concept Close-Up: Assessing Data (page 104) as a guide, answer the following question: How does this article turn information into knowledge? Specifically, how does it interpret the data from the survey so that readers understand what it means? ■

The Assignment

Compose an informative article that satisfies a readership's need or desire to know something. Depending on your instructor's requirements, your article can draw from personal experience (for example, a hobby, sport, or internship) and incorporate information gained from all forms of research (for example, print and online materials, interviews, and questionnaires).

What Can I Write About?

Promising informative topics can come from readings in any college class, from national and local news, from personal experience, or from online sources. Consider the following possibilities:

- **Personal experience.** Hobbies, sports, physical fitness, diets, gardening, cooking, and the like can be promising topics.
- **Work experience.** Businesses rely on the flow of information, so topics where you work are good possibilities. You may be an expert on something interesting to other people, such as how to get the best deal in purchasing a car.
- **Your community.** Community affairs are also a rich source of informative topics, such as the rules that govern home renovation in certain historical districts or the policies for coping with homeless people.

Consider writing in one of the common informative genres:

- **Book or movie review.** Provides guidance for what to read or see.
- **Technical description.** Explains how something works–for example, hydroponics, growing plants in liquid mediums rather than soil.
- **Cause-and-effect essay.** Explains why things happen, such as the increase in allergies when most other human health problems have declined in the United States.
- **Report.** Summarizes the findings of surveys, tests, or field observations–for example, how effective red-light cameras are or how well new software for class registration works.

How Do I Present Information? Questioning the Rhetorical Situation

Begin by picturing a **rhetorical situation** for your writing project, a real-world context for communicating. You should consider the *key variables in any act of communication:* a writer with something to say, a reader the writer wishes to reach, and a kind of text appropriate to the writing task. These three variables will affect many decisions in the composing process.

Writer: What Is My Purpose, and What Impression Should Readers Have of Me?

See Chapter 17, pages 372–78, for guidance on how to evaluate sources.

Your purpose is to provide accurate, current, and sufficient information to meet the needs and interests of your readers. "Accurate" and "current" simply mean that you should avoid, to the best of your ability, **misinformation,** *data that misrepresents reality or was once accurate but is not so now.* Because misinformation is common, both in print and Internet sources, check the information you find against other sources, especially if the content seems biased, is inconsistent with common sense or with what you know already, or is otherwise suspect. "Sufficient" is entirely relative to your reader: If you are an experienced stamp collector, for instance, you could easily overwhelm readers just taking up the hobby with too much information or assume that they know things beginners would not know.

Informative writing has a wide range of voices and styles, depending mainly on the topic and the readership. A light touch joined with humor might work well for informing amateur cooks about the amazing array of olive oils currently sold, but a piece for parents about the relative safety of car seats for young children must sound serious and concerned throughout.

An informative writer should be a helpful guide and therefore use **plain style:** *simple, direct sentence structure and ordinary, everyday vocabulary and illustrations.* Include technical information only as required, and be sure to explain what you include at the level your audience can comprehend.

Audience: Who Is My Reader?

The key question in selecting your readership is: **Who would profit most from knowing what I know?**

All good writing is reader aware, but informative writing is especially so because *what qualifies as information depends on who is reading it.* For example, an article describing ways to protect your computer from viruses might be informative for a new computer user but not informative to a technical expert or to someone who does not own a computer.

Select your readership with care, paying special attention to the background knowledge you assume readers have. If you assume too little, you will have to provide too much background; if you assume too much, you can have a readership you cannot reasonably expect to inform. An article about the latest computer game, for example, might be written for readers at an intermediate or advanced level of experience but not written for someone without experience or for people who create such games and thus know as much or more than you do.

Text: What Moves Can I Make?

The basic moves of informative writing are:

- Identify your topic.
- Define and illustrate key terms.
- Supply background information as needed, depending on the level of knowledge you assume your readers have.
- Provide a context for your topic, such as how common procrastination is, misinformation about historical events, or the costs of some problem in the workplace.

- Indicate why your topic matters–for example, it will help people cope better with procrastination; it will show that 40 percent of all young adults lack the education they need for satisfactory employment and why this matters; it will help people vote as well-informed citizens.
- Limit your topic as necessary to meet space requirements (for instance, discuss the amount of time wasted as a result of some workplace problem).
- Divide your topic into parts, and divide those parts into parts, so that your reader can concentrate on one large point or issue at a time and so that each large point or issue has a set of paragraphs that deal *only* with that issue or point.
- Depending on the nature of your topic, describe *how* it works, *what* motivates it, *how* to use it appropriately or safely, and so on, *going into detail in those places where your reader most needs the information.*

For examples of these strategies at work, consult Readings 6.1 and 6.2 or the revised student example at the end of this chapter.

How Do I Present Information? Engaging the Writing Process

No two people compose in exactly the same way, and even the same person may go through the writing process in different ways with different assignments. Nevertheless, because no one can attend to everything at once, there are phases in handling any significant writing task. You begin by preparing to write, generating content and finding your angle.

The next phase is planning and drafting your paper, getting a version, however rough it may be, on paper or screen so that you have something to work with during the next two stages: (1) revising your draft, making changes to the content, arrangement, and style of your writing, and (2) editing your draft to correct problems at the paragraph and sentence level, such as lack of focus and coherence, awkward or unclear sentences, and errors of grammar, spelling, and punctuation.

If you are assigned to write about a topic you know little about, organizing a "plan of attack" by answering some preparatory questions—such as, "What do I already know?" and "What do I still need to know?"—will help get the process rolling.
© Dean Drobot/123RF

Exploring Your Topic

In this phase you are *finding something to say,* generating ideas and content, which includes discovering your angle or point of view.

Let's assume the most challenging informative writing situation: a "cold" topic, one selected by someone else–a professor, a boss, the head of a committee you are on–and one that requires research because you know little or nothing about it. How do you begin? Organizing your efforts by answering the following questions will help.

What Does the Task Require?

Some informing situations call for only minimal interpretation. If your assignment is to trace sales patterns over the past ten years for a particular item your company makes, you can do that with charts and graphs combined with short commentary. In contrast, if your assignment is to write about potential power struggles among the various ethnic groups in Afghanistan, you will need to do more than tell your readers about the ethnic groups. You will need to analyze the potential for conflict, cooperation, and alliances, not only as they exist now but also as they are likely to exist in the future. Clearly, in this case, far more interpretation is necessary and appropriate.

However, make *a firm distinction between informing and arguing.* Informative writing typically avoids **open advocacy**–that is, *defending a position on a controversial issue with the intent to convince or persuade your readers.* Because many informative topics are controversial, you may need to describe the range of existing opinion. In interpreting existing opinion, you can say which point of view seems most acceptable to you and explain why. However, defending your opinion or someone else's at length would be inappropriate.

What Research Will I Need to Do?

We recommend brainstorming your topic first, writing down what you know and think about it in two or three fifteen-minute sessions separated by short breaks. Write whatever comes to mind without being concerned about how good it is. Step back and examine what you have; then ask, **"What do I need to know?"** Make a list in answer to this question, and you are prepared to get the most from research.

THE ART OF QUESTIONING Assessing News Stories

When you encounter a news story in doing research, use these questions to help you assess it.

1. **What is the writer's point of view?** Every news story is written by someone who has a point of view, a purpose for writing, and the potential for bias.
2. **Who would find this story worth reading?** Information is told to someone, some audience or readership.
3. **What makes this information newsworthy?** Information is published because it is newsworthy: that is, it is surprising, interesting.
4. All news stories include answers to the prime journalistic questions: **Who? What? When? Where? Why? How?** Answer these questions for the article you are assessing, being careful to distinguish what the writer says from sources cited.
5. **Who and what are mentioned and why?** News stories often mention people, books, organizations, conferences, and the like connected with the story. Use the references to pursue further research.

Information comes either from print and online sources or from **field research,** which involves *collecting your own information, such as conducting polls, interviewing experts, making firsthand observations, or carrying out simple experiments.* See Chapter 15, Planning a Research Project, and Chapter 16, Finding Sources, for guidance. Be sure to keep careful notes as you work your way through the source material (see pages 381–85) so you know which information came from what source and so you do not confuse your own comments about the source material with the material itself.

How Can I Evaluate the Research?

Answering the following questions will be especially useful when evaluating research.

1. **Is the data current?** Remember that a book or article published this year is likely to contain information that is at least two to three years old. Check it against more up-to-date sources of information, such as online data banks.
2. **How was the data generated?** In general we rely on a source's reputation for reliability, credentials, and qualifications. However, some information requires more. The Brookings article on the economic status of young adults provides the big picture, but cannot tell you what you need to know about how young adults are faring in your local community, what might be done to improve the situation, and so on.
3. **What sources did your source use?** Most published articles cite multiple sources of information. For information you are relying on most, go to the primary source: for example, the reporter who was an eyewitness to the event, the scientist who conducted the experiment, or the expert who recorded the observations. In short, *consult the sources your source cites.*
4. **What interpretations are consistent with the data?** The first three questions focus attention on assessing your information; this question asks you to assess your own response to it. No one can do research without forming conclusions about what the information means. Forming conclusions helps you interpret the information that matters most in informing your reader. However, *let the best information you have drive your interpretation rather than imposing an interpretation you had before researching the information.* Put another way, adjust your thinking to the information rather than the information to your thinking.

ACTIVITY 6.1 *Writer's Notebook*

Evaluating Sources

First, use the guidelines for evaluating sources (Chapter 17, pages 372–78) to assess your sources. Some might be too old, not directly relevant, or suspect because the writer may be biased by affiliation with a special interest group.

Second, sort the sources that are left into two groups by relevance and quality:

- The two or three you will rely on the most.
- The two or three you will probably use less, such as for only one section or paragraph in your paper.

As you assess your sources, be sure to preserve your thinking in notes to yourself. You may need to refresh your memory as you write and revise. ■

Preparing to Write

In evaluating your sources, you are already sorting out information you might use from all the information you have.

How Can I Decide Which Information to Include?

Consider the following questions:

1. **What do my readers know already?** You can either not mention such information or briefly refer to it to remind your readers.
2. **What do my readers need to know?** This is the key question. For most topics you can find much more general information than you can possibly include. However, what counts is only (1) what will be news to your readers, information they do not have, and (2) selecting from that news what is most relevant to how your readers will use the information. In a student essay about illegal immigration, for example, the writer selected information she considered most relevant to voters in the upcoming general election. That is, she asked herself, "Of everything I know about illegal immigration, what do well-informed voters need to know?" Ask yourself a similar question in deciding what information to include on any topic.

How Can I Find My Angle?

1. **What impact do you want your information to have?** In informative writing, what even qualifies as information depends on your readers. It makes sense, then, that your angle will also be reader-centered. The student example (pages 128–134) provides a good illustration of angle. The student wanted to impress upon her readers that not treating people kindly at work is not just a social or personnel problem but a big financial problem.
2. **In what framework is my information best understood?** In the case of illegal immigration, economics provided the best angle because supply-and-demand drives the entire process. There are usually jobs on our side of the border, well-paid jobs from a migrant worker's point of view, and grinding poverty and lack of opportunity on Mexico's side. Readers must understand the economics of illegal immigration to understand the topic at all. Hence, the student's choice of economics as her framework was ideal for her topic.

Drafting Your Paper

Begin by recalling what informative writing does: *It makes information relevant or interesting for readers; turns facts into something that matters, has meaning, a point.* What this means in practice is that selection depends on giving your readers "news"—things they do not know—and getting them to understand why the new information matters.

Select from all your information *what counts or is significant:* the results of the latest research, data your readers will not know, information that is surprising and/or that runs counter to what most people believe or imagine. Also select information *based on the story you can tell about it*—that is, in how it comes together to make a point, illuminate a problem, or clarify a cause or effect.

What Stance and Voice Are Appropriate for Presenting Information?

It is important to inform your readers, to provide facts or data they do not know or may have forgotten. Even more important, however, is interpreting the information you provide. *What you have to say about the information should be center stage.*

Consequently, reconsider your **stance** and angle, your point of view on your topic. For example, which of the following are you doing?

- Challenging beliefs and attitudes based on misinformation or disinformation?
- Enabling your readers to do something they otherwise could not do or not do as well?
- Explaining a cause-and-effect relationship?
- Describing a problem and ways to solve it?
- Giving advice based on experience with your topic?

There are many other possibilities—*what matters is that you know what you are doing and why.* Perhaps you will change your angle as you write; perhaps in assessing your draft you will find another angle you like better and write the second draft around it. Nevertheless, being as clear as you can about what motivates the information you are providing helps to focus and sustain your first draft.

Also consider what **voice** is appropriate for this aim and genre. Information requires your take on what the information means and why it matters, and therefore your voice will emerge mainly in your commentary. Eric Hoover's voice (see pages 106–111) emerges best in *commenting on his information,* as, for example, in the following sentences:

> Mr. Ferrari and other scholars from around the world are finding that procrastination is more complex—and pervasive—than armchair analysts might assume. And helping people climb out of their pits of postponement is not as simple as giving them a pill or a pep talk.
>
> The task is particularly challenging in the hothouses of procrastination known as college campuses. Free time, long-term deadlines, and extracurricular diversions conspire against academic efficiency. Students are infamous for not tackling their assignments until the jaws of deadlines are closing.

The underlined words convey Hoover's attitude toward procrastination, the seriousness of the problem, the urgent need to understand and attend to it.

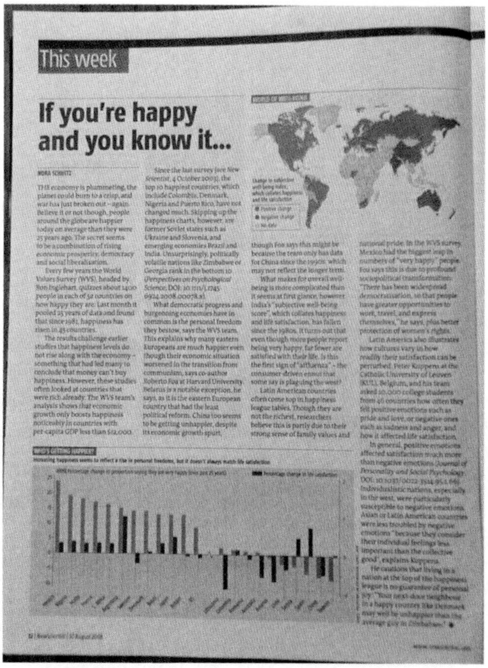

Images and graphics are an effective way to present information because they are easy for readers to understand and they add visual interest.

© Mark Dierker/McGraw Hill Education

How Might I Use Images and Graphics to Present Information?

When appropriate, plan to use photographs, drawings, maps, tables, and graphics for presenting readers with new information. Use graphics when you can because they:

- Take less space than giving information in prose.
- Are easier for readers to understand, remember, and refer to.
- Separate data from your commentary on what the data mean.

Here's the basic principle in deciding whether to use graphics: *When possible, use graphics to present information; use writing to tell your story about the information.*

Developing and Organizing Your Information

Develop an informative article effectively by doing the following:

- Pull together closely related material from several sources.
- Offer your own comments–explanations, illustrations, and ways of understanding the source material.

See Chapter 32 for detailed guidance on the design and use of visuals.

Consider this example from Hoover's article:

> Mr. Ferrari identifies two kinds of habitual lollygaggers. "Arousal procrastinators" believe they work best under pressure and tend to delay tasks for the thrill. "Avoidant procrastinators" are self-doubters who tend to postpone tasks because they worry about performing inadequately, or because they fear their success may raise others' expectations of them.
>
> Other findings complicate fear-of-failure theories. Some researchers say an inability to control impulses explains procrastinators best. And a recent study by Mr. Ferrari and Steven J. Scher, an associate professor of psychology at Eastern Illinois University, suggests that people who are typically negative avoid assignments that do not challenge them creatively or intellectually, whereas people who are typically positive more easily tackle less-stimulating tasks.
>
> Science is not likely to resolve the mysteries of procrastination anytime soon. After all, among researchers a debate still rages over the very definition of procrastination. Mr. Scher suspects there are different types of the behavior, especially if one defines it as not doing what one thinks one should do.

Passage pulls together information from two sources, defines two kinds of procrastinators, and indicates how complex the procrastination problem is.

Organizing information boils down to *answering reader questions in a sequence that makes sense.* The answer to one question implies another question, the answer to which implies yet another question, until you run out of questions that need answering to adequately inform your audience. In "Tomorrow, I Love Ya!" (pages 106–111), Hoover answers many questions, such as:

- What is procrastination? (paragraphs 1–6)
- What harm does it do? (paragraph 7)
- Why do people procrastinate? (paragraphs 18–21)
- What can be done about procrastination? (paragraphs 36–42)

ACTIVITY 6.2 *In Your Own Work*

Planning Your Draft

You have the information selected from the research you did for your topic. You know the readers you want to reach. Now imagine a conversation with your readers. Given your topic, what questions would they ask? List those questions as they occur to you. Look also at the information you have selected. What questions do they answer? List those as well.

Looking at your list of questions, ask, **"What question comes first?"** Often it will be the definitional question, **"What is it?"** Sometimes the first question is, **"Why does my topic matter?"** Or, **"What background knowledge does my reader need to understand or appreciate the importance of my topic?"**

Whatever you decide the first question must be, it will imply the next, which in turn will imply still another. Order your questions accordingly, and you have a plan for your draft. ■

Revising Your Draft

When you complete your draft, do a self-assessment. The revision questions that follow will help.

1. Early in the paper **have you indicated why your information is important?** How does it relate to your reader's life, crucial decisions, or topics she or he would find interesting?
2. Facts or data amount to misinformation if they are not reported accurately. **Are there any instances where the facts or data you report seem unlikely or contradictory?** Check what you say the facts are against your source.
3. Currency matters because information becomes misinformation if the data is seriously out of date. **Are there any instances where data cited might be too old?**
4. Information must be sufficient for the need at hand, which means there must be enough to satisfy your readers. **Are there places where you need more than you provide? Are there places where you offer too much,** which might confuse or bore your readers?
5. Information does no good if your readers cannot understand it. **Have you explained what the information means *at the level appropriate to your readership?***
6. Informative writers need to be consistent in their assumptions about what their readers know and think about the topic. **Have you assumed too much or too little about what your readers know before reading your paper?** Have you addressed misconceptions and unwarranted positive or negative attitudes they are likely to have?
7. **Have you adopted an angle, a single point of view, to help your readers follow your presentation?** Have you limited your discussion only to matters relevant to your angle?
8. **Have you organized your information into sections–major divisions of your topic– and structured each section to develop content relevant to that section only?** Would using headings, as Eric Hoover does (pages 106–111), help both you and your reader understand your paper's organization better?

9. **In reporting your data, have you mixed quotation, paraphrase, and summary? Have you identified the qualifications of your source?**
10. **Are there places where the information could be handled more efficiently by using visuals, such as photographs, drawings, and/or graphics?** If you have used graphics or plan to add them in revision, be sure to refer to each graphic and discuss what it means in your paper.

Excerpt from Student Amie Hazama's Draft

When writers use subheadings to identify the purpose of different sections of their papers, they still need to attend to the need for transitions as well, to show how each subdivision connects with the one before. This paper uses APA (American Psychological Association) style, so you will notice some differences from MLA style in the way sources are cited. Here is an example from the draft of the student paper printed in final form on pages 128–134.

Hazama's first subheading.

Introduction

A typical day at the office begins for Amanda. Walking to her cubicle, she passes Joe, who seems in a hurry and returns her "Good morning" with just a nod. Later, in a meeting, a phone goes off, distracting everyone. The owner shuts it off but does not offer an apology. On her lunch break, Amanda fills the empty coffee pot in the kitchen and throws out the empty sugar packages lying crumpled on the counter. After lunch, her boss asks her to make some copies, but first she has to spend extra time fixing the jammed photocopier. Back at her desk, she tries to concentrate on a project while two co-workers talk loudly in the next cubicle about a basketball game the night before. Finally, after a long day at work, Amanda is fatigued and stressed.

Hazama's second subheading.

What Is Workplace Incivility?

Workplace incivility is the subject of much research. Christine Pearson and Christine Porath (2005) define the problem as "low intensity deviant behavior that violates workplace norms for mutual respect and may or may not be intended to harm the target" (p. 8). It is called "low intensity" because it is subtle, often unconscious, and frequently not even recognized by managers and workers. Examples of uncivil behavior range from sending a nasty, demeaning note and publicly undermining an employee's credibility to not returning phone calls and failing to acknowledge others in the hall. More extreme examples include bullying by bosses (Hauser, 2011).

The problem with Hazama's draft is the writing's **flow,** its *movement from paragraph to paragraph.* In her revised version, she opened the second section with a short transitional paragraph to show the connection between the two subdivisions of the paper.

What Is Workplace Incivility?

Little acts of insensitivity like those described above are just part of the job for many employees. However, they are also part of a problem that is costing businesses in lost productivity and workers in lost job satisfaction.

Editing Your Revised Draft

A rule of thumb is that no more than 10 percent of the total words in your paper should be direct quotations. (See Chapter 18, pages 386–87 for more about when and when not to use direct quotations.) The solution is to use paraphrase, but when the source contains simple data, rewording it adequately takes some effort. In the original passage below, Hazama's wording is too close to that of the source.

Original Version of the Draft

In the book *Rude Awakenings,* Gonthier (2002), researchers found that as a result of workplace incivility 22% <u>decreased work efforts,</u> 10% <u>decreased the amount of time spent at work,</u> 37% <u>reduced their commitment to the organization,</u> and 12% quit companies to avoid rude instigators (p. 26).

The actual source wording was: "The researchers found that as a result of uncivil behavior at work:

- 22 percent of respondents intentionally decreased work efforts,
- 10 percent decreased the amount of time they spent at work (absenteeism),
- 28 percent lost time avoiding instigators, . . .
- 37 percent reduced their commitment to the organization, . . . and
- 12 percent actually quit companies to avoid rude instigators."

In the edited version Hazama made the wording more her own.

Edited Version

In her book *Rude Awakenings,* Gonthier (2002) reports that 22% of the victims of incivility decreased their work efforts, 10% increased their absenteeism, 37% felt less commitment to their employer, and 12% went so far as to quit their jobs to get away from the offenders (p. 26).

ACTIVITY 6.3 *In Your Own Work*

Editing for Adequate Paraphrasing

When editing, pay special attention to the passages of information you have taken from sources. You may need to do more rewording to avoid accidental plagiarism, which is just as serious as intentional plagiarism. You may want to recast some of the material into charts or other visuals, not only to avoid a poor paraphrase but also to present the information more vividly. ■

REVISED STUDENT EXAMPLE

1

Being Nice Is Good Business

Amie Hazama

Department of English

Southern Methodist University

COMP 101

Professor Channell

November 11, 2012

Being Nice Is Good Business

Hazama decided to use an anecdotal introduction just as Eric Hoover did in his article on procrastination. After reading through this paper, consider what other options would have made an equally effective opening to draw in readers.

A typical day at the office begins for Amanda. Walking to her cubicle, she passes Joe, who seems in a hurry and returns her "Good morning" with just a nod. Later, in a meeting, a phone goes off, distracting everyone. The owner shuts it off but does not offer an apology. On her lunch break, Amanda fills the empty coffee pot in the kitchen and throws out the empty sugar packages lying crumpled on the counter. After lunch, her boss asks her to make some copies, but first she has to spend extra time fixing the jammed photocopier. Back at her desk, she tries to concentrate on a project while two co-workers talk loudly in the next cubicle about a basketball game the night before. Finally, after a long day at work, Amanda is fatigued and stressed.

Hazama's angle is to show the wearing effects of incremental exposure to small acts of incivility. She wants to make readers care about the victims.

Level-one headings should be bold and centered. Hazama uses questions as headings to let the reader know what they will learn in each section of the paper.

What Is Workplace Incivility?

Little acts of insensitivity like those described above are just part of the job for many employees. However, they are also part of a problem that is costing businesses in lost productivity and workers in lost job satisfaction.

Workplace incivility is the subject of much research. Christine Pearson and Christine Porath (2005) define the problem as "low-intensity deviant behavior that violates workplace norms for mutual respect and may or may not be intended to harm the target" (p. 8). It is called "low-intensity" because it is subtle, often unconscious, and frequently not even recognized by managers and workers. Examples of uncivil behavior range from sending a nasty, demeaning note and publicly undermining an employee's credibility to not returning phone calls and failing to acknowledge others in the hall. More extreme examples include bullying by bosses (Hauser, 2011).

This paper is documented according to APA (American Psychological Association) style, which is commonly used in the social sciences. See pages 433–56 for a full treatment of APA style.

Hazama uses the comparison mode of development to define the concept of incivility.

Incivility is the opposite of civility, which is being aware of and respecting others. P.M. Forni is a civility expert and Professor of Italian Literature at Johns Hopkins University. In his book *Choosing Civility,* Forni states, "Courtesy, politeness, manners, and civility are all, in essence, forms of awareness. Being civil means being constantly aware of others and weaving restraint and consideration into the very fabric of this awareness" (Forni, 2002, p. 9). Forni's "Three R's" of civility are "respect, restraint, and responsibility" (as cited in Hauser, 2011). Saying a simple "please" and "thank you," putting trash in the proper receptacles, and signaling before making a right hand turn are examples of civility (Forni, 2002, p. 9). Civility is everywhere in daily life. Unfortunately, so is incivility.

As a transition into the causes of incivility, Hazama sets up a context for learning more about incivility—its prevalence in the workplace today.

What Are the Causes of Workplace Incivility?

Incivility has become common in the workplace. Pearson and Porath (2005, p. 7) surveyed close to 800 U.S. employees to find out about their personal observations of incivility while at work. Ten percent said they witnessed it on a daily basis, and twice that number, twenty percent, said they themselves were victims of it "at least once per week." Experts give several reasons for the increase. Oddly, one cause suggested by Giovinella Gonthier (2002), a civility consultant in Chicago, is the rise of equality in the workplace, caused by the feminist and civil rights movements of the 1960s. In the past, people who were superiors showed their high positions through manners and other "rituals of behavior" (p. 8), but in a more democratic society, we have dropped the manners that used to "prop up" unequal relationships (p. 9). In that same period, young people disillusioned by government and the Vietnam War "lost respect for tradition," and this generation went on to raise their children permissively. Everything just became more casual (Gonthier, 2002, pp. 4–5).

Pearson and Porath (2005) bring in a more recent cause: In our high-tech, fast-paced workplaces, people believe being nice takes too much time and "impersonal modes of contact do not require courtesies of interaction . . ." (p. 7). Also, there is the "me first" attitude common in the competitive workplace (p. 7) and the Gordon Gekko types, with the "impetuous, rude, 'everyone else be damned' personality" that many people associate with success ever since the movie *Wall Street* (Gonthier, 2002, p. 3).

Hazama now turns from the causes of the problem in business to the effects on business.

What Are the Ramifications of Incivility at Work?

All of this incivility is costly to businesses. Porath estimates that "stress and lost productivity" as a result of incivility costs the United States' total economy multi-billion dollars each year (as cited in Hauser, 2011). Pearson and Porath (2005) have found that "incivility corrodes organizational culture and that employees who are on the receiving end will respond in ways that are costly to their organizations" (p. 8). For example, two thirds of the victims of incivility reported that they put less effort into their work, four out of five said they lost time worrying about bad experiences, and 63% said they went out of their way to avoid being around the person who offended them (Hauser, 2011). In her book *Rude Awakenings,* Gonthier (2002) reports that 22% of the victims of incivility decreased their work efforts, 10% increased their absenteeism, 37% felt less commitment to their employer, and 12% went so far as to quit their jobs to get away from the offenders (p. 26). Incivility and disengagement go hand in hand, and they result in a very high level of people who are not actively engaged with their jobs. A Gallup study (2006) found that only 27% of workers reported feeling "engaged" while at work, while 59% described themselves as "not engaged." Still another 14% were "actively disengaged," which means they purposefully undermined the efforts of their co-workers.

There are additional costs to management. Resolving worker conflicts can take up 13% of executives' time, almost seven weeks of the year for any one boss (Pearson & Porath, 2005, p. 8). Replacing workers who leave can cost as much as 2.5 times the annual salary of the job if it is a high-profile job and interviewees have to be flown in and paid to move (Gonthier, 2002, p. 27). Replacing lost customers is another concern because sales will decline if disgruntled workers are in customer service positions and take out their frustrations on the customers, a common occurrence. Forni (2002) states, "A stressed, fatigued, or distressed person is less inclined to be patient and tolerant, to think before acting, and to be aware of the needs of others" (p. 139). Gonthier (2002) reports that 58 to 62% of customers will change to a different company if employees treat them rudely (pp. 30–31).

Note that Hazama has done a good job of synthesizing sources. This paragraph blends information from her three major sources.

A logical question to end this discussion is, "What can be done to solve the problem?"

What Can Be Done to Reduce Workplace Incivility?

In order to accomplish civility in the workplace, leaders must lead the way. Robert D. Ramsey (2008), who works in personnel administration and writes for management publications, says supervisors have the ability to do the most to turn around a bad working atmosphere (p. 4) and "create a culture of civility at work" (p. 5). Ramsey has devised a six-step action plan. First, managers must act as role models; they must represent civility in all their actions. Forni agrees, saying, "The attitude of the leader . . . has an enormous impact on the overall climate" of the workplace (as cited in Hauser, 2011). Programs like CREW (Civility, Respect, and Engagement in the Workplace) have shown that when leaders set the example, civility has a way of going viral, "infecting" other workers to act in equally courteous ways (Hauser, 2011).

Secondly, Ramsey (2008) says business relationships should become more personal, encouraging considerate and respectful behavior. A worker is more likely to act in a rude fashion through an impersonal encounter through the telephone or e-mail. Some businesses will not allow e-mails between workers who have offices on the same floor (p. 5). Next, issues between workers must be addressed. A leader needs to actively mediate disputes and remind workers of expectations and boundaries for behavior. Pearson and Porath (2005) echo this advice. They tell leaders, "When incivility occurs, hammer it" (p. 14). Ramsey's fourth step is about consequences. An authority figure must make policies and rules that delineate the proper conduct on the job, and carry through with the consequences when workers violate them. Ramsey says it is amazing how quickly people become more civil when their raise or promotion depends on it (p. 5). Fifth, business leaders can offer training programs, civility courses, and workshops on ethics, respect, responsibility, awareness, and etiquette. An example is the CREW program mentioned earlier and created for the Veterans Health Administration. Workers from all over the country fly to Cincinnati for three-day training sessions (Hauser, 2011). Ramsey's last step addresses how to develop trust among workers. Leaders should devise exercises that involve teamwork, even if they seem "childish," like "having an employee fall backwards into the arms of co-worker, counting on the other party to catch him safely" (p. 6).

Through their individual actions, employees can also maintain civility in their workplace. As Forni states, "Corporate responsibility does not erase individual responsibility" (Forni, 2002, p. 140). The little things add up to make either a bad day, like Amanda's, or a good one. Gonthier (2002) says, "Always say hello or good morning or good afternoon as you encounter co-workers on your rounds. And, of course, respond in kind if they initiate the exchange" (p. 110). A simple greeting shows a concern for their well-being. Also, compliments for a job well done will influence others to continue to work hard.

Listening properly will result in better teamwork and acceptance of each other's ideas. Being a cooperative listener includes responding in the right manner with questions and body language. A listener must show that he or she is listening by making eye contact, saying remarks to show engagement and repeating the speaker's thoughts to show comprehension (Forni, 2002, p. 52).

Other people's space must also be respected in a working environment. In order to maintain privacy, workers should keep noise levels down and distractions to a minimum (Forni, 2002, p. 102). Many tensions in the workplace arise from common facilities and resources. Resources at work are shared with all of the workers; therefore, if a worker creates a mess, he or she must clean it immediately so others do not have to clean up after them. Anyone who uses an appliance must make sure that he or she has left it in working condition (Gonthier, 2002, p. 125). If each worker takes responsibility for his or her actions, everything runs more smoothly and people are not tired and irritated by the end of the day.

Conclusion

Everyone benefits from a civil workplace. Joan Wrangler, an executive coach working at NASA's Goddard Space Flight Center, created a personal relations program there. She has discovered the huge difference that civility makes in productivity and creativity: "Civility is part of the foundation for bringing out people's brilliance. If you want to touch people's smartness and bring out their brilliance, then you need to be able to create a space where people feel safe enough to speak, to listen to one another, to be heard, to offer support, to coach one another" (as cited in Hauser, 2011). That sounds like the kind of place everyone would like to work.

This quotation sums up the civil workplace and points to its outstanding quality from the standpoint of both the employer and the employee: Every boss wants brilliant workers and every worker wants a chance to shine.

7

References

This student paper adheres to the APA style. Chapter 21 provides specific guidance on applying APA guidelines to an assignment.

Forni, P. M. (2002). *Choosing civility: The twenty-five rules of considerate conduct.* St. Martin's Press.

Gallup study: Feeling good matters in the workplace. (2006, January 12). *Gallup Management Journal.* http://gmj.gallup.com/content/20770/Gallup-Study-Feeling-Good-Matters-in-the.aspx

Gonthier, G. (2002). *Rude awakenings: Overcoming the civility crisis in the workplace.* Dearborn Trade Publishing.

Hauser, S. (2011, January 16). The degeneration of decorum: Stress caused by rude behavior in the workplace might be costing the U. S. economy billions of dollars a year. *Workforce Management,* 16–18. https://www.workforce.com/2011/01/16/the-degeneration-of-decorum/

Pearson, C., & Porath, C. (2005, February 1). On the nature, consequences and remedies of workplace incivility: No time for "nice"? Think again. *Academy of Management Executive, 19*(1), 7–18. https://doi.org/10.5465/ame.2005.15841946

Ramsey, R. (2008, December). The case for civility in the workplace. *Supervision, 69*(12), 3–6.

CREDITS

page 106: Eric Hoover. "Tomorrow, I Love Ya!" *Chronicle of Higher Education,* 9 Dec. 2005. Copyright © 2005 by The Chronicle of Higher Education. Reprinted by permission. **page 113:** Martha Ross and Nicole Bateman. (2017). "On Their Own Way? A Portrait of Young Adults." Washington, D.C.: Brookings Institute. Used with permission. All rights reserved. **page 128:** Courtesy of Amie Hazama

CHAPTER 7

Exploring a Concept

ENGAGING QUESTIONS

In this chapter, you will engage with the following questions:

- What does it mean to explore a concept?
- What is the purpose of writing to explore concepts?
- What questions stimulate thinking about a concept?
- How do writers identify appropriate topics for concept exploration?
- How do the elements of the rhetorical situation apply to the writing process for a concept exploration?
- How do writers apply the steps of the writing process to an assignment that explores a concept?

IN THE FIRST CHAPTER, WE INTRODUCED A KEY QUESTION FOR CRITICAL THINKING: What does that word mean? It is an especially valuable question because the meaning of many words is open to question. For example, when someone claims that the Internet is the most *democratic* communication technology ever developed, what does the person mean by "democratic"? Is the Internet any more democratic than, say, television? If so, in what ways? Question what the word *democratic* means and you begin thinking critically about a statement that usually passes as uncontroversial.

This chapter is about how to explore the meaning of words. We are most interested in exploring words that name concepts like "democracy"—words that we use in talking about ideas that are important to us. We use these words so often and in so many different contexts that we might wonder if they mean anything at all. Consequently, writers who use words responsibly often elaborate on their meaning, or they may write simply to explore the meaning of a concept.

ACTIVITY 7.1 *Collaborative Activity*

Thinking about the Core Meaning of Concepts

The **core meaning** of a concept refers to *what most people think of when the concept is mentioned.* It is therefore important in exploring concepts. The following chart depicts the results of two surveys of Americans, one in 1998 and one in 2013, who were asked what a middle-income household makes.[1]

1. American Enterprise Institute, "What Does Middle Class Mean?" *Political Report,* March 1, 2015.

A middle-income household is one making

September 2013

Less than $30,000	9%
Between $30,000 and $40,000	13
Between $40,000 and $50,000	23
Between $50,000 and $75,000	29
Between $75,000 and $100,000	16
Between $100,000 and $150,000	5
More than $150,000	2

December 1998

Less than $30,000	5%
$30,000–$39,999	22
$40,000–$49,999	24
$50,000–$74,999	35
$75,000–$99,999	7
$100,000 or more	2

Note: In each income category the pollsters supplied in 2013 up to $100,000, Americans were most likely to identify their own income bracket as middle-income.

In small group or class discussion, consider the following questions:

1. Compare the numbers from 1998 and 2013. What trend do you see?
2. How would you answer the question now?
3. "Working class" is another common category. What relation do you think it has to "middle class"?
4. In addition to income, what other characteristics do you associate with "middle class"?
5. What would you say the core concept of "middle class" is? ■

What Is Concept Exploration?

A **concept** is *a category, a way of grouping objects, attitudes, beliefs, and behavior that we consider related.* Cars, trucks, SUVs, and golf carts are all grouped as "vehicles." **Concept exploration** *examines concepts in an effort to understand what they mean and how they are used,* often with some practical question in mind. Should flag-burning count as "free speech"? The Supreme Court has ruled that it does, but many Americans believe that burning a flag is not speech and amounts to an unpatriotic act that should not enjoy constitutional protection.

CONCEPT CLOSE-UP The Nature of Concepts

- **Concepts can be concrete, like Barbie dolls, or abstract, like Barbie culture,** a set of values associated with the toys and studied by sociologists interested in gender roles.
- **Concepts are often value-laden, implying positive or negative judgments.** For instance, the concept of "empathy" designates something positive and good for people to have. The concepts of being "callous" or "uncaring" are the opposite of empathy and therefore negative.
- **Concepts vary across cultures.** What is "fashionable" in Paris can be "immoral" in certain Islamic societies and just "odd" in many places in the United States.

- **Concepts vary across time.** As a society's circumstances change, its concepts also change. "Exurb," for example, arose as a concept when people moved farther out from urban centers, beyond suburbs. We invent new concepts to characterize new realities and drop old ones as the realities they refer to cease to exist.

Why Explore Concepts?

We *define* concepts like "quark" to explain what they mean for readers unfamiliar with the terms, but we seldom explore scientific or technical concepts because of their precise, limited meaning. We *explore* abstract concepts like "democracy" and "empathy" because their meanings are not so precise and limited. Understanding them better matters because such words belong to our value systems and influence our behavior. For example, Mike Rose, now a distinguished professor of English, explains in his book *Lives on the Boundary* that he almost flunked out of college his freshman year. Influenced by the concept "individualism," he refused to seek help when he could not understand the assigned books. Similarly, Jamie Cummins, who explores "gender" at the end of the chapter, does so to determine whether we might be "trapped . . . by our ideas of appropriate behavior for men and women."

Concept exploration appears in newspaper stories and editorials, in scientific and philosophical books and articles, in blogs online, and in many other **genres,** or kinds of writing. It also appears in every context for writing. In a workplace setting we might need to assess how "democratic" the Internet is; in personal writing, we might explore what being a "friend" to someone ought to mean; and in academic writing, defining the word "novel" might be crucial to an essay exam.

Concepts can vary across cultures. What may be considered "fashionable" in one country may be considered odd or immoral in others.

How Do Writers Explore a Concept?

What should we ask when we want to think seriously about the meanings of a concept and its applications to life? Following are some basic questions that stimulate thinking about exploring concepts.

1. **What are the dictionary definitions of the concept?** Have definitions changed over time? Have the word's emotional associations changed, especially in a negative or positive direction? Four centuries ago, for example, "innovation" was a negative word, implying the work of a troublemaker, whereas now the word glows with all that is good and desirable.
2. **What are the root meanings of the word?** "Democracy," for example, comes from two Greek words

meaning "people rule." It is not surprising, then, that "democratic" now means for many Americans much the same thing as "popular."

3. **In what contexts do people use the concept?** In one situation, "fairness" means that everyone gets an equal share of something—as even young children know when a treat is being distributed. In another situation, "fairness" means *unequal distribution,* as when one person or one group has contributed more than another to a successful enterprise and therefore deserves a greater share of the reward.
4. **Is conflict or disagreement at hand when the concept is used?** "Freedom" often runs headlong into "social responsibility." Smoking in enclosed public spaces was once common in the United States; now it is rarely permitted.
5. **What is the practical impact of the concept?** "Subprime mortgages" and financial contracts called "derivatives" so damaged the American and global economy that the investor Warren Buffett called them "weapons of mass destruction." Many people do not understand that file-sharing of copyrighted materials is "theft" in the same sense as, for example, stealing someone's car.
6. **What company does this concept keep, and what distinctions are there among related ideas?** "Marriage," for example, connects with many other concepts, such as "soul mate," "monogamy," the "union of a man and a woman," "reproduction," and so on. Increasingly the connected concepts are being separated from the institution as the institution itself changes.
7. **What have other writers said about the concept?** About "justice," for example, a Supreme Court justice famously said, "Justice too long delayed is justice denied." What is the relation of "justice" to "timeliness"?
8. **What confusions or uncertainties surround the use of the concept?** For example, the concept of "preemptive war" is used to justify a surprise attack on an enemy who is about to attack you. Can we distinguish between "preemptive war" as self-defense and the use of the concept to disguise a motive like expanding a country's territory by attacking a weak neighbor?

READING 7.1

What Is a "System of Privilege"?

ALLAN G. JOHNSON

Allan G. Johnson (1946–2017) was a sociologist, a prolific writer, and a powerful speaker on college campuses. His theme was social justice, as the blog post reprinted here shows. "What Is a 'System of Privilege'?" explores one of the most important concepts required to understand American society—white privilege. But the implications of what he says apply to the understanding of any society that exists or has existed because all societies favor some groups over others.

The concept of privilege refers to any advantage that is unearned, exclusive, and socially conferred. For example, white people are generally assumed to be law-abiding until they show some sign that they are not, while people of color are routinely assumed to be criminals 1

Defines and illustrates the concept, so that, by the end of the first paragraph, we know what the whole blog post will be about.

or potential criminals until they show they're not. One way to see this is through a survey in which respondents were asked to close their eyes and picture a drug dealer. When asked to describe what they saw, almost 95 percent mentioned a black person, even though the vast majority of drug dealers in the U.S. are white.

So, when it comes to being randomly stopped and frisked by police, anyone identified as "white" has an advantage they did not earn and that is exclusive to whites. It is socially conferred in the sense that it depends on them being perceived in a particular way by the police—as "white"—before the advantage is given to them in the form of the assumption that they are not criminals. 2

It's important to note that privilege does not guarantee good outcomes for the privileged group or bad outcomes for everyone else. A white person, for example, can work hard and have little to show for it, can be mistreated by the police without cause, be denied a job they're qualified for. What privilege does is load the odds one way or the other so that the chance of bad things happening to white people as a category of people is much lower than for everyone else, and the chance of good things happening is much higher. Privilege is not something a person can *have*, like a possession, as in "Where's *mine*?" Instead, it is a characteristic of the social system—like a rule in a game—in which everyone participates. A system of privilege—a family, a workplace, a society—is organized around three basic principles: dominance, identification, and centeredness. 3

Helps us to understand that white privilege does not always result in success. Rather it stacks the cards unfairly, making the odds of success much higher. Note that by the end of this paragraph, we have three other concepts we can use to think about "systems of privilege": "dominance, identification, and centeredness."

A system of white privilege, for example, is white-dominated, which means the default is for white people to occupy positions of power. White-dominance doesn't mean that all white people are powerful, only that the powerful tend almost always to be white, and when a person of color occupies a position of power, that will be noted as an exception to the rule (as when Barack Obama is routinely identified as a black President and not just "the President"). 4

Elaborates on what privilege means: "White" is the standard for judging all other races and ethnicities in the U.S. Connects with the notion in the first paragraph that privilege is "unearned and exclusive," an arbitrary social preference.

White-identification means that the culture defines 'white' people as the standard for human beings in general. People of color, for example, are routinely identified as 'nonwhite,' a term that doesn't tell us what they are, but what they are *not*. 5

When a category of people is named the standard for human beings in general, the path of least resistance is to see them as superior, there being no other reason to make them the standard. Several things follow from this, including seeing the way they do things as simply "human" or "normal," and giving more credibility to their views than to the views of "others," in this case people of color. White-identification also encourages whites to be unaware of themselves *as* white, as if they didn't have a race at all. It also encourages whites to be unaware of white privilege. 6

An important aspect of privilege: the favored group sees itself as "just human," and partly for this reason is often unaware of the unearned advantages it enjoys.

White-centeredness is the tendency to put white people and what they do at the center of attention—the front page of the newspaper or magazine, the main character in the movie. 7

When you organize a society in this way, the result will be patterns of unearned advantage that are available to whites simply because they are socially identified as 'white.' A related consequence is patterns of oppression centered on 8

An extended example of the advantages being white in America confers. Note that the author moves back and forth between relatively abstract concepts and concrete illustration, one of the secrets to writing well about complex ideas.

people of color. Abundant research, for example, shows that whites and blacks are equally likely to use illegal drugs, which would lead us to expect them to be equally likely to wind up in prison for that offense. On top of that, young white males are the demographic most likely to sell illegal drugs. But a substantial majority of those in prison for drug offenses are people of color, in spite of their much smaller share of the overall population. The white privilege in this example, is the practice of the criminal justice system to overlook or respond less harshly to drug crimes committed by whites, while the corresponding oppressive consequence for people of color is the systematic selection of people of color for arrest, prosecution, and punishment.*

---

*For a detailed examination and documentation of the 'war on drugs' as a vehicle for mass incarceration, see *The New Jim Crow: Mass Incarceration in the Age of Colorblindness*, by Michelle Alexander. New Press, 2010.
For a more detailed discussion of these ideas, see Allan's book, *Privilege, Power, and Difference*. You might also want to read Allan's blog post, "The Luxury of Obliviousness."

Note that even blog posts use and should acknowledge sources.

Questions for Discussion

1. "Privilege is not something a person can have, like a possession, as in 'Where's *mine*?' Instead, it is a characteristic of the social system—like a rule in a game—in which everyone participates." Besides privilege based on race, what other inequalities result from our social "rules of the game"? How important would you say the "social system" is in our daily lives? Does it *determine* what we do or only *influence* it significantly?
2. Blog posts should not be too long if we want people to read them. Perhaps for this reason, Johnson does not say much about his "three basic principles [of systems of privilege]: dominance, identification, and centeredness." The role dominance plays is obvious, and he gives memorable examples. Less clear are the roles identification and centeredness play. What do these concepts mean to you? Do they help you understand systems of privilege? If so, how?
3. Examine the blog post to see how Johnson develops his concept. Besides definition, what other strategies or moves does he use to advance what he has to say?

Thinking as a Writer

What Is the Rhetorical Situation?

1. What Is the author's *purpose* in writing this article? What is his *angle* on the topic? How would you describe his *voice*?
2. Who is the intended *audience*? Who would read this publication? Is there anything you can point to in the article that implies the target readership?

3. Using the eight questions for how to explore a concept (pages 137–138) and the marginal annotations to the article, evaluate how the author develops his view of systems of privilege. That is, how does he define, illustrate, and explore this concept? ■

READING 7.2

Corn-pone Opinions

MARK TWAIN

Mark Twain, aka Samuel L. Clemens (1835–1910), is the most celebrated American author of all time. A prolific writer, he was also a master at entertaining the public in one-man shows all over the world.

"Corn-pone Opinions" is vintage Twain, an essay both funny and serious, both to be taken at face value as an exploration of conformity, and pondered for its underlying irony: Twain maintains that no opinion is really independent and thought-through, so are we to think that his opinion on corn-pone opinions is also, at bottom, just another way of conforming?

Establishes in first three paragraphs the context of corn-pone opinions: an experience the narrator had as a young man half a century before he wrote this essay. In so locating it, the narrator gives his concept a long history in his life, and therefore ample opportunity to ponder it.

1 Fifty years ago, when I was a boy of fifteen and helping to inhabit a Missourian village on the banks of the Mississippi, I had a friend whose society was very dear to me because I was forbidden by my mother to partake of it. He was a gay and impudent and satirical and delightful young black man—a slave—who daily preached sermons from the top of his master's woodpile, with me for sole audience. He imitated the pulpit style of the several clergymen of the village, and did it well, and with fine passion and energy. To me he was a wonder. I believed he was the greatest orator in the United States and would some day be heard from. But it did not happen; in the distribution of rewards he was overlooked. It is the way, in this world.

2 He interrupted his preaching, now and then, to saw a stick of wood; but the sawing was a pretense—he did it with his mouth; exactly imitating the sound the bucksaw makes in shrieking its way through the wood. But it served its purpose; it kept his master from coming out to see how the work was getting along. I listened to the sermons from the open window of a lumber room at the back of the house. One of his texts was this:

3 "You tell me whar a man gits his corn pone, en I'll tell you what his 'pinions is."

Corn pone is a simple, rustic kind of cornbread, without sugar or butter. It was a staple of army food during the Civil War.

4 I can never forget it. It was deeply impressed upon me. By my mother. Not upon my memory, but elsewhere. She had slipped in upon me while I was absorbed and not watching. The black philosopher's idea was that a man is not independent, and cannot afford views which might interfere with his bread and butter. If he would prosper, he must train with the majority; in matters of large moment, like politics and religion, he must think and feel with the bulk of his neighbors, or suffer damage in his social standing and in his business prosperities. He must restrict himself to corn-pone opinions—at least on the surface. He must

Definition of the concept of corn-pone opinions, or conformity.

get his opinions from other people; he must reason out none for himself; he must have no first-hand views.

I think Jerry was right, in the main, but I think he did not go far enough. 5

1. It was his idea that a man conforms to the majority view of his locality by calculation and intention. This happens, but I think it is not the rule.
2. It was his idea that there is such a thing as a first-hand opinion; an original opinion; an opinion which is coldly reasoned out in a man's head, by a searching analysis of the facts involved, with the heart unconsulted, and the jury room closed against outside influences. It may be that such an opinion has been born somewhere, at some time or other, but I suppose it got away before they could catch it and stuff it and put it in the museum.

Offers criticisms of his source, which radicalizes the slave orator's view of corn-pone opinions: adopting the prevailing opinions and fashions is not chosen and faked, but instinctive and heart-felt; there are no opinions that are independent, rational, without self-interest. Of course, such a view implies that, except for very rare instances, there is nothing but conformity to social approval in all our thinking.

I am persuaded that a coldly-thought-out and independent verdict upon a fashion in clothes, or manners, or literature, or politics, or religion, or any other matter that is projected into the field of our notice and interest, is a most rare thing—if it has indeed ever existed. 6

Paragraph expands the claim from opinions to fashion, expanding the range of corn-pone opinions to most of human behavior.

A new thing in costume appears—the flaring hoopskirt, for example—and the passers-by are shocked, and the irreverent laugh. Six months later everybody is reconciled; the fashion has established itself; it is admired, now, and no one laughs. Public opinion resented it before, public opinion accepts it now, and is happy in it. Why? Was the resentment reasoned out? Was the acceptance reasoned out? No. The instinct that moves to conformity did the work. It is our nature to conform; it is a force which not many can successfully resist. What is its seat? The inborn requirement of self-approval. We all have to bow to that; there are no exceptions. Even the woman who refuses from first to last to wear the hoop skirt comes under that law and is its slave; she could not wear the skirt and have her own approval; and that she must have, she cannot help herself. But as a rule our self-approval has its source in but one place and not elsewhere—the approval of other people. A person of vast consequences can introduce any kind of novelty in dress and the general world will presently adopt it—moved to do it, in the first place, by the natural instinct to passively yield to that vague something recognized as authority, and in the second place by the human instinct to train with the multitude and have its approval. An empress introduced the hoopskirt, and we know the result. A nobody introduced the bloomer, and we know the result. If Eve should come again, in her ripe renown, and reintroduce her quaint styles—well, we know what would happen. And we should be cruelly embarrassed, along at first. 7

Explains the tyranny of conformity by tracing it to self-approval gained from the praise of other people.

The hoopskirt runs its course and disappears. Nobody reasons about it. One woman abandons the fashion; her neighbor notices this and follows her lead; this influences the next woman; and so on and so on, and presently the skirt has vanished out of the world, no one knows how nor why, nor cares, for that matter. It will come again, by and by and in due course will go again. 8

Another expansion of the concept of corn-pone opinions: All social customs depend on mindless conformity.

Twenty-five years ago, in England, six or eight wine glasses stood grouped by each person's plate at a dinner party, and they were used, not left idle and empty; 9

to-day there are but three or four in the group, and the average guest sparingly uses about two of them. We have not adopted this new fashion yet, but we shall do it presently. We shall not think it out; we shall merely conform, and let it go at that. We get our notions and habits and opinions from outside influences; we do not have to study them out.

Our table manners, and company manners, and street manners change from 10
time to time, but the changes are not reasoned out; we merely notice and conform. We are creatures of outside influences; as a rule we do not think, we only imitate. We cannot invent standards that will stick; what we mistake for standards are only fashions, and perishable. We may continue to admire them, but we drop the use of them. We notice this in literature. Shakespeare is a standard, and fifty years ago we used to write tragedies which we couldn't tell from—from somebody else's; but we don't do it any more, now. Our prose standard, three quarters of a century ago, was ornate and diffuse; some authority or other changed it in the direction of compactness and simplicity, and conformity followed, without argument. The historical novel starts up suddenly, and sweeps the land. Everybody writes one, and the nation is glad. We had historical novels before; but nobody read them, and the rest of us conformed—without reasoning it out. We are conforming in the other way, now, because it is another case of everybody.

If fashion seems too trivial, Twain addresses "serious" matters like prose style—but it too is a matter of fashion, not eternal truth.

The outside influences are always pouring in upon us, and we are always 11
obeying their orders and accepting their verdicts. The Smiths like the new play; the Joneses go to see it, and they copy the Smith verdict. Morals, religions, politics, get their following from surrounding influences and atmospheres, almost entirely; not from study, not from thinking. A man must and will have his own approval first of all, in each and every moment and circumstance of his life—even if he must repent of a self-approved act the moment after its commission, in order to get his self-approval again: but, speaking in general terms, a man's self-approval in the large concerns of life has its source in the approval of the peoples about him, and not in a searching personal examination of the matter. Mohammedans are Mohammedans because they are born and reared among that sect, not because they have thought it out and can furnish sound reasons for being Mohammedans; we know why Catholics are Catholics; why Presbyterians are Presbyterians; why Baptists are Baptists; why Mormons are Mormons; why thieves are thieves; why monarchists are monarchists; why Republicans are Republicans and Democrats, Democrats. We know it is a matter of association and sympathy, not reasoning and examination; that hardly a man in the world has an opinion upon morals, politics, or religion which he got otherwise than through his associations and sympathies. Broadly speaking, there are none but corn-pone opinions. And broadly speaking, corn-pone stands for self-approval. Self-approval is acquired mainly from the approval of other people. The result is conformity. Sometimes conformity has a sordid business interest—the bread-and-butter interest—but not in most cases, I think. I think that in the majority of cases it is unconscious and not calculated; that it is born of the human being's natural yearning to stand well with his fellows and have their inspiring approval and praise—a yearning

Other "serious" concerns that many people consider too momentous not to have some kind of ultimate grounding. They are corn-pone opinions as well.

Spells out his thesis: There are no opinions except corn-pone opinions

Reflects on the causes of conformity: that it is not deliberate but based in human need for the approval of others.

which is commonly so strong and so insistent that it cannot be effectually resisted, and must have its way. A political emergency brings out the corn-pone opinion in fine force in its two chief varieties—the pocketbook variety, which has its origin in self-interest, and the bigger variety, the sentimental variety—the one which can't bear to be outside the pale; can't bear to be in disfavor; can't endure the averted face and the cold shoulder; wants to stand well with his friends, wants to be smiled upon, wants to be welcome, wants to hear the precious words, "He's on the right track!" Uttered, perhaps by an ass, but still an ass of high degree, an ass whose approval is gold and diamonds to a smaller ass, and confers glory and honor and happiness, and membership in the herd. For these gauds many a man will dump his life-long principles into the street, and his conscience along with them. We have seen it happen. In some millions of instances.

Twain develops the appeal of conformity to the point that we must recognize how much it controls us.

Men think they think upon great political questions, and they do; but they think with their party, not independently; they read its literature, but not that of the other side; they arrive at convictions, but they are drawn from a partial view of the matter in hand and are of no particular value. They swarm with their party, they feel with their party, they are happy in their party's approval; and where the party leads they will follow, whether for right and honor, or through blood and dirt and a mush of mutilated morals. 12

In our late canvass half of the nation passionately believed that in silver lay salvation, the other half as passionately believed that that way lay destruction. Do you believe that a tenth part of the people, on either side, had any rational excuse for having an opinion about the matter at all? I studied that mighty question to the bottom—came out empty. Half of our people passionately believe in high tariff, the other half believe otherwise. Does this mean study and examination, or only feeling? The latter, I think. I have deeply studied that question, too—and didn't arrive. We all do no end of feeling, and we mistake it for thinking. And out of it we get an aggregation which we consider a boon. Its name is Public Opinion. It is held in reverence. It settles everything. Some think it the Voice of God. 13

Concludes forcefully: Popular opinion is indistinguishable from the Voice of God.

Questions for Discussion

1. Try to doubt Twain's contention that all opinions are corn-pone opinions. What opinions have you encountered that you consider "coldly-thought-out and independent verdict[s]" about an important issue or question? Which of your opinions do you consider free of self-interest or love of approval from others?
2. Does Twain's view of opinions encourage or discourage critical thinking? Be prepared to defend what you decide.
3. Twain brings religion into the picture by mentioning various religious groups, Christian and not, and by concluding with "the Voice of God." Why does he do this? What impact did the allusions to religion have on your reaction to the essay?

Thinking as a Writer

What Is the Rhetorical Situation?

1. What is the author's *purpose*? What is his *angle* on the topic? How would you describe his *voice*?
2. Who is Twain's *audience* for "Corn-pone Opinions"? Is Twain writing for people who are already well informed about the nature of opinions or for people who might not have thought much about the concept? Is there anything in the essay you can cite that implies the author's target readership? ■

The Assignment

Write an essay exploring a concept. Depending on your teacher's instructions, you may draw from personal experiences, interviews, and observations as well as from reference works, books, and articles. Be sure to use the key questions for exploring a concept (pages 137–138). Some or all of them will help you see how to think critically about your concept and discover options for writing about it.

See Chapter 16, Finding Sources, pages 358–71, and Chapter 17, Evaluating Sources, pages 372–78, for kinds of sources you could consult.

What Can I Write About?

Your instructor may assign a concept to explore. When asked to choose your own, consider the following (see also Figure 7.1):

- **Personal experience.** Draw on your personal experience to select a concept for exploration. For example, seeing mothers interacting with their children in line at the bank or grocery store may prompt you to consider the concept "child rearing." An experience from childhood or adolescence that made you consider concepts such as "innocence" or "naïveté" could also be explored.

See Chapter 4, Narrating Experiences, for guidance.

- **Blog posts.** A student from Sweden described how the concept of "friendship" in his country differs from the concept in the United States. The post received many comments from other bloggers, opening up further exploration of a challenging concept.
- **Book reviews.** Nonfiction books especially can offer either new concepts or interesting analyses of familiar ones. You can respond to the author's exploration with comments of your own.

Here are some other sources for concepts to explore:

- **Class readings.** Concepts from the readings in this chapter—for example, "middle class" or "system of privilege" or in other texts you are reading for class could be concepts for exploration.

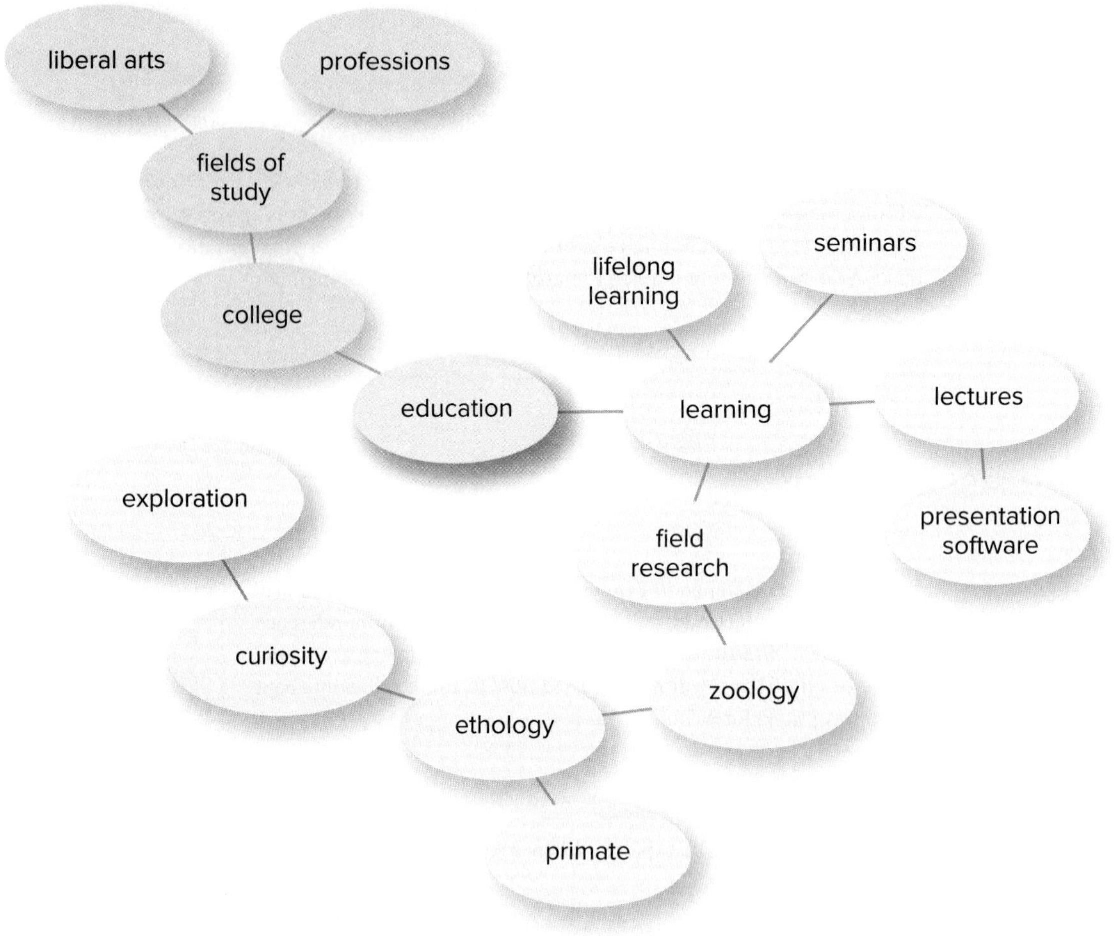

FIGURE 7.1

What Should I Write About?

Think of one interesting broad concept and then come up with as many concept "offshoots" as you can. Sometimes brainstorming with a visual diagram can help you come up with the perfect topic to write about.

- **Personal reading.** An article in your campus newspaper or in a magazine like *Time* or *Sports Illustrated* could provide a concept ("fairness in the media," "cheating in sports").
- **Campus issues.** For example, "plagiarism" or "going green" are good concepts for exploration. Speakers at your college or university may also discuss intriguing concepts.
- **Concepts in your community.** For example, "third place" is used to designate where people spend time besides home and work.

- **Concepts in your workplace.** For example, in a summer or regular job you may have encountered a concept such as "malware," a name for computer viruses, Trojans, and worms.
- **Concepts from foreign languages or cultures.** If you have studied a foreign language, you have probably encountered concepts unique to that language, which have no precise English equivalents. Such concepts can make interesting explorations, especially if you have lived in or visited countries where the language is spoken and can offer insight into how the concept is actually used.
- **Concepts from cultures in the United States.** Our country is in large part a collection of cultures, people of different races, ethnicities, nationalities, religions, languages, and so on. Perhaps you were raised in or have extensive experience with one of these cultures and can discuss a concept its people often use.

ACTIVITY 7.2 *Writer's Notebook*

Will It Work? Testing Your Concept

If you are in doubt about a concept you have chosen, try writing about it as fast as you can for about 15 minutes. If you find the ideas are flowing, you probably have a concept suitable for you to write about. As an alternative, write an e-mail to a friend or classmate explaining why you have chosen the concept and what you foresee saying about it. Ask for feedback. Either or both methods should help you test the concept before you commit yourself to a draft. ■

How Do I Explore Concepts? Questioning the Rhetorical Situation

Begin by picturing a **rhetorical situation** for your writing project, a real-world context for communicating. You should consider the key variables in any act of communication: a writer with something to say, a reader the writer wishes to reach, and a kind of text appropriate to the writing task. These three variables will affect many decisions in the composing process.

Writer: What Is My Purpose, and What Impression Should Readers Have of Me?

Exploratory writing is "thinking aloud"—for this assignment, putting on screen or paper how you have gone about trying to understand a concept. You may explain the concept and concepts related to it, but your primary purpose is to explore, not to inform or explain. You may also argue *for* your understanding of the concept—usually near the end of your essay, after your exploration is over—but your primary purpose is to explore, not to argue for your interpretation. The key to exploration is to **postpone closure,** which means *letting your mind play with the concept* rather than informing or arguing.

Consequently, your readers should see you as a *thoughtful guide* to the concept, someone asking and pursuing interesting questions. They should see you as someone with an open mind, not as someone who has all the answers.

Reader: Who Is My Audience?

As with all writing projects, you should imagine a group of people who might read your paper. Your instructor will evaluate your work, and part of that evaluation is how well you communicate with your reader. Beyond that, you need to write for a reader because doing so will help you decide what to say and how to order what you say. Therefore, one of the key questions you need to ask yourself often as you write and revise a draft is, **"What does my reader need?"**

Remembering this will help you imagine your reader: *Your purpose for writing determines your role as a writer, which in turn implies a role for your reader.* In this case, your purpose is exploration and your role is an explorer, someone engaged with the meaning of a challenging concept. You are displaying your thought process as you ponder the concept's dictionary definition, its root meanings, what other writers have said about it, how the concept is used, and so on. Without having to say it, you are inviting your readers to "come and think about this concept with me." You are saying, "Here's what I am thinking," which implies that you want what you say to stimulate their thinking.

Note how different this role for the reader is from informing or arguing. When you inform, your reader becomes somebody who needs or wants to know what you know. When you argue, your reader becomes someone you are trying to convince or persuade. Exploration is different: You want your readers to think through a concept with you.

Text: What Moves Can I Make?

The genre represented in Readings 7.1 and 7.2 and in the student example at the end of this chapter (pages 156–160) is the exploratory essay. The basic moves are as follows:

- Introduce the concept you intend to explore.
- Indicate why the concept needs to be explored.
- Cite the views of experts on the concept and comment on what they say, and/or . . .
- Cite dictionary meanings, root meanings, examples of how the concept is used, and so on (see the key questions on pages 137–138 for other possibilities) and comment on them, and/or . . .
- Cite your own experiences or observations that contribute to your thinking about the concept.
- Propose a core or basic meaning for the concept.
- Offer your view of what the concept means, including, when relevant, your evaluation of how the concept is used or misused.

How Do I Explore Concepts? Engaging the Writing Process

No two people compose in exactly the same way, and even the same person may go through the writing process in different ways with different assignments. Nevertheless, because no one can attend to everything at once, there are phases in handling any significant writing task. You begin by preparing to write, which includes generating content and finding your angle.

The next phase is planning and drafting your paper, getting a version, however rough it may be, on screen or paper so that you have something to work with during the next two stages: revising your draft by making changes to the content, arrangement, and style of your writing; and editing your draft to take care of problems at the paragraph and sentence level, such as lack of focus and coherence, awkward or unclear sentences, and errors of grammar, spelling, and punctuation.

Exploring Your Topic

In this phase you are *finding something to say,* generating ideas and content, which includes discovering your angle or point of view.

Generating Ideas and Gathering Materials

The following six questions will help you come up with ideas and more than enough content for your essay. Make handwritten notes as you work your way through these questions, or preserve your notes and comments on a computer file reserved for this assignment. Be sure to indicate the sources from which all your information comes.

See Chapter 15, pages 354–56, for guidance on keeping a working bibliography.

1. **What is the definition and history of the concept?** Start with the meanings of the concept as listed in a college-level dictionary. Distinguish the *concept's meanings* (called **denotation**) from the *implications of the concept* (called **connotation**). For example, "empathy" means the ability to feel what someone else is feeling (denotation); its connotations are always positive, implying a sensitive, caring person. Many dictionaries also show the word's **etymology** *(its derivation or root meanings).* The *Oxford English Dictionary (OED)* is particularly good for illustrating etymology because it gives example sentences showing how the concept has been used in the past.
2. **What other concepts are related to the concept you are exploring, and how are they related?** Concepts can be discussed only by using other concepts. What words were used to define your concept? What **synonyms** *(words that mean approximately the same thing)* did your dictionary supply? What synonyms can you think of? What synonyms are listed in a thesaurus?

   Consider also concepts closely related to your concept that are not synonyms. Johnson, for example, links "system of privilege" with "dominance, identification, and centeredness." You can find things to say about your concept by simply listing all the related concepts you can think of. Add to your list by writing down related concepts other writers have used to discuss your concept (see question 4).
3. **What metaphors are used to discuss your concept?** A metaphor is an implied comparison. People talk about "argument," for instance, using the concept of "war." Arguments are won and lost; we shoot down or demolish opposing views; evidence is ammunition. Consider how this metaphor influences how people think about argument and behave when they argue. It certainly works against listening thoughtfully to people we disagree with or empathizing with opponents in a dispute.

   Concepts are metaphorical more often than we realize. Expose and examine the metaphors in your concept. Remember also that language is full of **dead metaphors,** *comparisons used so habitually that people no longer recognize them as metaphors.*

The language of war used to discuss argument is a good example. When you encounter dead metaphors, invent fresh ones that might restore life to your concept. For example, why not present argument as dialogue or negotiation?

See Chapter 16 for advice on finding suitable print and online sources.

See Chapter 18 for advice on taking notes and making comments on source material.

4. **What has been written about my concept?** Using your library's online catalog and an all-purpose periodicals database, such as Academic Search Complete, InfoTrac, JSTOR, and ProQuest, find sources in which your concept is discussed. Then conduct a Google search on your sources' authors to learn about their background, their areas of expertise, and their perspectives on your concept. Keep copies of your sources, make notes about what the authors say, and add your own reactions and comments.

5. **Do different groups of people use the concept differently?** The most common sources of difference are race and ethnicity, gender, class, age, religion, and sex. "Equal opportunity," for example, may mean one thing to those born into privilege, something else to those born into poverty. "Community" may mean one thing to your grandparents and another thing to you. Consider how your concept may be understood by members of different groups. What conflicts or misunderstandings might result? How might your view of the concept help reduce conflict or misunderstanding?

See Chapter 15 for guidance on conducting field research.

6. **How do people actually use the concept?** Field research, such as surveys and interviews, can help you gain insight into your concept. One student exploring gender surveyed her fellow musicians' choices of instruments and found that instruments were "masculine" and "feminine"–that is, women tended to choose certain instruments (the flute, for example), while men tended to choose others (such as the drums). She was intrigued by how these gender concepts influenced musicians' choices. Consider conducting your own survey or interviewing a campus expert to learn more about your concept.

ACTIVITY 7.3 *Collaborative Activity*

Discussing Your Concept

If you keep a blog or if your class has an online discussion board, write a post about the concept you are exploring. Include any interesting results from answering the six questions above for generating ideas. Ask participants to post comments, contribute questions for exploration, and share their own experiences. ■

Drafting Your Paper

As you move toward writing your first draft, focus attention on angle, organization, and voice.

How Can I Find My Angle?

Angles are typically **contextual,** *derived from your life situation.* For example, the context for "Corn-pone Opinions" was most likely Twain's keen observations of ordinary people. He noticed that most people's opinions conform to those of their social

Finding an angle often means writing about what you know. For example, if you work at an indie radio station and have an opinion about what indie music is, write about it.

© Ilene MacDonald/ Alamy, RF

groups. His creative angle was to criticize this foible through a gentle satire, using the words of a slave who was good at imitating country preachers. The context for a college student wrestling with the concept "indie music" might be her own role as a DJ at the college radio station and the kinds of music her definition of "indie" would allow her to play. Concept exploration is usually motivated by practical needs, problems, or questions that arise at work, at home, in the community, or in one of many other contexts provided by life.

To determine your angle, consider the following questions:

1. **What context do I bring to the concept?** A student who surveyed fellow musicians about gender and instrument choice brought the context of playing in an orchestra. Any way that your concept can be connected with school, work, sports, family, or social life can help you find an angle.
2. **What outcome do I want for my exploration?** Johnson wanted us to appreciate how pervasive systems of privilege are and how blind the relatively privileged can be to their unearned advantages. Cummins explored "gender" to call attention to how limiting rigid notions of "masculine" and "feminine" can be.
3. **How can I challenge existing notions of the concept?** Everything you read about a concept can be questioned in some way, and often your angle can come from finding a particularly fertile question. When we read Twain's satire in "Corn-pone Opinions," for instance, we have to wonder just how independent any judgment is. Is Twain exaggerating to make a point, or is his dismissal of free and rational thought as self-deception justified?
4. **What distinctions might I make?** By their nature, concepts lump things together. Perhaps your angle can come from making one or several distinctions. The Swedish student who explored "friendship" thought Americans confused friend with acquaintance. That was his angle, and it worked well.

Organizing Your Exploratory Essay

Consider arranging your material as described below.

Introduction A good technique for opening exploration papers is to say what most people think about a concept and why it needs rethinking. Other options include:

- A quotation showing a particularly good or particularly bad understanding of the concept.
- A personal narrative about how your exploration got started.

Body One way to organize the draft is chronologically, beginning with your initial view of the concept and explaining the stages in which your understanding grew. See the student essay at the end of this chapter for an example. A chronologically organized draft would emphasize breakthrough moments, when your major insights occurred.

You can also organize around sources. Arrange your sources around a sequence of points they make or a set of questions they help to answer, and be sure to comment on them as they relate to your angle.

Conclusion Depending on your angle, conclude with the results of your exploration:

- How does your understanding of the concept work or fail to work in the context you brought to it? For example, the idea that band or orchestral instruments have a gender might end by considering boys who choose the flute and girls who choose the tuba. How do you explain choices that do not fit gender stereotypes?
- What outcome did you want from exploring the concept? Emphasize the results of your exploration, such as a clearer notion of friendship, a healthier view of romantic love, or an understanding of how much human society depends on civility.
- What challenge to the typical notion of your concept can you offer? For example, instead of the sharp contrasts that usually go with masculine and feminine gender categories, you could say that most people are a mix of the two genders, and therefore "masculine" and "feminine" tend only to distort reality.
- What distinctions seem important to you? For example, besides the usual distinction between friend and acquaintance, it might be interesting to discuss something relatively new—"friending," which can occur with people who are neither friends nor acquaintances.

Leave your readers with the feeling that your exploration made headway, but you need not resolve all issues or questions. Some explorations end by calling attention to problems, issues, and questions requiring further thought.

What Voice Is Appropriate for Exploring a Concept?

Saying what you mean involves voice, how you sound to your readers, so we need to consider voice in exploratory writing. Voice depends on function, on what a writer is doing. When we explore concepts, three functions are in play: informing, questioning, and asserting. All three functions and voices are present in "What Is a 'System of Privilege'?" (pages 138–140), but listen especially to the author's voice in the following passage:

> A system of white privilege, for example, is white-dominated, which means the default is for white people to occupy positions of power. White-dominance doesn't

> mean that all white people are powerful, only that the powerful tend almost always to be white, and when a person of color occupies a position of power, that will be noted as an exception to the rule (as when Barack Obama is routinely identified as a black President and not just "the President").

His voice sounds like the knowledgeable insider, who is sharing with us a precise and illuminating idea that we need to understand how society works.

Revising Your Draft

Because exploration depicts the thought process itself, laying it out for readers to follow, revision should not conceal or obscure the twists and turns of your thinking. Instead, *revise to highlight discoveries,* to expose how your thought unfolded. The Art of Questioning checklist below provides questions to guide assessment of your or another student's draft.

THE ART OF QUESTIONING Revision Checklist for Explaining a Concept

1. Does the paper explore the concept, opening it up to questioning rather than only informing or presenting an argument? Isolate passages that clearly explore. How can they be improved?
2. Is the author's angle on the concept clear, and does the writer provide a reason for exploring the concept in the introduction? What is the angle? Where is the reason discussed?
3. Does the author explain the context within which she or he will be exploring the concept? Recall that "context" for this paper means the concept's place in the writer's life. Where specifically are the connections with context made? What possible questions might a reader have that go unanswered?
4. Is the paper organized around the stages marking the writer's unfolding insights into the concept, around sources and the insights into the concept they provide, or in some other way that makes sense? If not, what changes in organization would help the reader follow the exploration better?
5. Has the author made the exploration specific enough to show how the concept is used, by providing examples and illustrations that demonstrate how people use the concept? Where in the paper does this happen? Where might the author provide additional supporting evidence?
6. If the author has used sources, how well are the authors of these sources introduced as people whose opinions on the concept should matter? To see how to incorporate sources, look at the student example (pages 156–160).
7. Is there too much quotation, paraphrase, and summary of sources and not enough commentary on the sources? Find places where the author has said

For more help on incorporating sources into your text, see Chapter 18, pages 379–400.

See Chapter 18, pages 386–91, for guidance on using quotations, paraphrase, and summary.

something about sources cited. To what extent do the comments express his or her own point of view and voice?

8. Has the author brought the exploration to some degree of closure by drawing a conclusion about what he or she learned? Should more be concluded? Why? Remember that closure in exploratory writing can include mentioning problems, issues, and questions that need further thought.

Student Example: Excerpts from Jamie Cummins's Draft

Student Jamie Cummins explored the concept of gender. He encountered specific challenges with his opening and using sources.

Problems with the Opening A paper's opening is important because it is the first thing your audience will read. In the rough draft of this chapter's featured student essay (see pages 156–160 for the revised draft), Cummins opened with a dictionary definition and then moved into a quotation from one of his sources, an expert on the topic of gender roles:

> Gender is defined in the dictionary as "kind, sort, class; also genus as opposed to species." And that's just it. Gender is a word meaning what *kind* of human are you. Most would say, "I am a male" or "I am a female." But the words "male" and "female" refer to their sex. Gender has nothing to do with one's biological make-up, but more of an element of one's identity—"'gender' is masculinity and femininity" (Kimmel 3).

Compare this opening with the opening of his second draft (page 156). Which do you like better? Why?

Problems with Using Sources Because your readers have not read the sources you cite, you need to comment on what sources say and set up quotations and paraphrases with enough context so readers can understand them. Here is Cummins's first effort to integrate a source:

> The idea that our gender is influenced and developed in elementary, middle and high school is explored by C. J. Pascoe, a sociologist at the University of California at Berkeley. Among many things, Pascoe explores the idea that school is "an organizer of sexual practices, identities, and meanings" (26) in her book, *Dude, You're a Fag: Masculinity and Sexuality in High School.* She also notes that "the heterosexualizing process organized by educational institutions cannot be separated from, and in fact is central to, the development of masculine identities" (27). Specifically, C. J. Pascoe refers to the "Mr. Cougar" competition in the high school she did her field work in. Candidates for the "Mr. Cougar" title performed short skits, usually mocking boys who are less masculine than the stereotypical "manly man." These skits reinforce the idea that the stereotypical "manly man" is strong, big and powerful. The "manly man" must also have a girlfriend and must

frequently have sex. The skits made being a "manly man" seem essential, and "male femininity [. . .] is coded as humorous" (4). Referring to one of the "Mr. Cougar" skits, Pascoe writes that "the skit fostered and encouraged masculinity as heterosexual" (45). The "Mr. Cougar" skits make it seem like one has to prove his own masculinity to be considered heterosexual. She reinforces the concept that because of "heterosexualizing" schools, gender is shaped and developed in elementary, middle and high school.

Compare this version to paragraphs in the revised version. Note how much better he handles context for and commentary on his source.

Editing Your Revised Draft

In working with sources, you often need to summarize what they say. A wordy summary can obscure the ideas rather than present them clearly. Compare the following two versions of a summary Jamie Cummins used for one of his sources. The original version reads like a list of disconnected points stated by author Michael Kimmel:

Original Version

Kimmel explains that "virtually every society known to us is founded upon assumptions of gender difference and the politics of gender inequality" (2). He believes that "gender difference is the product of gender inequality" (4) rather than the other way around. Kimmel focuses more on gender inequality and the "differences *among* men and *among* women" (9) rather than just explaining how they are different. He also mentions that "gender difference is the product of gender inequality" (4). Because of the inequality between men and women, their resulting gender is affected. Kimmel notices that "the organizations of our society have evolved in ways that reproduce both the differences between women and men and the domination of men over women" (15). His words reinforce that it is society that determines and develops our gender.

These sentences describe the original source by listing points Kimmel makes, but they do not show how the points relate to each other.

Passive voice obscures the point: Inequality causes gender differences.

The original passage is 132 words; in the revised version, Cummins cuts the word count down to 95. In the following passage, note how Cummins makes this summary both shorter and easier for readers to follow.

Edited Version

Kimmel explains that "virtually every society known to us is founded upon assumptions of gender difference and the politics of gender inequality" (2). While most people assume that inequality is caused by gender difference, Kimmel sees inequality as the cause, not the result, of gender difference. Gender inequality exists because "the organizations of our society have evolved in ways that reproduce both the differences between women and men and the domination of men over women" (15). In other words, societies dictate that the sexes have distinctly different roles in order to keep the sexes unequal.

The color coding in this revision shows the improved coherence in the revised summary, as each sentence picks up a point from the one before and carries it forward.

Sums up argument's main point.

REVISED STUDENT EXAMPLE

Cummins 1

Jamie Cummins

Professor Channell

Writing 205

24 August 2016

Exploring the Concept of Gender

In her book *Mindfulness,* Ellen J. Langer says that people can be "trapped by categories" or concepts from the past. One example she gives is "masculine/feminine" (11). I began to wonder how trapped we might be by our ideas of appropriate behavior for men and women. Many will say that because of men and women's biological makeup, our gender is simply something one is born with—an instinct, of sorts. But is this true? I decided to explore the concept of gender and gender roles to see how different the sexes really are. 1

Explains motivation for his exploration of "gender."

First, I looked into definitions of the word *gender.* I found that it can be interchanged with the word *sex* in common use, but social scientists use gender to refer to social roles and sex to refer to biological differences. According to the *Oxford English Dictionary,* gender is a "euphemism for the sex of a human being, often intended to emphasize the social and cultural, as opposed to the biological, distinctions between the sexes." If it is just a euphemism for sex, do we need it at all? Why should social distinctions need to be emphasized? 2

Results of dictionary information, including root meanings. Note his comments on the information.

I read the introduction to a book by a leading writer on gender, Michael Kimmel, titled *The Gendered Society.* He says, "'Sex' refers to the biological apparatus, the male and the female—our chromosomal, chemical, anatomical organization. 'Gender' refers to the meanings that are attached to those differences within a culture" (3). Kimmel believes that these meanings are socially constructed (9) in order to keep the sexes unequal. 3

Use of another writer's view of gender.

Kimmel explains that "virtually every society known to us is founded upon assumptions of gender difference and the politics of gender inequality" (2). While most people assume that inequality is caused by gender difference, Kimmel sees inequality as the cause, not the result, of gender difference. Gender inequality exists because "the organizations of our society have evolved in ways that reproduce both the differences between women and men and the domination of men over women" (15). In other words, societies dictate that the sexes have distinctly different roles in order to keep the sexes unequal. 4

This is an interesting theory, but I wonder how different are men and women, really? Kimmel acknowledges the biological differences but his social constructionist approach explores "the differences *among* men and *among* women" and has determined that "these are often more decisive than the differences between women and men" (9). A diagram in his book, shows that there is greater variation within the bell curve representing each sex than there is between the sexes. The shaded area in the middle is the overlap showing how similar men and women really are. Kimmel says the "interplanetary" view of men as from Mars and women from Venus just reinforces the myth of gender difference, but really, we are all from planet Earth (11). 5

So if men and women are not so different, where do they get the idea that they are? Kimmel says it is the social institutions of family, workplace, politics, and schools "where the dominant definitions are reinforced and reproduced and where 'deviants' are disciplined" (15). I saw gender roles at my high school, but I never thought school itself played a role. A recent book shows how this happens. 6

C. J. Pascoe, a sociologist, observed a typical public high school for an entire year and found that the school reinforced ideas of masculinity as white, athletic, and heterosexual. In her book, *Dude, You're a Fag: Masculinity and Sexuality in High School,* she describes a popularity contest called the "Mr. Cougar" competition. Candidates for the "Mr. Cougar" title performed short skits, in which they mocked boys who did not fit the stereotype of the "manly man." 7

Use of another writer as a concrete example of gender role conditioning.

In one skit, titled "The Revenge of the Nerds," the candidates for Mr. Cougar appeared at first as weak and effeminate, dressed in nerdy clothes. Pascoe says the audience thought this was hysterically funny because "male femininity . . . is coded as humorous" (4). The nerds' girlfriends were then kidnapped by other boys dressed as "gangstas." To get "their women" back, the nerdy boys had to bulk up by lifting weights. The girls were depicted as trophies awarded to the nerds once they had transformed themselves into manly men and proved their masculinity by rescuing the girls from the gangstas (45). When our class discussed this reading, many students reported that their high schools had similar contests, but they thought Pascoe was overanalyzing, and it was all just in fun. But I have seen all of this first hand. 8

Many different organizations promote male masculinity. At all levels of education, there is pressure to conform to the "normal" gender image. If one does not act "girly" or "manly," they are shunned. Most will eventually find out that one does not have to have sex, lift weights, or have a girlfriend to prove their masculinity. Actually, no one should ever have to *prove* their gender, especially since exaggerated gender roles reinforce inequality of the sexes. 9

Draws on his experience in this paragraph to illustrate gender role conditioning.

But women have made gains in equality, so it's logical to ask, since concepts of gender change with time, could our society's concept of masculinity be changing? Sharon Jayson, the author of the article "Guys Try to Read Society's Road Map for Behavior," says yes and no. Boys are getting mixed signals about sexuality and how to develop their masculine identity. An American Psychological Association study found 19% of the male high school students in the study received conflicting messages; some told them they had to be tough and others that they had to be nice. Andrew Smiler, an assistant professor of psychology at the State University of New York–Oswego, says boys learn that women are equals, but "we haven't changed masculinity" (qtd. in Jayson). Jayson quotes a professor of counseling who says "a large proportion of young males [still] view drinking and having sexual conquests as the appropriate way to begin to prove they are an adult male." Girls send boys the message they should be sensitive and show their feelings, but boys are still sending each other the old "macho" message. 10

Poses a significant question explored in the paragraph.

11 I was ready to accept that gender differences are totally social, but I still had to ask, "Is it possible that male and female brains are different in a way that would affect their behavior?" Some researchers believe that the sexes have innately different ways of thinking. Simon Baron-Cohen, a psychologist at Cambridge University, believes that "there are interesting differences between the *average* male and female mind. Recognizing these could lead to a mutual respect of difference" (77). He says studies show that females have more empathizing brains, while men have more systemizing brains (78). Women are more likely to share, take turns, show sensitivity to facial expressions, talk about emotions, and make eye contact. In contrast, a male brain is more likely to pay attention to relevant details, pursue math, science and physics, read maps, and show interest in mechanical systems. Even one-day old baby boys will "look longer at a mechanical mobile, which is a system with predictable laws of motion, than at a person's face, an object that is next to impossible to systemize" (86). This may be evidence that difference is innate, not learned.

Poses another key question he explores in this paragraph.

12 What disturbed me was that Baron-Cohen's article supports the idea that men are the dominant sex. Baron-Cohen tries to avoid discussing the politics of power and inequality in his article. He insists that the differences are "on average." Researchers found individual men with empathizing brains and individual women with systemizing brains; thus, "there is no scientific justification for stereotyping . . ." (92). However, by claiming that men have more systemizing brains, he shows why they are the dominant sex. We all know that those who are talented mathematicians, scientists and physicists get paid more than people in caretaking roles. And in today's society, money *is* power. If men are biologically stronger in these fields, they will be the ones who are more apt to make the money.

Calls attention to a disturbing implication of the innate difference view.

13 I have begun to think that gender is not a helpful concept for the human race, since as Kimmel argues, it is based in inequality. He says that if we could eliminate gender inequality, "we will remove the foundation upon which the entire edifice of gender difference is built" (4). Eliminating the concept of gender would be impossible, but we need to be aware of how it creates inequality and causes both men and women to be trapped in stereotypes.

Concludes with his tentative view of "gender" as the source of stereotypes.

Cummins 5

Works Cited

Baron-Cohen, Simon. "Does Biology Play Any Role in Sex Differences in the Mind?" *The Future of Gender.* Edited by Jude Browne. Cambridge UP, 2007, pp. 77–97.

Jayson, Sharon. "Guys Try to Read Society's Road Map for Behavior." *USA Today,* 26 Aug. 2008, p. 09D.

Kimmel, Michael S. *The Gendered Society.* 3rd ed. Oxford UP, 2008.

Langer, Ellen J. *Mindfulness.* Da Capo Press, Perseus Books, 1989.

Pascoe, C. J. *Dude, You're a Fag: Masculinity and Sexuality in High School.* U of California P, 2007.

CREDITS

CHAPTER 8

Comparing Perspectives

ENGAGING QUESTIONS

In this chapter, you will engage with the following questions:

- What is the role of synthesis in writing that compares perspectives?
- What are the purposes for comparing perspectives?
- What methods do writers use to investigate a topic for comparing perspectives?
- How do the elements of the rhetorical situation apply to the writing process for comparing perspectives?
- How do writers apply the steps of the writing process to an assignment that compares perspectives?

IN CHAPTER 1 WE DISCUSSED THE DIFFERENCE BETWEEN A QUESTION OF FACT AND A QUESTION OF OPINION. "Does playing video games improve visual response time?" is a question of fact. It can be answered by finding reliable current data. Questions of opinion, however, are open to debate. "Should sales of violent video games be restricted to people age eighteen or older?" is a question of opinion. On questions like this, we find a range of perspectives, all of which could be well informed.

Who is right? What should we think? When people encounter conflicting perspectives, two responses are common:

1. "It's just a matter of opinion." It *is* a matter of opinion, and to that extent the response is justified. However, this response usually implies that all opinions are equally sound.
2. "Since everyone is entitled to his or her opinion, I'll take whatever position appeals to me."

The problem with these responses is that they shut down further critical thought on the question.

A third response—one that opens up further thought—is to compare conflicting perspectives carefully, identifying the most intelligent perspective by asking questions like the following:

- Which opinion is backed by the best current information?
- Who offers the most convincing reasoning?
- How can I reconcile the best points in one opinion with the best points in another?

As we explore viewpoints, we accept some ideas and reject others. Eventually we draw our own informed conclusion about where the truth lies.

What Is Comparing Perspectives?

Comparing perspectives is the examination of the differences among **perspectives** *(opinions* or *points of view).* People have different perspectives because of different backgrounds and prior knowledge. For example, parents of young children are more likely to favor restricting the sale of violent video games, while people who work in the video game industry are more likely to favor open access.

Central to writing a comparison of perspectives is **synthesis,** a Greek word that means "putting together." An effective mash-up, for example, is a synthesis of different songs to create a new whole. In the academic world, most writing relies on synthesis, blending information and ideas from multiple sources to develop and support a single point of view.

Why Write to Compare Perspectives?

Your answer to any question depends on your perspective. For example, if someone asked you whether Facebook has been a positive social influence on young people, your answer would depend on your experience with Facebook. To get a broader perspective, you must move beyond your own knowledge and experience, deepening your understanding by comparing and evaluating the views of other people. On the Facebook question, for example, you might evaluate what psychologists and educators have had to say and compare their perspectives with those of your friends and classmates. The key questions for comparing perspectives, then, are the following:

- How do different people answer the question?
- Which perspectives seem most valid after careful examination?
- What can I use from these perspectives to answer the question more fully and thoughtfully for myself?

Finding what others think can complicate our thinking. But getting a mix of viewpoints stimulates thought. A good panel discussion can be more invigorating to an audience than a single person lecturing. Similarly, reading multiple perspectives opens your mind.

Why *write* to compare perspectives? Writing helps us do the following:

- Identify the specific points being discussed
- Analyze where opinions intersect and diverge
- Determine, point by point, the differences and similarities
- Reflect on the points under debate
- Formulate our own view

Writing a comparison of perspectives results in more precise and informed thinking about a question.

Comparisons of perspectives are common in business and community contexts, such as deciding which candidate to vote for, choosing a course of action after hearing a range of proposals, or soliciting the views of multiple consultants on some complicated issue or problem. In personal and academic contexts, people compare perspectives whenever they read reviews of colleges, books, and movies, and all researched writing involves exploring what experts have said.

Genres that compare perspectives include the introductions to books and scholarly articles in which the writer surveys previous scholarship on the topic, book reviews that compare how two or three books treat the same subject, and exploratory essays using multiple sources.

How Do Writers Compare Perspectives?

Like any kind of serious thinking, comparing perspectives works best if you have a method for your investigation:

1. Start by posing a question, not of fact but of opinion, a question on which reasonable people might disagree. It could be a question you wish to research, such as, "Do sports build character?" or "Do same-sex schools educate girls (or boys) better than coeducational ones?"
2. Next, ask how people have answered the question. This involves some kind of research.
3. Compare how people have answered the question.

THE ART OF QUESTIONING Some Ways Writers Compare Perspectives

1. **What is the central question addressed in all the readings?** What is the key question implied in each viewpoint you have read?
2. **What are the key terms or concepts used in discussing this question, and how do the writers define these terms?** Is there disagreement about the meaning of key terms?
3. **How do the authors answer the question, and where do their answers agree or disagree?** Which authors provide the best evidence in support of their views?
4. **What conclusions or insights into the central question have you been able to reach as a result of comparing perspectives on it?** Which perspectives do you want to incorporate into your own answer to the question?

For more on concepts, see Chapter 7, Exploring a Concept, pages 135–60.

The following reading is an example of comparing perspectives. Note that the author answers all four of the questions listed above.

READING **8.1**

The reading below is excerpted from an academic article in the social sciences by a psychologist at Florida State University. It is the introduction to a long article on the relationship between sports and character. In the social sciences, such as psychology, writers typically preface their articles with an abstract and a comparison of viewpoints uncovered through their research, a genre known as the "literature review."

Which Character Should Sports Develop?

ANDY RUDD

An *abstract* is an article summary common in scientific journals and databases. An abstract helps researchers decide whether an article is relevant to their research without having to read it.

Abstract

For years, strong claims have been made that sport builds character. Despite such claims, a "winning at all cost" mentality can frequently be seen within all of sport. The reason for this paradox may relate to confusion around what it means to demonstrate character. The purpose of this article is to show that there are indeed two distinct types of character that are espoused in the sport milieu. One type is related to social values (social character) the other related to moral values (moral character). Following an explication and comparison of these types of character, a recommendation is made for a needed emphasis towards the development of moral character.

Passive voice is customary in articles in the social sciences and natural sciences.

Explains and compares the views before making his recommendation.

Introduction

1 Typically when an athlete or team at any level of sport is considered to have displayed character, the word "character" is associated with a host of values such as teamwork, loyalty, self-sacrifice, perseverance, work ethic, and mental toughness. As a specific example, a high school athletic director defined an athlete's character as "a willingness to try no matter what the situation. An attempt to continually improve; a willingness to give all up for the cause; and sacrificing without expectations." In another example, a high school coach asserted: "Character is the belief in self-worth and your own work ethic. . . ." (Rudd, 1999).

Article uses APA (American Psychological Association) documentation style, common in the social sciences.

2 In professional sport, character has been defined similarly. For instance, consider a newspaper article that headlined, "The Arizona Diamondbacks Attribute Their Success to Character." Specifically, the article highlighted the Diamondbacks as players who work hard and don't complain about salaries (Heyman, 2000). Consider also an issue of *Sports Illustrated* in which New England Patriots' Troy Brown commented on former teammate Drew Bledsoe's ability to play with a broken finger and lead his team to victory. Brown stated, "It showed a lot of character" (Zimmerman, 2001, p. 162).

Presents more examples of *character* as a social value to demonstrate that this understanding of character is widespread.

3 However, in contrast to the notion that an athlete of character is one who displays values such as teamwork, loyalty, self-sacrifice, perseverance, work ethic, and mental toughness, sport scholars in the area of character development have defined character with a different set of values. Sport scholars, including sport philosophers and sport psychologists, more commonly define an athlete of character as one who is honest, fair, responsible, respectful, and compassionate (Arnold, 1999; Beller & Stoll, 1995; Gough, 1998; Shields & Bredemeier, 1995). For example,

Offers the other perspective of *character* as a moral value and cites several writers who hold it.

Arnold (1999) states, "In terms of moral goodness, or what I refer to as moral character, it involves a life that complies with such virtues as justice, honesty, and compassion" (p. 42).

Identifies patterns in the viewpoints and sums up the differences between the two.

It does indeed seem, therefore, that there are two distinct definitions of character maintained by two camps. The first camp consists of coaches, administrators, and players who may typically define character with social values such as teamwork, loyalty, self-sacrifice, and perseverance. This could be designated as "social character." The second camp consists of sport scholars, and people of earlier generations still alive, who typically define character with moral values such as honesty, fairness, responsibility, compassion, and respect. This is commonly referred to by many of them as "moral character." The existence of these two camps, each with their respective definitions of character, suggests that there is confusion and disagreement concerning the definition of character in sport. (Of course, there may be some "in the middle" who accept an overlapping, possibly conflicting set of values to describe the term "character.") 4

Offers an insight into what the comparison has revealed and why it matters. Concludes with view he favors.

As a result of the above, the differences in the way character is defined may provide strong evidence why many feel there is a lack of sportsmanship in competitive sport today. Similarly, these same people decry the "winning-at-all-cost" mentality that seems to prevail in athletics (see, for example, "A Purpose," 1999; Hawes, 1998; Spencer, 1996). Many coaches, athletic administrators, and parents may indeed place such a premium on social values such as teamwork, loyalty, self-sacrifice, and work ethic that they forget, or at least downplay, any emphasis on time-honored moral values such as honesty, fairness, responsibility, and respect. 5

References

A purpose pitch. (1999, May 17). *Sports Illustrated, 90*, 24.

Arnold, P. (1999). The virtues, moral education, and the practice of sport. *Quest, 51*(1), 39–54.

Beller, J. M., & Stoll, S. K. (1995). Moral reasoning of high school student athletes and general students: An empirical study versus personal testimony. *Pediatric Exercise Science, 7*(4), 352–363.

Gough, R. (1998). A practical strategy for emphasizing character development in sport and physical education. *Journal of Physical Education, Recreation, & Dance, 69*(2), 18–23.

Hawes, K. (1998). Sportsmanship: Why should anybody care? *NCAA News,* 1, 18.

Heyman, J. (2000, May 22). They're 'good guys, good players.' *Statesman Journal,* 3B.

Rudd, A. (1999). [High school coaches' definitions of character]. Unpublished raw data.

Shields, D., & Bredemeier, B. (1995). *Character development and physical activity.* Champaign, IL: Human Kinetics.

Spencer, A. F. (1996). Ethics in physical and sport education. *Journal of Physical Education, Recreation & Dance, 67*(7), 37–39.

Zimmerman, P. (2001, September 3). New England Patriots. *Sports Illustrated, 95*(9), 162–163.

Questions for Discussion

1. In the first and second paragraphs, what similar ideas connect the examples Rudd provides?
2. One of the keys to responding to anything we read is to evaluate it according to our own experience. What have you learned about character from participating in sports or from observing sports events?
3. Which of the two groups does your perspective on character in sports conform to, or does it include some of both views? If so, do you see conflict in your definition?

Thinking as a Writer

What Is the Rhetorical Situation?

1. What is Rudd's *purpose* in writing this literature review? What is his *angle* on the topic? How would you describe his *stance* and *voice*?
2. Who is this essay's intended *audience*? Is Rudd writing for his psychologist peers, for students with an interest in the topic, for athletes, for a more general public, or for another specific group? Is there anything in this essay you can cite that implies his target readership?
3. Using The Art of Questioning on page 163 and marginal annotations to the article, explore how the author develops his comparison of perspectives. What are the key moves he makes and in what order does he make them? ■

Portfolio of Readings on the Ethics of Eating Meat

The following three readings offer a range of opinions about how meat production and consumption could be more ethical than it currently is. These essays are arguments intended to provide an opportunity for you to explore and compare a range of perspectives. We will use these readings to demonstrate how to compare perspectives, which is the writing assignment for this chapter. As you work through each reading in the portfolio, use the critical reading skills covered in Chapter 2: awareness of the author and his or her purpose and audience; the claim and reasons (since most "perspective" pieces are arguments); and the key terms and assumptions. When preparing to compare texts, you should begin annotating them the first time you read them, noting similarities and differences as you go.

READING **8.2**

Eating Well vs. Being Good

DAVID KATZ

This perspective on the ethics of eating meat comes from David Katz, a medical doctor who is board-certified both in internal medicine and in preventive medicine and public health. He founded and directs the Yale-Griffin Prevention Research Center at Yale University. Katz is a frequent blogger on Huffington Post's *"The Blog," where he posted this reading, in which he carefully lays out the most common arguments about the ethics of meat consumption and subjects them to logical critique and evaluation.*

In my prior post about "best" diets, I promised to address the ethics of eating animals. I turn now to that topic. 1

On the basis of both health and ethics, the case for eating a mostly plant-based diet is strong. 2

The health case is all but irrefutable. It is impractical to cite all of the relevant evidence here. If one goes to the National Library of Medicine website and types "vegetarianism AND health" into the search box, more than 730 peer-reviewed articles pop up. I cite some portion of that evidence in the chapter on vegetarianism (chapter 43 for those who have the book) in my textbook, *Nutrition in Clinical Practice, 2nd Edition* (2008). In this pop culture forum, however, we may reasonably limit ourselves to the view from altitude and noting that relevant citations include intervention studies, nutrient studies, epidemiologic studies, trans-cultural comparison studies and ethnographic studies of cultural transitions. 3

But before the more zealous carnivores start sharpening spears or pitchforks, and despite my prevailing support for the vegans, I must add that neither on the basis of health, nor ethics, do I find a decisive case for only eating *only* plants. 4

The surest sign you're on the middle path is that people on both sides of you are telling you why you're wrong (often in terms unsuitable for prime time). In this instance, I anticipate the wrath of staunch carnivores and devout herbivores alike. Oh well. 5

I addressed in my prior post the evidence against veganism as the ONLY health-promoting diet. Rather than revisit that argument here, I will simply reassert the take-away message. Both entirely plant-based and mostly plant-based diets have been linked to powerful health benefits as compared to the typical American diet, the many glow-in-the-dark constituents of which might be hard to assign confidently to either the plant or animal kingdom. There have been no decisive, long-term comparison trials of optimal omnivorousness versus optimal vegetarianism, and perhaps never will be. The evidence available shows that eating only plants can reduce heart disease risk by 70 percent or more, and so can adopting a Mediterranean diet that includes animal foods. Impassioned arguments to the contrary notwithstanding, on the basis of evidence—it's a draw. 6

Eating only plants—whether vegetarianism or veganism—is generally a good idea, and when practiced well, an excellent idea—for health; for the kinder, gentler treatment of our fellow species; and for the preservation of our planet. That is a 7 trifecta if ever there was one, so I lend my very strong support to well-practiced vegetarianism.

8 But the fact that there are variations on the theme of eating well—both health-related and ethics-related variations—allows for more of us to opt in, and fewer to renounce the whole enterprise.

9 The ethical case against eating animals generally originates with our place in the animal kingdom. We are, of course, animals. We are not vegetables, or minerals and, in a time-honored, if admittedly simplistic cataloging of the universe, there's nowhere else to hide. Ethical arguments ensue from one of two fundamental assertions: We are like other animals, or we are different from them.

10 Let's start with being like other animals. I embrace this as the stronger claim not only on the basis of richly detailed renderings of evolutionary biology and molecular genetics, but on the basis of a far more intimate knowledge. Two animals—dogs, to be specific—are among the very best friends I have.

11 Living with these two animals and sharing friendship with them allows me to see just how much alike we are. I love them, they love me. I know joy, anxiety, fear, anticipation, delight and irritation—and so, very clearly, do they. I can be impatient, thankful, annoying, loyal, affectionate and contrite—and so can they. I can solve problems, and so can they—albeit less complex ones (of course, they also create less complex problems!). I like some people and dislike others—so do they. I remember what matters to me—and they remember what matters to them.

12 By any measure that counts—intelligence, resourcefulness, capacity to love, self-awareness, loyalty—I find that Bramble, Zouzou and I differ only by degree, not kind. We are much alike. And of course, this isn't only about my dogs, or dogs in general. All animals are related at one remove or another, and all life is a continuum.

13 The ethical case builds from there. It is inarguably wrong (at least in modern society) for humans to practice cannibalism and eat other humans. Other animals are members of the extended animal family. It is therefore wrong for, presumably, lesser versions of all the same reasons to eat other animals. Rationalizing the eating of some animals, but not others, is rank "speciesism."

14 But this argument quickly falls apart under scrutiny. If it is wrong for humans to eat animals because we are so alike, then what applies to us must apply to them. In other words, the logical extension of this thinking must be: It is wrong for *any* animal to kill and eat any other animal.

15 This is just silly. It is silly for many reasons, among them the fact that some animals are obligate carnivores and could not survive by any means other than killing and eating other animals (sometimes in drawn-out, painful and rather brutal ways). It is also the very height of presumption for creatures born into a natural world to declare that natural world in its normal workings "unethical." It would be as if carbon-based life forms decided it was unethical to use up carbon in making life forms. We could assert it, but it would be nonsense.

16 We should extend this reasoning a bit and note that it would be silly for modern humans to declare animal eating by pre-modern humans unethical. While there seem to

be some differences of opinion among anthropologists about the extent to which our forebears were hunters vs. gatherers, there appears to be universal consensus that they were both. Hunting extends even beyond the timeline of our species, to populate earlier entries into the genus Homo. Was it unethical for Homo *erectus* to hunt and eat what it killed?

There would be no modern ethical vegans had there been no Stone Age hunters feeding their ancestors, because those ancestors would have starved before ever making babies. (As I have noted on prior occasion, people who don't survive to make babies make very poor ancestors.) In contrast, there could certainly be modern meat-eaters whose meat-eating ancestors were fed by hunters, with no help required from ethicists. I am not sure it is reasonably in the purview of ethicists to declare as unethical something on which their existence depends. 17

It cannot be unethical for animals to kill and eat other animals. And it cannot be unethical for humans to have done so throughout their history. So can we make the ethical case based on how different we are from both other species, and our former selves? 18

In one sense, no. Biologically, we are the same as our former selves—at least the same as we have been for tens of thousands of years, if not far longer. And while we might argue we are fundamentally different from other animals, that might as readily destroy as make the argument against eating them. If animals are so different from us, why extend to them the same ethical considerations we apply to ourselves? 19

But in another sense, there is a case to be made based on how different we now are from other species, and our former selves. That sense is our impact on the planet. 20

In our voracious, resource-devouring multitudes, we are exerting a force no other species has ever approached, and which our Stone Age ancestors could not have imagined. In that sense, we are genuinely different. 21

The ethical issue has little to do with whether or not we eat animals. Instead, it has everything to do with how we turn them into food. Knowing, willful neglect or abuse of any creature by any other is unethical. It may be that only humans can be "knowing" about such things, which would give us a basis to limit ethical considerations to ourselves. It allows us to exonerate the occasional brutality of lions, or Komodo dragons. But if fully conscious, premeditated abuse of one creature by another is *not* unethical, it's hard to see how anything is. 22

A growing mass of humanity with a penchant for meat inexorably drives the supply side toward methods of mass production, involving cost-savings and corner-cutting. Animals are fed food unrelated to their native diets. They are crowded together. They are dosed with antibiotics and hormones. There are expedient means of turning creatures into chops and patties that, according to a litany of first-hand accounts, play out very cruelly. 23

In other words, the mass production of meat can obliterate the life of the animal whose meat it is. A steer is turned into something other than a creature—it's just a whole bunch of hamburgers on the hoof. By almost any defensible definition of ethics, the 24 practices that ensue from depending on animals for food to the extent that we do—are over the line.

Let's wrap up. Staunch proponents of veganism tend to over-interpret the evidence for plant-based eating, strong as it is. While it is clear that eating mostly plants is far better than hardly eating plants prevails in the U.S., it does not follow that eating only plants is the only way to eat well. Advocates of meat-eating who base their arguments on our ancestral consumption of meat overlook how radically different modern, domestic, mass-produced animal flesh is from the variety our ancestors ate. 25

As for the ethics, there are too many of us Homo sapiens on the planet already, and every reason to believe there will be many more of us before we control our population growth. Most of us who can, eat too many animals and animal products. The combination of our multitudes and our appetites results in the mass production of animal foods, which in turn results in—or at least invites—terrible abuses. 26

Perpetrating abuse while knowing it is abuse is unethical, if anything is. Eating animals may not be intrinsically unethical, but the means in this case may un-justify the ends. If we must maltreat animals to produce the volumes of animal food we demand, then we should stop demanding such volumes of animal food. 27

There is, however, some latitude left in the solution. 28

It would be fine if all of us were to eat only plants. But if most of us were to eat mostly plants, we could raise many fewer animals for food, and could treat those we do . . . ethically. There is more than one way to eat well and do good. The prevailing norm at present, however, isn't one of them. 29

READING **8.3**

The Ethics of Eating Meat

PAUL SCHWENNESEN

Like David Katz's piece, this one also appeared originally on Huffington Post's "The Blog." The author, Paul Schwennesen, after graduating from the U.S. Air Force Academy, went on to earn a master's degree in government from Harvard University. Now living in rural Arizona, he is a rancher who raises grass-fed beef in environmentally and ethically conscious ways, as he explains in this reading.

I kill animals for a living. 1

I do it so others, as well as myself, can eat them. This accident of circumstance probably disqualifies me from any serious ethical discussion of meat eating. After all, I can hardly claim objectivity. Then again, who can? I live very close to the forces of nature that give (and take) life and therefore have an informed, if undoubtedly nearsighted, sense of what it is I do. 2

But is it ethical? 3

Asking whether eating meat is "ethical" is like asking whether having sex is ethical. 4
Biological imperatives do not pander to such arbitrary distinctions.

My meat-eating is ethical, in the sense that it is not gratuitous; I understand 5
intimately the implications and contradictions of my consumption. I know how it is that my beeves are born, the grasses they like and the ones they don't. I've saved the lives of calves and butchered their mothers in the same afternoon. I thank each for the age-old sacrifice of prey to predator and I swear they understand. I neither rejoice in the blood nor shy from it. This is life. This is ethics.

For me, my proximate, deliberate understanding of what I do defines ethical 6
behavior as a whole: the social moderation of otherwise unrestrained individual yearnings. In my mind, eating #906 (a red mottle-face cow with upturned horns currently braising in the slow cooker) is an ethically different activity than eating a Big Mac on the run.

The fact that I feel comfortable making such a distinction indicates something 7
fundamental about ethics: they evolve. Our current handwringing over what we eat is clearly a privilege born of abundance. Room for such ruminations is only created after the belly hasn't room for anything else. We agonize over meat consumption because we can afford to. Lucky us.

"Ethics" exist as social shorthand; a distilled collective conscience that varies with 8
the social reality it reflects. Ethics do not stand like clean-cut traffic cops in the path of natural urges; they are more like cautionary rumble-strips as we careen down lives strewn with choices. Ethical consumption of meat, therefore, is based upon timing, circumstance, and conscientious understanding of what society deems appropriate. In modern Western culture at least, you are "unethical" if you cannot moderate a biological sexual urge. It is likewise "unethical" to fulfill biological carnivorous urges upon, say, kittens.

We have evolved from a society in which nearly everyone knew the intimate realities 9
and consequences of eating meat to one in which nearly no one does. We have commercially outsourced the twinge of guilt, the pang of discomfort, the heart-race of witnessing a death to just a handful among us. Is there an ethical distinction between the deaths caused by a yeoman farmer who grimly butchers a hog in the fall and a minimum-wage factory worker who mechanically butchers six thousand in a morning? Many of us now see an ethical nuance. Our physical capacities to produce and consume have altered dramatically in the last sixty years; our ethical capacity to accept these realities is altering as well.

My occupation, as a result, caters to omnivores and more than a few "recovering 10
vegetarians" who prefer (apparently) the conscientious killing I practice. I therefore raise my cattle with sentiment but cannot stray into the realm of sentimentality. I recognize that life rests upon the consumption of the unwilling. I obey this ecological truth while simultaneously working within the artificial, changeable lines society delineates. This too, is natural.

Eating meat, particularly #906, is ethical because most people think it is. That is, 11
perhaps, about all one can say.

READING 8.4

Reciprocity: A Foundation for Balance

CLARA SUE KIDWELL, HOMER NOLEY, AND GEORGE E. "TINK" TINKER

The final reading in our portfolio comes from a book about Native American religious views, written by three influential Native American scholars and theologians. Clara Sue Kidwell founded and directed programs in Native American studies at the University of Minnesota, University of California at Berkeley, and University of Oklahoma. Homer Noley is director of the National United Methodist Native American Center at Claremont Graduate University, and George E. "Tink" Tinker has been a member of the faculty at Iliff School of Theology since 1985, teaching courses in Native American cultures, history, and religious traditions. This selection, taken from their book, A Native American Theology, *explains the Native Americans' view of humans' ethical relationship to the earth, including plants and animals.*

The American Indian notion of reciprocity is fundamental to all human participation in world-balancing and maintaining harmony. Reciprocity involves first of all an understanding of the cosmos as sacred and alive, and the place of humans in the processes of the cosmic whole. It begins with an understanding that anything and everything that humans do has an effect on the rest of the world around us. Even when we cannot clearly know what that effect is in any particular act, we know that there is an effect. Thus, Indian peoples, in different places and in different cultural configurations, have always struggled to know how to act appropriately in the world. Indeed, this knowledge seems to be the consistent purpose of all Indian creation stories. Knowing that every action has its unique effect has always meant that there had to be some sort of built-in compensation for human actions, some act of reciprocity. 1

The necessity for reciprocity becomes most apparent where violence is concerned, especially when such violence is an apparent necessity as in hunting or harvesting. Violence cannot be perpetrated, a life taken, in a Native American society, without some spiritual act of reciprocation. I am so much a part of the whole of creation and its balance, anything I do to perpetrate an act of violence, even when it is necessary for the survival of our families and our communities, must be accompanied by an act of spiritual reciprocation intended to restore the balance of existence. It must be remembered that violence as a technical category must extend to all one's "relatives." Thus, a ceremony of reciprocity must accompany the harvesting of vegetable foods such as corn or the harvesting of medicinals such as cedar, even when only part of a plant is taken. The ceremony may be relatively simple, involving a prayer or song and perhaps a reciprocal offering of tobacco. 2

Many tribes maintained very extensive and complex ceremonies of reciprocation to insure continuing balance and plentiful harvests. Likewise, there is a tradition of mythic stories that accompany such ceremonies and function to provide the theoretical foundation for the ceremonies. Ultimately, all of these stories function further to insure the continuing respect of the communities who tell the stories for all the parts of the created world, all the relatives, upon which the people depend for their own well-being. 3

Even gathering rocks for a purification ceremony (sweat lodge ceremony) calls for care and respect, prayers and reciprocation.

4 In the same manner, ceremonies involving self-sacrifice (typically called "self-torture" or "self-mutilation" by the missionaries and early ethnographers) also come under this general category of reciprocation. In the Rite of Vigil, (vision quest), which is very widespread among Indian peoples of North America, as well as the Sun Dance,* the suffering the supplicant takes upon himself or herself is usually thought of as vicarious and as some sort of reciprocation. Since all of one's so-called possessions are ultimately not possessions but relatives that live with someone, an individual is not giving away a possession when he or she gives a gift to someone else. In actuality the only thing a person really owns and can sacrifice is one's own flesh. Thus these ceremonies of self-sacrifice tend to be the most significant ceremonies of a people.

5 While missionaries typically thought of these ceremonies as vain human attempts to placate some angry deity, Indian communities know that these ceremonies were much more complex than that. Rather, they are much more often thought of as vicarious sacrifices engaged in for the sake of the whole community's well-being. Moreover, they are thought of as ceremonies that came to the community as a gift from the Sacred Mystery in order to help the community take care of itself and its world. Thus, the Sun Dance is considered a ceremony in which Two-Leggeds† participate with the Sacred in order to help maintain life, that is, to maintain the harmony and balance of the whole. All these ceremonies, then, especially those that anthropologists call "world renewal," function as part of the constantly on-going process of creation.

6 Hunting and war, for example, typically involved a complex ceremonial preparation before a contingent of warriors or hunters left their home. The Osage War Ceremony (nearly identical to the ceremony performed before a buffalo hunt) involved an eleven-day ritual, allowing enough time to affirm the sacredness of life, to consecrate the lives that would be lost in war, and to offer prayers in reciprocation for those potentially lost lives.[1] In the hunt, most Indian nations report specified prayers of reciprocation, involving apologies and words of thanksgiving to the animal itself and the animal's spirit nation. Usually, this ceremonial act is in compliance with the request of the animals themselves as the people remember the primordial negotiations in mythological stories.‡ Thus, formal and informal ceremonies of reciprocation are a day-to-day mythic activity which has its origin in mythological stories in which human beings were given permission by the animal nations to hunt themselves for food. The

---

*Sun Dance:* Many tribes practiced some form of ritual, sacrificial dance in which young men attached themselves with leather straps to a pole. In many versions of the dance, the ends of the straps pierced the men's chests. The dancers' suffering was a sacrifice for the good of the whole community.

†*Two-Leggeds:* The Native Americans traditionally categorized animal life as two-legged and four-legged, rather than as human and non-human. These traditional categories maintained the belief that all life forms are kin to each other.

‡*Primordial negotiations in mythical stories:* Many Native American creation stories include an explanation of how the two-leggeds and four-legged animals determined which would eat the other. The question was settled by a race. There are many versions of the story. Paul Goble wrote and illustrated an outstanding children's book titled *The Great Race of the Birds and Animals,* based on the Cheyenne and Sioux legends.

resulting covenant, however, calls on human beings to assume responsibilities over against the perpetuation of violence among four-legged relatives. Even after the hunt or battle, those who participated must invariably go through a ceremonial cleansing before re-entering their own village. Not to do this would bring the disruption of the sacred caused by the perpetration of violence right into the middle of national community life and put all people at risk.[2]

Animals, birds, crops, and medicines are all living relatives and must be treated 7
with respect if they are to be genuinely efficacious for the people. The ideal of harmony and balance requires that all beings respect all other beings, that they respect life and avoid gratuitous or unthinking acts of violence. Maintaining harmony and balance requires that even necessary acts of violence be done "in a sacred way." Thus nothing is taken from the earth without prayer and offering. When the tree is cut down for the Sun Dance, for instance, something must be offered, returned to the spirit world, for the life of that tree. The people not only ceremonially and prayerfully ask its permission but also ask for its cooperation and help during the four days of the dance itself.

American technological and economic development cannot embody the Indian 8
ethic of reciprocity. It is not enough to replant a few trees or to add nutrients to the soil. These are superficial acts to treat the negative symptoms of development. The value of reciprocity which is a hallmark of Indian ceremonies goes to the heart of issues of sustainability, which is maintaining a balance and tempering the negative effects of basic human survival techniques. There is no ceremony among any people for clear-cutting an entire forest.

End Notes

1. See Francis La Flesche, *The War and Peace Ceremony of the Osage Indians,* Bureau of American Ethnography, Bulletin 101 (1939).
2. Leslie Silko's famous novel, *Ceremony* (New York: Viking, 1977), is precisely about such a situation. The novel deals with the healing and cleansing of a World War II veteran for whom a new ceremony had to be devised. Social and spiritual complexities of disintegration and alienation had made it much more difficult for the Laguna people and for himself. Thus, his healing has to do with the healing of the whole community and not just himself.

The Assignment

Read at least two perspectives addressing a topic of current interest. In an essay, explore the perspectives by noting where authors address the same or similar questions, and compare their answers. Decide which views seem most valid. Conclude by discussing how your exploration contributed to your understanding of the topic.

What Can I Write About?

If your instructor does not provide you with a set of readings that provide different views on a single question, you have several options for finding them:

- **Reviews of artistic works and performances.** You could compare reviews of a film, play, or musical performance.
- **Opinion columns assessing political candidates or proposed legislation.** If you are writing in an election year, you could compare candidates' positions on a single issue. Newspapers often run opinion columns where you can find at least two views on a current political issue.
- **Viewpoints on issues in current events or popular culture.** News articles often cite a few expert viewpoints on the topic, which you could use as a starting point. Use a library database to search for articles by these authors. You can also search using keywords for opinions and articles on an issue. Newspapers often run "debates," in which they publish two or more columnists' responses to a single question. The reference librarians at your school can also help you locate a variety of views on a topic.

See Chapter 16, pages 365–66, for guidance on using library databases.

See Chapter 16, pages 366–69, for guidance on Internet searches.

How Do I Compare Perspectives? Questioning the Rhetorical Situation

Begin by picturing a **rhetorical situation** for your writing project. Remember that rhetoric means *effective communication.* You are not just writing a paper; you are also communicating. You should consider the key variables in any act of communication: a writer with something to say, a reader the writer wishes to reach, and a kind of text appropriate to the writing task. These variables will affect many decisions you make during the composing process.

To get a broad perspective on a topic, compare and evaluate the views of other thinkers. Does everyone, for example, think that Facebook improves friendships? Which perspectives seem most valid after careful examination?

© mediaphotos/Getty Images, RF

Writer: What Is My Purpose, and What Impression Should Readers Have of Me?

The assignment in this chapter specifies a purpose for comparing perspectives: to explore the range of opinions on a single question and to draw an original conclusion informed by your reading and critical thinking. In college writing, this is a common purpose, since most research papers begin with an exploration of the research.

This project, then, will help you develop a crucial college skill you will also use regularly in daily life as you analyze competing bids, for example, or assess the arguments of political candidates vying for your vote.

Audience: Who Is My Reader?

As with all writing projects, imagining your audience will help you decide how best to represent the viewpoints you are comparing. You will need to place perspectives in context for your readers by identifying each writer and providing information about his or her background. Readers expect writers to represent the competing viewpoints fairly by providing accurate summaries of the various positions. Because the assignment requires comparing and evaluating viewpoints, your readers will need you to go beyond summary to identify the strengths and weaknesses of each position.

Text: What Moves Can I Make?

The basic moves are illustrated in Andy Rudd's comparison of views on character in sports (pages 164–66). The student example (pages 186–190) also illustrates the moves. In sum they are as follows:

1. Introduce a question upon which people take different positions.
2. Define any key terms central to the question.
3. Present the main point of each perspective in brief summary statements.
4. Look for patterns of agreement and disagreement, and compare what different people have to say on the same point.
5. Use quotation and paraphrase to show what different people say in defense of their viewpoints.
6. As you present your sources' viewpoints, respond with your own comments evaluating them.
7. Conclude with an evaluation of the viewpoints and what you learned from comparing them.

How Do I Compare Perspectives? Engaging the Writing Process

No two people compose in exactly the same way, and even the same person may go through the writing process in different ways with different assignments. Nevertheless, because no one can attend to everything at once, there are phases in handling any significant writing task. You begin by preparing to write, generating content and planning your draft. The next phase is drafting your paper, getting a version, however rough it may be, on screen or paper so that you have something to work with during the next two stages: revising your draft by making changes to the content, arrangement, and style of your writing; and editing your draft to take care of problems at the paragraph and sentence level, such as lack of focus and coherence, awkward or unclear sentences, and errors of grammar, spelling, and punctuation.

We will illustrate this process for comparing perspectives using this chapter's portfolio of three readings (pages 167–74) on the ethics of eating meat. We will guide you through strategies for finding points for comparison and organizing an exploratory essay around them.

Exploring Your Topic

Plan to spend at least half of the time allotted for this project on the preparation stage: careful reading and considerable informal writing, both in the margins and in notes either online or in a notebook.

Choosing and Narrowing Your Topic

As you choose readings on your topic, be sure that the authors are addressing not just the same topic but *the same question or questions* about the topic. For example, although some of our portfolio readings mention the health benefits of reducing meat consumption, the key question addressed in each case has to do with ethics, not health.

Read your selections critically, as described in Chapter 2 on page 12, and illustrated in the strategies and activities throughout the chapter. These strategies include the following preparations before reading:

1. Find out about the author and his or her likely bias.
2. Skim the reading to see the main ideas as evident in the introduction, paragraph openings, and the conclusion. Look for keywords that appear in other readings you are considering for your comparison.

What Does That Word Mean?

On any topic, certain words are central to the discussion, as in our reading about the concept of character in sports.

The keyword in our example about the ethics of eating meat is *ethical.* Critical thinking, as we say in Chapter 1, begins with a basic question: What does that word mean? Ethical does not simply mean "right" as opposed to wrong; according to the definition in the *Oxford English Dictionary,* it means that which "conforms to moral principles or ethics; morally right; honorable; virtuous; [and] decent." However, the closer we look at the word and how it is used, the more we see that people might disagree on what exactly makes an action, like eating meat, moral or immoral.

Many people argue that raising cattle in crowded conditions, as pictured here, makes eating meat unethical.

© sponner/Getty Images, RF

ACTIVITY 8.1 *Writer's Notebook*

Exploring Terms

List the key term or terms that are used in your question. Then look up the term(s) in a comprehensive dictionary like the *Oxford English Dictionary (OED).* Write a paragraph or two explaining what you discovered about the origins and definitions of your key term or terms. ■

When humans depended on hunting and gathering for survival, there could be no question about the morality of killing a deer, for example. Today, as David Katz argues, dietary science has proven that meat, while nutritious in moderation, is not essential for survival. If we could get by on tofu but prefer the taste of meat, are we as ethical in consuming it as were our Paleolithic ancestors? As rancher Paul Schwennesen says, "'Ethics' exist as social shorthand; a distilled collective conscience that varies with the social reality it reflects." The meaning of this term, *ethical,* will be crucial to the different answers people have today to the question, "Is it ethical to eat meat?"

Preparing to Write

Beyond gathering your readings and assessing them critically, the key step in preparing to write is to look for ways to synthesize what the perspectives say.

Finding Ways to Synthesize

Writing a good comparison depends on synthesis, bringing together what different people have to say on similar points. A useful strategy for finding connections among sources is to identify the main points in any one source and turn them into questions. Questions are helpful in making connections across readings because once you have identified a question, you can look to see how different writers answer it. For example, in the first of our portfolio readings, we see David Katz saying:

> A growing mass of humanity with a penchant for meat inexorably drives the supply side toward methods of mass production, involving cost-savings and corner-cutting. Animals are fed food unrelated to their native diets. They are crowded together. They are dosed with antibiotics and hormones. There are expedient means of turning creatures into chops and patties that, according to a litany of first-hand accounts, play out very cruelly.
>
> In other words, the mass production of meat can obliterate the life of the animal whose meat it is. . . . By almost any defensible definition of ethics, the practices that ensue from depending on animals for food to the extent we do—are over the line.

In this passage, Katz makes two important points:

- Industrialized meat production treats animals as things.
- This inhumane treatment is ethically indefensible.

By turning these statements into questions, we have a better tool for finding connections across the readings:

- How does mass production of meat "obliterate the life of animal[s]"?
- What, if any, practices would make meat production more ethical?

Besides Katz, who else has something to say about these questions?

ACTIVITY 8.2 *Collaborative Activity*

Turning Main Points into Questions

In groups of two or three, review the three readings on the ethics of eating meat, identifying the main points in each. State the question that each main point answers. Then find passages in two or more of the readings that answer the same question. What similarities and differences do you find among the answers? ■

BEST PRACTICES Advantages of Turning Key Points into Questions

1. Different sources will give different answers to the same question, but *stating the question* will help you bring the readings together.
2. **Questions can help you organize your essay point by point, showing how each question is addressed by different sources;** this approach is preferable to presenting entire perspectives, one after another. The latter organization results in summaries, whereas the former compares and comments on specific differences among the perspectives.

Mapping Ideas on a Comparative Grid

Another way to identify points of similarity and difference in multiple sources is to map the ideas on a grid, such as the one on page 180. Begin by identifying the questions answered by the main points in each selection. Then indicate where the answers can be found in the readings.

Additional Ways to Track Connections across Perspectives

As you read into a second or third person's perspective, try one or more of these suggestions to help keep control over your sources:

- Annotate each reading with references to page numbers in other sources that address the same questions.
- Use color-coded highlighters to mark passages addressing the same questions in different readings.
- Write informally to discuss where the authors agree or disagree and respond with your own opinion about who has the best viewpoint. See Chapter 2, pages 28–29, for a model. In the next section, we show an example of a student's informal writing in response to one question in common across the readings on ethical meat consumption.

Question	Katz (pages 167–70)	Schwennesen (pages 170–71)	Kidwell, Noley, Tinker (pages 172–74)
What is unethical meat production?	par. 22: "knowing, willful neglect or abuse of any creature"	par. 9: "factory worker" who "mechanically butchers" thousands a day	par. 7: "gratuitous or unthinking acts of violence" with no respect for life
What is unethical consumption?	par. 26: Consuming too many animals results in unethical production.	par. 5: "gratuitous" eating such as a "Big Mac on the run"; "Outsourcing" the killing and the guilt	par. 8: Failure to reciprocate with some prayer of thanks
What would have to change to make meat eating ethical?	par. 23: We would have to curb our "penchant for meat."	par. 9: People must moderate their natural urges according to changing ideas of ethics.	par. 8 We need to maintain a balance in the world by "temper[ing] the negative effects of basic human survival techniques."
How does Westerners' volume of meat consumption affect the ethics of eating meat?	par. 23: Abuses of mass production to satisfy the desire of too many people for too much meat.	par. 9: In the past 60 years humans have increased their capacity "to produce and consume," and these realities should affect our attitudes toward ethical consumption	par. 8: "[T]echnological and economic development cannot embody the Indian ethic of reciprocity"

Using Informal Writing to Join the Discussion

One of the best ways to generate content is to write informally about how different people answer the same questions and to say what you think about their answers. You can do this as freewriting, a notebook entry, or a post on a discussion board to share with classmates who might be reading and comparing the same sources.

The advantage of this kind of informal writing is that you can later use it as part of the draft of your paper. It will need cleaning up, but it will have two essential qualities:

- A comparison with specific references to the sources you have read
- Commentary showing your own thinking in your own voice

You need to be part of the synthesis, too, so it is never too soon to begin to evaluate the viewpoints. Following is an example of a freewriting from student Conner Kline, whose comparison of perspectives on the ethics of eating meat concludes this chapter (see pages 186–90). As Kline reads the first two of his three sources, he uses freewriting to draw some connections across the readings.

Student Example: Freewriting Comparing and Commenting

While my friends and I eat meat, I know that many people avoid it for ethical reasons. Some people take a stand for animal rights and say that humans should not eat animals at all. Only one author really deals with this question. David Katz, the doctor, says it is illogical to say that we should not eat animals because they are so much like us, when they really are not like us, since they are eating each other. This makes sense to me. Eating them is totally different, ethically, from eating other humans. So if it's OK to eat them, what *is* the ethical issue? Katz says that the real ethical problem with eating meat is the way it's produced, with "conscious, premeditated abuse." Then, when I read the blog post by the rancher, Schwennesen, I saw that slaughtering can be more humane. Schwennesen takes pride in running an ethical ranching business. He says he butchers his own cows and takes the time to think about what he's doing. He says he thanks each one for "the age-old sacrifice of prey to predator and I swear they understand." You have to respect him for caring and being personally involved with the death of his cows. Why should these two different ways of killing cows matter to us as consumers? One kind of killing is not ethical, not done with any moral principles; it's just about making money. The other kind of killing, also for profit, at least acknowledges that the animal made a sacrifice, for which we should be thankful. We should not support the kind of meat production that objectifies a living creature as if its life didn't matter, but the factory meat is everywhere and so it's hard to avoid it and be an ethical eater.

Begins with the big question of whether humans should eat animals and shows that one author answers it.

Paraphrases Katz's answer to the question.

Comments on Katz's argument.

Raises the second question: What is the real ethical issue?

Makes a connection to a second source, which shows an alternative to the assembly-line style of slaughtering.

Draws some conclusions about the questions raised by these three readings.

ACTIVITY 8.3 *In Your Own Work*

Respond to Ideas in Your Readings

As you read and reread each of the perspectives, record key points in a reading and respond to them with your own evaluations. Be sure to *refer to specific passages in the readings,* as in our freewriting example. ■

Drafting Your Paper

Begin by considering your own point of view or angle:

What Is My Angle?

Even though some of the writers agree on major points, each of the authors comes to the topic from a unique professional, personal, or philosophical background.

- David Katz is a medical doctor with a special interest in nutrition and disease prevention. His perspective is scientific and political. He founded Yale University's Yale-Griffin Prevention Research Center and he is interested in sustainability and sustainable eating habits. He is a writer with several news and magazine blogs, where he expresses his opinions and attempts to influence public policy decisions in the best interests of global health.

- Paul Schwennesen writes from the perspective of an environmentally conscious rancher and independent entrepreneur. He owns the Double Check Natural Grass-Fed Beef ranch in southern Arizona, which sells meat to local markets in Arizona. He was educated at the U.S. Air Force Academy, University of Arizona, and Harvard University, where he received a Master of Liberal Arts in Government. He is politically active and interested in conservation and land management.
- Clara Sue Kidwell is the primary author of the book *A Native American Theology* (Orbis, 2001). Although she holds a Ph.D. in history of science, she turned to an interest in Native American studies, which she taught at the University of Oklahoma and University of California at Berkeley, among other schools. She was joined on this book by two Native American theologians: Homer Noley, who is a retired director of the National United Methodist Native American Center at Claremont School of Theology, and George E. "Tink" Tinker, a prominent scholar at Iliff School of Theology in Denver. These authors are writing from a Native American and Christian perspective, and their angle here is not so much on the ethics of eating meat as on the ethics of living in harmony and balance with all of creation.

These three readings, however, are arguments, not explorations. How does a writer find an angle while keeping an open mind? *The answer is to think about why exploring the question matters to you personally.* What perspectives are you inclined to hold? As you read to discover and compare other perspectives, put your own attitudes to the same test. Consider the following questions:

1. **What context do I bring to the question?** A person exploring perspectives on the relationship between wealth and happiness began by considering how her own upbringing in a military family fostered frugality and self-discipline.
2. **What outcome do I want for my exploration?** Having an angle means believing that your exploration matters. What do you hope to learn from reading multiple viewpoints? Someone planning to become a teacher chose to read about different perspectives on how young children learn. Her interest in education gave her an angle.
3. **Which perspectives are commonly held, and should they be challenged?** On any given question, we can usually name some popular perspectives. An angle can derive from challenging popular perspectives. For example, many Americans believe that everyone should go to college. We can look for selections supporting this perspective, as well as perspectives that challenge it.

What Voice Is Appropriate for Exploratory Writing?

You do not want your essay to read like a list of points: "Source A says _____. On this question, Source B says _____." Such a paper would be monotonous. *You need to be present in the paper, speaking as someone thinking through the questions and evaluating the various viewpoints.*

Use the informal writing you did as you read, evaluated, and responded to the readings to get your own voice into your project. Ask yourself what you would say to the author if he or she were present and you were doing an interview. Challenging perspectives is a good way to put voice into your paper, but make sure that your challenges are well reasoned, not attacks. You should sound fair, thoughtful, and receptive, willing to consider points of view that you do not find persuasive but that may contain valuable points or insights.

Developing and Organizing Your Synthesis

Drafting the essay for this project should not be difficult if you have highlighted your sources to identify passages that answer the same questions, annotated your sources to note points in common, and written informally to compare and respond to the perspectives you have gathered. Review your notes and then consider the following advice:

1. **Introduction:** How might I begin the paper? For your introduction, you could do the following:
   - Open with your own view before reading. In the body and conclusion, indicate how your thinking changed.
   - Open with the question that is the focus of your exploration. State it clearly and explain its importance.
   - Open with the main question you will address, such as, "Can eating meat be ethical? If so, under what conditions or in what circumstances?" You could move directly into your paper this way.
2. **Body:** How can I introduce and compare the perspectives? You could devote one or two paragraphs to setting up all of the perspectives, summarizing the main position of each and introducing the key figures who hold that position, including full names and some background about their research. Or you could begin with the first question that cuts across at least two of the perspectives, introduce

BEST PRACTICES Tips for Organizing Your Paper around Questions

- Check the lists of questions you have made for each perspective. Put these lists together now and identify questions that appear in multiple readings.
- Consider whether narrowing the focus of your exploration might help. An exploration of the ethics of eating meat could have had a much larger focus, such as the rights of animals not to be eaten, but that focus would have been too large for a short paper.
- Based on length requirements for the paper and how much you have to say about the questions, select the ones you intend to address.
- Order the questions logically. For example, a definition question makes more sense at the beginning of the paper. Discuss causes and then effects.
- Plan on multiple paragraphs for each question. You could, for instance, devote one paragraph to one source's answer and another to what the others say on the same question.
- Create transitions so that your reader will know when discussion of one question is over and another is beginning.

the perspectives, and present what each says in response to that question. Then move on to another question.

The essential point is that a paper that synthesizes ideas from multiple authors *needs to be organized around the questions that cut across the readings,* not around the readings themselves. If you devote the first part of your paper to just one author's views, the second to the second author's views, and so on, your paper will read like a summary rather than an exploration.

3. **Conclusion:** Your conclusion should review your evaluations of the different perspectives. Whose reasons were the most persuasive? What evidence was the most compelling? Construct a perspective of your own using what you have found convincing and compelling from all the sources. Use your conclusion to explain how you developed deeper insight based on comparing your sources.

Revising Your Draft

Revising this kind of paper usually involves improving the organization, looking more closely at the perspectives to make your exploration more specific, and including more of your own reactions to the authors' views. The Art of Questioning lists specific activities for helping you revise.

THE ART OF QUESTIONING Revision Checklist for Comparing Perspectives

This checklist moves in descending order, from major challenges of this project to concerns to consider in every piece of formal writing.

1. **Did you explore?** Exploring means entertaining a question. To entertain a question means to hold it open and consider it thoughtfully. If you disputed a point before considering its merits, revise to show more open-mindedness before you declare that someone is wrong.
2. **How well did you represent the ideas of all the authors?** Did you draw on the sources to represent their views accurately and fully? Did you introduce the authors with full name on first mention and provide information about their credentials?
3. **How well did you organize the paper?** Check to see that you focus on one question at a time, not one source at a time. Did you bring in comparisons throughout your draft?
4. **How well did you work quotations into your paper?** Did you introduce quotations and follow up with explanation and commentary as needed?
5. **How well did you respond to the sources?** Did you provide enough commentary to show exactly what you agreed or disagreed with and why?
6. **How smoothly did the sentences flow?** Each sentence should prepare the reader for the one coming next. Read your draft aloud, listening for places where transitions are needed.

When you have limited time to revise a paper, you have to prioritize. Take care of the bigger problems first, the ones that alter your essay substantially. If smaller problems remain, solve as many as you can in the time you have. One common problem of drafts is inadequately developed paragraphs.

Student Example: Excerpt from Conner Kline's Draft

The following paragraph does not adequately introduce the authors of the source, and it jumps too quickly into the quotation about clear-cutting. In order to understand the point about forests and ceremonies, the readers need more background information about the Native American idea of ceremonies as reciprocation for taking anything from the Earth.

Draft Version

Clara Sue Kidwell, Homer Noley, and George E. Tinker would also agree that our industrialized system of mass-producing meat makes eating meat in our society unethical. In *A Native American Theology* they say, "There is no ceremony among any people for clear-cutting an entire forest" (44). This is because clear-cutting an entire forest is entirely wasteful, something that does not fall in line with the Native American belief of reciprocity. Reciprocity is the idea that balance has to be maintained in the world. Therefore, only what is necessary can be taken, otherwise balance in the cosmos will be thrown off. Clear-cutting an entire forest, or factory farming, is entirely wasteful, which is why the theologians say that "American technological and economic development cannot embody the Indian ethic of reciprocity" (19).

By opening the paragraph with the authors' names, Kline appears to be organizing his paper around his sources, not questions to explore. Also, he should include some information about the authors, who are experts on Native American religious beliefs.

The quotation about forests seems incoherent here because the analogy needs to be set up before the quote, not after it.

Revised Version

According to Native American spiritual beliefs, humans have kinship with animals, plants, and the Earth itself. This is in line with their religious belief that everything has spirit, even things we think of as inanimate, like mountains. Clara Sue Kidwell, a professor of Native American studies, and theologians Homer Noley and George E. "Tink" Tinker explain that the traditional belief is that everything is sacred and alive, and that "anything and everything that humans do has an effect on the rest of the world around us" (41). Therefore, they have to use restraint and not just take as much as they want. When they take anything, such as killing an animal or cutting down a tree, they compensate through a ritual offering or prayer to restore the balance in the world. Like Schwennesen, Native Americans give thanks to the animal, but in their case more formally, through ceremonies, gifts, and sacrifices to honor the spirit of the animal. They make "apologies and words of thanksgiving to the animal itself and the animal's spirit nation" (Kidwell, Noley, and Tinker 43). They do these ceremonies not just for the animal, to show respect, but for the "sake of the whole community's well-being" (42).

Although many Native Americans today are poor and probably have to eat factory farmed meat, their traditional attitudes would make them object to our industrialized system of mass-producing meat. With their belief in reciprocity, they would oppose taking anything from the Earth on such a large scale that the balance cannot be restored. As Kidwell, Noley, and Tinker say, "There is no ceremony among any people for clear-cutting an entire forest" (44). Clear-cutting

Paragraph opens with an idea that is central to understanding the concept of reciprocity.

In the revised version, the source authors are introduced, which is more important than naming the title of their book, which will be found in the Works Cited list.

By mentioning tree-cutting here, the revised version sets the reader up for the quote about clear-cutting in the next paragraph.

The revised paragraph explains the concept of reciprocation more thoroughly and draws a comparison to another perspective.

The quote is more understandable placed near the end of the discussion of reciprocity. A common revision move is to make two paragraphs out of one, opening up complex ideas instead of expecting readers to infer the connections between statements.

a forest, like factory farming, is unsustainable, wasteful, and disrespectful, which is why the theologians say that "American technological and economic development cannot embody the Indian ethic of reciprocity" (44).

Editing Your Final Draft

Nearly every draft can be improved by editing to reduce wordiness, vary sentence structure, and make word choices more specific. This is especially true in introductions. Once your writing project is complete, revisit the opening to see if it contains repetitions and other wordy sentence constructions, such as overuse of the verb *to be.*

Another common editing move is to trim direct quotations so that you do not include any of the quotation that is not relevant to your own point in using the quotation. For example, words that refer to material outside the quotation, such as words or phrases that worked as transitions in the original text, add clutter to your writing. Use ellipses to remove such expressions.

Original Version

This phrase provided a transition in Katz's essay that is not needed in Kline's paper.

David Katz, a medical doctor and Director of the Yale Prevention Center, agrees that the industrialized harvesting of animals is the real ethical problem. He says, "In other words, the mass production of meat can obliterate the life of the animal whose meat it is. A steer is turned into something other than a creature—it's just a whole bunch of hamburgers on the hoof" (23).

Edited Version

Kline trimmed the quote to fit into his paragraph.

David Katz, a medical doctor and Director of the Yale Prevention Center, agrees that the industrialized harvesting of animals is the real problem: he shows that the process objectifies the animal. Katz says, "[t]he mass production of meat can obliterate the life of the animal whose meat it is. A steer is turned into something other than a creature—it's just a whole bunch of hamburgers on the hoof."

REVISED STUDENT EXAMPLE

Kline 1

Conner Kline

Professor Channell

DISC 1312.014

4 December 2014

Making Meat Eating Ethical

Opening makes a personal connection with the issue.

Almost everyone I know eats meat. To be honest I would have a tough time 1
naming five people that I know personally who are vegetarians. Were my friends

Kline 2

Introduction clearly defines the scope of the exploration.

to know how their meat was obtained, however, I'm sure that I would know many more vegetarians. This is because animals are abused, disrespected, and have their lives carelessly thrown away in the industrialized system known as factory farming. Therefore, the question is how can we change our production of meat so that we can eat it ethically?

This is the question that the various sources will be addressing.

The paper is organized around questions on the topic.

Why has meat production become so unethical? David Katz, a medical doctor and Director of the Yale Prevention Center, argues that the industrialization of harvesting animals leads to unethical treatment. He says, "The ethical issue has little to do with whether or not we eat animals. Instead, it has everything to do with how we turn them into food." He shows that the process objectifies the animal: "[t]he mass production of meat can obliterate the life of the animal whose meat it is. A steer is turned into something other than a creature—it's just a whole bunch of hamburgers on the hoof" (23). Our mass production methods leave no room for respecting the lives of the animals that are being harvested, which ultimately leads to terrible mistreatment and abuse. Before they are killed, the animals suffer from abuse on the feed lots, where cost-cutting practices include crowding the animals, feeding them grain (instead of their natural diet of grass), and giving them antibiotics and hormones to make them grow bigger, faster. 2

Brings in the first perspective, introducing the author and his answer to this question.

This paragraph shows how Katz supports his view.

Introduces a second perspective by one who raises cattle for meat production.

Paul Schwennesen, a cattle rancher and owner of Double Check Ranch in Arizona, would agree that, unlike his small-scale operation, the industrialization of meat production is what makes eating meat unethical. People don't know where their meat comes from and how the animal died. He says, "We have evolved from a society in which nearly everyone knew the intimate realities and consequences of eating meat to one in which nearly no one does. We have commercially outsourced the twinge of guilt, the pang of discomfort, the heart-race of witnessing a death to just a handful among us." He sees a huge difference between the experience of a farmer who butchers a hog for his family's winter food and the "factory worker [who] mechanically butchers six thousand in a morning." Like Katz, Schwennesen sees mass meat production as the cause of ethical problems with eating meat. 3

Notes agreement between sources.

Kline 3

Introduces a second question: How could meat production be made more ethical?

Kline keeps the focus on ethics.

Meat production is unethical, but does it have to be that way? What would have to change? We as a society would have to change. We would have to choose to eat less meat, not just for health reason, but for ethical reasons. The corporations who employ factory farming are not the root cause of the problem. It's the fault of our society's massive demand for meat. Factory farms exist only because we demand that they do. They are not forcing their factory-farmed meat on us; we are demanding it. Katz points this out, saying, "A growing mass of humanity with a penchant for meat inexorably drives the supply side toward methods of mass production, involving cost cutting and corner cutting." The idea that we can eat as much meat as the factory farms and slaughterhouses can produce is unethical. Katz says, "By almost any defensible definition of ethics, the practices that ensue from depending on animals for food to the extent that we do—are over the line." 4

Note that Kline has returned to his first source to show how he answers this second question.

Introduces a third perspective on the question of how meat eating could be done more ethically.

We might learn to moderate our demands by studying the attitudes of traditional Native Americans. According to Native American spiritual beliefs, humans have kinship with animals, plants, and the Earth itself. This is in line with their religious belief that everything has spirit, even things we think of as inanimate, like mountains. Clara Sue Kidwell, a professor of Native American studies, and theologians Homer Noley and George "Tink" Tinker explain that the traditional belief is that everything is sacred and alive, and that "anything and everything that humans do has an effect on the rest of the world around us" (41). Therefore, they have to use restraint and not just take as much as they want. When they take anything, such as killing an animal or cutting down a tree, they compensate through a ritual offering or prayer to restore the balance in the world. This practice is known as reciprocity. Native Americans give thanks to the animal through ceremonies, gifts, and sacrifices to honor its spirit. They make "apologies and words of thanksgiving to the animal itself and the animal's spirit nation [other animals of its kind]" (Kidwell, Noley, and Tinker 43). They do these ceremonies not just for the animal, to show respect, but for the "sake of the whole community's well-being" (43) so that other animals will continue to allow humans to hunt them. 5

Kline 4

Kline takes two paragraphs to develop the perspective from his third source.

6 To Native Americans, any action that upsets the balance of the world is unethical. With their belief in reciprocity, they would oppose taking anything from the Earth on such a large scale that balance cannot be restored. They may cut down a tree, but as Kidwell, Noley, and Tinker say, "There is no ceremony among any people for clear-cutting an entire forest" (44). Clear-cutting a forest, like factory farming, is unsustainable, wasteful, and disrespectful, which is why the theologians say that "American technological and economic development cannot embody the Indian ethic of reciprocity" (44). David Katz also points to an imbalance in the world created by our current over-consumption of meat. He sees an ethical case for restraint based on "our impact on the planet. In our voracious, resource-devouring multitudes, we are exerting a force no other species has ever approached, and which our Stone Age ancestors could not have imagined."

Synthesis ties two sources' views together in one paragraph.

Asks a third question: What is the solution to the problem, in practical terms?

Returns to a source introduced earlier to develop him as an example of the solution.

7 Clearly our industrialized system severely disrespects not only the animals but the planet as well. How could we do less harm and still eat meat? We would have to pay more for meat produced in the way Paul Schwennesen does it. He does not crowd his cattle into feed lots like most of the meat industry, but instead lets them graze on their favorite grasses and live the best life possible. And when it is time to slaughter them, he is part of that process too. He says, "I thank each for the age-old sacrifice of prey to predator and I swear they understand. I neither rejoice in the blood nor shy from it. This is life. This is ethics." Schwennesen believes that his direct involvement with feeding and killing his cows makes his meat-eating ethical. He says, "For me, my proximate, deliberate understanding of what I do defines ethical behavior as a whole: the social moderation of otherwise unrestrained individual yearnings." His customers prefer to buy his beef over factory farmed meat because, as he says, they "prefer (apparently) the conscientious killing I practice" and are willing to pay more and eat less in exchange.

Introduces a fourth question that focuses on consumer behavior.

Returns to Native Americans as consumers of meat.

Returns to earlier source for example of ethical and unethical meat consumption.

8 Could the actual act of eating meat be done more ethically? We have seen that the traditional Native Americans ate with an awareness of the animal's life. For this reason, they thanked the animal and did not waste any part of it. Similarly, Paul Schwennesen is aware and grateful to the animal. He sees a big difference

between respectful and "gratuitous" meat eating: While writing this piece for the *Huffington Post* blog, he is in his kitchen, cooking a roast made from a cow that he remembers. He says, "In my mind, eating #906 (a red mottle-face cow with upturned horns currently braising in the slow cooker) is an ethically different activity than eating a Big Mac on the run." Fast food is the opposite of mindful eating. People eat and even toss away burgers with no thought of the animal's sacrifice.

Summarizes what the sources agree on.

Most informed people agree that the current way in which we obtain and con- 9
sume meat is unethical. Our society is constantly demanding more and more, to the point where 9 billion animals are killed each year to feed our demand. Stopping industrialized meat harvesting, as well as making the practices of Paul Schwennesen the norm in the meat industry, would all go a long way in making eating meat ethical.

Kline ends with his own conclusion on the question.

Works Cited

Works Cited list begins on a new page.

Katz, David. "Eating Well vs. Being Good: Can We Ethically Eat Animals?" *The Blog, The Huffington Post*, 20 Sept. 2011, www.huffingtonpost.com/david-katz-md/ethics-of-eating-animals_b_961242.html.

Kidwell, Clara Sue, Homer Noley, and George E. Tinker. *A Native American Theology.* Orbis, 2001.

Schwennesen, Paul. "The Ethics of Eating Meat." *The Blog, The Huffington Post*, 14 May 2012, www.huffingtonpost.com/paul-schwennesen/ethics-of-eating-meat_b_1510173.html.

CREDITS

CHAPTER 9

Critiquing an Argument

ENGAGING QUESTIONS

In this chapter, you will engage with the following questions:

- What role does context play in a critique?
- What is the difference between a reaction and a critique?
- How do writers analyze claims, reasons, and evidence?
- How do the elements of the rhetorical situation apply to the writing process for a critique?
- How do writers apply the steps of the writing process to a critique of an argument?

AN ARGUMENT IS A REASONED DEFENSE OF AN OPINION. When you hear or read an argument about a topic you find interesting, the first question you ask is, "What exactly did it say?" That is, you recall or reread the content. Then, depending on your reaction to the argument, you likely ask the following questions that respond to it: What do I agree with? What do I disagree with? Why?

When you answer these questions, you are engaging in **critique,** *offering a reasoned assessment of an argument.* We encounter critiques in letters to the editor in newspapers, in magazines that include reader responses to articles published in the previous issue, and in blogs devoted to some controversial issue or cause. The basic situation is always the same: First, someone writes an argument urging readers to believe or do something; next, a reader responds by agreeing or disagreeing (or doing some of both) and explaining why.

What Is a Critique?

A critique is a written assessment or review of the merits of someone's work. Reviews of concerts, for instance, are critiques; so are book reviews. When an instructor grades your work, he or she usually offers a brief critique of its strengths and weaknesses. In each case, the person evaluates the work according to a set of standards appropriate for the type of performance it is.

An argument offers reasons for believing or doing something. Therefore, a critique of an argument is a rational assessment of it, organized around one or more points of evaluation. It is not an attack or even necessarily negative. Critiques do not have to find fault; you can write to defend arguments, especially when you think others have wrongly criticized them.

Rational assessment includes understanding why people disagree. In large part, people disagree because they think about controversial issues or questions in different **contexts**—that is, *different frames of reference based on how they were raised; the life experiences they have had; what they know, believe, and value.*

CONCEPT CLOSE-UP Context and Critique

Arguments in newspaper opinion columns or magazines or websites are not actually the isolated pieces of writing they seem to be. They arise out of contexts, real-world situations as experienced and interpreted by their authors. People argue in response to things that happen in the news or in their lives. Real-world circumstances like economic class, political beliefs, or religious values influence people's arguments.

Context always matters for the following reasons:

- **Context is the key to understanding an argument as rhetorical communication.** Arguments are designed to move readers. We can understand an argument only by asking, "Who is the writer trying to convince or persuade?"
- **Context is the key to understanding why people disagree.** People look at issues from their own perspectives. An argument for making tuition loans easily available to college students might appeal to young people who cannot afford the cost of college. However, a student whose older sibling graduated from college and is now trying to repay a $20,000 debt might argue that easy loans are not the best solution to the problem.
- **Context is the key to understanding your response.** Arguments are also read within contexts—the background, knowledge, and experiences of the reader. Your initial reaction to an argument will depend on the point of view you bring to it. To judge an argument fairly, you will have to take this context into account.

Why Write to Critique an Argument?

Every day you hear or read the arguments of other people, in conversation, in books and magazines, on television, radio, and the Internet, in business meetings and community gatherings. There is no way to avoid arguments designed to influence what you think and do. Nor should we want to avoid them: Arguments and counter-arguments are democracy in action, one of the ways an open society works. However, good arguments must be distinguished from bad ones. This is the stake that you and all thoughtful people have in critique.

It is important to distinguish between a reaction and a critique. A reaction is just a "thumbs up" or "thumbs down" judgment, like responses to films we have seen. In responding to arguments, a reaction is simply agreement or disagreement without explaining why or offering any justification. In contrast, a critique offers reasons for agreeing or disagreeing. It attempts to defend an evaluation of an argument. Consequently, a critique can help us distinguish good arguments from bad ones.

How Do Writers Critique Arguments?

For more on the structure of argument, see Chapter 10, pages 219–20.

An argument advances a thesis or **claim,** *what the writer wants us to believe or do.* The claim is defended with reasons that explain and justify the claim, and the reasons are backed with evidence for accepting each reason. Critiques challenge the claim, the reasons, the evidence, or all three.

As you read the following arguments, focus on what the critiques challenge and why.

READING **9.1**

Why Sherry Turkle Is So Wrong

TOM STAFFORD

The book review is a common genre of argument critique. Tom Stafford, the author of this review of Sherry Turkle's Alone Together: Why We Expect More from Technology and Less from Each Other, *is a lecturer at the University of Sheffield in England. It appeared on his blog* idiolect. *The author of many influential books, Sherry Turkle is a distinguished professor at the Massachusetts Institute of Technology.*

1 *(Attention conservation notice: a rambling 1800 word book review in which I am rude about Sherry Turkle and psychoanalysis, and I tell you how to think properly about the psychology of technology.)*

2 This book annoyed me so much I wasn't sure at page 12 if I could manage the other 293. In the end I read the introduction and the conclusion, skimming the rest. Turkle's argument is interesting and important; I just couldn't face the supposed evidence she announced she was going to bring out in the body of the book.

First person, informal style, appropriate for a blog. Thesis in last sentence: Turkle's evidence is weak.

3 Psychoanalysts are conspiracy theorists of the soul, and nowhere is that clearer than in Turkle's reasoning about technology. Page after page of anecdotes are used to introduce the idea that communications technologies such as email, Facebook and Twitter offer an illusion of intimacy, but in fact drive us into a new solitude. This might be true, it's an important idea to entertain, but pause for a moment to think how you would establish if it really was the case or not.

Summarizes Turkle's position.

Anecdotes, short narratives about something experienced, are often not valued as much as evidence gathered from scientific studies.

4 For Turkle, the evidence is all around, discerned by her keen psychoanalytically-trained psychologist's eye. A young woman chats to her grandmother on Skype for an hour a week—touching example of a relationship deepened and sustained? No! Unbeknownst to the grandmother the young woman uses that hour to catch up on her emails, leaving her unsatisfied with the Skype conversation, with vague feelings of guilt

An example of evidence Stafford considers unconvincing.

and a failure to connect. Turkle combines stories like these of people she's met with sweeping generalizations about how "we" feel—increasingly disconnected, overwhelmed and unable to tell where the boundary between work and home life is. Text messages, originally a substitute of the phone call you couldn't make, "very quickly . . . became the connection of choice" she announces. Really? For everyone?

Questions assumptions not proven in the book.

Throughout Turkle seems to assume that this new age of communications technology has accelerated us into an age of dislocation and disconnection. This may be so, but a few anecdotes about people's unsatisfactory relationships and yearning for deeper intimacy and authenticity don't establish this. Here is the news: it was ever so. Now people wonder if their Facebook friends are true friends; previously we wondered if our friends on the team, or in the pub, were our true friends. Now we wish for romantic relationships without betrayal and inconvenience; previously this is what we wished for too. Ambiguity, failure and fear of disconnection are not a novel part of online relationships; they are part of the human condition and it is mighty irksome that Turkle assumes the novelty of these things. She is seeing what she wants to see in the world around her. There is also an inherent conservatism in her assumption that things were better before this anarchy of technology was loosed upon the world, the assumption that not only were things better before, but that this was the way they were "supposed to be." The comic thing is that her historical benchmark is just as arbitrary—as if phone calls were a good and proper means of communication, a ceremony of innocence drowned by the destructive forces of text messaging and Skype. When the phone was invented there was a moral panic about what this technology would do for relationships, the same as there was a moral panic when printed books became widespread. There's no reason why we shouldn't invent a new form of communication, such as the text message, and have it fill a niche in the ecology of how we relate to each other. People haven't stopped making phone calls; they have augmented the way they communicate with text messages, not substituted texting for phoning. 5

Critique can challenge the emotional appeal of an argument as well as its logical appeal.

Reading the book it is hard to shake the impression that everything Turkle says is in slightly dismayed and hysterical tones: "Oh no! The kids are using text messaging!" "Oh no! People underestimate the distracting effect of checking their email!" "Oh no! The kids find face to face conversations threatening; the little dears can't live in the real world!" 6

Again: it was ever so. And of course, with anything new, you can always find some genuinely misled and bewildered people. Turkle has some striking examples of people who wish for relationships—both romantic and sexual—with robots. This shows, she says, that we are in the "robotic moment." It is not that robots are ready for our desires, but that our desires are now ready for the idea for intimacy with robots. A young woman yearns for a robot lover, wanting to trade her human boyfriend for a "no risk relationship"; an elderly woman saying that her robot dog "won't die suddenly and abandon you and make you very sad"; the genuinely astounding argument of David Levy's "Love and Sex with Robots" which proposes that soon we'll be fighting for the right to marry robots in the same way we fought for the right to marry people of the same sex. Are we only discussing these possibilities, asks Turkle, because we are failing each other in human relationships? 7

The impression I get is of a very earnest anthropologist, speaking to the young people of an alien tribe, ready to be shocked and titillated by their revelations. Do the people speaking to Turkle really believe what they say, or are they egged on by her credulity, just as 8 the tribespeople compete to tell the anthropologist ever more outrageous things? Yes, yes I would prefer a robot lover. Yes, yes, real men are a disappointment—irritating, changeable—and the simulation of intimacy would be better than a risk of authentic intimacy.

My problem is not that people are seeking to escape human frailty and ambiguity with robots, but that Turkle seems to assume that there was ever a time when some people didn't try to escape human frailty and ambiguity. It isn't that we are newly dissatisfied with our relationships and newly struggling for authenticity. Rather it is that the old struggle has found a new form, that the eternal uncertainties we have about ourselves and each other are given a new light by technology. 9

Calls attention to the positive in Turkle's argument as well as the negative.

Turkle has an important point disguised by a boring pessimism. "Relationships with robots are ramping up; relationships with people are ramping down," she says—"Of every technology, we must ask, Does it serve our human purposes?" This later point is vitally important. The idea that Turkle has proven that human relationships are "ramping down" due to the current communications technology is the distraction. This is just a generational cry of despair, common to every age, when one age group realizes they don't understand or don't like how their children behave. 10

True, we must ask how technology can be built to enhance our relationships, and true intimacy and authenticity are endangered, but it was always so and Turkle's speculations of doom help only to muddy the waters. 11

Challenges the context Turkle brought to interpreting her evidence.

I find myself wondering why Turkle has this pervasive pessimism about our ability to sensibly navigate these new technologies. Perhaps it is related to the stance she seems to adopt to the characters that populate her anecdotes, which is of subjects under her microscope, an amorphous mass of "them" rather than unique individuals with stories and weaknesses just like all of us. This may just be my knee-jerk dislike of psychoanalysts but her stance towards these characters in her argument always felt condescending and arrogant, as if she alone possessed the objective stance, as if only she, with her psychoanalytic training, was expert enough to discern the loneliness and feel what they themselves didn't know they felt. Again, the tone reminded me of the naive anthropologist: Aren't they strange? Isn't their confusion fascinating? 12

I would have had more faith in Turkle's reasoning if she talked more about her experience, rather than relating anecdotes from people she met at conferences and at Parisian dinner parties. 13

An important counter-argument: Reality is always mediated in some way.

Turkle's underlying assumption is that technology is a thing separate from, or gets in between, authentic relationships. (There's a comparison to those who diagnose an addiction to the internet, as if the internet were a substance, when it is just a medium.) In fact, technology is part of relationships because it is part of our minds (see Andy Clark's book *Natural Born Cyborgs* for an exploration of this idea). Technology cannot get in the way of some kind of natural detection of reality because we never have direct contact with reality—it is always mediated by culture, history, language, expectations, and the whole architecture of our minds for understanding the world. As every psychologist should know, the idea of "virtual reality" is a misnomer because reality has always been virtual. A concrete example of this confusion is when Turkle assumes that she (alone) can tell the real (flesh and blood) encounters from the fake (technologically mediated) encounters. "The ties we form through the internet are not, in the end, the ties that bind" she says solemnly. This 14 is a ridiculous generalization, and must be confusing to all those who met over the internet, or have had relationships deepened because of the internet. Can you imagine how ridiculous Turkle would sound if she'd made such a generalization about another medium. "The ties formed through writing are not the ties that bind," "The ties formed by those speaking French are not the ties that bind." Nonsense! Again Turkle has been distracted by her pessimism and her conservatism. The problem of human bonds is not a new one; we've always struggled to find rapprochement with each other. The internet doesn't change that. It does give the problem interesting new dimensions, and I've no doubt that we'll struggle collectively with these new dimensions for decades, but I don't see Turkle doing anything to make clear the outlines of the problem or advance any solutions.

New technology is easy to think about, partly because the novel always stands out 15
against the background of the old, and partly because it is easier to think about the material aspects of things, and the material aspects of technology can be ubiquitous (like text messages and email) or particularly entrancing (like robots). But let me give an alternative vision to Turkle's Cassandra wail. Rather than technology, a far more real threat to intimacy and authenticity in the modern world is the continuous parade of advertising which tries to hock material goods with the promise that they can give access to transcendent values. Cars which give freedom, cameras which give friendship, diamonds that give love and clothes that give confidence. Here is a cultural force, with a massive budget and the active intention to make us dissatisfied with our possessions, our lifestyles, our bodies and our relationships. How about we worry a bit more about that and less about the essentially democratic technologies of communication?

A figure in Greek legend, Cassandra was a prophet or seer, someone who knew events before they occurred.

Another important counterargument: Not technology but rather consumerism is the problem.

Questions for Discussion

1. Any reader of this critique who has not read Turkle's book must depend on Stafford's summary of Turkle to judge his fairness. Do you think Stafford gives enough examples to show that her evidence is not sufficient or convincing? Do you have evidence from your own experience that technology is causing breakdowns in human interaction?
2. Do you believe that human relationships were better a generation or two ago? Why or why not?
3. What do you think about the impact of advertising on human relationships? Do you agree with Stafford (paragraph 15) that consumerism is the real threat to human relationships, not information technology?

Thinking as a Writer

1. What is Stafford's *purpose* in writing this essay? What is his *angle* on the topic? How would you describe his *voice*?
2. Who is Stafford's *intended audience*? Is he writing only for people who share his prejudice against psychoanalysis and the use of anecdotes as evidence? Is

he writing only for younger adults who grew up with information technology? Does he try to reach other readerships? Can you cite anything in the article that implies his target readership?

3. Using the Concept Close-Up box on page 193 and the marginal annotations to the article, show how Stafford uses *context* and the *conventions of critique* to raise doubts about Turkle's argument. If you were not convinced by his critique, what exactly did you resist in his arguments and why did you resist them? ■

The Assignment

If your instructor does not assign one, locate any short (750–1,000 words) argument on a controversial topic and write a critique of it. Your instructor may specify a length for your paper. If not, write a critique of about 500 to 1,000 words. Later in this chapter, we offer some arguments for critique, including David Fryman on responding to opinionated professors (pages 201–02) and Shikha Dalmia (pages 215–17) on birthright citizenship.

What Can I Write About?

This assignment could be written in many genres, the most common of which is a letter to the editor of a newspaper or magazine. But it could also be an op-ed piece; a response to a post on a blog; a short article for a newspaper, magazine, or newsletter; or an assessment of a classroom discussion, debate, chat room exchange, public speech, or some other oral argument.

We suggest that you pick an argument you disagree with or an argument you partly agree with and partly disagree with in almost equal measure. It is harder to write a critique of an argument you find wholly convincing.

You can locate suitable arguments by recalling something you read in a newspaper or magazine or on a website; by doing subject searches in online library indexes like ProQuest or Academic OneFile (see pages 365–66 for how to use these resources); and by using Google to search for information on a topic in the news. Consider also the following possibilities:

Asia Images Group/Getty Images

- **Class readings.** Class readings can provide arguments for critique, especially if the readings themselves are arguments.

- **Local news or observation.** Read your local and campus newspapers for arguments relating to your community. Sometimes these can be more interesting than overworked topics such as abortion or gun control.
- **Internet discussions.** Blogs are often good sources for arguments. Visit blogs on issues of public concern, such as National Public Radio's blog.

How Do I Write a Critique? Questioning the Rhetorical Situation

Begin by considering the **rhetorical situation,** *the key variables associated with you as writer; with your audience; and with the genre, conventions, and expectations of your text.* Understanding the rhetorical situation will give you a stable sense of the whole, something definite to hold in mind as you work your way through the process.

Writer: What Is My Purpose, and What Impression Should Readers Have of Me?

Your purpose in writing a critique depends entirely on the argument you are responding to and how you feel about it. Sometimes you agree with the argument and wish to offer additional reasons and evidence for it; sometimes you partly agree and wish to indicate why you cannot accept the argument entirely; and sometimes you disagree completely and wish to refute the argument. Regardless of your exact purpose, your readers should see you as someone who has listened carefully to the argument, understood it, and taken the time to write a well-considered response. Above all, you should be concerned that your readers understand what you agree and disagree with and why.

Audience: Who Is My Reader?

Most critiques address the same readership that the argument hoped to reach. Therefore, one of the more important questions you can ask is, **"Who is the reader for the argument I am responding to?"** The answer to that question tells you who your reader is. However, some critiques deliberately respond to an argument from the point of view of another possible audience, usually one the argument overlooked or chose not to address. For instance, a young adult might critique Turkle's book from the viewpoint of someone immersed in the Internet and social media for an audience of other young adults likewise situated—clearly not the scientific audience Stafford (pages 194–97) had in mind. When most of what you have to say would appeal to a different readership or when you want to call attention to reader concerns the argument fails to consider, shifting audience can be an effective strategy.

Text: What Moves Can I Make?

A critique is *a coherent evaluation of somebody else's argument from your point of view.* The moves you will make, therefore, depend on the argument you are responding to and your particular "take" on it. The following are common moves in critique, just to give you a general idea of what can be done:

- **Expose an assumption the argument makes that you consider doubtful or unjustified.** For example, arguments about gender often assume a simple masculine-versus-feminine contrast. You can show that most people are a mix of the characteristics we associate with masculine and feminine. Challenging assumptions is especially important in argument critique because, if you accept the author's assumptions, you tend to accept the argument.
- **Single out the claim for attention and show that it is unclear, contradictory, or too broad or too narrow.** Even claims that seem powerfully persuasive can be called into question. "Justice too long delayed is justice denied," though often quoted, is unclear until "too long delayed" is specified. How long is too long? Furthermore, how broadly should we apply the claim? Are there good reasons, for example, that some criminal trials involving the death penalty should, including appeals, go on for months or even years?
- **Call attention to reasons you consider weak.** For example, people argue against mercy killing or euthanasia because Nazi Germany used it to justify murder of people it considered undesirable. Clearly what the Nazis did was not euthanasia. Just as clearly, the five states that currently permit euthanasia are not motivated as the Nazis were.
- **Challenge evidence the author advances to back up reasons.** The most common move is to cite **counter-evidence:** *data or facts that call data or facts cited by the author into question.* You can also, among many other moves, expose an author's source as biased or otherwise untrustworthy. An argument against gun control, for example, is vulnerable if the writer relies heavily or exclusively on the National Rifle Association (NRA) website. When evidence comes from any organization that advocates a cause and lobbies Congress, it is likely to be distorted.
- **Oppose the values in the argument with values of equal or greater importance the author did not recognize.** Our enormous investment in counterterrorism efforts after 9/11 is justified by the value of national security. But if national security is important, so also is our greatest national value, liberty. How much liberty have we lost by all the counterterrorism measures? How much more could we lose? Does the threat of terrorism really justify the liberty sacrificed?
- **Expose the implications of an argument when you can show that they are impractical, undesirable, or unacceptable.** For example, good arguments have been made for reinstating the draft and/or for requiring a certain period of mandatory service for young adults. You can point to how extremely unlikely it is that such a policy could pass Congress and become law. You could also show that such a policy would disrupt education and therefore result in fewer college graduates.
- **Question analogies the argument relies on.** In the years before World War II, Britain, France, and other European countries tried to appease Hitler and prevent war by making concessions to his demands. Ever since, any effort under any circumstances to negotiate with countries and leaders considered our enemies has been likened to appeasing Hitler. You can show why the analogy is weak. Perhaps the enemy leader is not out to conquer other countries or lacks the military strength to do so.

How Do I Write a Critique? Engaging the Writing Process

No two people compose in exactly the same way, and even the same person may go through the writing process in different ways with different assignments. Nevertheless, because no one can attend to everything at once, there are phases in handling any significant writing task. You explore the topic to get a sense of whether it will work for you and what you might be able to do with it; if the topic is working out for you, then you move into preparing to write, generating more content and planning your draft.

The next phase is drafting your paper, creating a version, however rough it may be, on screen or paper so that you can work toward the final draft. Getting there involves two further phases: (1) revising your draft, making major improvements in it, followed by (2) editing your draft, taking care of errors, sentences that do not read well, paragraphs lacking focus and flow, and so on.

Exploring Your Topic

To see how to explore the argument you are about to critique, we need an example argument to illustrate the process. Here is one on an issue of some concern on most college campuses. Read it once or twice, just to understand what it says and to form a first reaction to it.

READING 9.2

Open Your Ears to Biased Professors

DAVID FRYMAN

David Fryman was a senior at Brandeis University when he wrote this opinion column for the school's newspaper, The Justice. *He is offering advice to younger college students who often encounter professors with political opinions different from those endorsed at home or in their local communities. Fryman's question is, How should they respond?*

One of the most important lessons I've learned in three years of higher education is the value of creativity and critical thinking, particularly when confronted with a professor whose ideology, political leanings or religious viewpoint fly in the face of what I believe. In fact, with a good professor, this should happen often. It is part of a professor's job to challenge you, force you to reconsider, encourage you to entertain new ideas and the like. My first year here, it bothered me. Some professors subtly endorsed certain ways of thinking over others without always justifying their biases. They offered opinions on issues beyond their academic expertise. Many showed partiality to the political left or right. 1

How should we react when a professor with a captive audience advances a perspective we find offensive, insulting or just ridiculous? Perhaps we would benefit 2 from treating our professors, who often double as mentors and advisers, the same way that we're taught to approach great works of literature: with critical respect.

3 The truth is many faculty members are at the top of their fields. They read, write and teach for a living. We're generally talking about the most well-educated and well-read members of society. So when a professor has something to say about politics, religion, war or which movie should win the Academy Award, I think it's a good idea to take him seriously.

4 It certainly doesn't follow, though, that there's a direct relationship between what a professor says and what's true. In fact, there may be no relationship at all. While our professors generally are leading scholars, some are also biased and fallible. I don't mean this as an insult. Professors are human beings and, as such, carry with them a wide array of hang-ups and prejudices.

5 Interestingly enough—if not ironically—our professors often teach us how to deal with biased and opinionated scholars like themselves. When we read novels, journal articles, essays and textbooks for class, we're taught—or at least this has been my experience—to be critical. We're expected to sift through material and distinguish between what holds water and what doesn't, what is based on reasoned analysis and what is mere speculation.

6 If we treat our professors similarly it should no longer bother us when they use the classroom as their soapbox. They have important things to say and we're here to learn from them. I've come to appreciate professors' opinions on a variety of issues not directly related to the subject at hand, and I think it helps us build relationships with them. While it's unfair for a professor to assign high grades only to students who echo their view or to make others feel uncomfortable to disagree, I prefer that professors be honest about what they think.

7 While it's a disservice to our own education to be intimidated or too easily persuaded by academic clout, it's just as problematic, and frankly silly, to categorically reject what a professor has to say because we take issue with his ideology, political leanings, religious views or cultural biases.

8 It's become popular, particularly among conservatives responding to what they perceive as a liberal bias in academia, to criticize professors for espousing personal views in the classroom. The ideal, they argue, is to leave students ignorant about their instructors' beliefs.

9 First of all, I think there's a practical problem with this strategy. It's more difficult to be critical if we're unsure where our professors stand. For the same reason that it's often helpful to have background information about an author before analyzing his work, it's useful to see our professors' ideological cards on the table. For instance, if I know my professor loves hunting and believes everybody should have firearms in his basement, then when I hear his interpretation of the Second Amendment, I'm better equipped to evaluate his thoughts.

10 Secondly, if we proscribe what views may or may not be expressed in the classroom, we limit our own access to potentially useful information. Even if most of the extraneous digressions aren't worthy, every once in a while we might hear something that goes to the heart of an important issue. To limit this because we don't trust our own critical abilities is cowardly.

11 To return to the question I posed above: How should we respond to politically-charged, opinionated, biased professors? I think we should listen.

Forming a First Impression

It is impossible to read an argument without having some kind of response to it. Start by asking yourself, **"What is my first impression?"**

ACTIVITY 9.1 ***Writer's Notebook***

State Your First Impression

State your reaction simply and directly. Write it down in your notebook or a computer file reserved for this assignment. Read the selection again. Is your reaction changing? How? Why? ■

Most of our students' first response to Fryman was favorable. He offered practical advice, and more appealing yet, *safe* advice. You may have had an entirely different reaction. First reactions cannot be right or wrong, good or bad. They just are what they are. The important thing is that *you* know what your reaction is.

Achieving Critical Distance through Analysis

Critiques require **critical distance** from first responses. "Critical distance" does not mean "forget your first response." On the contrary, first impressions often turn out to be sound. Critical distance does mean *setting your first response aside for a while so that you can think the argument through carefully.*

Use the questions for critiquing an argument in Best Practices to guide your analysis.

BEST PRACTICES Questions for Critiquing an Argument

1. **What is the context for this argument?** As we said earlier (page 193), arguments take place in contexts—situations that prompt people to write. Ask, therefore, "Who wrote this? What prompted him or her to write? What might explain his or her perspective?"
2. **What is the author claiming?** Find the main point or thesis that the writer wants you to believe and/or be persuaded to do. Sometimes the claim will be stated, sometimes implied. Then ask: Is the claim clear and consistent? Is it absolute, no exceptions allowed? Is it reasonable, desirable, practical?
3. **What reasons does the author provide for accepting the claim?** Reasons answer the question: Why? Given the claim, what explains or justifies it? Like the claim, reasons will be stated or implied. Then ask: Does each reason actually explain or justify the thesis? How convincing is the reason? If the author reasons by means of an **analogy** (*comparison, reasoning that what is true in one case should be true in a similar case*), does the comparison really stand up to inspection?
4. **What evidence has the author given to support the reasons?** Reasons need support using examples, data, or expert opinion. Look at the evidence offered for each reason and ask: Does the evidence actually support the

reason? How convincing is each piece of evidence, and how convincing is the evidence for each reason taken together?

5. **What are the key terms, and what do they mean?** Writers use words, often without defining them, that should be carefully examined. When a claim is justified, for instance, as the right or moral thing to do, we need to ask what "right" or "moral" means in this case.
6. **What is the author assuming?** It is impossible to argue without assuming many things, and "assumed" means "not stated." Ask: What must I believe to accept that claim, or reason, or piece of evidence? Is the assumption "safe," something that any reasonable person would also assume?
7. **What are the implications of this argument?** The implications are what the argument suggests or implies. Like assumptions, implications are usually not stated. To uncover them, ask: If I accept this position, what logically follows from it? Are its implications acceptable or not?
8. **What values motivate the argument?** What priorities does the author have? What other priorities or values conflict with those of the author?
9. **What voice and character are projected in the argument?** We talk about voice and presence in writing, and these are important to an argument's effectiveness. How would you describe the speaker and on what evidence from the text?
10. **Who is the audience for the argument?** Who is likely to agree with this argument? Who might want to refute it? What might an opponent object to and why?

Example: Critiquing an Argument

Here is a model of how some of these questions could be applied to Fryman's argument (pages 201–02):

1. **Thesis: What is the author's main claim?**
   Fryman: College students should listen with critical respect to biased and opinionated professors.
   Comment: Be clear about the argument's main point. Note that with this argument you have to piece together the thesis from several statements Fryman makes.
2. **Context: What prompted the author to write the argument?**
   Fryman: In paragraph 8, Fryman explains the situation that prompted him to write this argument. Conservative students had been protesting what they saw as an abuse of academic freedom by liberal professors.
   Comment: Fryman is not arguing directly to conservative activists. Whom do you think he sees as his audience? How would his argument be different if he were to address the more politically active protestors?
3. **Reasons: What are some reasons, and how well do they hold up to examination?**
   Fryman: One reason given is: "Many faculty members are at the top of their fields."
   Comment: Clearly, this statement is a reason—it explains why the author thinks students should accord professors respect. We can respond by saying, "Yes, some

professors are quite accomplished *in their fields.* But when they venture outside them, do their opinions count for more than any other relatively well-informed person's?"

4. **Key terms: What words are important to the argument, and would there be any confusion about what they mean?**
   Fryman: "How should we react when a professor with a captive audience advances a perspective we find offensive, insulting or just ridiculous? . . . with critical respect."
   Comment: It is important to note that Fryman is not saying that students have to agree or even be neutral but rather that they should think critically as they listen.
5. **Assumptions: Does the author make any assumptions you might question?**
   Fryman: He is assuming that professors airing their views in class will not take away from class time devoted to material that must be covered.
   Comment: We might respond by suggesting that Fryman should have qualified his argument by putting a limit on how much class time might be devoted to professors airing their biases.
6. **Implications: What happens in reality if we accept the argument?**
   Fryman: He implies that students should tolerate whatever the professor dishes out.
   Comment: We can respond by saying, "How much student toleration is too much toleration? Suppose that a professor is openly sexist, for instance? Shouldn't we not only reject the opinions but also report the behavior to university authorities?"
7. **Analogies: How well do comparisons hold up?**
   Fryman: He compares the approach students should take to opinionated professors with the critical respect accorded great works of literature (paragraph 2).
   Comment: We can respond by saying, "Great works of literature have typically survived for years. We call them classics. Does it make sense to meet the casual opinions of professors the same way that we approach Shakespeare?"

ACTIVITY 9.2 *In Your Own Work*

Exploring Your Argument

If you are working alone on an argument, use the ten questions in Best Practices: Questions for Critiquing an Argument (pages 203–04) to find possible content for your critique. Record the results in your notebook, your computer file for this assignment, or online—for example, as a blog that presents the argument and your analysis of it.

If all members of your class are critiquing the same argument, divide into small groups of about three or four people and do an analysis. Share what your group found with the class as a whole in discussion. Summarize what each group came up with in your notebook, computer file, or online as a blog entry or e-mail addressed to the entire class. Indicate which analytical comments you consider strongest. ■

Personal Engagement in Critiques

Critique focuses on *what an argument says.* The challenge of critique is to discover what you can say back.

Part of a good critique is to test the argument against what you know about reality. Test what the argument says against your experience with life and the world, and against what you know about the topic. Add to your knowledge of reality by gathering information through research.

What Information Is Relevant to My Critique?

The following questions should help you add insights about an argument:

1. **What is my own experience with the topic or issue or problem the argument takes up?** In the case of Fryman's argument, when have the comments of "biased teachers" been illuminating or helpful to you? When have they been boring, irritating, or useless? What's the difference between the two?
2. **What relevant information do I have from reading or from some other source?** Perhaps you have heard other students complain about professors pushing their political convictions on their students. What did the students say? Did their complaints seem justified? Why or why not?

See Chapter 16, pages 358–71, for detailed guidance on ways to research any topic.

3. **What could I find out from research that might be relevant to assessing the argument?** Most arguments suggest opportunities for at least checking up on information relevant to the argument. For instance, you might investigate the idea of academic freedom. How does it apply to professors? How does it apply to students?
4. **If the argument reasons from data, in what other ways might the data be interpreted? What other data might contradict the information given?** Research will often lead you to other arguments that interpret the same or similar data differently or that supply additional data the argument you are critiquing did not know or ignored. For example, arguments for stronger border patrol enforcement sometimes fail to mention that about 40 percent of undocumented immigrants came here legally and simply stayed. Enhanced border control obviously will have no effect on that group.

ACTIVITY 9.3 *In Your Own Work*

Assessing the Fit of Argument and Reality

In your notebook or computer file, sum up the results of applying the above questions. Freewrite about what you might add from your own experiences and observations or from research. Highlight the best insight you gained. It could be a major point in your critique, perhaps even the central point around which you structure it. ■

Preparing to Write

Thoughtful exploration of an argument—responding to what it says and pondering its fit with reality—results in much you could say. However, a critique is not a collection of comments or a list of criticisms. Rather it's *a coherent evaluation from a particular point of view*—your view. Consequently, formulating your position, your main point about the argument's validity, matters most.

Formulating Your Position

Your critique will need to focus on one main point: your position about the merits of the argument. You can reject an argument in general but see value in a part of it. You can accept an argument in general but with major reservations.

In response to Fryman's argument, a wide range of stances are possible. Someone in agreement could say:

> Fryman acknowledges that biased professors can be annoying, but he makes an effective argument that opinions have a role in the education process.

Someone disagreeing could say:

> Fryman would have a stronger argument if he did not imply that students should open their ears but not their mouths.

Or, among many other possible positions, someone could say:

> It is easy to agree with this argument in the abstract because Fryman avoids actually quoting any of the biased views he has heard.

ACTIVITY 9.4 *In Your Own Work*

Formulating Your Position

Using the suggestions above, write a position statement. If you are having difficulty, consider the following possibilities:

- **Return to your first impression.** Perhaps a revised version can be your stance.
- **Review the statements in the argument that you found open to question.** Is there a pattern in your criticisms? Or perhaps one statement stands out from the rest and seems central? Your position may be implied in your most important criticism.
- **Do you detect one place where the reasoning breaks down?** You could focus your critique on the major weakness in the argument's case, that is, its claim, reasons, and evidence.
- **Look for places where the author's view of reality and/or what is needed or desirable part company with yours.** Your position might be that the argument sounds logical but is not realistic or practical.
- **Talk through possible positions with another student or your instructor.** Just talking helps, and sometimes a comment from someone else can help your stance emerge.

Sometimes you will discover the best statement of your position only through writing a first draft. For now, try out the stance that appeals to you most. You can always revise and rewrite. ■

Drafting Your Paper

In your first draft, focus on organizing and voicing your main points fully and clearly.

What Voice Is Appropriate for a Critique?

See Chapter 10, page 240–41, for a discussion of voice in case-making.

Voice The voice of critique or analysis shares much in common with the voice of case-making: State your position clearly, directly, and forcefully, using a style more formal than conversation but less formal than a public speech. Remember that critique is not name-calling, insults, outrageous claims, or partisan bickering, but rather the calm voice of reason, opinions stated precisely and defended well.

Here is a good example of the voice for critique from Stafford:

> Psychoanalysts are conspiracy theorists of the soul, and nowhere is that clearer than in Turkle's reasoning about technology. Page after page of anecdotes are used to introduce the idea that communications technologies such as email, Facebook and Twitter offer an illusion of intimacy, but in fact drive us into a new solitude. This might be true, it's an important idea to entertain, but pause for a moment to think how you would establish if it really was the case or not.

This paragraph summarizes Turkle's position, something Stafford needs to do early in his critique so that readers know what he is talking about. But he also wants to convey his negative attitude toward psychoanalysis, so the paragraph begins with the memorable claim that "psychoanalysts are conspiracy theorists of the soul." That is, they claim to know, he thinks, what they have little evidence to support. It's all theory and guesswork. He combines this judgment with praise for the significance of Turkle's idea so that the reader can detect some balance and fairness in his criticism. At the same time, he is also preparing us for his extensive and confident attack on Turkle's evidence.

Your voice in critique, therefore, depends largely on how you assess the quality of the argument you are critiquing. Stafford boldly challenges Turkle's conclusions because he thinks her evidence would not convince a skeptical scientist. She needs real data, not anecdotes.

ACTIVITY 9.5 *Writer's Notebook*

Reader, Purpose, and Voice

Add notes about the key variables to your position statement. Answer these questions: **Do you intend to address the same readers that the argument does? Why or why not? How *exactly* does your version of the truth differ from the author's, and how great is the difference? How friendly to the author do you want to sound?** ■

Developing and Organizing Your Critique

Organization Whether you write first drafts in chunks and then fit them together or write from a plan more or less in sequence, have the following organizational principles in mind:

Introduction

- Begin by identifying the argument you are critiquing: who wrote it and for what group of readers, when and where it appeared, what it is about, and the position the author takes.
- Make your own stance clear and give it an emphatic position, near the end of your introduction.

Body

- From everything you found questionable in the argument, select *only* what is relevant to your stance. No one expects a critique to deal with everything an argument says or everything that can be said about it.
- *Don't let the order of the argument determine the order of your critique.* Organize around points that develop *your* position, and think about what order would have maximum impact on your readers.
- If you can say positive things, deal with these points first. Readers listen to the negative more willingly after hearing the positive.

Conclusion

Short critiques of short arguments do not need summarizing conclusions. Strive instead for a clincher, the memorable "parting shot" expressing the gist or main thrust of your response.

Development For each part of your critique, you have many options for development. Here are some of them.

Introduction

Besides identifying the argument and taking your stance, you can also include material about context, background information, and a preview of your critique. A critique of Fryman's argument, for instance, might place it in the context of efforts to restrict academic freedom; research about the author might reveal relevant background information, such as what was happening at Brandeis University when he wrote the article. Previews summarize the points you are going to make in the order in which you are going to discuss them.

Body

Take up one point at a time. Each point will challenge either the reasoning of the argument or its fit with reality. If the former, be sure to explain inconsistencies or contradictions fully so that your reader understands exactly where and why the reasoning went wrong. If you want to show that it is unrealistic, provide counter-evidence from personal experience, general knowledge, or research.

Conclusion

To clinch your critique, consider the following possibilities: a memorable quotation with a comment on it from you; a return to a key statement or piece of information in your introduction that you can now develop more fully; a reminder to the reader of your strongest point with additional support or commentary.

Revising Your Draft

Write a brief assessment of your first draft. Exchange your draft and assessment with at least one other student, and use the critique revision questions in The Art of Questioning below to help each other decide what you each need to improve.

THE ART OF QUESTIONING Revision Checklist for Critiquing an Argument

1. Look at all the places where you have summarized or paraphrased the argument. Compare them against the text. Are they accurate? Do they capture the author's apparent intent as well as what she or he says?
2. Locate the argument's context—the existing view or views the argument's author addressed. If the critique does not mention context, would it improve if it did? If so, where might a discussion of context work best?
3. Critiques seek the truth about some controversial issue or question. What is the issue or question the argument addresses? Is it stated in the critique? Does the difference between the argument's view of the truth and the view in the critique emerge clearly? If not, what could be done to make the difference sharper?
4. Underline the critique's main point or stance. Is it stated explicitly and early in the essay? Examine each critical point. How does it develop, explain, or defend the stance? Consider cutting anything not related to the stance.

Exchanging your draft with at least one other student and going over the Critique Revision Checklist together can help you decide what you each need to improve.

Creatas/SuperStock

5. Check the flow of the critical points. Does each connect to the one before it and the one after? If not, consider rearranging the sequence. How might one point set up or lead to another better?
6. What voice do you hear in the critique? The tone should be thoughtfully engaged, fair, balanced, and respectful, but also confident and forceful. Look for places where the tone might make the wrong impression. Consider ways to improve it.

Formulating a Plan to Guide Your Revision

The plan can be a single sentence or two: "I'll cut this, rearrange that, and add a section here." Or, if you work better from an outline, develop one now. The important thing is to have a definite, clear idea of what you want to do and what moves you will make to get the results you want.

Student Example: Excerpts from J. R. Solomon's Draft

The following passages are excerpted from student J. R. Solomon's draft critique of David Fryman's argument, "Open Your Ears to Biased Professors." These examples all illustrate common problems in first drafts of critiques.

Excerpt 1: Position statement not forceful enough

> Fryman believes that students should treat professors' personal opinions with critical respect. I agree, but think that his view is one-sided and therefore not fully persuasive.

All arguments present one position on an issue, so to say an argument is "one-sided" does not offer a valid critique. In fact, Solomon meant that the argument was unbalanced, tipping too far in favor of professors' powers. Here is the revised version:

> "Open Your Ears to Biased Professors," by David Fryman, a student writing for the Brandeis University paper, *The Justice,* deals with a common complaint among students: teachers who express their political or religious views in class. Fryman believes that students should listen to the personal opinions of professors with "critical respect." I agree, but the argument is not persuasive because Fryman describes an unbalanced situation where the professors have all the rights and the students have all the responsibilities.

Excerpt 2: Paraphrase or summary not accurate

> In my ethics class last year, my teacher . . . believed strongly in the right of homosexuals to marry. Some of the students, including myself, did not agree with her. Yet, when we tried to discuss our side of the issue, she cut us off. **Fryman neglects to discuss such instances when a teacher's opinions**

> **infringe on the students' right to open debate. I believe that if teachers can express their opinions openly in class, the students should be able to express theirs.**

The bolded sentences do not accurately represent Fryman's argument. Fryman also believes that students should feel comfortable expressing disagreement with the professor and says so in his paragraph 6. Here is the revised version:

> Unfortunately, some professors do not want students to form their own opinions but rather convert to the professor's ideology. In my ethics class last year, the teacher told us she was a lesbian. In one of our discussions we spoke about gay rights, and whether or not gay marriage should be legal. She believed strongly in the right of gay people to marry. Some of the students, including myself, did not agree with her. Yet, when we tried to discuss our side of the issue, she cut us off. Although Fryman says "it is unfair for a professor to assign high grades only to students who echo their view or to make others feel uncomfortable to disagree," he does not go far enough to emphasize professors' responsibility in ensuring students have a voice.

Excerpt 3: Unfocused and underdeveloped paragraphs

> Because he is writing only to students, Fryman has very little to say about how professors should conduct themselves. He deals with the problem of bias as if only what students should do matters. Actually, professors have more responsibility. They're older, more knowledgeable, and more experienced. I think if professors are going to express their political and religious views in class, they should do so in certain ways or not do it at all.

These sentences move from professors to students and back to professors, ending with a vague point about what professors should do. In the revised essay, Solomon used the two main points to organize his entire critique. You can see parts of this draft paragraph in paragraphs 2 and 5 of the revised draft.

Editing Your Revised Draft

There is almost no revised draft that could not improve with proofreading for habitual errors and editing to tighten up the writing and make some points more clear. The highlighted words below indicate where the passage could be tightened up.

Original Version

> In my ethics class last year, the teacher told us she was a lesbian. In one of our discussions we spoke about whether or not same-sex marriage should be legal. She believed strongly in marriage equality. Some of the students, including myself, did not agree with her.

The edited version that follows reduces the repetition and tightens up the style by using the pronoun *it*.

Edited Version

In my ethics class last year, the teacher told us she was a lesbian. When the class discussed the right of same-sex couples to marry, she expressed her view that it should be legal. Some of the students, including myself, did not agree with her.

One grammatical problem remains in the edited passage. The word *myself* is a reflexive pronoun; it should not be used unless the word *I* has already been used in a sentence ("I hurt myself"). However, the ethics class anecdote does not use the word *I;* the pronoun is treated as an object and should reflect this. This mistake–using *myself* instead of *me*–is common in casual talk; we tend to make it when we write too. Be alert to reflexives in your drafts.

Edited Version

Some of the students, including me, did not agree with her.

ACTIVITY 9.6 *In Your Own Work*

Editing Your Paper

Edit your own draft to eliminate errors, such as confusing plurals with possessives, using singular pronouns to refer to plural nouns, and misusing the reflexive pronoun *myself.* Exchange your edited paper with another student. Help each other find and correct any remaining errors. ■

REVISED STUDENT EXAMPLE

Solomon 1

J. R. Solomon

ENG 1301

Professor Crusius

12 October 2015

Indoctrination Is Not Education

The introduction sets up the argument to be critiqued with information about its author and publication.

1 "Open Your Ears to Biased Professors," by David Fryman, a student writing for the Brandeis University paper, *The Justice*, deals with a common complaint among students: teachers who express their political or religious views in class. Fryman believes that students should listen to the personal opinions of professors with "critical respect." I agree, but the argument is not persuasive because Fryman

The introduction ends with a strong stance, or position, on the validity or merits of the argument.

Solomon 2

describes an unbalanced situation where the professors have all the rights and the students have all the responsibilities.

The first point in support of the stance that the argument is unbalanced.

2 Because he is writing only to students, he has very little to say about how professors should conduct themselves. Fryman deals with the problem of bias as if only what students should do matters. They should listen and evaluate the professor's views just as they would a book or journal article assigned in the class. This is what he means by "critical respect." It sounds good; however, class readings are likely to be on-topic and written by experts, while the professor's personal opinions may be off topic and not as well thought out as something published. The professor's views may not deserve so much critical attention.

Questions the validity of the comparison between professors' opinions and the views in readings.

Questions an assumption about students at the heart of Fryman's argument.

3 Furthermore, the students might not be ready to take on the responsibility for evaluating the professor's opinions. Because professors know so much, they can appear very appealing to students who have not encountered an issue before. By leaving out other interpretations, the professor assures that students hear only the teacher's side, which does not allow students to form their own conclusions. I saw this happen in a government class which discussed the 2008 Presidential election. Most of the class did not know much about politics, and therefore accepted the professor's view completely. They didn't have the critical capacity Fryman assumes all college students have. Certainly professors should challenge students, but what my government professor did was convert.

The student connects the critique with his own experience of the issue.

Challenges an assumption about professors.

4 Unfortunately, some professors do not want students to form their own opinions but rather convert to the professor's ideology. In my ethics class last year, the teacher told us she was a lesbian. In one of our discussions we spoke about the right of same-sex couples to marry, and whether or not same-sex marriage should be legal. She believed strongly in the right of same-sex couples to marry. Some of the students, including me, did not agree with her. Yet, when we tried to discuss our side of the issue, she cut us off. Although Fryman says "it is unfair for a professor to assign high grades only to students who echo their view or to make others feel uncomfortable to disagree," he does not go far enough to emphasize professors' responsibility in ensuring students have a voice.

Personal experience showing the frustration when a professor does not allow disagreement.

Solomon 3

> Explains an alternative to "critical respect" and shows why that alternative is more educational.

5 Professors are responsible for educating, not indoctrinating. They are older, more knowledgeable, and more experienced. I think if professors are going to express their political and religious views in class, they should do so in a way that invites critical discussion, not just "critical respect." Students should hear about other viewpoints so they can think about all sides of the issue. The professor's views are one opinion, but not the only right one. Professors should encourage students to form their own opinions.

> Shows that Fryman's argument neglects another important responsibility of the professor.

6 Finally, Fryman fails to deal with the negative impact when teachers stray from the subject matter of the course. In my ethics class, the teacher was always returning to the issue of gay rights, even when the topic of discussion didn't relate to it. Because she lacked restraint, the class spent too much class time on one issue. It is the professor's responsibility to see that course material gets covered.

7 I agree that professors should share their opinions with the class and students should listen and learn from them. But the opinions should relate to the course content. Professors should not allow themselves to talk about just whatever happens to be on their minds. Most of all, education should not be indoctrination. Opinions should be discussed, not preached. A professor is a teacher, not a politician.

> Persuasive and memorable ending.

Sample Reading for Critique

READING **9.3**

The Bogus Case against Birthright Citizenship

SHIKHA DALMIA

Shikha Dalmia is senior analyst at the Reason Foundation, a think tank advocating free markets and free thinking. She won the 2009 Bastiat Prize for Online Journalism.

1 Like gout, anti-immigration restrictionism[1] is a perennial affliction that comes and goes with the seasons. And with Republicans gaining ground this political season, get ready for a particularly painful bout of it.

Texas Rep. Lamar Smith, a committed restrictionist who now chairs the House Judiciary Committee, is already planning a big push to clamp down on undocumented aliens, especially by denying automatic or birthright citizenship to their children—a right enshrined in the 14th Amendment. Meanwhile, Republicans in five states—led by Arizona—are launching their own offensive to force Congress to repeal this right. 2

Such calls are not new. What is new is that they are gaining traction beyond a shrill nativist[2] minority. Some conservative libertarians are arguing that birthright citizenship is bad for the country—and some progressive libertarians are arguing that it is bad for immigrants. Not only are both wrong, they can't reconcile this position with their broader commitment to the constitution and limited government respectively. (In this column I will address only the conservatives, saving the progressives for the next.) 3

The most famous representative of the conservative view is George Will, whose recent column is an odd hagiographic[3] exercise lauding Smith—obviously calculated to pave the ground for Smith's birthright crusade that Will has openly embraced. 4

Smith is pushing a law in Congress to scrap this right, even though literally no one believes that it would pass constitutional muster. That's because the 14th Amendment is unusually clear about extending citizenship rights to everyone born on American soil except for children of foreign diplomats and American Indians (who belong to sovereign tribes). Eliminating these rights for anyone else will require three-quarters of the states to ratify another amendment. 5

Remarkably for someone who counsels deference to the original Constitution, Will has few qualms about this. Why? Because the authors of the 14th Amendment could not possibly have meant to extend birthright citizenship to illegal aliens given that no laws restricting immigration existed in 1868 when it was passed, he maintains. "Is it reasonable to presume they would have wanted to provide the reward of citizenship to the children of the violators of those laws? Surely not," he declares. 6

It's even more plausible, however, that if the authors failed to foresee something, it was not the law-breakers but the laws themselves. Hostility toward immigrants, especially the Irish who arrived in the wake of the potato famine, was certainly around in their time. But they still didn't pass such laws—perhaps because they thought that a country that had borne the sin of slavery to get cheap foreign labor should not erect barricades to keep out voluntary cheap foreign labor! 7

But if the failure to foresee events offered sufficient grounds for amending the Constitution, then we might as well throw out the whole document and begin anew. Would the Founders have written the First Amendment enshrining the freedom of press if they had known that the Internet would one day allow Wikileaks to release classified documents and jeopardize soldiers on the battlefield? Or the Second Amendment guaranteeing the right to bear arms in a world of cop-killing bullets? Or the Fourth Amendment's injunction against improper searches and seizures in an age of terrorism? Or the Fifth Amendment's prohibition against government takings of private property when rare species are allegedly facing extinction? 8

The 14th Amendment was written, among other things, to prevent Confederate states from denying citizenship to newly freed blacks. What comparable injustice would amending this amendment prevent? Restrictionists claim that birthright 9 citizenship encourages pregnant women to illegally sneak into the U.S. for a just-in-time delivery so that their newborns can gain citizenship and later sponsor the parents for citizenship. They call these kids "anchor babies."

But *Time* magazine reported last year that of all the babies born in 2008 to at least one unauthorized parent, over 80 percent were to moms who had been in the United States for over one year. Actual instances of "birth tourism," where moms expressly came here to deliver babies on American soil, accounted for about two-tenths of 1 percent of all births in 2006. And most of these moms were not poor, illegal Hispanics—Smith's target group. They were rich Chinese moms on tourist visas. 10

Nor is it plausible that their intention was to use their kids to gain citizenship for themselves. Kids have to wait until 21 to seek legal status for illegal parents and the parents must typically then wait outside the U.S. for at least 10 years before they can obtain their green cards. About 4,000 unauthorized parents with kids who are citizens can avoid deportation every year. This, then, is the grand illicit citizenship racket that Will & Co. want a constitutional amendment to crack! 11

Conservatives argue that this amendment is necessary to enforce the rule of law. But the first principle of conservatism, constantly deployed against liberal reformers, is that it is not wise to make radical changes to long-standing laws and institutions for small gains. As Aristotle warned in the *Politics* two-and-half millennia ago: "[W]hen the improvement is small, and since it is a bad thing to habituate people to the reckless dissolution of laws, it is evident that some errors of both legislations and of the rulers should be let go; for the city will not be benefited as much from changing them as it will be harmed through being habituated to disobey the rulers . . . The easy alteration of existing laws in favor of new and different ones weakens the power of law itself." 12

Yet, here are conservatives now, disregarding their own wisdom and subverting the rule of law in the name of the rule of law to fight bogus causes. 13

Notes

1 **Restrictionism**—This term refers to the belief that laws should put strict limits on immigration to the United States.
2 **Nativism**—This more extreme term refers to the belief that the culture of a country's founding citizens should remain the dominant culture. Nativists thus oppose immigration by different racial and ethnic groups.
3 **Hagiography**—While the word originally refers to the biography of a saint, it is now often used pejoratively to describe any writing in which the author heaps excessive and uncritical praise upon some person.

CREDITS

CHAPTER 10

Making an Argument

ENGAGING QUESTIONS

In this chapter, you will engage with the following questions:

- What does it mean to make an argument?
- What are the purposes, or motives, for making an argument?
- Why is case structure necessary for making a convincing argument?
- How do writers identify appropriate topics for making an argument?
- How do the elements of the rhetorical situation apply to the writing process for making an argument?
- How do writers apply the steps of the writing process to an assignment that asks them to make an argument?

YOU HEAR OR READ ABOUT SOME TOPIC THAT INTERESTS YOU (CALL IT "X"), and soon enough you form an opinion about it. Nothing much happens until someone asks you a key question, "What do you think about x?" This question starts many serious conversations, but it leads to stating opinions, not to **argument,** which means *a reasoned defense of an opinion.* To get to argument, you need a question with a sharper edge, a critical thinking question: "*Why* do you think this about x?" That is, "What reasons do you have to explain and justify what you think? What evidence do you have to back up your opinion?"

When you answer these questions, you are making a **case,** *arguing for a position by advancing reasons and evidence in defense of it.* Making a case occurs in many genres, including newspaper editorials, letters to the editor, blog posts, speeches, and personal letters.

What Is a Case?

A **case** develops an opinion about a controversial issue or question. It has three parts:

1. A **claim,** or thesis
   Example: College costs are unjustifiably high.
2. One or more **reasons** that explain or justify the claim
   Example: They have increased much more than inflation over the last thirty years.
3. Appropriate **evidence** to back up each reason
   Example: Data comparing the cost of living in general with increases in tuition and fees over the last thirty years.

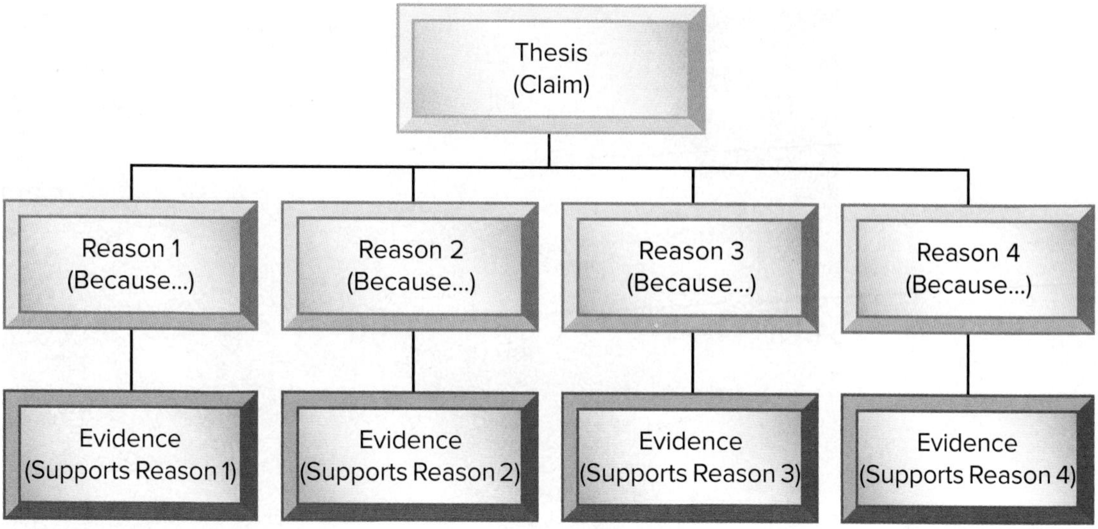

The flow chart above shows the structure of a case. A claim can be supported by one or more reasons.

CONCEPT CLOSE-UP Visualizing the Structure of a Case

A case has the following structure:

The claim answers the question, **What are you asserting?**

Reasons answer the question, **Why do you make this claim?**

Evidence answers the question, **What information confirms your reasoning?**

Why Make a Case?

An issue is controversial when reasonable people take different positions on it. One reason to make a case is to convince readers to accept one of those positions. For example, perhaps you feel that texting and talking on a handheld cell phone while driving should be banned. In an editorial or a blog you could make the case by pointing out how dangerous it is.

Convincing other people, however, is not the only motivation for making a case. We all have casual opinions we have never thought through. How valid is one of the unexamined opinions you have? The best way to answer that question is to attempt to make a case for it. If you cannot make a good one that other people find convincing, it may be time to change or modify your opinion. Making a case, then, is not only a challenge to convince others but also a testing of how sound your own opinions and reasoning are.

Proposing a ban on texting and driving is a good example of an issue you could make a case for.

© jinga80/Getty Images, RF

How Do Writers Make a Case?

Cases combine structure (claim, reasons, and evidence) with a strategy for engaging with the readers you most want to convince. For example, many people are in favor of lowering the drinking age from twenty-one to eighteen because they believe the higher drinking age is at least partly to blame for binge drinking. On the other hand, organizations such as Mothers Against Drunk Driving (MADD) support the legal age of twenty-one. They point to thousands of people who die each year in traffic accidents caused by drunk drivers and say that lowering the drinking age will only make a serious problem worse.

Suppose that you wanted to convince supporters of the current drinking age (twenty-one in most states) to alter their opinion. *You have to think as they think.* Everyone agrees that abusing alcohol is a big problem. You could argue that the issue is not age but rather moderation and responsibility whenever people drink. Moderation and responsibility are exactly what the current law cannot promote; prohibition cannot encourage moderation and responsibility. You could allay concerns about drunk driving by advocating stronger enforcement of the law. Without such a strategy, any case you make is likely only to strengthen the views of people who already share your position–not convince those whose view you want to change.

READING 10.1

Building a Better Life through Greenways and Trails

TRAILS AND GREENWAYS CLEARINGHOUSE

An issue that matters to many people is the preservation of trails and greenways in cities and suburbs. Of course, economic incentives sometimes work against using space for these purposes because homes and businesses cannot be built where green spaces exist already or others are being created. Are the green spaces worth the land devoted to them? This article makes the case that they are.

To make a greenway is to make a community.
—Charles E. Little, *Greenways for America*

Necessary background information.

1 Greenways are corridors of protected open space managed for conservation and recreation purposes. Greenways often follow natural land or water features, and link nature reserves, parks, cultural features and historic sites with each other and with populated areas. Greenways can be publicly or privately owned, and some are the result of public/private partnerships. Trails are paths used for walking, bicycling, horseback riding, or other forms of recreation or transportation.

Stresses diversity and nationwide extent of green spaces.

Some greenways include trails, while others do not. Some appeal to people, while 2
others attract wildlife. From the hills of inland America to the beaches and barrier islands of the coast, greenways provide a vast network linking America's special places.

Why Establish Trails and Greenways?

Summarizes reasons taken up in order in subsequent headings.

There are many reasons for preserving and improving the trails and greenways we have 3
and for creating new ones. They improve the economy, promote good health, protect the environment, and preserve our rich and diverse American heritage.

Economic Benefits

First reason.

Trails and greenways provide countless opportunities for economic renewal and growth. 4
Increased property values and tourism and recreation-related spending on items such as bicycles, in-line skates and lodging are just a few of the ways trails and greenways positively impact community economies.

Evidence defending first reason. Note evidence includes data from two different sources and the testimony of a local official.

In a 1992 study, the National Park Service estimated the average economic activity 5
associated with three multi-purpose trails in Florida, California and Iowa was $1.5 million annually.[1]

According to a study conducted by the U.S. Fish and Wildlife Service, bird watchers 6
spend over $5.2 billion annually.[2]

The impact on local economies can be significant. As Chris Wagner, Executive 7
Director of the Greater Connellsville Chamber of Commerce, Pennsylvania, remarked,

1. "The Impacts of Rail-Trails, A Study of Users and Nearby Property Owners from Three Trails." *National Park Service, Rivers, Trails and Conservation Assistance Program*, 1992.
2. "Economic Impacts of Protecting Rivers, Trails, and Greenway Corridors." *National Park Service, Rivers, Trails and Conservation Assistance Program*, 4th ed., 1995.

Three new gift shops have recently opened, another bike shop, a jewelry store, an antique and used furniture store, a thrift shop, a Wendy's Restaurant and a pizza and sandwich shop. All this is happening, and only with the *prospect* of the trail opening in July. There is an air of excitement and anticipation now within this community, something Connellsville has not felt for many years.

Promoting Healthy Living

Second reason.

Many people realize exercise is important for maintaining good health in all stages of life; however, many do not regularly exercise. The U.S. Surgeon General estimates that 60% of American adults are not regularly active and another 25% are not active at all.[3] In communities across the country, people do not have access to trails, parks, or other recreation areas close to their homes. Trails and greenways provide a safe, inexpensive avenue for regular exercise for people living in rural, urban and suburban areas. 8

Environmental Benefits

Third reason.

Specific example used as evidence.

Greenways protect important habitat and provide corridors for people and wildlife. The preserved Pinhook Swamp between Florida's Osceola National Forest and Georgia's Okefenokee National Wildlife Refuge protects a vital wildlife corridor. This important swampland ecosystem sustains numerous species, including the Florida black bear, timber rattlesnake, and the Florida sandhill crane. 9

Trails and greenways help improve air and water quality. For example, communities with trails provide enjoyable and safe options for walking and bicycling, which reduces air pollution. By protecting land along rivers and streams, greenways prevent soil erosion and filter pollution caused by agricultural and road runoff. 10

Evidence connects with news stories of almost annual floods, something readers know about and can easily appreciate.

Greenways also serve as natural floodplains. According to the Federal Emergency Management Agency, flooding causes over $1 billion in property damages every year. By restoring developed floodplains to their natural state, many riverside communities are preventing potential flood damage. 11

Appeals to feelings of alienation from nature in metropolitan America.

Finally, trails and greenways are hands-on environmental classrooms. People of all ages can see for themselves the precious and intriguing natural world from which they often feel so far removed. 12

Preserving Our History and Culture

Fourth reason.

Trails and greenways have the power to connect us to our heritage by preserving historic places and by providing access to them. They can give people a sense of place and an understanding of the enormity of past events, such as Native American trails and vast battlefields. Trails and greenways draw the public to historic sites. For example, the six-mile Bethabara Trail and Greenway in Winston-Salem, North Carolina draws people to the birthplace of the city, the original Moravian Christian village founded in the late 1700s. 13

3. "Physical Activity and Health: A Report of the Surgeon General." U.S. Department of Health and Human Services, 1996.

Other trails preserve transportation corridors. Rail-trails along historic rail corridors provide a glance at the importance of this mode of transportation. Many canal paths, preserved for their historic importance as a transportation route before the advent of railroads, are now used by thousands of people each year for bicycling, running, hiking and strolling. Many historic structures along canal towpaths, such as taverns and locks, have been preserved. 14

Building a Better Life

Strong conclusion appeals to quality-of-life issues and sentiments.

As new development and suburbs are built farther and farther from cities, open spaces have disappeared at an alarming rate. People spend far too much time in traffic, detracting from time that could be better spent with their families and friends. 15

Through their votes, thousands of Americans have said 'yes' to preserving open spaces, greenways, farmlands and other important habitat. During the 1998 election, voters in 44 states approved over 150 conservation-related ballot initiatives. Trails and greenways provide what many Americans seek: close-to-home recreational areas, community meeting places, historic preservation, educational experiences, natural landscapes and beautification. Both trails and greenways help communities build pride by ensuring that their neighborhoods are good places to live, so that children can safely walk or bike to a park, school, or to a neighbor's home. Trails and greenways help make communities more attractive and friendly places to live. 16

Questions for Discussion

1. This case appeared on a website where arguments are usually kept short to encourage online readers not to skip over them. Besides its brevity, what other features of this case should appeal to online readers?
2. Why does the case begin with the economic benefits of trails and greenways?
3. How does the case appeal to the values and feelings of readers? Were you moved by these appeals? Why or why not?

See Chapter 3, pages 39–44, for definitions of purpose, angle, and voice.

Thinking as a Writer

What Is the Rhetorical Situation?

1. What is the *purpose* of the case? What is its *angle* on the topic? How would you describe its *voice*?
2. Who is the intended *audience*? Is there anything you can cite that implies the target readership? How do the four reasons appeal to various interest groups and points of view in the United States?
3. Using the chart on page 219 and the marginal annotations, discuss the organization of the case as a claim supported by reasons and backed by evidence. How is the case framed in the opening paragraphs? How does it close or conclude the argument in the last two paragraphs without just summarizing it? ■

READING **10.2**

The Need for More Teachers of Color

JOSÉ LUIS VILSON

A math teacher in New York City, José Vilson is also a blogger, public speaker, and author of a book, This Is Not a Test: A New Narrative on Race, Class, and Education *(2014). The following case arguing for more teachers of color, especially more male teachers, is based in part on this book. Vilson's argument, like most long arguments, offers more than the basic case of thesis, reasons, and evidence. Note, for example, that Vilson avoids alienating white readers by affirming the value of white teachers for minority students even as he makes the case for more teachers of color.*

If I've done the math correctly, out of the 50 or so teachers I've had in my lifetime, only two or three of them were men who were black and/or Latino. For someone who is 33 years old and was born and raised in New York City, a place often celebrated for its diversity, that's staggering. 1

You're allowed to wonder why that's so important. After all, teachers of all races, backgrounds, sexes, and ages have proven to be effective educators of urban youth. In fact, I love that many white people care enough about the plight of black and Latino students that they seek to work in the neighborhoods in which these students live. Throughout my own education, many of my white teachers were excellent. I understand that there needs to be a diversity of experiences; our students have to survive in the same world as everyone else. A small part of me also thinks: Who better to teach students of color the tools needed to survive in a predominantly white country than white people? 2

But as a teacher of color, I'd be lying if I told you I wasn't disturbed by the lack of representation of black and Latino people, especially males, as teachers. Some work as principals and district administrators. Others are third-party vendors, education lawyers, and professors in institutions of higher education. Effective (and ineffective) teachers often leave the classroom in favor of these occupations; while plenty of men do great work in administration, many use it as a steppingstone to stay in education without grounding themselves in the educational practice of the classroom. 3

Because about 75 percent of our nation's teachers are women, many in society also view teaching as "women's work," a category that often leads to demeaning and obtuse ways of dismissing teachers' contributions. This dynamic compounds the already existing problem of society talking down to educators in our schools. Too many people don't see the need to pay teachers well or to ensure they have proper working conditions because educators are regarded as caretakers, not professionals. While male-dominated professions like computer science or medicine garner respect, the teaching profession still has to combat patriarchy. 4

The fact that so many people view teaching as a second-class profession speaks volumes about our society's values. Plenty of men talk favorably about teachers, but when asked if they'd ever be teachers themselves, they respond, "I don't have the patience," and "You guys don't get paid enough." In our society, money means stature, whether we value the occupation or not. It's not just coming from the younger 5 generation, either. My mom, whom I love dearly, on occasion wonders aloud why, with all the stress I endure as a teacher, I would put up with my job when I could make far more as a computer programmer.

There are those who have left the profession because it's really easy to become jaded about the school system *and* the human experience. I don't know any fellow black or Latino teachers who think that every student in their school is getting properly served by this system. Some conclude that the system is hopeless. Others say, "We'll continue to fight." The latter are crucial: when our students see more black or Latino sports figures populating a multimillion-dollar basketball court or football field, yet see only one black or Latino teacher in their whole grade, or two or three in their whole school, then they're probably less inspired to take their own education, inside and outside the classroom, seriously. 6

To be clear, I'm not speaking for every person of color here, but I'm calling things like I see them. I'm black and Latino. I'm a guy who grew up in public housing on the Lower East Side of Manhattan. You may or may not share any of these characteristics, and whether you share all of them, some of them, or none of them, you may or may not agree with me. No one group of people—people of color included—is monolithic in their thinking or experience. And just because someone is a person of color does not mean he or she grew up poor. But based on my experiences as someone who came of age in a pretty tough neighborhood, and then shocked everyone, including myself, by becoming a middle school teacher, I have some insights into schools and teaching as both a student and an educator of color. 7

Making a Contribution

For a decade, I have been a New York City public school teacher, teaching students math at Inwood Intermediate School (IS 52) in the neighborhood of Washington Heights. I hadn't always intended to become an educator. I attended Syracuse University seeking to graduate with a bachelor's degree in computer science, but then my college roommate showed me the movie *Office Space* and I realized I didn't want to spend my life longing for my stapler or beating up dysfunctional printers. Instead, I wanted to teach students whose backgrounds were similar to mine. A few years after earning my undergraduate degree in computer science from Syracuse, I enrolled in the New York City Teaching Fellows program, which places candidates in schools in three high-poverty regions of New York City. I chose to work in the Manhattan neighborhood of Washington Heights/Inwood, which is predominately inhabited by people who speak Spanish. 8

When I started teaching there, the neighborhood had already become a mostly Dominican (as in Dominican Republic) stronghold, a little DR in the United States, so to speak. But it was still home to a hodgepodge of cultures, a conglomeration of Puerto Rican, black, and Chinese blue-collar workers. As someone who grew up in similar circumstances, I came to the Heights because it's where I thought I could make a contribution. 9

With only seven weeks of pre-service training under my belt, I, like so many bright-eyed, bushy-tailed teachers, was filled to the brim with hope and enthusiasm. Such feelings usually fade fast, partly due to the strain of the school year, but also due to 10 the pressure to perform miracles under deplorable learning conditions and the lack of agency to make things better. Challenges such as lack of autonomy, teacher isolation, and inadequate administrative support are easier to solve than teacher pay, yet they also fall under the top reasons why many teachers, especially teachers of color, leave, and why those of us who *do* stay learn to temper our zeal.

My first adviser in the NYC Teaching Fellows program predicted that I wouldn't survive my first year of teaching because of the passion I exuded during my pre-service teaching. Ten years later, I tell others what I told him. I thrived then, and continue to do so now, not because of my idealism but because of my idealistic realism. 11

The difference between idealism and idealistic realism is that the former suggests a wishful dream far removed from reality. The latter, which I've often found with teachers of color (and those who have worked in high-poverty schools with a student body that's predominantly of color), is that we hold fast to the vision of a better country, a better town, a better neighborhood, where students find success in positive and enlightening ways. Yet, we do this in the context of their lives, and not based on our projections of what success looks like for them. We're not trying to mold them into what we believe they should be. We're trying to open doors to show them alternatives for what they could be. 12

In *The Teacher Wars: A History of America's Most Embattled Profession*,* journalist Dana Goldstein suggests that we recruit more teachers of color, saying "A half century of research and 150 years of practical experience show teachers of color are more likely to hold high expectations for students of color." 13

Yet the number of teachers of color still lags far behind the number of white educators. Of the nearly 3.4 million public school teachers in the United States in 2011–2012, the year for which most recent data are available, nearly 82 percent were white, and approximately 18 percent were of color.† Only about 4 percent were men of color.[1] For that same year, nearly 52 percent of public school students were white and approximately 48 percent were of color.[2] 14

With a predominantly white profession and a student body that's now majority nonwhite, we must consider the importance of recruiting teachers of color, especially male teachers of color. Just as integration by socioeconomic status can promote racial diversity while narrowing the achievement gap between low-income and more-affluent students,‡ increasing the percentage of teachers of color would narrow what I call the vision gap—the gap that can arise in how low-income and more-affluent students view themselves as future professionals. 15

After all, children can't be what they can't see. By hiring more teachers of color (in particular, those who grew up economically challenged, like I did), students of color can form relationships with professionals who may share their cultural background *and* possess powerful narratives for success. 16

---

*For an excerpt, see "Quieting the Teacher Wars" in the Spring 2015 issue of *American Educator*.
†The National Center for Education Statistics identifies teachers of color as black, Hispanic, Asian, Pacific Islander, American Indian/Alaska Native, and two or more races.
‡For more on socioeconomic school integration, see "From All Walks of Life" in the Winter 2012–2013 issue of *American Educator*.

A Genuine Connection

When I first walked into the classroom as a teaching fellow, my students were mostly from low-income families and were Dominican and black. Just like me. They raised their eyebrows the first time I stood in front of them; they looked as if they had never before seen a teacher of color. At the time, most of the male adults of color at the school were deans and administrators, who had been quickly shuffled out of the classroom into their positions. My students may have had a few women of color as teachers as well, almost all of whom were veterans with strong content and pedagogical knowledge and classroom management skills. 17

With only a month and a half's worth of training, I relied heavily on my ability to connect with students through their culture to survive that first year. I didn't yet have the experience that my older colleagues possessed, and I was not as sure of my teaching ability, so I was probably harder on myself than I needed to be. But according to others, I fared just fine. Some teachers in my first year approached me to ask for advice on how to handle certain situations, and I couldn't tell them because I didn't have the words for it. I usually referred them to veteran teachers in the building, who they seemed to be afraid of. I didn't understand it then, but all those times that I called my students' parents and spoke to them in Spanish, used my students' home language to help them understand math, and followed them from class to class, my genuine connection to their backgrounds was enabling me to develop a positive relationship with them. I had an instant leg up because I could see things through their eyes, and because I'd been where they'd been and still found success. 18

My colleagues acknowledged that my efforts were paying off. When I came into the school building one morning, a dean spotted me in the hallway as I was escorting my students to lunch and said in his burly growl, "Vilson, you're doing a yeoman's job!" 19

I said, "Huh?" 20

"A yeoman's job!" 21

"What?" 22

"You're doing a HELLUVA job, Vilson!" 23

"Thanks." 24

Despite the fact that many white teachers (like that dean) acknowledge the important contributions made by teachers of color, some still doubt the need for a diverse educator workforce. Here, I want to state clearly that we need more research, including quantitative research, on the effects of black male educators on student outcomes. For instance, a recent study suggests that teachers of color specifically could help to improve the academic achievement of students of color.[3] Based on my own experiences, I believe it's important for children of color, especially male children of color, to see teachers of color, especially male teachers of color, as role models. 25

Whenever someone like me suggests that public schools do in fact need more teachers of color, the first question inevitably asked is, "Do you think we need to get rid of white teachers?" and, as a corollary, "Are you saying white teachers can't teach children of color?" That's not what I'm saying at all. If anything, balance matters for our students. 26

I would suggest that children of color need access to the ways and means of the dominant culture, and who better to teach that than white teachers and teachers of color who have mastered it? As Lisa Delpit writes in her book *Other People's Children: Cultural Conflict in the Classroom*, "Teachers need to support the language that students bring to school, provide them input from an additional code, and give them the opportunity to use the new code in a nonthreatening, real communicative context." Survival in this country often depends on understanding the code to success (the phrase "college and career ready" comes to mind here), and if white teachers and teachers of color can show children of color the values and norms of our dominant culture, then we can close the vision gap for those students. 27

Educators of color can also make a positive impact on white students. Often, the onus of developing cultural competence falls solely on teachers of color. A more diverse teaching population can help white students interact with and understand people of different races and cultures. It would also enable them to see people of color in positions of authority. Exposure to peers and adults with different experiences and worldviews helps all children develop empathy for others and assess their own humanity. 28

Yet, the hiring of white teachers, which historically resulted in the removal of teachers of color, has often been, for all intents and purposes, a matter of public policy. For instance, when the Supreme Court began to mandate that southern states comply with *Brown v. Board of Education*, more than 30,000 black teachers and administrators were fired to ensure that white teachers kept their jobs. Even the 1966 merger of the National Education Association and the American Teachers Association, a historically black teachers union, didn't sway many teachers of either race to see the common struggle of teaching in America.[4] However well intentioned, the merger didn't ultimately improve the racial and gender dynamics that continued to play out in schools and union meetings.[§] 29

Fast-forward to this century, and a closer look at teacher demographics in New York City speaks volumes as to why we need to hire teachers of color. According to a report published by the New York City Independent Budget Office, the share of teachers staffing high-poverty schools in 2011–2012, the year for which most recent data are available, was approximately 44 percent white, 25 percent black, 24 percent Hispanic, and 5 percent Asian, with other subgroups not reported.[5] In low-poverty schools, the percentage of white teachers is substantially higher, at approximately 73 percent, while the percentages of black and Hispanic teachers are only 12 percent and 8 percent, respectively. Asian teachers' share is about the same, at 6 percent. The report also noted that "teachers in high-poverty schools transfer to other New York City public schools in larger numbers, suggesting that student characteristics might be an important factor in turnover decisions." 30

When I ask some of my colleagues of color why they stay in high-poverty schools, they often say it's because they feel as if they're paying their successes forward, opening doors for their students, and teaching them to succeed. Few, if any, ever point to job protections and benefits, though both help to ensure that teachers make a career of the profession. 31

---

§In 1957, the American Federation of Teachers expelled locals that refused to desegregate.

To further complicate matters, teachers of color leave the profession at a faster rate than their white peers,[6] not due to salaries or benefits but because of learning and working conditions. Too often, the high-poverty schools where teachers of color typically work are either overmanaged by outside consultants or in the process of being shut down by their mayor or governor. While it's certainly true that poor management and lack of funding can negatively affect teachers at any school, such problems hit our high-poverty schools the hardest and often make professional concerns personal for teachers of color. 32

Professional and Cultural Competence

To truly transform our education system and recruit and retain teachers of color, we must push multiple levers. One lever is ensuring the cultural competence of *all* educators. In October 2014, 11 civil rights groups ranging from the NAACP and the Mexican American Legal Defense and Educational Fund to the National Urban League and the Southeast Asia Resource Action Center came together to lay out a handful of reforms and principles that would help narrow achievement gaps and push education in America into the 21st century. One of these principles focused on professional competence: 33

> Systems of preparation and ongoing development should ensure that educators have the time, investments, and supports necessary to acquire the knowledge about curriculum, teaching, assessment, linguistic and cultural competence, implicit bias, and student support needed to teach students effectively. This should include additional supports for education professionals who serve children and families in historically under-resourced and disadvantaged classrooms and schools. School systems should recognize educators' abilities, particularly in working with diverse learners and students of color. They should not only create incentives for education professionals to develop or acquire additional skills, but also require professional learning to ensure their effectiveness in the classroom.[7]

Thus, professional competence and cultural competence go hand in hand. We don't just teach subject matter; we teach the students in front of us. And if we share the same skin color and cultural and socioeconomic background as they do, we can serve as immediate models for success. From an administrative standpoint, having more teachers of color in a school means there may be more teachers whom students can turn to and feel comfortable having conversations with about certain situations. I've often joked that some teachers of color could earn loads of professional development credit for all the racial situations they must address in schools, and perhaps that's a benefit administrators should consider in hiring a diverse faculty. With more teachers of color in buildings with students of color, administrators and teachers alike can turn to one another to foster a more inclusive school community and advocate for all children. 34

* * *

In 2011, I had the privilege of attending an event in Tarrytown, New York, held by the organization Today's Students Tomorrow's Teachers. The program was founded by Bettye Perkins to encourage more teachers of color to enter the profession through an 35 eight-year program that provides mentorship for high school students and scholarships for college tuition; all candidates have to do is earn their certifications and become teachers. I wish such a group had existed when I first came into my own, but I'm excited that people like me have this opportunity now. I was invited to share a few remarks, which I titled "It's Not about a Salary, It's All about Reality," a quote from rapper and producer KRS-One's classic "My Philosophy":

> Who gets weaker? The king or the teacher?
> It's not about a salary; it's all about reality
> Teachers teach and do the world good
> Kings just rule and most are never understood

I shared these lines to encourage the attendees to consider the ways educators inspire students to think for themselves. I also gave a few words of advice—for example, "Sample the best teachers from your past, but make your own story."

In my first month of teaching, I told them, I had this crazy idea that I would transform 36
my students' lives and that they would change for me the way that students of famed educator Jaime Escalante did in the movie *Stand and Deliver*. They didn't. But that first class was probably my favorite, and the one from which I learned the most.

One time, we did a lesson on percentages. I wrote my lesson using the technical 37
aspects of finding percentages. As I began to teach it and saw the bored looks on my students' faces, I had an idea. I wrote the word "percent" out and asked my students, "Does anyone recognize a word in here?"

"Cent!" 38

I said, "Oh, good! Now, has anyone ever heard of the word somewhere else, even in 39
Spanish?"

Students jumped out of their seats, they were so excited to answer. 40

A few shouted, "Ooh! Ooh! *Centavo*!" 41

"So what does *centavo* mean?" 42

"A penny!" 43

"And how many pennies do you need to get a dollar?" 44

"A hundred!" 45

"So when we say *percent*, we mean we're comparing one thing out of a possible 46
hundred."

"OOHHHHH!!" 47

That piece of my lesson took a few more minutes than I had planned for, I explained. 48
But it also made a huge difference. Teachers who can relate to their students on a cultural level can reach their students in important ways.

I'm not saying people from other cultures can't help us, but every student of color 49
could use a role model. If that role model just happens to be the teacher in front of them, that's a good thing.

Endnotes

1. "Number and Percentage Distribution of Teachers in Public and Private Elementary and Secondary Schools, by Selected Teacher Characteristics: Selected Years, 1987–88 through 2011–12," in National Center for Education Statistics, *Digest of Education Statistics*, 2013, table 209.10.

2. "Enrollment and Percentage Distribution of Enrollment in Public Elementary and Secondary Schools, by Race/Ethnicity and Level of Education: Fall 1998 through Fall 2023," in National Center for Education Statistics, *Digest of Education Statistics*, 2013, table 203.60.
3. Anna J. Egalite, Brian Kisida, and Marcus A. Winters, "Representation in the Classroom: The Effect of Own-Race Teachers on Student Achievement," *Economics of Education Review* 45 (2015): 44–52.
4. David Cecelski's *Along Freedom Road: Hyde County, North Carolina, and the Fate of Black Schools in the South* (Chapel Hill: University of North Carolina Press, 1994) provides a detailed account of the devastation visited upon African American educators in North Carolina in the wake of *Brown v. Board of Education*. Cecelski estimates that more than 30,000 southern African American educators lost their jobs in the process of school desegregation. See also chapter 10 of Adam Fairclough, *A Class of Their Own: Black Teachers in the Segregated South* (Cambridge, MA: Belknap Press, 2007).
5. New York City Independent Budget Office, *Demographics and Work Experience: A Statistical Portrait of New York City's Public School Teachers* (New York: Independent Budget Office, 2014), 4.
6. Richard Ingersoll and Henry May, *Recruitment, Retention and the Minority Teacher Shortage* (Philadelphia: Consortium for Policy Research in Education, 2011), 24.
7. "Civil Rights Groups Demand Accountability for Equity in Public Education," National Opportunity to Learn Campaign, October 28, 2014, www.otlcampaign.org/blog/2014/10/28/civil-rights-groups-demand-accountability-equity-public-education.

Questions for Discussion

1. "The Need for More Teachers of Color" is more than an argument for the proposition that we need more teachers of color. It is also a highly informative piece about teaching, and our society in relation to teaching. What did you learn from the article? What is the relation between what you learned and the need for greater teacher diversity?
2. In some arguments, such as "Building a Better Life through Greenways and Trails" (pp. 221–223), the case is explicit, sometimes even labelling the thesis, reasons, and evidence as such. Vilson's case is much more implicit, requiring the reader to dig out the parts of the case before assessing its cogency. Find his thesis, reasons, and evidence. How convincing is his case? In your view, which is more effective, the explicit or the implied case?
3. Based on what Vilson says, and your own experience and intuitions, what will have to change before more people of color will become teachers? What will have to change before more *males* of color will enter the classroom? Is it really important to have more men? Why or why not?

Thinking as a Writer

What Is the Rhetorical Situation?

1. What is Vilson's *purpose* in writing this essay? What is his *angle* on the topic? How would you describe his *voice*?
2. Who is Vilson's intended *audience*? What strategies does he use to counter and disarm objections some in his audience might have to his claim?
3. The Vilson article illustrates cause-and-effect reasoning in case-making, a common strategy in arguments that examine a problem and propose a solution. How does Vilson understand the problem of too few teachers of color? What does he say causes the problem? How does he link his solution to the cause? ■

Collaborative Activity

Examining Cause-and-Effect Reasoning

Working in groups of two or three, use the chart on page 219 to create a diagram that shows how Vilson uses the *conventions* for organizing an argument to structure his claim, reasons, and supporting evidence. How does Vilson frame his case? In what rhetorical situation did Vilson present his case? How might it affect his ability to reach his audience? ■

The Assignment

Make a case for or against a position on a controversial topic, problem, issue, or question. You may propose a solution or criticize someone else's proposed solution. Be sure to analyze your audience, to build common ground, and to offer reasons and evidence that not only support your claim but also respond to readers' concerns.

What Can I Write About

Your topic must be controversial, something about which reasonable people could disagree. Matters of fact are not controversial. For instance, it is a tragic fact that many veterans of the wars in Iraq and Afghanistan have committed suicide. People do not disagree about this fact but rather about whether enough is being done to help prevent more suicides.

Besides selecting a controversial issue, pick one you know something about from personal experience. Civic activities, internships, and jobs can be rich sources of topics. Here are some other places to find topics:

- **Class readings.** Class readings may suggest possibilities. For instance, reading Vilson's article may lead you to other issues and questions regarding education.
- **Local news.** Read your local and campus newspapers (especially the editorial page) or examine online news sources for controversial topics.
- **Internet discussions.** Visit blogs on topics that interest you. Many newspapers, magazines, and radio shows sponsor blogs that address controversial issues.

As you settle on a topic and begin to organize your thoughts, keep in mind the conventions of the argument described earlier in this chapter.

Topics for case-making must be controversial, such as how to reduce suicide among veterans of the wars in Afghanistan and Iraq.

JEWEL SAMAD/AFP/Getty Images

How Do I Make a Case? Questioning the Rhetorical Situation

Begin by considering the **rhetorical situation,** *the key variables associated with you as writer, with your audience, and with the genre, conventions, and expectations of your text.* Understanding the rhetorical situation will give you a stable sense of the whole, something definite to hold in mind as you work your way through the process of writing your essay.

Writer: What Is My Purpose, and What Impression Should Readers Have of Me?

The *purpose* of a case is to seek assent through logic in the form of a carefully worded claim supported by compelling reasons and accurate, convincing evidence. Your readers need to feel that you have thought your opinion through and that you are knowledgeable about your topic. You may feel passionate about your position, but your stance should be dispassionate, calm, and fair. Treat other opinions and arguments with respect, even as you show that your evidence and reasons are stronger.

Audience: Who Is My Reader?

Cases aim to convince two groups: people weakly inclined to agree with your thesis and those inclined toward another position but willing to consider alternatives. Your case should strengthen the adherence of those favorably disposed to your thesis by giving them good reasons and strong evidence they may have lacked before. Your reasons and evidence should also appeal to readers entertaining other positions, but reaching them requires strategy. (See pages 240–41.)

You cannot expect to convince readers unalterably opposed to your opinion. For example, there is nothing you could say in favor of people living together before marriage that would convince readers who believe it is a sin prohibited by their faith.

Text: What Moves Can I Make?

A case requires a central contention, also called a thesis or a claim. It requires that the claim be explained and defended with reasons. It also requires that the reasons be backed by evidence of one kind or another. These moves are required because readers expect them when they are reading a case.

Other moves, however, are more a matter of choice, and include some or all of the following:

- **Define the key terms in your thesis.** If you use a word or phrase your readers may not understand or may understand in a way you do not intend, define the word or phrase. For example, *sustainable farming,* though now often used, has a range of meanings and is not well understood by people not involved in agriculture. Define it as you want it understood in your thesis.
- **Provide background information as needed for readers to have an adequate grasp of the context of your case.** Most people do not know, for instance, that the vast majority of criminal cases do not come to trial but are handled by a process called plea bargaining. Among other bad results of plea bargaining is pressure on the person accused of a crime to plead guilty even if he or she is innocent. In a case that targets plea bargaining for reform, this context of abuse of the procedure needs to be presented and explained.
- **Anticipate obvious objections to your case and respond to them.** For example, if your case requires an increase in taxes to finance the measures you support, you should recognize that many readers will not be convinced on this count alone. You can say that the tax increase will be small and the benefits great as compared to the cost.
- **Show awareness of and toleration of those who would argue against your case.** The tendency in too much argumentation now is to see the opposition as the enemy. This is bad strategy if you want to convince people who do not already agree with you. Whenever you can, then, show solidarity with the other side. Except for criminals who want to steal information, we all have a stake, for example, in online security. People differ not about the value of security but rather about how to achieve it.
- **Pay special attention to opening and closing your case.** Openers should create interest and motivate the reader to keep reading, as well as connect strongly to the case you are about to make. Endings should leave the reader with something memorable. Remember: Readers tend to recall best what they read first and last.
- **Maintain a voice throughout that is calm and reasonable.** Just as too many people demonize their opponents, too many arguers seem to think that sounding hysterical wins assent. It doesn't.

How Do I Make a Case? Engaging the Writing Process

No two people compose in exactly the same way, and even the same person may go through the writing process in different ways with different assignments. Nevertheless, because no one can attend to everything at once, there are phases in handling any significant writing task. You **explore the topic** to get a sense of whether it will work for you and what you might be able to do with it; if the topic is working out for you, then you move into **preparing to write,** generating more content and planning your draft.

The next phase is **drafting your paper,** getting a version on screen, however rough it may be, so that you can work toward the final draft. Getting there involves two further phases: **revising your draft,** where you make major improvements in it, followed by **editing your draft,** taking care of errors, sentences that do not read well, paragraphs lacking focus and flow, and so on.

Exploring Your Topic

For case-making, exploring your topic means examining the issues involved in it. If your assignment calls for research, do some general reading about your topic to discover what the issues are. See Chapter 15, pages 352–57, for how to find and take notes on source material. If your assignment does not call for research, rely on your general knowledge about the topic to formulate the issues.

Find the Issues

An **issue** is *a point of controversy always or frequently raised in connection with a particular topic.* For your topic, begin by asking, **"What are the questions that people disagree about when discussing this topic?"** For instance, the primary purpose of prisons is always an issue when prison reform is discussed. Some see prisons as primarily punishment for crime; others see them as primarily institutions that should rehabilitate criminals. "What should prisons do?" is the question. Other questions include the following: What should be done about prison overcrowding? How can we reduce assaults on inmates by other, violent inmates? Is prison a breeding ground for more criminal behavior after inmates are released? If so, what can be done to prevent this from happening?

ACTIVITY 10.1 ***Collaborative Activity***

Isolating the Issues

List the issues connected with your topic. The key question is, **"What do people argue about whenever this topic is discussed?"**

If your class is working with a common topic or you share your topic with at least one other student, you could collaborate to answer the following exploratory questions:

- What issues were you unaware of before you formulated them?
- What positions do people take on these issues?
- What is your view of these issues?

Consider your view of the topic now. If you had no opinion before examining the issues, are you beginning to form one now? If you had an opinion, is it changing significantly? Which issue interests you most? Consider focusing your essay on that issue. ■

Order the Issues (Stasis)

Discussing the issues is an important step in exploring a controversial topic. Ordering them can help as well. Here is an example that illustrates one way of ordering the issues involved in committing American troops to combat in a foreign country:

- Are vital American interests at stake?
  - If you say no, make a case against committing the troops.
  - If you say yes, move on to the next question.
- Have nonmilitary alternatives been exploited fully?
  - If you say no, make a case for increased diplomatic effort or some other measure not requiring American troops on the ground.
  - If you say yes, move on to the next question.
- Do the announced objectives make sense?
  - If you say no, make a case for changing the objectives.
  - If you say yes, move on to the next question.
- Can we realize our objectives in a reasonable amount of time with minimal loss of lives?
  - If you say yes, make a case for military intervention.
  - If you say no, make a case against it based on impracticality.

Ordering the issues in this way is sometimes called **stasis,** a Latin word that means "stop" or "stay." That is: If you think a proposed military intervention would not secure vital national interests, you stop with the first question and make a case against it. If you think nonmilitary options have not been pursued enough, you argue for more diplomacy, economic sanctions, or some other alternative. You "stay" with the second question—and so on, through the whole list.

You can order the issues connected with any controversial topic this way. Doing so can clarify your own thinking as you work toward an opinion or assess the one you have.

ACTIVITY 10.2 *Writer's Notebook*

Committing to an Opinion

Cases require a considered opinion—that is, an opinion thought through carefully. Consequently, after finding and ordering the issues, you need to decide what your opinion is on the issue or issues you choose to address. Your opinion may change as you write and assess your first draft, but you cannot write a draft at all without one.

In a blog post or notebook entry, state your opinion about the issue you have settled on and the reasons you have for holding that opinion. ■

BEST PRACTICES Working with Sources in Making a Case

If your assignment involves research, consult Chapter 18, 379–400 on how to engage with sources and 386–92 pages for how to assess and incorporate source material in your paper. Keep the following points in mind as you work with your sources:

- Distinguish evidence from interpretation, or "spin." For example, in 2018, more than 30,000 people were killed in Mexico as a result of gang violence by local drug cartels. Citing this figure, your source might argue that American tourists should avoid Mexico. There is no reason to doubt the figure, but the interpretation is disputable: Drug-related violence seldom involves American tourists, and many destinations in Mexico are no more risky than some cities in the United States.

- Distinguish information from speculation. **Facts** are *uncontested, established data.* How the stock market performed over the last month is a matter of fact, as measured, for example, by the Dow Jones Industrial Average. Speculations are at most probabilities. How the stock market will perform over the next year is anyone's guess. You cannot ignore the facts, but you can use or not use speculation, depending on whether it helps you to make your case.
- Strive to maintain intellectual independence from the view your source has of the subject. Avoid distorting or misrepresenting the information in a source to fit what you want to believe, but feel free to interpret the information your own way, as you see the subject. For instance, you may support the screening of passengers before boarding commercial airliners as a necessary counterterrorism measure. If so, you cannot ignore considerable evidence that screening often fails to detect prohibited items that could be used for a terrorist act. Instead of ignoring or denying the evidence, you might argue that screening technology must improve.

Preparing to Write

Some writers prefer to go straight to drafting, working out their cases in several drafts. We recommend going through the following steps first, which most writers find helpful:

1. State your opinion as a claim or thesis.
2. Analyze the thesis to determine what you must argue to defend it adequately.
3. State the reasons you will use to explain or justify your thesis.
4. Select and order the evidence you will use to back up each reason.

These steps, described in more detail below, yield a **brief,** *an outline of your case.* Add ideas for an introduction and a conclusion, and you have all you need to guide your first draft.

State Your Opinion as a Claim or Thesis

You are still testing your opinion when you write a first draft of your case, because the value of any opinion depends on how strong a case you can make for it. Writers often change or modify their opinion as they compose or when they evaluate their first draft.

However, your first draft will be stronger if you attempt to state your opinion as a claim in a thesis statement before you begin drafting. An opinion is a general stance or point of view. For instance, in the second reading in this chapter (pages 224–31), Vilson argues that more teachers of color are needed in the classroom; more specifically, he says they are needed as role models and as adults who understand the cultures of minority students with similar backgrounds.

In preparing to write a case, the advantage of a thesis over an opinion is a *sharper focus, with carefully selected key terms.* It is therefore worth your time and effort to work toward a thesis before you draft.

To write a defensible claim or thesis, keep the following in mind:

- Your claim is a statement you will defend, not just a description of something that is factual.

  Not a claim: Student debt for government loans has grown to almost $30,000 for the average graduate, a heavy burden for young people just entering the workplace.

  Claim: The economy as a whole would benefit if the federal government would forgive student debts for higher education, which now average almost $30,000 per graduate.

  The first in this pair describes a problem. The second makes an assertion for doing something about the problem.

- The claim should be focused, specific, and directed at a particular audience, or readership.

  Too general: Many professors do not know how to make effective use of technology in teaching.

  Better: Professors who use presentation technology such as PowerPoint too often stifle creativity and student involvement in the class.

  The second example in this pair is more refined, indicating specific directions that the argument will take. It is also clearly directed at educators. The more specific your claim, the easier it will be to decide what your paper will include.

- Some claims may need to be qualified.

  Too absolute: Professors should openly state their opinions on political issues in classes where such opinions are relevant to course content.

  Qualified: Provided that they encourage students to discuss their own opinions freely, professors should be able to state openly their opinions on political issues so long as the issue is relevant to course content.

- Think of objections your readers might have to your claim, and modify it to eliminate the possible objection.

Analyzing Your Thesis

To analyze a thesis means to detect the key terms that make the assertion. For example, consider this thesis: "*Huckleberry Finn* should be required reading in all American high schools." To defend the thesis adequately requires addressing all the key terms: why this *particular book* should be a *required* title on American literature lists and why *high school* is the best place to teach it.

Thinking about Reasons

The reasoning that led you to your claim will supply the reasons you will offer to explain and justify it to your readers. In listing your reasons, however, you can avoid potential problems by thinking carefully about the following questions:

- **Does the statement of each reason say *exactly* what I mean to say?** The wording of your reason or reasons matters as much as the wording of your thesis.
- **Do I need all the reasons I am thinking of using?** As a general rule, two or three reasons are better than four or five because they are easier for the reader to remember. *Concentrate on developing your best reasons well rather than offering all the reasons you can think of.*
- **Does each reason clearly connect to the thesis by either explaining or justifying it?** Imagine your reader asking, "Why do you believe your thesis?" Each reason should answer this question.
- **Are there advantages in taking up my reasons in a particular order?** In general, begin and end your argument with your strongest reasons. But also consider the possibility that one reason will lead naturally to another and therefore should come before it.
- **If I have more than one reason, are they consistent with each other?** Make sure, for instance, that your first reason does not contradict your third reason.

Thinking about Evidence

Just as the reasoning that led you to your thesis supplies the reasons you will develop to convince your readers, so any information that led you to or confirmed your reasons will supply the evidence. Arrange the evidence you have under each reason.

Select and order your evidence in response to the following questions:

- **What kind of evidence does each reason require?** For example, if you are arguing for making cell phone use by drivers illegal, one of your main reasons will be the link of cell phone use with accidents. You'll need data–facts and figures–to back up your reason. If you also argue that such a law would not restrict personal freedom unduly, you will need other kinds of evidence–for example, laws banning the use of cell phones while driving are no more restrictive than laws against driving while intoxicated.
- **How much evidence do I need?** The answer is: *enough to overcome the degree of resistance your reader is likely to have.* Many Americans, for instance, assume that the federal government is already too big, too intrusive, and too expensive. Defending any proposal that would increase its role requires significant evidence for both need and positive results.
- **Have I mixed evidence types?** For example, when a reason requires hard data, you must supply it. But if you also have a statement from a respected expert confirming your reason, consider using it as well. Some readers are convinced more by authoritative statements than by hard data. You could also offer anecdotes, stories from people involved in an event, to confirm a reason. Stories from wounded soldiers who have served in Afghanistan or Iraq, for example, offer strong evidence for improvements in Veterans Health Administration hospitals. Many people find testimony more convincing than any other kind of evidence.
- **Have I selected the best pieces of evidence from all that I could use?** Just as it is better to develop two or three reasons well than four or five poorly, so it is better to offer two or three strong pieces of evidence than four or five that vary in quality. More is not necessarily better, and too much evidence can confuse and overburden your reader.

Student Example: Noelle Alberto's Brief

A brief, like the argument it summarizes, has a three-level structure: a statement of the thesis you intend to defend; a statement of each reason that explains why you hold your thesis; and a statement of the evidence that supports each reason.

In the following student example, Noelle Alberto develops a case that urges her fellow students to stop multitasking when they study.

Claim: **Multitasking between recreational technology and studying impairs students' learning and does not prepare them for the real world of work.**

Reason: *Multitasking increases the amount of time spent studying.*

Evidence: Homework takes twice as long to complete with multitasking. (Source: Tugend)

Evidence: Switching tasks makes you have to relearn information to get back on track. (Source: Hamilton)

Reason: *Switching tasks requires relearning.*

Evidence: It prevents students from being able to store information learned through studying. (Sources: Rosen, Jarmon)

Reason: *Multitasking is poor preparation for the workplace.*

Evidence: Businesses don't want people who multitask, they want people who prioritize. (Source: LPA)

Evidence: Multitasking decreases production ability of workers. (Source: Rosen)

Reason: *Multitasking decreases worker productivity.*

Evidence: Ability to pay attention to one thing at a time is a mark of mature thinking. (Source: Rosen)

Drafting Your Paper

Using your brief as a guide, write your first draft. Focus on the following concerns as you write.

What Stance and Voice Are Appropriate for a Case?

The conventional stance and voice for arguing a case has been the **middle style,** in contrast to the plain style common in informative texts and the passionate style of some public speaking. What does middle style sound like? Here it is in a passage from the Vilson reading (pages 224–31):

> We don't just teach subject matter; we teach the students in front of us. And if we share the same skin color and cultural and socioeconomic background as they do, we can serve as immediate models for success. From an administrative standpoint, having more teachers of color in a school means there may be more

teachers whom students can turn to and feel comfortable having conversations with about certain situations.

Read these sentences aloud and you can hear the voice of middle style: *It states its position clearly, directly, and forcefully.* It is more formal than chatting but not as formal as most public speaking.

Avoid the phony, overheated sensationalism of much talk radio and TV. Case-making has nothing to do with name-calling, insults, outrageous claims, and partisan bickering. Rather, argument is the calm voice of reason, one of the voices most admired and respected wherever productive interaction among people occurs: at universities, in business meetings, in community gatherings.

Finding Common Ground

To convince people who do not already agree with you requires not only that you supply good reasons and strong evidence–your case–but also that you find common ground with them and acknowledge their reasonable concerns and counterarguments. In short, strategy always matters in convincing, and strategy always means engaging with your reader. What can you do as you compose your draft to connect with your reader?

- **Make a concession.** For example, if you are writing against multitasking as a study habit, you can concede that multitasking may be fine–or even an advantage–with other, less demanding tasks than studying.
- **Offer a refutation or a counterargument.** For example, if you are writing in favor of lowering the legal drinking age to eighteen, you can provide evidence that doing so would not increase the number of drunk-driving accidents–a central belief of those who support the legal drinking age of twenty-one.
- **Show understanding of and sympathy for other positions.** For example, if you advocate maintaining a U.S. military presence in Afghanistan for still more years, you can acknowledge the consequent cost in lives and treasure. If you can show that the results justify the costs, your argument is strengthened by confronting the facts directly.

See the Art of Questioning box for other strategies for reducing resistance and creating the common ground that case-making requires.

THE ART OF QUESTIONING Finding Common Ground

To convince your readers, first ask these two questions:

1. **What are the opinions of people who differ from me?**
2. **Why do they hold these opinions?**

Then, based on your answers to these questions, ask three more:

1. **Do we share any goals, values, attitudes, or beliefs?**
2. **Can I agree with at least some of what they say?**
3. **What reasons and evidence can I present to change their viewpoint?**

Your answers to these questions can reduce the "us versus them" mentality that can make reasoning with those who hold alternative viewpoints frustrating and pointless. Furthermore, connecting with your readers does not mean weakening the case you are making; on the contrary, connecting strengthens your case by taking away objections and reducing resistance to the thesis you are defending.

Developing and Organizing Your Case

Start off by orienting your reader, providing what she or he needs to know to understand your topic and why it is significant. Establish the point of view toward the topic you want your readers to share with you. Make your own position clear. Divide the body of your paper into subheadings. The Best Practices box offers more suggestions to help you as you write.

BEST PRACTICES Drafting Your Case

1. Openers are important. Start your essay by putting your case in context. For example, the trails and greenways case (pages 221–23) opens by telling us what green spaces are and how they function—important because we can easily take their existence for granted.
2. Your reader may need background information to understand your case. Part of this will come from establishing the context in the opening, but sometimes additional information your reader lacks or may not remember will be necessary or desirable. Vilson (p. 224, paragraph 4) reminds us that public school teaching is associated with women, which helps to explain the relatively low percentage of men of color in the public schools.
3. Avoid summarizing, "in conclusion" conclusions. Strive instead for a memorable "parting shot," something with impact. Vilson's last sentence is a good example: "I'm not saying people from other cultures can't help us, but every student of color could use a role model. If that role model just happens to be the teacher in front of them, that's a good thing."
4. Strive to maintain the dispassionate, calm, and fair voice of the middle style throughout your essay. Simple, forceful statements allow the thesis and its supporting reasons and evidence to stand out for your reader.

Revising Your Draft

Write a brief assessment of your first draft. Exchange your draft and assessment with at least one other student, and use the revision questions in the Art of Questioning box to help each other decide what you each need to improve.

THE ART OF QUESTIONING Revision Checklist for Arguing a Case

1. **Who is the target audience?** How is the case framed—introduced—to reach that audience? **Does the writer keep this audience in mind throughout the essay?**
2. Locate the claim as stated or implied. **Is the claim held consistently throughout the essay?**
3. Locate the line or lines of argument and the reasons that explain and justify the claim. Does the writer focus on one reason at a time, staying with it until it is completely developed? How effectively does each reason appeal to the audience? **Is each reason clearly connected to the line of argument it defends?**
4. **Do you detect a logical progression in the ordering of the reasons, so that the first reason leads to the second, the second to the third, and so on?** Is there a better way to order the reasons? Can you find weak reasons that should be cut? Can you suggest reasons not included that would make the case stronger?
5. **How much will the audience resist each reason?** Is there sufficient evidence to overcome the resistance? Is the evidence for each reason clear and relevant to the reason it supports?
6. **Do you see a better way to order the evidence for any of the reasons?**
7. Look at the conclusion. **How does the conclusion clinch the case, leaving the reader with something memorable?** Can you see a way to make the conclusion more forceful?

Formulate a Plan to Guide Your Revision

The plan can be a single sentence or two: "I will cut this, rearrange that, and add a section here." Or, if you work better from an outline, develop one now. The important thing is to have a definite, clear idea of what you want to do and what moves you will make to get the results you want.

Student Example: Excerpts from Noelle Alberto's Draft

The introduction from Noelle Alberto's first draft illustrates a common problem with arguments. It opens with generalizations that do not grab the readers' attention and show how the topic of the paper will matter to them.

> Long before the computer, people have always needed to multitask. Mothers dressed their children while getting ready for work and making breakfast. Men drank their morning coffee and ate breakfast on their drive to work. Multitasking has long been a part of our society, and now, technology has granted us new means of multitasking. This multitasking is now crucial to the younger generation's way of life, but it may be hurting them academically.

Alberto did a good job of creating a context for her case against multitasking, and her thesis is clearly stated in the last sentence. However, she could have used a specific example to connect with her intended audience: college and high school students. By using a source, she was able to revise her introduction to more effectively engage her readers' attention.

> A recent National Public Radio program described the study habits of a modern teenager, Zach Weinberg of Chevy Chase, Maryland. On a typical evening, he worked on French homework while visiting his e-mail and Facebook, listening to iTunes, messaging a friend, and playing an online word puzzle (Hamilton). According to the story, Zach is a successful student, but many studies of multitasking suggest that he could be better if he focused on one thing at a time. While human beings are capable of doing two things at once if one of those things does not require much attention, like driving and drinking your morning coffee, there are some things that require a single focus, like school work. Multitasking between studies and recreational technology is not an effective way to study.

Another common problem in arguments is using sources to support and develop points but not using enough from the source to make the evidence clear and convincing. Here is an example:

> David Meyer, a professor at University of Michigan, found that when you switch to a new task, the parts of the brain that are no longer being used "start shutting things down—like neural connections to important information" (Hamilton). The work you were focusing on isn't as understandable, and when you finally get back to it you "will have to repeat much of the process that created [the information] in the first place" (Hamilton).

The source actually provides additional detail that could help Alberto more clearly explain the issue she is addressing. (Alberto's revised version of this passage appears in paragraph 3 of her final paper on page 246).

To catch this kind of revision problem, ask a friend to read your draft and to be completely honest about evidence from sources that you have not explained clearly.

Editing Your Revised Draft

Alberto's revised draft was well written. Most of her paragraphs were effective; each had an appropriate length and made a single point. In one case, however, a paragraph needed editing for wordiness and unnecessary repetition.

Original Version

This sentence repeats the idea in the first two sentences.

> Another misconception is that multitasking prepares you for the business world. "Able to multitask" used to be considered a positive on employee résumés. Now, according to the U.S. Departments of Labor and Education, businesses want an employee who "selects goal-relevant activities, ranks them, allocates time, and prepares and follows schedules" ("Skills and Competencies"). Businesses are no

longer looking for people who can multitask. They want people who can separate their tasks for the most efficient use of time. School is about preparation for the real world, and if multitasking is not functional there, it is also not functional in school. Furthermore, multitasking in the business world has been found to be completely inefficient. Christine Rosen of *The New Atlantis* writes how multitasking is "a serious threat to workplace productivity" and actually "costs the U.S. economy $650 billion a year in lost productivity" (Rosen 106). A study conducted at the University of London found that "workers distracted by e-mail and phone calls suffer a fall in IQ more than twice that found in marijuana smokers" (qtd. in Rosen 106). Multitasking has no business being in the workplace, and if multitasking is difficult and harmful in the business world, it has no place in a university either.

This sentence repeats the point of the third sentence.

The connection between sentences 5 and 6 is not tight.

Before concluding that multitasking is not functional in the business world, the writer should present the evidence for saying so.

The concluding sentence also repeats a point made earlier.

The edited version is more tightly organized and concise.

Edited Version

Another misconception is that multitasking prepares you for the business world. "Able to multitask" used to be considered a positive on employee résumés. However, multitasking has been found to be completely inefficient. Researchers found that "extreme multitasking—information overload—costs the U.S. economy $650 billion a year in lost productivity" (Rosen 106). A study conducted at the University of London found that "workers distracted by e-mail and phone calls suffer a fall in IQ more than twice that found in marijuana smokers" (qtd. in Rosen 106). Future employers do not value multitasking. Now, according to the U.S. Departments of Labor and Education, businesses want an employee who "selects goal-relevant activities, ranks them, allocates time, and prepares and follows schedules" ("Skills and Competencies"). If multitasking is difficult and harmful in the business world, it has no place in a university either.

ACTIVITY 10.3 *In Your Own Work*

Editing Your Revised Draft

We called attention to one problem in Alberto's draft: paragraph structure and flow. Look for long paragraphs in your own draft and edit in ways similar to those demonstrated here. Go on to look for other problems, especially ones you know about from previous papers. ■

Every writer has editing problems. Keep a checklist of yours. For instance, list words that you misspelled. If you did not punctuate a sentence correctly, write down the sentence and circle or underline the correct punctuation mark. If you need examples to remember other types of problems–like editing for flow–take one from your paper. Check your revised draft for your most common problems.

Study your instructor's marks and comments on every paper. Add new editing problems to your list as needed. *Always check your next paper for the problems you have listed.* In this way you can reduce your characteristic editing problems.

REVISED STUDENT EXAMPLE

Alberto 1

Noelle Alberto

Professor Channell

English 120

29 April 2016

Multitasking: A Poor Study Habit

A recent National Public Radio program described the study habits of a modern teenager, Zach Weinberg of Chevy Chase, Maryland. On a typical evening, he worked on French homework while visiting his e-mail and Facebook, listening to iTunes, messaging a friend, and playing an online word puzzle (Hamilton). According to the story, Zach is a successful student, but many studies of multitasking suggest that he could be better if he focused on one thing at a time. While human beings are capable of doing two things at once if one of those things does not require much attention, like driving and drinking your morning coffee, there are some things that require a single focus, like school work. Multitasking between studies and recreational technology is not an effective way to study. 1

Claim.

One misconception that students may have about their multitasking is that they are saving time. Some say that they feel they get more done in a shorter amount of time, but they are actually not doing two things at once. They are switching from one task to another, and constant task switching takes more time. Gloria Mark of the University of California Irvine conducted a study in which business workers were interrupted approximately every 11 minutes while working on a project. Each time, it took them about 25 minutes to return their attentions to the original project (Tugend). In study terms, if you interrupt yourself to check e-mail every ten minutes, a chapter that would take thirty minutes straight through takes over an hour to complete. 2

First reason.

What happens when people shift from one demanding task to another? David Meyer, a professor at University of Michigan, found that when you switch to a new task, the parts of the brain that are no longer being used "start shutting things down—like neural connections to important information." If a student is studying 3

Paragraph 3 gives more evidence for the first reason.

Alberto 2

French and interrupts to click open a message, the neural connections to the French homework start to shut down. To restore his level of understanding, Meyer says the student, "will have to repeat much of the process that created [the connections] in the first place" (qtd. in Hamilton).

This frequent reconnecting to prior levels of focus and understanding is a waste of time. It is time lost that could be used more efficiently. If students eliminated technological distractions during study time, they would be able to complete more work in a shorter amount of time with greater understanding. There is always time to socialize after homework and studying have been completed. 4

Paragraph 4 is a transitional paragraph that wraps up the first reason.

Another misconception is that multitasking prepares you for the business world. "Able to multitask" used to be considered a positive on employee résumés. However, multitasking has been found to be completely inefficient. Researchers found that "extreme multitasking—information overload—costs the U.S. economy $650 billion a year in lost productivity" (Rosen 106). A study conducted at the University of London found that "workers distracted by e-mail and phone calls suffer a fall in IQ more than twice that found in marijuana smokers" (qtd. in Rosen 106). Future employers do not value multitasking. Now, according to the U.S. Departments of Labor and Education, businesses want an employee who "selects goal-relevant activities, ranks them, allocates time, and prepares and follows schedules" ("Skills and Competencies"). If multitasking is difficult and harmful in the business world, it has no place in a university either. 5

Second reason.

Besides wasted time and money, another unfortunate effect of multitasking is the serious damage to students' ability to learn. Studies by psychology professor Russell Poldrack show if you multitask while learning, "that learning is less flexible and more specialized, so you cannot retrieve the information as easily" (qtd. in Rosen 107). Studies of blood flow in the brain show why. When people are task-switching, they use the "striatum, a region of the brain involved in learning new skills" (Rosen 107). In contrast people who are not multitasking "show activity in the hippocampus, a region involved in storing and recalling information" 6

Third reason.

Alberto 3

(Rosen 108). Amy Jarmon, dean at Texas Tech's School of Law, recalls a study comparing two groups of students in a large lecture class. One group of students was allowed to use laptops in class; they performed much more poorly on a memory quiz of lecture content than students not permitted to use laptops. The students who were able to check their e-mail and update their web pages during class were less capable of recalling because they were not using the hippocampus section of their brains.

This is the last reason because it has weight in showing how multitasking undermines intellectual potential.

Finally, if students get into the habit of multitasking, they could miss out on developing a personality trait prized by the most highly successful people. As Christine Rosen writes in *The New Atlantis,* that trait is "a finely honed skill for paying attention" (109). The great British scientist Sir Isaac Newton said his discoveries owed "more to patient attention than to any other talent" (qtd. in Rosen 109). The American psychologist William James wrote that the ability to pay attention marked the difference between a mature and an immature person: "The faculty of voluntarily bringing back a wandering attention, over and over again . . . is the very root of judgment, character, and will" (qtd. in Rosen). Maturity means recognizing that there is a time and place for everything. In meeting the challenges of college, I have realized the truth of this saying. When I go to the library to study, I leave my computer behind so that I will not be tempted to multitask. After an hour of focused school work, I have accomplished a great deal. It is also a good feeling to know that I have practiced self-discipline by not allowing my mind to wander. 7

Brings author's personal experience into the paper to confirm a reason.

Multitasking is now part of every student's life. The facts indicate that we need to resist it more. Multitasking is not as helpful as many people think, and its very appeal is part of the problem. It is inefficient, reduces intelligence, and impairs recall. Zach Weinberg's mother worries that Zach's multitasking study habits will cause him to "[lose] out on other skills" like the ability to concentrate (Hamilton). To think deeply rather than shallowly, we need to be able to concentrate. Therefore, the best approach is to divide study time from social time. Focusing on one thing at a time will produce better outcomes now and in the future. 8

Brings the paper back around to the student introduced in the opening, as a way to frame the argument.

Alberto 4

Works Cited

Hamilton, Jon. "Multitasking Teens May Be Muddling Their Brains." *National Public Radio,* 9 Oct. 2008, www.npr.org/templates/story/.php?storyId=95524385.

Jarmon, Amy L. "Multitasking: Helpful or Harmful? Multitasking Has Been Shown to Slow Learning and Reduce Efficiency." *Student Lawyer,* vol. 36, no. 8, 2008, pp. 33–35.

Rosen, Christine. "The Myth of Multitasking." *New Atlantis*, Spring 2008: pp. 105–110.

"Skills and Competencies Needed to Succeed in Today's Workplace." North Central Regional Education Laboratory, Learning Point Associates, n.d. Accessed 7 Apr. 2009.

Tugend, Alina. "Multitasking Can Make You Lose. . .Um. . .Focus." *The New York Times,* 25 Oct. 2008, www.nytimes.com/2008/10/25/business/yourmoney/25shortcuts.html.

CREDITS

page 221: "Building a Better Life through Greenways and Trails." Trails and Greenways Clearinghouse. Courtesy of Rails-to-Trails Conservancy, www.railstotrails.org/. **page 224:** Vilson, Jose Luis. (2015). "The Need for More Teachers of Color." The Professional Educator. Used with permission of American Educator and Jose Luis Vilson. **page 246:** Courtesy of Noelle Alberto

CHAPTER 11

Arguing to Persuade

ENGAGING QUESTIONS

In this chapter, you will engage with the following questions:

- What does it mean to persuade?
- What are the practical purposes of persuasion?
- What role do appeals play in persuasion?
- How do writers identify appropriate topics for writing that appeals for action?
- How do the elements of the rhetorical situation apply to the writing process for an appeal for action?
- How do writers apply the steps of the writing process to a persuasive writing assignment?

ARGUING TO PERSUADE, BELONGS TO THE ANCIENT DISCIPLINE OF RHETORIC, established by the Greek philosopher Aristotle about 2,500 years ago. The purpose of rhetoric, he said, was "to discover the available means of persuasion in any given case." Its driving question is, How can I move this person (or those people) to do what I believe is good, right, or desirable?

We began to practice rhetoric as children, when we persuaded our friends to play one game rather than another, or when we worked on our parents to persuade them to buy something we wanted. Persuasion has worked on us all our lives, through advertisements; sermons; editorials; and speeches, books, articles, and videos, as well as other genres that address controversial topics. Entire careers, such as those in communications or marketing, are devoted to persuasion. Persuasion plays a major role in personal and family life, in business, and in the community. It is important to examine more closely what persuasion is and how it works.

What Is Persuasion?

Advertising is one of the most common examples of moving people to action. We can learn a great deal about persuasion by studying advertisers' creative use of persuasive appeals, both verbal and visual, to market their products to targeted audiences.

Persuasion asks us to do something: spend money, give money, join a demonstration, recycle, vote, enlist, convict, or acquit. Like convincing people to change their perspective on an issue (see Chapter 10, pages 218–20, for an explanation of convincing), persuading them to take action for a cause also involves providing reasons and evidence for doing something, but it also appeals in other ways, especially by gaining people's trust and confidence and by arousing emotions favorable to the action advocated.

CONCEPT CLOSE-UP When Should You Persuade?

Pay close attention to what your course assignments call for, because the full range of persuasive appeal is not always appropriate. The more purely intellectual your topic and the more academic your audience, the more you should emphasize logical appeal, or making a good case. A clear thesis, supported by good reasons and backed by solid evidence, is usually what professors want.

When the issue is public, for example, matters of policy or right and wrong, persuasion's fuller range of appeal is typically appropriate. Making an argument for the creation of a homeless shelter in your community requires establishing your good character and personal involvement with the project as well as appealing to the emotions of your readers. *Persuasion appeals to the whole person:* mind, emotion, the capacity for trust and cooperation, even the appreciation for things said well.

College assignments calling for persuasion will often ask you to take knowledge gained from a course and use it to persuade others who lack it. For example, using what you learned from a course in environmental science, you might write an article urging Americans to buy smaller, fuel-efficient automobiles to reduce carbon dioxide emissions and oil consumption.

See page 252 for a discussion of the full range of appeals.

Why Write to Persuade?

Persuasion brings about change in the world, whether in national or local politics, in neighborhoods, on campus, in the workplace, or in personal relationships. For example, persuasion

- Sways elected officials to favor one policy over another.
- Induces people and nations to resolve conflicts peacefully rather than by violent means.
- Affects business decisions of all kinds, including how to promote a product or service.
- Influences college officials who set tuition rates and housing costs on campus.

No other kind of writing has more practical impact. If you want to make a difference in the larger world or your own community, learning how to persuade other people is the key.

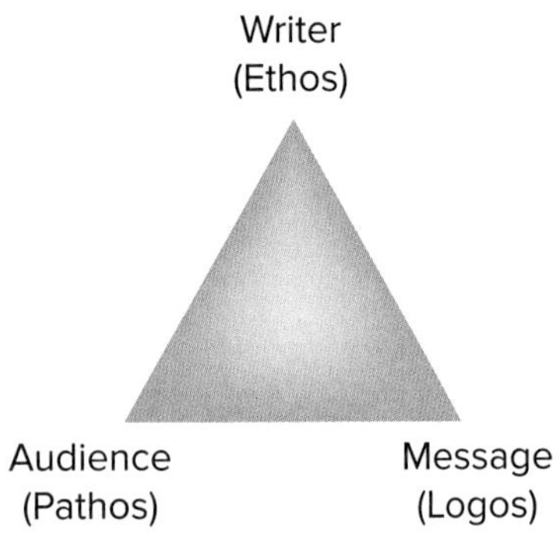

FIGURE **11.1**

The Rhetorical Triangle

Aristotle identified three types of appeals used to persuade.

How Do Writers Persuade?

Getting people to take action requires more than good reasoning. Aristotle identified three kinds of appeal (Figure 11.1):

- *Logos,* or appealing to reason
- *Ethos,* or appealing to the character of the speaker
- *Pathos,* or appealing to the emotions of the listeners

In all three, you adapt your argument to the interests, beliefs, and values of a target audience.

For example, to save money and for other reasons, Americans are looking for alternatives to cars. One of these alternatives is the motorcycle or scooter. Suppose you were writing an essay entitled, "Getting around on Two Wheels."

First, what might you say to appeal to your readers' sense of reason, or logos? You could argue that

- Motorcycles cost far less than cars to buy and maintain.
- They use on average about one-third as much gas.
- They take up only about half as much parking space.
- With proper training and equipment, they are not as dangerous to operate as many people think.

Motorcycles could help solve many problems, including reduction in traffic, greenhouse gas emissions, and American dependence on oil.

Next, how could you use pathos, or emotional appeals? The main value here is the fun of motorcycling. Motorcycles are the mechanical horse–you do not drive them, you ride them–and it should be fairly easy to appeal to the American love for freedom and adventure.

Finally, how could you appeal to ethos, or character? If you are a motorcyclist yourself, you could draw on your own experience. If not, interview friends who ride and cite what they say: You can borrow *ethos* from others, particularly if they are subject experts.

THE ART OF QUESTIONING What Really Persuades Us?

Many people say they are persuaded only by reasons and evidence. That is, *logos* matters most. Aristotle thought that *ethos* might be more powerful: If we think that a writer is intelligent, well informed, and trustworthy and has genuine concern for our needs, we will tend to believe most of what that person says. Look at advertising and you will probably conclude that *pathos* is the prime persuader. Nearly all ads appeal to emotions and attitudes most of all.

What do you think? Consider the last important decision you made. How did you persuade yourself to do one thing rather than another? If someone tried to persuade you, what kinds of appeal did the person use? Which of these appeals had the most impact on the decision you made?

READING 11.1

Soaking It All In

NICOLAS BRULLIARD

"Soaking It All In" testifies to the contribution of "forest bathing" to both physical and mental health, especially for people who live in big cities. The purpose of the article, which appeared in National Parks *magazine in 2017, is to move readers to partake in forest therapy.*

Nicholas Brulliard is a writer, a geologist, and associate editor of National Parks.

The woods are lovely, dark and deep—perfect for forest bathers searching for a little peace of mind. 1

2 We walk off the trail, careful not to crush brand-new saplings and spring blossoms that dot the forest floor of Rock Creek Park. After Melanie Choukas-Bradley finds a suitable clearing, she instructs us to set up our folding stools in a circle ("Just make sure it's stable before you sit on it"). She then reads a particularly fitting quote by naturalist John Muir—"Another glorious day, the air as delicious to the lungs as nectar to the tongue"—given that the rains that soaked the Washington, D.C., region the day before have given way to a bright, chilly April morning. Next, Choukas-Bradley asks us to share why we are here.

3 There are two Environmental Protection Agency workers coping with a new boss who had been one of the EPA's most vocal nemeses in his previous job as attorney general of Oklahoma. There is one recovering Clinton campaign worker. Many others in the group of 17 say they are suffering from the negative side effects of a fast-paced life in the nation's capital. "I need to find ways to chill out—I'm being told by everyone around me," says Lisa Hyland, an energy and national security analyst at a local think tank.

Because most people feel overburdened at least some of the time, most readers will identify with the people who have come to experience Choukas-Bradley's forest therapy. Identification is fundamental to persuasion.

4 We have come to the right person: Choukas-Bradley is a certified forest therapy guide. A naturalist who has been leading walks in and around Washington, D.C., for decades, she's also the author of several books on local green spaces, including one chronicling the seasons in Rock Creek Park, the urban forest that stretches through the city and is managed by the National Park Service. As soon as Choukas-Bradley learned about forest therapy—known also as forest bathing—in 2014, she found a certification program in Santa Rosa, California, and signed up for a weeklong workshop.

Appeals to ethos. The guide is not just anybody, but someone who is "certified," educated to guide people looking for the peace of natural places.

Studies show that slow, contemplative walks in forests, such as Washington, D.C.'s Rock Creek Park, help reduce blood pressure and boost immunity.

© Tony Bowler/Shutterstock

5 "It just resonated with me immediately," she says.

One kind of evidence for the value of forest bathing: the testimony of an expert.

6 Shinrin-yoku, which translates as taking in the forest atmosphere or forest

Historical background shows that forest bathing is not a fad. It has serious origins and purposes.

bathing, was developed by Japan's Forestry Agency in 1982 as a way to promote well-being in an overworked population that has one of the highest suicide rates in the world. The practice, which focuses on soaking up the good vibes of the forest through a slow walk or simply sitting quietly in the woods, has now spread globally. The Association of Nature and Forest Therapy Guides and Programs conducts training in the United States as well as in countries such as France and Australia.

> Note that the walks are slow and contemplative, not at all like typical aerobic exercise. This too appeals as something that will lead to getting in touch with what matters.

In Japan, the government set up dozens of forest bathing trails that people can follow on their own or under the guidance of a forest therapy ranger. Ranger stations allow people to measure their blood pressure before and after their walks, and it can take as little as 20 minutes of forest bathing for blood pressure to go down, says Florence Williams, the author of "The Nature Fix," a book about nature's health benefits. "By engaging all your senses, you can have kind of a shortcut to relaxation and a restorative state," she says. 7

> Another kind of evidence as proof of the value of forest bathing: It lowers blood pressure.

Most of the scientific research on forest bathing has come out of Japan, and much of it is good news for those who like to soak up the greenery. In addition to experiencing a drop in blood pressure, forest bathers exhibit lower levels of cortisol, a stress-related hormone. Their heart rates slow, and they see an increase in natural killer cells, which are a critical component of the immune system. Also at play are phytoncides, volatile chemicals that plants produce and people inhale on their forest walks. These substances have been linked to lower heart rates and reduced activity in the prefrontal cortex of the brain, which suggests relaxation. 8

> More quantitative or "hard" evidence for the value of forest bathing. The benefits are not merely subjective.

"All that health research really backs up what it feels like to be out in nature," Choukas-Bradley says. "It feels good. We belong there." 9

She recently took 25 high school students on a forest bathing walk on Sugarloaf Mountain in Maryland and was amazed to see how comfortable they were. They quickly relaxed, lounging on rocks and sharing their thoughts with each other and with the nature around them. "What really impressed me was how they just seemed to be soaking up the quiet," she says. "They just took to it like fish to water." 10

> Returns to the "feel good" benefits, but this time with the social interaction among participants emphasized.

Choukas-Bradley structures her walks around a series of "invitations" designed to help participants pay close attention and use all their senses. "The more tuned in you are, the more you see, the more you experience," she says. 11

Her first invitation to us is to feel the "pleasures of presence." She asks us to close our eyes, "just relax and breathe deeply into your belly and feel the goodness of the air." A woodpecker drums insistently in the distance, and the soft steps of a jogger on packed dirt echo nearby. After a few minutes, she tells us to open our eyes "and imagine that you're seeing the world for the very first time." She then picks up a "talking stick," and asks us to pass it around and take turns saying one thing we are grateful for. Many appreciate the calm and quiet of the forest, and are thankful for the people who protect it. (The walk was organized by the Rock Creek Conservancy.) "I feel grateful for the vivid shades of the green and the blue," says Kimberley Raue, an education consultant. "It's so beautiful." 12

> Persuasion often makes use of sensory descriptions of places. As in poetry, concrete details here evoke emotions.

Other invitations include paying attention to motion (one forest bather notices "tiny flecks of pollen catching the sunlight," while another has to look closely to figure out that a slug on the trail is indeed moving) and spending 10 minutes 13

> More specific images and sounds allow the reader to experience some of what forest bathing could offer them.

looking for treasure. Choukas-Bradley brings us to attention each time by ringing her small Himalayan singing bowl. One participant's treasure is "just staying put," and someone else discovers "a perfect spot of warm sun."

After each invitation, we pick up our light stools and walk a couple hundred yards at most. By the end of the three-hour walk, we probably have covered less than a mile. We form our circle one last time and pass around a thermos of warm maple sap and tea cups that Choukas-Bradley has brought with her. We read poems by Mary Oliver ("Wild Geese") and Wendell Berry ("The Peace of Wild Things"), and we each take a final turn with the talking stick to share what we'll take with us from the experience. Calm and stillness is the consensus. One participant promises to notice beauty more. As parting advice, Choukas-Bradley urges us to find a patch of nature close to where we live and return to it often. As we rise and fold our stools, she asks: "Are you ready to go back to the world?" 14

Concludes with the high value of "calm and stillness" in a world that has too little.

No one says yes. 15

Questions for Discussion

1. Using the marginal annotations and the discussion of the kinds of appeal in persuasion earlier in this chapter (pp. 252), list everything you can find from "Soaking It All In" that appeals to reason, emotion, and the character of Choukas-Bradley. What did you find most persuasive? What moved you the least?
2. What does the photo the author included with his article contribute to persuading the reader to give forest bathing a try?
3. In paragraphs 12–14 especially, the article appeals with concrete detail, sensory experience from the therapy session. Here is the appeal of style in persuasion, the use of language to create vivid impressions. How much are you moved to assent to the value of forest bathing by the style of the writing alone?

Thinking as a Writer

What Is the Rhetorical Situation?

See Chapter 3, pages 39–44, for definitions of purpose, angle, and voice.

1. What is Brulliard's *purpose*? What is his *angle* on the topic? How would you describe his *voice*?
2. Who is the intended *audience*? Is there anything you can cite that implies the target readership? How do the rational, emotional, and ethical appeals work separately and together to persuade his readers?
3. Using the marginal annotations to the reading, discuss the organization of the article. How is it framed in the opening paragraphs? How does it close or conclude the argument in the last two paragraphs without just summarizing it? ■

READING **11.2**

Grocery bags and takeout containers aren't enough. It's time to phase out all single-use plastic.

LOS ANGELES TIMES EDITORIAL BOARD

This editorial from 2017 is truly an editorial—that is, a statement from the editors of a paper (in this case, the Los Angeles Times*) expressing the opinion of the paper on a controversial issue. Editorials are one of the many ways newspapers influence public perception and opinion, and one of the major kinds of persuasive writing.*

Note that editorials usually address well-known issues already being debated. The emphasis is not on something new, but rather on contributing to the existing conversation

Faced with an unholy tonnage of chip bags, soda bottles, takeout containers and other disposable plastic items flowing into our landfills and our waters, winding up in wildlife, drinking water and food, policymakers in California have tried reining in plastic waste bit by bit. For example, more than 100 cities have adopted restrictions on polystyrene takeout containers, and the state has banned single-use plastic grocery bags. 1

Considering the magnitude of the problem, however, this item-by-item, city-by-city approach isn't going to cut it. 2

The state and local rules certainly have raised public awareness about the problem. Denying free plastic bags at checkout or providing plastic straws only on request sends consumers an important message that there's a bigger cost to these everyday items than they may have considered. But the actual flow of trash has been disrupted only modestly. 3

It's going to take more than a smattering of bans on single items to cure society of its disposable-plastic habit. The sheer volume of plastic trash now littering Earth has become impossible to ignore. It's time for environmentalists, policymakers and elected officials to start planning a broader response: phasing out *all* single-use plastic, not just the most pernicious. 4

That's right, all of it. 5

If that sounds like a pipe dream, consider what's happening across the pond. Last month, British Prime Minister Theresa May outlined a plan to eliminate plastic waste by 2042. Queen Elizabeth II kicked it off this month by banning plastic straws and bottles from royal estates, and the Church of England supported a nascent social media campaign, #plasticlesslent, to encourage its flock to give up plastic for Lent this year. Simultaneously, the European Union announced its own plan to significantly reduce plastic waste, including adopting a possible plastic tax, in a direct response to the news that China, the largest importer of plastic recyclable material, was no longer accepting "foreign garbage." 6

We don't expect President Trump or Congress to follow suit, even though it's impossible to pretend that the trash filling up in the ocean is naturally 7 occurring. That leaves it to states like California to step in. One strategy is for lawmakers to adopt a reduction goal, as they did for greenhouse gas emissions and energy derived from fossil fuels, and then to adopt specific programs to meet that goal. It's a simple but effective approach to tackling such a formidable environmental threat. Also, it puts makers of disposable plastic on notice, so they can't complain they didn't have time to adapt or move into other, less harmful product lines.

If we don't cut back now, there will eventually be more plastic than fish in 8
the ocean.

Plastic makers spent millions of dollars trying to stop the state from banning 9
single-use plastic bags. Imagine what they might unleash if all their disposable plastic products were threatened. As part of that, they will no doubt argue, as they did in the plastic bag fight, that the efforts to clean up plastic waste would mean lost jobs. But even forewarned, the plastic industry isn't likely to take an assault on its bottom line well.

But it's not a zero-sum game. Cutting jobs on a disposable plastic product line 10
doesn't automatically translate into fewer people employed. If the door closes on polystyrene takeout containers, for example, it will open for cardboard and other biodegradable alternatives.

No one expects consumers to give up convenience completely. In fact, the 11
market for bio-plastic alternatives, which are made from corn starch and other biodegradable sources, is already growing thanks to public awareness and the sporadic efforts to curb plastic waste.

Opponents will insist that the answer is just to encourage more recycling. Not 12
only is recycling not the answer (see China's diminished appetite for imported plastic trash), it has only enabled our addiction to convenient, disposable plastic packaging to deepen for some 60 years.

Yes, it's scary to think about a world where one has to carry around a reusable 13
bag or worry about a paper drinking straw falling apart mid.... Oh, wait. No, it's not. Knowing that every piece of plastic manufactured on Earth is still with us and that if we don't cut back now, there will eventually be more plastic than fish in the ocean—that's the truly frightening thought.

Questions for Discussion

1. "It's time," the authors say, "to start [. . .] phasing out all single-use plastic, not just the most pernicious. That's right, *all* of it" (paragraph 4, our emphasis). One way to get attention and stimulate interest is to advance a claim that is more extreme than one usually encounters on an issue. How did you react to this claim? Did you resist it because it is extreme or respond to it favorably because you think that plastic pollution is so dire that only an extreme claim is an adequate response to the situation?

2. How do the authors support and justify the extreme claim they advocate? That is, what do they say that makes any gradual, piecemeal approach less persuasive? What do they say that makes eliminating all plastic use a necessary and compelling position?
3. The authors are aware that their extreme position will encounter resistance on practical grounds: Can it be done at all? How much will the economy be damaged? What alternatives exist to plastic? These are among the questions thoughtful and well-informed readers will ask. What do the authors say in response to the practical objections? Do you find what they say persuasive? Why or why not?

Thinking as a Writer

What Is the Rhetorical Situation?

1. What is the editorial's *purpose*? What is its *angle* on the topic? How would you describe the writers' *voice*?
2. Who is the intended *audience*? What can you cite that implies the target readership?
3. Discuss the organization of the editorial. That is, in what order do the authors tell us what we need to know? How does the argument close without just summarizing what has been said? ■

Collaborative Activity

Using Implied Judgments

Persuasion often depends on *implied judgments, on statements that imply the writer's judgments without stating them.* For instance, the *LA Times* editorial board admit that, despite the actions taken in Europe to eliminate plastic waste, "We don't expect President Trump or Congress to follow suit, even though it's impossible to pretend that the trash filling up in the ocean is naturally occurring." The statement implies a judgment about the attitudes of some politicians toward global warming: They ignore the evidence that human behavior contributes significantly, just as they ignore the problem of plastic pollution, which is indisputably caused by human actions.

In class discussion or small group work, locate other instances of implied judgments in this chapter's readings (pp. 253–55, 256–57). Spell out in each case what the judgments imply. In each case, consider why the writer or writers chose not to make the implicit explicit. That is, why is the reader left to draw out the implied judgment?

The Assignment

Write an essay on any disputed topic that asks your readers to take action. Your topic must be something about which reasonable people could disagree. In some cases, you might advocate doing nothing when other people want to take action or stop doing something that causes more harm than benefit.

What Can I Write About?

Remember that your topic must be controversial: Various courses of action are possible, and genuine choice exists. Matters of fact are not controversial. For instance, it is a tragic fact that many veterans of the wars in Iraq and Afghanistan have committed suicide. People disagree not about this fact but rather about whether enough is being done to help prevent more suicides.

Besides selecting a controversial issue, pick one you know something about from personal experience. Civic activities, internships, and jobs can be rich sources of topics. Here are some other places to find topics:

- **Class readings.** Class readings can suggest topics for persuasion, especially if the readings themselves are persuasive, like the examples in this chapter. For instance, if the forest therapy article interests you, do further research into its practices and benefits.
- **Readings in other classes.** In a political science class, for example, you might study how presidential candidates are selected by the Democratic and Republican parties. The process is highly controversial, and many proposals for reform have been advanced. Perhaps one of the reforms struck you as especially desirable. Do some more reading about it; perhaps you have found your topic.
- **Local news or personal observations.** Read your local and campus newspapers for issues and problems of concern to your community. Take a walk around your neighborhood or campus, looking for problems that need solutions, such as wasted energy in offices, dorms, and classrooms.
- **Charities and advocacy groups.** An advocacy group is an organization that seeks to influence government decisions and gather public support for social change. Examples are the American Civil Liberties Union, the NAACP, and the Anti-Defamation League. For more examples, see the website of the National Association for Multicultural Education <https://www.nameorg.org/advocacy_groups.php>

How Do I Appeal for Action? Questioning the Rhetorical Situation

Begin by picturing a rhetorical situation for your writing project, a real-world context for communicating. You should consider the key variables in any act of communication: a writer with something to say, a reader the writer wishes to reach, and a kind of text appropriate to the writing task. These three variables will affect many decisions in the composing process.

Writer: What Is My Purpose, and What Impression Should Readers Have of Me?

The general purpose of persuasion is to move your readers to take action. Given your topic, consider exactly what action your readers can reasonably take. As readers of the *LA Times* editorial, for instance, we can stop or greatly reduce using disposable plastic items, but we cannot take the collective, political action required to eliminate all plastic waste, as the editorial advocates.

Audience: Who Is My Reader?

In many cases, what you want done implies your audience so strongly that virtually no choice exists. For instance, the *LA Times* editorial requires an audience of people already committed to environmental causes. In some cases, however, you could reasonably choose between two groups of readers or among or across several. For instance, if your topic is charter schools (privately owned and operated alternatives to public schools), your readers could be students, their parents, local political leaders, state legislators, officials directly involved with educational policy in your state, or some combination of these. In such a case, *choose the readership you know best* because it is difficult to appeal to an audience you know only as an abstract entity, such as state legislators. Once you make your choice, be sure to advocate action your readers can actually take. Parents cannot pass laws, but they can influence educational policy by voting for a candidate in your local district who favors the action you favor toward charter schools.

Text: What Moves Can I Make?

Persuasion joins the appeal of reasoning well to the appeal of the writer's character and to your reader's emotions. The moves of reasoning are discussed in Chapter 10, on page 234. Possible moves for appealing to character and to emotion include the following:

Character

- If you have personal experience with your topic, share your experience with your reader. For example, an article encouraging your readers to become involved with Habitat for Humanity will be more persuasive if you have helped build a house for a poor family and can talk about how satisfying your participation was.
- Provide background and explanatory information as needed. For example, the Habitat for Humanity article could include information about the organization itself and how people can get involved. Readers respond positively to writers who are well informed.
- Show that you are thinking about your reader's concerns and interests. Advocating the purchase of a car powered by an electric motor obviously benefits the environment. But it also has benefits for an owner, which you can specify in detail. Readers tend to trust writers whose self-interest is either absent or subordinate to doing something that benefits them.

Emotion

- Share your emotional reactions through simple, direct statements of how you feel or felt. If you are writing about date rape, for example, and you are a victim, readers will sympathize with feelings of anger and helplessness. They will also expect to read about your emotional responses.

- Arouse appropriate emotional responses in your readers by depicting a situation that made you happy, sad, grateful, resentful, and so on—whatever emotion or emotions you felt and want your readers to feel. If you are writing about police profiling and you were stopped and interrogated, describing that experience can help readers who have never been "shaken down" to understand the damage profiling does.
- As a rule, it is not a good idea to say that people should not feel what they feel. However, sometimes common emotional responses to your topic can be inappropriate and an obstacle to persuasion. For example, influenced by the "Welfare Queen" stereotype, too many people see all people on welfare as lazy and dishonest. Counter these negative judgments by describing the actual circumstances of most recipients and/or by citing data that indicate that welfare fraud is the exception rather than the norm.

How Do I Write Persuasively? Engaging the Writing Process

No two people compose an appeal for action in exactly the same way, and even the same person may go through the writing process in different ways for different projects. Nevertheless, because no one can attend to everything at once, there are phases in handling any significant writing task. You **explore the topic** to get a sense of whether it will work for you and what you might be able to do with it; if the topic is working out for you, then you move into **preparing to write,** generating more content and planning your draft.

The next phase is **drafting your paper,** getting a version, however rough it may be, on screen or paper so that you can work toward the final draft. Getting there involves two further phases: **revising your draft,** where you make major improvements in it, followed by **editing your draft,** taking care of errors, sentences that do not read well, paragraphs lacking focus and flow, and so on.

Exploring Your Topic

The following questions will help you delve into your topic and begin writing about it.

1. What do you want your readers to do?
2. Who are your readers? Describe them as specifically as you can. What about them will be relevant to your argument? Consider age, religion, income bracket, occupation, political orientation, education, and gender.
3. Reader awareness is important: How much will readers know about the problem, question, or issue you intend to address? What is their likely attitude?
4. Why do you care about this topic? What makes you a credible writer on behalf of your position?
5. What is the best reason you can give your readers for doing what you want them to do? State it as a sentence. Do you have a second reason in mind?

6. What additional ideas do you have for appealing to your readers? What values and beliefs can you appeal to?
7. If your topic requires more than general knowledge and personal experience, what sources have you found to support your argument? What additional material might you need?

See Chapter 10, page 220 for more information on case structure and strategy.

ACTIVITY 11.1 *Thinking as a Writer*

Responding to the Exploration Questions

Write answers to the seven questions above. Consider whether your topic may be too large for the space you have; limiting your topic can save time later, when you have to rewrite a draft that takes on too much. If you have good reasons in mind, write them down. If you have ideas for appealing to reader emotions, values, and beliefs, write these down too. Include whatever insights you have gained from personal experience. Exchange them with a partner via e-mail and/or in small group sessions in or out of class to help each other refine and develop ideas for and approaches to the first draft. ■

Preparing to Write

Some writers prefer to go straight to drafting, working out their appeals in several drafts. We recommend going through the following steps first, which most writers find helpful.

Strategies for Appeals

As the readings above (Readings 11.1 and 11.2) and the student example at the end of the chapter (pages 272–76) show, you have many options in persuasive writing. Ask yourself the following questions as you begin to develop your essay:

- Is there an opportunity to tell a personal or a historical story? Brulliard provides a good model for storytelling as persuasion.
- How can I make a **case,** *an argument with reasons and evidence,* to support the action I advocate?
- How can I join the case to ethical and emotional appeals, persuading my audience through self-presentation and appropriate feelings?
- When I encounter good reasons for another course of action, how can I refute or use those reasons to favor my own? *The LA Times* editorial is a good model for how to make this move.
- How can I defend my course of action as the best alternative in an imperfect world? Student Natsumi Hazama (see pages 272–76) does not offer a perfect solution to the problem of too much pressure from Asian parents, only an approach that reduces the harm it does.
- How might I use photos and other visual means of persuasion effectively? For examples, see the photo in "Soaking It All In" (page 253).

Doing Research

If the assignment calls for research, use the techniques for finding and evaluating sources (see Chapters 16 and 17, pages 358–71, 372–78) to find articles, books, and online materials about or related to your topic.

Thinking More about Persuasive Appeals

Thinking through the appeals to reason, character, and emotion helps many writers build up confidence, energy for drafting, and a more detailed plan to guide the first draft.

The Appeal through Logic: Articulating a Claim

You know what you want your readers to do; try formulating it as a claim. These suggestions will help. Your claim is a statement you will defend, not just a description of something factual.

Original Version (not a claim)

Students are choosing majors based on future income instead of interests and abilities.

Revised Version (claim)

Students should find a major that excites their desire to learn rather than one that promises only financial rewards.

The claim should be focused and specific and directed at a readership.

Original Version (too general)

Parents need to be stricter.

Revised Version (better focused)

Parents need to teach children to be sensitive to other people in restaurants, stores, and other public places.

The claim uses concrete nouns and verbs, rather than vague and indirect wording, to make its point.

Original Version (vague)

One's natural abilities cannot grow into an established intelligence unless a person learns how to control their attention and concentration.

Revised Version (more concise)

Even highly talented people need to learn to control attention and concentration to develop their full potential.

Some claims may need to be qualified.

Original Version (too absolute)

High schools need a vocational track.

Revised Version (qualified)

Unless they send all their students to college, high schools should offer a high-quality vocational track.

■ ACTIVITY 11.2 *In Your Own Work*

Refining Your Claim

Share several versions of your claim in class or by an e-mail exchange with one or several other students. Ask for feedback based on which version best states your thesis and creates least resistance in your audience. ■

Developing Reasons for Your Claim

Once you have a working version of the claim, begin to formulate reasons for it—why your readers should take the action you are arguing for. Focus on the fit between your reasons and the values and beliefs of your readers.

See the Best Practices box that follows for some places to find reader-oriented reasons.

BEST PRACTICES Places to Find Audience-Based Reasons

- In the audience's *beliefs and values.* Think about their politics and the values of their culture or subculture.
- In *traditions and traditional texts.* What books, ceremonies, ideas, places, and people do they revere?
- In *expert opinion and/or data.* Draw on the reasoning of qualified experts your audience will respect—mention them by name and cite their credentials. Construct reasons from information and statistics taken from sources your readers will know and trust.
- In *comparisons or analogies* your audience would accept. Analogies work because they liken the less familiar and known to the more familiar and known. Those who oppose genetic engineering, for example, often reason that altering human genes is like altering nature—it has bad side effects.
- In establishing *cause and effect.* If you can show the action you would like the audience to take will lead to positive consequences, you have a good reason. Of course, you will need evidence to show that the cause-and-effect relationship exists.

Making a Brief of Your Case

The brief is a concise version of a logical argument. It has three levels:

1. The claim, what you want your readers to do
2. A reason or reasons explaining why
3. Evidence to support each reason

Briefs can help in preparing to write, but keep in mind that new ideas will come to you as you draft. Also bear in mind that a brief is not a plan for the whole paper, only its logical appeal.

Student Example: Natsumi Hazama's Brief

Student Natsumi Hazama wrote a persuasive paper urging Asian parents not to push their children so hard in school. Here is the brief she developed for her argument:

Claim: Asian-American parents need to moderate their demands for high career goals and obedience to parents, allowing their children to find goals and challenges that are right for them.

Reason: Too much pressure can lead to depression and even suicide.
Evidence: CNN.com article on college student suicides; *Chronicle of Higher Education* online article about depression and suicide at Cornell

Reason: Overprotective parenting does not prepare children for the independence of college life.
Evidence: Asian Outlook website quotes

Reason: Students will be more successful at careers they prefer, not the limited choices of engineering and medicine preferred by their parents.
Evidence: My personal experience

Reason: Constant pressure to do better rather than praise for what has been accomplished leads to low self-esteem.
Evidence: Class reading by Csikszentmihalyi

ACTIVITY 11.3 *In Your Own Work*

Formulate Your Brief

Outline the logical case you will make. If possible, include supporting evidence for each reason. ■

The Appeal through Ethos: Presenting Good Character

Ethos is self-presentation. In general, you should

- Sound informed and engaged with your topic.
- Show awareness of your readers' views.
- Treat competing courses of action with respect but show that your solution is better.
- Refer to your values and beliefs, your own ethical choices.
- When appropriate, reinforce your ethos by citing information and expert testimony from sources your readers respect and trust.

See the Art of Questioning on the next page for a more specific list of ideas for establishing good ethos.

THE ART OF QUESTIONING Establishing Ethos with Your Readers

1. Do you have a shared local identity—as members of the same organization, the same institution, the same town or community, the same set of beliefs?
2. Can you get your audience to see that you and they have a common cause or perspective?
3. Are there experiences you might share? These might include dealing with siblings, helping friends in distress, caring for ailing family members, struggling to pay debts, or working hard for something.
4. Can you connect through a well-known event or cultural happening, perhaps a movie, a book, a political rally, or something in the news?

ACTIVITY 11.4 *Writer's Notebook*

Establishing a Persuasive Ethos

Write about what attitudes you could convey in your paper that will show your good character and values. What can you talk about that will get these appeals across to your readers? ■

The Appeal through Pathos: Using Emotional Appeals

Sharing your own emotions is the most honest way to appeal to your audience's feelings. However, simply saying what your feelings are will not arouse emotion in others. How can you arouse emotions?

Show the audience the *concrete images and facts* that aroused the feelings in you. Brulliard used a photo and **testimonials, comments from people supporting his viewpoint,** to appeal to his readers' desire for peace and relaxation.

In short, *give your readers a picture,* in words or otherwise.

ACTIVITY 11.5 *Writer's Notebook*

Resources for Emotional Appeal

Freewrite to identify specific details and images related to your topic that move you. If you can, make lists of what you recall. Visit or revisit places relevant to your topic and take notes or pictures. ■

Drafting Your Paper

By now you have generated many ideas for appealing to your readers. As you move toward drafting, first focus attention on two main concerns:

- **Your angle and your voice,** how you want to sound to your reader
- Your draft's **development and organization**

What Stance and Voice Are Appropriate for Persuasion?

Appealing for action is in part the calm voice of reason described in Chapter 10 (see the section, Writer: What Is My Purpose and What Impression Should Readers Have of Me? on page 233): your opinion stated clearly, directly, forcefully, and with confidence. To this, persuasion adds the *controlled passion* of emotional appeal, designed to arouse appropriate feelings in your readers.

Look at paragraph 12 in Brulliard's "Soaking It All In." Here is the voice of controlled passion:

> Her first invitation to us is to feel the "pleasures of presence." She asks us to close our eyes, "just relax and breathe deeply into your belly and feel the goodness of the air." A woodpecker drums insistently in the distance, and the soft steps of a jogger on packed dirt echo nearby. After a few minutes, she tells us to open our eyes "and imagine that you're seeing the world for the very first time." She then picks up a "talking stick," and asks us to pass it around and take turns saying one thing we are grateful for. Many appreciate the calm and quiet of the forest, and are thankful for the people who protect it. (The walk was organized by the Rock Creek Conservancy.) "I feel grateful for the vivid shades of the green and the blue," says Kimberley Raue, an education consultant. "It's so beautiful."

Brulliard wants to share the feelings of calm and uplift, the positive feelings of being out in the forest on a good day, but he does so without excessive emotion and in the context of the actual happenings of forest therapy.

Developing and Organizing Your Appeal

Here are some answers to common questions that will help with both development and organization.

1. **How might I open the paper?** Here are some possibilities:
   - An anecdote (short narrative) based on your own experience or something you found in a source.
   - A surprising fact or opinion relevant to your topic.
   - A question that will stimulate reader interest.
   - A description of a person or place relevant to your claim.
   - A memorable quotation, with commentary from you.

   Introductions are often more than one paragraph, and your claim can appear anywhere in the paper.
2. **What background material should I provide?** Here are two principles:
   - Offer *only* what your readers need.
   - Place it just before the section or sections of your essay where the background is relevant.
3. **Where will I show my connection to the topic?** The introduction is often a good place. In the second paragraph of "Soaking It All In," Brulliard places himself in the scene simply by using the word "we." From then on, we think of the author as a participant as well as an observer.

4. **Will I present opposing views and, if so, where?** How you handle opposing views depends on your reader's relationship to them. If you think your readers will have an opposing view, the best strategy is to engage it first in several paragraphs. Otherwise handle opposing views after your case and with less space devoted to them.
5. **How will I order my reasons?** If your case has three or more reasons, starting and ending with your stronger ones is good strategy. In developing your reasons, *remember that multiple paragraphs are often necessary to develop a reason.*

See Chapter 32 for more on using visuals.

6. **What visuals might I use and where should they go?** For example, a student who wrote against wearing fur added much to the *pathos* of her argument by including photographs of animals injured by trappers.
7. **How will I conclude my paper?** Try one of these ending strategies:
   - Look back at your introduction. Perhaps some idea you used there to attract your reader's attention could come into play again—a question you posed has an answer, a problem you raised has a solution.
   - End with a well-worded quotation, and follow it up with comments of your own.
   - Repeat an idea you used earlier in the essay, but with a twist. The *LA Times* editorial repeats the idea of "frightening thought" in the last paragraph effectively.

Revising Your Draft

The strongest revisions begin with assessing the draft yourself. Put it aside for a day or two. *Take the point of view of someone reading your paper.* Ask the questions in the Art of Questioning box to assess it.

THE ART OF QUESTIONING Revision Checklist for Appealing for Action

1. Is it clear what the author wants the readers to do? Where is it stated most clearly? Is this the best place to state it?
2. Does the paper have a shape and sense of direction? Does it have parts that clearly play their individual roles in making the argument? Could you make any suggestions for rearranging the parts to make it easier to follow?
3. Do the reasons for taking this action stand out as such? Are they good reasons for the intended audience? Is there a better way to order the reasons?
4. Has the author given enough evidence to support each reason?
5. Has the author shown awareness of and sympathy for the audience's perspective?
6. Are the individual paragraphs unified, and is their contribution to the section in which they appear clear?
7. Can you hear the author's voice in this paper? Do you think readers would find this voice appealing? Does the author exhibit a personal connection with the topic?
8. Where do you see the author using emotional appeals? Are they appropriate? Do they move you?
9. Do you have suggestions to improve the introduction and the conclusion?
10. Has the author smoothly integrated the sources used or just dropped them in?

ACTIVITY 11.6 *In Your Own Work*

Revising Your Draft

After getting a second opinion, formulate a revision strategy:

1. Decide what you think are the useful criticisms and comments. Reassess your self-criticisms—do you still see the same problems? Make a list of specific items you intend to work on. "The first point on page 3 needs more development" is an example of what we mean by specific.
2. Divide your list into two categories: big revisions that will change all or much of the paper and smaller revisions requiring only adding, deleting, or rewriting a paragraph or two.
3. Ponder the best order for doing big revisions. For example, suppose that you need to rearrange the order of your reasons and improve your tone throughout. Rearrange first because attending to tone will require changing many sentences, and each sentence revision can have an impact on the flow of ideas from sentence to sentence.
4. Finalize your plan with a step-by-step list. Usually the spot revisions can be done in any order, but tackle the ones requiring the most work first, leaving the easier ones for last. ■

Student Example: Excerpts from Natsumi Hazama's Draft

Common revision problems include improving opening paragraphs and making points more persuasive.

Revising Opening Paragraphs

A revised draft of Natsumi Hazama's paper appears on pages 272–76. To see how revision improved it, read the following excerpts from her first draft.

Original Version

One night in 1990, Eliza Noh got off the phone with her sister in college. Eliza knew her sister was depressed and something bad might happen. She sat down to write a letter to support and encourage her. But it was too late. By the time the letter arrived, her sister was dead. She had taken her own life. Eliza believed that too much pressure to succeed contributed to her sister's death. This tragedy led Noh to pursue a career in studying the effects of pressure on Asian-American students.

Revised Version

Growing up in an Asian-American family I was raised to stay close to my family and always to strive to be number one in my classroom. My parents were both born in Japan and came to America for my father's work. My father was a very intelligent man who wanted me to go into either medicine or engineering. My parents also made me go to Japanese School every Saturday to learn to read and write my native tongue. Going to school six days a week left no time for a social life. The girls at my English school would always have sleep over parties on Friday nights, but I was studying for my next Japanese test. I excelled in school, but that wasn't good enough. Even if I scored a 98 on my math test, my parents would say, "Why didn't you get a 100?"

Do you agree that opening with Hazama's own story is more effective? The original opening moved to paragraph 15; do you think this arrangement is better?

ACTIVITY 11.7 *In Your Own Work*

Revising the Introduction

Look at the opening of your own draft. Why did you choose to open the paper as you did? If you are not happy with the opening, do you see material elsewhere in the draft that might work better? If not, review opening strategies discussed above (page 267) and try one of those instead. ■

Revising to Bring Out the Structure of the Argument

Here is a body paragraph from Hazama's first draft, offering a reason and evidence in support of her claim.

Original Version

Dr. Henry Chung, assistant vice president for student health at New York University and executive director of the NYU student Health Center, says "Asian-American/Asian students, especially males, are under unique pressures to meet high expectations of parents by succeeding in such traditional predetermined careers as medicine and engineering" (qtd. in Ramanujan). Asian students feel that even though they aren't interested in these fields they must major in them and they end up stressing themselves out. Because students major in fields that they aren't interested in they end up not doing as well in school as they could. If you don't have a passion for your job you feel like you are working twice as hard with loads of work on your shoulders.

Revised Version

Along with bringing home straight "A's," parents also urge their children to major in a subject that they see as respectable. Dr. Henry Chung, assistant vice president for student health at New York University and executive director of the Health Center, points out that "Asian-American/Asian students, especially males, are under unique pressures to meet high expectations of parents by succeeding in such traditional predetermined careers as medicine and engineering" (qtd. in Ramanujan). Even if these fields are not areas of strength or interest, Asian-American students feel that they must major in them. Their grades may start to slip, but as Nguyen at Berkeley says, "Some stay in these majors because they think that they need to. They're reluctant to leave because their parents don't understand: 'If you're not a doctor or engineer, then what are you?'" (qtd. in "Mental").

In the revised version, how has the argument emerged better in the opening sentence? How has it been supported better?

ACTIVITY 11.8 *In Your Own Work*

Evaluating the Structure of Your Case

Look over the body paragraphs of your draft. Open with a point of your own; use your sources to support and develop it. Look over your entire draft. How could revising make your reasons stand out more? ■

Editing Your Revised Draft

A common editing problem is integrating source material into your own writing.

Integrating Sources

Using sources responsibly means not only citing the source but also identifying the source by name. Hazama noticed that she was not always clear about whose words were in quotation marks. Here is an example of the problem:

See Chapter 18, page 386, for more on this important research skill.

Original Version

When kids come to college they receive conflicting messages. "The message at home is that their priority should be to look after their parents and take care of their families" ("Mental"). But the message you get at college and from your friends is that you need to learn to think for yourself and be who you are and do what is best for you. This is a different value than the Asian culture so Asian students feel guilty for not doing what they are supposed to be doing ("Mental").

As the underlined phrases in the edited version show, identifying your sources by name and qualifications not only helps your reader understand who is saying what, but also increases the authority of the quoted statements.

Edited Version

According to Diem Nguyen, a UC Davis student affairs officer, when Asian American students come to college, they sometimes end up partying too much because they are not used to this freedom (qtd. in "Mental"). Also, when kids come to college they receive conflicting messages. Nadine Tang, a psychotherapist who has counseled students at UC Berkeley, says they get the message at home that family is their top priority, but the message at college is "to be who you are, learn to be yourself and do what is best for you. . . . You feel guilty for not doing what you're supposed to and not fulfilling your obligations" (qtd. in "Mental").

ACTIVITY 11.9 *In Your Own Work*

Citing Sources

If you are using the words of someone quoted in your source, are you *identifying the actual speaker of the words* as well as citing the source? If not, identify this person as Hazama did in the revised version above. ■

REVISED STUDENT EXAMPLE

Hazama 1

Natsumi Hazama

English 1301

Professor Channell

25 August 2017

Is Too Much Pressure Healthy?

Hazama uses paragraphs 1, 2, and 3, to tell her personal story, allowing non-Asian readers to understand the issue more concretely and the author to build her authority *(ethos).*

1 Growing up in an Asian-American family I was raised to stay close to my family and always to strive to be number one in my classroom. My parents were both born in Japan and came to America for my father's work. My father was a very intelligent man who wanted me to go into either medicine or engineering. My parents also made me go to Japanese School every Saturday to learn to read and write my native tongue. Going to school six days a week left no time for a social life. The girls at my English school would always have sleep over parties on Friday nights, but I was studying for my next Japanese test. I excelled in school, but that wasn't good enough. Even if I scored a 98 on my math test, my parents would say, "Why didn't you get a 100?"

Creates sympathy *(pathos)* for children treated this way.

2 When I was in 8th grade my father was diagnosed with colon cancer. He grew very ill, and my parents actually knew that he was dying but didn't tell my sister and me. One week, all my relatives from Japan flew in; at the end of that week he passed away. It was a horrible experience, but my mother, sister, and I helped each other, and with the support of all of our family and friends we got through it.

3 Starting high school was completely different. Because my mother knew growing up without a father was hard enough, she just wanted me to be happy. Coming home with a few B's on my report card was okay now. My mother didn't pressure me to get good grades; she basically let me do whatever I wanted. I wasn't in the top 10% of my class, didn't get straight A's or take all AP courses. However, I was completely satisfied with my high school experience. I was part of the nationally ranked cheerleading team. I had higher self-esteem. I would give anything to have my father still alive, but I have learned to think for myself and to set my own goals.

Strong emotional appeal to American belief in the value of a balanced approach to school and extracurricular activities.

Hazama 2

Shows good reader awareness: author not rejecting her culture—especially important for her Asian-American parent audience.

Thesis: Note that it asks for a course of action Asian–American parents can take.

My situation before the death of my father is common among Asian-American 4
families. I understand it is part of my culture, which I value. However, Asian-American parents need to moderate their demands and allow their children to find goals and challenges that are right for them.

Important section for explaining cultural norms to non-Asian audience—shows reader awareness again.

Wenju Shen and Weimin Mo, experts on educating Asian-Americans, describe 5
our ways as rooted in Confucianism: “The Confucian ethical code. . .holds that the first loyalty is to the family, even above their allegiance to their country and religion.”

This closeness to family can bring pressures. In an Asian family the most 6
important thing is to always keep your “face.” “Face” means family pride. “Family” means not only immediate relatives, extended relatives, dead ancestors, but also anyone with my last name. To fail in any obligation to the family is to “lose face” and bring shame to myself, my parents, my relatives, and all my ancestors.

First reason to reduce excessive pressure: escape stereotypes.

While family should be important, this cultural pressure to succeed helps to 7
create harmful stereotypes. As Shen and Mo point out, the “whiz kid” stereotype of Asian-American students encourages their parents to maintain practices “not compatible with the values and beliefs of American society.” Asian-American parents need to learn how to balance obligations to the family with the more individual values of Americans.

Second reason to reduce excessive pressure: greater personal fulfillment.

A more balanced approach to parenting will lead children to more fulfilling 8
lives. Mihaly Csikszentmihalyi, a psychologist at University of Chicago, is noted for his work on happiness, creativity, and subjective well-being. His book, *Finding Flow,* describes the kind of family that leads children to develop their full potential: “they combine discipline with spontaneity, rules with freedom, high expectations with unstinting love. An optimal family system is complex in that it encourages the unique individual development of its members while uniting them in a web of affective ties” (88). Asian-American parents should raise their children more like this. Too much parental pressure hinders what Csikszentmihalyi calls “flow,” a state of mind where the person is fully engaged in what he or she is doing for its own sake (29–32).

Hazama 3

Third reason to reduce excessive pressure: not good preparation for independence of college.

9 For most Asian students, college is the first time they have spent a significant amount of time away from home. Because they aren't used to this responsibility and freedom that they have at college, these students don't know what to do with themselves. They are exposed to new experiences and as a result, they sometimes end up partying too much because they are not used to this freedom that they have.

Fourth reason for reducing excessive pressure: puts young people in a bind.

10 They also receive conflicting messages. Nadine Tang, a psychotherapist who has counseled students at UC Berkeley, says the message at home is that family matters most, but the message at college is "be who you are, learn to be yourself and do what is best for you. . . . You feel guilty for not doing what you're supposed to and not fulfilling your obligations" (qtd. in "Mental").

11 That is what life is all about, fulfilling your own potential, as Csikszentmihalyi says. Unfortunately, even if Asian American students receive excellent grades in school, they tend to have a lower self-esteem than other students (Csikszentmihalyi 24). I think this is because their parents never praise them. Asian-American parents see success as a duty, so children should not receive praise; instead they are told to do even better and aim still higher (Shen).

12 Along with bringing home straight "A's," parents also urge their children to major in a subject that they see as respectable. Dr. Henry Chung, assistant vice president for student health at New York University and executive director of the Health Center, points out that "Asian-American/Asian students, especially males, are under unique pressures to meet high expectations of parents by succeeding in such traditional predetermined careers as medicine and engineering" (qtd. in Ramanujan). Even if these fields are not areas of strength or interest, Asian-American students feel that they must major in them. Their grades may start to slip, but as Nguyen at Berkeley says, "Some stay in these majors because they think that they need to. They're reluctant to leave because their parents don't understand: 'If you're not a doctor or engineer, then what are you?'" (qtd. in "Mental").

Evidence for fourth reason: Asian-American expert opinion.

Fifth reason to reduce excessive pressure: better mental health.

13 The result can be destructive to a student's mental health, often leading to anxiety and depression. These problems are more common in Asian-American students than in the general population ("Mental"). When Asian-American students

Hazama 4

are unhappy, they usually don't seek help, even though the best way to recover is to get counseling. Chung at NYU explains that in Asian culture "suffering and working hard are accepted as part of life, a cultural paradigm" (Ramanujan). Asian-American students don't get counseling because discussing emotional problems is a sign of weakness ("Mental"). They also do not tell their parents about their problems. As a psychologist at Baylor University, Dr. Dung Ngo, says, "The line of communication in an Asian culture goes one way. It's communicated from the parents downward" (qtd. in Cohen). If students can't express their anger and frustration, it turns into helplessness; they feel like there is no way out.

Use of Asian-American authorities to back up fifth reason, sources her audience must respect.

Suicide is therefore common among Asian-American students. According to CNN, Asian-American women age 15–24 have the highest suicide of any ethnic group. Suicide is the second-leading cause of death (Cohen). At Cornell University, between 1996 and 2006 there were 21 suicides; 13 of these were Asian or Asian-American students (Ramanujan). 14

CNN tells the story of how Eliza Noh, a professor of Asian-American studies at California State University at Fullerton, decided to devote her studies to depression and suicide among Asian-American women. One night in 1990, she had been talking to her sister, a college student, on the telephone. She knew her sister was depressed. She sat down to write a letter to encourage her. It was too late. By the time the letter arrived, she had taken her life. Noh believes that the pressure to succeed contributed to her sister's death (Cohen). 15

Strong evidence for the harm of excessive pressure, both data and an actual instance of suicide.

I have lived both sides, living with pressure and without. Living without pressure has enabled me to think for myself and be happier. Parents need to give their children support and encouragement, allow them to make their own decisions about goals, and most of all, stop pressuring them so much. 16

Hazama 5

Works Cited

Cohen, Elizabeth. "Push to Achieve Tied to Suicide in Asian-American Women." *CNN.com/Health*, 16 May 2007, www.cnn.com/2007/HEALTH/05/16/asian.suicides/.

Csikszentimihalyi, Mihaly. *Finding Flow: The Psychology of Engagement with Everyday Life.* Basic Books, 1997.

"Mental Health of Asian Youth a Growing Concern." *Asian Outlook—Challenges for Today's Asian American Students.* Asian Pacific Fund, Fall/Winter 2007.

Ramanujan, Krishna. "Health Expert Explains Asian and Asian-American Students' Unique Pressures to Succeed." *Chronicle Online,* Chronicle of Higher Education, 19 Mar. 2006, www.news.cornell.edu/stories/2006/04/health-expert-explains-asian-students-unique-pressures-succeed.

Shen, Wenju, and Weimin Mo. "Reaching Out to Their Cultures: Building Communication with Asian American Families." *ERIC*, n.p., 1990. Accessed 15 Apr. 2008, archive.org/stream/ERIC_ED351435/ERIC_ED351435_djvu.txt.

CREDITS

page 250: Edward P. J. Corbett. *The Rhetoric and Poetics of Aristotle*. Modern Library, 1984. **page 253:** National Parks Conservation Association, "Soaking It All In." Used with permission. **page 256:** Times Editorial Board. (2018, Feb. 20). "Grocery Bags and Takeout Containers Aren't Enough. It's Time to Phase Out All Single-Use Plastic." Used by permission of the Los Angeles Times. **page 272:** Courtesy of Natsumi Hazama

CHAPTER 12

Writing an Evaluation

ENGAGING QUESTIONS

In this chapter, you will engage with the following questions:

- What does it mean to evaluate a subject?
- What are the purposes for writing evaluations?
- How do writers use criteria when evaluating?
- How do writers analyze the rhetorical situation for an evaluation?
- How do writers apply the steps of the writing process to an evaluation assignment?

TO SURVIVE, HUMAN BEINGS HAVE ALWAYS ASSESSED THE WORLD AROUND THEM, asking, "How good is x?" and posing answers to that question, such as, "This plant was good to eat, or this place was good for hunting." In today's consumer-driven culture, anything can be evaluated and almost everything is; "x" could be a movie, a car, a company, or a health care plan.

Evaluation is so common that every genre of writing evaluates in some way or another: Editorials evaluate politicians and policies; consumer reports (including online reviews on sites like Yelp and Hotels.com) evaluate virtually every good and service; and reviews and journal articles evaluate literary works, scientific research, engineering designs, public opinion, and how well people behaved in the past—in short, anything people can study. In business, we assess how well a corporation did in the last quarter; in public life, we debate the value of a speech; in personal writing, we exchange e-mails or texts that judge yesterday's social event; and in academic writing, we compare solutions to a particular problem, such as how best to feed an overpopulated world projected to exceed nine billion people by 2050.

What Is an Evaluation?

An evaluation is always *someone's* judgment about the quality, utility, value, or beauty of something, so personal or subjective experience comes into play. We can acknowledge the subjective aspect of our judgments in many ways. For example, when warning a friend that a restaurant we recommend serves highly spiced food, we say something like, "You know me–I like hot food," which implies, "Don't go there if you don't."

Magazines like *Consumer Reports* offer evaluations of everything from small electronics to cars, providing reliable information for us to make the best choices possible.

NetPhotos/Alamy Stock Photo

Open societies like ours–in which people are free to offer opinions about anything–provide and encourage methods for making evaluations less subjective. For example, we are careful to compare "apples and apples" rather than "apples and oranges." We can usefully compare Miami Beach with other beach vacation destinations but not with the mountains of Colorado, where people go to ski, hike, or breathe mountain air.

Why Write to Evaluate?

Evaluations are *guides to conduct, ways to make informed choices about something.* Sometimes nothing less is at stake than survival, as when evaluations we consult lead us to drive a safe car, seek medical treatment from a highly-rated hospital, or buy nutritious food that promotes health. More often evaluations enhance the quality of life, making it more pleasurable, or more efficient, as when we consult *Consumer Reports* or online user reviews before purchasing a refrigerator or laptop. Because some manufactured items are made better than others of the same type, reliable information matters in our selection.

Indeed, when we stop to consider all the evaluations we encounter every day and in every dimension of our lives, little else we can write or read is likely to have more practical impact. Our choices largely determine our present and shape our possibilities for the future, so making good choices matters deeply.

How Do Writers Evaluate?

People are inclined to ignore or dismiss evaluations that seem merely subjective. "It's just his or her opinion," we say. Some judgments, however, just *are* subjective by nature, such as questions of fashion or aesthetic taste. The fashion blogger Scott Schuman of "The Sartorialist" photographs people on the street that he deems fashionable, including the woman in Milan shown on this page.

Subjective judgments can have value. Someone's verdict about a style may be a reliable indicator of what is fashionable to people who care about fashion. Most of the blog's readers agreed that this woman has style.

In any case, we cannot exclude subjective judgments from evaluation, nor should we wish to, because they express an individual's **sensibility,** a *mostly nonconscious "feel" for what matters most or has high or low interest or value in his or her experience.* We all have sensibilities, and they matter to us. Tact and civility require us to respect them.

At the same time, we need evaluations that go beyond subjective impressions. The writer needs them for judgments to carry weight so that readers will listen and take an evaluation seriously. Readers need them to guide their conduct—to decide, for instance, if a book is worth reading. How can we offer an evaluation that is more than subjective?

Some evaluations are subjective but still valuable to those who care about the subject, such as opinions on fashion or taste. The fashion blog "The Sartorialist" features photographs of people on the street whom the blogger deems fashionable, such as this woman.

Eugenio Marongiu/Getty Images, RF

CONCEPT CLOSE-UP Using Criteria for Evaluating

Criteria, a concept that originated in the Greek word for "judge," refers to *standards for evaluating something.* The singular form of the word is *criterion,* but the plural is more common because people usually have more than one standard in mind when making an evaluation.

Often we do not think consciously of the criteria we use when passing judgment. But when we rank some products or performances, such as Olympic diving, criteria assume great importance. Setting up criteria when writing an evaluation shows your engagement with whatever you are evaluating, implying that your judgment is not casual, hasty, or superficial. It shows that you have asked this important question: **What qualities define excellence in this and similar items?**

An evaluation is a form of argument because the writer makes a claim about the quality of something and supports the claim by showing how it meets or fails to meet the criteria. Evaluators may disagree about which criteria should be used when judging some things, such as a film or a travel destination. Considering the audience for a written evaluation will help the writer choose criteria that readers would find acceptable.

READING **12.1**

Samsung Galaxy S9 Review

JULIAN CHOKKATTU

Julian Chokkattu is the Mobile and Wearables Editor for Digital Trends, *an online guide to the digital world. This evaluation of the Galaxy S9 cellphone comes from* Digital Trends' *website. The mix of product assessment and promotion, evaluation and advertising, is common online, making* Digital Trends *and similar sites quite different from such traditional mediums as* Consumer Reports.

Note summary of evaluation, included both for readers who only want the gist of the article and as a memory-jogger for those who have read it. Some readers may use the summary to decide whether to read the entire article.

HIGHS

- Excellent display
- Great 5.8-inch size
- Good speakers
- Strong performance
- Stunning low-light camera

LOWS

- Battery life is lower than competition
- Slow Android updates
- Camera not as versatile as S9 Plus

Small smartphones tend to not get much love. They often aren't as feature-packed as their larger counterparts, which is why it was refreshing to see the only differences between the original 2016 Google Pixel and Pixel XL, as well as last year's Samsung Galaxy S8 and S8 Plus, were the size and battery. 1

Unfortunately, trends show things are quickly going back to the norm. The Pixel 2 XL differentiated from the Pixel 2 with a bezel-less design, and the Sony Xperia XZ2 Compact doesn't have wireless charging or the new Dynamic Vibration System found in the larger Xperia XZ2. And with the new Galaxy S9, you won't find the versatile dual-camera system that's present in the larger Galaxy S9 Plus. Are the extra features in the Galaxy S9 Plus worth the money, or will you be satisfied with a smaller phone? Let's take a closer look. 2

The key question: Is more really worth the money?

Small and Compact

The Galaxy S9 is the perfect-sized phone. It's easy to wrap our palms around this smooth 5.8-inch device, and our fingers ergonomically rest on the curved edges along the S9's frame. The power button on the right edge sits in an easy-to-access position, as does the Bixby button on the left edge. It's a shame we've turned off Bixby's functionality, so the button remains useless—more on that later. 3

Note the thoughtful attention to detail throughout this evaluation. The writer goes far beyond general impressions to assess the S9's features—in this way educating the reader as well as advising him or her on a possible purchase.

Despite the small size, the volume rocker on the left edge is still a little too hard to reach, just like it is on the Galaxy S9 Plus. We have to shuffle the phone a little lower to tap it. 4

On the bottom edge of the phone is a USB-Type C charging port, with a bottom-firing speaker and a headphone jack. You'll be pleased to learn that Samsung finally uses stereo sound—the top earpiece works with the bottom-firing speaker for AKG-tuned, Dolby Atmos audio. Music is easily room-filling, with rich, 5

The mix of positives and negatives helps to make this evaluation believable.

clear sound, but weak bass. It's a step up from Samsung's previous smartphones, but dual front-facing speakers like those on the Pixel 2 would be an even better addition—we often end up covering the bottom-firing speaker when holding the phone in landscape mode.

The back of the S9 isn't drastically different from years past. Samsung has essentially flipped its horizontal camera and fingerprint sensor setup vertically, making it easier to place your finger. Sadly, it's still easy to touch the camera sensor because the fingerprint module isn't distinguished enough from the camera frame, and both are still too close to each other. Speaking of fingerprints, get ready to carry a microfiber cloth or use a case with the S9—otherwise you'll spend countless minutes getting rid of smudges and fingerprints off the glossy, glass back. 6

Size is the Galaxy S9's strength here. The S9 is slightly shorter than last year's S8, but you get the same 5.8-inch screen thanks to the smaller bezels surrounding the display. After going between the S9 Plus and the S9, we much prefer the smaller phone. It's comfortable and easy to hold, while still being a great entertainment device with a large display and great sound. 7

In terms of colors, a Sunrise Gold version is now available, alongside Midnight Black, Coral Blue, and Lilac Purple. 8

This evaluation has two audiences in mind: the average consumer and readers who are more technologically sophisticated. The author supplies technical information, but he also tells the reader what such information means—in this case that, because the smaller phone has the same number of pixels as the larger one, its screen image is sharper. The need to reach at least two audiences is common in evaluations; the author shows us how to do it.

Sharp, Colorful Display, Plus Speedy Performance

It may have been around for a year, but we still can't stop gazing at Samsung's Infinity Display. Samsung has taken the effort to mask all the cameras and sensors sitting in the bezel of the phone, making it look like the screen blends in with the edges, which creates a more immersive viewing experience. 9

The 5.8-inch screen size is the same as the S8, but there are some improvements in the AMOLED panel. Colors are incredibly vibrant, but still accurate, and the screen gets brilliantly bright. The S9 has a Quad HD+ (2,960 × 1,440 pixel) resolution, just like the Galaxy S9 Plus, which means it's even sharper than its larger brother because it packs more pixels (570 pixels-per-inch to be exact). 10

The end result is a beautiful screen that's perfect for binge-watching the new season of *Jessica Jones*. The S9 supports HDR10 after all, so apps like Netflix, YouTube, and HBO with HDR10 content look their absolute best on this phone. Sure, the Galaxy S9 Plus has more screen real estate, but we're happy watching shows and movies on the smaller S9 as well. 11

The Galaxy S9 and S9 Plus are the first phones we've tested with Qualcomm's Snapdragon 845 processor, and we're happy to announce the new chipset delivers great performance. Apps open quickly, and moving throughout the user interface is mostly smooth. We say mostly because we have encountered the occasional stutter, which reminds us of Samsung's TouchWiz launcher days. 12

What impressed us more is gaming performance. The Snapdragon 845 chip boasts bigger graphics improvements, and it shows. Games like *Tekken* and *The Sims: Mobile* run without a hitch, and the phone doesn't get too warm after we were playing for a while. 13

The author is aware of what his audience wants to know about most and, therefore, comments on how the phone handles gaming.

14 Here are a few results from benchmark tests:

- AnTuTu 3D Bench: 261,876
- Geekbench 4 CPU: 2377 single-core; 7,982 multi-core
- 3D Mark Slingshot Extreme: 468 OpenGL; 3,617 Vulkan

15 The scores are slightly lower than what we received on the Galaxy S9 Plus, and that may be due to the 6GB of RAM in the larger phone—the regular S9 only has 4GB. More RAM is beneficial when you're doing a lot of multitasking, and it also helps future-proof the phone. Still, 4GB is plenty for most people, and the S9's scores are way higher than the Pixel 2 and almost all Android flagship smartphones from 2017. Needless to say, the Galaxy S9 can easily handle multitasking, gaming, and everyday tasks without issues. You'll be satisfied with performance on this phone.

16 The S9 comes with 64GB of storage, but there's a 128GB model and a 256GB model available as well. A MicroSD card slot lets you add in more space if you need it.

Who Needs a Second Camera?

17 The biggest difference between the S9 Plus and the S9, other than size, is the extra camera on the rear of the S9 Plus. Like many other flagship smartphones, the dual-camera system offers features like 2x optical zoom and a Portrait Mode for a blurred background effect, as well as a wide-angle camera on certain devices like the LG V30. You won't get any of that on the small Galaxy S9, but you do get a killer single 12-megapixel camera with variable aperture.

Note that the writer returns often to the central question posed in the first paragraph: Is more really worth the price? Here he contends that for most people the camera of the S9 is more than adequate.

18 That doesn't sound as cool, but you'll undoubtedly be more than satisfied and impressed with the photos—specifically the low-light photos—the S9 captures. As we've explained before, variable aperture is when the camera can switch between two apertures: In the S9's case, it can switch between f/1.5 and f/2.4.

19 The aperture is the hole in the camera that lets light into the sensor. The S9's f/1.5 is the widest aperture available on a smartphone currently, and that means it can absorb a lot of light because the hole is larger (the lower the number, the wider the aperture). The problem with having such a wide aperture is that the details in the photograph are not as sharp. So if you compare a daylight photo taken with the f/1.5 aperture versus the f/2.4 aperture, the latter photo will be far more detailed.

Assures the reader that the camera technology is easy to use.

20 Thankfully, you don't need to think about any of this because Samsung hides all this complicated mechanical machinery away from the user interface. Simply open the camera app, tap the shutter icon, and the S9 will take a great photo. It will default to the f/2.4 aperture most of the time, so your photos remain sharp, but when it detects poor lighting, it will automatically switch to the f/1.5 aperture. These photos are noticeably brighter than the S9's competitors, and while they may be a little fuzzy, they're still excellent considering the lighting conditions. You can also manually switch apertures in the camera's Pro mode.

21 What's even more impressive is Samsung's multi-frame noise-reduction image processing, which may not sound interesting, but is important. We've all taken

photos at night only to find a lot of grain or "noise" ruining the picture. When you tap the shutter icon on the Galaxy S9, the phone captures 12 photos it then compiles to eliminate as much noise as possible. When you compare low-light photos with the Google Pixel 2, for example, the difference in noise is astounding, and it always makes for a better photo.

There's also the Super Slow Motion feature, where you can take 720p videos that are 32 times slower than real life. It's a fun addition into the camera app, though it does take some getting used to when trying to capture fast-moving scenes. Samsung has also taken a page out of Apple's book with AR Emojis, mimicking Animojis that debuted on the iPhone X. We're not fans of how AR Emojis look—though some people on our staff think they look great. More importantly, the motion-capture technology used to create and send AR Emoji videos is not good at all. Animojis remain far superior. Like Animojis, however, we expect no one to talk about this feature after a month. 22

We're genuinely impressed at the low-light achievements here with Samsung's "reimagined" camera, and the Super Slow Motion addition is genuinely fun. We do still think the Galaxy S9 Plus' second camera is worth the extra money, though. We kept trying to use the S9-exclusive 2x optical zoom on the regular S9, only because taking detailed photos of objects further away makes the camera so versatile. Live Focus is also a handy and fun feature to have, and the "Selective Focus" software version feature on the S9 doesn't compare. 23

Summarizes this relatively complex section, leaving the reader with what matters most to remember.

If those two latter features aren't important to you, then you'll still be overjoyed with the Galaxy S9's camera. 24

Customizable Software, but You Can't Erase Bixby

The Galaxy S9 runs Android 8.0 Oreo, but it's layered with the Samsung Experience 9.0 user interface. The software looks far better than Samsung's old TouchWiz UI, and there's plenty of customization options to personalize your S9. 25

Again the author shows reader awareness in calling attention to how easy and extensive the customizing options are.

For example, you can change the exact color of the clock on the lock screen, not to mention choosing a clock design from a variety of options. The sheer amount of customization options are great, and they don't feel overwhelming. Most people won't touch a lot of these settings, but we're happy to know they are there. 26

With all this customization, however, you would think Samsung would let people remap the Bixby button. Bixby is Samsung's artificially intelligent assistant first introduced in the Galaxy S8. It's meant to be an easy way to perform traditional touch functions on your phone with your voice. It can be handy sometimes, but we've generally found the experience to be slower and not as reliable as Google Assistant, which you can access by pressing and holding the home button. Sliding the home screen to the right to open Bixby Home is sluggish, and there never really seems to be any useful information here. 27

There are a few new additions to Bixby Vision—the camera part of Bixby—including Makeup, Food, and improved instant language translation. The latter two are wonky, and never completely reliable, but we've found Makeup to be fun and useful. It leverages technology from a company called ModiFace, and it lets you 28 layer makeup products over your face. If you like the way a product looks on your face, tap the link and you can purchase it from the website. Right now, Makeup has Sephora products, but Samsung said to expect more, like Cover Girl, soon.

While Bixby can be annoying, the biggest disappointment in terms of software is updates. It's why the Pixel 2 XL remains our top Android phone, because version and security updates are important to us, and Samsung has taken its sweet time to update its devices to the latest version of Android. Android 8.0 Oreo came out back in August 2017, and the Galaxy S8 and S8 Plus are still on a beta. With Android P's first developer preview now available, don't expect to have it on the S9 or S9 Plus until early 2019. If you care about fast software updates, get a Google Pixel. 29

Calls attention to a significant limitation of the S9, the need for frequent charging. An indication that it is not the best choice for "heavy hitters."

Daylong Battery Life

If you're a power user, don't expect to get through a day without charging up the Galaxy S9. After using it heavily for watching YouTube videos, taking photos, playing video games, and browsing the web, we reached 7 percent by 6 p.m. That's not good at all, and you can easily find better battery life with the competition, especially the Huawei Mate 10 Pro. 30

If you don't use the phone as much, you'll obviously see better battery life. You can also head to the device manager settings to optimize the battery and get as much time out of it as possible. On a light day of use, we managed 38 percent by 5 p.m., starting with a full charge at 7:30 a.m. 31

The phone supports fast wireless and wired charging, so you have plenty of ways to charge it back to full strength quickly. 32

Price, Availability, and Warranty Information

The Galaxy S9 costs $720 from Samsung, or you can purchase it on a monthly payment plan. You can also buy it through carriers and other retailers, and you can check out our buying guide for more details and deals. 33

Samsung offers a one-year limited warranty that protects the phone from manufacturing defects. You can purchase Samsung Premium Care for an extended warranty, as well as other features. 34

OUR TAKE

Two sentences encapsulate the entire evaluation.

The Galaxy S9 is a comfortable and compact phone that offers a fantastic camera and great performance, but is it one of the best smartphones on the market? We do think the S9 Plus is worth it for the second, versatile camera, but the S9's perfect size makes it hard to ignore. 35

Anticipates and answers a question readers will surely ask and want answered

Is There a Better Alternative?

Maybe. The Google Pixel 2 is another small phone with fluid performance and an excellent camera, and you get fast Android version and security updates. The problem is that it doesn't feature a bezel-less design, so it looks quite dated. 36

If you don't care about operating systems, there's always the iPhone X, which is smaller than the iPhone 8 Plus, or the iPhone 8. Both are excellent phones with similar strengths as the Google Pixel 2, and the iPhone X has that contemporary, stylish look you want. Check out our best small phones guide for more. 37

How Long Will It Last?

Expect the Galaxy S9 to last you three or more years. It's IP68 water- and dust-resistant, so it will survive dips in the pool, but it's covered in glass, so you might want to protect it with a case. Samsung issues software updates for two years, so you will start to see performance dips by then, especially since the battery will start to depreciate. 38

Should You Buy It?

Poses and answers the "bottom line" question.

Yes. If you don't care about the extra camera on the Galaxy S9 Plus, the Galaxy S9 is an excellent device with a stellar camera, great performance, and brilliant hardware. 39

Questions for Discussion

1. Both online and in print subheadings are the norm in most publications. Beginning with the first subheading, "Small and Compact" (see paragraph 3), discuss how they work in this evaluation. Imagine the article without subheadings. What would be lost?
2. All evaluations, but especially those that deal with technology, have the problem of too much or too little. On the one hand, if you don't provide enough information, some of it "hard data" (that is, quantified, very specific data), readers will feel unsatisfied. On the other hand, if you provide too much, readers will become bored or confused or both. Did Chokkattu strike a good balance? Is there any place or places where you wanted more information? Is there any place or places where you got more than you wanted?
3. There's a difference between a mere gimmick and genuinely useful features in many manufactured products. Assess the Samsung S9 review from this standpoint. That is, what does this cell phone offer the potential user that is truly functional, worth having?

Thinking as a Writer

What Is the Rhetorical Situation?

1. What is Chokkattu's *purpose* in writing this essay? What is his *angle* or point of view? How would you describe his *voice*—that is, how does he sound to you?
2. Who is Chokkattu's intended *audience*? That is, who would read *Digital Trends*? What in the article's content best reveals the interests and values of the website's readers?
3. Chokkattu makes a strong claim: The S9 is one of the best smaller cell phones currently available. Such a strong claim requires strong support. How does he attempt to justify his claim? What different kinds of evidence does he use? ■

READING 12.2

The Promises and Pitfalls of Online Education

ERIC BETTINGER AND SUSANNA LOEB

This evaluation of the effectiveness of online college education was prepared for the Brookings Institute by Eric Bettinger, Associate Professor of Economics of Education at Stanford Graduate School of Education, and by Susanna Loeb, Associate Professor of Education, also at Stanford. Like the Samsung cell phone evaluation in this chapter, this report notes both positive aspects of taking college courses online and negative aspects for some students whose success may depend on more personal interaction than is afforded by many current learning platforms.

EXECUTIVE SUMMARY

Online courses have expanded rapidly and have the potential to extend further the educational opportunities of many students, particularly those least well-served by traditional educational institutions. However, in their current design, online courses are difficult, especially for the students who are least prepared. These students' learning and persistence outcomes are worse when they take online courses than they would have been had these same students taken in-person courses. Continued improvement of online curricula and instruction can strengthen the quality of these courses and hence the educational opportunities for the most in-need populations. 1

Online courses offer the promise of access regardless of where students live or what time they can participate, potentially redefining educational opportunities for those least well-served in traditional classrooms. Moreover, online platforms offer the promise, through artificial intelligence, of providing the optimal course pacing and content to fit each student's needs and thereby improve educational quality and learning. The latest "intelligent" tutoring systems, for example, not only assess students' current weaknesses, but also diagnose why students make the specific errors. These systems then adjust instructional materials to meet students' needs.[1] 2

Yet today these promises are far from fully realized. The vast majority of online courses mirror face-to-face classrooms with professors rather using technology to better differentiate instruction across students. As one new study that we completed with our colleagues Lindsay Fox and Eric Taylor shows, online courses can improve access, yet they also are challenging, especially for the least well-prepared students. These students consistently perform worse in an online setting than they do in face-to-face classrooms; taking online courses increases their likelihood of dropping out and otherwise impedes progress through college.[2] 3

Online college courses are rapidly growing. One out of three college students now takes at least one course online during their college career, and that share has increased threefold over the past decade.[3] The potential for cost savings and the ease of scaling fuels ongoing investments in online education by both public and private institutions.[4] Online courses have grown in the K-12 sector as well. Florida, for example, requires each high school student to take at least one online course before graduation and the Florida Virtual School offers over 150 classes to students across the state.[5] An estimated 1.5 million K-12 students participated in some online learning in 2010,[6] and online learning enrollments are projected to grow in future years.[7] 4

Non-selective and for-profit higher education institutions have expanded online course offerings particularly quickly. These institutions serve a majority of college-aged students, and these students typically have weaker academic preparation and fewer economic resources than students at other more selective colleges and universities. As such, their ability to provide useful course work, engage students, and build the skills necessary for economic success is particularly important. Their use of online coursework is promising to the extent that it can reach the most students in need and serve them well. 5

While online course-taking is both prevalent and growing, especially in non-selective higher education institutions, relatively little evidence has examined how taking a course online instead of in person affects student success in college. Our new study is the first of which we are aware to provide evidence on the effects of online courses at-scale at non-selective four-year colleges. It is also the first to assess the effects of online course taking at for-profit institutions. Nearly 2.4 million undergraduate students (full-time equivalent) enrolled at for-profit institutions during the 2011–12 academic year, and the sector granted approximately 18 percent of all associate degrees. 6

Our study uses data from DeVry University, a large for-profit college with an undergraduate enrollment of more than 100,000 students, 80 percent of whom are seeking a bachelor's degree. The average DeVry student takes two-thirds of her courses online. The remaining one-third of courses meet in conventional in-person classes held at one of DeVry's 102 physical campuses. The data include over 230,000 students enrolled in 168,000 sections of more than 750 different courses. 7

DeVry University's approach to online education makes it particularly well suited for estimating the effects of taking online courses. Each DeVry course is offered both online and in-person, and each student enrolls in either an online section or an in-person section. Online and in-person sections are identical in most ways: both follow the same syllabus and use the same textbook; class sizes are approximately the same; both use the same assignments, quizzes, tests, and grading rubrics. Many professors teach both online and in-person courses. The contrast between online and in-person sections is primarily the mode of communication. In online sections, all interaction—lecturing, class discussion, group projects—occurs in online discussion boards, and much of the professor's "lecturing" role is replaced with standardized videos. In online sections, participation is often asynchronous while in-person sections meet on campus at scheduled times. In short, DeVry online classes attempt to replicate traditional in-person classes, except that student-student and student-professor interactions are virtual and asynchronous. 8

Using variation in course-taking that arises both from changes in course offerings at particular campuses in a particular term and from variation across students in the distance that they have to travel to take in-person courses, we find that taking a course online reduces student grades by 0.44 points on the traditional four-point grading scale, approximately a 0.33 standard deviation decline relative to taking a course in-person (See **Figure 12.1**). To be more concrete, students taking the course in-person earned roughly a B- grade (2.8) on average while if they had taken it online, they would have earned a C (2.4). Additionally, taking a course online reduces a student's GPA the following term by 0.15 points; and, if we look only at the next term GPA for courses in the same subject area or courses for which the course in question is a pre-requisite, we find larger drops of 0.42 points and 0.32 points respectively, providing evidence that students learned less in the online setting. 9

FIGURE 12.1
Benefit of in-person course taking

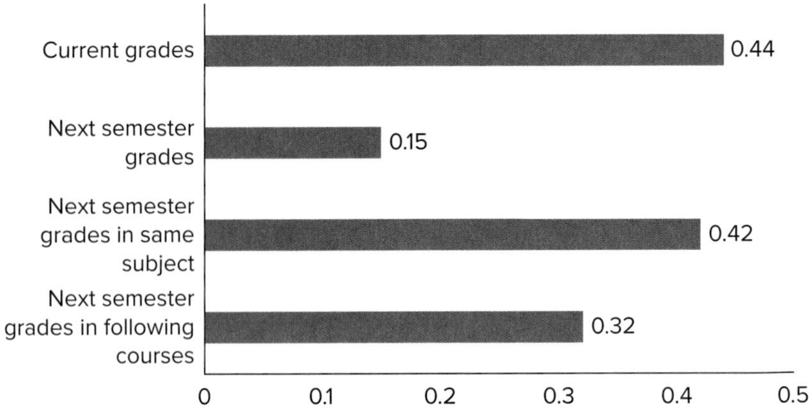

We also find that taking a course online, instead of in person, increases the probability that a student will drop out of school. In the semester after taking an online course, students are about 9 percentage points less likely to remain enrolled. This reduction is relative to an average of 88 percent of students remaining enrolled in the following term. Moreover, taking a course online reduces the number of credits that students who do reenroll take in future semesters. While this setting is quite different, we can compare the effects on online course taking to other estimates of effects of on college persistence. For example, the literature on financial aid often finds that $1000 in financial aid increases persistence rates by about three percentage points[8] and college mentorship increases persistence rates by five percentage points.[9] 10

The negative effects of online course taking are concentrated in the lowest performing students. As shown in Figure 12.2, for students with below median prior GPA, the online classes reduce grades by 0.5 points or more, while for students with prior GPA in the top three deciles we estimate the effect as much smaller and, in fact, we cannot tell whether there is negative effect at all for this higher-achieving group. Thus, while online courses may have the potential to differentiate coursework to meet the needs of students with weaker incoming skills, current online courses, in fact, do an even worse job of meeting the needs of these students than do traditional in-person courses. 11

These analyses provide evidence that students in online courses perform substantially worse than students in traditional in-person courses and that experience in these online courses impact performance in future classes and their likelihood of dropping out of college as well. The negative effects of online course-taking are far stronger for students with lower prior GPA. The results are in line with prior studies of online education in other settings such as community colleges and highly competitive four-year institutions that also show that online courses yield worse average outcomes than in-person courses.[10] 12

The current negative effect of online course taking relative to in-person course taking should not necessarily lead to the conclusion that online courses should be discouraged. On the contrary, online courses provide access to students who never would have the opportunity or inclination to take classes in-person.[11] As one indication, of the 5.8 million students taking online courses in the fall of 2014, 2.85 million took all of their courses online.[12] Moreover, advances in AI offer hope that future online courses can respond to the needs of students, meeting them where they are in their learning and 13

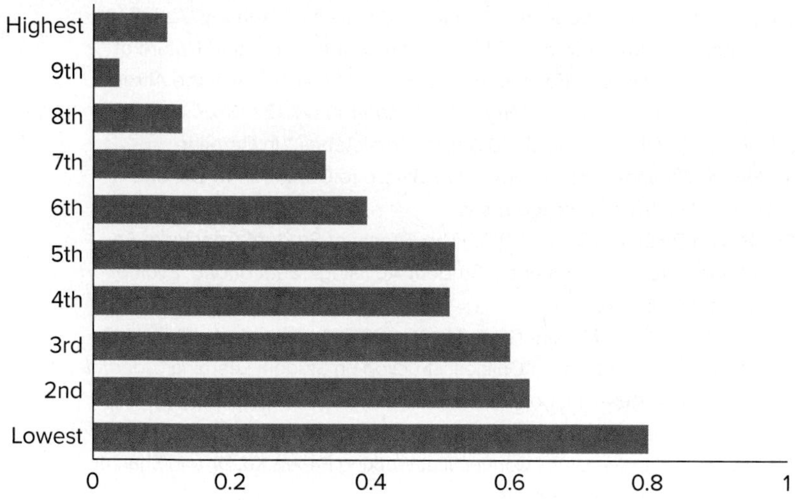

FIGURE **12.2**

Benefit of in-person course taking by prior GPA

engaging them in higher education even better than in-person courses are currently able to do.[13] Nonetheless, the tremendous scale and consistently negative effects of current offerings points to the need to improve these courses, particularly for students most at risk of course failure and college dropout.

The authors did not receive financial support from any firm or person with a financial or political interest in this article. They are currently not officers, directors, or board members of any organization with an interest in this article.

End Notes

1. Graesser, Arthur C., Mark W. Conley, and Andrew Olney. 2012. "Intelligent tutoring systems." In *APA Educational Psychology Handbook, Vol. 3: Application to Learning and Teaching*, edited by Karen. R. Harris, Steve Graham, and Tim Urdan. Washington, DC: American Psychological Association.
2. Bettinger, E., Fox, L., Loeb, S., & Taylor, E. (Forthcoming). Changing Distributions: How Online College Classes Alter Student and Professor Performance. *American Economic Review.*
3. Allen, I. Elaine, and Jeff Seaman. 2013. *Changing Course: Ten Years of Tracking Online Education in the United States*. Newburyport, MA: Sloan Consortium.
4. Deming, David J., Claudia Goldin, Lawrence F. Katz, and Noam Yuchtman. 2015. Can Online Learning Bend the Higher Education Cost Curve? *American Economic Review, Papers & Proceedings*, 105 (5):496–501.
5. Jacob, B., Berger, D. Hart, C. & Loeb, S. (Forthcoming). "Can Technology Help Promote Equality of Educational Opportunities?" In K. Alexander and S. Morgan (Editors), *The Coleman Report and Educational Inequality Fifty Years Later*. Russell Sage Foundation and William T. Grant Foundation: New York.
6. Wicks, Matthew. 2010. "A National Primer on K–12 Online Learning. Version 2." Vienna, VA: International Association for K-12 Online Learning.
7. Watson, John, Amy Murin, Lauren Vashaw, Butch Gemin, and Chris Rapp. 2012. "Keeping Pace with K-12 Online Learning: An Annual Review of Policy and Practice

2011." Durango, CO: Evergreen Education Group. And Picciano, Anthony G., Jeff Seaman, Peter Shea, and Karen Swan. 2012. "Examining the Extent and Nature of Online Learning in American K-12 Education: The Research Initiatives of the Alfred P. Sloan Foundation." *The Internet and Higher Education* 15 (2): 127–35.

8. Bettinger, Eric P. 2004. "How Financial Aid Affects Persistence." In Caroline Hoxby (Ed.), *College Choices: The Economics of Where to Go, When to Go, and How to Pay for It*. University of Chicago Press.
9. Bettinger, Eric P., and Rachel B. Baker. 2013. "The Effects of Student Coaching: An Evaluation of a Randomized Experiment in Student Advising." *Educational Evaluation and Policy Analysis* 36 (1): 3–19.
10. See for examples: Figlio, David, Mark Rush, and Lu Yin. 2013. "Is It Live or Is It Internet? Experimental Estimates of the Effects of Online Instruction on Student Learning." *Journal of Labor Economics*, 31 (4):763–784; Couch, Kenneth A., William T. Alpert, and Oskar R. Harmon. 2014. "Online, Blended and Classroom Teaching of Economics Principles: A Randomized Experiment." University of Connecticut Working Paper; Xu, Di, and Shanna Smith Jaggars. 2014. "Performance Gaps Between Online and Face-to-Face Courses: Differences Across Types of Students and Academic Subject Areas." *The Journal of Higher Education*, 85 (5): 633–659; Hart, Cassandra, Elizabeth Friedmann, and Michael Hill. 2014. "Online Course-Taking and Student Outcomes in California Community Colleges." Working Paper; and Streich, Francie E. 2014. "Online and Hybrid Instruction and Student Success in College: Evidence from Community Colleges in Two States." University of Michigan Working Paper.
11. See, for example, Joshua Goodman, Julia Melkers, and Amanda Pallais, "Can Online Delivery Increase Access to Education?" National Bureau of Economic Research working paper 22754, October 2016.
12. *Online Report Card—Tracking Online Education in the United States*, the 2015 Survey of Online Learning conducted by the Babson Survey Research Group and co-sponsored by the Online Learning Consortium (OLC), Pearson, StudyPortals, WCET and Tyton Partners.
13. See, for example, the Open Learning Initiative at Carnegie Mellon University.

Thinking as a Writer

What Is the Rhetorical Situation?

1. How would you describe the purpose of "Promises and Pitfalls of Online Education"? Do you think Bettinger and Loeb are aiming this evaluation at college students or some other audience of readers? If so, who might those readers be?
2. If you have read the evaluation of the Samsung Galaxy S9 cell phone earlier in this chapter, you will notice the difference in voice and tone between that evaluation and this one published by the Brookings Institution, a nonprofit public policy organization that employs experts in government and academic institutions from around the world. How would you describe the voice in Bettinger and Loeb's evaluation?
3. Besides voice, what other features of this evaluation would make it convincing to more scholarly readers? ■

The Assignment

Write a review evaluating a product, service, cultural event, institution, or anything else your instructor considers appropriate. You should be familiar with the subject of your evaluation and with other, similar products, services, events, and so on, so that you can knowledgeably set up criteria for assessment. If your instructor wants you to support your judgment of the subject with sources such as surveys and expert opinion, you should consider whether such sources are available.

What Can I Write About?

Your instructor may assign your topic. If you are asked to choose your own topic for this assignment, select something you know well from personal experience. Consider the following categories and examples:

- **A manufactured item:** a car, electronic device, item of clothing, office machine, sports equipment, home, apartment, or condo.
- **A service:** a restaurant, travel agency, tax preparation service, online dating service, university or college dining hall or exercise center.
- **A cultural item or place:** a television show, film, stage play, museum, musical performance, or sports event.
- **A print or online publication:** a novel, business report, textbook, advertisement, magazine, newspaper, website, blog, or social networking site.
- **Software:** a video game or computer program.
- **Travel destination or other place of interest:** a foreign city, attraction in your home town or near your campus, historical memorial, national park, or model community.
- **Proposed legislation or policy changes:** proposals to remedy on-campus problems such as parking, off-campus problems such as inadequate public transportation, ecological problems such as clean diesel engines in cars to reduce pollution, or national problems such as the dropout rate in education.

To explore additional topic ideas and see additional models for evaluation, read articles from *Consumer Reports,* book and movie reviews in magazines and newspapers, and online evaluations in blogs and on consumer sites.

How Do I Write an Evaluation? Questioning the Rhetorical Situation

Begin by picturing a rhetorical situation for your writing project, a real-world context for communicating. You should consider the key variables in any act of communication: a writer with something to say, a reader the writer wishes to reach, and a kind of text appropriate to the writing task. These three variables will affect many decisions in the composing process.

Writer: What Is My Purpose, and What Impression Should My Readers Have of Me?

Your purpose is to make a convincing case for your judgment of something. Beyond that, your judgment may serve a variety of purposes, such as helping readers appreciate a movie or a new album, or recommending–or warning against–a restaurant or hotel. You want to sound knowledgeable and be able to justify your opinion since readers may encounter other opinions the opposite of yours. Your readers should see you as someone who has arrived at an assessment thoughtfully. They will need to have confidence in the good reasons you offer for evaluating your topic as you have.

Audience: Who Is My Reader?

As with all writing projects, you should imagine a group of people who might read your paper. Having a readership in mind for your evaluation will help you decide what to say and how to order it. **"What does my reader need to know?"** is therefore one of the key questions you need to ask yourself often as you write and revise a draft.

Readers come to evaluations wanting to know about whatever you are assessing. You can assume interest; what readers want is information, including your assessment and what led you to it, which they will use to help them decide whether to buy the product, use the service, visit the local attraction, and so on. Clearly, readers of *Digital Trends* want and expect technical details such as the choice in lens aperture for the Samsung S9's camera. Select the information you think will be most relevant to your readers.

Text: What Moves Can I Make?

The genre represented in the readings above (pages 280–90) and in the student example at the end of this chapter (pages 299–302) is the review or evaluation. Basic moves include the following:

- Indicate what you are evaluating immediately. Catch the readers' attention with an interesting move in the introduction. For example, the Samsung S9 evaluation opened with a memorable claim: "Small smartphones tend to not get much love."
- Provide background information the reader needs to put your topic in an appropriate context–the reviewer of the S9, for example, placed his evaluation in the context of full-size versus smaller cell phones by competing makers.
- Explicitly lay out the criteria for your judgment and explain any criterion whose relevance may not be obvious.
- Use the criteria to structure your essay.
- State your overall assessment, usually early in your review, remembering that it can be positive, negative, or some mix of the two.
- Offer supporting details or specifics to justify and support your assessment, which may be observations from experience, research data, expert opinion–indeed, anything appropriate to your topic that meets your readers' need to know why you have assessed your topic as you have.
- Especially if you offer a negative review of something most people like or a positive review of something most people dislike, offer a defense of your evaluation–acknowledge that you are going against the popular judgment and explain why.

When selecting your evaluation topic, choose something familiar and interesting to you, such as a dining experience at a favorite restaurant.
monkeybusinessimages/ Getty Images

How Do I Write an Evaluation? Engaging the Writing Process

No two people compose in exactly the same way, and even the same person may go through the writing process in different ways with different assignments. Nevertheless, because no one can attend to everything at once, there are phases in handling any significant writing task. You **explore the topic** to get a sense of whether it will work for you and what you might be able to do with it; if the topic is working out for you, then you move into **preparing to write,** generating more content and planning your draft.

The next phase is **drafting your paper,** getting a version, however rough it may be, on screen or paper so that you can work toward the final draft. Getting there involves two further phases: **revising your draft,** where you make major improvements in your draft, followed by **editing your draft,** taking care of errors, sentences that do not read well, paragraphs lacking focus and flow, and so on.

Exploring Your Topic

Readers read evaluations to know more about a topic, not just how you rate it. Consequently, your task is partly informative, providing facts about your topic. Where will you find this information?

Many evaluations are based entirely on the author's experience with the product, service, vacation destination, and so on–with whatever you are evaluating. Begin, then, by brainstorming what you know from personal experience and observation. Write a list or a notebook entry with facts about your topic. How much do you actually know that is factual? If you cannot generate much by listing or freewriting, you may need to choose a different topic or dig further into the one you plan to write about.

Go back to your topic. If it is a film, watch it again. If it is a product, examine it more thoroughly. You may need to gather some information from sources, such as product information, film credits, and other basic facts appropriate to your topic. You may want to read what other experts have said, but bear in mind that you should make your own judgment aimed at your own audience, based on your experiences and opinions. However, another reviewer might remind you of points or criteria for evaluation.

Finding Criteria for Evaluating

Which comes first: making a subjective judgment about the quality of something or making a list of criteria and then deciding how well something meets the criteria? Human nature being what it is, most likely we form our opinions and then think of ways to justify them.

Whether you start with a set of criteria or a gut opinion, your evaluation should show that you have thought about reasonable standards of excellence for items similar to your topic, or your readers will not find your opinion credible. Asking questions will help you generate a list of criteria for judging your topic.

When your evaluation of something is solicited, such as when your college asks you to evaluate a course, you usually receive a list of questions: How well was the class organized? Was the professor prepared? How available was the professor for help? For this project, you will have to generate a list of questions appropriate to evaluating your topic.

ACTIVITY 12.1 *Collaborative Activity*

What Makes Something Good?

Begin by listing the questions that people usually ask when evaluating items similar to your topic. If members of your class are writing about similar topics, get together to compare your lists of questions. Even if you are not writing on shared topics, a classmate or two can help you think of good points upon which to rate your topic. ■

ACTIVITY 12.2 *Writer's Notebook*

Evaluating Your Criteria and Main Points

After you have generated a list of criteria for evaluating your topic, write informally in your writer's notebook to rehearse the main points you want to make in an evaluation of your topic. If you want to be able to see other classmates' ideas, everyone might post their ideas on an online discussion board. On your list of criteria, are there points upon which you would give your topic the highest rating? Are there other points where your topic falls short? How would you sum up your rating of your topic? ■

Preparing to Write

Some writers prefer to go straight to drafting after having explored a topic thoroughly. Others prefer to lay out a plan for the organization of the paper. Either way, it is good to take stock of the notes you have made and write a tentative thesis for your evaluation.

Stating Your Evaluation as a Thesis

The thesis of an evaluation is simply the main point about the quality of the topic. It does not have to go into all of the criteria used in the evaluation itself, but it should sum up the writer's opinion. For example, consider this sentence from an example earlier in the chapter.

- **From the evaluation of the cell phone:** "The Galaxy S9 is a comfortable and compact phone that offers a fantastic camera and great performance."

ACTIVITY 12.3 *Collaborative Activity*

Trying Out Thesis Sentences

Look over your prewriting notes and lists. What criteria do you think most contributed to your overall estimate of the quality of your topic? Try out some thesis sentences that express your opinion and point to a specific direction that your evaluation might emphasize. In groups of two or three, go over each other's ideas for the thesis and discuss what specific reasons each writer could use to defend that opinion. ■

Drafting Your Paper

Focus on angle, voice, and organization in drafting your paper.

What Angle and Voice Are Appropriate for an Evaluation?

As you begin drafting your evaluation, you should be conscious of your angle on the topic. A writer's angle is his or her point of view. Angle makes writing original and interesting and gives the writing personality, or what we have called voice. Two writers could give the same item equally excellent reviews based on the same criteria, but their written evaluations will likely have different angles and voice, depending on each writer's attitude toward his or her topic and relationship with his or her readers.

Knowing your topic well enough to have an angle on it and picturing readers who would find your angle interesting–these are the keys to writing with voice.

Developing and Organizing Your Evaluation

Write a first draft of your evaluation. In planning your draft, consider the suggestions in the Text: What Moves Can I Make? section on page 292, which will help you generate material to develop your thesis and organize the evaluation.

Revising Your Draft

Think of the first draft as raw material that could be rearranged for a better flow of ideas or improved emphasis. Have you put your points in the best order to make your evaluation forceful and easy for readers to follow? First drafts often need more development–specific details that readers cannot be assumed to know. Sometimes you will need to take out material that readers would find either too general or common knowledge or too specific and not relevant to their interest and level of knowledge on the topic. Consider who your readers are and what you might need to explain more or say less about, given their interest in your topic.

THE ART OF QUESTIONING Revision Checklist for Evaluation

Use the following questions to review your own draft or to help classmates find ways to improve theirs.

1. Does the evaluation have an interesting opening that would engage readers' interest? What is the opening move, and what other options are possible?
2. Does the writer have an angle on the topic? What is the angle? Does the opening show enough personal engagement with the topic? How could the writer show more connection with the topic?
3. Is the main point about the topic clearly stated as an opinion about the quality of the topic? Does the thesis suggest the author's angle on the topic?
4. Who is the audience for this evaluation? Where might this essay appear if it were to be published online or in print? How much would this audience already know about the topic? Can you think of anything not covered in the draft that these readers might want to know?
5. How well-developed is this evaluation? Does it contain enough specific evidence to support the judgments made about the topic? Where might the draft need more specific development?
6. What other options are there for arranging the main points? Would any other arrangements offer an advantage, such as a more logical progression from minor to major criteria for evaluation?
7. How smoothly do the sentences flow? One common problem in first drafts is organization, including organization within paragraphs. It is especially hard for writers to find gaps in the train of thought because the writer knows how the ideas connect in his or her mind, even if the connections are not tight or clearly signaled on the page. Read through the draft again, paying attention to connections between sentences and the flow of ideas. (Read the section that follows, Student Example: Excerpts from Collin Dobmeyer's Draft, for more help with checking for coherence.)

Student Example: Excerpts from Collin Dobmeyer's Draft

One of the most common problems in first drafts is poor *organization of ideas,* or **coherence.** The writer thinks of several ideas, all worth developing, and wants to get them down in writing. Realizing that there is more to say on some point, the writer comes back to it later in the paragraph—or even in a later paragraph. The reader feels a gap in the train of thought when this happens.

Many drafts can be improved by simple rearrangement of ideas, with clear transitions to signal the reader about turns in the train of thought. The following example of revising for coherence comes from student Collin Dobmeyer's review of the video game *Halo: Reach.* The full revised paper appears on pages 299–302.

Excerpt from First Draft

Bungie really went out on a limb with *Halo: Reach.* They abandoned their previous faceless, emotionless, super soldier hero Master Chief in favor of a squad of Spartan super soldiers with faces and personalities. Among your teammates there is the able commander Carter, the emotional George, the introverted Emile, the snide engineer Kat, and the talkative sniper Jun. However, Bungie had better make us care about these characters if they want the player to care about their deaths. The extent to which they can make these characters relatable is a major deciding factor in the success of the game, which makes it a letdown that it doesn't quite work out. The problem stems from the gameplay. *Halo: Reach* is a game that centers on "run and gun" fighting. It is downright difficult to create sympathetic characters when all we see them doing is murdering every alien life form within 500 yards. It is also a problem because these characters lack depth. Every one of them is an unstoppable, immortal superman that doesn't even flinch when it comes time for their own deaths. The only character with human vulnerability is George, who ironically dies first.

> Dobmeyer assumes his readers know who produced the game.

> In the draft, Dobmeyer repeats the point about needing to care about the characters.

> In the draft, Dobmeyer turns to the problem of the game play style before completing the point about the lack of human characteristics.

Note how much better the flow of thought is after Dobmeyer revised for coherence.

Excerpt from Revised Draft

Bungie really went out on a limb with *Halo: Reach.* They abandoned their previous faceless, emotionless, super soldier hero Master Chief in favor of a squad of Spartan super soldiers with faces and personalities. Among your teammates there is the able commander Carter, the emotional George, the introverted Emile, the snide engineer Kat, and the talkative sniper Jun. However, Bungie had better make us care about these characters if they want the player to care about their deaths. The game fails to do so because nearly all the characters lack depth. Every one of them is an unstoppable, immortal superman that doesn't even flinch when it comes time for their own deaths. The only character with human vulnerability is George, who ironically dies first. From then on it becomes difficult to generate any strong emotional attachment to the characters.

This isn't to say that the characters are completely mindless robots; in fact many of them have developing personalities, but the game just doesn't spend enough time developing them beyond the super soldier demeanor. For this, I blame the game play. *Halo: Reach* is a shooter that centers on "run and gun" fighting. It is downright difficult to create sympathetic characters when all we see them doing is murdering every alien life form within 500 yards.

> Sets up the team.

> After setting up the team, Dobmeyer moves to the need for deeper character development.

> Dobmeyer's revision adds a transition into the role of the game style in failing to allow for the characters' development.

Editing Your Revised Draft

Editing for style can help you emphasize main points and bring out your voice and attitude. The coordinating conjunction *and* often causes a main point to almost disappear or seem like an afterthought. In his earlier drafts, Dobmeyer found a few places where he overused "and," as in the following passage:

Original Version

Will the game successfully build the story to a satisfying climax through a coherent series of events, or will it fall prey to a mindless open season on aliens? These are the factors that will determine *Halo: Reach*'s quality, and sadly Bungie missed the mark.

In the edited version, separating the verdict from the setup makes it a more forceful statement.

Edited Version

Will the game successfully build the story to a satisfying climax through a coherent series of events, or will it fall prey to a mindless open season on aliens? These are the factors that will determine *Halo: Reach*'s quality. Sadly Bungie missed the mark.

Consider the value of short sentences when you want to stress a point.

Another stylistic mistake is to put a main point into a dependent clause, especially one beginning with a pronoun like *that* or *which.*

Original Version

Instead of a coherent story, it's more like a series of isolated cut scenes strung together with violence. This problem ties in with a more general issue with *Reach,* which is the general lack of polish.

In the edited version, an appositive set off with a strong punctuation mark gives the second sentence a more forceful ending.

Edited Version

Instead of a coherent story, it's more like a series of isolated cut scenes strung together with violence. This problem ties in with a more general issue with *Reach:* the general lack of polish.

In the final example below, the point about Alex is first made with a dependent "that" clause.

Original Version

It's because she seems like a human with real emotions that Alex becomes an integral, and welcome, part of the story.

In this revision, the point about Alex is promoted to the main clause–and main point–of the sentence.

Edited Version

Because she seems like a human with real emotions, Alex becomes an integral, and welcome, part of the story.

REVISED STUDENT EXAMPLE

Dobmeyer 1

Collin Dobmeyer

Professor Channell

English 1301-010

27 October 2014

Is Classic Status Out of *Reach*?

The evaluation opens with the topic clearly stated and an interesting specific fact about it.

Halo: Reach represents the culmination of the Bungie *Halo* franchise, which has run for nine years. Sales of *Reach* hit $200 million on the first day of its release in September 2010. Its popularity suggests it will be a classic, but will it? The series consists of four games: *Halo: Combat Evolved,* which was released back in 2001; *Halo 2; Halo 3;* and *Halo: Reach. Reach* brings the Bungie series to a close with a prequel whose events tie closely with the beginning of the first game. The player joins a group of elite soldiers known as Noble Team as they fight a losing battle to save the planet Reach from aliens. Normally this is where a reviewer should have written "SPOILER ALERT," but the outcome of the battle is quite clear from the outset with your character's helmet sitting in a smoldering crater with a bullet hole through the visor. Because the ending is known, the only chance this game has to make a huge impression on the player is how well Bungie can deliver the story line and personify the human characters. 1

This question suggests the writer's angle on the topic: Will it be a classic?

Gives an overview of the game's plot.

Shows the two main criteria that the writer will use as the basis of the evaluation.

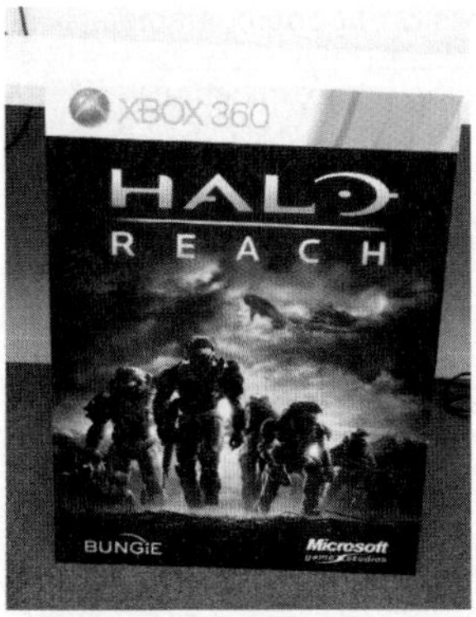

Mike Coppola/Getty Images

The question is: did Bungie manage to pull this game off well enough that *Halo: Reach* deserves the title of "classic"? If the characters are not able to engage the players' emotions, then *Reach* will fail to reach classic status because the story is built around their deaths. The other indicator is how well the story unfolds. Will the game successfully build the story to a satisfying climax through a coherent series of events, or will it fall prey to a mindless 2

Dobmeyer 2

The thesis or main point that the evaluation will prove. Memorable summary judgment.

open season on aliens? These are the factors that will determine *Halo: Reach*'s quality. Sadly Bungie missed the mark. *Halo: Reach* fails to deliver both characters and plot; as a result it will never be remembered for anything but its sales figures.

Bungie really went out on a limb with *Halo: Reach.* They abandoned their previous faceless, emotionless, super soldier hero Master Chief in favor of a squad of Spartan super soldiers with faces and personalities. Among your teammates there is the able commander Carter, the emotional George, the introverted Emile, the snide engineer Kat, and the talkative sniper Jun. However, Bungie had better make us care about these characters if they want the player to care about their deaths. The game fails to do so because nearly all the characters lack depth. Every one of them is an unstoppable, an immortal superman that doesn't even flinch when it comes time for their own deaths. The only character with human vulnerability is George, who ironically dies first. From then on it becomes difficult to generate any strong emotional attachment to the characters. 3

Major criticism.

This isn't to say that the characters are completely mindless robots; in fact many of them have developing personalities, but the game just doesn't spend enough time developing them beyond the super soldier demeanor. For this, I blame the game play. *Halo: Reach* is a shooter that centers on "run and gun" fighting. It is downright difficult to create sympathetic characters when all we see them doing is murdering every alien life form within 500 yards. 4

Further develops the reason for the lack of character development in the game.

Looking at other classics like *Half-Life* brings the necessity of good characterization into sharp relief. For those of you who have played the game, think for a moment about how tedious the experience would have been in *Half-Life 2* if your supporting character Alex was just one step up from a help screen. Because she seems like a human with real emotions, Alex becomes an integral, and welcome, part of the story. The supporting characters in *Reach* just don't work in this position because the player does not see them as anything more than ordinance support. *Halo: Reach* will be remembered for trying to develop good characters, but they fall short of really making those characters human. 5

Compares the game to other games with better character development that have reached classic status.

The writer knows that his audience is other game players. He speaks to them as a fellow gamer in a voice that includes appropriate sarcasm.

Dobmeyer 3

Shows how the game fails to meet the second criterion.

Finally we come to the most important part of *Reach:* the story. Too bad that there really isn't much to it. *Reach* is built around the simple premise of super soldiers fighting an alien invasion, a story that in the game world is only slightly less common than trees. *Halo: Reach* pretty much boils down to killing whoever is in front of you and progressing by finding more to kill. Nothing else actually happens during the game itself; all of the important dialogue and characterization occur during animated cut scenes, which gives the game a detached feeling. Instead of a coherent story, it's more like a series of isolated cut scenes strung together with violence. 6

Gives more development about why the game fails to meet the second criterion.

This problem ties in with a more general issue with *Reach:* the general lack of polish. Polish in game creation is like editing and revising for a book, and just as essential. Having a polished game means that levels flow smoothly from one set to another, the Artificial Intelligence works without feeling artificial, and the scenes impart a feeling of wonder. 7

Qualifies the review by stating ways in which the game excels. This move adds credibility to the writer, showing his knowledge and fairness.

I do have to give credit to Bungie for delivering the set. The scenery in *Reach* is unlike any other shooter to date. With vast backdrops of war raging in the distance, they almost manage to give the player the feeling of being part of something greater. I also give credit to Bungie for the A.I. Enemies in *Reach* react almost like real people and the Elites are downright cunning in their strategies. Too bad that after you have killed a few thousand of them as part of the campaign they cease to be scary or menacing in any way, shape or form. 8

Explains why the game did not succeed as a story.

What it amounts to is that Bungie liked the run and gun tactics a little too much. They allowed the game to become nothing more than a straight road between the same boring fight. The gameplay requires the player to keep his eyes glued to the action. As a result there is very little time to dwell on that wondrous feeling of being an integral part of a global mission. Polish could have taken care of that. If Bungie had taken the time to balance, or better yet, incorporate the scenery into the flow of the game *Halo: Reach* could possibly reach that elusive classic status. As it stands, it feels like Bungie made a set for *Lord of the Rings* just to perform a puppet show. The general lack of polish 9

Dobmeyer 4

damages *Reach*'s case for classic status to the point where slamming out patches isn't going to fix the problem. Bungie really dropped the ball on this one.

Sums up the reviewer's judgment.

Despite my despairing tone, *Halo: Reach* is not the worst game on the market 10
today, but it isn't deserving of such massive hype either. The game is mediocre. It is another generic shooter with some pretty backgrounds and won't be remembered in a different light in a decade. Games like *Half-life* and *Deus Ex* with their wonderfully complex stories and in-depth character development will always trump *Halo: Reach* when it comes to classic status. For all of the people who are considering buying *Halo: Reach,* I advise putting it on the rent list for now and saving your money for *Half-life: Episode 3* if Valve ever gets around to making it.

Stays with the angle of classic versus mediocre games.

CREDITS

page 280: Chokkattu, Julian. "Samsung Galaxy S9 Review." Digital Trends (2018), https://www.digitaltrends.com/cell-phone-reviews/samsung-galaxy-s9-review/ . Used with permission of YGS Group.

page 286: Betttinger, Eric and Susanna Loeb, (2017, June 9). "Promises and Pitfalls of Online Education", Brookings, Used by permission. **page 299:** Courtesy of Collin Dobmeyer

CHAPTER 13

Choosing Modes of Development

ENGAGING QUESTIONS

In this chapter, you will engage with the following questions:

- What are modes of development?
- How do the various modes help writers achieve specific aims?
- How do writers use these modes to develop their work?
- How do writers develop a repertoire of modes to use when developing a piece of writing?

SUPPOSE YOU ARE WRITING AN INFORMATIVE PAPER ABOUT EARTHSHIPS, the sustainable houses that people build in remote areas off the power grid. You have to get your essay off the ground somehow; you need an idea for an introduction. What are your options?

- You could describe an earthship, giving specific details about the natural and recycled building materials and the ground-hugging architecture.
- You could define the term *earthship* and explain the ways in which such houses are self-enclosed environments like spaceships.
- You could narrate, or tell the story, of a typical day in an earthship, comparing the experience to a day in a nonsustainable house.

These three options (among other possibilities) are **modes of development.** The modes are *moves that writers make when constructing a piece of writing.*

What Are the Modes?

In this chapter, we will examine eight modes of development.

1. **Exemplifying:** Giving instances or examples
2. **Narrating:** Telling a story or recounting a process
3. **Describing:** Showing the parts or features of something
4. **Evaluating:** Assessing how good something is
5. **Defining:** Telling what something means
6. **Classifying:** Putting something in a group with similar things
7. **Comparing-contrasting:** Saying what something is like and not like
8. **Showing cause and effect:** Explaining why something exists or happens

We list the modes one by one, but in practice they work in combination, two or three at a time. For example, you might define and exemplify to explain "communism": citing a dictionary definition and providing examples of communist nations, such as Cuba and North Korea. You might also compare and contrast communism with capitalism. The following text shows how modes work in combination.

READING 13.1

Repatriation Raises Questions That Resist Sweeping Answers

IOANNIS D. STEFANIDIS

Ioannis D. Stefanidis is Professor of Diplomatic History at Aristotle University of Thessaloniki in Greece. The following article, which appeared in History Today *in 2019, contributes to a heated and ongoing debate about* repatriation*—that is, the return of artifacts and art stolen from relatively powerless countries or from native people by colonial powers and private collectors.*

Mode: Exemplification. The entire article uses a single example to explore the problems that repatriation can raise.

Mode: Narrative. The author gives us a brief history of the Horses of Saint Mark.

Mode: Description. All narratives use description, in this case, references to the many places where the statues have resided or been displayed to the public.

Mode: Evaluation. This paragraph begins to assess the competing claims of Greece, Italy, Turkey, and France to "own" the Horses of St. Mark.

1 Few artifacts encapsulate the intricacy of this question better than the "Horses of Saint Mark." Variously dated to classical Greek or Roman antiquity, these copper statues of four horses found their way to the Hippodrome of Constantinople in the fourth century AD, were looted and shipped to Venice after the sacking of the Byzantine capital by the Crusaders in 1204, removed from St. Mark's Basilica and placed on the Arc de Triomphe in Paris by Napoleon in 1797 and, following Waterloo, returned to Venice, where they remain. More recently, one or more of them were displayed in various cities abroad and in Milan, before, in 1982, they were relocated inside St. Mark, as a precaution against further damage from air pollution.

2 The fate of the horses raises a number of issues, common to innumerable cases of claimed cultural property around the world. First, one needs to establish their place of origin: this could be either some part of Greece or, more plausibly, Italy. A case could be made that, irrespective of where their foundry lay, they were intended for display in Constantinople. There for nearly nine centuries they symbolized

Rick Elkins/Getty Images

Mode: Evaluation. Continues to assess competing claims, the point being that one cannot say which claim is best.

equestrian prowess. True, they were moved to Venice as spoils of war, but they became an integral part of that city's religious life for another nine centuries. Their forced Parisian sojourn seems to underscore their identification with the lagoon city, whose environment has, however, proved corrosive.

Who, then, is entitled to claim "repatriation" before the UNESCO Intergovernmental Committee? Could the second looters, the French, qualify? Under international law, looting is illegal today and was widely deprecated in 1797, though one might wonder about the difference between Napoleon's pilfering of the horses and the Venetians' misappropriation since 1204. Time offers an easy answer. This would suggest that Constantinople or its modern incarnation, Istanbul, should be considered. Could the Turks claim the horses "back," on the basis of their connection with an existing monument, the Hippodrome, despite their nine-century long absence and the fact that they are not exactly associated with the Ottoman or Turkish cultural heritage? The repatriation of artifacts removed from their place of origin before such practice was progressively outlawed during the 20th century raises questions that resist sweeping answers. 3

How Do Writers Choose Modes?

Modes are means of development, ways of saying something. They make sense, therefore, only in relation to the aims a writer is trying to achieve. What does Stefanidis' article try to do? Clearly, it informs. But Stefanidis also has an angle, a definite point of view he wants us to share: Repatriation is not always, or even usually, a simple matter. Where a work of art belongs, what nation or people can be said to "own it," typically is controversial.

Stefanidis chose his modes based on the aims (informing and persuading) of his article. His writing task is to address the large question of whether works of art, once removed from their home countries, ought to be repatriated, or returned. He chooses exemplification as his main mode of development, his example being the statue titled "The Horses of Saint Mark," which illustrates well the complications involved in determining where a work of art should belong. Finally, he evaluates, assessing the competing claims of each country who has claimed the "Horses of Saint Mark" as its own.

In sum, *select modes that help you realize your aims.*

BEST PRACTICES When Should You Apply the Modes?

The eight modes are always at work. As you draft, you are using them without thinking about them. However, there are times when thinking about them can help.

1. *After planning your current writing project*

   Ask these questions:

   What aim or aims do I want my essay to achieve?

   Who are my readers? What will they need and expect from me?

Based on your answers to these questions, look again at your plan and sketch out the modes you will need for each section. What might you need to define? What must you describe?—and so on, considering all eight options. This will help to keep you from getting stuck or bogged down with no ideas about where to go next.

2. *When revising a paper*
   When you have a paper in first draft, examine it for underdeveloped points. Ask the same questions as in item 1, and sketch out additional or different moves to solve whatever developmental problems you detect.
3. *When assessing graded papers*
   Look at the instructor comments. Did they single out places where development could improve? Do you see ways to develop more fully what you said, either by adding modes or using different ones?

What Do the Modes Look Like in Detail?

In this section, we look more closely at examples of the modes in action.

Exemplifying

When you exemplify, you give the reader instances or examples to answer the questions **Who? What?** and **Which?**

Types of examples include

- Brief examples
- Extended examples

Brief Examples

Use brief examples to provide instances of an abstract category or idea. Our first illustration comes from Al Gore's influential book, *An Inconvenient Truth* (see Figure 13.1). It consists of seven photographs showing examples from the category of green technology.

Imagine that Gore had omitted Figure 13.1. Readers would not *see* the technologies and would therefore have a less concrete idea of what is meant by green technology.

How do you choose examples when many are available? Look at the ones Gore chose. He chose examples *to persuade* readers to buy environmentally responsible products and to become advocates of green technologies. *When you write, choose examples that will help you achieve your aims.*

Even a brief example should be specific. Details make examples memorable and effective. Consider this paragraph that describes the consumer tastes of a well-off class of people known in the 1980s as yuppies. Consider how the details add up to convey the author's angle or point of view:

> Here are just a few of the yuppie badges: yellow ties and red suspenders, Merlot, marinated salmon steaks, green-bottle beer, Club Med vacations, stuff with ducks on it, Gaggenau stoves, Sub-Zero refrigerators, latte, clothing from Ann Taylor or Ralph Lauren, designer water . . ..
>
> —JAMES B. TWITCHELL, "HOW I BOUGHT MY RED MIATA"

FIGURE **13.1**

Kinds of Green Technologies

In his influential book *An Inconvenient Truth,* Al Gore chose examples like these to persuade readers to buy environmentally responsible products and to become advocates of green technologies.

a) Koichi Kamoshida/Getty Images; b) huangcolin/Shutterstock; c) Jose Gil/Shutterstock.com; d) David Burton/Beateworks/Corbis; e) Kyu Oh/iStock Exclusive/Getty Images; f) Corbis Premium Collection/Corbis/Alamy; g) Car Culture/Getty Images

The more specific your description of something (or someone) is, such as Twitchell's very detailed description of yuppies, the better idea your readers will have of what you are talking about.

Dynamic Graphics Group/Getty Images

Twitchell might have said: "Yuppies like fancy clothes, wine, broiled fish, special beer, and expensive vacations." Instead, he got very specific. Not fancy clothes, but "yellow ties and red suspenders," not wine, but "Merlot." He is poking fun at the yuppies by showing us how predictable and brand-specific their consumption habits were.

When your instructor asks you to "be specific" when giving examples, think about how you can move down from general words like "car" to words that bring to mind a picture of a particular car: "a fifteen-year-old, lipstick-red, '91 Ford Thunderbird," as Katherine Krueger-Land described her car in "Driving Away." (See her essay in Chapter 4, pages 57–60.)

Extended Examples

The mode of exemplification can be used to develop a paragraph or several paragraphs of your writing. These extended examples usually incorporate other modes such as description or narration. Here is an example from a student paper on gender roles in which the author uses a source to provide an extended example of one way in which high school traditions promote gender stereotypes. (See his essay in Chapter 7, pages 158–60.)

> Pascoe (2007) observed a typical public high school for an entire year and found that the school reinforced ideas of masculinity as white, athletic, and heterosexual. A popularity contest called the "Mr. Cougar" competition is an example of how the process works.
>
> Candidates for the "Mr. Cougar" title performed short skits in which they mocked boys who did not fit the stereotype of the "manly man." In one skit, titled "The Revenge of the Nerds," the candidates came on stage looking weak and effeminate, dressed in nerdy clothes. The audience thought this was hysterically funny because, as Pascoe explains, in our culture, "male femininity . . . is coded as humorous" (p. 4). The nerds' girlfriends were then kidnapped by other boys dressed as "gangsta's." To get "their women" back, the nerdy boys had to bulk up by lifting weights. The girls were depicted as trophies awarded to the nerds once they had transformed themselves into manly men and proved their masculinity by rescuing the girls from the gangsta's (p. 45).
>
> —Jamie Cummins, "Exploring the Concept of Gender"

The example is specific in describing the details and smoothly integrates quotations and paraphrases. You might compare this version with the draft in Chapter 7, pages 154–55.

Narrating

When you narrate, you tell a story or recount a process. Narratives answer the question **"What happened?"** A narrative usually sticks to chronological order, and it can be combined with other modes. The extended example of the high school skit, above, combines exemplification and narration to show what happened that reinforced gender stereotypes. Narrative is the primary mode used in telling stories, whether fiction or nonfiction. When used to develop parts of a larger piece of writing, narrative can play a variety of roles.

Types of narratives include

- Anecdotes
- Dialogue
- Summaries
- Process narratives

Personal anecdotes, like the story of a boy's father catching Joe DiMaggio's foul ball, are a great way to open or close an essay and make important connections.

AP Images

Anecdotes

The most common narrative is the **anecdote,** *a short personal account of something that happened,* commonly used to open essays, conclude them, and illustrate important points in between. Below is the first paragraph from an essay about one of the most remarkable accomplishments in baseball, Joe DiMaggio's 1941 56-game hitting streak. The author was a distinguished scholar in the field of evolutionary biology.

> My father was a court stenographer. At his less than princely salary, we watched Yankee games from the bleachers or high in the third deck. But one of the judges had season tickets, so we occasionally sat in the lower boxes when hizzoner couldn't attend. One afternoon, while DiMaggio was going 0 for 4 against, of all people, the lowly St. Louis Browns, the great man fouled one in our direction. "Catch it, Dad," I screamed. "You never get them," he replied, but stuck up his hand like the Statue of Liberty—and the ball fell right in. I mailed it to DiMaggio, and, bless him, he actually sent the ball back, signed and in a box marked "insured." Insured, that is, to make me the envy of the neighborhood, and DiMaggio the model and hero of my life.
>
> —STEPHEN JAY GOULD, "THE STREAK OF STREAKS"

This anecdote connects the writer's childhood experience to his fascination with a baseball record and the man who set it. The result is an effective opener. Anecdotes, like most stories, benefit from the use of dialogue. Dialogue helps to catch the drama of the moment, as in the brief exchange between the son and his father in the example above. Although in this example, both speakers' words are in the same paragraph, it is preferable to make a new paragraph with each change of speaker. Use common identifying tags such as "I said" and "she asked" unless the speaker's identity is so obvious from the context that tags are not needed.

Dialogue

Dialogue is a narrative mode that helps in many genres, such as informative articles, where you might interview an expert and use his or her *exact words* to supply some of the information. Or an entire piece of writing could take the form of an interview or discussion. Ideas can be explored through dialogue. Plato wrote his great works of philosophy as dialogues between his teacher, Socrates, and other characters. Consider using dialogue in your writing when appropriate to add realism and voice, as in the example below from David Herbert Donald's Pulitzer Prize–winning biography of Abraham Lincoln.

> At three o'clock he broke away from his desk to take a ride with Mary in an open carriage. As they started out, she asked whether he wanted any guests to accompany them, but he said, "No—I prefer to ride by ourselves today." They drove about the city and went out to the Navy Yard [. . .]. Throughout the afternoon he was "cheerful—almost joyous," his wife recalled, and his spirits were so high that she said to him, laughing, "Dear Husband, you almost startle me by your great cheerfulness."
>
> "And well may I do so, Mary," he responded, "I consider *this day,* the war has come to a close." He then added, in what was as close to a reprimand as he ever offered to his wife, "We must *both* be more cheerful in the future—between the war and the loss of our darling Willie—we have both been very miserable."
>
> —David Herbert Donald, *Lincoln*

Summaries

Narratives also work well in creating a **summary** of a complex history or situation, as in the following example:

> Humankind has been steadily transforming Earth's surface for some 8,000 years, initially in Eurasia and later on all continents. Initially, we caused these transformations by clearing land for farming; later, other aspects of civilized life joined farming as important causes of this transformation. Well before the industrial era, the cumulative result over many millennia was an enormous loss of what had been "natural" on this planet.
>
> During the 1800's and 1900's, human population increased from 1 billion to 6 billion, an explosion unprecedented in human history. This rise came about because new sanitary standards and medicines reduced the incidence of disease and because human ingenuity led to innovations in agriculture that fed ever-larger numbers of people. As a result, our already sizable impact on Earth's surface increased at a much faster rate.
>
> By most estimates, the explosive population increase still under way will end near AD 2050 as global population levels out at some 9–10 billion people, or roughly 50 percent more people than now. A major reason for the predicted stabilization will be the increase in affluence that has historically resulted in fewer children per family.
>
> —William F. Ruddiman, "Consuming Earth's Gifts"

Writers often use narrative summaries to recap key points made earlier. In this case, Ruddiman sums up key points he made in the preceding chapters of his book, *Plows, Plagues, and Petroleum.*

Note these features:

- Summaries often take more than one paragraph.
- These narratives often help writers make a case. Ruddiman argues that human impact on the environment is nothing new. You can see why, then, he starts his story with the beginnings of agriculture 8,000 years ago. Narratives often emphasize cause and effect. That is, they are efforts to explain why something happens or happened.

See Chapter 10, pages 218–20, for guidance.

Process Narratives

Use **process narratives** to *describe how something is done, how something works, or how something changes over time.* Examine Figure 13.2, an example of a **flowchart,** *a common visual tool that depicts the steps in a process.*

Even simple processes are easier for readers to follow and remember with a flowchart. For complicated processes, such as computer troubleshooting, flowcharts can be indispensable.

A flowchart is a visual example of a process narrative, but many process narratives rely solely on words. This paragraph explains how muscles in the eye respond to light and darkness:

> Our pupils naturally expand in darkness and shrink in bright light through the actions of the two opposing iris muscles, the iris dilator and the iris sphincter. The dilator muscle, which extends radially through the iris, contracts to pull the iris outward, bunching it up like an open curtain. The iris sphincter is arranged in a circular pattern, similar to a purse string. Its constriction pulls the iris inward and flattens it, like a curtain drawn closed.
>
> —Donald Mutti, "How Our Pupils Dilate"

Writers use process narratives to explain how something works, how to assemble and operate machines, how legislation makes its way through the U.S. Congress, and for a host of other purposes.

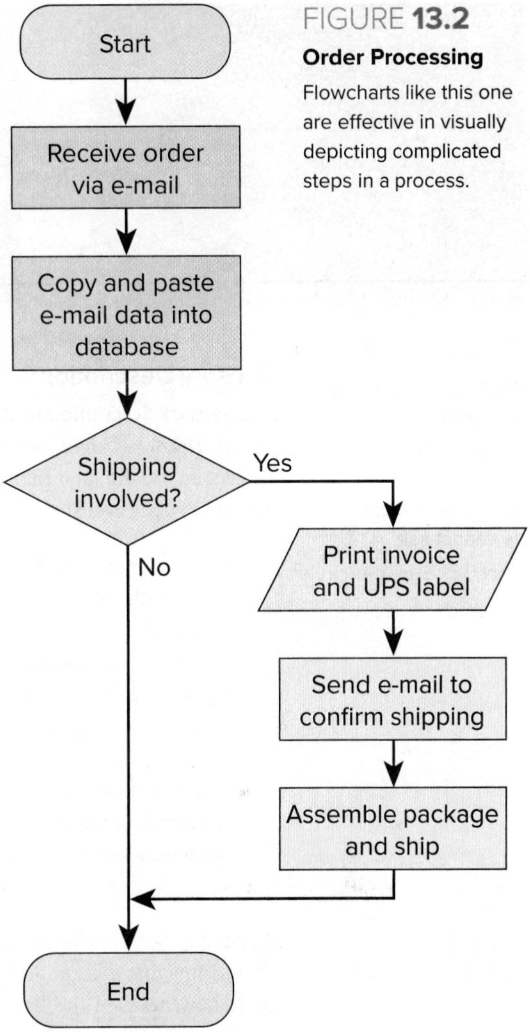

FIGURE **13.2**
Order Processing
Flowcharts like this one are effective in visually depicting complicated steps in a process.

Describing

When you describe, you discuss the parts or features of something to answer questions such as **"How does something look, feel, sound, taste, and smell?"** Descriptions can also show readers how the parts of something are related, and description is often used in evaluations to tell readers why something is good or bad.

Types of description include

- Sensory
- Conceptual
- Scientific

Figure 13.3 shows the two primary ways description works. First, as in the photograph of a hurricane, it helps readers see your subject matter or recall what they have seen before. Second, as in the drawing of a hurricane, it reveals what readers cannot see, such as the internal structure of something.

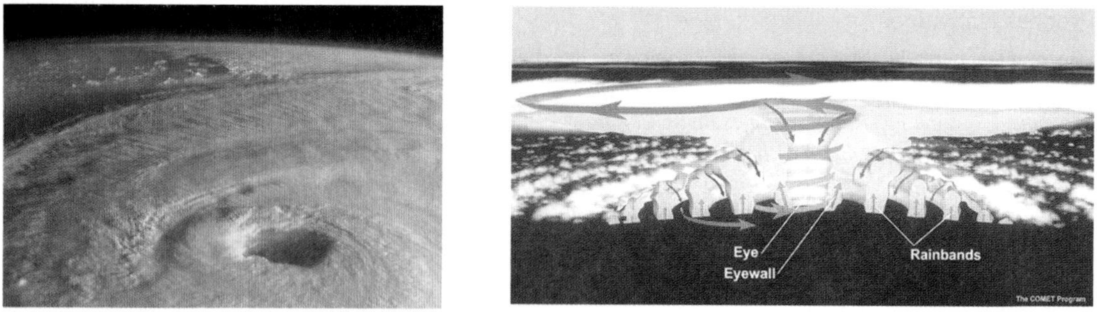

FIGURE **13.3**

Photograph versus Drawing

Photographs capture what we can see; drawings depict structures we cannot see.

Purestock/SuperStock

Sensory Description

Use **sensory description** to communicate the concrete details of something you experienced. *Details of sight, sound, touch, smell, and taste* help the reader experience your subject as you did, and thus share your feelings about it. Here is a description that both depicts a scene and shares a feeling:

> It is Easter Sunday, 1950. I am dressed in a green, flocked scalloped-hem dress (handmade by my adoring sister, Ruth) that has its own smooth satin petticoat and tiny hot-pink roses tucked into each scallop. My shoes, new T-strap patent leather, again highly biscuit-polished. I am six years old and have learned one of the longest Easter speeches to be heard that day, totally unlike the speech I said when I was two: "Easter lilies / pure and white / blossom in / the morning light." When I rise to give my speech I do so on a great wave of love and pride and expectation. People in the church stop rustling their new crinolines. They seem to hold their breath. I can tell they admire my dress, but it is my spirit, bordering on sassiness (womanishness), they secretly applaud.
>
> —Alice Walker, "Beauty: When the Other Dancer Is the Self"

Appealing both to the eye and ear, this paragraph is effective sensory description, letting us imagine a scene from long ago and the sense of community that went with it. Note how detailed the description is: "tiny hot-pink roses tucked into each scallop." Such detailed descriptions are known as ***images*** because they paint a picture with words.

Most description leans heavily on sight because human beings rely so much on vision. In your descriptions, do not neglect the other senses: hearing, taste, smell, and touch. They can also contribute to sensory detail in description.

Conceptual Description

Use **conceptual description** to *communicate ideas and categories. We learn to distinguish greenways from trails especially, but also from "nature reserves, parks, cultural features and historic sites . . . and . . . populated areas."*

> Greenways are corridors of protected open space managed for conservation and recreation purposes. Greenways often follow natural land or water features, and link nature reserves, parks, cultural features and historic sites with each other and with populated areas. Greenways can be publicly or privately

owned, and some are the result of public/private partnerships. Trails are paths used for walking, bicycling, horseback riding, or other forms of recreation or transportation. Some greenways include trails, while others do not. Some appeal to people, while others attract wildlife. From the hills of inland America to the beaches and barrier islands of the coast, greenways provide a vast network linking America's special places.

—"BUILDING A BETTER LIFE THROUGH GREENWAYS AND TRAILS," TRAILS AND GREENWAYS CLEARING HOUSE

The description in this passage is conceptual, depicting categories rather than things we see, hear, touch or taste. First, we get a definition of greenways: "corridors of protected space," then, second, concepts associated with greenways, such as "nature reserves, parks, cultural features and historic sites." Third, we encounter the distinction between "publicly and privately owned," two more concepts that appeal to the mind rather than the senses, as does the difference between greenways with trails versus those without.

As with sensual description, the details of conceptual description convey an angle or attitude toward what is being described. "Greenways" is a celebration of human-managed natural places, rich in variety, each greenway having its own makeup and appeal. Clearly, the writers love greenways and want us to share in their enthusiasm.

Writers are sometimes taught to keep their attitudes and judgments out of writing, especially for school papers. For some assignments, like lab reports, that is good advice. For others, however, loaded description is not only appropriate but necessary. For example, an assignment that asks you to take a stance (argue or persuade) will call for a certain amount of loaded description. How strong should your language be? That depends on the topic, how you see it, and how you want your audience to see it.

Scientific Description

Use scientific description to report the methods and findings of research. For example, the following passage describes the apparatus required to conduct an experiment:

Methods and Materials

A 1,000-milliliter flask fitted with a three-hole rubber stopper, separatory funnel, and a measuring pipette was used. First, fill an Erlenmeyer flask with 250 milliliters of distilled water. Put the glass tube with a right-angle bend into one hole of the three-hole stopper. Place stopper in flask making sure no air bubbles are trapped.

–DEBORAH A. SMITH, "TRANSPIRATION"

Much scientific description is far more technical, including research methods and statistics, but we can note some common features of description that reports on research:

- Maintains an objective tone
- Avoids first person
- Refers to other researchers and gives credentials
- Draws conclusions about the meaning of the observations or results described

Evaluating

When you evaluate, you assess how good something is. Use the evaluation mode to answer questions such as these: **How well does this work? How bad would it be if that happened? How should we measure this? Why does this thing work so well?**

Types of evaluation include

- Personal evaluation
- Formal evaluation

Personal Evaluation

Use personal evaluation to offer your judgment or opinion. Most political and social commentary cartoons offer briefly stated evaluations, such as the example in Figure 13.4. Computers have brought us the "information superhighway," but at the price of making wisdom as scarce as water in a desert. That is the cartoonist's view of the Internet, shown in a simple drawing.

When warranted, don't shy away from personal evaluations. Below is an example in which a student expresses his disapproval of the dating culture of his peers.

> The hook-up culture is very deceptive. Hooking-up promises to be liberating and strengthening. Yet people find themselves needing more and more "liquid courage" to even make the first move. Hooking-up promises fun and fulfillment and no regrets, but when morning comes it delivers the "walk of shame." The hook-up culture has tricked us. It has led us to believe that our emotions are disconnected from our bodies, that love is divorced from sex.
>
> —JACK GRIMES, "HOOK-UP CULTURE"

When you think that something is either good or bad, say so and then explain why, as Grimes does here. The evaluation need not be a moral judgment; it can be any assessment of anything, such as the quality of a movie, the impact of a policy, and so on.

FIGURE **13.4**

Where Is Wisdom in the Information Age?

Most political and social commentary cartoons like this one offer clear evaluations. Do not be afraid to make such judgments in your writing.

Mike Keefe. InToon.com.

Formal Evaluation

Use **formal evaluation** when you have done some research and serious study of a topic. Like personal opinions, formal evaluations are also *your judgment on a topic, but they are more thought through and are supported with evidence.* They are often mixed judgments that balance the pluses against the minuses, as in the following example.

> I acknowledge the many positive things that the [online] network has to offer: enhancing friendship, family connections, education, commerce, and recreation. The triumphalist narrative of the Web is the reassuring story that people want to hear and that technologists want to tell. But the heroic story is not the whole story. In virtual words and computer games, people are flattened into personae [made up roles]. On social networks, people are reduced to their profiles. On our mobile devices, we often talk to each other on the move and with little disposable time—so little, in fact, that we communicate in a new language of abbreviation in which letters stand for words and emoticons for feelings. We don't ask the open-ended "How are you?" Instead we ask the more limited "Where are you?" and "What's up?" These are good questions for getting someone's location and making a simple plan. They are not so good for opening a dialogue about complexity of feeling. We are increasingly connected to each other but oddly more alone: *in intimacy, new solitudes.*
>
> SHERRY TURKLE, *ALONE TOGETHER: WHY WE EXPECT MORE FROM TECHNOLOGY AND LESS FROM EACH OTHER*

The author here is a professor at MIT, a person who has done much research on the social effects of technology. Her stance is critical of information technology, but she knows enough to concede that there are social benefits. Her strategy is to devote a few sentences to the positive side and then, with a transition like "but" or "however," devote a few sentences to the negative side. When you opt for the positives-versus-negatives structure, be sure to leave no doubt what your stance is. Turkle clearly thinks genuine intimacy and friendship matter more than experimenting with identity.

Defining

When you define, you tell what something means. Definitions primarily answer *who* and *what* questions: **Who is this person? What is that? What does this mean?** A good definition educates the reader by specifying exactly what the writer means. There are many uses for the defining mode in writing.

Types of definitions include

- Simple definition
- Complex definition
- Negative definition
- Stipulative definition

Simple Definition

Use simple definitions to provide the meaning of words readers might not know. For example:

> Solar cells, also known as photovoltaics, use semi-conductor materials to convert sunlight into electric current.
>
> —DANIEL M. KAMMEN, "THE RISE OF RENEWABLE ENERGY"

Kammen defines solar cells because he is writing for a readership that includes people who may not know much about solar energy.

Use simple definitions also to specify the meaning of terms that readers might understand differently or less precisely than you need them to be understood. For example:

> I'm talking about teardowns—the practice of purchasing and demolishing an existing house to make way for a new, much bigger house on the same site.
>
> —RICHARD MOE, "BATTLING TEARDOWNS, SAVING NEIGHBORHOODS"

Moe wants to distinguish the most general meaning of "teardowns," which includes old, condemned houses, from the meaning he intends: the destruction of sound but smaller houses in older neighborhoods to make way for McMansions.

Complex Definition

Some words defy simple definitions. *Love, friendship,* and *wisdom* are good examples of concepts that require complex definitions. Use complex definition to show your understanding of a word that has many meanings. Here is an example of one of the most complex concepts in the English language, a word uttered millions of times every day:

> What is love really? What does it mean to love someone?
>
> . . . In *Altruism and Altruistic Love,* Post, Underwood, Schloss and Hurlbutt (2002) raised an important question: "What is at the very core of human altruistic love?" Their answer was that love might be conceptualized as "affirmative affection."
>
> We all know what it feels like to be valued in this way, and we remember loving persons who conveyed this affective affirmation through tone of voice, facial expression, a hand on the shoulder in time of grief, and a desire to be with us. . . . Love implies benevolence, care, compassion, and *action.* (p. 4)
>
> In our view, actions that fit the description of a loving relationship are expressions of affection, both physical and emotional; a wish to offer pleasure and satisfaction to one's mate; tenderness, compassion, and sensitivity to the needs of the other. . . .
>
> —ROBERT W. FIRESTONE, LISA A. FIRESTONE, AND JOYCE CATLETT, "WHAT IS LOVE?"

This kind of definition is also called **operational,** *which means that something is defined by telling how it works.* Regardless of the name, the purpose is clear: to make vague abstractions, with many meanings, into something more precise, with something closer to a single meaning.

Negative Definition

Use negative definitions, saying what a word does not mean, to argue that the common understanding of a word is not correct. Negative definition is especially useful with abstract concepts like love. This use of negative definition comes from the same article as the example cited in the previous section:

> To better understand what genuine love is, perhaps we should also describe what it is not. Love is not what we mean when one is told by a family member that "mommy or daddy really loves you but he/she just doesn't know how to show it."

> Love is not selfish, possessive, or demanding, or a proprietary right over the other. Love is never submission or dominance, emotional coercion, or manipulation. Love is not the desperate attempt to deny aloneness or the search for security that many couples manifest in their desire for a fused identity.
>
> —ROBERT W. FIRESTONE, LISA A. FIRESTONE, AND JOYCE CATLETT, "WHAT IS LOVE?"

The authors say what love is not because people routinely think that "real love" includes some or all of the situations and motives described. The authors want us to see that much "real love" is not genuine love at all.

Stipulative Definition

In a stipulative definition, a writer gives a specific and often original meaning to a term, usually as part of an argument that challenges conventional thinking about the word.

When you stipulate a definition, you redefine words to suit your purpose. In this example, the author is talking about the use of style in the design of everyday objects:

> In this context, "aesthetics" obviously does not refer to the philosophy of art. Aesthetics is the way we communicate through the senses. It is the art of creating reactions without words, through the look and feel of people, places and things. . . .
>
> Aesthetics shows rather than tells, depicts rather than instructs. The effects are immediate, perceptual and emotional.
>
> —VIRGINIA POSTREL, "THE AESTHETIC IMPERATIVE"

Postrel is arguing for the value of beauty in ordinary, everyday experience, like the design of a bathroom. Because aesthetics is most commonly used in the fine arts, she has to spell out how she is using the word for her topic.

The second type of stipulative definition calls into question the connotations of a word, the emotional overtones it has. Barry M. Goldwater (1909–1998), a U.S. senator from Arizona, was the Republican candidate for president in 1964. Accused of being a dangerous extremist, he made the following remark near the end of his acceptance speech for the nomination that has since often been quoted by conservatives and libertarians:

> I would remind you that extremism in the defense of liberty is no vice. And let me remind you also that moderation in the pursuit of justice is no virtue.
>
> —BARRY M. GOLDWATER

In his use of stipulative definition, Goldwater takes the word "extremism," used to criticize and condemn, and recasts it as something acceptable at least, even worthy of praise.

Classifying

When you classify, you put something in a group with similar things. Classifications can answer several questions: **What kind of thing is this? How is this related to that? Where does that fit in a larger scheme?**

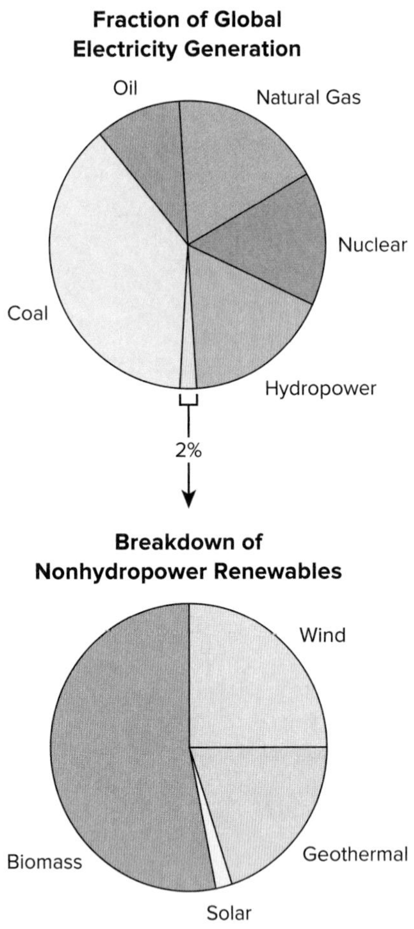

FIGURE **13.5**

Dividing and Subdividing

Organizing information into chunks and dividing and subdividing as needed is a very effective and straightforward way to convey information.

Types of classification include

- Simple classification
- Mixed classification
- Questioning classifications

Among the modes of development, classifying has special importance because how we divide things into groups has much to do with how we think. Examine Figure 13.5, the two pie graphs that appeared in an article about sources of renewable energy.

Both graphs are examples of classification. We have one big category, Global Electricity Generation: all the ways to generate electricity. This category is divided into six types, one of which is nonhydropower renewables (wind, solar, and so on).

The top pie chart shows us how much of each type the world uses; the bottom pie chart examines one category from the top pie chart by dividing it into four subcategories. Taken together, the graphs show that, despite the vast energy-generating potential of renewables, they do not as yet supply much of our energy.

Organizing information this way is straightforward: Divide something into chunks, then divide the chunks into smaller chunks, and so on, dividing and subdividing as much as you need to.

Simple Classification

Use **simple classifications** to *make distinctions between items in one category and items in another,* as in the following example. The author is pointing out a sharp contrast between Native American views of the human condition and those of most major world religions.

> One aspect of many Native American worldviews involves their concept of the human condition at the beginning of life. Generally the central image is that of a person starting out on the "path of life" and striving to follow this path without falling off or straying from it throughout one's allotted time on earth. The central idea is keeping one's balance on the path by honoring the traditional teachings and practices of one's people. It is believed that such a life is full of harmony and health, and enables a person to be useful to his or her family and community.
>
> According to this way of thinking, every person starts out already on the proper path and simply strives to remain on it. This stands in marked contrast to the way nearly all the major "world religions" depict the human condition at the beginning of life. According to the dominant world views of both the West and the East, humans either come into a world that is illusory and/or evil, or they arrive on the scene already out of harmony with the goals and values of divine reality. In either case, something is deemed to be drastically wrong at the very beginning of life and needs to be set right before humans can enter into the fullness and bliss for which they are intended.
>
> —JERRY H. GILL, *NATIVE AMERICAN WORLDVIEWS: AN INTRODUCTION*

Two categories—Native Americans in contrast with most other people—are set apart by the difference between seeing the world as good versus seeing it as "illusory and/or evil."

The human mind works largely by "this versus that" distinctions, and therefore simple classification is a common mode of development.

Mixed Classification

Use **mixed classifications** to depict complex situations in which *objects, or in the case of the next example, people, can be grouped in different ways according to different classification schemes.*

> One in nine Americans is an immigrant. And half the laborers entering the American workforce in the 1990s were foreign-born. Add in their families and extended families and the picture grows more dramatic still. Together, immigrants and their children now account for one in five Americans. Hispanics, at nearly 14 percent of the population, are already the largest minority, outnumbering blacks. Asian-Americans are still a relatively small share of the nation—at only 4 percent. But despite their numbers, they, too, are going to play a major part in the country's future: already, they make up between 15 and 20 percent of the students at most Ivy League colleges.
>
> Where do these new arrivals come from? Just over half the foreign-born are Hispanic and a little more than a quarter are Asian. They hail from all the corners of the globe, though more from some countries than from others. Mexicans, by far the largest category, account for roughly one in three first-generation immigrants—almost ten times more than any other nationality. The next largest groups are Filipinos and Indians, followed by Chinese, Vietnamese, Koreans, Cubans and Salvadorans—but none of these account for more than 3 or 4 percent of the total.
>
> —Tamar Jacoby, "The New Immigrants and the Issue of Assimilation"

Jacoby's topic is the new immigrants, the wave of people entering our country now. Their diversity is not easy to grasp. To depict it, she needs to mix some of the many ways new immigrants are classified. First, she contrasts immigrants with all Americans. Then she shifts to two large groups of immigrants in particular, Hispanics and Asian Americans, and compares these to various populations of all Americans. Finally, her third classification is immigrant groups based on national origin.

Any writer can do what Jacoby does *so long as group contrasts are clear.* Notice how Jacoby helps us follow what she has to say by staying with the Hispanic/Asian classification from the fifth sentence on. If she had made the groups she was talking about much more complex, readers would have trouble following her meaning.

Questioning Classifications

Call classifications into question to challenge entrenched or habitual ways of thinking about something. Look at Figure 13.6, an ingenious poster from an organization called the Southampton Anti-Bias Task Force. Its message: "Many skin colors fall into a single category: 'flesh.'" Our humanity is much more important than the shade of our skin.

In the 1950s, boxes of Crayola crayons included a peach-colored one, labeled "Flesh." The company renamed it "Peach" in 1962. So the poster also says: "That crayon is long gone, and with it the assumption that 'white' is normal and all other skin colors deviate from the norm."

Unfortunately, classification leads to stereotypes, which in turn lead to discrimination. Following is another potent example of questioning a stereotype that causes many

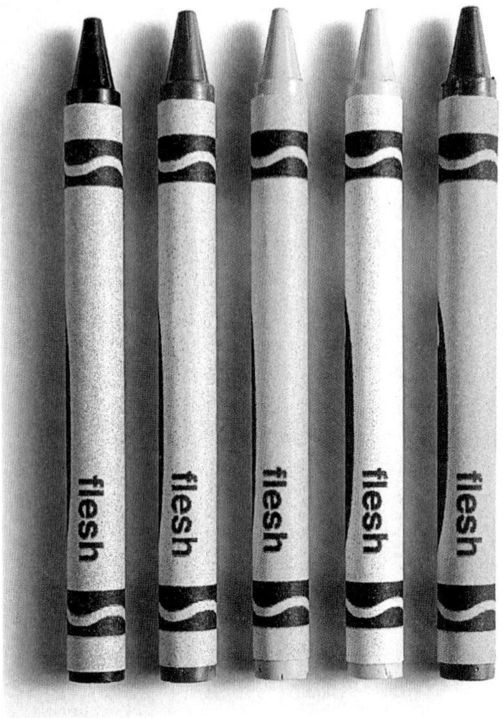

FIGURE 13.6

The Many Colors of "Flesh"

The above image from a poster recalls Crayola boxes that once labeled the center crayon "Flesh," now renamed "Peach." The bias toward white skin as "normal" is clearly the poster's target.

Bret Willis

neighborhoods in the United States to remain highly segregated. The author, an African American, had been turned down for a mortgage to buy a house in a white neighborhood.

> The bank was proceeding according to demographic data that show any time black people move into a neighborhood in the States, whites are overwhelmingly likely to move out. In droves. In panic. In concert. Pulling every imaginable resource with them, from school funding to garbage collection, to social workers who don't want to work in black neighborhoods to police whose too frequent relation to black communities is a corrupted one of containment rather than protection. It's called a tipping point, this thing that happens when black people move into white neighborhoods. The imagery is awfully catchy, you must admit: the neighborhood just tipping right on over like a terrible accident, whoops! Like a pitcher I suppose. All that nice fresh wholesome milk spilling out, running away . . . leaving the dark, echoing, upended urn of the inner city.
>
> —PATRICIA J. WILLIAMS, "THE DISTRIBUTION OF DISTRESS"

Afraid of the "tipping point," banks find ways to deny loan requests or impose terms so unfavorable that the applicant cannot afford to accept them. Clearly, our habitual ways of thinking about race as a classification still need to be exposed and challenged.

Comparing-Contrasting

When you write to compare or contrast, you are answering these questions: **How are these things similar? How do they differ?**

Types of comparing-contrasting modes include

- Comparison
- Contrast
- Analogy

Comparison

To develop a point on any topic, you might compare by drawing parallels between your subject and another to help make your point. For example, the following paragraph compares the landscape of a New Jersey industrial site to a Mediterranean vista.

> Kearny Marsh reminds James of a trip he took many years ago to the South of France. For a photographer, the Meadowlands present what he describes as "the Mediterranean problem." On one side we have the Alps (in our case, mountainous landfills, industrial landscape), and on the other, the Mediterranean (Kearny Marsh,

> the Hackensack). The challenge, then, was to compose a series of photographs that conveys both: river and skyline, habitats and trash piles, reedbeds and radio towers.
>
> —"PERPETUAL MEADOWLANDS: AMONG THE REEDBEDS OF THE HACKENSACK," BY ELIZABETH MURPHY AND JAMES WRONA

The strategy is to take two items in the same classification–in this case, two landscapes located in different parts of the world–and compare them, show how they are alike.

The similarities are emphasized effectively with a pattern of parenthetical lists: "On one side we have the Alps (in our case, mountainous landfills, industrial landscape), and on the other, the Mediterranean" (Kearny Marsh, the Hackensack). The author draws these parallels in order to illustrate what it means to encounter "the Mediterranean problem." In doing so, she is also bringing out contrasts in the landscape's features.

As with other modes, how comparison and contrast work in any particular case *depends on what a writer is trying to do.* In their photo essay in Chapter 5, Murphy and Wrona want to bring together elements of a landscape typically viewed in isolation–to capture seemingly disparate features within a single composition.

Contrast

Use contrast to emphasize the differences between things that are similar in some other ways. Contrasting items that most readers would assume are interchangeable can help you make a case for choosing one over the other.

Showing stark contrasts can make a dramatic statement. Consider Figure 13.7, a photo taken to illustrate a student's paper arguing that tearing down older homes in order to build bigger new ones destroys the character and charm of a neighborhood. (The essay appears in Chapter 33, on pages 575-76.) Notice how the contrasts in size and building style help to make the point that the new construction is a poor fit with the older homes on the street.

FIGURE **13.7**

Development in the Suburbs

Use contrast to make a point. In this case, the point is that the new construction is cheap and lacking in style, compared to the smaller house on the right.

Carolyn Channell

In the following example of simple contrast, the writer sets the ethics of reciprocity practiced by Native Americans against the greed and waste of American industry:

> To Native Americans, any action that upsets the balance of the world is unethical. With their belief in reciprocity, they would oppose taking anything from the Earth on such a large scale that balance cannot be restored. They may cut down a tree, but as Kidwell, Noley, and Tinker say, "There is no ceremony among any people for clear-cutting an entire forest" (44). Clear-cutting a forest, like factory farming, is unsustainable, wasteful, and disrespectful, which is why the theologians say that "American technological and economic development cannot embody the Indian ethic of reciprocity" (44).
>
> —Conner Kline, "Making Meat Eating Ethical"

Analogy

An analogy is an explicit comparison used to bring out similarities in apparently unrelated items or ideas. Writers often use analogies to help readers understand concepts and other complicated points. You can ask, "How is the thing I am talking about, which my audience does not understand, similar to something else that my audience does understand?" In other words, **"What is this like?"** is the key question.

Many common analogies help us to picture information, remember things, solve problems, and make decisions. For example, what analogy describes the structure of the Internet? The World Wide Web, of course. Even if the Internet does not closely resemble a spider's web, the analogy gives us a concept we can understand.

Analogies can also help us make arguments, as in the overworked analogy between alcohol and marijuana that argues if the former is legal, the latter should be also since it is so similar. But analogies can also be fresh and creative, as in the following review of *Harry Potter and the Sorcerer's Stone:*

> This overly familiar movie is like a theme park that's a few years past its prime; the rides clatter and groan with metal fatigue every time they take a curve. The picture's very raggedness makes it spooky, which is not the same thing as saying the movie is intentionally unsettling.
>
> —Elvis Mitchell, "The Sorcerer's Apprentice"

Someone who liked the movie might not like Mitchell's analogy, but it makes a strong impression. We do not usually associate movies and theme parks. How did he think of the analogy? Perhaps he thought about the film's primary audience, children, who also love theme parks. Maybe Mitchell happened to recall taking children to a rundown theme park and found enough similarities to the movie to make the link. And so an analogy is born: Likeness suddenly emerges in seemingly unrelated things.

No writer can simply decide to use an original analogy. Rather, analogies come to us or they do not. When something we are writing about reminds us of something else, we can stop and wonder why, and try to uncover the resemblance we sense is there. Being receptive to the working of our own minds is about all we can do.

Overused Analogies

Challenge overused analogies when they block good thinking. Some analogies are so common because people use them too much and without serious thought about what they mean. We can call the value of such analogies into question, as in this example.

> Thirty-five years ago, at the beginning of a twelve-year Senate inquiry into the drug industry, Senator Gaylord Nelson opened the session on psychotropic drugs by comparing them to the drugs in *Brave New World*. . . . Thirty-five years later, *Brave New World* is still invoked, time and again, as a warning against the dangers that await us if we embark on new enhancement technologies. News stories about psychotropic drugs, stem cells, reproductive technologies, or genetic engineering inevitably appear with headlines reading Brave New Medicine, Brave New Babies, Brave New Minds, or Brave New People. It is as if we have no other metaphors for these technologies, no competing visions of possible futures.
>
> —CARL ELLIOTT, "THE TYRANNY OF HAPPINESS"

Elliott goes on to point out that most of the new technologies are not like the "happy pills" of *Brave New World,* designed to tranquilize a population into accepting totalitarian government. People choose them; they aren't imposed; they choose most of them to gain an apparent competitive advantage, not for escapism.

Writers are often told to avoid overused or trite analogies. That is good advice, but we can also do what Elliott does—challenge them.

Cause and Effect

Cause and effect explains *why something exists or happens.* It answers *how* and *why* questions: **How did this happen? Why is this the case?** The mode often arranges information in a chronology to show causation or to suggest an effect: **What happened in what order? What might happen next?**

Types of cause-and-effect modes include

- Simple causation
- Complex causation

Simple Causation

Writers use simple causation to show why something happened. What happens when you mix blue and yellow paint? Green paint, of course. *The effect must be an inevitable result of the cause* and not just related to it. For example, a study of the dairy industry and federal crime data found that increased ice cream production correlated to an increase in rape cases. The statistics were correct, but the study was created to show how statistics can be used improperly. Increased ice cream production does not cause rape to increase. Both result from seasonal changes in temperature.

Complex Causation

Use complex causation to explain events that have many contributing causes. The typical situation we face in explaining human behavior is **multiple causation,** *many interacting forces and motivations,* as in the following example.

> While television has long been suspected as a promoter of consumer desire, there has been little hard evidence to support that view, at least for adult spending. After all, there's not an obvious connection. Many of the products advertised on television are everyday low-cost items such as aspirin, laundry detergent, and deodorant. Those TV ads are hardly a spur to excessive consumerism. Leaving aside other kinds of ads for the moment (for cars, diamonds, perfume), there's another counter to the argument that television causes consumerism: TV is a *substitute* for spending. One of the few remaining free activities, TV is a popular alternative to costly recreational spending such as movies, concerts, and restaurants. If it causes us to spend, that effect must be powerful enough to overcome its propensity to save us money.
>
> Apparently it is. My research shows that the more TV a person watches, the more he or she spends. The likely explanation for the link between television and spending is that what we see on TV inflates our sense of what's normal. The lifestyles depicted on television are far different from the average American's: with a few exceptions, TV characters are upper-middle-class, or even rich.
>
> —JULIET SCHOR, "WHEN BUYING BECOMES YOU"

Note how carefully Schor prepares us for her determination of cause. Instead of creating resistance by claiming "TV causes excessive consumerism," she disarms us by first calling her view into doubt. TV is not *self-evidently* related to excessive spending. It might even work against it, she says. Then, when she asserts the connection between television and spending, she calls it a "link" rather than a cause. In social science terminology, the link would be called *correlation–a relationship in which two things vary in concert, but without evidence of causality.* We do not know and often cannot know for sure. Schor supports the plausibility of her link by attempting to explain why television has the effect she says it has: We watch so many well-off people on television that we come to think of wealthy as normal.

How Can I Develop a Repertoire of Modes?

This chapter has been just a start for exploring options you have as a writer. The eight modes covered here do not exhaust the range of possibilities for inventing and developing ideas in your papers and other writing. Like a good vocabulary, modes for development are part of a writer's toolbox, and the more you use them, the better you become at your craft.

In the long run, what matters most is that you continue to learn from the writers you admire. As you read, note the moves made by good writers, and take time to reflect on why they used a particular mode and how they put it into sentences, paragraphs, and multiparagraph sections. When working on a project of your own, feel free to imitate the modes of other authors–in your own way, with your own content, audiences, and purposes. All good writers learn to write this way, by becoming interested in how a better writer handles something. Over time you will internalize the modes, combine them with others, and transform them in dozens of different ways so that what started as someone else's skill becomes your own.

CREDITS

CHAPTER 14

Editing Fundamentals

ENGAGING QUESTIONS

In this chapter, you will engage with the following questions:

- What does it mean to edit a piece of writing?
- Why do writers edit their work?
- How do writers evaluate their work for coherence and flow?
- What key points can writers keep in mind when editing their work?

IF YOU HAVE EVER GOTTEN A PAPER BACK COVERED WITH CORRECTION MARKS—for example, with comments in the margins like "What does this mean?" or "Don't follow you here"—and marked with a grade lower than you anticipated, then you know what happens when you do not edit well. Instead of responding to what you have said, your instructor is responding to problems with how you have said it.

Look and listen for problems in the following sentence from a student's paper:

> One route that companies have already taken, and been successful, is to have meditation when something like sexual harassment occurs.

If your ear heard how awkward the sentence sounds, you know it needs editing. If your eye saw that the writer meant "mediation" not "meditation"—one little "t" makes a big difference—you can eliminate a significant mistake.

Looking and *listening* are two essential editing skills. A third skill is *rewriting* to solve problems. Consider this edited version of the sentence:

> One successful route companies have already taken is to mediate sexual harassment disputes.

No one will be irritated or distracted by this sentence. It says what the writer meant, and the reader will understand its meaning immediately. In short, *nothing interferes with the meaning coming through.* That is what editing is all about.

You can learn to edit. A little knowledge about grammar can help, but you will need practice above all. Editing is a skill, learned as you do it. This chapter provides the fundamentals:

- Understanding the process of editing and how it fits into the writing process
- Knowing common problems to look and listen for
- Applying strategies for solving problems you find

Once you get into the habit of editing, with each paper you will find it easier to make your writing more clear, concise, and coherent. You will not need instructors' comments to find and correct the rough spots.

What Is Editing?

Editing is an intense effort to find and solve whatever problems remain in a piece of writing after revision. It amounts to paying attention to small details you may have missed earlier in the process. Editing includes

- Checking for **flow and focus within individual paragraphs**
- Checking for **flow and focus from one paragraph to the next**
- Reworking **awkward, wordy, or unclear sentences**
- Correcting **errors of grammar, spelling, and punctuation**
- Attending to **formalities,** such as parenthetical notation and works cited pages

Why Edit?

Perhaps you feel that editing should not matter very much. After all, it is content that counts. Saying something worth reading is the whole point of writing. However, *content cannot be separated from the way it is expressed.* Have you ever been irritated or distracted because background noise or a bad connection interfered with a cell phone conversation? A poorly edited paper is like a bad connection: It irritates and distracts readers. More seriously, if your sentences do not say what you mean, if readers struggle to understand your sentences, if your paragraphs wander, your thoughts and your message get lost.

Edit, then, *to communicate better with your readers.* Edit also because the impression other people have of you matters. An unedited or poorly edited paper says that the writer lacks either the skill or the discipline to attend to details. Judgments like "incompetent" or "careless" or even "illiterate" are common. Such judgments may seem unfair, but the consequences are real: poor grades, lukewarm recommendations, being stuck in low-level jobs.

BEST PRACTICES Where Does Editing Belong in the Composing Process?

Focus on editing only when you have a draft you consider "final," the best you can do. Why?

First, editing requires undivided attention. Some writers edit as they compose, even while writing first drafts. We do not recommend it. Editing as you write slows down composing and takes attention away from where it ought to be, on saying what you have to say. In subsequent drafts, you can attend to **revision,** which deals with *large-scale changes in a draft* to achieve your purpose or meet the requirements of an assignment, develop your points more adequately, connect with your readers more consistently, improve your organization, and so on. **Revise first; then edit.**

Second, editing too soon is not efficient. If you edit a sentence or a paragraph in the first draft and then delete it during revision, you have wasted time and effort.

Still worse, you might resist throwing out a sentence you have edited so carefully when it should be cut. Editing too soon can actually get in the way of something more important—revising and rewriting to solve major problems.

Finally, compulsive editing can easily lead to **writer's paralysis,** *being so critical of everything you write that you can hardly write at all.* When you are composing, let go, let thoughts and words flow. Save editing for later.

How Do Writers Edit?

Every semester students come to us with papers covered with correction marks and marginal commentary. They are shocked, puzzled. "But I read it over several times," they say, sometimes adding, "I even had a _____ [tutor, parent, or friend] look it over." To this we say, "But editing is not 'reading' or 'looking over.' You cannot edit a paper by scanning through it."

When we read something, we *look through* the sentences to what is being said. To edit, you have to *look at* the sentences and paragraphs to see *how* things are said.

If you are working on paragraphs, take it one paragraph at a time; if sentences, one sentence at a time. Linger over each one, looking and listening for signs of problems. A good method for slowing down and listening is to read your draft out loud. Your ear will catch things that your eye might miss. Mark anything that bothers you. Then go back and rework the sentence or the paragraph until it does not bother you anymore. In short, **slow down.**

You may be thinking, "Won't this take a long time?" The answer is "Yes, much longer than reading over a paper." If you are working on a five-page, double-spaced paper, expect to spend at least forty-five minutes to an hour editing it. You will get faster with experience, but "fast" and "editing" never go together.

- Budget downtime. Try to get away from a paper for a day or two before editing it. You will be fresher and more detached from your writing.
- Avoid trying to do all the editing at one time. Try fifteen- to twenty-minute sessions, with breaks in between. Otherwise it is hard to maintain the high level of concentration required.
- After editing on your own, find a classmate who is also committed to editing. Exchange papers and help each other find the problems self-editing missed.

The most important thing to remember when editing your work is to *slow down.* Linger over paragraphs and words, and rework anything that bothers you.

© scibak/Getty Images, RF

What Is the Spiraling Down Method?

We strongly advocate a **spiraling down method** of editing. That is, first address the flow from paragraph to paragraph; then the flow within paragraphs; and finish with attention to individual sentences, word choice, and errors. You will need to make several passes through your paper, once or twice at the paragraph level, once or twice at the sentence level. Spiraling down offers several benefits:

- It keeps you from being overwhelmed by all the details; you can "divide and conquer."

- A key principle of editing is: *The more you look for at one time, the less you find.* If you are examining paragraphs or sequences of paragraphs for coherence and flow, you are not likely to detect individual sentences that need work and vice versa.
- It allows some problems to solve themselves. If you work on paragraphs first, any changes you make may fix or eliminate bad sentences, so you will not have to bother editing them. When you are working at the sentence level, some typos and grammatical errors may simply disappear during rewriting. Why hunt for errors before you give them a chance to go away on their own?

Working on Paragraph Sequences

The first focus of editing is working on paragraph sequences. Paragraphs are the building blocks of any piece of writing. Paragraphs, either singly or in groups, make up the sequence of moves that an author makes while composing. The sequence of paragraphs should create a smooth train of thought and a logical development of points.

Paragraphs may look like independent units, but actually *they mark off a move within a set of connected moves* that make up a section in a paper. A **move** is *an answer to an implied question,* something the reader needs to know. It is common in long essays and book chapters for multiple paragraphs to work together in making any one move. When two or more paragraphs work in unison to make a single move, we refer to them as paragraph groups.

Consider the following passage from Julian Hoffman's "The Wonder of Ordinary Places," a longer excerpt of which appears in Chapter 23. We have indicated the implied question each move answers.

Move 1: What makes a child's experience of nature so unique?

When it comes to wonder and the natural world, children are the true specialists. They are particularly open to that state of astonishment that we associate with awe. A child, in the most common of landscapes, is capable, through a combination of intense perception and imagination, of discovering an entire world in the smallest fragment of nature. It might be among wildflowers and weeds at the edge of a scrubby field where an iridescent emerald beetle or the bright flight of a butterfly can hold a child's attention for several minutes. It could be along a river bank where a child excitedly follows an oak leaf as it travels downstream. It might simply be the prints of an animal, perfectly preserved by snow, that captures a child's imagination.

Move 2: If intense perception and imagination characterize a child's experience with nature, is there anything else special about the perceptions of children?

What is so remarkable about children's perception, even more so than its intensity, is that it is characterized by an equality of interest. Everything a child encounters in nature, no matter how small, offers possibility and is therefore equally fascinating. Children make little distinction between major and minor motifs. A feather found on the beach is as wondrous as the creature it belonged to.

Move 3: What do adults lose from the childhood experience of nature that they most need to revive?

> As childhood is left behind, adults tend to shed that capacity for curiosity, that spirit that animates the smallest of things. We yearn for greater and faster excitements; we seek larger vistas, grander views. But in a contemporary Western world increasingly obsessed by speed, style and seduction, there is perhaps all the more need to reclaim the ordinary, to celebrate the everyday. Because the ordinary, when perceived in the spirit of curiosity, is actually extraordinary.
>
> —JULIAN HOFFMAN'S "THE WONDER OF ORDINARY PLACES"

Here is the principle at work: *Every paragraph, or paragraph group, implies and answers a key question.* The purpose of each paragraph is to move the line of thought forward, in order, 1, 2, 3. . . . Once you see the logic, it is hard to imagine any other paragraph sequence for presenting the information.

Successful paragraph sequences work this way. Consequently, here is how to edit your own paragraph sequences:

1. Isolate each major section of your paper. If the paper is short, treat the whole paper as one section.
2. Check to see if each paragraph, or paragraph group, makes a *single* move in a sequence of connected moves. Use the implied-question-and-answer test demonstrated above.
3. If this is not happening, ask, **"What are the 1, 2, 3 (and so on) moves you need to say what you want to say?"**
4. Rewrite the section, making paragraphs that correspond to each move.

BEST PRACTICES Editing Paragraph Sequences

Moving section by section through your paper, concentrate first on the *sequence* of paragraphs. Ask these questions:

1. **Does each paragraph or paragraph group have a definite function or purpose?** If you cannot say what function some paragraph performs, you may need to delete it or reconsider what moves you want to make in your paper.
2. **Do my paragraphs follow a logical sequence in building a train of thought for my reader to follow? Do I need to add more to the sequence or rearrange parts of it?** Add what is needed to existing paragraphs or add a new paragraph.
3. **Are there smooth transitions from one move to the next?** How could you signal the reader where a paragraph or paragraph group makes a new move or takes on a new function in the sequence of your paper?

ACTIVITY 14.1 *Collaborative Activity*

Paragraph Sequencing Practice

The following passage looks like one paragraph but should actually be two. The sentences in both paragraphs have been scrambled and intermixed. Working with one or two other students, sort out the sentences and make them into two separate paragraphs. Be able to say what question each of the two paragraphs answers on the topic of underage drinking.

> The laws in Europe do not limit alcohol consumption to people twenty-one or older. People experience alcohol in their earliest years, and therefore Europe does not experience the same problem that the U.S. has. According to Elizabeth Whelan, alcohol-abuse researcher at Harvard, "prohibiting the sale of liquor to reasonable young adults creates an atmosphere where binge drinking and alcohol abuse becomes a problem." Enforcing a younger drinking age is not a way of extending the party to people of all ages, but an attempt to fix our present situation. Those that oppose the age eighteen legal drinking age have two major arguments to support their position. The first is that lowering the drinking age will only increase alcoholism. However, studies indicate that alcoholism is mostly a genetic disease. Furthermore, children imitate their parents. If children grow up in families where alcohol is abused, the chances are high they will misuse it too. The second argument is that drunk driving will increase. Drunk driving is certainly a major problem, but the vast majority of those arrested for it and who get into accidents are not illegal drinkers. The twenty-one drinking age is not the cure; young adults who drink responsibly is. ■

ACTIVITY 14.2 *In Your Own Work*

Editing Paragraph Sequences

Select any recent paper you have revised. Next to each paragraph, write down the question it implies and answers. Edit the order of the paragraphs to achieve a 1, 2, 3, and so on sequence. When you are done, print out your edited version and read through it carefully. Does it read better than before? What did you change, and why did you make the changes? ■

Working on Individual Paragraphs

Editing paragraphs is the second focus of editing. At the paragraph level, editing focuses on coherence, meaning how well the sentences cohere, or stick together. When sentences cohere, we say the writing flows well, with no gaps in the train of thought.

BEST PRACTICES Editing Paragraphs

Moving paragraph by paragraph through your paper, ask these questions:

1. **Does the first sentence indicate what the entire paragraph will be about?**
2. **Did you provide explanations, comments, and examples that *develop* the first sentence?**
3. **Is there flow, a smooth movement from sentence to sentence?**
4. **Does the paragraph connect to the previous one and to the following one?**

Individual paragraphs function much like paragraph sequences: They are a sequence of connected moves. The difference is that a paragraph is a sequence of connected sentences. Consider the following example, a paragraph from student Lauren Knazze's blog:

> An interesting concept came up in Wellness class today. My instructor used the example of circus elephants to explain the idea. From their youth, circus elephants are trained to be helpless and hopeless. When they are little, they are chained to large boulders so that they cannot escape. Although they try, their efforts prove to be futile. When they grow larger, the elephants believe that they cannot escape, so they don't try. Even though they could pull the rocks and move away, the failures from before are enough to keep them stuck in place, with no resistance. My instructor's point was that people too become so stuck in their ways or so fearful because of past failures that they don't realize that they could change their lives for the better.

Notice how each sentence picks up the idea of the sentence before it and answers the question most likely posed in the reader's mind. In coherent paragraphs, the writer anticipates what the reader is likely to ask–and provides the answer in the very next sentence.

> An interesting concept came up in Wellness class today. (Introduces the topic.)
>
> My instructor used the example of circus elephants to explain the idea. (Answers the question: **What happened in Wellness class?**)
>
> From their youth, circus elephants are trained to be helpless and hopeless. (Answers the question: **What was the example?**)
>
> When they are little, they are chained to large boulders so that they cannot escape. (Answers the question: **What happens to the elephants?**)
>
> Although they try, their efforts prove to be futile. (Answers the question: **Then what happens?**)
>
> When they grow larger, the elephants believe that they cannot escape, so they don't try. (Answers the question: **What happens next?**)

> Even though they could pull the rocks and move away, the failures from before are enough to keep them stuck in place, with no resistance. (Answers the question: **What is the point of the example?**)
>
> My instructor's point was that people too become so stuck in their ways or so fearful because of past failures that they don't realize that they could change their lives for the better. (Answers the question: **Why was this idea important in a Wellness class?**)

Of course, neither writer nor reader is normally aware of the questions that each sentence answers. But when you find a paragraph that is not working, try making the reader's questions explicit and test the next sentence to see if it answers the question. Sometimes the answer comes in a later sentence, and rearranging the sentences solves the problem.

A good paragraph coheres and flows. It **coheres,** *holds together,* because it is about *a single focus or theme*—for example, explaining an idea about personal empowerment. It **flows** because *each sentence answers a question the reader is likely to have asked in response to the previous sentence.*

How Transitions Connect Paragraphs

In addition to editing for the focus of each paragraph, we have to ensure that the beginning and end of each paragraph connect to previous and subsequent ones. These links, called "transitions," function much like turn signals on a car. Imagine that, as a writer, you are taking readers somewhere they have not been, and they are following you. Transitions, like turn signals, tell the reader you are about to turn down another road.

Look back at the three paragraphs from the Hoffman example, p. 329. The first sentence claims that in appreciating nature "children are the true specialists." As a reader you expect the author to develop this claim—to explain why children respond to nature better than older people. The rest of the paragraph does that well: The child combines perception and imagination to respond to nature. Then the paragraph concludes with three examples in three sentences of what a child might see, beginning with "It might be among wildflowers . . ." The examples provide concrete illustrations of the two most important abstract words: perception and imagination.

Then the next sentence—the first sentence in the following paragraph—creates a transition by repeating the key word—perception—and then stating the new theme or focus: "equality of interest."

Transitions are not all alike. Sometimes the last sentence of the preceding paragraph does the linking, while the first sentence of the next one announces the new focus. How transitions happen matters less than making sure that they do. Look at all endings and beginnings of your paragraphs to make sure the transitions work as smoothly as possible.

ACTIVITY 14.3 *Collaborative Activity*

Paragraph Editing Practice

In groups of two or three, edit the following paragraph to make a sequence of sentences with both a single theme or focus and development or movement.

Use the implied question-and-answer method we have discussed to help discover a good sentence order. Feel free to cut, add, rearrange, and rewrite sentences. If you think a single paragraph should become two or more, do that as well. Create any needed transitions.

> My day at the Boys and Girls Club of Greater Houston consisted of running around, playing, and laughing a lot. I graduated from St. Agnes Academy, where one hundred hours of volunteer work were required for graduation. The Boys and Girls Summer Day Camp is a day-care facility where families pay two dollars for an entire summer of supervision of their children while they are at work. From my experiences as a camp counselor I realize that some people you meet leave a strong impression. The children I worked with in the summer of 1997 were underprivileged minorities. I will never forget any of the children, but one little boy was special to me. ■

■ ACTIVITY 14.4 *In Your Own Work*

Editing Paragraphs

Select any recent paper you have written and edit the paragraphs for focus and movement. Look at each indentation. Is there a sentence near the opening of each paragraph that contains the main idea and keyword(s) that unites the paragraph? Look at the flow or connection between each sentence and the next. Does each sentence pick up an idea or key word from the sentence before it? ■

Working on Sentences

Working on sentences is the third focus of editing.

Sentences are the basic unit of expression. We speak mostly in sentences. With few exceptions, we write in sentences. Therefore, *reworking sentences is the heart of editing itself.*

BEST PRACTICES Editing Sentences

1. Moving sentence by sentence through your paper, read each one aloud or subvocalize, "hearing" it in your head. Your ear is the key to detecting sentences that need editing. Mark sentences that sound bad to you.
2. Rework your sentence so the doer of the action comes first, followed by the action itself, the verb.
3. Look for sentence-level errors—for example, fragments, using a comma when you need a semicolon or vice versa, putting a comma after "although," incorrectly punctuating clauses beginning with the word *which.*

What a Sentence Must Do

It is no mystery. A sentence must

- Say precisely what we mean
- Make it easy for our readers to grasp what we mean

A sentence must do these two things; otherwise we have not *communicated.* Anything else takes a back seat. Writing correctly, for example, does not matter if communication has failed.

Why Do Sentences Go Wrong?

Sometimes we are not sure what we mean; we are confused or conflicted. Sometimes we know what we mean but lack confidence in what we want to say. Sometimes we have a general idea of what we want to say but cannot find the words. And sometimes we think we have said what we mean until somebody interprets our sentence in a way we did not intend or points out that our meaning is unclear.

Sentences go wrong because we do not have the point we want to make clearly in mind. Sentences also go wrong because it is difficult to see our own sentences as readers will see them. A sentence that seems perfectly clear to us puzzles or confuses our readers.

Editing is the time to detect uncertainties about what you want to say. You know the sentences you struggled with in writing your drafts and the feeling "this is still not quite right" even after you have revised. Step back and ask, "Why am I confused or conflicted here? What is keeping me from having confidence in what I want to say? What is wrong with that idea that keeps eluding the words to express it?" If you can diagnose the problem, you can get "in here" to line up with "out there." You will not always succeed, but give it your best effort.

Editing is also the right time to seek input from others. When we write a sentence, we get no immediate feedback–nobody is there to look puzzled or ask for clarification as there is in conversation. Instead, we have to *imagine* a reader's response, *anticipate* problems a reader might have, and rework sentences so that he or she will understand. We try, but even the most talented writers cannot always see their sentences "from the outside," as a reader will in responding to them. Therefore, all writers need an actual reader's response, and that is especially true for those sentences that are still bothering us after self-editing.

Edit your own writing first, but then seek out another set of eyes and ears to help you detect more of what you missed.

What Matters Most in Editing Sentences?

In a word: clarity. The first step is to make your writing sound more like something you would say. For example, read this sentence:

> The cessation of the employment of extraordinary means to prolong the life of the body when there is irrefutable evidence that biological death is imminent is the decision of the patient and/or the immediate family.

What does this thirty-five-word sentence mean? It sounds impressive and authoritative, but no one would say it. More likely, you would say something like this:

> Only the patient or the patient's family can decide to stop life support.

This thirteen-word sentence says what the writer means without making readers struggle to understand it. How did we arrive at this much better sentence? First, *simplify*. The two most important moves you can make in editing are to simplify and find an active verb.

- The "cessation of the employment of extraordinary means to prolong life" equals "stopping life support." What else could it be?
- If we are talking about life support, we must be talking about a patient who would otherwise be dead or likely to die, so why say anything about death at all?
- We found the subject performing the action–"the patient or the patient's family."
- We found the verb, the action the subject was performing, in the noun "decision," so we used the verb "decide."

BEST PRACTICES Editing for Wordy Phrases

One way to write more plainly, simply, and directly is to look for the following common phrases, each of which has a more concise equivalent.

For these phrases . . .	**Use . . .**
at all times	always
biography of the life	biography
close proximity	near
due to the fact that	because
final result	final
first and foremost	first
for the purposes of	to
for the reason that	because
green in color	green
in order to	to
in spite of the fact that	although
in the event that	if
in the not-too-distant future	soon
in this day and age	today
is able to	can
is necessary that	must
mix together	mix
refer back	refer
repeat again	repeat
until such time as	until

We pick up these and many other phrases from conversation and use them without thinking about them. In editing we should weed them out of our sentences.

ACTIVITY 14.5 *Collaborative Activity*

Sentence Editing Practice

Working in groups of two or three, cut the excess verbiage from the following sentences. First, step back and ask: What is the writer trying to say? Find a plain, simple, direct way to say what the writer really means. Delete what you do not need to say it. Find the subject and combine it with an action, a verb.

1. Willy is so frustrated in his futile quest for riches and failure to achieve social approval due to the dreadful reality of his limitations that he consequently turns to a dream world.
2. The lessons I have learned and continue to learn of hard work and entrepreneurship are a great value and truth that shall be passed from me to my kids and to their kids and so on.
3. Americans are starting to worry again, because certain aspects of immigration, such as overpopulation and lack of education, which results in poverty, are beginning to affect America as a whole.
4. On many campuses, gays and lesbians have formed their own fraternities and sororities, not only coming out of the closet, but also benefiting from the social as well as the academic education a school offers.
5. I can only hope by the time my children grow up in this country that affirmative action will no longer be an issue so that they will be looked at as a student for academic ability, character, and personal attributes to do the best they can. ■

ACTIVITY 14.6 *In Your Own Work*

Eliminating "Deadwood"

Select any recent paper you have written and revised. Edit the sentences as you did in the previous exercise.

Tip: Read your sentences aloud to find the ones that need work. They'll sound like something nobody would say. Get rid of "deadwood" and your prose will immediately improve. ■

How Do We Detect Sentence-Level Errors?

Use your ear in editing: Listen to what you have written either in your head or by reading it aloud.

However, certain norms in speech are considered errors in writing, and you cannot rely on your ear to pick them up. In fact, the most common sentence-level errors relate to speech patterns we cannot carry over into writing. For instance:

> As we've moved toward greater equality, a new struggle has emerged in America. New in that it focuses on sexual preference rather than race or gender.

The second sentence is a fragment, common in conversation, but usually considered an error in writing. Fragments are easy to fix. Many fragments can be eliminated simply by adding a comma and attaching them to the preceding sentence.

> As we've moved toward greater equality, a new struggle has emerged in America, new in that it focuses on sexual preference rather than race or gender.

Proofreading

Proofreading is the fourth focus of editing. In publications, editors read the final page "proofs" or set type, looking for little errors. In writing a paper, proofreading similarly means looking very closely at the final manuscript to find the small, but nevertheless still important, errors.

By errors we mean, for example, the following:

- Typing "minorities" (plural) when you mean "minority's" (possessive), or vice versa
- Confusing "there" with "their" and "they're"
- Confusing "to" with "too" and "two"
- Typing "it's" (contraction for "it is") when you mean "its" (possessive form of "it"), or vice versa
- Misspelled words
- Typos
- Omitting a word you meant to include, or typing a word or phrase twice
- Not putting titles in quotation marks or italics

These are the kinds of mistakes that proofreading must catch. You will find some of them as you "spiral down," working first with paragraphs and then with sentences. But if you do not proofread, you will miss too many. Furthermore, in reworking paragraphs and sentences, you will probably make a few more errors. Therefore, *proofreading is an essential, last focus of editing.*

BEST PRACTICES Proofreading

Move sentence by sentence through your paper, *looking* for errors like misspelled words, typos, and word choice problems. *Look because most errors have to be seen, not heard, detected by the eye and not the ear.* Mark the errors. Go back and correct each one.

Proofreading cannot be omitted or done hastily because errors like these are easily and routinely detected by people assessing your writing. Nor can you rely on spell checks and grammar checks to find all such errors for you. Use the programs, but remember that they will miss many mistakes and sometimes tag something as an error that is not wrong.

Our general advice is to approach errors systematically. You will make mistakes. Some of these you will miss even with diligent proofreading. The ones you miss professors marking your papers will usually detect. *It is what you do with the marks on your papers that can make all the difference.*

What matters most are errors that occur regularly. They indicate that you do not recognize the error as an error or do not understand how to correct it in all cases. Talk to your instructor. Or look for the relevant section in the Connect Composition handbook available online. Then, having grasped the nature of the error, *make a note about it in an editing checklist you keep for yourself.* Write down a description of the error, what you typically do wrong and how to correct it. You might include an example or two, with corrections. Save this list in a notebook or in a computer file. Keep this editing checklist to consult the next time you have to proofread.

ACTIVITY 14.7 *Collaborative Activity*

Error Editing Practice

Working with two or three students, correct the errors in the following sentences. If you detect other editing problems, attend to them as well.

1. The administration has done everything they can to improve race relations, now we students must do our part.
2. Looking back at the foundling fathers of our country, they had very similar views about the federal government.
3. Parents install morals in there children; hoping they will make the right decisions as adults.
4. Once she escaped her strict upbringing at college, she lost all restraints, the perfect example of a girl who goes crazy her first year of freedom.
5. The book The Beauty Myth, by Naomi Wolf dedicates itself to the fact that women are controlled by their looks.
6. I was perfectly content living in a closed knit community, where everyone felt they were at home.
7. The worst part of the advertisement was their was a girl next to the man, messaging him. ■

ACTIVITY 14.8 *In Your Own Work*

Proofreading

Select any recent paper you have revised. Edit the sentences to eliminate errors like the ones discussed and illustrated above. Listening to your sentences can help, especially with some punctuation errors, but concentrate on *looking* for errors. What writing errors have you made in the past? Be sure to check for those in a separate step.

Tip: A good way to proof is by working backward, starting with the last sentence. Reading backward slows the process down and disrupts the flow from sentence to sentence so that you can *look at* the sentences for the errors you need to detect. ■

What Matters Most in Editing? Three Key Points

- **Editing is not just "cleaning up."** Cleaning up is proofreading, and that is important but is only the last step in editing. The purpose of editing is to detect and eliminate *everything* that gets in the way of communicating with your reader–and that means attending to much more than error. You need to work on your paragraphs and sentences even when they have no mistakes.

- **Editing requires time and concentration.** It is not "reading over" your final draft. It is working through your final draft methodically, first focusing on paragraph sequences and paragraphs, then on sentences, and finally on errors.
- **Keep an editing checklist** that helps you pay special attention to your particular editing problems. Study the marks and comments on every graded paper. When they relate to editing, add them to your list. If you do not understand an error or problem, ask your instructor to explain or consult our handbook. Add any notes you need to help remember the error or problem and how to fix it. Use the checklist as you edit your next paper.

Do these things, and your editing problems will diminish and you will gain fuller control over the ones that remain. You will be amazed at how much your writing will improve.

CREDITS

PART III

Researching Writing

CHAPTER 15

Planning a Research Project

ENGAGING QUESTIONS

In this chapter, you will engage with the following questions:

- What types of research do writers do?
- What distinguishes primary and secondary sources?
- What distinguishes popular and scholarly sources?
- How do writers plan research projects?
- How do writers choose appropriately focused topics for research?
- How do writers formulate research questions?
- What methods help writers effectively manage sources throughout a research project?

RESEARCH BEGINS WITH QUESTIONS, NOT JUST WITH A TOPIC. Without questions, research would be a haphazard and aimless task. One question is always relevant: "Given what I already know about my topic, what more do I need to know?" Asking it exposes the gaps in your existing knowledge and tells you what you need to focus on when doing research.

Research, however, is more interesting and creative than just gathering facts. For example, research can help us ask and answer a more important question: "What do the facts mean?" This question calls for critical thinking, which requires more questions and answers. For example, history textbooks are filled with facts, but they might have different facts or different interpretations of the same facts. A researcher might ask *why* textbooks' explanations of an event might differ. Could the differences have to do with the political climate of the time in which each was published? The writer could attempt to answer this question by finding textbooks published at different times, comparing their depictions of an event, and then relating them to what was going on politically when the books were written.

As a researcher what you are seeking most is *a question that you and your readers will find engaging, worth writing about, and worth reading.* We know, for instance, that wolves thrive in some environments and struggle in others. Why? One question we could ask is, "How does hunting by humans affect the behavior of species that are hunted?" Animal behaviorists are researching how wolf packs behave depending on whether they live in protected areas or in areas where hunting is permitted. What they have learned is worth writing about and sharing with readers—and if we have the opportunity, can even get us out into the field ourselves to do our own firsthand research.

If we think of research as just finding facts and quotations to add to a draft, we have missed what research is all about. *Research is about finding a question worth pursuing. Then it is about finding information and interpreting it in order to answer the question.* Put simply, research builds the foundation for writing.

When Is Research Necessary?

Research is needed whenever general knowledge and common sense are not enough. Most college writing requires research because instructors want students to go beyond assigned readings to increase the depth of their knowledge, analyze conflicting interpretations, and develop their own understanding of the course subject matter. After college, people conduct research on the job (for example, to analyze markets or prepare proposals for clients) and in community life (for example, to support their claim that a neighborhood should be rezoned or that school funding should be increased).

Research goes on throughout the writing process. In a college writing class, depending on the assignment, you may

- Conduct *preliminary research* to get basic information on a topic and stimulate your curiosity about it.
- Pursue *in-depth research* to satisfy that curiosity, answering your questions and acquiring the solid evidence you need to convince others.
- Continue your research as needed in revision to add support when a point is underdeveloped, your focus shifts, or new questions arise.

What Kinds of Sources Do College Researchers Use?

Most assignments encourage students to consult a variety of sources featuring different opinions on and approaches to a topic. The following discussion offers an overview of the kinds of sources available.

Primary Sources versus Secondary Sources

To learn how to conduct observational studies, surveys, and interviews, see Chapter 16, pages 370–71.

Primary sources are *data or artifacts, works of art or literature, before they have been interpreted by another researcher.* In the natural sciences and social sciences, primary sources may include data from observational studies, surveys, and laboratory experiments. In the humanities, they may include historical documents (the *Mayflower Compact,* the *Declaration of Independence*), works of art and film, novels and poetry, or letters, diaries, and manuscripts. In all disciplines, researchers may interview experts to learn about their research or their experiences firsthand. Primary sources provide raw materials for your own analysis and specific evidence for developing your points and supporting your reasoning.

Primary sources, such as the *Declaration of Independence*, are documents or works of art or literature that have not been interpreted by another researcher. They are uninterpreted works in their original form.

© Comstock/PunchStock, RF

For more on how to compare sources, see Chapter 8, especially pages 162–63 and 178–80.

Secondary sources, in contrast, *result from someone else's research.* For example, in a British literature course, your primary source might be Samuel Taylor Coleridge's poem "The Rime of the Ancient Mariner." Secondary sources would be interpretations of the poem by literary critics. Secondary sources also include general and specialized encyclopedias, most books, and articles in magazines and scholarly journals. They provide useful background or historical information; they communicate other people's ideas and conclusions about a topic, to which you can compare your own thoughts and conclusions. Also, in secondary sources you will find expert opinions that you can use to help formulate your own opinions and to support and develop your opinions. You may also use secondary sources to provide opposing views and opinions you would like to refute. Comparing the perspectives of secondary sources can help you construct a position of your own.

Popular versus Scholarly Sources

Secondary sources have a wide range of audiences; they may be magazine articles directed to the general public or highly specialized texts written by scholars for other professionals in their field.

Secondary sources, like *National Geographic* magazine, demonstrate other people's ideas and conclusions about a topic, to which you can compare your own thoughts and conclusions.

© FRANCISCO GARCÍA VELASCO/NOTIMEX/Newscom

Popular works offer accessible introductions to a topic and include the following:

- **Textbooks** Textbooks offer surveys of a field, such as this guide to writing. They can be a good place to begin research.
- **General Encyclopedias** Like textbooks, general encyclopedias (such as *Britannica Online* and *Wikipedia*) offer an overview of the basic information on a topic and therefore can serve as starting points for research. However, keep in mind that most assignments will require that you move on to more specialized sources. Footnotes and links in general encyclopedia entries can take you deeper into scholarship on the topic.
- **Magazines and Newspapers** Magazines and newspapers offer a wide range of information, from celebrity gossip to scientific discoveries. For most college research, instructors prefer that students avoid light reading titles such as *Cosmopolitan* and *USA TODAY* in favor of publications that offer more in-depth articles such as *Women's Health Weekly* and *The New York Times.*
- **Trade Books** Trade books are published by commercial presses (like Harper Collins, Knopf, and Simon & Schuster) and aimed at an educated segment of the general public, including students and professors. Trade books are typically more accessible than books published by scholarly presses, but the authors are often experts in their field who also publish more academic works.

Scholarly works include the following:

- **Specialized Encyclopedias and Dictionaries** Specialized encyclopedias and dictionaries are works devoted to specific topics and written by experts. You will find many in the reference section of your library; others, like *The New Palgrave Dictionary of Economics* and *The Blackwell Encyclopedia of Sociology,* can be accessed through your library's database offerings. Entries are written by experts and peer reviewed, which means that other scholars have had to approve the credentials of the writer and the accuracy of the material. Entries in specialized encyclopedias and dictionaries provide background information, define terms, and include suggestions for further reading.
- **Scholarly Journals** Articles in scholarly journals are written by experts and reviewed by other subject specialists before publication. Scholarly journals are specialized sources, so undergraduates might find reading their articles challenging. Such articles are highly reliable sources of in-depth information, however, so perseverance will pay dividends. See "How Do I Deal with the Difficulties of Scholarly Texts?" on pages 29–35 of Chapter 2.
- **Scholarly Books** Scholarly books are written by experts in the field and published by university presses. They are rigorously reviewed by other experts in the field (a process known as peer review) before publication, and they are intended for an audience

Magazines such as *The Atlantic* are popular sources intended for an intelligent and well-informed readership.
Robert Alexander/Getty Images

CONCEPT CLOSE-UP Comparison of a Scholarly Journal Source with a Magazine Source

You can distinguish scholarly journals from popular magazines in several ways. First, scholarly journals do not include glossy advertisements. Second, the titles of scholarly journals, and the articles they publish, usually indicate specifically what they cover. For example, in the *American Journal of Family Therapy,* you will find articles such as "Understanding Online Gaming Addiction and Treatment Issues for Adolescents," whereas an article in a popular magazine such as *Psychology Today* will have a catchier title like "Why Johnny Can't Stop Playing Video Games." The examples in Figure 15.1 reveal the typical design features, vocabulary, and reading level of academic journal articles and articles in popular magazines.

FIGURE **15.1**

Understanding How Different Sources Work

How does the treatment of the same topic differ in scholarly and popular sources?

Source: Young, Kimberly. (2009). Understanding Online Gaming Addiction and Treatment Issues for Adolescents. The American Journal of Family Therapy. Taylor & Francis Group.

The American Journal of Family Therapy, 37:355–372, 2009
Copyright © Taylor & Francis Group, LLC
ISSN: 0192-6187 print / 1521-0383 online
DOI: 10.1080/01926180902942191

Routledge
Taylor & Francis Group

Understanding Online Gaming Addiction and Treatment Issues for Adolescents

KIMBERLY YOUNG
The Center for Internet Addiction Recovery, Bradford, Pennsylvania, USA

Massive Muti-user Online Role-Playing Games or MMORPGs as they are often called are one of the fastest growing forms of Internet addiction, especially among children and teenagers. Like an addiction to alcohol or drugs, gamers show several classic signs of addiction (Grusser, Thalemann, and Griffiths, 2007). They become preoccupied with gaming, lie about their gaming use, lose interest in other activities just to game, withdrawal from family and friends to game, and use gaming as a means of psychological

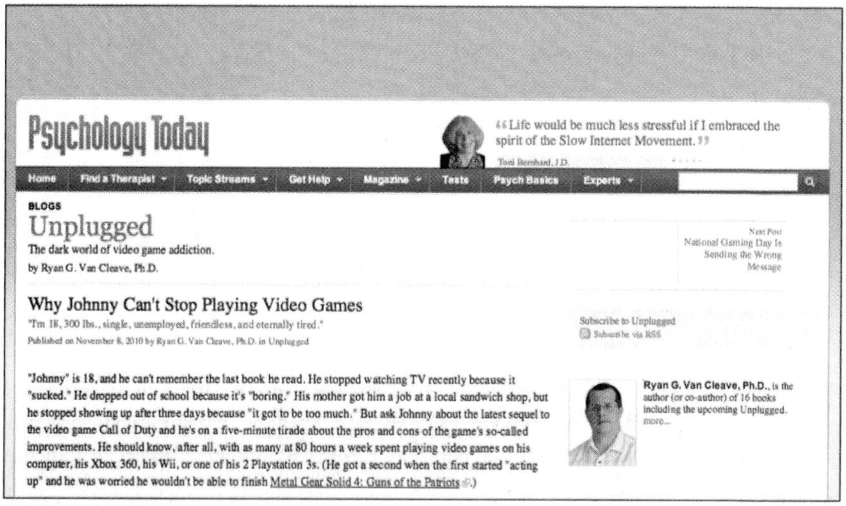

Source: Psychology Today

of other scholars in the same field. You can depend on authors of scholarly books to cite their sources and to include a bibliography at the end of the book. The style of the writing can range from accessible at the undergraduate level to highly technical.

We will talk later about how to find these and other sources (see Chapter 16, pages 358–71) and how to evaluate such sources (Chapter 17, pages 372–78), but this overview should give you an idea of the main kinds of sources available to you.

Print Sources versus Digital Sources

The distinction between online and print sources is not as relevant as it used to be since most print sources, even older ones, have become available digitally. Libraries subscribe to databases that provide online the full text of many magazine and journal articles. Increasingly, e-books are available through libraries' book catalogs.

How Do I Plan a Research Project?

Writing a research project can be a big undertaking. To minimize anxiety and keep your progress on track, first break the project down into stages.

Stages of a Research Project

The stages of research include preliminary thinking and research; focused research; informal writing, drafting, and revising; and, finally, editing and proofreading (Figure 15.2).

1. Preliminary Thinking and Research

- If you are writing in response to an assignment prompt, reread it to make sure you understand your instructor's guidelines for the project.
- Brainstorm appropriate topics for questions or problems that interest you personally; confer with your instructor for advice if needed.
- Begin a research log, which is a record of your progress (see Best Practices: Habits of Successful Researchers, page 349).
- Brainstorm possible research questions, and then browse a variety of sources, bibliographies, and indexes to test the availability of resources for answering these questions.
- Decide on a research question, or determine if you need to do more preliminary research before forming a research question.

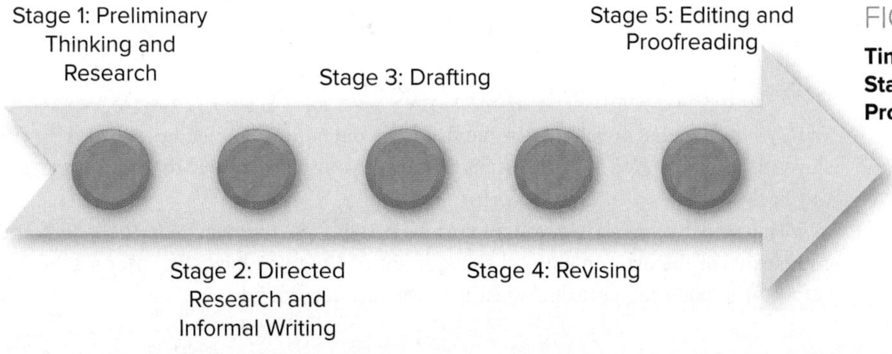

FIGURE **15.2**

Timeline for the Main Stages of a Research Project

2. Focused Research and Preliminary Writing

- Identify keywords to use as search terms.
- Find and evaluate sources and begin your working bibliography.
- Consult a librarian if you need help.
- Write notes about all relevant materials; make printouts and photocopies of the sources you will rely on the most.
- Refine your research question.
- Write a preliminary version of your thesis.

3. Planning and Drafting

See Chapter 32, pages 548–54, for guidance on using photographs, drawings, tables, and graphs.

- Work out a plan for developing your thesis, such as an outline or flowchart.
- Decide which sources you will draw on to develop each part of the plan.
- Consider what information you could best present visually.
- Begin drafting; *incorporate and cite your sources as you draft.*
- Decide what additional information you need, and do more research.

4. Revising Your Draft

See Chapter 14, pages 327–40, for a systematic approach to editing.

- Refine your thesis if necessary. Rewrite as required to improve your first draft.
- Confer with peers or your instructor to discuss organization and development.
- Do additional research to make underdeveloped sections more specific.

5. Editing and Proofreading Your Draft

For keeping a list of your common errors, see Chapter 14, page 340.

- Read your draft aloud for style, flow within and across paragraphs, and conciseness.
- Review suggestions in Chapter 18 for help with smoothly integrating paraphrases and quotations; edit as needed.
- Run spelling and grammar checks.
- Proofread again, paying special attention to your list of common errors.
- Check the correct MLA or APA formats for in-text and end citations.

Scheduling Your Research Project

With your calendar or planner in hand, assign dates for completing each task in the stages described above. You may want to start at your project's due date and work your way backward.

How much time should you allot to each stage? That depends on the length and complexity of the assignment and the amount of time you have. We offer a schedule below for a four-week project. Adjust the schedule accordingly.

- **Week 1:** Choose a topic, develop a research question, and begin to find and evaluate potential sources.
- **Week 2:** Continue preliminary research, reading and analyzing sources; finalize your research question, and draft a preliminary thesis.
- **Week 3:** Outline and write your first draft. Be sure to incorporate and cite your sources as you draft. Decide what further research you will need to develop this draft, and conduct additional research.
- **Week 4:** Reread and (if possible) get feedback on your draft from a writing tutor, your instructor, or peers; revise your thesis (if necessary), rewrite as needed, edit for style and integration of quotations; proofread and prepare your paper according to your instructor's submission guidelines.

BEST PRACTICES Habits of Successful Researchers

Following the suggestions below, you can remain in control of any research project.

1. **Plan your work and work your plan.** If you stay on schedule and do some work every day, you will greatly reduce the stress of doing a major research assignment. *Consistent work is the key.*
2. **Take initiative.** The difference between an outstanding research project and a poor one often comes down to motivation. *Get engaged and stay engaged* from the time you get an assignment until it is ready to turn in.
3. **Keep a research log.** Doing research is like making your own path through a forest; if you do not keep track of where you have gone and what you have found, you can waste too much time retracing the same territory. *Keep a log or daily record of your research* as described later in this chapter on page 352.
4. **Employ a range of reading skills.** Researchers change reading styles to suit their purposes. They browse indexes, bibliographies, and the Internet to scout out possible sources. They skim articles and books to get the gist and determine the writer's angle. But when they find a suitable source, they slow down and dive deeper, reading critically and annotating and taking notes.
5. **Avoid premature closure on research and thinking.** The best resources are not necessarily the first ones you find. If your instructor suggests a minimum number of sources, you will need to gather more so you can pick the best ones. Keep an open mind. Do not decide you know the answer to your research question and seek out only the information that supports your answer.
6. **Ask for help.** Librarians want to help, but you have to initiate contact. If you look for information for more than thirty minutes without success, ask a librarian.

See Chapter 2, pages 12–29, for guidance on critical reading.

How Do I Choose and Narrow a Topic?

An effective research project must focus on a topic that you can do justice to in the allotted space. A typical research project cannot meaningfully examine topics as broad as animal rights, bank regulation, global warming, health care reform, or terrorism. Many complete books have been published on narrower topics than these. To narrow a topic to one that you can usefully explore in a brief assignment, look in some of the places listed below.

- **Course Readings** Many topics for research papers come from course readings. Look at chapter headings and subheadings for ideas about subtopics, and take note of narrower topics while reading. If your text has an index, look at entries and subentries. For example, students researching the dangers faced by illegal immigrants in the Southwest wanted to find out more about the people engaged in human smuggling. To narrow the topic, they looked at the entry for the smugglers, called *coyotes,* and found subentries on coyotes as gangsters, the macho image of coyotes, and the operations of coyotes.
- **Catalogs and Databases** In Chapter 16, Finding Sources, we show how to find resources using library databases and Internet search tools such as Advanced Search in Google. (See pages 359–61 and 365–68 for help with searching databases and using Web search engines.) Reading the titles of articles and other sources on your general topic is a good brainstorming technique, as the titles alone can suggest interesting ways to focus a research question. For example, some titles that came up in a search about college student debt suggest possible questions for further research:

Article Titles Found in a Database	Questions for Research Inspired by the Article Titles in a Database
"A Lifetime of Student Debt? Not Likely" "College Students' Knowledge and Use of Credit"	Should colleges offer courses in budgeting and managing personal finances?
"Credit Card Debt, Stress and Key Health Risk Behaviors among College Students"	Is there a relationship between excessive credit card debt and other high-risk behaviors?
"When Life Gets in the Way of Paying for College"	How are high college costs affecting the life choices of young adults?

- **Specialized Reference Sources and Research Guides** You can also find inspiration and background material on your topic in reference works such as specialized dictionaries and encyclopedias (in print and online) and in research guides on college library websites. For more on specialized encyclopedias and reference guides, see pages 362–63 in Chapter 16, Finding Sources.
- **Your Own Interests** Topics for research can be found in your own backyard. For example, a student needing to write a paper on small businesses

noticed that a restaurant he frequented had closed recently. He found his topic: the difficulties of running a restaurant. Another student had to write on a class-assigned paper having to do with the environment. Looking around her neighborhood, she noticed many smaller, older homes being torn down, only to be replaced by much larger, new homes that removed existing trees and grass and required more energy to heat and cool. She had found her topic: the teardown epidemic.

How Do I Turn a Topic into a Research Question?

No matter how narrow your topic, you will not write an interesting paper without *a meaningful question that you and your readers will want answered.* Your research question will give you an angle on your topic, something that matters to you.

To turn your topic into a research question, try the following:

- **Use the reporter's questions.** Ask yourself *who, what, where, when, why,* and *how.* On this list, the words most likely to produce a good question are *why* and *how* because these lead to analysis and evaluation. "How did the national debt become so enormous?" is a good example. But do not rule out the other question words because they can also lead to thought-provoking questions like "What personality types are most attracted to social networking sites?"
- **Use critical thinking questions.** Critical thinking is analytical. With "x" being your topic, you might ask
  - What are the causes of "x"? (For example, why are rural areas in the United States losing population?)
  - What are the implications or effects of "x"? (For example, what happens to children's learning when letter grades are abolished?)
  - What larger context or contexts does "x" belong to? (For example, is graffiti in public places art or vandalism?)
  - What issues are people debating about "x"? (For example, on the topic of drug wars in Mexico, people are debating the possible entry of United States contract employees to assist the Mexican government. Is this a good idea?)
  - What do most people think about "x"? How could you question the conventional thinking? (For example, conventional thinking about curing traffic congestion on freeways is to widen them. Is there any evidence that this thinking is wrong?)
- **Look at your topic from different perspectives.** Consider how different groups of people might look at your topic from different angles. On the topic of tearing down houses to build bigger ones: How do developers look at an older neighborhood with small homes, many in disrepair, sitting on valuable land? How is this perspective different from that of a young couple with children who want a large home in a close-in neighborhood? What about members of the neighborhood who want to see their property values go up? Any of these perspectives can furnish an angle on the topic.

Student Example: Turning a Topic into Research Questions

In the case of the student who wanted to write on the topic of teardowns, she could approach research by asking:

- What are the causes of the teardown epidemic?
- Why do people want to replace traditional small homes with giant new ones?
- Why do Americans think they need such large houses?
- How does this change impact the neighborhood?
- Who is hurt by this trend and who gains?
- What is the environmental impact of replacing the smaller houses with bigger ones?

How Do I Manage the Sources I Find?

Once you have your research question, begin gathering sources, assessing their relevance and considering how you might use them. We recommend that you not gather a massive pile of materials to look through later. Instead of one long round of gathering sources, think of this stage as alternating between gathering and reading, note-taking, and reflecting on what you have, and then returning to find more sources as you follow up on leads and questions you encounter. Reading sources as you gather them allows you to develop more interesting research questions and refine your focus. It also helps in developing an understanding of how sources relate to each other and therefore a sense of the big picture you will need to make your own contribution to the topic. Some sources will also direct you to others as you consult the footnotes and bibliographies they provide.

To manage the sources you uncover during this stage, develop a research log, make copies of sources to annotate, and maintain a working bibliography so you can cite sources fully as you draft your project.

Create a Research Log

See Chapter 19, pages 405–06, for help with avoiding accidental plagiarism.

Keeping track of the sources you consult and the notes you take from them is crucial to avoiding plagiarism and writing a successful research project. Maintaining a research log can help you work more efficiently by making it easier for you to keep track of sources and by helping you to avoid having to retrace your steps.

A research log should contain the following:

- Your research question, which you might revise as you move through the research process.
- Ideas and questions that occur to you while browsing and reading.
- Search terms you used, added as you find new terms.
- Notes about catalogs and indexes you searched on any particular day.
- A working bibliography with *complete bibliographical information about each source and notes about what the source contains,* why it is credible and worthy of your and your readers' trust, and how you might use it. See more on working bibliographies on pages 354–56 in this chapter.

Your research log could be a notebook, a computer file, or a series of file folders, or it could be housed online in an electronic source management tool like *Zotero*. You may have folders for different kinds of notes (such as search terms or responses to readings).

Make Copies of Sources

Many sources can be downloaded and stored on your computer. However, we advise that you also print out electronic sources and make photocopies of print sources as well. With paper copies you will be able to read more critically, marking up and annotating the more difficult sources. Making copies also helps you avoid problems when sources are no longer available, as when someone else checks out the book you need or an online source is taken down or moved. Student researchers may also need to submit copies of their sources with their project.

BEST PRACTICES Storing Copies of Your Sources

1. When photocopying or using your cell phone to photograph a printed source, be sure to capture all the information you will need later: Avoid cutting off page numbers. Be sure to copy not only the chapters or sections of print sources that will help answer your research question but also the title page and copyright page for books, the front cover or table of contents for magazines and journals, and the top portion of newspaper pages (where the name of the newspaper, the date of publication, and the edition are located). You will need the information on these portions of your sources in order to cite your source fully and accurately.
2. Clip or staple your printed copies, label them clearly, and keep them in a file folder or binder.
3. For electronic magazine and journal articles, save PDF files, rather than HTML files, whenever possible. PDF files include the source's page numbers and illustrations, which you will need when creating your works cited list (sometimes called a references list or bibliography). HTML files include the text but not the page numbers from the original article. The pages will not match up with the pages of the original.
4. Keep all electronic copies of articles in a file folder; label the files and folders clearly so you know at a glance what it contains. Doing so will save you a good deal of time and trouble later.
5. Bookmark your online sources. Keep a list of websites you want to return to in an Internet browser's Bookmarks or Favorites folders. Make one file for all your bookmarks on a single project. Library databases usually also provide some means for storing links to sources, bibliographic information, and even notes on the source. Check the tools or visit the database vendor's website to learn more.

Keep a Working Bibliography

A working bibliography is a list of the publication information for your potential sources, including books, articles, websites, and any other type of source. Keep a separate entry in your working bibliography for each source you might possibly use. The entries in a working bibliography are the same as those in the works cited page or references page that you will eventually include in your final draft. The working bibliography, however, keeps track of all potential sources and all of the sources that you've read regardless of whether you actually use them in the research project itself. It should also include an annotation with notes about the content of the source and your personal responses, such as how you might use the source and how different sources compare or contrast on the same topic or issue.

To save yourself time later on, construct your working bibliography in the appropriate documentation format (see Chapter 20, pages 407–32, for MLA style, and Chapter 21, pages 433–56, for APA style). Doing this will reduce the time and effort required at the end of the project. It will also prevent you from having to track down books and articles you no longer have or search for bibliographic information that you did not know you needed (such as volume numbers or reprint dates).

Citation software like *Zotero* (free on the Web) and *RefWorks* and *EndNote* (sometimes available through your library's webpage or through your school's computer center) can help you format your citations. Be aware, however, that citation software is not perfect. Be sure to check the format against the models in this book or in the style guide you are using in your course before submitting your research project.

Table 15.1 shows the essential information needed for the most common categories of sources.

Annotate Your Working Bibliography

As you skim, evaluate, and read potential sources, annotate your working bibliography by explaining how the source addresses your research question and how you might use the source in your paper. Entries might include the following information:

- **Genre, or Type, of Writing** Is it, for example, an informational article or an argument, an opinion column or an article in a scholarly journal, a book review or an abstract?
- **Author's Credentials** Is the author a reporter, a journalist, or a professor? What are the author's areas of expertise, educational background, credentials, and affiliations?
- **Use of Source** How would you use the source? To answer your research question, provide background information, stimulate thought, represent an alternative viewpoint?

TABLE 15.1

Basic Citation Information for Working Bibliography Entries

Print Sources	Electronic Sources
Book • Author(s), full name • Book title, subtitle • Publisher • Year published	**E-book** • Author(s), full name • Book title, subtitle • E-book edition (Kindle ed., etc.) • Publisher • Year published • Website title if found online (e.g., *Google Book Search* or *Bartleby.com*) • URL of website
Selection from a book or anthology • Author(s), full name • Article or essay title • Book title, subtitle • Editor's name (or editors' names) • Publisher • Year published • Inclusive page numbers of the article	**Selection from an online book or anthology** • Author(s), full name • Article or essay title • Book title, subtitle • Editor's name (or editors' names) • URL of website • Publisher • Year published • Inclusive page numbers of the article (if fixed) • Website title if found online (e.g., *Google Book Search* or *Bartleby.com*)

Magazine article
• Author(s), full name
• Article title
• Title of the periodical
• Date of publication (day, month, and year for weekly or biweekly magazines, month and year for monthly magazines)
• Page numbers on which article appears
	Online magazine or journal article
	• Author(s), full name
	• Article title
	• Website title (e.g., *TheAtlantic.com*, *TIME.com*)
	• Site sponsor (e.g., The Atlantic Monthly Group, Time Inc.; look for this at the bottom of the webpage)
	• Date of publication (day, month, and year). (Skip this information if the name of the website is similar to the sponsor's name.)
	• Name of the database (e.g., Academic OneFile)
	• For an article accessed through a database, also include the following:
	    • Name of the database (e.g., Academic OneFile)
	    • URL or DOI of article

TABLE **15.1**
continued

Print Sources	Electronic Sources

Journal article
• Author(s), full name
• Article title
• Journal title
• Volume and issue numbers
• Date of publication (year)
• Article page numbers (inclusive)
	Online journal article
	• Author(s), full name
	• Article title
	• Journal title
	• Volume and issue numbers
	• Date of publication (year)
	• Article page numbers; use *n.p.* ("no page numbers") if not available or permanent
	• For an article accessed through a database, add the following:
	  • Name of the database (e.g., Academic OneFile)
	  • DOI or URL for the article

Newspaper article • Author(s), full name, if listed • Article title • Newspaper title (include city name if not included in title) • Date of publication (day, month, and year) • Edition (such as late edition), if specified • Section name or number, if paginated separately • Page numbers on which article appears	**Online newspaper or magazine article** • Author(s), full name, if listed • Article title • Newspaper or magazine website title (e.g., *NYTimes.com, LATimes.com*) • Site sponsor (e.g., The New York Times Company, Los Angeles Times; look for this at the bottom of the webpage). (Skip this information if the name of the Web site is similar to the sponsor's name.) • Date of publication (day, month, and year) • URL of the article without "http//:" **Webpage, website, discussion list, blog** • Author(s), full name • Webpage or post title, or subject line (if any) • Title of website, discussion list, or blog • Edition, version (if any) • Site sponsor • Date of publication (day, month, year or whatever is available) • URL • Date last accessed

Student Example: Working Bibliography

Following is an example from a student's working bibliography. The research question was: Is there a difference in the experience of reading online versus reading in a printed book? This entry is for an article in an online journal.

- **Author(s):** Not given
- **Article title:** “Bye Bye Books”
- **Journal title:** *Wilson Quarterly*
- **Volume, issue numbers:** 33:2
- **Publication date (year):** 2009
- **Article page number(s):** 69
- **Date last accessed:** Aug. 8, 2009
- **Database:** Academic OneFile
- **URL:** http://www.wilsonquarterly.com/page.cfm/About_Wilson_Quarterly

Notes: This unsigned review article in a journal published by Woodrow Wilson International Center for Scholars assesses two essays in other magazines. The essay by Christine Rosen in *The New Atlantis* magazine is relevant to my question. (The other is not—it’s about libraries.) The most interesting point is that Rosen thinks that reading printed books and reading online sources are creating two different classes of people, one with book-reading abilities and the other without. The people with only screen-reading abilities have more dopamine, blocking activity in the part of the brain that “controls judgment and measures risk.” Both adults and children who read online books wind up becoming more interested in using the technology than in deep reading. I could use this source to argue that the switch is making people less thoughtful. It doesn’t have many facts or references about the dopamine studies, but I could go to Rosen’s original article for more of her argument. Rosen is a respected writer and editor.

The advice so far should give you an overview of the research process and how it unfolds. In the next chapter, we take you more deeply into the many options for finding good sources.

CHAPTER 16

Finding Sources

ENGAGING QUESTIONS

In this chapter, you will engage with the following questions:

- How do writers use keywords to pursue research questions?
- How do Boolean operators improve keyword searches?
- What role do libraries and librarians play in the research process?
- When and why do writers use reference works?
- What kinds of resources are available through library catalogs?
- How do writers use library databases to find periodicals?
- How do writers use the Web to find reliable sources?
- Which types of interactive online sources are useful and appropriate for college research projects?
- Which types of field research can be useful for college research projects?

ONE OF THE PURPOSES OF A RESEARCHED WRITING PROJECT IS TO INTRODUCE YOU TO THE WIDE ARRAY OF RESOURCES available to anyone who wants to learn more about virtually any topic. An Internet search engine like Google is just one of many resources. Public, college, and government-sponsored libraries and websites offer resources for finding everything from general information to specialized data and scholarly articles. In addition to finding information, you may want to generate your own through interviews, experiments, and observations. This chapter shows you how to stretch your research skills and take advantage of the variety of resources that will help you find not just any sources but the best sources for your project.

How Do I Conduct a Keyword Search?

No matter what kind of index or database you are searching, you will need to think about the words to use. Begin by thinking of *terms that people commonly use to name or describe your topic.* These are known as **keywords** in searching. Keyword searches are good when starting research because databases look for them not only in titles but anywhere in the text of an article.

Develop a List of Keywords as You Find Them

"McMansion" describes a large house of cheap construction. Typical of a McMansion, the house on the left lacks architectural details except on the front.
Carolyn Channell

Start generating a list of keywords by examining your research question for words that name and describe your topic. Add words you encounter when reading as well as synonyms or related concepts, and soon you will have a list of words with which to begin. For example, one student's topic was the replacement of older homes in her neighborhood by huge new ones. Julie Ross began her search with the term "teardowns," which she had picked up in neighborhood discussions. She also thought of "neighborhood preservation." As she did preliminary research, she uncovered two more terms she would not have thought of on her own: "McMansions" and "mansionization," which describe the houses built after the tearing down. An abridged version of Ross's completed essay appears in our online Chapter 33, Claiming Voice.

List your keywords in your research log. You will add to this list as your reading takes you more deeply into your topic. Using research to find more keywords is just one example of the ways research is like a branching tree. One good search term leads to more.

Know How to Narrow or Broaden Your Search

See pages 352–53 in Chapter 15 on keeping a research log.

Keywords should be specific to your topic, such as the word "teardowns" in the search described above. If the student had begun her search with a word like "houses" or "neighborhood," she would have found hundreds of irrelevant sources. On the other hand, a term like "McMansion" might be too specific as a starting point and yield few results.

- **Combining Search Terms** Most search engines and library databases use what are called Boolean, or logical, operators to narrow or broaden your search. The operators AND and NOT narrow your search, and the operators OR and the wildcard character–usually an asterisk (*) or a question mark (?)–broaden your search. Table 16.1 shows how these operators work.
- **Advanced Searching** Search engines like Google and online indexes and databases such as those on your library's website offer an advanced search option to help you do more precise searching. In Google, Advanced Search is especially helpful in filtering the vast amounts of material on the Web. By going to the Google Advanced Search screen you can choose webpages by keywords, phrases, and possible alternatives to your keywords. You can also filter out pages with words that you know would be irrelevant to your search, and you can limit the search to certain languages, reading levels, websites, or domains. Figure 16.1 shows an example of an advanced search in Google.

See pages 376–77 in Chapter 17 for more about domains.

TABLE 16.1

Use Boolean Operators to Narrow or Broaden a Search

Boolean Operator	Search Results
AND	Narrows your search. Use to find sources that cover two different concepts. Example: (gas-powered cars) AND (electric-powered cars)
OR	Broadens your search. Use to search for sources using one or more synonyms. Example: (electric cars) OR (fuel cell cars)
NOT	Narrows your search. Use to eliminate irrelevant material. Example: (gasoline-powered cars) NOT (natural-gas powered cars)
*	Broadens your search. Use to search multiple versions of a term (photograph, photographs, photographic, photography) simultaneously. Example: Civil War AND photograph*

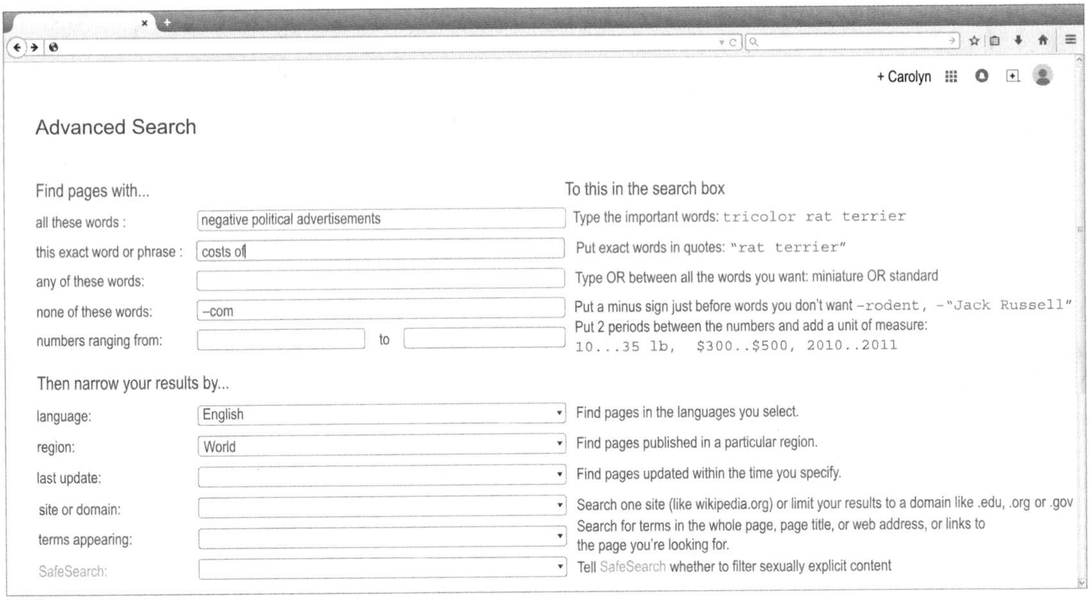

FIGURE 16.1

Advanced Search

The screen above shows an advanced search narrowed to find sources about the costs of negative political campaign advertisements, eliminating all commercial sites known as "dot-com" sites, and written at an intermediate reading level.

Keywords versus Subject Words

Many databases will give you the option of searching by keywords as well as subject words. What is the difference? The subject word option limits the search to the vocabulary preferred by the database; it is less forgiving if you do not know whether the database prefers the word "car" or "automobile," just to give an example. However, most databases provide a thesaurus tool that will direct you to the preferred terms. Once you know the right subject words to search by, the results are going to be good sources, highly relevant to your topic.

What Resources Can I Find through My College Library?

For starting a research project, your most valuable resource is your college library and its staff of librarians. If you don't even know where to begin, ask a librarian. You can find them at the reference desk of any library.

The Internet has not caused libraries and librarians to become extinct. In fact, librarians are more necessary than ever as technology keeps adding to the reserves of information available online.

For online help, your school's library home page is the gateway to all the resources available to you in print and online, including films, audio recordings, artworks, and other media. The example home page in Figure 16.2 gives you an idea of the resources available at one school library; many college libraries, such as this one, have subject-specific research guides composed by staff librarians.

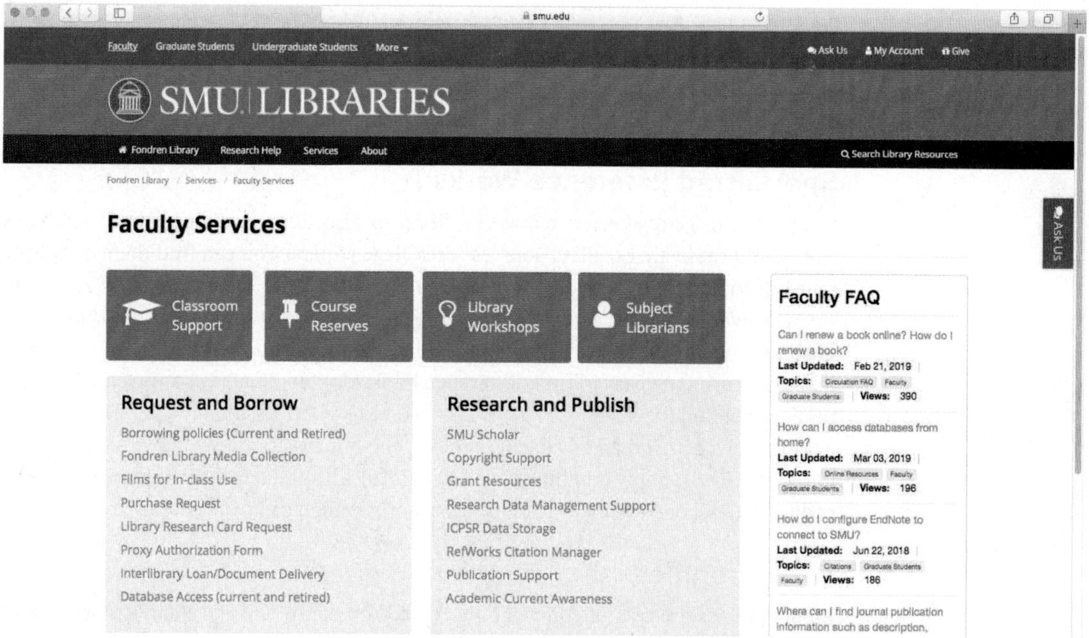

FIGURE **16.2**

Example of a College Library Home Page

Reprinted by permission of the Fondren Library and Southern Methodist University (SMU)

How Do I Find Reference Works through My College Library?

To many people, research suggests books, but the library online catalog offers other great resources to inspect before heading across campus to cart home a load of books. For example, consider beginning with **reference works.** Reference works can be books or websites but regardless of the media, *they are compilations of information organized for easy reference.* They are therefore excellent entries into any topic. Too often, students overlook reference works or are unaware of their existence, except for the common encyclopedias.

General Reference Works

Before digging into more detailed books and articles, you can get entry-level knowledge on a topic through general reference works such as encyclopedias, dictionaries, and almanacs. Some examples of general reference works are

Oxford English Dictionary

The World Almanac and Book of Facts

Encyclopædia Britannica

Wikipedia

Many professors prefer that you use general reference works only as starting points for increasing your background knowledge about a topic. General reference works are seldom cited in college writing because the information there is **common knowledge.** That does not mean that everyone knows it; common knowledge is technically defined as *information easily available to anyone from at least three sources.* In the case of *Wikipedia,* many professors advise students to double-check its information because, although it is usually accurate, it is a group-sourced work to which anyone can contribute.

Specialized Reference Works

In contrast to general reference works, libraries also offer more specialized reference works, and these are excellent sources for college papers. You can find them on a wide range of topics, as is evident from these sample titles: *The Almanac of New York City, Encyclopedia of 20th-Century American Humor,* and *Encyclopedia of Multimedia Technology and Networking.* Many are available online through the library, and those that are in print are easy to find. Reference books do not circulate, so you can count on finding them on the shelf.

To find them, do an advanced search in the library's online catalog. As illustrated in Figure 16.3, simply combine your keyword(s) with the term "dictionary," "encyclopedia," "atlas," or "almanac" to find these works online or in your library.

Bibliographies

Bibliographies are lists of sources on a topic. You can often find them in the back of books, where authors list works that they have consulted or that other readers may wish to consult to get more information. You can also search for bibliographies in your library's catalog using the method described above for specialized encyclopedias, or ask your librarian if there are research guides on the subject of your research. Many will be bound books, but increasingly bibliographies are available online, as in Figure 16.4.

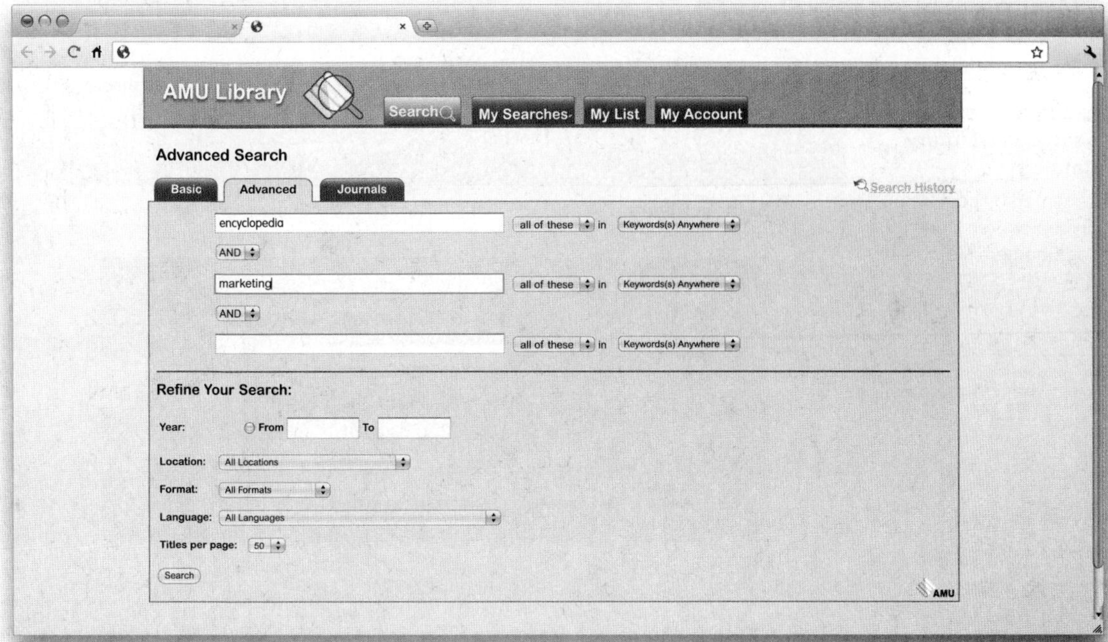

FIGURE **16.3**

Example of a Search for a Specialized Encyclopedia

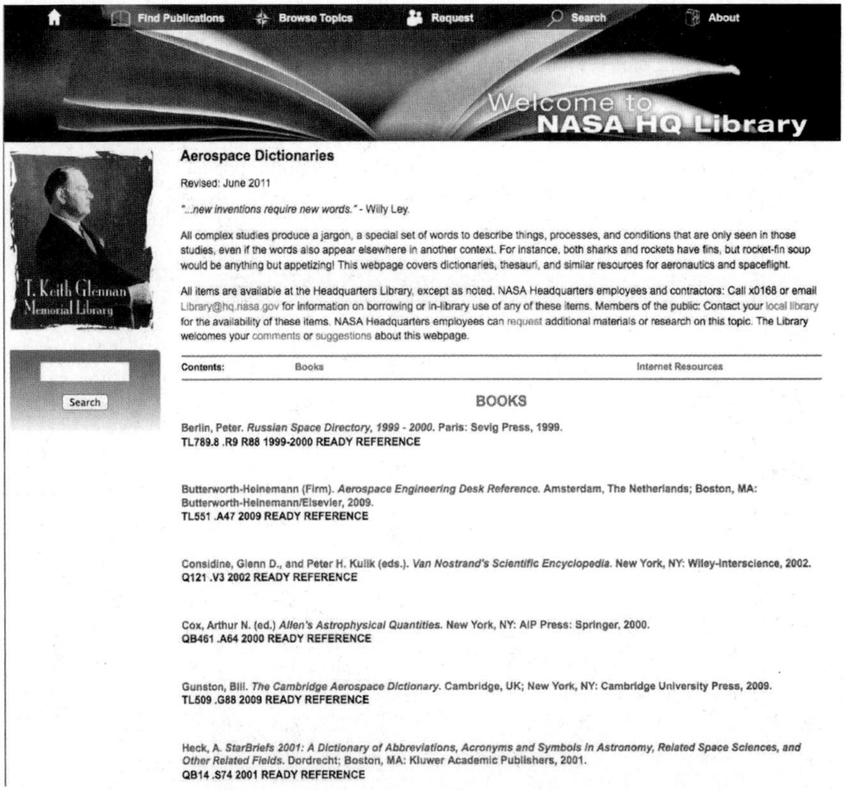

FIGURE **16.4**

Example of an Online Bibliography

NASA Headquarters Library

FIGURE **16.5**

Example of a Quick Search in a Library Catalog

Reprinted by permission of the Fondren Library and Southern Methodist University (SMU)

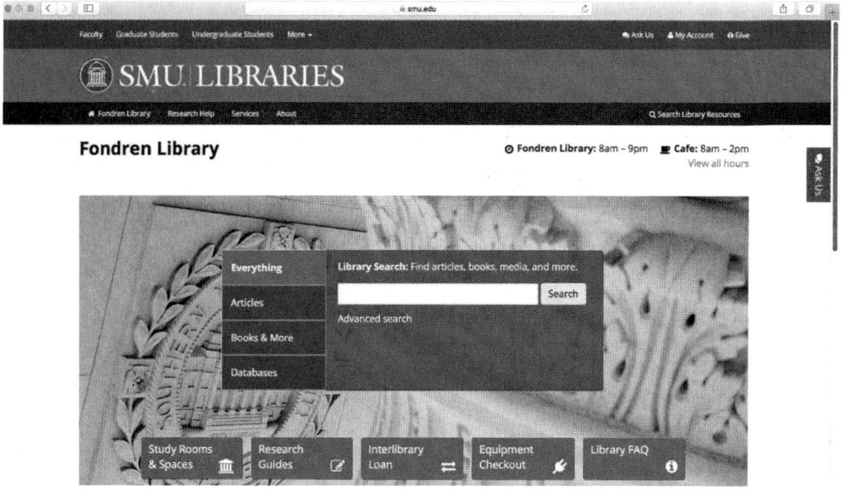

How Do I Use a Library Catalog to Find Books and Other Resources?

Your library's home page will have a link to the library catalog, which is an index of all the library's holdings in all media: print, film, digital, and so on. The home page in Figure 16.5 shows what you can expect to find.

Two main categories of resources are books and audiovisual materials.

- **Books** You can search for books by subject, author name, title, keyword, and call number, as shown in the advanced search screen in Figure 16.6.
- **Audiovisual Materials** Audiovisual materials are also found through the catalog and sometimes through a link on the library's home page.

FIGURE **16.6**

Example of an Advanced Library Search

Reprinted by permission of the Fondren Library and Southern Methodist University (SMU)

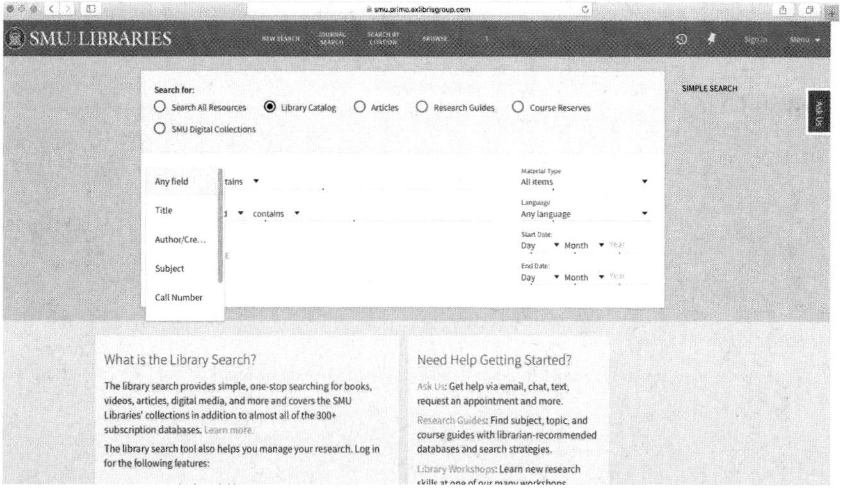

How Do I Use Library Databases to Find Articles?

The best route to finding reliable articles is through your library's online databases, which are typically accessed through the library's home page. Look for a link under categories like "Find," "Search," or "Research," or look for labels like "articles," "databases," "e-resources," or "online resources."

Thousands of databases are available to researchers, and libraries subscribe to a range, both general and subject-specific. Some of the most popular databases are listed in Table 16.2.

A library's databases will often be listed alphabetically, by title and by subject area, and by popularity. Other search options may also be available, as illustrated below.

Anatomy of a Database Search

Finding articles in subscription databases is a multistep process.

Step 1: Search. Choose one of the databases, and type your keywords in the search field. Advanced search options allow you to narrow or broaden a search.

TABLE **16.2**

Popular Library Databases

Database	Useful for Accessing . . .
Academic OneFile	Articles in both popular and scholarly periodicals for a broad range of disciplines
Academic Search Complete	Articles in both popular and scholarly periodicals for a broad range of disciplines
America: History and Life	Index of literature covering the history and culture of the United States and Canada
Engineering Village	A database of engineering research literature, with references to more than 5,000 engineering journals and conferences
ERIC	Resources on education from a wide range of sources
Factiva	Articles on current international economic and financial news, produced by Dow Jones
General Science Index	Index of scholarly and popular articles in biology, chemistry, and other sciences
JSTOR	Full text of more than 2,600 academic journals and more than 1 million images, letters, and other primary sources, most of them in the humanities and social sciences
MLA International Bibliography	Indexes articles on topics in literature and languages
Project Muse	Database of peer-reviewed academic journals and electronic books
ProQuest	Indexes a mix of scholarly journals, trade publications, magazines, and newspapers
PsycINFO	Articles on topics in psychology, published by the American Psychological Association

FIGURE **16.7**

Example of Results of an Advanced Search

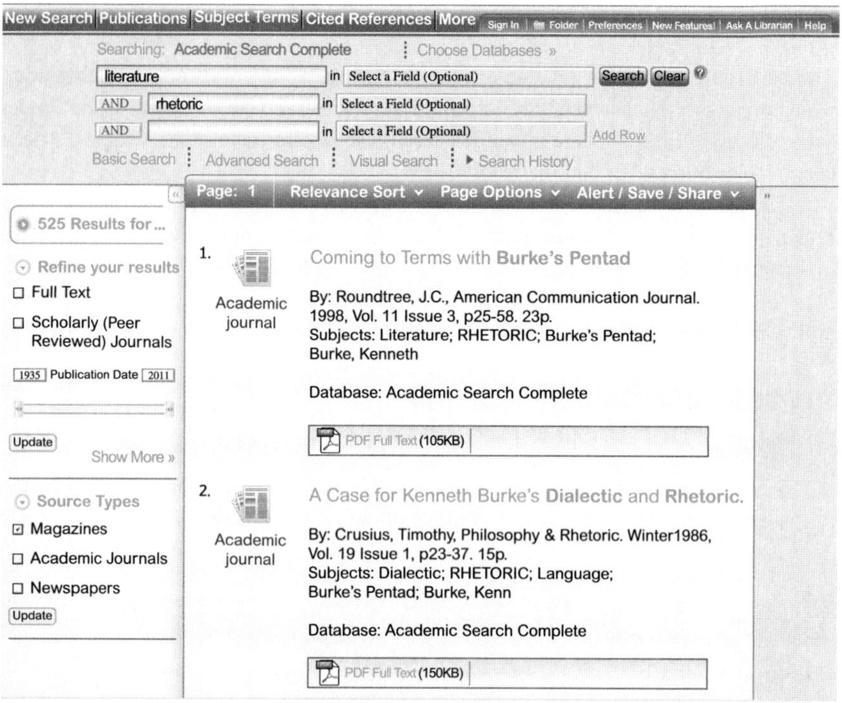

(See Table 16.1 to learn more about Boolean searching.) In a hypothetical search, we wanted to find out if reading literature made people more empathetic. In an advanced search of Academic Search Complete, we combined the keywords "literature" and "rhetoric" to get the results shown in Figure 16.7.

Step 2: Survey the results of your search. Figure 16.7 shows some of the titles this search turned up. Some things to note are

Details of the search query appear at the top of the page.

Each entry tells you if the article is available in full text online, and if so, whether in HTML or PDF files.

Results may be filtered further by publication type or by date.

Step 3: Open and examine the entries. Click on a title to find out more about that source. A typical article entry will include useful information such as an abstract of the article and links to related subjects (see Figure 16.8).

How Do I Use the Web to Find Reliable Websites and Online Journals?

The Internet provides access to a vast and ever-changing assortment of files: commercial advertising, personal webpages and blogs, newspapers and magazines, videos and podcasts, images, archives, university projects, government documents, and on and on. In short, the Internet is an unfiltered mass of information. However, it can be an

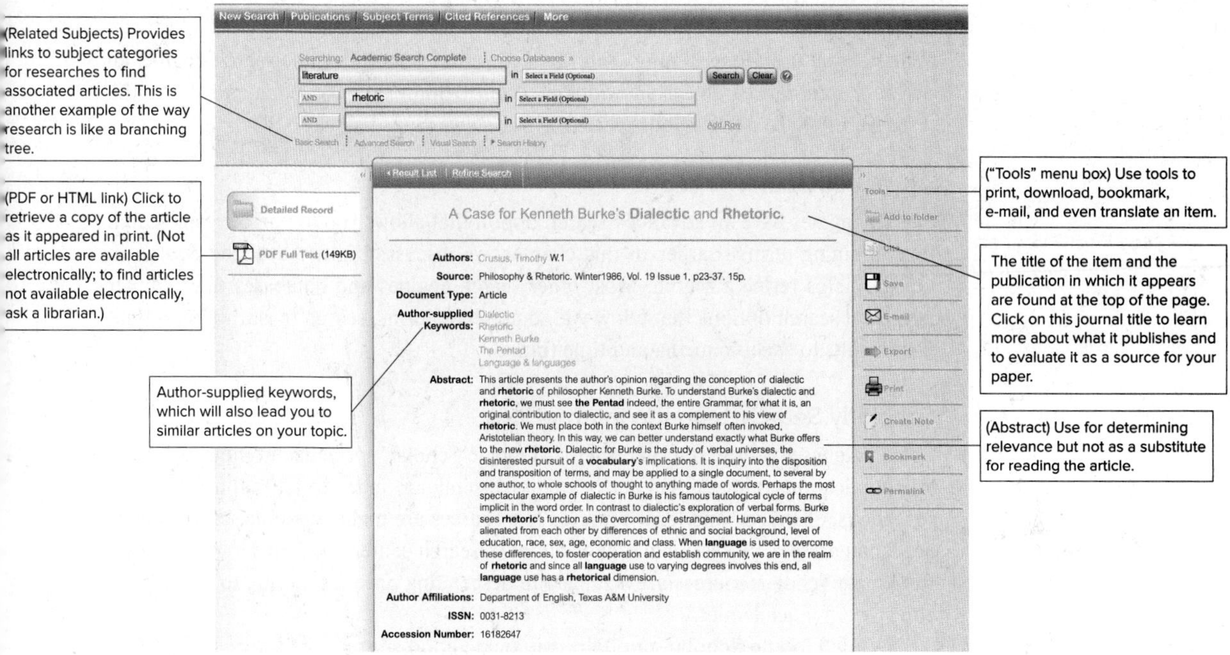

FIGURE **16.8**

Example of an Article Entry

(Abstract): Reprinted by permission of Timothy Crusius.

excellent source of free, high-quality information if you know how to use the search engines efficiently and assess the reliability of your results carefully.

CONCEPT CLOSE-UP Why Care Is Needed in Internet Searching

While the Internet is a great resource, researchers should see it as a complement to the library rather than a substitute, for several reasons:

- Because anyone can publish online, Web sources must be assessed carefully.
- The quantity of information can be overwhelming. The Internet is so large—estimated to contain hundreds of billions of webpages—that one can easily waste valuable time sifting through the mass.[1]
- Many excellent sources are available for free through libraries, but you may have to pay to access them on the Internet.

See the criteria for evaluating websites in Chapter 17, pages 375–78.

1. Alon Amit, "How Many Pages Are in Google's Web Index in 2017?" *Quora.com*, November 5, 2017, www.quora.com/How-many-pages-are-in-Googles-web-index-in-2017.

Use Web-Based Databases and Search Engines

Whether you use Google, Bing, Yahoo!, Exalead, or another online search engine, an ordinary Internet search casts a wide net, often yielding an overwhelming list of unfiltered websites. To narrow your search, try the suggestions below.

Advanced Search Options

See Figure 16.1, page 360, for an example of a Google Advanced Search.

Search engines have an advanced search option that allows you to narrow your search by combining terms. Earlier in this chapter, we discussed how Advanced Search in Google helps refine a search. Most other search engines and databases offer similar advanced search options that allow you to combine terms, search by author, and limit your results to specific media and time frames.

Scholarly Searches on the Internet

Some databases on the Internet, such as Google Scholar, specialize in indexing scholarly publications. Google Scholar is a cross-disciplinary index to journal articles, theses, books, abstracts, and legal sources. The sources are highly credible, coming from academic presses, professional organizations, research centers, and university websites. In Google Scholar, sources are arranged in descending order according to those most cited by other academics.

While Google Scholar can help you locate good sources, be aware that not all the results of your search will be available for free. Many scholarly journals require that you subscribe or pay a onetime fee for single articles. However, if you are enrolled at a school that subscribes to the journal or publishing house, you will have free full-text access through your school library. Many library online resources pages contain a link to Google Scholar so students can use it to search their own library's resources.

Online Periodicals (Newspapers, Journals, and Magazines Not Published in Print)

Articles in some scholarly journals, such as *Kairos: A Journal of Rhetoric, Technology, and Pedagogy,* and magazines, such as *Slate* (www.slate.com), are "born digital" (online only). As such, these sources may or may not be indexed in your library's databases. If you are having trouble finding sources in periodicals that are online-only, ask your school librarian for help. Online periodicals, such as your campus newspaper, are usually searchable by author.

Audiovisual and Archived Materials

Resources available online include the following:

- **Smithsonian Institution** (www.si.edu/researchcenters/). This is a searchable website of the Smithsonian's holdings, museums, encyclopedia, and research projects. You can find podcasts at the Smithsonian Institution site at www.si.edu/podcasts/.
- **Library of Congress** (www.loc.gov). This is also a searchable website. Go to www.loc.gov/library/libarch-digital.html to search the digital collections.

Online Reference Works and Bibliographies

You can find some specialized reference works available free online by searching in the same way we advised searching your library's catalog. In a Google Advanced Search, for example, you could type "encyclopedia" and one or more of your keywords.

An excellent source of online bibliographies is available through the Library of Congress website at www.loc.gov/rr/program/bib/bibhome.html.

How Do I Find Interactive Online Sources?

Many intelligent discussions take place on blogs, e-mail discussion groups, podcasts, and comment threads in online journals. Online communication can provide you with timely and stimulating debate on a topic. Although the style of this writing is less formal than in published work, these writers often have professional credentials and may be considered experts in their field. Always evaluate interactive sources carefully, however; sources in which anyone can join the conversation or in which participants remain anonymous are unlikely to be reliable. Below is a list of source types that may be useful in a college research project:

- **E-Mail Discussion Lists** People subscribe to these lists to participate in conversations on topics of interest. For a good list of groups in the humanities and social sciences, go to H-Net: www.h-net.org/lists/.
- **Blogs** For academic blogs in the humanities, social sciences, sciences, and many other disciplines and subject areas, go to Academic Blogs wiki at academicblogs.org/index.php?title=Main_Page. Nearly all online versions of newspapers have opinion blogs by their columnists. You can also google respected authors and scholars to see if they publish a blog by inserting the author's name (in quotation marks) and adding the word "blog."

How Do I Generate My Own Information?

Sometimes a research question will take you out of the library and into the world—into "the field" as researchers call it—to observe some aspect of the world around us: people and other living things, places, nature, buildings, social behavior, institutions, media, and anything that can be observed, measured, drawn, recorded, photographed, or filmed.

The need for field research arises when a researcher simply cannot answer her or his research question with existing sources. Perhaps the research question involves traffic flow in a village center, but the city has collected no traffic data. Or the question examines employee responses to changes in health care coverage, but no one has surveyed the workers yet. In such cases, the researcher may need to perform his or her own field research.

The methods for performing field research depend upon the researcher's question and the type of information available to answer that question. Can the information be observed? A researcher could observe and record information about traffic flow in a village center. Can the information be collected? In the case of employee responses to changes in health care coverage, the researcher might conduct surveys or even interview individuals.

Field research is a time-consuming and challenging venture. For example, how many days of traffic would the researcher need to observe—or how many employees

This photograph illustrates part of an experiment conducted through Massachusetts Institute of Technology that began when one woman in Seattle asked the question: "Where does my trash go when I toss it out?" Students attached electronic transmitters to trash in order to trace its journey to its ultimate destination.

Kevin P. Casey/The New York Times/Redux

would need to be surveyed—before readers would consider the field research complete and accurate? Guidance about research methodology is beyond the scope of this chapter, but it should be required reading for those planning a serious field research project. We offer some brief advice about conducting observations, surveys, and interviews.

Observational Studies

Depending on your topic, firsthand observations can be useful in developing a response to your research question.

Earlier, we described one student's research topic, the tearing down of old homes and their replacement with newer, larger ones. To do research for the project, the student walked the streets of her own neighborhood, noting specifics and taking photographs. More dramatically, a writer can observe undercover, like the anthropologist who posed (with the university's approval) as "Rebekah Nathan," a first-year student living in the dorms and attending classes. Her book, *My Freshman Year* (Cornell UP 2005), aims to give professors an understanding of college from the student's perspective.

Surveys

You may be able to get information on some topics, especially if they are local or campus-related, by doing a survey. Be forewarned, however, that it is difficult to conduct a reliable survey questionnaire. First, there is the problem of designing a clear and unbiased survey instrument. If you have ever filled out an evaluation form for an instructor or a course, you know how problems of clarity can arise. An evaluation might ask whether an instructor returns papers "in a reasonable length of time"; what is "reasonable" to some students may be too long for others.

Second, there is the problem of getting a representative response, that is, a response that represents the whole group the survey is intended to represent. A survey of undergraduates taken at the entrance to the library in the evening might have vastly different results from one taken at the gym in the afternoon.

Surveys can be useful, but seek additional advice on how to design and administer them. You might consult a book like T. L. Brink's *Questionnaires: Practical Hints on How to Avoid Mistakes in Design and Interpretation* (Heuristic Books 2004.)

Interviews

Depending on your topic and research question, personal interviews can be a wonderful source of information. Many people in your community, in your workplace, or at your school are experts on specific topics–from city leaders, to environmental activists, to bank presidents. Most will happily share what they know.

Interviews require time from people's often busy schedules, so it is only polite to ask well in advance for their participation, explain what you will be asking them, and give them an estimate of how much of their time you will need. Once you have determined possible sources, begin a courteous round of phone calls and carefully composed e-mails, continuing until you connect with the right person. If necessary, let the person know that you are willing to conduct the interview by e-mail or phone as well as face-to-face.

Prepare for the interview by having questions ready; if you want to record it, be sure to gain permission. Begin the interview by acknowledging the value of the person's time. Tell the person about your research project but withhold your own position on controversial matters. Take careful and complete notes, including the spelling of the person's name as well as the person's title and credentials. Later, follow up with a thank-you note or e-mail. If multiple people in your class are researching the same topic, avoid flooding any one person with requests for interviews. One or two students could conduct the interview and report to the class, or the interview could take place in the class either in person or through live chat or video.

For more about how to do interviews, see Chapter 5, Describing People and Places, pages 74–102.

We suggest that you evaluate sources, covered in Chapter 17, as you do your research rather than making evaluation a separate step. You might spend a day gathering possible sources, and then, before going on to more databases and indexes, look over the ones you have at hand. Evaluating can be as simple as checking a website's home page for information about the credibility of its author or sponsor, or it can be a more time-consuming process of skimming or reading an article or book. Considering the credibility, focus, and angle of the sources you find will help you decide if they are a good fit with your proposed research question and the scope of your project.

CHAPTER 17

Evaluating Sources

ENGAGING QUESTIONS

In this chapter, you will engage with the following questions:

- How do writers use questions to evaluate a source's usefulness?
- How do writers use questions to evaluate a source's reliability?
- How can websites be evaluated for credibility?
- How do writers recognize sources of false information?

OF THE HUNDREDS OF POTENTIAL SOURCES THAT TURN UP IN A SEARCH, how do you select the ones that will be the best for your project? This is an important question because, like a gourmet dish, your paper will be only as good as the ingredients that go into it. Asking two questions will help you make smart choices: (1) How useful will a source be in helping me achieve my purpose for writing? (2) How credible or reliable are the contents of the source? These two questions are equally important. Although we take them up separately here, you should have both of them in mind as you inspect each possible source.

How Do I Decide If a Source Is Useful?

For a source to be useful, it has to fit well with your topic and purpose. The contents need to be relevant to your research question. You cannot always make that determination from the title alone, but there are other ways to predict usefulness. If an article abstract is available, read it; if one is not, skim the article for subheadings or major subdivisions of the content. For a book, read the introduction, preface, or book jacket; skim the index at the back to see what topics are covered. If a book looks promising, you might want to read a couple of reviews to find more about its coverage and the author's angle on your topic.

Below are a few more questions to ask yourself for determining the usefulness of a source.

- **Is the source's angle on your topic a good fit for your purposes?** For example, a search on the topic of bullying in schools might turn up articles on specific kinds, such as bullying of children with autism or bullying of immigrants. You may decide that you want to take your research in that direction, but be aware that doing so may make other sources you already have irrelevant to the new angle. Also, many databases and search engines will turn up articles and websites from foreign countries. Research from and about foreign countries may or may not be relevant to your topic. The point is: Be aware and make an informed decision.

- **Does the source offer the kinds of information you need in order to accomplish your purpose?** Do you need case studies, experts' analyses of a situation, or arguments on an issue? Do you need statistics or other kinds of data? How in-depth is the information? Does the source go beyond the level of what is considered common knowledge–that is, information readily available from multiple other sources? For any source that looks promising, do a preliminary reading and take some notes about how and where it could contribute to your research project.
- **If your topic requires up-to-date information and expert opinions, is the source current enough?** There is no "date of expiration" on a source, and you may want to use a classic or historic work, but if your topic needs recent sources, do enough research to find them before settling on a source that may no longer be relevant.
- **Is the source a good fit with your ability, not just to read but to read critically on your chosen topic?** Sources for college research projects should be challenging, but if a source is so specialized or technical that you have to skip over parts of it, you may not be able to write confidently and clearly about the ideas and information in it. Titles can often clue you to levels of difficulty. For example, a database search for articles on school bullying turned up a title that contained the phrase "longitudinal consequences of adolescent bullying perpetration." If a title contains unfamiliar concepts, chances are the article will too.

See Chapter 2, pages 12–27 for an explanation of critical reading.

How Do I Decide If a Source Is Reliable?

The reliability of a source is as important as its usefulness. A source that your readers will not respect and find credible is not a useful one. A reliable source will provide you with credible information, authoritative opinions, and responsible research.

Journals and books that are published by universities can usually be assumed to be reliable. If a book or journal is published by a university press, it has gone through a process known as "peer review," which means it has been critiqued and approved by other scholars working on the topic. You may trust that the books and journals available through your college or university library are credible because they have been selected by librarians and professors.

However, you will also find many sources from publications more broadly available to the public, such as books from popular presses, magazines, and materials on the Internet. Making responsible choices from these more popular sources requires careful scrutiny and critical thinking. For any source, the following questions will help you decide if you should use it.

Who Is the Author?

Information about the author is one of the best clues to a source's credibility. Whether your source is a book, an article, or a website, you should be able to find some information about the author's credentials, such as

- Educational background, advanced degrees
- Professional affiliations, honors, and awards
- Other publications

Information about the author should not be difficult to find. It is usually printed as a headnote or footnote in articles and in the back pages of books and anthologies. For Internet sites, a tab titled "About Me" or "Biography" provides a link to this important information. Consider whether the person's education and affiliations would indicate that he or she is an authority on the subject. Be suspicious if you cannot find information about an author on the source itself.

If the author is a journalist rather than a scholar or professional in the field of your research, you should consider the credibility of the publication itself, as described below.

Who Published the Source?

Every book, periodical, primary source, and website has a person or organization responsible for its existence. That person or group may be a university press, a government agency, or an organization with an agenda to push or a product to sell. Sometimes a publisher's goals might conflict with the purported topic in a way that may lessen the credibility of the information. To determine the credibility of publishers, ask the following questions:

- **Is the publisher well recognized and respected, such as a major city's newspaper or a newspaper with nationwide circulation?** For books, is the publisher an established house or has the author self-published the book? If the latter, you need to look further into his or her credentials.
- **Who is the sponsor behind the publication?** Is it an institution, like the Smithsonian? Is it an independent research center or a university?
- **Does the publication list its editorial board, including members' credentials?**
- **What other types of articles or other authors does this publisher publish?**
- **What is the purpose or goal of the publication?** You can often find the mission statement of magazines and newspapers near the masthead inside, and websites also provide descriptions of their purpose through an "About" link on the home page. If you are using a library database like Academic Search Complete, the journal or magazine title in the detailed record is a link that takes you to information about the publication, including bias, audience, and topics typically covered.

How Recent Is the Source?

We mentioned this criterion earlier in the chapter, but the date of a source's publication is as important to its credibility as it is to its usefulness. Especially in the social science and science disciplines, information that is more than five years old may well be outdated by more recent research. Although older sources may provide a history of the subject, more recent sources provide more credible information.

How Good Are the Source's Sources?

Just as your instructor expects you to provide documentation for information in your writing, you can expect to find documentation in your sources. When a source includes facts, information, statistics, or quotations, the author should tell you where that information came from. Naming one's sources gives scholarly credibility to the work and

FIGURE **17.1**

Government Website Dedicated to Prevention of Bullying

Source: Stopbullying.gov/U.S. Department of Health and Human Services

helps readers in their own research, a professional courtesy. Even if a source does not include footnotes, endnotes, or a list of works cited, you should find specific references to books, articles, and experts woven into the body of the writing.

Will Your Readers Find the Source Authoritative?

Your search may turn up books, articles, and websites aimed at readers of high school age or younger. The information may be perfectly correct, but in making the topic accessible, writers may provide a simplified, less specific treatment than they would give to an older readership. Or the audience for the source may simply be the general public. The information in such sources is often common knowledge. In a paper for a college class, you need to go beyond common knowledge to information that justifies citing your source.

Clues to audience are the level of vocabulary and specialized terminology as well as visual elements such as graphics. In Figure 17.1, the titles, links, and visuals should clue you to the fact that this government website on bullying is aimed at the general public. The website gives basic information and does not acknowledge its sources since the information is common knowledge.

To find websites that go beyond common knowledge and offer lists of sources more acceptable for college research papers, you will want to go to academic websites such as those hosted by universities. On bullying prevention, for example, the University of Virginia's Curry School of Education offers an annotated bibliography of scholarly articles from publications such as the *Journal of School Psychology* and the *Journal of School Violence*. The authors of these articles will have cited their sources. Using these sources will make your research paper more credible to serious readers than a government website aimed at the general public.

How Do I Evaluate a Website?

No one oversees the reliability or truth of material posted on the Web. Anyone can post almost anything, so users have to take the responsibility for assessing credibility unless the source is a digital version of a reliable print source. All of the questions listed on pages 372–75 are relevant to evaluating both print and online sources; however, the questions below are specific to evaluating websites.

What Is the Domain Name Extension?

You can use a website's URL (uniform resource locator) to help you judge reliability. Every URL ends with a period followed by an abbreviation indicating its domain. Some of the more common domain types are

- **Commercial (.com and .net).** "Dot-com" and "dot-net" sites include businesses and their publications and other commercial publications. Magazines on the Web usually are dot-com sites, as are many personal webpages and blogs.
- **Nonprofit organizations (.org).** Most nonprofit organizations use the "dot-org" extension. These organizations include charities and advocacy groups, such as Autism Speaks (www.autismspeaks.org), which supports research, fund-raising, and general awareness of the facts about autism. Be aware, though, that use of the dot-org extension is open to anyone. On its own, the fact that a website ends in .org does not guarantee that the site is operated by a nonprofit organization or that it is reliable.
- **Educational institutions (.edu).** The "dot-edu" extension is associated with schools, colleges, and universities, including the pages and e-mails of individuals associated with these institutions.
- **Government agencies (.gov and .mil).** "Dot-gov" sites are useful for getting the latest information about any aspect of American government and its agencies. The U.S. military has its own extension, "dot-mil."
- **Foreign countries (for example, .ca or .uk).** These examples are the domain abbreviations for Canadian and United Kingdom sites, but all countries outside the United States have URLs ending in an abbreviation for the name of the country.

In general, sources located on educational (.edu) and government (.gov or .mil) sites are most likely to be reliable. However, an article posted on a website ending in .edu could be the paper of a first-year student or even a student in high school, so you always need to look further into the source. Sources with other domain name extensions, such as .org, .com, .net, or .biz, should be carefully evaluated to determine if they are credible.

Who Is the Publisher of the Website?

A website that serves as the official online presence of a reputable commercial or nonprofit organization is also likely to be reliable. You will need to use critical thinking and reading skills to determine which websites are legitimate. One way to verify that the website is legitimate and reliable is to consider how you arrived at the URL; being directed to a website by a source you already trust indicates that the site is reliable. For example, if the *New York Times* publishes the URL for a company in an article, that's an indication that the website is official and credible. Printed material produced by an organization will also usually include the URL of the organization's website.

The definitive way to determine whether the site is the official arm of the entity it purports to represent is to perform a WHOIS Lookup on the domain and verify that the registration information is real contact information for the organization. Go to www.whois.net and enter the domain name in the WHOIS Lookup box. You can verify that the contact information returned by the lookup corresponds to the organization's real contact information by using phone books or other directories. Be wary of any site for which information about the registered owner is not available.

What Is the Purpose or Agenda of the Website?

Websites of reputable institutions and organizations will provide information about the sponsoring person, organization, or body, as well as their mission and funding, on a page with a name like "About Us," "Philosophy," or "Biography." Links to these pages should be available on the home page, which is usually easily accessible by a link on every page on the site.

Does the Author Have Appropriate Credentials?

If articles on a website are signed, check to see if the author has credentials that would ensure he or she has some authority on the topic. If the article is unsigned, the credibility rests on that of the publisher.

Has the Website Been Updated Recently?

Look for the date of the most recent update, commonly located at the bottom of the page. If no one has updated a website in more than a year, it may be abandoned or at least neglected. Avoid websites that offer undated information.

Has the Author Cited Sources for His or Her Information?

Has the author documented his or her sources with links or with footnotes and a works cited or references list? If there are links, do they work? Do the links take you to high-quality sources?

Is the Website Possibly a Hoax?

It is always possible that on the face of things, a website will appear legitimate but actually be satirical or deceitful (see Figure 17.2). You should not be fooled if you have carefully answered the above questions and used some common sense. Having a slightly skeptical attitude is good insurance against fraud.

How Do I Recognize False Information?

A hoax website might be a joke, but there is nothing funny about the intentional dissemination of false information. It is common today to hear of "fake news" or "alternative facts," but no matter what you call it, it is lying and a serious threat to our nation and communities. As a college student, you have the responsibility to become information literate, to be able to know fakes from facts.

This chapter has already provided much advice about how to evaluate sources of many kinds. Using sources that you have found through your school's library is one way to guard against finding and using bad sources. Checking the author's or publisher's credentials is another. However, because the problem of fake news has been exacerbated by the rise of agenda-driven news, social media, and the ease of posting anything on the Internet, we offer additional advice on telling truth from lies.

FIGURE **17.2**

This hoax website fooled at least one professional writer who included it as a legitimate source. What clues indicate that it is satire?

Source: Mavav.org

1. Use your critical reading skills. Read for tone and bias in sources. If you react strongly to the emotional tone of voice in a source, it may not be objective or credible. Insulting language about opposing views should be a warning that you need to pay special attention to the people or institutions responsible for putting it in print or online. Name-calling and fear-mongering is often just "clickbait," intended to create revenue for a website.
2. Know the difference between facts and opinions. Opinions are subjective points of view about which people may differ. Facts are objectively verifiable. As an American politician, Daniel Patrick Moynihan, said, "Everyone is entitled to his own opinion, but not his own facts." Some news sources use selective sourcing to stack the deck toward one point of view; some media mislead by presenting opinion as factual news.
3. Use fact checkers to verify information, especially when you find contradictory information in different sources. Some good places to check facts are Snopes, FactCheck.org., Politifact, Hoax Slayer, and Truth or Fiction.
4. Use lateral searching, looking at a wide range of sources, rather than vertical searching into one website or news source.
5. Take advantage of nonprofit organizations that evaluate news for bias and fact, such as AllSides, Politifact, FactCheck, and Media Bias/Fact Check.
6. Recognize that good reporting follows ethical standards, represents multiple viewpoints, identifies sources, and uses reputable authorities.

CHAPTER 18

Incorporating Source Materials

ENGAGING QUESTIONS

In this chapter, you will engage with the following questions:

- How is conducting research like entering a conversation on a topic?
- How does informal writing allow writers to engage in the conversation?
- How do writers draw connections between different sources?
- What roles can sources play in writing?
- What methods do writers use to incorporate source material?
- Why is it important for writers to acknowledge, integrate, and cite their sources?
- What methods do writers use to acknowledge sources?
- What are the guidelines for integrating source materials?
- What are the steps to follow when documenting sources?
- How do writers maintain their voice when using source material?

SOURCE MATERIALS ARE INTEGRAL TO RESEARCHED WRITING. Reading sources generates questions, helps you find an angle, and gives you information and ideas for developing your paper. While some sources will make major contributions and others play lesser roles, all the sources taken together form a foundation for writing with your own voice and purpose. As you read about your topic, a big picture starts to take shape, and your knowledge and confidence grow. Eventually, you are ready to enter the conversation, asserting your own thesis and bringing in sources to develop and support it.

What Does It Mean to Enter the Conversation?

Beginning research is like entering a conversation on your topic. When you write using sources, you join a conversation that includes ideas from the sources you cite, your interpretation of what these other voices are saying, your presentation of your own views, and the responses of people who read your completed paper.

Reading while you research can start lightly with skimming, getting a quick overview of the genre, author, and angle of each potential source. Following are some questions you could ask while skimming, or previewing, sources. Chapter 2 (pages 15–16 and 19–21) gives you more information about how to preview sources and how to read them critically if you decide to use them in your writing.

BEST PRACTICES Read While You Research

Take time to read *while* you research. Reading is a part of research, not something you do after you have gathered up a stack of sources. The following are good reasons to read the sources as you find them:

1. One good source leads to another. Writers will refer to others who have written on your topic. You will find these references in the body of a reading and/or in a bibliography at the end.
2. You will gradually learn the angles and range of opinions on your topic, so when it is time for you to form your own thesis, you will be operating with full knowledge of the conversation already out there.
3. You will be able to compare the sources, deciding which have the best information and arguments to use in your paper.

THE ART OF QUESTIONING Previewing a Source

In deciding whether and how to use a source, the most important questions are the following:

1. **What is the genre (kind of writing) of this source?** For example, is the source an informative and relatively objective entry in a reference book, or is it an argument in an academic or popular journal? Is it an article in a magazine or on a website?
2. **Who is the author of this source?** Is the author an important figure with expertise on your topic?
3. **What are the focus, purpose, and angle of this source, and what is its bias?** After skimming the source, think about how the author's angle compares with that of other sources you have found or your own angle on the topic, if you have formed one.
4. **How might you use this source?** Does it contain good facts and data? Does it analyze or explain information? Does it cite experts you could use to support a point?

How Does Informal Writing Engage Me in the Conversation?

When you are involved in an oral conversation, you listen to what others have to say, you respond, and you ask questions. In much the same way, while you are reading, you should not simply read to hear what a writer is saying but think about it, respond to it, and question it. Writing informally helps you engage with sources by preserving your responses and questions before, during, and after you read.

How Do I Annotate to Engage with a Source?

Annotating means taking notes on the source itself–in the margins, between the lines, or on sticky notes if you prefer not to mark up your copy. Annotating supports critical reading, as explained in Chapter 2, in the Art of Questioning box on pages 20–21. When annotating, you interact with the source, firming up your understanding of what it says as well as what it implies. Students who mark up their sources have better comprehension than those who don't and therefore are able to use sources more competently.

Annotations support research by helping form the big picture of the conversation on your topic, especially if you mark up passages with notes about how author "X" compares with authors "Y" and "Z" on similar points. Annotations can point to places in a text that offer leads to other sources you might want to consult.

The reading that follows is an excerpt from a book by a specialist in information technology.

Our annotations show common kinds of notes readers make to themselves in the margins to help make good use of a source.

Indeed/Getty Images

READING **18.1**

The Slow Movement and Slow Reading

JOHN MIEDEMA

John Miedema has worked for IBM as a specialist in Information Technology. He studied Information Science at the University of Western Ontario, with special interests in reading research and open source for libraries. This reading is excerpted from his book Slow Reading, *published by Litwin Books, 2009.*

Note that the idea of slow reading goes back to the 1970s.

Quotable words, and note contrast between this and screen reading.

1 After a pressured day in his world of advertising there seemed to be no solution to the problems thrashing around in the head of Sydney Piddington. In *The Special Joys of Super-Slow Reading* (1973), Piddington recounts his decision to relax by spending three hours on two chapters of a book: "I lost myself in the author's world, *living* his book. And when I finally put it down, my mind was totally refreshed" (157). Ironically, this article was published in *Reader's Digest*. On the back flap was an advertisement directed to women for the magazine's condensed books: "To every Miss, Mrs. and Ms. Who has no time to

This is Miedema's main point.

read—READ THIS!" Piddington understood what his publishers did not, that slowing down is essential in the rush of modern culture.

2 Piddington wrote his article in 1973 before the mainstream integration of the personal computer and other digital technologies into our lives. Technology does make life easier in many ways but we tend to accept it unreservedly, forgetting that each solution comes with its own set of problems. As an information technology professional, I appreciate how web access allows me to work from home, but I also find it difficult to mentally let go at the end of the work day. I wind up checking work email when I would rather be playing ping-pong with my son. No doubt every generation has felt rushed, the accelerating presence of technology in our lives comes with escalating costs. We pay for the constant speed with reduced performance, burnout, impaired relationships, and sometimes even our lives.

This book might be worth looking into for my paper.

3 Increasing numbers of people are getting fed up with the rush of modern life and are choosing instead to slow down. [Carl] Honoré (2004) is the author of the book *In Praise of Slow: How a Worldwide Movement is Changing the Cult of Speed,* which documents the rise of the Slow Movement. In 1986, McDonald's opened another one of their restaurants in Rome. Fed up with fast food, Carlo Petrini protested by starting Slow Food, an organization that promotes the pleasures and payoffs of eating fresh local foods produced in season by sustainable farming practices. Slow Food International currently claims over 85,000 members in 132 countries (2008). Honoré traces the development from Slow Food to other movements. Slow Cities is intended to recreate urban life based on the principles of Petrini. Others practice slow exercise, slow sex, slow work, slow parenting and so on. It's a global reaction against acceleration.

This strikes me as laughable. What is the purpose of a bedtime story anyway?

4 Honoré's interest in the Slow Movement began with reading. One day in an airport he spotted a newspaper article on a series of condensed fairy tales called *The One-Minute Bedtime Story.* At first it struck him as brilliant—the cure to his nightly tug-of-war with his son's demands for more stories; then the absurdity of his fast lifestyle called him to his senses. These days (2007), he goes into his son's room, leaving his watch behind and his computer speaker turned off so does not hear the pings of email deliveries, and slows down to his son's pace, talking about whatever as they read a story. It has changed from a task to be hurried to a reward to be cherished.

An important concession.

Important benefits of slowing down.

Milton wrote the great epic poem *Paradise Lost* in 1667. Waters means these children will not be prepared to read the great works of literature.

A quotable passage from the Harvard editor.

5 Speed is not anathema to the Slow Movement. Not everything should be done as slowly as possible. It is only that our obsession with speed has turned into an addiction. Slowing down tends to improve life. At work, a slower pace tends to increase overall performance. Slow reading increases literacy skills. [Lindsey] Waters, executive editor for the humanities at Harvard, declared a worldwide reading crisis resulting from our global push toward productivity. Young children are learning to read faster, skipping phonetics and diagramming sentences; these children will not grow up to read Milton. Foreseeing the end of graduate English literature programs, he advised re-introducing time into reading: "People are trying slow eating. Why not slow reading?" (2007) The benefits of slow reading can be

academic or more pedestrian. Mid-afternoon at work, I get a lift just thinking about the escapist novel I have waiting for me at home.

References

Honoré, C. (2007). Slowing down in a world built for speed. TED: Ideas worth spreading. http://www.ted.com/index.php/talks/carl_honore_praises_slowness.html

Piddington, S. (1973, June). The special joys of super-slow reading, *Reader's Digest, 52,* 158.

Slow Food (2008). Our philosophy. https://www.slowfood.com/about-us/our-philosophy/

Waters, L. (2007, February 9). Time for reading. *Chronicle of Higher Education, 53*(23). https://www.chronicle.com/article/Time-for-Reading/10505

How Can a Research Log or a Notebook Help Me Engage with My Sources?

Although marginal annotations can include personal responses, it is better to use a notebook or file on your computer to write more expanded informal responses. The more you write to interact with your sources before you use them in your own writing, the more comfortable you will be when it comes time to weave their voices and ideas into your paper. Following are some examples of the kind of background writing that helps you rehearse your use of sources. Performing these actions immediately after reading a source will save you time later because you will have generated raw material for some of your draft.

THE ART OF QUESTIONING What Do I Think about What the Source Is Saying?

Assert your own voice by freewriting in your research log or writer's notebook in response to questions such as the following:

- What do I agree with here, and why? What do I know that causes me to agree?
- What do I disagree with here, and why?
- What would I like to know more about, checking for the accuracy of the writer's information?
- What other context or perspective might be possible on the views expressed here?
- What other sources or writers have I found that speak on the same topics, and how do these sources compare?

Below are some example notebook entries in response to Miedema's chapter:

I wonder what book might give me this same refreshed feeling if I took three hours to read two chapters. What novel would I want to live in?

Notes can pose a question.

I agree that reading for speed is not compatible with reading for pleasure.

Notes can agree or disagree with a writer or speaker.

This reading reminds me of how Nicholas Carr ("Is Google Making Us Stupid?") compares digital reading to jet skiing and deep reading to scuba diving.

Notes can show your observations of similarities between sources.

In a good research paper, the writer weaves material from multiple sources into a coherent whole.

Tony Sweet/Digital Vision/ Getty Images

How Do I Draw Connections between Sources?

To use your sources well, you must not use each in isolation, taking them up one at a time. You will need to blend them, a critical thinking skill known as **synthesizing,** which means *bringing together.* A good research paper uses multiple sources in any one section, even any one paragraph. (Synthesis is covered in Chapter 8, Comparing Perspectives, pages 162–83.)

As you read a second source, a third, a fourth, and so on, use informal writing to note where authors talk about the same topics. Notice places where they agree or disagree. It is possible that sources will contradict each other; this too, is worth noting and pursuing in further research.

Many kinds of informal writing can help you manage the job of synthesis: We have already suggested annotations and notebook entries. You could also create a chart, like the one shown on page 180 in Chapter 8. All of these methods can help you with the difficult task of organizing ideas across sources.

The example notes that follow illustrate how writers can use their notebooks to make connections between points in multiple sources. The student paper in Chapter 20, pages 426–32 shows how these notes helped the writer synthesize his sources.

STUDENT EXAMPLE **Notes**

Note: Two English professors and an information technology expert bring up this idea: Education and books should help us escape the hectic pace of life and slow down and reflect on our lives.

Mark Edmundson, English professor, U. Va.
Says students "skate fast over the surfaces of life." But "To live well, we must sometimes stop and think, and then try to remake the work in progress that we currently are. There's no better place for that than a college classroom where, together, we can slow it down and live deliberately, if only for a while." (no pages)

A good way to draw connections between sources is to paraphrase and directly quote passages from different sources that touch on similar points. The highlighting here shows specific points that run across the three sources.

John Miedema, Information Technology specialist
Not everything should be done as slowly as possible. It is only that our obsession with speed has turned into an addiction. Slowing down tends to improve life. At work, a slower pace tends to increase overall performance. Slow reading increases literacy skills. [Lindsey] Waters, executive editor for the humanities at Harvard, declared a worldwide reading crisis resulting from our global push toward productivity. Young children are learning to read faster, skipping phonetics and diagramming sentences; these children will not grow up to read Milton.

Mark Bauerlein, English professor, Emory U.
Says that reading should be a relief from stress and a way to help us put our lives into better perspective: "Books afford young readers a place to slow down and reflect, to find role models, to observe their own turbulent feelings well expressed, or to discover moral convictions" (58).

Writing informally to note where sources converge in their thinking, or where they diverge, will help you put them together in a plan of your own. The next sections of this chapter address the many ways you can employ sources, working them gracefully into your own writing and documenting them correctly.

What Roles Can Sources Play in My Writing?

As you prepare to start drafting, think of the ways you can use your sources. Remember that sources are integral to the construction of your thinking and the development of your ideas. Bring your sources in as you draft, and cite them correctly so you do not have to find the needed bibliographic information later. Consider the many contributions sources make to academic and workplace writing:

1. Sources provide the background knowledge you need in order to know if your research question is important or already settled.
2. Sources provide awareness of the climate of opinion on an issue, so you can explain opposing views.
3. Sources provide detailed information that makes any kind of writing specific and interesting. Your readers may need background information, concept explanations, and examples that illustrate your topic.
4. In an argument, sources provide evidence and opinions that the writer may use for support.
5. The sources we use not only provide evidence and opinions but also give legitimacy to our writing. Without sources, writing appears untrustworthy.
6. Using a range of sources shows the writer has inquired thoroughly into a topic and considered a wide spectrum of evidence and opinion in order to arrive at a thesis.

What Are My Options for Bringing in Source Material?

To incorporate source information into a paper or project, a writer has three options: direct quotations, paraphrases (also called indirect quotations), and summaries. In the first method, words are taken exactly as they appear in the source, with any alterations noted. In the second, paraphrase, the source material is reworded, and in the third, source material is both reworded and shortened. Each method is appropriate to specific circumstances; making the right choice depends on your purpose as well as the content of the material you plan to include.

Using Direct Quotations

Direct quotations are an efficient way to present material from a source. However, of the three options, direct quotation is the one you should use least. A great deal of source material is not worth quoting directly, and overuse of direct quoting can create a patchwork of voices in your paper, drowning out your own voice. It can also create a choppy, incoherent style if you don't set quotations up with enough context from the source. A good rule of thumb is that no more than 10 percent of a paper should be direct quotations: 100 words in a 1,000-word paper. So when should you use them?

Reserve direct quotations for the words of people whose credentials and opinions will lend weight to your paper or for the words of sources you want to dispute or analyze. You might also use direct quotations for

- Strongly or uniquely worded statements of opinion where capturing the colorful voice of the speaker matters to the point you are making.
- Literary turns of phrase, such as metaphors and analogies, where the style is part of the message.
- Highly technical language, such as professional jargon, where no easy translation is possible.

The example passage below makes good use of a direct quotation.

Appropriate Use of Direct Quotation to Present an Opinion from a Source

Mark Bauerlein, an Emory University professor of English, believes teenagers have stunted their intellects by limiting their use of the Internet and other information technology to peer-to-peer socializing. Although he has called them "the Dumbest Generation," he says, "These kids have just as much intelligence and ambition as any previous cohort, but they exercise them too much on one another. They are building youth culture into a ubiquitous universe, and as ever youth culture is a drag on maturity" (22).

Bauerlein, Mark. "Generation Text." *America,* 12 Oct. 2009, americamagazine.org/issue/710/new-media/generation-text.

Using Paraphrases

Paraphrases are more common in professional researched writing than direct quotations. Unlike quoting, paraphrasing and summarizing let you maintain your role as the paper's dominant voice. Also, readers find direct quotations distracting when there is no good reason for using someone else's exact words instead of your own.

Paraphrase Facts or Background Information

Paraphrase when presenting information such as facts found in reference books, websites, and newspaper articles where the writer is a reporter or journalist, not an expert whose credentials would bolster your paper's credibility. Rewriting an informative passage in your own words may seem like extra work, but it is better to make the effort than to use direct quotations for passages that simply provide information. The following box gives advice on how to write a good paraphrase.

BEST PRACTICES Writing Paraphrases

Follow these steps to create your own paraphrase:

1. Read the entire source or section. You cannot write a good paraphrase of a passage you have taken out of context. Surrounding sentences will provide information essential for understanding the sentence you are paraphrasing; to make the idea clear to your readers, you will need to set up the context so that your readers will understand how the passage fits into the source.
2. Read the passage and surrounding sentences several times, including surrounding text, until you understand it and its context. Annotate it. Look up any words that are even slightly unfamiliar to you.
3. Put the text away so you will not be able to look at it while you try to say it in your own way. Recall the main ideas, and try to put each one into your own words and your own wording. A paraphrase must not be an echo of the original's sentence patterns with synonyms plugged in. That is really a form of plagiarism since it involves "stealing" the author's sentence pattern. You may want to break up complex sentences into shorter, simpler ones that make the idea easier to comprehend.
4. If the passage refers to or depends on surrounding material for meaning, put that information into your paraphrase. For example, you may need to replace a pronoun with a noun for clarity.
5. Do not feel that you must find a substitute word for every ordinary word in the passage. For example, if a passage has the word *children,* don't feel you have to say *kids.*
6. Go back and check your paraphrase against the original to see if you have accurately represented the full content of the original passage. Make adjustments as needed.

See Chapter 19, pages 405–06, for examples of plagiarism in poorly written paraphrases.

A paraphrase should not retain the same syntax, or sentence patterns, as the original, even if the vocabulary is different. A paraphrase that imitates the original sentence is technically plagiarism and does not improve comprehension of the ideas. A good paraphrase is likely to be as long as, or even longer than, the original passage, especially if it expresses the same meaning.

Below is an example of a passage from a draft in which the writer uses a long direct quotation. Note that the quoted material is not memorable in style. The wording is not worth reproducing as a direct quotation.

> Food writer Mark Bittman argues that people should take a more sustainable approach to eating: "To reduce our impact on the environment, we should depend on foods that require little or no processing, packaging, or transportation, and those that efficiently convert the energy required to raise them into nutritional calories to sustain human beings" (19).

A revised version uses all of Bittman's point but not any of his exact wording. As you see here, paraphrasing allows you to keep your own voice, vocabulary, and style in the writing. When you paraphrase, you "own" the material, explaining it as you understand it.

> Food writer Mark Bittman believes people need to take a sustainable approach to eating. We should shrink our environmental food footprint by choosing locally grown foods that require minimal processing and packaging. And, in order that energy not be wasted in the production of junk food, he says we should choose nutritious foods that give us a good return in energy for the energy it takes to produce them (19).

Bittman, Mark. *Food Matters: A Guide to Conscious Eating.* Simon & Schuster, 2009.

In the two examples below, the draft passage uses a direct quotation to present purely factual information, while the revised version uses a paraphrase of the basic information in the quoted material. Writers should avoid direct quotations of facts.

Draft Version: Inappropriate Use of a Direct Quotation

> Human invention of laws resulted from the need to regulate water use in dry areas such as the Tigris-Euphrates Valley. According to Michael Mares, "our very system of written laws dates back to Hammurabi, king of Babylonia from 1792 to 1750 B.C., whose first laws were written to deal with the use of water for agricultural purposes" (xxix).

In the revision below, the information has been paraphrased.

Revised Version: Appropriate Use of Paraphrase

> The human invention of law began under King Hammurabi, who ruled Babylonia from 1792 to 1750 B.C. In the arid region of the Tigris-Euphrates Valley, the Babylonian people needed laws to regulate their use of water, a precious commodity for the development of agriculture (Mares xxix).

Mares, Michael A. *Encyclopedia of Deserts.* U of Oklahoma P, 1999.

A paraphrase must completely rework the wording and sentence patterns of the original passage. Students can commit plagiarism inadvertently if they do not double-check paraphrases for too much similarity to the wording of the source.

For additional guidance on paraphrasing, see Chapter 19, pages 402–06, and Chapter 2, page 24.

Blend Direct Quotations with Paraphrases

A good way to avoid overly long quotations and to blend your own voice with some key phrases from a source is to embed the quotable bits into paraphrases, as shown in the example below. When you blend paraphrase and direct quotation so that the quoted words are integral to your own sentence, no punctuation is needed to set off the quoted words.

> Bauerlein disdainfully describes the world of thirteen- to seventeen-year-olds as a "dynamic 24/7 network" in which "teen activity accrues more and more significance" as the events of the day "are recorded and circulated" (22).

Using a Summary

When you are working with the extended ideas of one of your major sources, you may need to include more than a few quotations and paraphrases in your paper to do the idea justice. In books, it is common to find passages that summarize the entire argument of a source, often with some discussion woven in. Therefore, it is reasonable in some cases to devote one to two paragraphs to a summary, depending upon the length of your paper and the relevance of the source. If you do choose to summarize, make sure that the summary contains only content relevant to your paper and that you comment upon the relevance of the source.

The following Best Practices box gives advice on the steps necessary to writing a good summary. Summary writing is also covered in Chapter 2, pages 26–27.

BEST PRACTICES Summarizing a Source

In your notebook, first write down the author, title, and other source information you'll need for your works cited list (for MLA—Modern Language Association) or list of references (APA—American Psychological Association). Then follow these suggestions for writing summaries.

1. Read and annotate the entire source, noting the main points and the key supporting points.
2. For long texts, break them into subdivisions. Working with one subdivision at a time, write paraphrases of the main ideas in each. Try working from memory as you write, and check the original later for accuracy. Decide which specific facts would be appropriate to include, depending on the purpose of your summary.
3. Make sure that your sentences restate the points; do not just describe the original passage, as in "The author talks about. . . ." Instead, say what the author's point is.

4. You may include brief direct quotations, but avoid quoting whole sentences. That is not efficient.
5. Do not try to include all of the figurative language and tone of the original. Write the summary in your own voice, not in imitation of the author's voice and style.
6. Keep your summary objective; reserve your commentary for follow-up if you use the summary as part of your paper.
7. Edit your summary to reduce repetition and to combine points into single sentences where possible.

A good summary restates the author's points rather than simply describing what the author does. It provides enough detail so that the readers of the summary have something close to the experience of reading the original, but in a more concise version.

Below we offer a passage from a source that is represented in summary form in the student example paper in Chapter 20 on pages 426–32. If the passage is long and difficult, as is the one below, it helps to annotate it with notes to yourself, as we demonstrate here, before attempting to draft the summary.

Refresh memory on Socrates: 469–399 B.C. Philosopher who engaged the young men of Athens in debating philosophical questions about virtue and truth. Felt the unexamined life is not worth living.

Original Passage with Annotations from "Dwelling in Possibilities" by Mark Edmundson

I think he means the order of things, how things are on campuses.

This section of the reading introduces the question of how well young people know themselves, really, versus how others have defined them.

If Socrates looked out on the current dispensation, what would he see? He'd see the velocity and the hunger for more life, faster, faster—sure. But given his interests, he'd notice something else, too. He'd see that by the time students get to college, they have been told who they are and what the world is many times over. Parents and friends, teachers, counselors, priests and rabbis, ministers and imams have had their say. They've let each student know how they size him up, and they've let him know what they think he should value. Every student has been submitted to what Socrates liked to call *doxa*, common sense, general belief.

The source of orthodox?

Socrates encouraged questioning common beliefs, for which he was seen as stirring up trouble.

This paragraph acts as a transition into the role of college in finding identity.

And a student may be all the things the people who raised her say she is; she may want the things they have shown her are worth wanting. She may genuinely be her father and mother's daughter. But then again, she may not.

Here, the author is suggesting that reading the great authors helps students see beyond the common views they may have grown up believing.

The primary reason to study Blake and Dickinson and Freud and Dickens is not to become more cultivated, or more articulate, or to be someone who at a cocktail party is never embarrassed (but can embarrass others). The ultimate reason to read them is to see if they may know you better than you know yourself. They may help you to cut through established opinion—*doxa*—about who you are and what the world is. They may give you new ways of seeing and saying things, and those ways may be truer for you than the ones that you grew up with. Genuine education is a process that gives students a second chance. They've been socialized once by their parents and teachers; now it's time for a second, maybe a better, shot. It's time—to be a little idealizing about it—for Socrates to have a turn.

This is clever. He knows that some people read books for superficial reasons, for the status.

Should college change you, and make you question prior beliefs?

This section shows why students should read the great writers for wisdom and new understandings of the world.

After noting the major subdivisions and writing paraphrases of them, the student put the paraphrases together smoothly to make the summary below. (The bibliographic information for this essay by Mark Edmundson appears in the works cited list of the student's paper, on page 392.) Note how the following summary also makes use of several direct quotations to convey some of the original language of the source.

Summary

Edmundson imagines that if Socrates were around today, he would worry about the same thing Edmundson worries about—the fast pace of college students' lives and how well they really know themselves and the world. All through their years of school, they've been influenced by adults in their lives—parents, teachers, and clergy—who have told them how to define themselves and interpret the world. Edmundson says these interpretations may be true, but then again, they may not. That is why education and books are important. They challenge "established opinion" and what seems like "common sense" but may not be true. Thus, books give students new perspectives about themselves and the world that may be truer for them than what they had always been told was true.

How Do I Acknowledge, Integrate, and Cite My Source Materials?

When using source information, whether factual data or the opinions and arguments of other people, writers must acknowledge each source and integrate the material smoothly into their own surrounding text. In scholarly and professional writing, they must also cite their sources.

Acknowledging sources means *giving credit to a source for paraphrased ideas, direct quotations, and any information that is not common knowledge.* Acknowledging can include citing, as discussed below, but in some genres that do not include documentation, just mentioning a name serves as an acknowledgment. To fail to acknowledge a source is to steal from it, to plagiarize. In magazines, newspapers, trade books, and online writing, authors must acknowledge their sources of information. Authors who do not are considered unethical and irresponsible.

Integrating sources means *blending in source material alongside your own words* so that your paper flows, with no gaps in thought or expression. Smooth integration requires writing in your own voice and signaling readers when you introduce others' words and ideas.

Citing sources (also called documenting) means *providing written information about a source's author, title, date, and place of publication,* in some cases including when and how you found the source. Documentation is not a standard feature in the popular press, but it is usually required in academic articles and scholarly books. While there are many documentation styles, this book covers the two most common ones: those of the Modern Language Association and American Psychological Association.

The following paragraph demonstrates the basic elements of acknowledging, integrating, and citing sources. It uses the MLA documentation form.

Integrates the source material by leading into the history of zombie films.

Documents, or cites, the source by giving the page number.

Integrates the source by paraphrasing factual information rather than overrelying on direct quotations.

Acknowledges the source by giving the expert's full name on first mention, along w[ith] some identification o[f] credentials.

Integrates the upcom[ing] source by setting up [the] context of social unre[st] in the 1960s.

Unique words taken from a source must b[e] in quotation marks.

Citations can be placed before the en[d] of a sentence to sho[w] precisely what was taken from the sourc[e].

Documents, or cites, t[he] source of this informa[tion] by title because there [is] no author.

The modern zombie movie has been around for almost forty years and, like other genres, it has gone through periods of feast and famine. According to film scholar Darryl Jones, the genre was born in 1968 with the release of George A. Romero's *Night of the Living Dead* (161), in which a motley group of people, led by an African American antihero named Ben (Duane Jones), must spend the night in a besieged country house, waiting for the authorities to arrive. When the county militia finally does show up, its first response is to shoot and kill Ben, the only survivor of the supernatural abattoir. The violence and graphic images in this low-budget horror film were unprecedented at the time, and the movie functions largely as a metaphor for the atrocities of Vietnam and racism. Called "hippie Gothic" by film theorist Joseph Maddrey (51), *Night* protests the war by graphically confronting audiences with the horrors of death and dismemberment and by openly criticizing those who use violence to solve their problems. The politically subversive film gained a cult following and eventually made more than $30 million worldwide ("Business Data for *Night*").

Works Cited

"Business Data for *Night of the Living Dead*." *Internet Movie Database.* amazon.com, 3 May 2006, www.imdb.com/title/tt0063350/.

Jones, Darryl. *Horror: A Thematic History in Fiction and Film.* Arnold, 2002.

Maddrey, Joseph. *Nightmares in Red, White and Blue: The Evolution of the American Horror Film.* McFarland, 2004.

What Are the Options for Acknowledging Sources?

Acknowledging means giving credit. The first time you introduce an important speaker, give the person's first and last name; thereafter, use last names only. Give credentials such as publications or university affiliations.

Acknowledge Sources with Short Phrases or Sentences

You can acknowledge a source in a short phrase, known as a signal phrase because it signals the connection between the material and its source. You can also use a complete sentence to acknowledge a source. (The examples below include citations in MLA form.)

The two introductory phrases below, each followed by a comma, provide the name and expertise of the source. (Citations are explained in detail in Chapter 20, pages 407–32 for MLA and Chapter 21, pages 533–56 for APA.)

Signal Phrase to Identify a Source

According to Maryanne Wolf, a reading expert from Tufts University, "Typically when you read, you have more time to think" than when you look at images or listen to stories (qtd. in Dzubow).

You should also use signal phrases to acknowledge paraphrased material from a source.

According to Maryanne Wolf, a reading expert from Tufts University, reading is an activity that allows the brain more time for thinking than does listening to a story or watching it in a movie or television show (qtd. in Dzubow).

In this example, Wolf is not the author of the source. See Chapter 20 (page 410) and Chapter 21 (page 437) for how to cite sources used by your sources, known as indirect sources. Dzubow is an online source, so no page number is available.

Even if you have paraphrased the words or ideas of a source found in your source, MLA requires that you use "qtd. in" in your parenthetical citation.

You can also acknowledge sources with a complete sentence. In this case, however, you must use a colon rather than a comma between your words and those of the source. The colon is needed here to prevent a comma splice. A comma splice before a quotation is a common punctuation error.

Complete Sentence to Identify a Source

Maryanne Wolf, director of the Center for Reading and Language Research at Tufts University, explains why reading is more stimulating to the brain than hearing speech or looking at images: "Typically when you read, you have more time to think" (qtd. in Dzubow).

In this example, the complete sentence provides more context for the quotation than would a simple signal phrase, making a smooth transition between the quotation and the preceding discussion of the mental benefits of reading.

Vary the Placement of Acknowledgments

To add variety to your writing style, you can place the acknowledgment of a source before the material, after it, or in the middle.

Acknowledgment before a Source

In an *Atlantic* article, Nicholas Carr, an expert on information technology, describes how using the Internet has changed his reading style: "Once I was a scuba diver in the sea of words. Now I zip along on the surface like a guy on a Jet Ski."

Acknowledgment after a Source

"Once I was a scuba diver in the sea of words. Now I zip along on the surface like a guy on a Jet Ski," writes information technology expert Nicholas Carr in an *Atlantic* article about the effects of the Internet on people's reading styles.

Acknowledgment Surrounded by a Source

"Once I was a scuba diver in the sea of words," says information technology expert Nicholas Carr in an *Atlantic* article. "Now I zip along on the surface like a guy on a Jet Ski."

Use a Variety of Verbs to Indicate Acknowledgment

Using the word "says" to lead into quotations becomes repetitive. Think about how you are using the quotation and which verb would best describe the function of the quotation. Here are some options for changing things up:

admits	finds	points out
argues	holds	remarks
claims	insists	shows
comments	maintains	states
contends	observes	suggests

Follow Conventions When Choosing Verb Tenses to Use When Acknowledging Sources

It is customary to use present tense when leading into a quotation or paraphrase from a text you are using as a source. Use past tense only when referring to a past action, as in this example:

The author refers to Wilson's action of speaking.

In the 1940s, Edmund Wilson declared that "detective stories [are] simply a kind of vice that, for silliness and minor harmfulness, ranks somewhere between smoking and crossword puzzles."

How Can I Integrate Source Material into My Writing?

Integrating sources means blending them smoothly into your own writing. If you've ever received a paper back from your instructor and found the comment "choppy" or "needs to flow" in the margins, then you can understand the difficulties writers face when they bring outside material into their own writing. Making ideas flow can be tricky enough when they are all your own ideas, so adding other voices can make it even trickier.

Researched writing sounds choppy and even incoherent if the writer has not led into quotations, anchored them with a signal phrase, and followed up on quotations with some commentary. Even paraphrases need some setting up, and if your paraphrase is not specific enough, your reader will have trouble getting the point.

BEST PRACTICES Guidelines for Integrating Sources

Source material should not be dropped into a researched paper like items into a shopping cart. Your paper does not simply contain the sources; it is constructed using the sources.

- Organize around your own points; use sources to develop those points in depth.
- Cite as you write. Do not try to draft without including your source material, correctly worked in and cited.
- Lead up with enough explanation to show your readers how the source fits into your discussion.
- When presenting an authority's viewpoint, introduce the person first, with full name on first mention and any relevant credentials or affiliations. This formality is more common in MLA style than in APA.
- When quoting directly, anchor the words from the source to the surrounding text with a phrase or sentence that introduces the speaker. You should also indicate how the quotation relates to the surrounding text.
- Prefer paraphrase to direct quotation when presenting factual information. Keep direct quotations to approximately 10 percent of your paper.
- Follow up by commenting on the ideas or information to show how the source relates to a point of your own.

Avoid Dropped-In Quotations

Direct quotations need to be set up, not dropped into your paper. Provide enough of the original context to fit the quotation coherently into your paragraph. You may need to paraphrase some of the surrounding sentences from which the quotation was taken. If you have not done so already, you may need to introduce the speaker of the words, along with his or her credentials if the speaker is an important writer or authority. If the author is a staff writer, it is sufficient simply to put the last name in a parenthetical citation.

In the following example, the student did not do enough to connect the speaker's words to the idea in the preceding sentence.

> Some people claim that reading on computer screens is the same as reading on paper. "Are you not exercising the same cognitive muscles because these words are made out of pixels and not little splotches of ink?" (Johnson).

The revised version below does a better job of setting up and integrating the quotation.

> Some people claim that reading on computer screens is the same as reading on paper. In an online newspaper column titled "Dawn of the Digital Natives," Steven Johnson, a best-selling nonfiction author, asks his readers, "Odds are that you are reading these words on a computer monitor. Are you not exercising the same cognitive muscles because these words are made out of pixels and not little splotches of ink?"

Set Off Long Quotations in Block Style

See Chapter 20, page 410, and Chapter 21, page 437.

The two main documentation styles differ slightly on the rules for block quotes, but they agree that it is necessary to set off longer quotations in order to distinguish them from your own words, as in the example below.

For block style quotes only, the period at the end of a sentence precedes the parenthetical citation.

> When the Nielsen researchers used an eye tracker to see how people read on the Internet, they discovered a surprising pattern that creators of websites need to know:
>
> > The pattern looks like the capital letter F. At the top of the page, users read all the way across, but as they proceed their descent quickens and horizontal movement shortens, with a slowdown around the middle of the page. Near the bottom of the page, the eyes move almost vertically, forming the lower stem of the F shape. . . . Whatever content businesses want to communicate to visitors better not be concentrated in the lower-right portions of the screen, Nielsen advised. (Bauerlein 144)

For an overview of the guidelines for formatting quotations in both APA and MLA styles, see Table 18.1.

TABLE **18.1**

Formatting Quotations

Length	Spacing
MLA If a quotation extends to more than four lines in your paper, use the block form. **APA** If a quotation is forty words or longer, use the block form.	**MLA** Begin a new line and indent it one inch (ten spaces) from the left margin. If you are quoting only one paragraph or part of one, do not indent the first line any farther. If the quotation runs more than one paragraph, indent the first line of each new paragraph by three spaces. **APA** Begin a new line and indent it one-half inch (five spaces) from the left margin. If the quotation runs more than one paragraph, indent the first line of each new paragraph by one-half inch (five spaces).

Guidelines for Both MLA and APA	
How to space it	Double space the quotation. Do not add extra spacing at the top or bottom.
How to cite it	With block quotations, any parenthetical citation follows the final punctuation mark.
How to treat internal quotations	Internal quotations within block form quotes receive the standard double quotation marks.
How to lead into long quotations	Depending on the context, you may need no punctuation between your lead-in or attributive tag and your quotation; however, it is common to lead in with a full sentence and a colon.

To Delete Parts of Direct Quotations, Use Ellipses

Sometimes a direct quotation goes into more detail than is necessary for your purpose or contains references or transitional expressions that had a purpose in the original passage but would only be confusing to your readers. When you remove these words from a quotation, you replace them with ellipses. An ellipsis is a series of three spaced periods. When removing words from the end of a sentence, you add a fourth period.

This is the original passage from Steven Johnson's book *Everything Bad Is Good for You:*

> Tools like Google have fulfilled the original dream of digital machines becoming extensions of our memory, but the new social networking applications have done something that the visionaries never imagined: they are augmenting our people skills as well, widening our social networks, and creating new possibilities for strangers to share ideas and experiences.

If you wanted to use only the underlined section of the passage, you should remove the transitional expression "as well" since it no longer serves the purpose of relating the two points in the original passage.

> Some people think that because online communication is not face-to-face, it is causing a decline in our social skills. But Steven Johnson argues that the social networking sites "are augmenting our people skills . . . , widening our social networks, and creating new possibilities for strangers to share ideas and experiences" (124).

In most cases, writers use ellipses to remove passages that are too detailed or irrelevant to the purpose of their own paper.

Use Square Brackets to Change Wording for Clarity and Grammatical Correctness

You can change quotations to make them fit more smoothly into your sentence, provided that you use square brackets around the words you alter. If you take words out and replace them with words in brackets, the brackets will signal to the reader that you have made a substitution, so there is no need for an ellipsis.

Sometimes you need to change the tense of verbs, as in this example from the student paper that appears on pages 426–32 in Chapter 20. The original passage by University of Virginia professor Mark Edmundson quoted Ralph Waldo Emerson and read

> The idea is to keep moving, never to stop. . . . "In skating over thin ice," Emerson says, "our safety is in our speed." . . . Skate fast over the surfaces of life and cover all the extended space you can, says the new ethos.

In the passage from a student's paper, below, to combine his own words smoothly with the quoted passage, the student writer had to change the form of the verb *skate:*

> Too many students are connected to everything and everyone but themselves, as Edmundson says, "[skating] fast over the surfaces of life," depending on energy drinks or someone else's Adderall.

You can also use brackets to alter a word to make a quotation clearer in the context of your sentence, as in the following example. Steven Johnson's book contained this sentence about one drawback of the Internet compared with books:

> But it is harder to transmit a fully fledged worldview.

To fit Johnson's words into his own sentence, the writer had to change the article *a* to *the:*

> Steven Johnson admits in his book *Everything Bad Is Good for You* that the Internet is not so good at "training our minds to follow a sustained textual argument" (187) or to "transmit [the] fully fledged worldview" of another person (186).

Avoid Stringing Sources Together with No Commentary

In the following example, the author has used many short quotations without showing enough of their original context and how the quotations connect with each other. The result is a paragraph that contains *words* from the sources but not enough of the *ideas* from the sources, as in the revised example below.

> Native Americans have always shared a strong traditional relationship with the Earth. To the Native American, the Earth is "sacred and itself a spiritual entity" (Kidwell, Noley, and Tinker 127). The Earth was not thought of as merely real estate, but rather a "gift from the Creator given for the care of creation" (Kidwell, Noley, and Tinker 127). As Jerry H. Gill says, "The Native American seeks to fit in with nature rather than alter it" (175). Native Americans view the Earth as their "mother" and the sky as their "father" (Momaday 33). This is why a plan to build a gondola ride into the Grand Canyon has met opposition from the Hopi, Zuni, and some Navajo people. The contractors of the Grand Canyon Escalade Project seek to build the tramway and other tourist attractions near the confluence of the Colorado and Little Colorado rivers, an area that these tribes see as a place of their emergence from the earth and sky (Cart). As one Navajo said, "This is the heart of our Mother Earth. This is a sacred area. It is going to be true destruction" (Yellowhorse qtd. in Nagourney).

A revised version introduces the important authorities used as sources and fills in the gaps with more explanation of the origin story and its relationship to the goal of conserving and respecting the Confluence area as a sacred place.

> Native Americans have traditionally shared a strong spiritual relationship with the Earth. Historians and theologians Clara Sue Kidwell, Homer Noley, and George "Tink" Tinker explain that while the Native Americans do not worship the Earth, they do see it as alive, "a spiritual entity" given by the Creator "for the care of creation" (127). For this reason, the Native Americans have a conservation ethic toward the land, wanting to preserve the gift as it was made by the Creator. As sociologist Jerry H. Gill says, "The Native American seeks to fit in with nature rather than alter it" (175). Further, the Earth is seen as sacred because many tribes believe that they emerged from worlds below or

above. The Kiowa-American author N. Scott Momaday explains that the Native Americans' "investment" in the Earth begins with a concept central to their worldview: "The earth is our mother. The sky is our father" (qtd. in Momaday 33). For these reasons, a plan to build a gondola ride into the Grand Canyon has met opposition from the Hopi, Zuni, and some Navajo people. The contractors of the Grand Canyon Escalade Project seek to build the tramway and other tourist attractions near the confluence of the Colorado and Little Colorado rivers, an area that these tribes see as a place of their emergence from the earth and sky (Cart). Renae Yellowhorse, a Navajo woman, told a reporter, "This is the heart of our Mother Earth. This is a sacred area. [The development] is going to be true destruction" (qtd. in Nagourney).

How Do I Document My Sources?

Documentation is a two-step process. The first step, which appears in the paper itself and is therefore called an in-text citation, is to identify the author (or title if there is no author) and the page number if one is available. Acknowledgment of an author by name does some of the work of citing but not all of it.

Chapter 20, pages 407–32, covers in-text citing and works cited lists in MLA style. Chapter 21, pages 433–56, covers in-text citing and reference lists in APA style.

The second step, which appears at the end of the paper, is to provide a full bibliography, an alphabetical list of sources (articles, books, websites, and so on) that are referenced in the paper. This bibliography is called a list of works cited (MLA) or a list of references (APA). In academic writing, every source quoted or paraphrased must appear in the bibliography. These lists appear at the ends of books, articles, and sometimes chapters.

The important point to make here is that when a project calls for documentation, you must have two matching citations: one in the text of your paper and its partner in the list of sources at the back. For every source used in the paper, there must be an item on the list at the back. For every item on the list, there must be a corresponding reference to it in the body of your paper.

How Do I Incorporate Sources without Losing My Own Voice?

To wrap up our advice on incorporating source materials, we want to remind you of the importance of keeping your own voice and perspective in your writing. When a writer brings other people's voices into a paper, one danger is those sources may try to dominate the conversation and determine how the paper develops. The source authors are often, after all, experts on the topic. However, your job as the writer is to politely control the conversation.

Imagine that writing a research paper is like hosting a dinner party. You need to plan the meal and invite the guests. Your sources are like guests who should not monopolize the conversation or take over the dinner. In a paper, you are in charge, organizing around your goals and presenting your perspective. Your thesis drives the paper; your sources are there to help support your points.

Maintain Your Own Angle and Plan

Writers sometimes feel intimidated about asserting their own voices in a conversation of published experts. When you encounter this situation, ask these questions:

- What are my angle and purpose?
- How does this source's information serve my angle and purpose?
- What is the smallest amount of information that I need from this source to make my point?

The following example, illustrating APA documentation style, shows how nutritional scientist Sera L. Young kept her voice in a paper about how attitudes have changed over time on a peculiar type of human behavior. Notice how the writer's tone differs from the tone of her sources' quoted words. Notice also how little of each source's words she needs to convey her point.

> Earth-eating, or geophagia, has always incited strongly negative reactions. Even scientists have done little to conceal their "disgust" for such a "vile habit" (Cragin, 1835) and denounce geophagists: "[W]ith the tenacity of ignorance these people cling to their filthy habits" ("The clay eaters," 1897, p. 150). Positive or even neutral regard for geophagia has only emerged in the last few decades. Yet the grounds for the proclamation of geophagia as "good" or "bad" are limited, even today.
>
> Young, Sera L. (2007). A vile habit? The potential biological consequences of geophagia, with special attention to iron. In J. MacClancy, J. Henry, & H. Macbeth (Eds.), *Consuming the inedible: Neglected dimensions of food choice* (pp. 67–79). Berghahn Books.

By maintaining a neutral tone, Young shows the contrast between her modern perspective and the outdated attitudes of the sources' voices. Also note that Young has successfully acknowledged her sources, integrated their words smoothly into her own sentences, and cited both in text and in a bibliographic entry at the end.

Chapters 20 and 21 continue our advice about how to cite sources in the text of your papers and in the works cited (MLA) and references (APA) lists at the end of the paper.

CREDITS

page 381: Miedema, John. Slow Reading. Used by permission of Litwin Books. **pages 384, 390:** Edmundson, Mark. 2008. Dwelling in Possibilities. Chronicle of Higher Education. https://www.chronicle.com/article/Dwelling-in-Possibilities/7083. **page 385:** Bauerlein, Mark. (2009). The Dumbest Generation: How the Digital Age Stupefies Young Americans and Jeopardizes Our Future (Or, Don't Trust Anyone Under 30). TarcherPerigee. **page 392:** Kyle Bishop. "Dead Man Still Walking: Explaining the Zombie Renaissance." *Journal of Popular Film and Television*, vol. 37, no. 1, 2009, pp. 16–25. **page 394:** Carr, Nicholas. 2008. Is Google Making Us Stupid. Atlantic Magazine. https://www.theatlantic.com/magazine/archive/2008/07/is-google-making-us-stupid/306868/ Page 397: Johnson, Steven. 2005. Everything Bad Is Good for You. Riverhead Books.

CHAPTER 19

Using Sources Responsibly

ENGAGING QUESTIONS

In this chapter, you will engage with the following questions:

- What is plagiarism, and what forms can it take?
- What materials must be quoted and cited?
- What methods do writers use to avoid plagiarism?

RESEARCHERS BUILD THEIR WORK ON FOUNDATIONS LAID BY OTHERS. However, the structure falls apart when a researcher steals material. Whether on purpose or not, using another person's work without acknowledging or giving credit to the source is theft.

Word processing software and the Internet have made it easy to copy and paste the words and visual images found in sources. The interactive nature of creative content on the Internet makes borrowing and mashing up seem perfectly acceptable. However, *anytime you put your name on something and claim it as your own work, borrowing without acknowledging is plagiarism.* Universities, the business world, and the law take it very seriously.

Writers who steal not only lose the reader's trust, but they also often face criminal charges. Cases of copyright infringement often make the news, and they damage the careers of popular novelists, song writers, newspaper reporters, and sometimes even professors who have been careless while taking notes or been too trusting of assistants' research skills.

By citing your sources, you earn your readers' respect. Readers are more likely to accept your views if you project good character, what the ancient rhetoricians called *ethos.* Honesty is part of good character. Part of writing honestly is distinguishing your ideas from the ideas of others. Therefore, *when in doubt, always cite.*

What Is Plagiarism?

Ethical use of sources requires paying careful attention to the texts of sources, whether written, audio, video, or works of art. Failure to acknowledge sources is plagiarism.

Intentional plagiarism occurs when a student knowingly submits work containing the words, ideas, images, or other intellectual property of another person without acknowledging and citing the source of the material. Note that plagiarism does not have to consist of word-for-word copying of another person's work. Rewording another person's ideas without acknowledging the source of the ideas is every bit as much plagiarism as copying and pasting material from a source into your paper.

Many professors and institutions regard unintentional or accidental plagiarism as seriously as the intentional kind and give it the same penalties. Unintentional plagiarism occurs when a researcher has been sloppy about note-taking and paraphrasing, not realizing that even a single phrase or word group taken verbatim needs quotation marks and a citation. It occurs when a researcher fails to distinguish an opinion found in a source from common knowledge or common facts, which may not need to be cited, as we will explain below. Unintentional plagiarism may not be as unethical as intentional plagiarism, but it is nevertheless serious and can result in an "F" for a paper.

In college, punishment for plagiarism can include failure in the course or even suspension or expulsion from the university. Many universities will indicate on a student's transcript if there has been an honor violation, something that potential employers will see.

When Do I Need to Cite My Sources?

The point of using sources is to combine other people's ideas and knowledge with your own, and the point of citing sources is to distinguish between your sources' knowledge and your own knowledge and ideas. Specifically, acknowledging (giving credit) and citing (with appropriate documentation) are required in the situations described below.

Cite and Quote Exact Words, Phrases, and Sentences

It is easy to understand that you need to put quotation marks around whole sentences that you take from one of your sources. For example, a complete sentence from a book is cited below.

> Yale law Professor Steven L. Carter is concerned about the future of democracy. Noting that many people vote without bothering to inform themselves on the issues, he argues, "Living in a democracy requires hard work that we seem less and less willing to do" (17).

If you wanted to take just a few words from this sentence, the words that express Carter's opinion of Americans' voter apathy, you would still have to enclose the words in quotation marks, as in the example below.

> Yale law Professor Steven L. Carter is concerned about the future of democracy. Noting that many people vote without bothering to inform themselves on the issues, he argues that Americans "seem less and less willing" to carry out the "hard work" of responsible citizenship (17).

Cite Ideas Found in Your Sources

See Chapter 18, pages 387–91, for guidance on paraphrasing.

Even if you rework someone else's writing into a paraphrase, *if you use someone else's idea, then you need to cite the source because ideas are intellectual property.* When you paraphrase, you must also acknowledge the source, or you are plagiarizing.

Cite Paraphrased Ideas from Your Sources

It is a standard practice for writers to draw upon the work of others, including both the information they have gathered and the ideas they have formulated. Whether you quote them directly or put them into your own words, you need to give credit to the source, so you do not appear to be claiming these ideas as your own.

The following passage comes from a book by Jeffrey Sachs on the decline of civic engagement by Americans today. Note that he opens with his own point but develops it with the research of an authority, Robert Putnam. Sachs paraphrases the research in his own words and acknowledges Putnam as the source by naming him.

> TV also shifted the center of gravity of society from the public park and the bowling alley to the privacy of our own homes, as couch potatoes in front of a giant screen. Over time, the single screen in the living room migrated into separate TV screens in each bedroom. Families retreated from other families, and then family members eventually retreated from one another. The political scientist Robert Putnam, in *Bowling Alone*, his magisterial account of the decline of civic engagement, found that time in front of the TV screen is the most powerful single characteristic accounting for the long-term decline in the time devoted to civic activities.

Cite Ideas That Coincide with Your Own

You may encounter ideas in sources that coincide with your own. For example, suppose you think that optimistic people do better in life than pessimists. This is a belief you have concluded from observations of family and friends–and perhaps your own attitudes in meeting challenges. Then you read Gregg Easterbrook's book *The Progress Paradox,* and on page 223 you see the following:

> Lisa Aspinwall, a psychologist at the University of Utah, has shown that as a group, the optimistic do better in life than the pessimistic. . . . [O]ptimists . . . are actually better at overcoming negative experiences because they can bounce back rather than be dragged under.

Easterbrook is acknowledging Aspinwall as his source. Easterbrook is your source, but do you need to cite the source of something you could have said on your own? If you do not use Easterbrook's exact words, is it plagiarism to use Aspinwall's opinion without acknowledging Aspinwall's research and citing Easterbrook's book?

A classic book on research, *The Craft of Research,*[1] advises you to take the cautious approach and cite: "In the world of research, priority counts not for everything, but for a lot. If you do not cite that prior source, you risk having people think that you plagiarized it, even though you did not" (203). You do not have to check to see that all of your own ideas are not already out there; however, if you encounter one of your own in a source, you should acknowledge that source. This also strengthens your case: Not only do you believe optimists tend to be more successful in life, but others think so too.

---

1. Wayne C. Booth, Gregory G. Colomb, and Joseph M. Williams, *The Craft of Research*, 2nd ed. (U of Chicago P, 2003).

Cite Even a Single Significant Word or Phrase

Verbatim use of some words and phrases cannot be avoided; it would not be necessary to put quotation marks around common words and phrases, such as *fifth-graders* and proper nouns like *White House* or *Secretary of State John Kerry.* However, *when a single word expresses a writer's opinion or judgment, it should go in quotation marks and the source should be acknowledged.*

For example, in this passage from Steven L. Carter's book *Civility,* the word "diabolical" is significant enough to merit a citation:

> As for the automobile itself, it seems an almost diabolical tool, in the traditional sense of the word—a thing of the devil, made to bring out the worst in us.

In your paper, you might put the idea into your own words, acknowledge Carter as the source, and quote the single word.

> Under the cover of anonymity within their cars, drivers become not just uncivil but, as Steven Carter puts it, even "diabolical" once behind the wheel (7).

Cite Factual Information That Is Not "Common Knowledge"

Facts that can be easily obtained through multiple sources such as reference books, Google searches, and standard textbooks do not have to be cited. A rule of thumb is that *if the reader could fact-check your information in at least three easily accessed sources, it can count as common knowledge.*

Common knowledge generally includes factual information not in dispute, such as dates or authors of books. For example, a historical date like the bombing of Pearl Harbor on December 7, 1941, is common knowledge. However, the equally important historical date September 6, 1941, when Japanese leaders decided to take the country to war, is not common knowledge, so it is information that must be documented.

If you already knew something that shows up in your research, that is a good indication it is common knowledge, but also consider whether your *readers* would already know it. If your readers know less about your topic than you do, it is good to cite the source, especially if the information might surprise them. Citing sources is a courtesy to readers who may want to pursue their interest in your topic.

It is also not necessary to cite the exact source location for commonly known quotations, such as Martin Luther King Jr.'s declaration "I have a dream," or commonly available sources, such as the *Declaration of Independence*. Again, the rule of thumb here is that if readers could easily find a copy of the document, it is not necessary to cite it. However, the motto for research remains important: *When in doubt, cite your source.* You can also consult your professor for advice on when to cite.

Comstock/Jupiter Images/Getty Images

Cite Debatable or Unique Information

Some information is disputed or still open to debate. For example, some research has shown that gas and oil production using hydraulic fracturing, known as fracking, is more likely to pollute groundwater than traditional methods such as mining. However, other studies show no greater levels of pollution caused by fracking.

If information is not generally agreed upon, then the source of the information should always be cited. When in doubt, imagine one of your readers asking, "But how do you know that?" If readers can pose this question, it is best to point them to a source.

Cite Charts, Artwork, and Graphics

Any time you include artwork, photographs, graphics, charts, diagrams, maps, and other audiovisual materials that you got from another source rather than creating the image yourself, you must acknowledge and cite the source.

How Can I Avoid Plagiarizing?

It is easy to avoid blatant forms of plagiarism, such as buying a paper, having someone write your paper for you, or copying and pasting from the Internet into your paper without acknowledging the source. You simply choose not to do it.

However, writers can accidentally plagiarize if, for example, they are careless when taking notes and fail to place quotation marks when they copy something from a source into their notes and then transfer that passage into their paper. Writers are responsible for double-checking paraphrases against the original passage. *Make sure the words and sentence patterns are your own to avoid accidental plagiarism.*

Consider the example of accidental plagiarism below.

Original Passage from *iBrain* by Gary Small and Gigi Vorgan[2]

> Our high-tech revolution has plunged us into a state of *continuous partial attention,* which software executive Linda Stone describes as continually staying busy—keeping tabs on everything while never truly focusing on anything. . . . When paying continuous partial attention, people may place their brain in a heightened state of stress. They no longer have time to reflect, contemplate or make thoughtful decisions. Instead they exist in a sense of constant crisis—on alert for a new contact or bit of exciting news or information at any moment. Once people get used to this state, they tend to thrive on the perpetual connectivity. It feeds their ego and sense of self-worth, and it becomes irresistible.

In the example on the next page, the underlined words and phrases have been taken directly from the source. *This is plagiarism even though the authors and the page have been cited.*

2. Gary Small and Gigi Vorgan, *iBrain: Surviving the Technological Alteration of the Modern Mind,* (New York: HarperCollins, 2008).

Some features of good paraphrasing to note: The paraphrase is set up with the authors' names and credentials; the sentences are new, some longer, some shorter. The words "continuous partial attention" are quoted the first time they appear to show that those are the words of the source. It would be optional to use quotation marks the second time since the term has been established as a technical phrase.

Irresponsible (Plagiarized) Paraphrase or Short Summary

Our high-tech revolution has put us into a state of continuous partial attention. According to software executive Linda Stone, this is a state of continually staying busy—paying attention to everything while never really focusing on anything. In continuous partial attention, people place their brain in an increased state of stress or constant crisis, without time to reflect or make thoughtful decisions. They are always on alert for exciting tidbits of news. Once they get accustomed to this state, they thrive on being constantly connected because it feeds their ego and gives them a sense of self worth (Small and Vorgan 18).

Responsible Paraphrase or Short Summary

According to Gary Small and Gigi Vorgan, authors of the book *iBrain,* technology has caused some people to experience "continuous partial attention," a state in which people divide their attention among many things at once but never really focus their mind on any one thing at a time. They are always seeking the next exciting piece of information. Small and Vorgan say continuous partial attention is stressful because it leaves people with no time to reflect. But it is also addictive, because once people get used to it, they like the feeling of self-importance they get from being connected at all times (18).

The best way to avoid inadvertent plagiarism is to pay close attention whenever you are using material from sources:

See Chapter 2, pages 24–27, on paraphrasing and summarizing.

See Chapter 18, pages 379–85, on using and documenting sources.

- Take careful notes.
- If you ever cut and paste from an online source into a draft with the intention of reworking the passage into a quotation or summary/paraphrase later, highlight or shadow the entire passage in some bright color so it will stand out as writing that is not your own.
- Summarize fairly and accurately.
- Paraphrase by putting ideas fully into your own words and sentences.
- Choose quotations that accurately depict ideas in the source and carefully use quotation marks to indicate use of exact wording.

CREDITS

pages 402, 404: Stephen L. Carter. *Civility: Manners, Morals, and the Etiquette of Democracy.* Basic Books, 1999. **page 403:** Jeffrey Sachs. (2012). The Price of Civilization. New York: Random House. **page 403:** Gregg Easterbrook. *The Progress Paradox.* Random House, 2004.

CHAPTER 20

Documenting Your Sources: MLA

ENGAGING QUESTIONS

In this chapter, you will engage with the following questions:

- How do I create in-text citations using MLA style?
- How do I create a works-cited list using MLA style?

THE MODERN LANGUAGE ASSOCIATION (MLA) STYLE OF DOCUMENTATION IS USED IN THE ARTS AND HUMANITIES—in particular, by researchers in the fields of language and literature. MLA documentation uses in-text parenthetical citations that are matched to a list of works cited at the end of the paper. This chapter covers the basics of using MLA documentation style. You can find detailed explanations of MLA guidelines for documenting your sources and formatting your papers in the *MLA Handbook*, 8th edition.

How Do I Make In-Text Citations Using MLA Style?

See Chapter 18, pages 387–91, for guidance on summary and paraphrase.

For an explanation of what is considered common knowledge, see Chapter 19, page 404.

When you quote from, summarize, or paraphrase the work of someone else–and when you provide information that is not common knowledge–cite your sources in the text by providing the author's last name and, if available, the exact page number(s) where the quoted or paraphrased material was found. If the author's name appears in your signal phrase (for example, "As Smith said"), omit it in the parenthetical citation. All in-text citations must match the citations in your works cited list. The examples that follow illustrate the most common ways to cite sources in the text of your papers.

Direct Quotation with Source Named in Signal Phrase

> As part of his argument that popular culture makes us smarter, Steven Johnson argues, "The rise of the Internet has challenged our minds in three fundamental and related ways: by virtue of being participatory, by forcing users to learn new interfaces, and by creating new channels for social interaction" (118).

Punctuation Alert: Use a comma between a signal phrase and the opening of a quotation that is a complete sentence.

Punctuation Alert: Close direct quotations before parenthetical citations. Place a period after the parenthetical citation unless you have a block quotation (see page 410).

Direct Quotation with Source Named in Parentheses

> Popular culture can be mentally stimulating. The Internet, for example, "has challenged our minds in three fundamental and related ways: by virtue of being participatory, by forcing users to learn new interfaces, and by creating new channels for social interaction" (Johnson 118).

Punctuation Alert: In MLA style, there is no comma between the name of the author and the page number. Do not use the word *page* or any abbreviation for it.

Summary or Paraphrase with Source Named in Parentheses

> Reading is unlike other natural human functions of seeing, moving, speaking, and thinking. Reading is an invented cognitive function, and understanding how it works illustrates the amazing plasticity of the brain (Wolf and Barzillai).

When you are citing online sources with no page numbers and no numbering of paragraphs, as in the example above, you will not be able to cite a page. You also do not need to cite a page if the source is only one page long or if you are referring to it in its entirety.

Source with Two Authors

If your source has two authors, give both last names.

> In their book *iBrain,* Small and Vorgan claim that Internet use can be addictive, as people get a rush of the brain chemical dopamine when they turn on their computers (48–49).

For three authors or more, give the first author's name followed by the abbreviation *et al.* (not in italics, but ending with a period).

> The nativist opposition to immigration in the 19th century was fueled by the rising numbers of immigrant voters who cast their votes against temperance, antislavery, and other reforms favored by the Protestant native-born majority (Maier et al. 481).

Two or More Works by the Same Author

When you are citing more than one work by an author, you need to specify which one you are referring to; do this by using shortened versions of the titles:

> Mark Edmundson believes that people should read good literature with the hope or goal of being influenced by it ("Narcissis Regards"). He argues that this goal is especially important for college students because college reading opens doors to ideas different from the ones students grew up with ("Dwelling" 28).

Two or More Authors with the Same Last Name

If you have sources by two or more authors with the same last name, use initials for first names in parenthetical references (or full names if the initials are also the same). In your discussion, you should use full names the first time you mention an author.

> Although some researchers (C. Smith) have found that this particular gene plays a significant role in promoting cancer cell growth, others (R. Smith) have not been able to discover a link.

Organization or Agency as Author

Treat an organization or government agency the same way you would treat an individual author; the name may be used in a signal phrase or in a parenthetical reference. Try to introduce long names in a signal phrase. If you use the name in a parenthetical citation, you may shorten or abbreviate it, but be certain that it matches the reference list entry. For example, in parentheses you may use Natl. Public Radio instead of National Public Radio.

Work with No Author or Editor

If no author or editor is named, use the title of the work in both in-text citations and works cited entries. If the title is long, abbreviate it. Begin the title or its abbreviation with the first word that is not an article (*the, a, an*) because your works cited list will be organized alphabetically according to the first significant word in the title. The following example is from a page on a website.

> The Law School Aptitude Test (LSAT) measures ability to read and comprehend in-depth texts with insight, to draw "reasonable inferences" from readings, and to analyze and evaluate the reasoning of others' arguments ("About the LSAT").

More than One Source in a Parenthetical Citation

If you have more than one source to cite for a piece of information, list them alphabetically, separated by a semicolon:

> Several researchers believe that reading books puts the brain to work in ways that reading on the Internet does not (Bauerlein; Wolf and Barzillai).

Reference to an Entire Work; Work with No Page Numbers

> Mark Bauerlein's *The Dumbest Generation* argues that people under thirty are not taking full advantage of the Internet's resources for gaining knowledge.

When you do not have page numbers to cite because you are referring to an entire work, try to put the author's name in the text of the sentence rather than in parentheses. The works cited list would contain full bibliographic information for this source. A reference to a source with no page numbers is treated in the same way.

Use of Quotation Marks within a Quotation

In the source from which the following example comes, "truth" appeared in quotation marks. When you quote the entire passage yourself, *truth* should have single quotation marks:

> According to Wolf and Barzillai, "[Socrates] worried that the seeming permanence of writing would delude young people into thinking that they had learned the 'truth,' when they had just begun the search for it."

> **Punctuation Alert:** In the above example, "he" was used instead of "Socrates" in the source. You need to substitute Socrates because otherwise your reader would not know who "he" was. Use square brackets to substitute proper names for pronouns that have no clear reference in your own sentence.

Long Quotations (Block Quotations)

For direct quotations that will be more than four lines in your paper, omit quotation marks and display the quotation as a block of text set in from the left margin by one inch. Double-space the entire block quotation. In a block quotation, the final period precedes the parenthetical citation. Here is an example of a block quotation:

> In his best-selling book, *The Dumbest Generation,* Mark Bauerlein describes the studies of Jacob Nielsen, who runs a consulting group that designs Web pages for corporations. This group does eye-tracking studies to show how people read on computer screens. The researchers' conclusion was "They *don't*" (qtd. in Bauerlein 143). The eye tracker revealed a surprising pattern that creators of Web sites need to know:
>
> > The pattern looks like the capital letter F. At the top of the page, users read all the way across, but as they proceed their descent quickens and horizontal movement shortens, with a slowdown around the middle of the page. Near the bottom of the page, the eyes move almost vertically, forming the lower stem of the F shape. . . . Whatever content businesses want to communicate to visitors better not be concentrated in the lower-right portions of the screen, Nielsen advised. (Bauerlein 144)

Indirect Source (a Source Your Source Used)

Sources quote and document their own sources. How do you treat a source within a source? First, do not cite anything that you have not consulted yourself. Second, use *qtd. in* (not italicized) for "quoted in" and cite the source in which you found the quotation. In the example below, the student's source was an article by William Major.

> Students today are always connected, always in touch. When a professor asked his students to give up cell phones for a few days, they responded as if he had asked them to take off their clothes (Major). In contrast to Thoreau, who wrote, "I never found the companion that was so companionable as solitude," (qtd. in Major), today's students seem more frightened by than enthusiastic about the possibilities offered by solitude.

> **Punctuation Alert:** As in the example above, use double quotation marks around direct quotes. If your quotation itself contains words or phrases that should be in quotation marks, put these in single quotation marks. *Do not use quotation marks around block quotations* unless they are themselves quotations (dialogue from a novel, for example).

A Work in an Anthology

Cite the author of the individual work, not the editor or compiler of the anthology.

> In "Toadstools," the narrator suspects that the food in supermarket aisles "hold[s] stories of other people's houses" (Nguyen 130).

A Multivolume Work

If your citation requires page numbers, list volume number, followed by a colon and the page numbers. If you are not referring to specific pages, then use the abbreviation for volume: vol. 2.

> In his narrative history of the Civil War, Shelby Foote devotes the chapter "Beleaguered City" to the Battle of Vicksburg (2: 323–427).

Work of Literature or Classic Work

Because works that are out of copyright (such as nineteenth-century novels) can be found in many editions, citing a page number alone will not help your reader. Along with the page number, provide chapter numbers, section numbers, or even paragraph numbers if that is the only way the work is divided. Use abbreviations for parts of books.

> Elizabeth Bennet expresses her recognition of her own pride and prejudice to her sister: "I have courted prepossession and ignorance, and driven reason away. . . . Till this moment I never knew myself" (Austen 136; ch. 36).

Punctuation Alert: Use a semicolon after the page number and before any additional material.

Poetry is cited by line numbers. The first time you cite a poem, use the word *line* or *lines;* after that, give just the numbers.

> He did not touch the shroud, or raise the fold
> That hid my face, or take my hand in his,
> Or ruffle the smooth pillows for my head:
> He did not love me living; but once dead
> He pitied me; and very sweet it is
> To know he still is warm though I am cold. (Rossetti, lines 9–14)

Punctuation Alert: Use a comma after the author's name if what follows is not a number.

Use Arabic numerals to cite act, scene, and lines (if needed) from a play; use periods to separate them.

> The warrior Fortinbras has the final words in *Hamlet:* "Take up the bodies; such a sight as this / Becomes the field, but here shows much amiss. / Go, bid the soldiers shoot" (5.2.386–88).

Punctuation Alert: If you are using fewer than four lines of poetry, use a slash (virgule) to separate lines; the slash is preceded and followed by a space.

Religious Texts

Do not italicize the name of sacred texts in your sentences: the Bible, the Koran, the Bhagavad Gita. However, the names of specific editions should be in italics. In parenthetical references, abbreviate the names of biblical books, and separate chapter and verse with periods. The titles of biblical books are not italicized.

> The translation in the *New Oxford Annotated Bible* reads: "Now the manna was like coriander seed, and its appearance like that of bdellium. The people went about and gathered it, and ground it in mills or beat it in mortars, and boiled it in pots, and made cakes of it; and the taste of it was like the taste of cakes baked with oil" (Num. 11.7–8).

How Do I Make Entries in the Works Cited List Using MLA Style?

Your works cited list should include complete bibliographic information for all sources you refer to in your paper. The examples in this section indicate how to cite the kinds of sources commonly used in first-year writing assignments.

General Guidelines for Your Works Cited List

All the guidelines described below are illustrated in the example research paper at the end of this chapter, pages 426–31.

- The first word of each entry on the works cited list must match the in-text citation. If you refer, for instance, to Edward Hoagland's essay on aging in your paper, there should be an entry in the works cited list that begins with "Hoagland, Edward."
- Put *all* entries in alphabetical order according to the first word in each entry. Usually the first word will be the lead author's or editor's last name or–if no author is named–the first word in the title not including articles (*a, an, the*).
- Do not number the entries.
- Double-space within and between entries.
- Begin each entry at the left margin and indent all subsequent lines by one-half inch. The hanging indent feature of your word processing program will help you.
- Italicize titles of books, periodicals (such as magazines and journals), films, and other major works like websites and blogs.
- Put quotation marks around titles of articles and essays from periodicals or books of collected works (such as anthologies) and around pages or posts found on a website.

- Capitalize all words in titles and subtitles except for articles (*a, an, the*), coordinating conjunctions (*and, or, but*), and prepositions. Always capitalize the first and last word of a title, regardless of its part of speech.
- Include subtitles of works. Separate them from the title with a colon.
- If some publication information is not given, use the following abbreviations (not italicized) in place of the missing data: *n.p.* for "no place" or "no publisher," *n.d.* for "no date," and *n. pag.* for "no pagination."

Printed Books

Your entries for printed books should contain the following:

1. Name of author or editor, last name first, followed by a period (unless no author or editor is listed)
2. Title of the work, italicized, followed by a period
3. Publisher, followed by a comma
4. Year of publication, followed by a period

In the works cited list, do not cite page numbers for chapters or portions of books. Do include page numbers for items in an anthology or collected set of works.

Last name, First name. *Title.* Publisher, date.

Book by a Single Author

Urrea, Luis Alberto. *The Devil's Highway: A True Story.* Little, 2004.

Two or More Books by the Same Author

Instead of repeating the author's name in your works cited list, give the name in the first entry only. For subsequent works, use three hyphens in place of the name, followed by a period. Arrange the works in alphabetical order according to the first word in the title of the work, excluding articles (*a, an, the*).

Obama, Barack. *The Audacity of Hope: Thoughts on Reclaiming the American Dream.* Crown, 2006.

---. *Dreams from My Father: A Story of Race and Inheritance.* 1995. Three Rivers, 2004.

Note: For reprinted works, include the original date of publication immediately following the title, as in the second citation above.

Book by Two Authors

Put the name of the lead author first, beginning with his or her last name. Begin with the first name for the second author. Use commas between names.

Small, Gary, and Gigi Vorgan. *iBrain: Surviving the Technological Alteration of the Modern Mind.* HarperCollins, 2008.

Suárez-Orozco, Carola, Marcelo M. Suárez-Orozco, and Irina Todorova. *Learning a New Land: Immigrant Students in American Society.* Belknap-Harvard UP, 2008.

If the title page shows an imprint (for example, Belknap, an imprint of Harvard University Press, in the citation above), include both it and the publisher's name, separated by a hyphen.

Book by Three or More Authors

Use only the first author's name and the Latin abbreviation *et al.* (not italicized), meaning "and others."

Chambers, Mortimer, et al. *The Western Experience.* 9th ed., McGraw, 2007.

In the works cited list, use a comma between the author's first name and *et al.* The parenthetical in-text citation would read (Chambers et al. 2007), with no comma.

Book by a Corporate Author or Government Agency

Treat the corporation or agency as an author.

Modern Language Association. *MLA Handbook for Writers of Research Papers.* 8th ed., MLA, 2016.

If you abbreviate publisher names, use abbreviations that your readers will understand.

Book with No Author or Editor

Begin the citation with the title. In the works cited list, ignore articles *a, an,* and *the* when placing entries in alphabetical order; the following example would be alphabetized under *New.*

The New York Times Guide to Essential Knowledge: A Desk Reference for the Curious Mind. 3rd ed., St. Martin's, 2011.

Later Edition of a Book

Directly after the title, add the edition number without italics. Use numerals; abbreviate *edition.*

Williams, Joseph M. *Style: Ten Lessons in Clarity and Grace.* 9th ed., Pearson, 2007.

Reprinted Book

Include the original date of publication before current publication information.

Adams, Henry. *The Education of Henry Adams: An Autobiography.* 1918. Houghton, 1961.

Translation

For a translated work, follow the title of the work with the name of the translator, followed by a comma and current publication information. Include this information before current publication information.

> Vargas Llosa, Mario. *The Bad Girl.* Translated by Edith Grossman, Farrar, 2007.

Preface, Introduction, Foreword, or Afterword Not by the Book's Author or Editor

Start the entry with the name of the author of the part of the book; then provide the name of the section, followed by the title of the book. Use the word *By* before the author of the book. If the book is a reprint, include the original date of publication. Indicate the inclusive page numbers for the part of the book you used as your source.

> Bellow, Saul. Foreword. *The Closing of the American Mind.* By Allen Bloom, Simon & Schuster, 1987, pp. 11–18.

If the section has a title of its own, use the following format:

> Mochulsky, Konstantin. "Dostoevsky and *The Brothers Karamazov.*" Introduction. *The Brothers Karamazov.* By Fyodor Dostoevsky. Translated by Andrew R. MacAndrew. 1970, Bantam, 2003, pp. xiii–xxii.

Scholarly Edition

Important works are often published in scholarly editions, and the scholarship of the editor (on the text, introduction, and footnotes, for example) might be what you cite in your paper. Use the following format if most of your citations are to the work itself:

> Melville, Herman. *Moby Dick.* 1851. Edited by Tony Tanner. Oxford UP, 2008.

Use this format if most of your citations are to the editor's work:

> Tanner, Tony, editor. *Moby Dick.* By Herman Melville. 1851. Oxford UP, 2008.

Anthology or Edited Compilation

Place a comma after the editor's name, and add editor.

> Shreve, Susan Richards, editor. *Dream Me Home Safely: Writers on Growing Up in America.* Houghton, 2003.

Work in an Anthology

For works in collections of essays, poetry, and short stories, put the author of the individual work first, followed by its title in quotation marks, and then the title of the collection in italics. The editor's name follows. Note that entries for works in anthologies do cite the inclusive page numbers of the selection.

Nguyen, Bich Minh. "Toadstools." *Dream Me Home Safely: Writers on Growing Up in America,* edited by Susan Richards Shreve, Houghton, 2003, pp. 129–132.

The MLA rule for inclusive page numbers is to include all digits for numbers 1-99 but only the last two digits of the second number when the range starts at 100 or higher (unless more are needed for clarity): 23-67, 79-102, 107-23, 1859-75, 1859-917.

Two or More Works from the Same Anthology

If you are using more than one selection from an anthology, you will need at least three entries in your works cited list, one for the entire work, opening with the name of its editor, and one for each of the items, opening with the name of its author. The editor's last name follows the title of the selection and refers your readers to the entire book; it is followed by the inclusive page numbers of the selection. Place each entry in its alphabetically determined spot on the works cited list, as illustrated below.

Griffith, Patricia. "The Spiral Staircase." Shreve, pp. 73–81.

MacDonald, Michael Patrick. "Spitting Image." Shreve, pp. 112–22.

Shreve, Susan Richards, editor. *Dream Me Home Safely: Writers on Growing Up in America.* Houghton, 2003.

One Volume of a Multivolume Work

Directly after the title of the work, indicate the volume number you used.

Foote, Shelby. *The Civil War: A Narrative.* Vol. 2. Random, 1963.

More than One Volume of a Multivolume Work

After the title, indicate the total number of volumes in the work. If the work was published over multiple years, indicate the range of years.

Foote, Shelby. *The Civil War: A Narrative.* 3 vols. Random, 1958–74.

Book That Is Part of a Series

Open with the name of the series and a series number for the work if available. End with the name of the series. Do not italicize the series title.

Horning, Alice, and Anne Becker, editors. *Revision: History, Theory, and Practice.* Parlor, 2006. Reference Guides to Rhetoric and Composition.

Signed Article in a Reference Book

Cite the name of the author, the title of the entry, the title of the reference work, name of the editor, and publication information. Do not include page numbers if entries are arranged in alphabetical order in the reference book itself.

Zangwill, O. L. "Hypnotism, History of." *The Oxford Companion to the Mind,* edited by Richard L. Gregory. Oxford UP, 1987.

Unsigned Article in a Reference Book

Open with the title of the entry. Include page numbers if entries do not appear in alphabetical order.

"A Technical History of Photography." *The New York Times Guide to Essential Knowledge: A Desk Reference for the Curious Mind.* St. Martin's, 2004, pp. 104–12.

Edition of a Religious Text

Italicize the title and provide names of editors and/or translators and the publication information.

The New Oxford Annotated Bible with Apocrypha. New Revised Standard Version. Edited by Michael D. Coogan et al. 4th ed., Oxford UP, 2010.

The Bhagavad Gita: According to Paramhansa Yogananda. Edited by Swami Kriyananda. Crystal Clarity, 2008.

Art Reproduction

Treat art found in books in the same way you treat selections found in edited collections. Open the entry with the artist's name, followed by the title of the work and the date it was created, if available. Before you list publication information, indicate where the original work of art may be found.

O'Keeffe, Georgia. *Light /17: Evening Star, No. V.* 1917. McNay Art Museum, San Antonio. *O'Keefe and Texas.* By Sharyn R. Udall. The Marion Koogler McNay Art Museum, 1998, p. 51.

Articles in Print Periodicals

Your works cited entries for articles in print periodicals should contain the following:

1. Author's name, followed by a period
2. Title of the article, followed by a period, all in quotation marks
3. Title of the periodical, italicized, followed by a comma
4. Volume number (if given); issue number (if given)
5. Date (if given), followed by a comma
6. Inclusive page numbers, followed by a period

Article in a Journal with Volume Numbers

Put the volume number (for example, "71" in the example below), a period, and the issue number (if there is one) after the title of the article. Put the year in parentheses.

Last name, First name. "Article Title." *Journal Title,* vol., issue, date, pages.

Bracher, Mark. "How to Teach for Social Justice: Lessons from *Uncle Tom's Cabin* and Cognitive Science." *College English,* vol. 71, no. 4, 2009, pp. 363–88.

Some journals are not published by volume. In this case, use issue number only.

Article in a Monthly Magazine

Last name,	First name.	"Article Title." *Magazine Title,* date, pages.

Abbreviate all months except May, June, and July.

Walter, Chip. "First Artists." *National Geographic,* Jan. 2015, pp. 32–57.

Article in a Weekly Magazine

Levy, Ariel. "Nora Knows What to Do." *The New Yorker,* 6 July 2009, pp. 60–69.

Article in a Newspaper

Last name, First name.	"Article Title."	*Newspaper Title,* date, edition, pages.

Give the day, month, year, and edition if specified; use abbreviations. Give section and page number. If pages are not consecutive, put a plus sign after the first page number.

Keller, Julia. "Sticks and Stones and Presidential Speeches." *The Chicago Tribune,* 23 Jan. 2011 final edition, sec. 4, p. 4.

Yoon, Carol Kaesuk. "Reviving the Lost Art of Naming the World." *The New York Times,* 11 Aug. 2009, natl. ed.: D1+.

If the page number does not include the section number or letter, indicate the section in another way: for example, sec. A, sec. 6, Arts and Entertainment sec. If the city is not named in the newspaper title, add it (not italicized) in brackets after the title, but before the date: *Times Union* [Albany], 13 Jan. 2011.

Editorial in a Newspaper—No Named Author

If no author is named, begin the citation with the title.

"Poverty-Busting in Dallas." Editorial. *Dallas Morning News.* 19 Jan. 2015, p. A20.

Letter to the Editor of a Newspaper or Magazine

Add *Letter* (not italicized) following the author name to indicate a letter to the editor.

Black, Antony. Letter. *Economist,* 22 Jan. 2011, p. 20.

Lyon, Danny. Letter. *New Yorker,* 19 Jan. 2015, p. 3.

Review

Open with the name of the reviewer and the title of the review, if there is one. Add the words *Review of* (not italicized) followed by the title of the work being reviewed, and its author or performer.

Hofferth, Sandra. "Buying So Children Belong." Review of *Longing and Belonging: Parents, Children, and Consumer Culture,* by Allison J. Pugh. *Science,* vol. 324, no. 5935, 26 June 2009, p. 1674.

Advertisement in Print Medium

Open with the name of the item or service being advertised.

Canon. Advertisement. *National Geographic,* Jan. 2015, p. 3.

Digital Sources

When the information is available, your works cited entries for digital sources should contain the following:

1. Name of author, editor, performer, or translator, followed by a period
2. Title of work, followed by a period
3. Title of website, followed by a comma
4. Publisher or sponsor of the site, followed by a comma
5. Date last updated (or n.d), followed by a comma
6. The URL (without "http://"), followed by a period.

Last name, First name. "Title of article or page." *Title of website,* Sponsor/ publisher, date of update, URL.

Example Entry for Entire Website

See Figure 20.1. Begin with the title of the site if there is no author named. If the source no longer exists, provide the date of your last access to it.

Pew Hispanic Center. Pew Research Center, 2015, www.pewhispanic.org/.

Example Entry for a Webpage or Document Found on a Website

Author. "Title of Page." *Title of Site,* Sponsor, date of publication, Location (URL).

This format for an individual webpage or document, such as the one displayed in Figure 20.2, is the basis for many different types of MLA works cited entries, including news stories on television network sites, documents in online archives, online video and audio, and even online performances. Some of the variations on this format follow.

Personal Website

If the site has no title, use *Home page* or some other descriptive title, not italicized. If there is no sponsoring organization, use *N.p.* (not italicized) to indicate no publisher.

Alexie, Sherman. Home page. Falls Apart Productions, 2015, fallsapart.com/.

Books Accessed Online

Begin as you would for any book, but after the publication information, include the online library or retrieval service, and the URL.

Austen, Jane. *Pride and Prejudice.* 1895. *Project Gutenberg*, www.gutenberg.org/files/1342/1342-h/1342.htm.

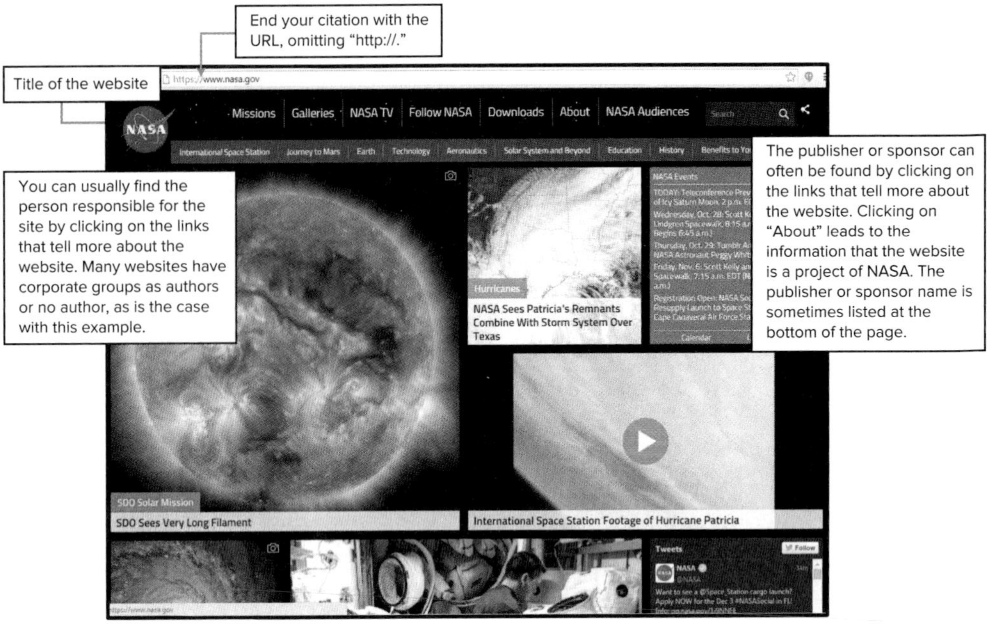

FIGURE **20.1**

Example of a Website or Independent Online Work

Source: National Aeronautics and Space Administration

FIGURE **20.2**

Webpage or Document Found on a Website

Source: National Aeronautics and Space Administration

Use the digital publication date. If the Web source gives print data for the edition used, include it.

Austen, Jane. *Pride and Prejudice*. Vol. 3 1813. Interactive Media, 2012. *Google Books,* books.google.com/books?id=aFbCdW8CcuAC&printsec=frontcover&dq=pride+prejudice&hl=en&sa=X&ved=0ahUKEwjfl-Oyo_3LAhXKPCYKHawXA5QQ6AEIJjAA#v=onepa.

For books published before 1900, the publisher's name is not needed.

Article in an Online Journal

Follow the print format, but add the URL. The following periodical is published annually, so it has a volume number only.

O'Dwyer, Kathleen. "Nietzsche's Reflections on Love." *Minerva—An Internet Journal of Philosophy,* vol. 12, 2008, pp. 37–77, minerva.mic.ul.ie/vol12/Nietzsche.pdf.

If no pages are given, use *n. pag.* (not italicized).

Article Accessed through a Library Subscription Database

Give print information and then database information. Italicize the database name.

Wolf, Maryanne, and Mirit Barzillai. "The Importance of Deep Reading." *Educational Leadership, Academic Search Complete.* vol. 66, no. 6, 2009, pp. 32–37.

Article in an Online Magazine

Wilson, A. N. "Leo Tolstoy, Russia's Thunderous Prophet." *Real Clear Politics,* The Slate Group. 20 Nov. 2010, http://www.realclearpolitics.com/2010/11/20/leo_tolstoy_russia039s_thunderous_prophet_246117.html.

Article in an Online Newspaper

Put the website in italics; follow with the name of the sponsor or publisher, not italicized.

Hotz, Robert L. "Creative Destruction on a Cosmic Scale: Scientists Say Asteroid Blasts, Once Thought Apocalyptic, Fostered Life on Earth by Carrying Water and Protective Greenhouse Gas." *The Wall Street Journal.* Dow Jones & Company, 14 Aug. 2009, www.wsj.com/articles/SB125020578491030557.

Editorial in an Online Newspaper or Magazine

Cite as you would online articles in periodicals, but add the designation *Editorial.*

"Pre-K Must Be Texas Priority." Editorial. *San Antonio Express-News,* Hearst Newspapers, 16 Jan. 2015, www.expressnews.com/opinion/article/Your-Turn-Jan-15-6015616.php.

Online Letter to the Editor

Open with the author of the letter and the designation *Letter*.

Talley, Penelope. Letter. *San Antonio Express-News,* San Antonio Express-News. Hearst Newspapers, 14 Jan. 2015, www.expressnews.com/opinion/article/Pre-K-must-be-a-Texas-priority-6021304.php.

Online Review

Use *Review of* (not in italics) to introduce the title of the book being reviewed. If the review has a title of its own, include it.

Garner, Dwight. "Engagements with History Punctuate a Lifetime in Books." Review of *Outside Looking In,* by Garry Wills, *The New York Times,* 2 Nov. 2010, mobile.nytimes.com/2010/11/03/books/03book.html?.

Article in an Online Reference Work

If unsigned, open with the title of the article. When alphabetizing, ignore opening articles (*a, an, the*).

"The Philosophy of Dance." *Stanford Encyclopedia of Philosophy.* Metaphysics Research Lab, Stanford U, 12 Jan. 2015, plato.stanford.edu/entries/dance/.

Blog Post

Put the title of the post in quotation marks and the blog title in italics.

Jerz, Dennis. "Writing School Papers: Does Your First Version Say It All?" *Jerz's Literacy Weblog,* 12 Jan. 2015, learningenglish.voanews.com/content/writing-school-papers/2569201.html.

Government Document on the Web

United States Congress, Senate Special Committee on Aging. *Social Security Modernization: Options to Address Solvency and Benefits Adequacy.* 111th Cong., 2nd sess. S. Rept. 111–187. 13 May 2010. Government Printing Office, 2010. 111th Congress, 2nd session, Senate Report 111-187.www.congress.gov/111/crpt/srpt187/CRPT-111srpt187.pdf.

Broadcast or Published Interview

Open with the names of the interviewee or interviewees, followed by the title of the interview, if there is one; if not, provide the interviewer's name.

Fahim, Kareem. "How Does Al-Quaida Continue to Grow?" Interview by Arun Rath, *All Things Considered,* Natl. Public Radio, WBUR, Accessed 10 Jan. 2015.

Tweet

Open with the user's Twitter handle (in place of the author's name). Include the tweet in its entirety, enclosed in quotations. Provide the date and time of the posting, followed by the URL.

@B_Ehrenreich. "Zombie debts to US govt are crushing US seniors. Brought to you by the Economic Hardship Reporting Project." Twitter, 15 Oct. 2019, 10:54 a.m., https://twitter.com/B_Ehrenreich/status/1184165692662263809.

Discussion Groups and Online Forums

MLA suggests that postings to online forums and discussion groups are not appropriate sources for research papers and does not provide a format. But there might be a reason for you to cite them in a paper that examined Internet communication, for example.

Perlstein, Arnie. "A Novelist's Progress." Message to Austen-L. 26 Jan. 2011, www.pemberley.com/janeinfo/austen-l.html.

Wiki

"Herman Melville." *Wikipedia.* Wikimedia Foundation, 13 Jan. 2015, en.wikipedia.org/wiki/Herman_Melville.

E-Mail Message

Crusius, Timothy. "Procedural Suggestions." Received by Carolyn Channell, 9 April 2016.

Other Sources

E-Book

Use the format for a print book, modifying as necessary.

Erdrich, Louise. *The Painted Drum*. Kindle ed., HarperCollins, 2005.

Motion Picture

Begin with the title of the film followed by the director and performers.

The King's Speech. Directed by Tom Hooper, performance by Colin Firth, Geoffrey Rush, and Helena Bonham Carter, Weinstein, 2010.

Television

For an individual episode:

"Cleaning House." *How I Met Your Mother.* Created by Pamela Fryman, directed by Steven Lloyd. CBS. WBBM, Chicago, 28 Sept. 2010.

For a series:

Monk. Created by Andy Breckman, performance by Tony Shalhoub, Jason Gray-Stanford, Ted Levine, and Traylor Howard. USA Network. 2002–2009.

Play or Other Live Performance

In the Heights. By Lin-Manuel Miranda. Directed by Thomas Kail. Choreographed by Andy Blankenbuehler. Richard Rodgers Theatre, New York. 9 Jan. 2011. Dance performance.

Add a description of the performance if not otherwise obvious. If you want to emphasize an individual's contribution, use this format:

Sher, Bartlett, director. *South Pacific.* By Richard Rodgers and Oscar Hammerstein II, performance by Kelli O'Hara and Paulo Szot. Vivian Beaumont Theater, Lincoln Center, New York. 3 Apr. 2008.

Musical Composition and Sound Recording

If your emphasis is on the work, start with the composer. If it is on the performance, start with the conductor or performers. Song names are in quotation marks; longer works are italicized. Add the production company and release date.

Baez, Joan, performer. "Simple Twist of Fate." By Bob Dylan. *Diamonds and Rust.* A&M, 1988.

Barenboim, Daniel, conductor *Symphony No. 5.* By Gustav Mahler. Chicago Symphony Orchestra. Rhino, 2006.

Cooder, Ry. *Paradise and Lunch.* Reprise, 1990.

Podcast

Cite as you would a radio program.

"Fearless." Narrated by Lulu Miller and Alix Spiegel. *Invisibilia.* Natl. Public Radio, 16 Jan. 2015.

Cartoon

Designate the cartoon genre, as these examples show.

Batiuk, Tom. "Funky Winkerbean." Comic strip. *The Chicago Tribune* 19, Jan. 2011, p. 12.

Wilson, Gahan. Cartoon. *The New Yorker* 24, Jan. 2011, p. 24.

Work of Visual Art

For works of visual art, state artist, title (italicized), date of composition (or n.d.), the work's medium, the location (such as the museum, gallery, collection), and city.

Seurat, Georges. *A Sunday on La Grande Jatte.* 1884, Art Institute, Chicago.

If your source comes from the Web, use the following format:

Seurat, Georges. *A Sunday on La Grande Jatte.* 1884, School of the Art Institute, Chicago, www.artic.edu/aic/collections/artwork/27992.

Map

Olivebridge, New York. Map, *Mapquest,* www.mapquest.com/us/ny/olivebridge-282894452.

A map from a book would be cited this way:

"The Pusan Perimeter, August 4, 1950." Map, *The Coldest Winter: America and the Korean War.* By David Halberstam. Hyperion, 2007, p. 165.

Use this form only if the map was your only source from the book; otherwise, list the entire book under works cited and indicate in a signal phrase that you are referring to a map.

Oral Presentations

This category includes papers presented at professional conferences as well as readings, speeches, and keynote addresses. Use quotation marks around titles.

Laurence, David. "The Condition of the Modern Languages in Higher Education: What the Data Tell Us." Rocky Mountain Modern Language Association Conference, Albuquerque, 15 Oct. 2010. Address.

Pamphlet

Set up works cited entries for pamphlets and brochures as if they were books.

Museum of Indian Arts and Culture. *Turquoise—Water—Sky: The Stone and Its Meaning.* New Mexico Department of Cultural Affairs, 2014.

Use *n.p.* (no italics) if no place of publication is listed; use *n.d.* (no italics) for "no date."

Legal Sources

Open citation with the title of the act or case, followed by numerical details.

Griswold v. Connecticut. 381 US 479. Supreme Court of the US. 1965. *FindLaw.* Thomson Reuters, 2011, caselaw.findlaw.com/us-supreme-court/381/479.html.

The names of legal cases are italicized in your text: *Griswold v. Connecticut.*

Personal Interview

Give the name of the person interviewed, and the date it took place.

Amsel, Stephanie. Personal interview. 20 Oct. 2014.

YouTube Video

Include name of uploader and the author, if different from the uploader. If the author is the uploader, cite only the author.

Clarke, Frank. "Simply Painting Galway Bay." *YouTube*, 9 Jan. 2018, www.youtube.com/watch?=yFY9lbtIX3o.

SAMPLE RESEARCH PAPER **MLA Style**

1"

½" 1"

Van Buskirk 1

Header

Put your name and the page number at the right top corner of every page.

Kyle Van Buskirk

Professor Channell

English 1302

April 25, 2010

Identifying information (double spaced)

Double space between date and title

The Benefits of Slow Reading Lost in Our Fast-Paced Culture

Double space between title and 1st line

½"

For many young adults today, reading anything in depth almost seems like an ancient pastime. In English class, high school students will search online for the Cliff Notes rather than actually read the book. When we want news, instead of reading newspapers, we check the headlines on MSNBC. Doing research, we surf the Internet. A study of computer activity in the British Library found that researchers skim and "bounce" from site to site. "It almost seems that they go online to avoid reading in the traditional sense," concluded the authors of the study (qtd. in Carr). People have lost sight of the many benefits of reading because we live in such a fast-paced, technology-driven culture. We have become too impatient to read.

Carr is quoting the authors of the study, but Carr is the source. Use the abbreviation for "quoted in" for indirect sources.

Our pace of life makes everything that takes time seem like a burden. Even sitting down to drink a cup of coffee takes too long, so we use the drive-through at Starbucks. What people do not realize is that life is short, and it will be shallow and unsatisfying if we refuse to slow down to think and reflect. Reading books provides us with that opportunity, enriching our lives in the long run, but also giving us many immediate, practical benefits.

Some people claim that we read just as much as ever, only we do it on computer screens. In an on-line newspaper column titled "Dawn of the Digital Natives," Steven Johnson, a best-selling nonfiction author, asks his readers, "Odds are that you are reading these words on a computer monitor. Are you not

Lead into an opinion by first introducing the person who holds that opinion, giving full name on first mention and some identification or credentials.

1"

Van Buskirk 2

exercising the same cognitive muscles because these words are made out of pixels and not little splotches of ink?"

But there is evidence that on-line reading and on-paper reading are not the same. In his best-selling book, *The Dumbest Generation,* Mark Bauerlein describes the studies of Jacob Nielsen, who runs a consulting group that designs Web pages for corporations. This group does eye-tracking studies to show how people read on computer screens. The researchers' conclusion was "They *don't*" (qtd. in Bauerlein 143). The eye tracker revealed a surprising pattern that creators of Web sites need to know:

Use block form for quotations of more than four lines of type. Double-space as normal before, after, and within block quotations.

> The pattern looks like the capital letter F. At the top of the page, users read all the way across, but as they proceed their descent quickens and horizontal movement shortens, with a slowdown around the middle of the page. Near the bottom of the page, the eyes move almost vertically, forming the lower stem of the F shape. . . . Whatever content businesses want to communicate to visitors better not be concentrated in the lower-right portions of the screen, Nielsen advised. (Bauerlein 144)

Use ellipses to show where parts of quotations have been deleted. An ellipsis is a series of three spaced periods. The first period here is not spaced because it ends the sentence before the deleted portion.

Period ending a block quotation goes before the parenthetical citation.

This study gives scientific evidence that on-line readers could be missing a lot of content. But if people do not read books, they also miss out on important mental exercise.

Work quotations into a paraphrase to present key ideas concisely. Use square brackets where you have had to alter a quotation to fit it into your sentence.

Even though Steven Johnson defends screen reading as making "Digital Natives" highly informed, he admits in his book *Everything Bad Is Good for You* that the Internet is not so good at "training our minds to follow a sustained textual argument" (187) or to "transmit [the] fully fledged world view" of another person (186). Johnson writes a blog to exchange ideas with readers, but he writes books to present his arguments in full.

Can we get the benefits of book reading from watching the movie version of a novel or listening to an audio book while we drive? According to reading experts, we cannot. Oprah Winfrey, who has promoted book reading on her TV show,

Van Buskirk 3

Cite the source of paraphrased information that is not common knowledge.

Use a colon before a direct quotation if you lead into it with a complete sentence instead of a phrase.

published an article in her magazine *O* about the mental benefits of reading. Reading gives your brain more of a neurobiological workout than hearing speech or looking at images (Dzubow). Maryanne Wolf, director of the Center for Reading and Language Research at Tufts University, explains why: "Typically, when you read, you have more time to think. Reading gives you a unique pause button for comprehension and insight. By and large, with oral language—when you watch a film or listen to a tape—you don't press pause" (qtd. in Dzubow). In a more technical article, Wolf explains that experienced readers' brains have developed "streamlined" circuits that allow them to go far beyond just decoding the words. As they read, experienced readers can also "question, analyze, and probe" and "go beyond the wisdom of the author to think their own thoughts," a process that involves "all four lobes and both hemispheres of the brain" (Wolf and Barzillai 34). Reading gives our brains a workout, but because on-line readers click on links and allow their eyes to jump around in the F-shaped pattern described earlier, they are not developing these critical reading skills.

However, even when a person sits down with a book, he or she may not take the time to hit the pause button and read deeply. In an article for *Atlantic Monthly* titled "Is Google Making Us Stupid?" Nicholas Carr, who writes about information technology, describes how switching to the Internet as his main source of information has changed his style of reading. He went from loving to read long books to having to struggle to pay attention to them: "I get fidgety, lose the thread, begin looking for something else to do. I feel that I am always dragging my way-ward brain back to the text." Carr has lost the ability to immerse himself in a book. As he describes it, "Once I was a scuba diver in the sea of words. Now I zip along the surface like a guy on a Jet Ski."

One would think that schools would encourage reading for pleasure, but too often they encourage reading for speed. This bothers Thomas Newkirk, Professor of English at University of New Hampshire. He criticizes the Accelerated Reading Program, which awards points for numbers of books read, and standardized testing "in which reading is always 'on the clock.'" A slow reader himself, Newkirk

Van Buskirk 4

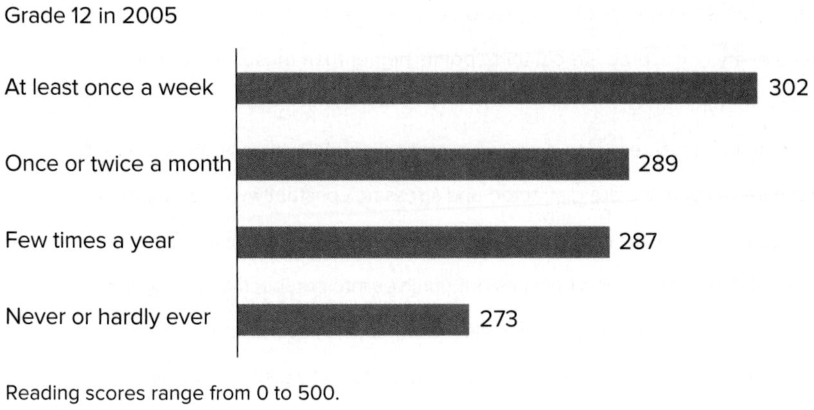

FIG. **1**

Average Reading Scores by Frequency of Reading Fiction Books or Stories Outside School

Source: United States, Department of Education, National Center for Education Statistics, reported in United States, National Endowment for the Arts, *To Read or Not to Read: A Question of National Consequence,* Nov. 2007, 71, www.arts.gov/sites/default/files/ToRead.pdf.

says fast readers miss out on a lot, just as riders on high-speed European trains miss out on the details of the scenery and see the distant landscape as a blur. Newkirk says that "there is real pleasure in downshifting, in slowing down. We can gain some pleasures and meanings no other way." The pleasure is not just a result of going slow, explains John Miedema, who wrote a book on slow reading. "To me," he says, "slow reading is about bringing more of the person to bear on the book" (qtd. in Ramer). This is what people mean when they say they "got into" a book. Getting lost in a book is fun.

Setting aside time to read for pleasure also pays off in practical ways. Students who read for pleasure have distinctly higher reading comprehension scores and better writing scores. Fig. 1 shows the correlation between twelfth graders' reading scores and the amount of time they spend reading fiction for fun.

Van Buskirk 5

Fig. 2 shows the results of a slightly older study on writing ability. Students who read every day scored almost thirty points higher than those who did almost no reading for fun.

Reading for pleasure is also a way of improving mental wellness. Most students live at too fast a pace. We are distracted and stressed, constantly worrying about the next quiz, test, project, or research paper. Bauerlein believes leisure reading provides relief from stress and helps us put our lives into perspective. He explains, "Books afford young readers a place to slow down and reflect, to find role models, to observe their own turbulent feelings well expressed, or to discover moral convictions" (58). Slowing down to think is necessary in college, when students are making important decisions about their morals, goals, and identity.

Likewise, Newkirk argues that schools should encourage slow reading to show students "an alternative to an increasingly hectic digital environment where so many of us read and write in severely abbreviated messages. . . ." Encouraging slow rather than fast reading would be one way to help students keep their lives in balance. Even before the Internet, media critic Neil Postman argued that a

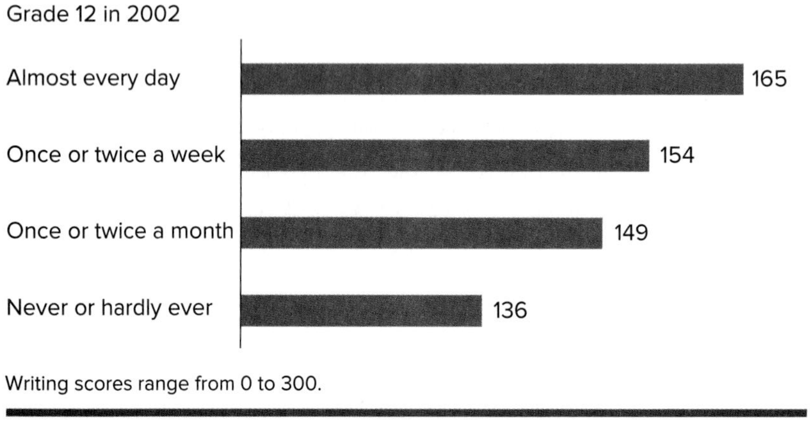

FIG. **2**

Average Writing Scores by Frequency of Reading for Fun

Source: United States, Department of Education, National Center for Education Statistics, reported in United States, National Endowment for the Arts, *To Read or Not to Read: A Question of National Consequence,* Nov. 2007, p. 72, www.arts.gov/sites/default/files/ToRead.pdf.

Van Buskirk 6

"major role" for schools "is to help conserve that which is necessary to a humane survival and threatened by a furious and exhausting culture" (qtd. in Newkirk). In other words, reading quality literature at a leisurely pace helps to keep us human.

Another English professor, Mark Edmundson, at the University of Virginia, is also concerned that the lifestyle of college students is too hectic. He sees that his students are always connected through their cell phones and laptops, working too hard, playing too hard, and taking ADD drugs to keep going. Edmundson worries that the fast pace of his students' lives keeps them from really knowing themselves and reflecting on the world. He imagines that Socrates would worry that today's students do not slow down enough to question what they have been told is true, what Socrates referred to as "*doxa,* common sense, general belief". All through their years of growing up, adults in their lives—parents, teachers, and clergy—have told them how to define themselves and interpret the world. Edmundson says these interpretations may be true, but then again, they may not. That is why education and books are important. Edmundson wants professors to slow their classes down: "to live well, we must sometimes stop and think, and then try to remake the work in progress that we currently are."

Use summary to present a large section of a source, citing pages for paraphrases as well as where brief quotations help to preserve the voice of the source's author.

We do a disservice to ourselves when we do not take time to read slowly. In addition to preparing us for success in our careers, deep reading helps us put our lives into perspective. Too many students are connected to everything and everyone but themselves, as Edmundson says, "[skating] fast over the surfaces of life," but not thinking about where we are going and why." Reading books for leisure helps to connect us with our own lives because books contain wisdom, not just more information, which we are already drowning in. To read for wisdom, we have to slow down the pace.

Use brackets when changing verb tenses to make them fit grammatically into your sentence.

Works Cited

Bauerlein, Mark. *The Dumbest Generation: How the Digital Age Stupefies Young Americans and Jeopardizes Our Future.* Tarcher-Penguin, 2008.

Carr, Nicholas. "Is Google Making Us Stupid?" *TheAtlantic.com*, July-Aug. 2008, www.theatlantic.com/magazine/archive/2008/07/is-google-making-us-stupid/306868/.

Dzubow, Lauren. "Watch This. No. Read It!" *Oprah.com,* Harpo Productions, June 2008, www.oprah.com/health/How-Reading-Can-Improve-Your-Memory.

Edmundson, Mark. "Dwelling in Possibilities: Our Students' Spectacular Hunger for Life Makes Them Radically Vulnerable." *The Chronicle of Higher Education,* 14 Mar. 2008, chronicle.com/article/Dwelling-in-Possibilities/7083.

Johnson, Steven. "Dawn of the Digital Natives." *guardian.co.uk.* Guardian News and Media Ltd., 7 Feb. 2008, www.theguardian.com/technology/2008/feb/07/internet.literacy.

---. *Everything Bad Is Good for You: How Today's Popular Culture Is Actually Making Us Smarter.* Riverhead, 2005.

Newkirk, Thomas. "The Case for Slow Reading." *Educational Leadership,* vol. 67, no. 6, 2010, www.ascd.org/publications/educational-leadership/mar10/vol67/num06/The-Case-for-Slow-Reading.aspx.

Ramer, Holly. "NH Professor Pushes for Return to Slow Reading." *Seattle Times,* 17 June 2010, www.seattletimes.com/nation-world/nh-professor-pushes-for-return-to-slow-reading/.

United States. Natl. Endowment for the Arts. *To Read or Not to Read: A Question of National Consequence.* Nov. 2007, www.arts.gov/sites/default/files/ToRead.pdf.

Wolf, Maryanne, and Mirit Barzillai. "The Importance of Deep Reading." *Educational Leadership,* vol. 66, no. 6, 2009, pp. 32–37. *Academic Search Complete,* search.ebscohost.com.proxy.libraries.smu.edu/login.aspx?direct=true&db=a9h&AN=36666622&login.asp&site=ehost-live&scope=site.

CREDITS

page 408: Steven Johnson. *Everything Bad Is Good for You.* Penguin Group USA, 2006. **page 409:** Maryanne Wolf and Mirit Barzillai. "The Importance of Deep Reading." *Educational Leadership,* vol. 66, no. 6, 2010, pp. 32–37. **page 410:** Mark Bauerlein. *The Dumbest Generation: How the Digital Age Stupefies Young Americans and Jeopardizes Our Future (Or, Don't Trust Anyone Under 30).* Penguin Group USA, 2008. **page 410:** Henry David Thoreau **page 411:** Jane Austen. *Pride and Prejudice.* Vol. 3, 1813. **page 411:** Christina Rossetti. "After Death." **page 411:** William Shakespeare. *Hamlet.* **page 412:** *New Oxford Annotated Bible.* Num. 11.7–8. **page 426:** Courtesy of Kyle Van Buskirk

CHAPTER 21

Documenting Your Sources: APA

ENGAGING QUESTIONS

In this chapter, you will engage with the following questions:

- How do I create in-text citations using APA style?
- How do I create a reference list using APA style?

THE AMERICAN PSYCHOLOGICAL ASSOCIATION (APA) STYLE OF DOCUMENTATION is used not only in the field of psychology but also in education, anthropology, social work, business, and other behavioral and social sciences. In APA documents, it is common to find authors referred to by their last name only rather than their full names, as in Modern Language Association (MLA) documents.

Like MLA style, APA documentation requires that a writer acknowledge the source of all direct quotations, paraphrased and summarized ideas from sources, and information that is not common knowledge. Citing is a two-step process that includes a brief in-text reference to the author and date of publication and a longer entry with complete bibliographical information in the reference list at the end of the article or book.

How Do I Make In-Text Citations Using APA Style?

For direct quotations and paraphrases of information that is not common knowledge, the basic in-text citation provides the last name of the author of the source, directly followed by the year the source was published. Citing page numbers is required for direct quotations and highly specific data but not for summarizing or paraphrasing ideas found throughout a text. The following examples show options for citing in text.

Summary or Paraphrase with One Author Named in Your Sentence

> The playground is a space where gender identities are constructed. Paechter (2007) argues that boys who are physically passive on the playground move into the marginal spaces occupied by girls and younger children and thus become stigmatized by other boys as effeminate.

Summary or Paraphrase with One Author Named in Parentheses

> The playground is a space where gender identities are constructed. Boys who are physically passive on the playground move into the marginal spaces occupied by girls and younger children and thus become stigmatized by other boys as effeminate (Paechter, 2007).

> **Punctuation Alert:** Place a comma between the author's name and the date of publication.

The parenthetical citation does not include page numbers because the information is a summary.

Direct Quotation with Author Named in the Sentence

> According to Yoon (2009) anthropologists have found that people around the world create remarkably similar categories when labeling plants and animals, a phenomenon known as folk taxonomy. Yoon finds consensus about such categories as trees, vines, and bushes especially interesting "since there is no way to define a tree versus a bush" (p. D4). In naming the world around them, people appear "unconsciously to follow a set of unwritten rules" (p. D1).

Use the abbreviations *p.* or *pp.* (not in italics) for in-text page references. Also cite figure numbers, table numbers, or other parts of a book if they are the source of specific information. If the source does not use page numbers, give readers another way to locate the passage, such as a heading name or paragraph number. See page 436 for an example.

> **Punctuation Alert:** Close direct quotations before parenthetical citations. Place periods after the parenthetical citation unless you have a block quotation (see page 437).

Direct Quotation with Author Named in Parentheses

Unless the author is named in a sentence, all references in parentheses must include the last name and the year.

> Anthropologists have found that people around the world create remarkably similar categories when labeling plants and animals, a phenomenon known as folk taxonomy (Yoon, 2009). Consensus about such categories as trees, vines, and bushes is especially interesting "since there is no way to define a tree versus a bush" (Yoon, 2009, p. D4). In naming the world around them, people appear "unconsciously to follow a set of unwritten rules" (Yoon, 2009, p. D1).

Source with Two Authors

Give both authors' last names each time you refer to the source. If you name them as part of your sentence, use *and* to join them.

> Wolf and Barzillai (2009) describe the cognitive work of the reading brain.

If you name them in parentheses, use an ampersand (&).

> Reading is very much unlike our other natural human functions of seeing, moving, speaking, and thinking. Reading is an invented cognitive function, and understanding how it works illustrates the amazing plasticity of the brain (Wolf & Barzillai, 2009).

Source with Three or More Authors

For three or more authors, give the name of the first author only, followed by *et al.* (not in italics). Use this format in every citation, including the first, unless doing so would cause ambiguity.

> Radeloff et al. (2005) argue that rural sprawl has more impact on forests than urban sprawl because even though rural sprawl is less dense, its effects are spread over larger areas that once were forests.

More than One Publication by an Author in the Same Year

When you are citing more than one publication by an author with the same year of publication, label the years *a, b, c,* and so on (not italicized); the letter *a* would be assigned to the publication that comes first alphabetically. See the reference list example on page 444.

> Developmental psychologists often focus on the stresses of adolescence rather than on the positive aspects of that stage of life (Steinberg, 2005a, 2005b).

Punctuation Alert: Works by the same author are separated by commas.

Two or More Authors with the Same Last Name

Include identifying initials before each last name.

> S. Young (2007) complains that scientists study earth-eating, or geophagia, only from the standpoint of their own disciplinary interests. Thus, there is no "global perspective of all the possible benefits and all the possible negative consequences of geopaghia" (p. 67).

Organization or Agency as Author

Spell out the name of the organization the first time you use it.

> According to the National Collegiate Athletic Association (2015), the Academic Progress Rate is a way to measure academic performance for college and university sports teams.

If the name is long and has a familiar abbreviation, you may use that in subsequent citations.

> (NCAA, 2015)

Always spell out brief names or names that do not have familiar abbreviations.

Work with No Author or Editor

If no author or editor is named, use the title of the work in both in-text citations and reference list entries. If the title is long, abbreviate it in the text but not on the reference list. Use double quotation marks around the title of an article, a chapter, or a webpage in your discussion, but not in the reference list. Italicize the title of a periodical, book, or report. The example below shows a webpage.

> The Law School Aptitude Test (LSAT) measures ability to read and comprehend in-depth texts with insight, to draw "reasonable inferences" from readings, and to analyze and evaluate the reasoning of others' arguments ("About the LSAT," 2019).

More than One Source in a Parenthetical Citation

If you have more than one source for the same information, include all sources in the parenthetical citation, in alphabetical order, as they would appear in the reference list. Use a semicolon to separate sources by different authors.

> (Steinberg, 2005a, 2005b; Stewart, 1987)

Work with No Page Numbers (Including Webpages and E-Books)

If online material, e-books, or even print material is unpaged and you need to cite a specific passage, use chapters, paragraphs, headings, or whatever other indicators will help readers find the passage.

> According to Friend (2009), "Extraordinary oddities of conduct are tolerated among Wasps so long as you show up for Christmas" (Chapter 4, para. 78).

If the chapters have further numbered subdivisions, include them. For example,

> (Chapter 5, Section 5, para. 4)

Reprinted Works

When you cite a work that has been republished, give both the original date and the date of the version you are using. The in-text citation for the example on page 441 would be (Obama 1995/2004). The date of original publication comes first, although on the reference list the date following the author's name will reflect the edition you used (2004, in this case).

Citations within Quotations

You will often find that your source cites other sources. Do not put these sources on your reference list unless you also read them and used them in your paper. When quoting, include the citations as they appear in the passage you are quoting.

> Hunters seldom wear protection for their hearing, resulting in hearing loss among practitioners of the sport, as Flamme et al. (2010) explain:
>
>> Firearm impulse sound exposure contributes to the poorer hearing ability and hearing handicap evident in sports hunters when compared to nonhunters (Taylor & Williams, 1966; Stewart et al., 2002). Nondahl et al. (2000) calculated a 7% increase in the likelihood of having a marked high-frequency hearing loss for every 5 years of hunting.

Long Quotations

For direct quotations of forty or more words, omit quotation marks and display the quotation as a block of text set in from the left margin by one-half inch (in the same place as a new paragraph's opening). Double-space the entire quotation. See the example above on citations within quotations.

Punctuation Alert: With block quotations, place the final period before the parenthetical citation.

Indirect Sources

A good researcher relies on primary sources. But if your only source for information was cited in another source, use this format.

> . . . as noted by Conley (as cited in McMaster, 2009).

Include McMaster on your reference list, not Conley.

Work in an Anthology

If you are citing a selection from an anthology, list the author of the selection. If you are citing the collection as a whole, list the editor or compiler of the book.

Classics and Religious Works

When you are citing a work whose original publication date is not known or is not relevant, show the date of the version you are using–(Defoe, 2005 version), for example, for a modern version of *Robinson Crusoe,* first published in 1719. For a translation of a classical work, show the date of translation. If the work is ancient, use an approximate date preceded by *ca.* (meaning *circa*), and followed by *B.C.E.* Provide the date of translation following a forward slash (Sophocles, ca. 429 B.C.E./1911). Religious works are cited only in the text, not in the reference list. Instead of page numbers, cite books, chapters, verses, lines, and so forth. Use standard abbreviations for biblical books: Num. 11.7–8, for instance.

A Multivolume Work

Cite all the years of publication if you are referring to the entire work.

> (Foote, 1958–1974)

If you have used all the volumes but are citing from just one, include the volume number.

> (Foote, 1958–1974, Vol. 2, p. 165)

If you used only one volume, cite only that volume's year of publication.

> (Foote, 1963, Vol. 2, p. 165)

An Entire Website

When your source is an entire website, cite it in the text by providing the uniform resource locator (URL), but do not provide a reference list entry.

> The PsychCentral website, sponsored by mental health professionals, offers news, information, and support group hosting for people interested in or affected by mental health disorders (http://psychcentral.com).

Personal Communications

Personal communications such as letters, emails, text messages, online chats, telephone calls, and personal interviews are not listed in the reference list; they are cited in text as in the following example.

> Carolyn Coman described her use of storyboarding to focus on the emotional impact of significant scenes in her fiction (C. Coman, personal communication, August 15, 2009).

Note that the names of months are not abbreviated in APA style and that month precedes day.

How Do I Make Entries in a Reference List Using APA Style?

This section includes examples of how to cite the most common kinds of sources in papers using the APA style of documentation.

General Guidelines for Your Reference List

- Begin the list on a new page and center and bold the word *References* at the top. (Do not italicize.)
- The first word of each entry must match the in-text citation.
- Put all entries, regardless of genre and medium, in alphabetical order according to the author's (or editor's) last name, followed by the initials of the author's first name or names. Use an ampersand before the last author's name.
- If no author is named, use the first word in the title that is not an article (*a, an, the*).
- Do not number the entries.
- Double-space within and between entries.
- Begin each entry at the left margin and indent all subsequent lines by one-half inch. The hanging indent feature of your word processing program will help you do this.
- Italicize titles of books and periodicals.
- Do not enclose titles of articles in quotation marks, although you do use quotation marks for article titles when you refer to them in text.

- Capitalize only the first word of titles and subtitles of books and articles; however, capitalize all proper nouns in any title or subtitle (for example, a person's name).
- Capitalize the full names of periodicals, journals, and newspapers.
- Include a retrieval path in your citation. When a citation closes with a retrieval path, do not include end punctuation.

Retrieval Paths: DOIs and URLs

Whenever possible, include a retrieval path in your citation. Doing so will allow readers to easily access the work you are citing. Retrieval paths take the form of either a DOI or a URL.

A **DOI,** or *digital object identifier*, is *a string of numbers and letters that identifies a source and provides a stable link to it.* DOIs are commonly assigned to journal articles and, in some cases, to books. For example, the following DOI identifies an academic article on adolescent friendships: 10.1353/mpq.0.0035. DOIs are usually located near the copyright date in an article. You can also find them in the bibliographic information in the library's full-record display. When you include DOIs in a reference list, they should appear as live links, unless your instructor prefers otherwise.

A **URL,** or *uniform resource locator, can also be used to guide readers to a source on the Internet.* Unlike DOIs, URLs are not stable and may change over time, so they are not the preferred information to use in a reference list. They are, however, the only way to link to many online sources, such as websites, newspaper and magazine articles, and social media posts and comments. For example, the following URL links readers to a tweet by author and environmentalist Bill McKibben: https://twitter.com/billmckibben/status/1184825236098699265. Like DOIs, URLs should also display as live links in your reference list.

The following guidelines will help you decide when to include a DOI or URL in your references:

- Always include a DOI, if one is assigned. This applies even if the source you are citing is a print source.
- If you are citing a print source that does not have a DOI, do not include a URL in its place.
- If you are citing an online source that does not have a DOI, apply the following guidelines for when and how to include a stable URL in your reference:
    - For a website (excluding databases), provide a URL that links directly to the article or piece you are citing.
    - For a work from a database with no DOI assigned, do not include a URL. Most academic databases are widely available and easily accessed by readers.
    - For a work for which the URL is no longer functional, cite as you would a work with no recoverable source, such as a personal communication. See page 449 for an example.

DOIs and URLs should appear as hyperlinks in your reference list, so that readers can easily access the sources you cite. To convert a DOI to a live link beginning with https://, use the link provider available at https://www.doi.org/. If a URL is long and unwieldy, you may use a site like Bitly or TinyURL to shorten it. Do not include end punctuation following a DOI or URL, as punctuation could interfere with the link's functionality.

See the following list of examples for more help with citing specific kinds of sources.

Books and Reference Works

Your entries for books (whether print or e-books), as well as for reference works such as dictionaries, encyclopedias (including *Wikipedia*), and diagnostic manuals, should contain the following:

1. Name of author (or editor) in inverted order, followed by a period (unless no author or editor is listed)
2. Date of publication in parentheses, followed by a period
3. Title of the work, in italics, followed by a period
4. Publisher, followed by a period
5. Retrieval path, if available, hyperlinked with no end punctuation

Last name, Initial(s). (Date). *Title.* Publisher. retrieval path

Book by a Single Author

Paechter, C. F. (2007). *Being boys, being girls: Learning masculinities and femininities.* McGraw-Hill.

Use a brief form of the publisher's name. Do not include words like *Company, Corporation,* or *Inc.* Words like *Books* and *Press* should be retained. Do not use abbreviations. If you are citing an e-book, do not list the platform or format in the reference. Do include a DOI, if one is available. If not, include a stable URL, as is done in the following example:

Dewey, J. (1891). *Outlines of a critical theory of ethics*. Register Publishing. https://www.gutenberg.org/files/60422/60422-h/60422-h.htm

Two or More Books by the Same Author

List the works in order of publication, with the earliest first. Repeat the author's name for each entry.

Obama, B. (2004). *Dreams from my father: A story of race and inheritance.* Three Rivers Press. (Original work published 1995)

Obama, B. (2006). *The audacity of hope: Thoughts on reclaiming the American dream.* Crown.

Book by Two or More Authors

List all authors by last name and initials, separated by commas. Use an ampersand (&) before the final name. If a work has up to twenty authors, list them all. If there are more than twenty authors, list only the first nineteen authors' names, followed by an ellipsis (three spaced dots), then the last author.

Booth, W., Colomb, G., & Williams, J. (2008). *The craft of research* (3rd ed.). University of Chicago Press. https://doi.org/10.7208/chicago/9780226062648.001.0001

Small, G., & Vorgan, G. (2008). *iBrain: Surviving the technological alteration of the modern mind.* HarperCollins. https://doi.org/10.1109/MSPEC.2009.47954

Book by a Corporate Author or Government Agency

Treat the corporation or agency as an author. If the author and publisher are the same, omit the publisher.

American Psychological Association. (2019). *Publication manual of the American Psychological Association* (7th ed.). https://doi.org/10.1037/0000165-000

Book with No Author or Editor

Start with the title of the work. Use "Anonymous" only if that is what the title page says.

The Chicago Manual of Style (17th ed.). (2017). University of Chicago Press. https://doi.org/10.7208/cmos17

Later Edition of a Book

Put the edition number in parentheses after the title.

Williams, J. M. (2013). *Style: Ten lessons in clarity and grace* (11th ed.). Pearson.

Reprinted Book

Indicate the original date of publication in parentheses.

Obama, B. (2004). *Dreams from my father: A story of race and inheritance.* Three Rivers Press. (Original work published 1995)

Note: The in-text citation should include both dates, with the original publication date first (1995/2004).

Anthology or Compilation

Between the editor's name and the date, put the abbreviation for editor(s) in parentheses, followed by a period.

MacClancy, J., Henry, J., & Macbeth, H. (Eds.). (2007). *Consuming the inedible: Neglected dimensions of food choice.* Berghahn Books.

Selection in an Anthology or Compilation

For articles in edited works, put the author of the individual work first, followed by the year of publication, and then the title of the article, followed by the word *In* and the editor or editors' names (not in inverse order) and the title of the collected work. The inclusive pages of the selection follow the title of the book, in parentheses. End the citation with name of publisher.

Young, S. (2007). A vile habit? The potential biological consequences of geophagia, with special attention to iron. In J. MacClancy, J. Henry, & H. Macbeth (Eds.), *Consuming the inedible: Neglected dimensions of food choice* (pp. 67–79). Berghahn Books.

Note that APA style for inclusive numbers uses all digits.

Translation

Put the translator's initials and last name, followed by the abbreviation for translator (*Trans.*) in parentheses after the book's title.

Ariès, P. (1965). *Centuries of childhood* (R. Baldick, Trans.). Vintage Books. (Original work published 1962)

Sophocles. (1911). *Oedipus Rex* (G. Murray, Trans.). Ruskin House. https://www.gutenberg.org/files/27673/27673-h/27673-h.htm (Original work published ca. 429 B.C.E.)

For classical works, such as *Oedipus Rex,* cite both the date of translation and the date of publication in your text: (Sophocles, ca. 429 B.C.E./1911).

Preface, Introduction, Foreword, or Afterword Not by the Book's Author or Editor

Open the entry with the name of the author of the part of the book; then put the date in parentheses and write out the name of the section written by this author. Follow with author or editor, title, and publication information for the entire book.

Gore, A. (2008). Foreword. In B. McKibben (Ed.), *American earth: Environmental writing since Thoreau.* Library of America.

Multivolume Work

Directly after the author, indicate the inclusive dates of the volumes. After the title of the work, indicate in parentheses the number of volumes.

Churchill, W. (1956–1958). *A history of the English-speaking peoples* (Vols. 1–4). Cassell.

One Volume of a Multivolume Work

If the individual volumes in a multivolume work have their own titles, use the following format when only one of them should be included in your reference list.

Churchill, W. (1957). *A history of the English-speaking peoples: Vol. 3. The age of revolution.* Cassell.

If the volume does not have its own title, then put the volume number in parentheses after the title, as when citing all volumes.

Signed Article in a Reference Book

Include inclusive page numbers for the entry in parentheses after the title of the book.

Zangwill, O. L. (2004). Hypnotism, history of. In R. L. Gregory (Ed.), *The Oxford companion to the mind* (pp. 330–334). Oxford University Press. https://doi.org/10.1093/acref/9780198662242.001.0001

Unsigned Article in a Reference Book

Open with the title of the entry.

A technical history of photography. (2004). In *The New York Times guide to essential knowledge: A desk reference for the curious mind* (pp. 104–112). St. Martin's.

Article in an Online Encyclopedia or Reference Work

If the entry is unsigned, open with its title, as in the first example below.

The philosophy of dance. (2015, January 12). In E. N. Zalta (Ed.), *Stanford Encyclopedia of Philosophy.* http://plato.stanford.edu/entries/dance/

Botstein, L. (2005). Robert Maynard Hutchins and the University of Chicago. In J. Reiff, A. D. Keating, & J. R. Grossman (Eds.), *Encyclopedia of Chicago.* http://www.encyclopedia.chicagohistory.org/pages/2190.html

Wikipedia Entry

Sigmund Freud. (2019, September 17). In *Wikipedia.* https://en.wikipedia.org/w/index.php?title=Sigmund_Freud&oldid=916212260

Because the material published on *Wikipedia* is likely to change frequently over time, cite the archived version of the page you referenced. Provide that date in parentheses following the title of the entry. If you are citing a wiki that does not archive its pages, use the word *Retrieved* followed by the retrieval date and a comma. Then use the word *from* followed by the URL.

Articles in Periodicals

Your reference list entries for periodicals, which include journals, magazines, newspapers, newsletters, and professional blog posts, should contain the following:

1. Name of author (or editor) in inverted order, followed by a period (unless no author or editor is listed)
2. Date of publication in parentheses, followed by a period
3. Title of the article, not in italics, followed by a period
4. Title of the periodical, in italics, followed by a comma (and, for a journal, further publication information)
5. Inclusive page numbers, followed by a period
6. Retrieval path, hyperlinked with no end punctuation

Article in a Journal with Volume and/or Issue Number

Last name, Initial(s). (Date). Title of article. *Title of Periodical, vol. no*(issue), pages. retrieval path

Place a comma after the journal title, followed by the volume number in italics; then (without inserting a space) put the issue number, if one is included, in parentheses, followed by a comma and inclusive page numbers. The following examples demonstrate how to cite a journal article with a DOI and without.

> Bracher, M. (2009). How to teach for social justice: Lessons from Uncle Tom's Cabin and cognitive science. *College English, 71*(4), 363–388. https://doi.org/10.2307/25472333
>
> Wolf, M., & Barzillai M. (2009). The importance of deep reading. *Educational Leadership, 66*(6), 32–37.

Journal Article—with DOI

> Mottron, L., Mineau, S., Martel, G., St.-Charles Bernier, C., Berthiaume, C., Dawson, M., Lemay, M., Palardy, S., Charman, T., & Faubert, J. (2007). Lateral glances toward moving stimuli among young children with autism: Early regulation of locally oriented perception. *Development and Psychopathology, 19*(1), 23–26. https://doi.org/10.1017/S0954579407070022

Journal Article—without DOI

When no DOI is available for a periodical, do not include a URL.

> O'Dwyer, K. (2008). Nietzsche's reflections on love. *Minerva—An Internet Journal of Philosophy, 12,* 37–77.

Source Accessed through a Database

Cite books and periodicals according to the guidelines already given. Only include the name of the database if you think it would be difficult to find the source in any other way. If no DOI is given, include an accession number or article number provided by the database in parentheses following the article's title.

> Brown, M., Ray, R., Summers, E., & Fraistat, N. (2018). #SayHerName: A case study of intersectional media. *Ethnic and Racial Studies, 40*(11). https://doi.org/10.1080/01419870.2017.1334934

Multiple Publications by the Same Author in the Same Year

Use letters to distinguish works by the same author in the same year; assign the letters according to the alphabetical order of the titles of the works.

> Steinberg, L. (2005a). Cognitive and affective development in adolescence. *Trends in Cognitive Sciences, 9,* 69–74. https://doi.org/10.1016/j.tics.2004.12.005
>
> Steinberg, L. (2005b). *The ten basic principles of good parenting.* Simon & Schuster.

Article in a Magazine

For magazine articles, put the volume number in italics followed by the issue number in parentheses, a comma, and page numbers. Because magazines are paged by issue, the issue number is required. However, if you are citing an online magazine that does not have volume, issue, or page numbers, omit these from the reference. Include a DOI or URL if one is available.

Davies, A. (2019, September). Speed is killing the planet. Time to focus on efficiency. *Wired, 27*(9), 128–133. https://www.wired.com/story/speed-is-killing-the-planet-focus-on-efficiency/

If the magazine publishes weekly, list the day as well as the month and year.

Gladwell, M. (2009, October 11). Offensive play: How different are dogfighting and football? *The New Yorker,* 50–59. https://www.newyorker.com/magazine/2009/10/19/offensive-play

Article in a Newspaper

Give the day, month, year, and edition if specified. For newspaper articles, use the abbreviations *p.* and *pp.* (not italicized) before the page number. List all page numbers if the article appeared on discontinuous pages. If the article is from an online newspaper, as in the following example, you can omit the edition and page numbers.

Carrington, D. (2019, October 21). Ocean acidification can cause mass extinctions, fossils reveal. *The Guardian.* https://www.theguardian.com/environment/2019/oct/21/ocean-acidification-can-cause-mass-extinctions-fossils-reveal

If the article appeared in an online news site that does not have an associated daily or weekly newspaper, follow the format for a webpage. See page 446 for an example.

Newspaper Article with an Anonymous Author

Start with the title of the article. When alphabetizing, ignore opening articles (*a, an, the*).

Nuns' numbers dwindling. (2015, January 25). *Dallas Morning News,* p. 4A.

Editorial in a Newspaper—No Author Given

Put the genre (editorial) in square brackets. Unlike citations for other periodicals, those for newspapers have *p.* or *pp.* before the page number or numbers.

Poverty-busting in Dallas [Editorial]. (2015, January 19). *Dallas Morning News,* p. 20A.

Letter to the Editor of a Newspaper or Magazine

Put the genre (letter to the editor) in square brackets. If the letter appears in a newspaper, use the abbreviation *p.* and *pp.* (not italicized) before the page number; if it appears in a magazine, as in the following example, this is not required.

Schlosberg, J. (2015, January 26). Clickbait [Letter to the editor]. *The New Yorker,* 5.

Review

Open with the name of the reviewer, the date, and the title of the review, if there is one. Include *Review of* (not in italics), followed by the item being reviewed, in square brackets.

Menand, L. (2019, September 30). Is meritocracy making everyone miserable? [Review of *The Years that matter most: How college makes or breaks us* by Paul Tough, and The meritocracy trap by Daniel Markovits]. *The New Yorker,* 75–80. https://www.newyorker.com/magazine/2019/09/30/is-meritocracy-making-everyone-miserable

Hofferth, S. (2009, June 26). Buying so children belong [Review of the book *Longing and belonging: Parents, children, and consumer culture* by A. J. Pugh]. *Science, 324*(5935).

Although *Science* is a scholarly journal, it is published weekly; APA style treats it and similar journals like a magazine.

Website

Do not list entire websites in the reference list. Give the URL in your discussion. See the example on page 438.

Webpage

If the source is something unusual, such as a lecture, a data file, or a video, put that in square brackets after the title. If the source is one that is designed to change over time, and the page itself is not archived, include a retrieval date, as in the example below.

Tartakovsky, M. (2010). Asperger's syndrome. Retrieved October 5, 2018, from http://psychcentral.com/lib/aspergers-syndrome/0004226

Abstract

Sweeten, G., Bushway, S. D., & Paternoster, R. (2009). Does dropping out of school mean dropping out into delinquency? [Abstract]. *Criminology, 47,* 47–92. https://doi.org/10.1111/j.1745-9125.2009.00139.x

Other Types of Sources

Blog Post

Cite a professional blog post, as in the following example, the same way you would an article in a periodical. If citing an informal blog, or micro-blog post, cite as you would a social media post.

Agapakis, C. (2010, December 8). Making blind mice see. http://scienceblogs.com/oscillator/2010/12/making_blind_mice_see.php

Social Media Post

Provide the name of the individual or group posting. If citing a tweet or Instagram post, provide the handle in square brackets followed by a period. Include the date of the post in parentheses followed by a period. For the title, include the first twenty words of the post. If a tweet includes an image, a video, or a thumbnail image with a link, indicate that in brackets after the title (e.g. [Thumbnail with link attached]).

McKibben, B. [@BillMcKibben]. (2019, October 17). *Last month tied for the hottest September on record. There's no massive El Nino underway—this is just what happens as we pump more greenhouse gasses into the air* [Tweet]. Twitter. https://twitter.com/billmckibben/status/1184825236098699265

Discussion Groups and Online Forums

Begin with the author of the post, the date, the title, the genre in brackets, the source, and the retrieval path.

Mendez, J. O. (2014, October 27). First-year seminars and academic advising [Online forum comment]. Penn State Division of Undergraduate Studies. http://dus.psu.edu/mentor/2013/08/first-year-seminars-academic-advising/

Bracketed labels could also include:

[Discussion list message]
[Newsgroup posting]

Published or Broadcast Interview

Published and broadcast interviews follow the same format. For an interview recording in a digital archive, list the name of the archive as the source and include the label *[Interview]* (not in italics) after the title, followed by a period.

Fahim, K. (2015, January 10). Interview by Arun Rath. NPR. http://www.npr.org/2015/01/10/376381082/how-does-al-qaida-continue-to-grow

Podcast

List the name of the host as the author and specify that person's role in parentheses. After the title, list the episode number in parentheses. If the podcast does not number episodes, omit. Specify the type of podcast in square brackets. Then provide the name of the podcast, preceded by the word *In*. The URL follows the source information.

Jad Abumrad (Host). (2019, June 14). Problem Space [Audio Podcast]. In *Radio Lab*. NPR. https://www.wnycstudios.org/podcasts/radiolab/articles/g-problem-space

Film, YouTube Video, or Other Streaming Video

For films, open with the director of the film followed by the date, title, format (how you watched the film), and production company. For online video sources, open with the producer or the person or group who uploaded the video and end with a URL.

Gonzalez, A. (Producer & Director). (2014). *Birdman or (The unexpected virtue of ignorance)* [Film; DVD]. Fox Searchlights Pictures.

Hirsh, M. (2010, December 16). Richard Holbrooke: A friend to journalists [Video]. YouTube. http://www.youtube.com/watch?v=leGGGEUsCI0

Television Program (Episode or Webisode from a Series)

Fryman, P. (Writer), & Lloyd, S. (Director). (2010). Cleaning house (Series 6, Episode 2) [TV series episode]. In C. Bays, P. Fryman, R. Greenberg, & C. Thomas (Executive Producers), *How I met your mother.* CBS.

If you want to cite the entire series, list the creators and producers first, along with inclusive dates.

Paper Presented at a Professional Conference

Jones, S. L., and Yarhouse, M. A. (2009, August 9). *Ex-gays? An extended longitudinal study of attempted religiously mediated change in sexual orientation.* Paper presented at the meeting of the American Psychological Association, Toronto, Canada. https://doi.org/10.1080/0092623X.2011.607052

Live Performance

Include location information when a work is associated with a specific location, such as with a live performance or a conference presentation.

Rickson, I. (Director). (2014, November 28). *The river* [Live performance]. Circle in the Square, New York, NY.

Musical Compositions and Sound Recordings

Cooder, R. (1990). *Paradise and lunch* [Album]. Reprise.

Mahler, G. (Composer), & Barenboim, D. (Conductor). (2006). *Symphony no. 5* [Song recorded by Chicago Symphony Orchestra]. Rhino.

Map

Dynamically created maps (such as a Google Maps map) are likely to change over time, and so do not have titles or publication dates. The abbreviation *n.d.* (meaning "no date") is used in such cases. Provide a description in square brackets and a retrieval date. If the URL is long, you can use a URL shortener, as in this example.

Google (n.d.) [Google Maps road map of Kingsville, Texas]. Retrieved January 21, 2019, from https://tinyurl.com/y6spp6bg

Advertisement

Open with the sponsor of the advertisement, followed by the date of publication, its title, and the page number.

New York City Ballet. (2015, January 26). [Advertisement]. *The New Yorker,* 5.

Visual Art

Seurat, G. (1884). *A Sunday on La Grande Jatte* [Painting]. Art Institute of Chicago, Chicago, IL, United States. https://www.artic.edu/artworks/27992/a-sunday-on-la-grande-jatte-1884

Give the medium and the location. If you cite a work of art in a book, indicate what you are referring to (painting, sculpture, etc.) in your text and list the entire book in the reference list.

Dissertation or Thesis Retrieved from a Database

For a published dissertation from a database, include in parentheses the words "doctoral dissertation" and the name of the university.

Warner, A. (2018). *Writing new boundaries for the law: Black women's fiction and the abject in psychoanalysis* (Doctoral dissertation, University of Massachusetts, Amherst). https://scholarworks.umass.edu/dissertations_2/1303/

Unpublished Dissertation or Thesis

Pendleton, R. (2005). *Teaching biography: History as lives, lives as history* [Unpublished master's thesis]. University of Rochester.

Legal Sources

Griswold v. Connecticut, 381 U.S. 479 (1965).

Patient Protection and Affordable Care Act, Public Law 111-148, 124 Stat. 119-1025 (2010). http://housedocs.house.gov/energycommerce/ppacacon.pdf

Your in-text citations should italicize the names of court cases.

Personal Communications

Personal communications such as interviews, emails, text messages, and letters, and any reference lacking a recoverable source, are not included in the list of references in APA style. However, you need to cite them in the text as described on page 438.

SAMPLE RESEARCH PAPER **APA Style**

½" 1"

1

Papers written for most courses do not require running heads. However, if your instructor requires them, include your title, but not your subtitle, in the top left of every page. Number all pages, starting with title page.

Popularity's Downside:

Valuing Quantity over Quality in Friendship

Audra Ames

Department of English

Southern Methodist University

COMP 101

Professor Channell

November 11, 2012

Center the title, author, department, name of college or university, course, professor, and date submitted in the upper half of the page.

½" 1"

2

1" 1"

Heading (centered and bolded), new page

Abstract

Do not indent first line of abstract.

Abstract is an objective summary of the main points in the essay or article.

Adolescents commonly value popularity over having a few high-quality friends, as they see popularity as a mark of status. However, making popularity one's main goal causes young people to miss out on the benefits of real friendship because the values and behavior required for popularity conflict with those that would allow true friendships to form. True friendship encourages personal growth and deep intimacy while an obsession with popularity encourages aggression, mean competition, and conformity to peer group preferences. It also causes young people to keep personal problems to themselves and to become self-absorbed to the point of narcissism. Young people with poor self-image and values may seek the security of groups whose friendship can be destructive, but most settle for superficial friendships that are not harmful, but do not promote personal growth or offer the deep rewards of true friendship. Popularity itself is good but should be seen as a means for finding potential friends with whom to form deep relationships.

Abstract should be between 150 and 250 words.

Keywords: popularity, competition, peers, friendship

3

Popularity's Downside:

Valuing Quantity over Quality in Friendship

Indent 5 spaces or 1/2"

Double space between title and opening of the essay.

⟷In middle school, junior high, and high school, social hierarchies are very important, with the top rungs of the ladder usually occupied by cheerleaders, athletes, and the physically attractive people. There is a high correlation between these sources of status and being popular. Popularity itself is a source of status. Even after high school, some people want to continue to play the popularity game; they seek quantity of friends, not quality in friendships. Studies show that this is a mistake. Having large quantities of friends is not as worthwhile as having a few high quality friendships. Real friendships are based not on status and hierarchies but on shared interests and equality. Making popularity one's main goal causes young people to miss out on the benefits of real friendship because the values and behavior required for popularity conflict with those that would allow true friendships to form.

Thesis states the main point derived from the findings of the research.

Level-one headings are bolded and centered.

The Value of Friendship

High-quality friendships have been described as relationships in which people are willing to put aside some of their own self-interests to invest attention in each other's goals and personal growth. Friendships support mutual growth. Relationships with friends are not static and unchanging because friends keep each other moving forward, as described by Csikszentmihalyi (1997): "We try new things, activities, and adventures; we develop new attitudes, ideas, and values; we get to know friends . . . deeply and intimately" (pp. 81–82). Similarly, Berndt (2004) found that "friendships are higher in quality when friends feel free to disclose their most intimate thoughts and feelings to each other" (p. 1). With true friends, no one feels the need to hide who they are, or what they really think and feel, or fear being seen as weak if they confide about insecurities and doubts.

The rewards of friendship are great; studies have shown that people's most positive experiences occur with friends, and this is "especially true for adolescents" (Csikszentmihalyi, 1997, p. 81). Growing up is just easier with a good friend. Studies have found that having a close friend and being in a reciprocated friendship helps children of middle-school age adjust to their changing environment with less stress and depression (Dittmann, 2004).

How Popularity Conflicts with Friendship

However, a problem for many adolescents is the importance of popularity over having a few quality relationships. A study of middle school girls found that although they highly valued friendship as a source of trust and intimacy, "friendship was seldom a serious contender with popularity when girls had to choose" (Merten, 2004, p. 362). Similarly, Closson (2009) found that clique members were willing to give up their personal preferences in friends to comply with the leaders' preferences. He concluded that "the desire for popularity may be stronger than the desire for a stable, high-quality friendship in early adolescence" (p. 429).

1"

1"

It seems that young people are torn between their desire for friendship and their desire for status. Studies confirm what most people know from personal experience: Social status is "a central aspect of daily life" for young adolescents (Closson, 2009, p. 407). The desire for status conflicts with the desire for friendship because young people choose to associate with those who can help boost their status rather than those who share their interests and goals. Csiksentzmihalyi (1997) argued that "friendships are expected to provide mutual benefits, with no external constraints that might lead to exploitation" (p. 82). The desire for status puts constraints on the choice of friends, and young people might act friendly to someone simply for the social benefits that person brings.

Too much concern for popularity can keep young people from discussing personal problems, and thus getting the benefit of a peer's sympathy and support. In his study of junior high girls, Merten (2004) noted that true friendships encouraged sharing of all experiences (inclusion), while the desire for popularity caused girls to exclude from conversations any experiences that might cause them to be judged as weak. In friendships, Merten saw girls "respecting and valuing each other's experiences, rather than having the demands of popularity select which experiences were worthy of inclusion in a relationship" (p. 364). Basically, the girls seeking popularity had to filter what they said around their popular friends in order to not have a vulnerability exploited. Popularity is accompanied by a fear of vulnerability. If you show weakness, you are picked apart or criticized for it.

The Downside of Popularity

The fact is that popularity is associated with some bad traits, such as aggression and gossip. Even within cliques, Closson (2009) found that members act aggressively to gain and keep status, and this happened most frequently in cliques that were recognized as having high status within the school:

> Compared to members of lower status cliques, those in perceived popular cliques used more instrumental relational aggression. Some researchers have suggested that peer-directed relational aggression may be used intentionally to damage another peer's social reputation, thereby . . . maintaining or

> increasing one's status within the clique by decreasing the social position of others. (p. 428)

Closson (2009) also found that popular people were described by their peers as "cool, nice, and funny yet also conceited, exclusionary, and mean" (p. 408). But conceited people are not usually happy because they are too self-absorbed.

A desire for popularity inspires narcissism, which can be described as overly high self-esteem and self-absorption. Narcissistic people are "looking for happiness by way of what they can draw toward themselves, rather than what they can share with others" (Schumaker, 2007, p. 175). People who are obsessed with being popular are buying into a system that almost rules out the possibility of real friendship because as Merten (2004) found, "Popularity was based on hierarchy, public recognition, and self-interest [while] friendship was based on equality . . ." (p. 363). The main focus of popularity seems to be popularity in itself, and especially the attributes that go along with being popular, like physical attractiveness (p. 363). It is not surprising that narcissism has been connected with aggressive behavior, including bullying. Schumaker (2007) described narcissists as aggressive, with a tendency to bully (p. 168). When their self-esteem is threatened, narcissists put others down in order to build up their egos again.

Sometimes people can be popular in another way that creates malignant growth. They can be popular with the wrong crowd, and this can inspire aggressive, antisocial behavior. Interactions with a certain group of people may change a person or encourage violence and aggression, so that the person is more willing to commit unlawful, harmful acts in order to impress his peers. Berndt (2004) summarized studies related to "the three A's of friendship: adjustment, attachment, and aggression." In one study done on aggression in children, surprising data was collected. "Students higher in relational aggression actually had higher quality friendships, perhaps because these students needed friends to join them in attacking or excluding their victims" (Berndt, 2004, p. 2). These relationships are of high quality, but only because peers bond over acts of violence, which does not create a stable, high quality life. An extreme example of destructive friendship would be gangs, in which individuals support each other in a kind of "malignant growth" (Csikszentmihalyi, 1997, p. 82).

Putting Popularity in Its Place

More commonly, people of all ages settle for superficial "friendships" that are more like high school cliques. Csikszentmihalyi (1997) describes these groups as "safe cocoon[s]" for people not seeking to change: "The superficial sociability of teenage peer groups, suburban clubs and coffee klatches, professional associations, drinking buddies, gives a soothing sense of being part of a like-minded set of people without demanding much effort or growth" (p. 82). Having a large circle of acquaintances is not a bad thing if people do not see it as sufficient for the real happiness of true friendship.

One argument in favor of popularity is that it enables people to find friends and to be friends: Nangle, Erdley, Newman, Mason, and Carpenter (2004) found that popularity laid the groundwork for children with good social skills to find potential friends from a large "pool" of others with similarly good social skills (p. 551). Most important, these researchers found that young people with good social skills were able to form deep and long-lasting close friendships. Popularity is not a substitute for real friendship, just a stepping stone to it.

Conclusion

When you have a few good quality friendships versus a lot of acquaintances, you are able to explore, challenge and push yourself into becoming a better person. Equally important is the social support of a good friend. Studies have shown that the most frequent complaint of people dealing with an emotional crisis is that they do not have any true friends to turn to (Csikszentmihalyi, 1997, p. 83). People that do not have social support when they experience a rough patch are more likely to become depressed. Young people need to make it through adolescence with an appreciation for real friendship, and not give in to an immature obsession with popularity as a status symbol. Overall, quality over quantity in friendship is a much more successful route through all of one's life.

Always include a DOI, if one is assigned. This applies even if the source you are citing is a print source.

Begin references on a separate page.

8

References

Berndt, T. J. (2004). Friendship and three A's (aggression, adjustment, and attachment). *Journal of Experimental Child Psychology 88*(1), 1–4. https://doi.org/10.1016/j.jecp.2004.03.004

Closson, L. M. (2009). Aggressive and prosocial behaviors within early adolescent friendship cliques: What's status got to do with it? *Merrill-Palmer Quarterly: Journal of Developmental Psychology, 55*(4), 406–435. http://dx.doi.org/10.1353/mpq.0.0035

Csikszentmihalyi, M. (1997). *Finding flow: The psychology of engagement with everyday life.* Basic Books.

Dittmann, M. (2004, July). Friendships ease middle school adjustment. *American Psychological Association.* http://www.apa.org/monitor/julaug04/friendships.aspx

Merten, D. E. (2004). Securing her experience: Friendship versus popularity. *Feminism & Psychology, 14,* 361–365. https://doi.org/10.1177/0959353504044635

Nangle, D. W., Erdley, C. A., Newman, J. E., Mason, C. A., & Carpenter, E. M. (2004). Popularity, friendship quantity, and friendship quality: Interactive influences on children's loneliness and depression. *Journal of Clinical Child and Adolescent Psychology, 32*(4), 546–555. https://doi.org/10.1207/S15374424JCCP3204_7

Schumaker, J. F. (2007). *In search of happiness: Understanding an endangered state of mind.* Praeger.

Note that for a periodical, the volume number is provided in italics. The issue number is enclosed in parentheses with no italics. There is no space between them.

When citing an online article with no DOI, provide a functional URL that links directly to the article or piece you are citing. If no such URL exists, omit it from the reference.

For a book, the first word of title is uppercase; same for the first word following the colon, and for any proper nouns in the title. Note that entries for books do not include page ranges; however, page numbers must appear in your in-text citation.

If a source has one to twenty authors, list all in the order given. Use an ampersand (&) before the final name.

CREDITS

page 434: C. K. Yoon. "Reviving the Lost Art of Naming the World." *New York Times* 11 Aug. 2009: D1+. **page 435:** Sera L. Young. "A Vile Habit? The Potential Biological Consequences of Geophagia, with Special Attention to Iron" in J. MacClancy, J. Henry, & H. Macbeth (Eds.), *Consuming the Inedible: Neglected Dimensions of Food Choice*. Berghahn Books, 2007. 67. **page 436:** T. Friend. *Cheerful Money: Me, My Family, and the Last Days of Wasp Splendor.* Hachette Book Group, 2009.

PART IV

Writing in the Genres

CHAPTER 22

Writing a Rhetorical Analysis

ENGAGING QUESTIONS

In this chapter, you will engage with the following questions:

- How is rhetorical analysis different from other types of analytical writing?
- What are the purposes of rhetorical analyses?
- What types of texts are typically chosen for rhetorical analyses?
- How do writers prepare to write rhetorical analyses?

IN A TYPICAL ANALYSIS OF A TEXT—A LITERARY PIECE, A SPEECH, A CONVERSATION, a commercial, an image—you carefully examine the text, often to figure out what it means. In a rhetorical analysis, you study the text to determine not only what it means but how it creates and communicates this meaning.

What Is a Rhetorical Analysis?

Rhetorical analysis involves *taking apart or breaking down a text; separation of the parts from the whole enables understanding and evaluating how the strategies being used work together to achieve the text's purpose.* First, you read the text to understand its purpose: to explain an idea, to share information, to convey a feeling or emotion, to argue a position–whatever you think the text was created to do. Second, you read the text to see how it works: for example, its tone, choice of words and kinds of sentences, the emotion created, the context implied, or the relationship to the audience.

THE ART OF QUESTIONING Anatomy of a Rhetorical Analysis

Ask and answer the following questions:

- Description: **Who wrote or created the text? When? Where?**
- Reader identification: **Who is the target audience? How does the author try to reach the audience?**
- Stated or implied goal: **What is the text's purpose?**
- Strategies: **How does the text appeal to logic, emotion, or credibility?**
- Structure: **How are the ideas or images put together?**
- Keywords: **What language choices do you find?**

Why Write a Rhetorical Analysis?

People do rhetorical analysis whenever they want to understand the way an idea is presented to them. At halftime during the Super Bowl, you might think about the similar ways that commercials try to convince you to buy a product and wonder about the assumptions those businesses have made about who their audience is. While walking across campus, you might notice a flyer that catches your attention, post its image on your Facebook page, and offer your rhetorical analysis in the caption.

In college and in your work life, you will be expected to analyze the rhetorical situation whenever you read critically, whether it is a piece of literature or a letter from the CEO to the company's stockholders. When you write a rhetorical analysis, your task is not simply to state all of the elements of the situation (author, purpose, and audience) or to itemize all of the ways that the writer or creator uses language, images, or emotions. *Your task is to make a point or come to a conclusion about how the text communicates meaning to its audience.*

EXAMPLE Rhetorical Analysis

Rhetorical Analysis of the Section on the Church in "Letter from Birmingham Jail"
Ginny Norton

Introduction: explains context and background of text analyzed.

The text of "Letter from Birmingham Jail" is available online. Search by the title to read the entire text. The analysis deals with paragraphs 33–44.

1 On April 12, 1963, eight Alabama clergymen published a letter in the local newspaper as a response to the protests being enacted to affect the desegregation of Birmingham, Alabama, in which they asked the African Americans to wait for a more opportune time to begin their protests. Meanwhile, Martin Luther King had been arrested and imprisoned in the Birmingham jail for his participation in one of his non-violent action campaigns. While in jail, he read the letter from the clergymen and was inspired to write a rebuttal, which asserted why African Americans have waited long enough to receive equality and freedom, and also why it is the moral responsibility of the Church, which has remained uncharacteristically silent "behind the anesthetizing security of stained glass windows" to endorse racial equality. This rebuttal became known as his "Letter from Birmingham Jail." In this letter, Martin Luther King masterfully uses rhetorical appeals . . . to convince the American public that African Americans need the support of the Church as they act immediately to eradicate racial inequality.

Transitional sentence: alerts reader analysis about to begin.

Focuses on the appeal of character *(ethos)*, moving an audience by generating respect for the writer. Provides specific citations from the text as evidence.

2 King uses ethos early in his section on the complacency of the Church on racial issues, which serves to build his credibility as a minister and civil rights leader. Dr. King demonstrates his long-standing relationship with the Church by telling us he is a third generation preacher. He then adds to his credibility by praising a few notable examples of churches that have taken a stand for racial equality, such as Reverend Stallings, who held a non-segregated Sunday worship service the previous Sunday. King also demonstrates his worthiness as a civil

rights leader by nonchalantly mentioning that he "was suddenly catapulted into the leadership of the bus protest in Montgomery [Alabama]." He once again emphasizes how experienced he is in matters involving the Southern Church, by exclaiming that he has heard "numerous religious leaders of the South" implore their congregations to conform to desegregation merely because it is a law. However, Dr. King laments that those Southern religious leaders do not encourage desegregation because it is the morally right thing to do, which lays the foundation for King's logical argument. King's use of *ethos* is a very effective tool for establishing him as a knowledgeable, veteran preacher and civil rights leader.

Transitional word moves reader from paragraph 2 to 3.

Additionally, King's impassioned, potent word choice creates several instances of *pathos*. At the beginning of his argument about the Church, he first explains that he is critiquing the Church as someone who deeply loves and respects it and will continue to do so "as long as the cord of life shall lengthen." This beautiful explanation of King's relationship with the Church has the effect of making readers sympathize with a man whose dearest institution has let him down. Midway through his critique, King uses deliberately short, adamant sentences to point out that the early Christians were once so fired up for the Lord that they were not intimidated by the masses. During this period, the Church used its influence to bring an end to infant sacrifice, as well as brutal conquests. Next, King shifts his focus to the modern Church, and acerbically asserts that the Church of today "is so often a weak, ineffectual voice with an uncertain sound." This accusation leads into King's main argument as it emotively demonstrates that the Church has fallen from its powerful position of setting the moral agenda on issues to an outdated, fruitless institution. 3

Focuses on the appeal to feeling or emotion *(pathos)*. Note: last example of emotional appeal linked to discussion of the appeal to reason in next paragraph.

Lead sentence is topic sentence signaling to the reader what the entire paragraph is about.

Dr. King concisely uses logos throughout his argument about the ineffectual nature of the contemporary Church on the topic of immediate racial equality. King succinctly reminds his audience that the early Church frequently occupied towns and rearranged their entire power structure with the conviction that "they were a 'colony of heaven' and had to obey God rather than men." King shows that the contemporary Church is conversely an "arch supporter of the status quo." In fact, King illuminates how the power structures of today's cities are reliant upon the Church's placating, "silent . . . sanction of things as they are." Lastly, King ardently explains that the civil rights movement will succeed, because, as he so eloquently proclaims, "the sacred heritage of our nation and the eternal will of God are embodied in our echoing demands." As a minister, King hoped that the Christian values of morality and universal brotherhood in Christ would be incentive enough for the Church to realize the dire need for immediate action in favor of racial equality. Dr. King expresses disappointment in the Church's uncharacteristic silence on the issue of racial injustice, when it is so clearly morally wrong. King goes on to express fears that if the Church fails to regain the sacrificial spirit of the bygone era, it will soon be "dismissed as an irrelevant social club with no meaning for the twentieth century." 4

Focuses on the appeal to reason or logic *(logos)*. Note: backed by citation from the text and commentary by the author.

Thinking as a Writer

Understanding the Moves in a Rhetorical Analysis

Using The Art of Questioning: Anatomy of a Rhetorical Analysis (page 458) and the marginal annotations to the reading, work through Norton's rhetorical analysis. What function or functions does each paragraph have? That is, describe *what each paragraph does and how it contributes to the analysis as a whole.* Finish your study by making a list of the possible moves you can make when you write your rhetorical analysis. ■

What Can I Write About?

You could write a rhetorical analysis of virtually anything–a political speech, a newspaper editorial, a blog, a literary passage, a scene in a film or play, an overheard conversation. When choosing a text to analyze for an assignment, look for something that intrigues you, that you want to comment on or explain the workings of. Here are some possibilities:

- **An advertisement.** Print ads in magazines are often good choices. Because magazines have definite, well-defined readerships, you can assess the ad's effectiveness especially well.
- **A commercial or institutional website,** especially the home page. Because online access matters so much to businesses, universities, government agencies, museums, and so on, special effort goes into creating the right impression.
- **A song lyric,** if the words are interesting enough to make analysis worthwhile.

How Do I Prepare to Write a Rhetorical Analysis?

When preparing to write a rhetorical analysis, consider what the task requires, voice and style, and development and organization.

Task Requirements

First read the text carefully and critically. Before drafting your analysis, examine all of the elements of the text by asking yourself the following questions:

- **What is the writer's or speaker's overall point (thesis) and purpose** (to persuade, to shock, to criticize)?
- **Who is the intended audience?**
- **What kind of emotion or tone does the text create,** and how do you respond to it on an emotional level?

- **What kind of language is used** (slang, technical jargon, formal, conversational), and how are sentences structured (short and choppy, questions or exclamations)?
- **Are there any significant shifts in pattern and structure or in tone and language?**

As you answer these questions, think about the details in the text that helped you answer them and why the author chose them. This will help you make a strong argument in your analysis.

Voice and Style

The voice and style of your analysis need to match the context. For example, an overly formal tone when analyzing a singer's connection to the audience in a hip-hop song might diminish your credibility, creating questions in your audience's mind about your ability to understand the song. Similarly, an angry tone in an analysis of a political speech might lead your readers to question whether you are unbiased enough to assess the speech fairly.

Development and Organization

A key feature of a good rhetorical analysis is demonstrating where the text itself supports your claims. This means you cannot simply state that a pop song is targeted at an audience of teenage girls; you need to include quotations from the song to show how you have arrived at this conclusion. Good ideas need details to back them up.

What Are the Steps in Writing a Rhetorical Analysis?

Because a good rhetorical analysis requires very close examination of the text it discusses, you will need to move back and forth between writing your analysis and rereading the text. Keep an open mind throughout this process, and you might discover new angles and points to develop in your analysis.

1. **Draft your analysis.** As you write your first draft, you will begin building the argument for the thesis of your analysis, which is the point that you want to make about the rhetorical situation in your text. Work your way through the text, gathering evidence to support your thesis and all points you make in developing your thesis. Careful reexamination of the text can result in discovering a different or better point you want to make. Allow yourself time, then, to draft and revise so that you can change the direction when a new idea comes to you.
2. **Revise your analysis.** Read your analysis critically by asking these questions:
   - **Does the opening introduce the text and make my main point clear?**
   - **Am I moving from point to point based on the needs of my argument?** Does the logic of my essay too closely follow the sequence of the text? Structure your analysis to meet the needs of your argument.

- **Does my analysis offer more than a summary of the text?** A brief summary at the beginning of the analysis is fine, but after that you should be making points about how the text works and providing evidence and commentary about the evidence.
- **Have I offered enough detail to support my claims?** Are there any comments that I have made but not supported? Have I used the best evidence in the text to support each point?

3. **Edit your analysis.** A rhetorical analysis needs to integrate its own ideas with the ideas from the text it is examining. Be sure to link what you are saying to whatever you are citing from the text to back up your point. That is, your reader must understand clearly which point your evidence supports and how it supports each point.
4. **Proofread your analysis.** Any paper should be proofread carefully for errors. In a rhetorical analysis, you need to pay extra attention to quotations to ensure that you have cited them accurately.

BEST PRACTICES Writing a Rhetorical Analysis

When you are writing a close analysis of a text, you must refer to details from the text, quote it, and describe it. A fine line exists between enough detail and too much. You must draft, revise, and edit with this in mind to ensure that you are not flooding your audience with too much information not relevant to the point you are making.

A good rhetorical analysis is itself rhetorical, an effort to convince others that your analysis has merit. Assume the audience has read the text you are analyzing but lacks information that will help in understanding the text better and needs your interpretation to grasp how the text works.

CREDIT

page 459: Courtesy of Ginny Norton

CHAPTER 23

Writing a Reflection

ENGAGING QUESTIONS

In this chapter, you will engage with the following questions:

- What is the relationship between reflection and thinking?
- What are the purposes of reflection?
- How do writers identify appropriate topics for reflection?
- How do writers prepare for writing reflections?

"IT MAKES YOU STOP AND THINK," WE SAY, WHEN SOMETHING HAPPENS THAT DISTURBS OUR NORMAL EXPECTATIONS, our usually half-awake approach to the world around us. Stopping and thinking is the essence of exploratory writing. The genre that best represents what we can do when we take time to think is reflection.

What Is a Reflection?

In a **reflection,** a writer explores or ponders a subject, examining ideas or feelings about the subject or contemplating connections with related subjects. Rather than making an argument or persuading an audience, reflections offer writer and readers a space to think about experience. Reflections reveal an individual's thought process to others.

THE ART OF QUESTIONING Anatomy of a Reflection

Ask and answer the following questions:

1. Topic: **What do I wonder about?** A reflection focuses on one subject that opens further avenues of thought.
2. Personal connection to the topic: **How am I involved with my topic?** Reflection demonstrates the writer's curiosity and ideas; thus, the writer refers to his or her thinking in the writing.
3. Details: **What examples, cases, and details help connect my thoughts with my own and my readers' lived experiences?** Reflection moves back and forth between abstract thoughts and concrete experiences.
4. Conclusion: **Where has my thinking led me?** A reflection is like a journey; your thinking should take you and your readers to a destination, or conclusion. The ending should provide a sense of focus and closure.

Why Write a Reflection?

People write reflections in a wide variety of settings: private journals, public blogs, newspaper or magazine columns, and portfolios–basically any place where ideas or subjects can or need to be contemplated. Reflections allow writers to think through any topic that concerns them and to invite readers to comment on what they have written or respond with their own reflections on the same or similar themes.

In your coursework, you might be asked to write reflective essays or journal entries that respond to course readings or class discussions. At the end of a course, you might be asked to reflect on all of the essays that you wrote, on your own writing process, or on what you learned during a class project. You could also be asked in a writing class to write a reflection on whatever interests you. In any of these tasks, the goal is the same: *Explore the subject and demonstrate the thinking that you have done.*

EXAMPLE Reflection

The Wonder of Ordinary Places (Blog Post, May 13, 2011)
Julian Hoffman

Julian Hoffman is an award-winning nature writer. Originally from England and Canada, he now lives in northern Greece, on the shores of Lake Prespa, where his careful observations of his surroundings inspire reflective writing such as this excerpt from a blog post.

Announces topic immediately.

Clarifies the special awareness of children, lost too often in adults.

1 When it comes to wonder and the natural world, children are the true specialists. They are particularly open to that state of astonishment that we associate with awe. A child, in the most common of landscapes, is capable, through a combination of intense perception and imagination, of discovering an entire world in the smallest fragment of nature. It might be among wildflowers and weeds at the edge of a scrubby field where an iridescent emerald beetle or the bright flight of a butterfly can hold a child's attention for several minutes. It could be along a river bank where a child excitedly follows an oak leaf as it travels downstream. It might simply be the prints of an animal, perfectly preserved by snow, that captures a child's imagination.

The shore of Lake Prespa photographed in the mist by the author.
Julian Hoffman

2 What is so remarkable about children's perception, even more so than its intensity, is that it is characterized by an equality of interest.

Everything a child encounters in nature, no matter how small, offers possibility and is therefore equally fascinating. Children make little distinction between major and minor motifs. A feather found on the beach is as wondrous as the creature it belonged to.

> Note how the writer moves from an abstract idea to a concrete example that explains the idea.

3 As childhood is left behind, adults tend to shed that capacity for curiosity, that spirit that animates the smallest of things. We yearn for greater and faster excitements; we seek larger vistas, grander views. But in a contemporary Western world increasingly obsessed by speed, style and seduction, there is perhaps all the more need to reclaim the ordinary, to celebrate the everyday. Because the ordinary, when perceived in the spirit of curiosity, is actually extraordinary.

> A good move in reflective writing is to point out a problem and explore its causes.

> Reflective writing has a focus, a point. Here is the main idea in Hoffman's blog post.

4 The American writer and naturalist, Barry Lopez, once wrote that "with the loss of self-consciousness, the landscape opens." This, I believe, can be understood in two ways. First, when we let go of our constant self-awareness and regain something of a child's immense curiosity and interest in the world 'out there,' the world around us, we become more attuned to its wonders. Leaving something of our self behind, other lives arise in its place. That is when the ordinary transforms into the extraordinary, and a landscape like the shore of Great Prespa Lake becomes something else.

> Reflection often comments on what others have said.

> Great Prespa Lake is near the author's home in Greece. Note that the writer ties his reflection to his own life experiences.

. . .

5 Barry Lopez's assertion about landscapes, however, provides a second clue to engaging more deeply with place. To be self-conscious means not only to be aware of one's own mind and actions, but to be conscious of being observed and therefore embarrassed as a result. Self-consciousness prevents us from doing many things, but in the case of a landscape it can stand in the way of knowing it.

6 Landscapes are best learned through proximity. Wherever children go, they are tempted to climb trees. They slither through long grasses like snakes, eyeing up insects excitedly from their own height. They make hide-aways in dense shrubs. Children catch frogs in their hands and then slowly open their fingers to reveal them. They collect caterpillars in jars, fascinated by the coming transformation. Children's inquisitive experience of the natural world is hands-on, intimate and utterly without self-consciousness. They are part of a place, not distinct from it.

> Note how the author uses details to make the curiosity of children concrete and real.

7 When we approach similarly, with a sense of freedom unburdened by embarrassment, we open ourselves to the quieter aspects of a landscape. How the light falls through the willow leaves, passing through them like waves. How bear prints and otter tracks lead us first along the beach and then into their lives. The way tiny, resplendent butterflies gather around a flower. There are the curious sounds of water and reptiles in the marsh. How the wind breathes mysteriously through the reeds, their seeds catching the light as they float above the river. The way the bark of a silver birch feels like ancient paper in our hands. Walk into any pocket of the shoreline landscape and there is a world of new moments unfolding.

The conclusion arrives at a persuasive point about the consequences of the failure to appreciate the wonders of the ordinary.

All landscapes contain the seeds of astonishment. Whether we let them take root or not is up to us. But if we become aware of the wonders within easy reach, those close at hand and part of our daily experience, then the everyday places that we live amongst become less easy to dismiss. The greatest threat facing many landscapes is their assumed irrelevance. When a place is perceived to hold little of interest or importance then a whole landscape can turn invisible, and be treated accordingly. Though any child will show you there is no such thing as a place without interest. 8

Thinking as a Writer

Understanding the Moves in a Reflection

Using The Art of Questioning: Anatomy of a Reflection (page 464) and the marginal annotations to the reading, discuss "The Wonder of Ordinary Places" in class. How does the author establish his subject? How does he develop it? The photograph is beautiful and eye-catching, but what does it contribute to what the author wants us to think about? How does he connect adult life with the neglect of nature and with indifference to the environment? The blog post is primarily exploratory, but how does it also inform and persuade? ■

What Can I Write About?

You could write a reflection on anything, from what you ate at breakfast to the best way to avoid nuclear warfare. Whatever topic you choose, remember that a reflection is more than a report or summary of what happened or what you know. It has a goal: To explore an interesting thought, confront a dilemma, prove you read and thought critically about an assigned text, or share an experience. For example, no one really cares what you ate for breakfast, but the process of pondering the statement on your cereal box that no genetically modified organisms (GMOs) are contained in it might lead you on an interesting mental journey. Perhaps thinking about food labeling, GMOs, organic foods, and pesticides makes you wonder whether you need to be trained as a scientist simply to know what to eat for breakfast.

Therefore, whether you have an assigned topic, such as the novel you read for class last week or the essay you just finished revising, or whether you can write on any topic you choose, you can come up with stronger and more interesting ideas by asking yourself the following questions:

- **What interests me? What gets my brain working?** To have something to say in a reflection, you need to be thinking about the topic in a personal and interesting way. So if you are searching for a topic, consider topics you often think about, things that intrigue or bother you, make you angry, or puzzle you. For an assigned topic, such as reflecting on a book or a movie, focus on the moments in the text or film that you reacted to strongly, that connected with your life and concerns, or that stuck in your head for some other reason or reminded you of something else.
- **What are my own experiences? What is happening around me? What concepts do I know about that will help me evaluate a situation?** Reflective writing comes from you, and so it is crucial to bring your experiences and knowledge to bear. If you try to write about something you have no knowledge of or connection to, your reflection will lack depth. Maybe you are reading Jane Austen's *Emma* and could not care less whether or not she finds a husband. However, you are also taking an economics class and are intrigued by how the whole process of selecting a spouse in this novel seems more like business than love. "Love as Economics" would be a good angle on the novel, a way to reflect on what it shows us about courtship and marriage.

How Do I Prepare to Write a Reflection?

Consider what the task requires, voice and style, development and organization, and visual appeal.

Task Requirements

Regardless of what your topic is, you need to think about the following intertwined questions in order to help you shape how you write about that topic.

- **What is my purpose in writing? Why am I reflecting on this topic?** The purpose of your writing will influence what aspect of your subject you discuss. If you're writing for an assignment that is designed to measure the thoughtfulness you have put into a required reading, then reflecting only on how it reminds you of what happened to you last week would not achieve your goal. You would instead need to focus on isolating and exploring particular moments from the reading—even if part of how you explore them relates to what happened last week. In contrast, if your goal is to entertain your readers, you would need an angle that opens your subject to humor or a combination of humor and serious insight.
- **Who is my audience?** Your audience will shape not only how you write your reflection but also what direction it takes. If your reflection is just for you, then

it might focus on things that only you know. If it is for your instructor or a school magazine, then you will need to think about what others might think about the topic and how you need to connect your ideas and reflection to that broader view.

Voice and Style

The most crucial aspect of the voice and style for reflection is that it should represent you and the mental exploration in which you are engaged. As long as you are sharing this reflection with an audience, then you are inviting them into your mind, and so you want the writing to reflect your personality. Based on what your purpose is and who your audience is, however, you might need to showcase different aspects of your personality: Are you questioning and speculative about this topic? Are there feelings that need to be evoked when you explore this topic, such as joy, amazement, sorrow, or frustration? Is your attitude on this subject humorous and witty? Let your angle determine your voice and style.

Development and Organization

Although a reflection may resemble a mental journey through a topic, our minds work in messy and confusing ways we cannot preserve entirely in writing. We free-associate, have random ideas pop into our heads, or have partial images or a vague feeling about events or moments that stand in for more detailed and complete ideas or descriptions. Therefore, when we translate mental contemplation into writing that will be shared with others, we have to *identify the connections that move from one point to the next and develop our ideas and discussions more completely.*

A reflection can be organized rather conventionally: Introduce the topic, explore the several aspects that you want to discuss, and offer a final thought on what this mental journey reveals. Or you may find that you need to move from point to point less predictably, introducing the main idea, following one path of discussion that might lead to a new path, but then coming back to the original idea before beginning again along a new idea. In all cases, the reflection needs to move in directions that will make sense to your audience and offer them something to think about.

Visual Appeal

Depending upon the goal of your reflection, consider graphics and how your writing will appear on the page. If it is in a blog, you may want the look of the page to be an expression of yourself. If you are writing about an image or a scene, it can help to include a photograph.

What Are the Steps in Writing a Reflection?

The first step is to devote time to thinking, because reflection is thought. The question is: When do you move from thinking about your subject to thinking through your subject as you write about it? Depending upon the topic and goal, you might want to try to preserve the initial thought process as much as possible. In this case, the writing is the thinking. In other cases, the reflection might be more of a looking backward—after the fact—in which case you may want to spend a larger chunk of time recalling and thinking before you begin your draft.

1. **Draft your reflection.** Once you begin your draft for a reflection, you should allow your ideas and thoughts to move more freely than you would for an informative or argumentative essay. Even if you are writing your reflection after much thought, the process of writing is a continuation of that thought. Writing without editing your ideas or restricting where they go has the potential to lead you to new ideas or connections. Use the draft as a space for thinking and developing ideas; use the revision as a space for streamlining, reordering, and shaping the ideas.
2. **Revise your reflection.** If you have used your draft as an exploratory space, you might well need to revise to make the logic clearer and the ideas more coherent. However, in a reflection, revision should not eliminate speculation, multiple and even contradictory or overlapping ideas, and, in general, an open-ended quality. Therefore, focus on making the reflection as interesting, as thoughtful, and as coherent as possible. To do that, ask yourself the following questions:

   - **Do I introduce my subject in a way that will interest the reader?** The focus of a reflection should be something that someone would want to join you in contemplating.
   - **Is there logic in the move from one point to another?** Are the connections between the ideas clear? Remember that free association without transitions makes reflection hard for a reader to follow.
   - **Are there any ideas that seem to detract from the reflection or that do not add much to its content or interest?** You do not need to include everything that you think about your subject; even a reflection needs to choose the most relevant and important ideas. Do not be reluctant to cut a line of thought that seemed promising but failed to pay off.
   - **Are there shifts in voice or style?** Have a good reason if your voice and style changes. For example, you could begin a reflection with a humorous scene that leads to a serious point and becomes the focus of what you have to say.
   - **Are there any ideas that need to be more fully developed?** Be attentive to what you have said, for often better ideas will come to you when you let your mind play with what you already have on the page. If you have the sense that "I did not quite arrive at what I wanted to say there," give such places special attention after allowing a day or two to pass. You will be surprised how often what is missing will suddenly occur to you.

3. **Edit your reflection.** Reflections have a more personal or casual style, but when you share them with others you need to edit as you would with any other piece of writing. Look especially for awkward sentences, wordiness, and transitions

between paragraphs. The key question is: Does this sentence say what I mean, not almost, but exactly? Work with it until it does.

4. **Proofread your reflection.** Make sure that your reflection reflects well upon you. Check for misspellings and grammatical errors.

CREDIT

CHAPTER 24

Writing a Visual Analysis

ENGAGING QUESTIONS

In this chapter, you will engage with the following questions:

- What does it mean to analyze a visual text?
- What are the purposes of visual analysis?
- How do writers choose appropriate subjects for visual analysis?
- How do writers prepare to write a visual analysis?
- How do writers apply the steps of the writing process to a visual analysis assignment?

"IMAGE IS EVERYTHING," A WELL-KNOWN COMMERCIAL TOLD US, and if that has some truth to it, then images have everything to do with creating the public perception of an organization, company, university, or individual. The amount of time and money devoted to creating and managing visual impressions is hard to imagine though we see the results everywhere: in the body design of automobiles, clothing, the architecture of buildings, store windows, college catalogs, and so on. Surfing the Internet exposes us to a sea of images, all designed to catch our attention, sell products and services, and form a favorable impression of whoever created each website.

With images everywhere, and image control so important, it is hardly surprising that assessing visuals has also become crucially important. Part of assessment is **visual analysis,** *taking an image apart to see how it works.*

What Is a Visual Analysis?

A visual analysis examines visual "texts," such as print, billboards, online advertisements, photographs, and paintings—anything you can examine that was created by people. It also includes visual aspects that are part of other texts, like the images and graphics on television, in movies, and in printed texts such as books and magazines. A visual analysis examines an image to see how it is constructed, the purpose being to understand its parts and how they work together. Usually an evaluation is at least implied; that is, analysis answers the question, **"How well does the image work?"**

THE ART OF QUESTIONING Anatomy of a Visual Analysis

Ask and answer the following questions:

1. The visual text: **How can I represent the visual in my writing?** If possible, include a copy of the image you are assessing in your paper. The size and quality of the image matter, especially if you are calling attention to details the reader must be able to see to follow your discussion.
2. Description of the image: **What do I see that matters?** Complex images cannot be fully described, so you have to decide what matters, what you want your reader to notice. In this way, you show the image to your reader through your eyes.
3. Identification of purpose: **What is the image trying to accomplish?** We have already mentioned commercial purposes, the most common motivation for creating an image, but images are also created for critical and artistic purposes, such as the one in the example of visual analysis below.
4. Identification of audience: **Whom does the image hope to reach?** Because images are so widely distributed and anyone can view them, it is easy to neglect an important fact: *They always have a target audience in mind.* Becoming aware of the target audience, therefore, is important for analysis.
5. Analysis of key aspects: **What impact do the image's details have? What do they add up to or mean?** You need to say what impact or meaning the image has and how the details relate to impact or meaning.

Why Write a Visual Analysis?

Learning to understand how visual texts work helps you observe them critically rather than simply passively receiving the messages. It can also help you understand how to create such images successfully.

Writing a visual analysis amounts to, first, thinking about what comprises the image and how the elements work together to present an idea and, second, writing an explanation of your assessment. Art scholars and critics write visual analyses of paintings and photographs all the time, as do columnists or bloggers who write about contemporary culture, and marketing professionals who are working on new advertising campaigns.

You might be asked to write a visual analysis for a variety of different classes, from history and politics to art and business, because visual images are so important in our culture. Writing a visual analysis, like writing any analysis, helps develop skills important to critical thinking generally: the habit of taking things apart to see how they work and the ability to explain their relationships. The following student paper analyzes an artistic photograph using close observation, personal insights, and secondary sources for information about the photographer and his work. The photograph is housed in the collections of Duke University Library, but can be viewed online here: https://crashinglybeautiful.tumblr.com/post/1131486438/william-gedney-three-girls-in-kitchen.

EXAMPLE Visual Analysis

Jarol 1

Ashley Jarol

ENGL 1302

Professor Channell

4 October 2017

Three Girls in a Kentucky Kitchen

Background on photographer: part of context for analysis.

William Gedney was a documentary photographer whose best-known photographs are of poor people in India and in the Appalachian coal fields of Kentucky. He received little recognition for his work until after his death of AIDS at age 56 in 1989, even though he had managed to get a one-man show of his work at the Museum of Modern Art in New York in 1968. This picture of three girls in a kitchen was featured in the New York exhibition, and it is now part of its permanent collection (William Gedney Photographs). 1

He took the picture in July 1964 during a visit to the mining town of Leatherwood, Kentucky. Gedney lived for eleven days in this family's house. They welcomed him into their home even though the father had been laid off from his job in the mines, and they had twelve children at the time. Gedney kept notebooks and journals about his travels and his pictures, and he recorded the names and ages of everyone in the family. He and the family kept in touch through letters. He sent them Christmas presents, and he visited them again in 1972 and took more pictures of them. In 1977, he sent them $35 with a note that said, "I made myself a promise that if I ever sold any of the pictures I took of your family I would split any money with you. I sold my first picture from those I took. It is of the three girls in the kitchen" (Sartor and Dyer 74). 2

More context for the analysis: the family of the girls in the photo and artist's relationship with them.

Gedney's photographs of the Cornett family capture everyday aspects of their lives. In this picture, we see the simple interior of a miner's kitchen and three young girls peeling potatoes. The picture seems to illustrate Gedney's belief that the lives of ordinary people made the best subjects for his pictures. "I prefer the ordinary action, the intimate gesture, an image whose form is an instinctive reaction to the material" ("Short Distances"). Gedney saw something beautiful and intimate in this simple moment and instinctively took his picture. The picture shows that in contrast to the stereotypical view of the never-ending poverty and hopelessness of the Appalachian coalfields, there is grace and beauty in these people's lives. 3

Connects characteristics of photo to artist's interests and intentions.

Main claim: photo counters stereotypes about Appalachian people.

Even though many details in the kitchen show how poor the family was, there is a cheerful feeling to the room. We see the bare wood floor, the window with no curtain, and the dishes piled up as if there is no cabinet to store them, but the walls are papered with a cheerful floral print that made me think of angels flying upward. 4

Jarol 2

Everything is worn, but the floor and table top seem clean and well cared for. The room could be dark and dreary on a different day but at the moment of the picture it is filled with light. The natural sunlight illuminates the room and gives the picture warmth and lightness. Rays of sun fall on the refrigerator and the floor, and there is even a prism of reflected light on the floor in the right foreground. The sun reflects off of the painted ceiling and makes the single bare light bulb look transparent. Gedney chose to put a lot of ceiling into the picture, maybe because the ceiling was so filled with light. If you took away the ceiling, the picture would lose some of its lightness. Also, through the bright window, the viewer can see out into the sunny backyard. This gives the picture a feeling of lightness and openness.

Close attention to details of photo in relation to what the author sees as "lightness and openness." Note organization: first, the scene, then the girls.

But it is the girls themselves that give the feeling of summer and lightness. 5
Each of them stands on one foot. They look so animated and graceful. They wear summer dresses, and with their knees pulled up, their skirts look like sails on a boat. But their poses also make me see them as dancers. I have been dancing nearly all my life, and when I first looked at the three girls, I noticed that each one has a natural balance and grace. The tallest and probably the oldest of the sisters stands on the right with a straight back and excellent posture. The sun outlines the curve of her slender arm. The girl in the center balances on the side of her foot. She has positioned her body so that the sunlight falls over her shoulder, making it easier to see what she is doing. I like to imagine that the summer sun is warming her back as she works. The youngest girl is taking a break from peeling her potato and seems to be in the midst of telling a story. She leans against the refrigerator with her back arched, so that only her head and shoulders touch the refrigerator. Although the position might make another person seem clumsy and off balance, she looks perfectly at ease. Her arms are flung outward and behind her, as if she has just reached a point in her story that needed extra body expression.

Good connection of analysis to the author's experience as a dancer.

As Gedney said in the quotation cited above, he wanted to capture the 6
intimate moments in the lives of his subjects. There is an intimacy to the kitchen. Because of the frame of the picture, the viewer seems to be in the room. The girls are surrounded by the ceiling, floor, and walls. We feel like we are looking into their lives, just as Gedney did, but what is interesting is that they don't seem to be even aware that he is there. One critic noted that this is common in Gedney's photographs: "William Gedney's subjects rarely acknowledge the photographer's presence. They appear to ignore the viewer too, frequently showing us their backs. . . . In only a few portraits does the subject lift a wide-eyed gaze to the camera. For the most part, Gedney's people act out the rhythms of unobserved lives" (Gunnell).

Good use of source to confirm author's analysis.

Most middle-class people don't see the everyday lives of people as poor as 7
the Cornetts. If we don't see them, we make assumptions about them that may not be true. The Cornett family did live a hard life, but Gedney wanted to show through his photographs that even the poorest families have grace and beauty.

Short conclusion reminds us of author's main point.

Jarol 3

Works Cited

Gunnell, Barbara. "Simple Truth." *New Statesman,* 7 Feb. 2000.

Sartor, Margaret, and Geoff Dyer, editors. *What Was True: The Photographs and Notebooks of William Gedney.* W.W. Norton, 2000.

"Short Distances and Definite Places: The Photographs of William Gedney." San Francisco Museum of Modern Art, 8 Oct. 2011, documentarystudies.duke.edu/exhibits/past-exhibits/short-distances-and-definite-places-the-photographs-of-william-gedney.

William Gedney: Photographs and Writings. Digital Collections, Duke University Libraries, 12 Oct. 2009, library.duke.edu/digitalcollections/gedney/.

Questions for Discussion

Why does Jarol provide the amount and kind of background information she does? How does she understand the point, meaning, or impact of the photograph? What details did she call attention to and why did she select those? How does she connect those details to meaning and impact? How did her analysis help you better understand how the photo works? ■

What Can I Write About?

You can find an image to analyze simply by looking around you: online resources, magazines, newspapers, advertisements, art galleries, and so on. Choose a visual whose content interests you, either because you know something about the subject or because the subject allows you to talk about other topics that interest you. For example, if you were interested in fashion, you might want to analyze an advertisement for Diesel sportswear—but even if you choose your jeans and t-shirts based on comfort over fashion, you might still analyze the advertisement from a different angle, such as ideas of masculinity and femininity.

Ask yourself the following questions as you look for an image to analyze:

- **Is this an image (or series of images) that deals with a topic I am interested in, a topic that I have some knowledge about, or a topic that I want to think more about?** If you could not care less about advertising, for instance, analyze an image from a photographic essay, a painting, or the architecture of a building.
- **Is this an image with complexities?** Although any image can be analyzed, some are so simple that a written analysis would not be worthwhile. You want an image

complex enough to provide an opportunity for substantial analysis. Bear in mind, however, that an image can *appear* to be simple and become quite interesting and complex as you begin to see more and more in it. The Gedney photograph above is a good example. It is a simple composition that becomes more interesting as you read the student essay and contemplate its details.

- **Is this an image with rich cultural connections and implications?** Sometimes the image itself is less interesting than the cultural context in which it functions. For example, for years the "food pyramid" was the standard image for representing good nutrition. However, evidence accumulated to show that many people did not understand the message of the image. Nutritional experts also began to doubt the accuracy of the information it displayed. And so recently the "food plate" has begun to replace it. In itself, the food plate is not an especially interesting image, but the cultural context of the obesity epidemic makes the image worth analyzing as a way of conveying information effectively.

How Do I Prepare to Write a Visual Analysis?

Consider what the task requires, voice and style, development and organization, and visual appeal.

Task Requirements

Preparation for writing a visual analysis first requires spending time with the image and thinking about everything you see in it and everything that it brings to mind. Write down what you see and what you are thinking about with each detail. Then analyze the rhetorical situation of the image by asking the following questions:

- **What is the purpose of this image?** Is it an artistic representation, an ad to make you buy something, a photograph of war that argues for peace? You must understand what the goal of the image is before you can assess whether and how it achieves its purpose.
- **Who is the intended audience?** An ad in a magazine, for instance, will often target the magazine's readership. A car company will stress the practicality of a car in a consumer publication and the fun of driving it in a car magazine.
- **What are the most important elements of the image?** In any image there will be foreground and background. Study both carefully. What you are looking for is pattern, how the elements that make up the foreground and background work together as a whole and how each element contributes to the image's meaning and impact. Remember: You are not just describing the image. You are sharing *your understanding* of it, which means showing readers part-whole relationships.

Voice and Style

The tone and style of your analysis depend first on why you are writing it. A visual analysis written for a blog will be different in tone from a visual analysis for an art history class. Second, even within those different purposes, how you relate to the image makes a big difference. Are you an objective observer of an artifact from popular culture? Are you a suspicious critic of an advertisement that is trying to push your buttons? Are you interpreting art for an audience unfamiliar with the artwork?

Development and Organization

The structure of Jarol's visual analysis (pages 474-76) offers a good idea of organization:

1. **Example visual analysis:** Offers your reader information about who created the image and/or the image's function and context.
2. **Image description:** Calls your reader's attention to features of the image worth close attention.
3. **Image explanation:** Relates details to a central meaning or intended impact.
4. **Conclusion:** Leaves the reader with a memorable sense of how the image works.

Of course, this general idea of structure permits many variations, depending on what your image requires for analysis and the particular angle you have on it. For example, analyzing a television ad or a movie scene might require isolating its key moments—perhaps presented as stills—and repeating 2 and 3 above with each key moment.

Development amounts to repeating these four key moves: point to a feature; describe it; comment on the impression you have of it or what you think it means; and connect with related features. Remember that description of an image is not an analysis; you have to explain how the whole image relates to its parts or features. You have to interpret it or show how it works. Having an interpretation without commenting on the details of the image also is not an analysis; you need to show that your understanding of the image can explain what the reader sees.

Visual Appeal

Whenever possible, include a copy of the image that you are analyzing. You might need to take a photograph of a painting or billboard, scan a print ad, or save a screen image from the Web. Remember that your readers need to see an image large enough and clear enough to see what you want them to see. If you are comparing the image to other similar ones, include an example or two to help you make the comparisons.

What Are the Steps in Writing a Visual Analysis?

A good visual analysis requires a very close examination of the image it discusses. Therefore, you need to make sure to keep the image in front of you as you write, thinking about how all of the details of the image work together.

1. **Draft your analysis.** As you write your first draft, you will begin building the argument for the thesis of your analysis, which is the overall point that you want to make about the image. Build your analysis around this point, working your way through the ideas that support your overall analysis with in-depth discussion of specific elements in the composition of the image. Keep an open mind throughout the initial draft process, and you might discover new angles and points to develop. You can adjust your main point in revision as you incorporate new insights.

2. **Revise your analysis.** Read your analysis critically by asking these questions:
   - Does the opening introduce the text and make my main point clear?
   - Am I moving from point to point based on the needs of my argument? Or does the logic of my analysis seem more like a list of points?
   - Does my analysis offer more than a description of the image? Do I need to highlight why these moments are important and identify what they achieve in the text?
   - Have I offered enough detail to support my claims? Are there any comments that I have made but not supported?
3. **Edit your analysis.** A visual analysis needs to smoothly develop its own ideas as it examines and describes the image. Look for lack of transitions between your points and descriptions of the image.
4. **Proofread your analysis.** Any paper should be proofread carefully for errors. Carefully check spelling and punctuation to ensure that your writing is as clear as your point.

CREDIT

page 474: Courtesy of Ashley Jarol

CHAPTER 25

Writing a Literary Analysis

ENGAGING QUESTIONS

In this chapter, you will engage with the following questions:

- What does it mean to interpret a text?
- Why do readers interpret literary works?
- How do readers interpret literature?
- How do the elements of the rhetorical situation apply to the writing process for a literary analysis?
- How do writers apply the steps of the writing process to a literary analysis?

THE GREAT NATIVE AMERICAN NOVELIST AND POET N. SCOTT MOMADAY speaks of the power of language to allow us to realize our greatest potential as human beings. In his book *The Man Made of Words*, he writes, "Language is the stuff of the imagination. The imagination is the creative aspect of language. It enables us to use language to its highest potential. It enables us to realize a reality beyond the ordinary, it enables us to create and recreate ourselves in story and literature."[1]

Momaday is talking about creative writing and its predecessor, oral storytelling, and all the many forms in which language allows creative expression in both fiction and nonfiction, prose and poetry: stories, novels, poems, plays, and essays, to name just some of the kinds of language we categorize as literature. As literature, these genres (or types of writing) are not merely entertainment (although they can be highly entertaining.) Literature entertains, but its purpose is the purpose of all art: to **reveal**—that is, *to draw back the curtain and show some significant part of (or angle on) reality.*

Once we find ourselves thinking about what a work of literature reveals, the question of all interpretation, "What does it mean?" arises. Works of literature usually do not interpret themselves; they do not tell us what they mean. Rather, they show us something, and it is up to us, as readers, to say what they mean. The novelist Annie Proulx said that her stories are not finished until a

1. N. Scott Momaday, *The Man Made of Words* (New York: St. Martin's, 1997), 1–3.

reader reads them: Her role is to create the story; our role is to interpret it. This chapter is about how to do that, how to go about answering the what-does-it-mean question.

What Is Interpretation?

We will rarely disagree about what a work of literature reveals, the part of reality it depicts or shows us. However, we will normally answer the key question, "What does it mean?" differently.

Consequently, because works of literature can be interpreted in different ways, an interpretation is an argument. That is, you offer your view of what the work means and cite evidence from the text itself to back it up. In effect you are saying, "Try seeing the story or poem as I see it" or "Here is how I understand it." You want your reader to share your interpretation, to find it convincing, but whether other interpreters agree with you matters less than contributing to their understanding and appreciation of meanings in the story or poem. If you help them to see the significance of parts of the work they may have missed, for instance, you have accomplished what an interpretation ought to do. The same purpose applies to anything else you might interpret, such as an essay, a film, a podcast–or, as in this chapter, a poem. If you are answering the question, What does it mean? you are interpreting, and you answer the question by arguing for your understanding of the text.

Why Interpret Literature?

First, *literary works make our sense of reality*. Essays, plays, poems, and stories show us, as Momaday says, "a reality beyond the ordinary." Serious literature expands our horizons by showing us the world through a creative lens and helps us imagine other possibilities for our lives.

Second, literature helps to make our sense of identity. Just as we know ourselves through the family stories we hear and tell, we know who we are through the literature of our people's culture.

Third, literature connects us with other ways of being human. To the extent that we can understand places, times, people, and events remote from our own experience, we grasp them through novels, plays, and personal narratives. Reading about others' experiences expands our understanding and empathy for people we may know only through common stereotypes.

In short, serious literature challenges our natural tendency to interpret our experiences and think more deeply about our lives. In literature, we sense there is something intriguing or profound going on, some special insight that we cannot fully grasp without interpretation. Literature of high quality rewards interpretation. When we begin to see why an author has crafted a work and what it shows us about human beings and life, suddenly we have a new way of seeing our own experiences.

How Do Writers Interpret Literature?

The key idea in literary interpretation is to help readers see meaning in a literary work, not "The Meaning," but *a* meaning that you have discovered through careful reading and close observation of features of the text.

- Reading can include gathering some background information about the author and the circumstances of the work's creation.
- Careful reading is slow and attentive, noting and marking what seems significant and interesting to you. Another reader may notice other features of the text, but your paper will have its own angle on the work because of what strikes you as important.
- Interpretation requires engaging with the text and asking questions such as why certain details were included or why certain words were chosen rather than others. Think about the effect of the author's choices.
- Interpretation usually involves looking for patterns and repetitions in the work, such as repeated ideas, themes, and images and sounds. Reading poetry aloud helps you notice the effects of word choice and sentence structures.
- Interpretation can involve reading what other critics have said about a particular work. You do not want to echo what they have said, but you might find something of your own to say in response to their ideas, even to disagree with their interpretation.
- Note that your analysis is not a summary. While you will need to provide evidence from the text for your thesis about what the work means, you should assume that your readers have also read the work and do not need you to inform them about what it says. Use quotations and paraphrases in service of your thesis and reasons only.

Your essay will have all or most of the following features:

- Background information necessary for understanding the work.
- A thesis, or central contention, about what the work means.
- Points that clarify, explain, or confirm the thesis.
- Evidence–brief summaries, paraphrases, and quotations from the text–that supports each point.

Your instructor may stipulate that you interpret a poem or story, possibly a particular one. The following reading and its discussion illustrate one way of approaching a poem. The chapter also includes an example of how one student went about the process of writing an interpretation of a short story.

READING 25.1

Stopping by Woods on a Snowy Evening

ROBERT FROST

Robert Frost (1874–1963) was one of the most celebrated American poets, winning four Pulitzer Prizes and the Congressional Gold Medal. This poem is one of his best-known and loved works. As you read, consider what has made it a classic work.

Whose woods these are I think I know.
His house is in the village, though;
He will not see me stopping here
To watch his woods fill up with snow.

My little horse must think it queer
To stop without a farmhouse near
Between the woods and frozen lake
The darkest evening of the year.

He gives his harness bells a shake
To ask if there is some mistake.
The only other sound's the sweep
Of easy wind and downy flake.

The woods are lovely, dark, and deep,
But I have promises to keep,
And miles to go before I sleep,
And miles to go before I sleep.

The key question in all interpretation is *Why this*? It is the question we should ask of anything said or done in a short story or a poem (or a play, film, blog, tweet, and so on). So the speaker in the poem might have told us any number of things about the experience of stopping by woods on a snowy evening. But he chooses to open the poem by sharing information with us: that he may know whose land the woods are on; that, because the owner lives in the village, he will not observe the speaker's behavior.

Why this, then? Why does it matter that the owner of the woods is not around to see the speaker stop with no other purpose except "to watch his woods fill up with snow"? It matters because of the way people think when they own property. When people own land, they feel justified in watching for suspicious behavior from strangers. The speaker knows he is doing something that the owner would question if he were present. If he simply rode by on his way to keep the "promises" he mentions in line 14, no one would notice or care. That's normal behavior in our society, something we seldom are asked to explain. But if we stop for no apparent reason, that exposes us to such questions as, *Who are you? Why are you here? What are you doing?*—questions that we usually feel obligated to answer. If we answer the last question by saying "I am contemplating the beauty of the woods and the snow," such an answer may not convince because both the behavior and the reason for it are barely acceptable, too close to odd or deviant to be taken at face value. Even the speaker's horse knows something "wrong" is going on: "He gives his harness bells a shake/To ask if there is some mistake."

Questions for Discussion

Continue to explore the meaning of "Stopping by Woods" by discussing the following questions.

1. If the key question of interpretation is *Why this?* then *What is this*? can also be important. The poem refers to "the darkest evening of the year." The reference is to the winter solstice. What is the winter solstice? Why is it an appropriate setting in time for pondering this place?
2. Appreciation of natural beauty often does not get beyond how pretty it is. What tells us that the speaker has moved beyond the postcard beauty of woods in falling snow? What do you think he is seeing beyond or through its beauty?
3. The repetition in the last line, "And miles to go before I sleep," has led some interpreters to say that the speaker is thinking about death. What do you think?

But there is no mistake. There's only the speaker doing something most people are too busy or too distracted or too oblivious to do—be mindful in the present moment.

The Assignment

If your instructor does not assign a short story or poem, pick one you find interesting and write an interpretation intended to help your readers understand it better. Among many others, our students have found the following works engaging and worth interpreting:

Short Stories

James Baldwin, "Sonny's Blues"

Raymond Carver, "Are These Actual Miles?"

Sandra Cisneros, "Woman Hollering Creek"

Bharati Mukherjee, "The Management of Grief"

Amy Tan, "Two Kinds"

Tobias Wolff, "Say Yes"

Poems

Gwendolyn Brooks, "The Bean Eaters"

e.e. cummings, "anyone lived in a pretty how town"

Emily Dickinson, "Tell all the truth, but tell it slant"

Pablo Neruda, "If You Forget Me"

Deborah Paredeza, "The Gulf"

Tracy K. Smith, "Don't You Wonder Sometimes"

Using Google or other search engines, you can find information about these stories and poems online; perhaps one of them will work for you.

How Do I Write an Interpretation? Questioning the Rhetorical Situation

Begin by considering the **rhetorical situation**, *the key variables associated with you as writer; with your audience; and with the genre, conventions, and expectations of your text.* Understanding the rhetorical situation will give you a stable sense of the whole, something definite to hold in mind as you work your way through the process of writing your essay.

Writer: What Is My Purpose, and What Impression Should Readers Have of Me?

Your purpose is to write a convincing interpretation that will help your reader understand the literary work better. Consequently, they should see you as a helpful guide, someone who provides needed background knowledge they may not have and relates it directly to understanding the work and who calls their attention to significant details and what these details mean.

Audience: Who Is My Reader?

Think of your readers as other students who have read the work and found it interesting enough to want to know what it means. You can summarize all or parts of the work, but do so briefly either as background information at the beginning of your interpretation or as preparation for making a major point. *Otherwise, avoid summary*—remember that you should assume your readers have read the work—and concentrate instead on answering the key questions, **"What does it reveal? What does it mean?"**

Text: What Would Be an Appropriate Work for Me to Interpret?

If your instructor assigns a story, move on to How Do I Write an Interpretation? Engaging the Writing Process. If you have a choice among several, choose the one that intrigues you the most—perhaps because of what it is about or your interest in understanding it better. If you are asked to select your own piece for analysis, we suggest picking one you enjoyed reading recently or one by an author you especially like.

How Do I Write an Interpretation? Engaging the Writing Process

No two people compose in exactly the same way, and even the same person may go through the writing process in different ways with different assignments. Nevertheless, because no one can attend to everything at once, there are phases in handling any significant writing task. You explore the text to get a sense of whether it will work for you and what you might be able to do with it; if it is working out for you, then you move into preparing to write, generating more content and planning your draft.

The next phase is drafting your paper, getting a version, however rough it may be, on screen or paper so that you can work toward the final draft. Getting there involves two further phases: revising your draft, making major improvements, followed by editing your draft, taking care of errors, sentences that do not read well, paragraphs lacking focus and flow, and so on.

Our illustration shows the process of drafting, revising, and editing an analysis of a short story, so we will be referring to that story from here, going forward.

Exploring the Story

Interpretation requires multiple readings. Begin by reading the story for pleasure, as you would with any piece of fiction. This chapter demonstrates the process of interpreting fiction with an analysis of a story by Kate Chopin. You can find the story, titled "Désirée's Baby," on pages 499–503 of this text. Read it now so that you can see how one student worked through the process of writing his analysis.

ACTIVITY 25.1 *Writer's Notebook*

First Impressions

Jot down your first impressions about the story's meaning. Post your notes on the class website or bulletin board. You can also share first impressions by bringing printouts to class, where they can be exchanged and discussed. If classmates are writing on the same story, read their reactions and respond to them in at least one additional posting. Is your interpretation of the story changing? ■

Establishing the Facts of a Story

Reading a story is like being an eyewitness to a significant event. We see some things, do not see other things, and our memory of the whole experience can be unreliable. The difference is that we cannot revisit the event, whereas the story is always there. Simply by returning to the text we can always see more and refresh our memory as often as we feel the need.

On your first return to the text, use the questions in Concept Close-Up: The Features of Stories below to help you establish the facts of the story.

CONCEPT CLOSE-UP The Features of Stories

Narrator: Who is telling the story?

When writing a literary analysis, it is important to distinguish the narrator from the author. Authors create a **persona**, *an invented voice*, to tell the story. Because everything in the story comes from the narrator, it is important to understand his or her point of view. Is the story told in **third person**? That is, does *the narrator refer to the characters as "he" or "she"*? If so, how much does the narrator know about the characters and events? Third-person narrators range from all-knowing (omniscient) to highly limited (knowing only what any observer could see or hear). The other common narrative strategy is **first person**, *a story told by a person who was part of the action and refers to herself or himself as "I."* In first-person narration we must consider the bias and limitations of the character telling the story.

Internal Audience: To whom is the story told?

Just as we must not assume that the narrator is the author, so in many stories the narrator is speaking to an audience that is, to varying degrees, different from us, the readers. Ask: **What group of people would understand the narrator's story best?** Chopin's story is set during the period of slavery in American history. It would be understood best by Americans, especially those with some understanding of life on plantations in the South prior to the Civil War.

Conflict: What are the opposing forces or motives?

Stories are structured around some kind of conflict or tension. Sometimes the conflict is external, between characters or between one group of people and another, or between contrasting locations (scenes) where events occur. Sometimes the conflict is internal, within a character or characters or implied by the scene in which the events occur. Ask also: **To what extent is the conflict resolved at the end of the story?**

Action (or Plot or Story Line): What happens and in what order?

Stories are told either in chronological order, beginning to end, or by departing from chronology by moving to something that happened before the action and/or to events in the future related to the action. In either case, you need to know *precisely* what happened where and when to interpret a story. Note also references to the past or to the future not depicted in the story but mentioned or implied by something the narrator or a character says. From details revealed by the narrator, we learn that Armand grew up in France until the age of eight, when his mother died and his father brought him to America. This is when he met Désirée as a young girl. He knew her before he fell in love with her.

Characters: Who are the major and minor characters, and how are they connected to each other?

Even when stories are told in third person, usually the narrator favors one character or group of characters in telling the story. In Chopin's story, Désirée is a major character, but the narrator does not know, or does not say, much about her past. She was found by chance by the Valmondés at their plantation gate. The local people say that she may have been abandoned by people passing through to Texas. Armand's family are neighbors to the Valmondés. Ask: **Which character or characters are featured in the story? Why are the minor characters in the story? What functions do they serve?**

Setting: Where and when does the action take place?

The scene or setting may be stated or implied; when you are not told in so many words where and when, look for statements in the story that indicate setting or for editorial notes or other background information easily accessible on the Internet to help establish it. The setting matters. For instance, to understand "Désirée's Baby," it is important to know about the caste system of the Old South in the time of slavery. The masters were seen as superior because of their pure white blood lines, while the slaves were seen as inferior if they had even a small percentage of black blood. Thus, one slave character is known as La Blanche because her skin is white. It also helps to know that Louisiana was settled by the French and was a French colony, named after King Louis XIV, until it was passed to Spain in 1763. This explains the French names and vocabulary in the story.

Theme: What is the story about?

Short fiction rarely tells you what it is about; theme must be inferred from events and comments on the events from the narrator and the characters. In specifying the theme, try to move beyond a summary of what happens. "Désirée's Baby" is about the culture of the Old South, a slave culture that depended on a belief that the master class was racially superior to the slave class. The theme has to do with the false assumptions and lies that went into maintaining the belief in racial superiority of whites over anyone with any amount of black ancestry.

ACTIVITY 25.2 *In Your Own Work*

List the Facts of Your Story

In your computer file for this assignment or in your writer's notebook, answer the questions in the Concept Close-Up: The Features of Stories. Don't trust your memory. Be sure to check your answers by referring to the text. ■

Close Reading: Interpreting the Details

In a second return to the text, pay special attention to the story's opening, conclusion, and all key passages where the most important things happen. For example, here's an important passage revealing that Madame Valmondé, and perhaps others, suspect that Désirée's baby is of mixed race:

> Madame Valmondé had not seen Désirée and the baby for four weeks. . . . The young mother was recovering slowly, and lay full length, in her soft white muslins and laces, upon a couch. The baby was beside her, upon her arm, where he had fallen asleep, at her breast. The yellow nurse woman sat beside a window fanning herself.
>
> Madame Valmondé bent her portly figure over Désirée and kissed her, holding her an instant tenderly in her arms. Then she turned to the child.
>
> "This is not the baby!" she exclaimed, in startled tones. French was the language spoken at Valmondé in those days.
>
> "I knew you would be astonished," laughed Désirée, "at the way he has grown. The little cochon de lait! Look at his legs, mamma, and his hands and finger-nails,—real finger-nails. Zandrine had to cut them this morning Isn't it true, Zandrine?"
>
> The woman bowed her turbaned head majestically, "Mais si, Madame."
>
> "And the way he cries," went on Désirée, "is deafening. Armand heard him the other day as far away as La Blanche's cabin."
>
> Madame Valmondé had never removed her eyes from the child. She lifted it and walked with it over to the window that was lightest. She scanned the baby narrowly, then looked as searchingly at Zandrine, whose face was turned to gaze across the fields.
>
> "Yes, the child has grown, has changed;" said Madame Valmondé, slowly, as she replaced it beside its mother. "What does Armand say?" (paragraphs 6–14).

The passage contains many significant details that alert the reader to the increasing tension in the story. Madame Valmondé is clearly disturbed by the appearance of the baby, taking it to the window to look more closely. The nurse, who is described as "yellow," or of mixed race, turns her face to look out the window while Désirée speaks of the baby with a new mother's pride. When she speaks of Armand hearing the baby crying "as far away as La Blanche's cabin," the reader is reminded of another mixed-race slave, and wonders too about Armand's presence at that woman's cabin. Is he perhaps being unfaithful?

It is also significant that Armand is described as "dark" in several places, such as a reference to his "dark, handsome face" (paragraph 17) and in the scene where Armand sends Désirée away, she protests that her skin is whiter than his. He responds that hers is "as white as La Blanche's" (paragraph 26). These details show the hypocrisy of the slave system, depending as it did on racism, and the damage it is doing to the innocent Désirée.

Close reading, in sum, involves three actions:

1. Select key passages for special attention.
2. Note significant details.
3. Draw inferences from these details.

ACTIVITY 25.3 *In Your Own Work*

Close Reading

Explore the story you're interpreting in the way illustrated above. Remember that the goal of close reading is *plausible*, *supportable* inferences from the details of the story. If you can explain your understanding of the story and back it up with references to the text, you are doing what an interpreter should do. ■

Preparing to Write

To write an interpretation you'll need the following:

1. An angle (point of view) expressed as a thesis about meaning
2. A set of points that develop your angle
3. Evidence from the story to back up each point

THE ART OF QUESTIONING Asking Questions: Finding an Angle

Any interpretation of a story will be about its theme or subject matter. Because you cannot discuss everything in a story, your angle is *some aspect or part of the story* that you find interesting, worth discussing.

Sometimes you find your angle in reading it, in reflecting on the facts of the story, or in close reading of important passages. If you are still struggling to find an angle, consider the following suggestions:

1. Return to your first impressions, the notes you wrote after reading the story. **Is there a key idea or insight that emerged from reading the story, interacting with other students, or discussing it in class that could become your angle?**
2. Look again at Concept Close-Up: The Features of Stories. **Does one of the seven features seem especially promising as an angle?**
3. Consider what emerged in close reading of your story. **Do you see patterns or connections in the details of the story that converge in an angle?**

ACTIVITY 25.4 *In Your Own Work*

Planning Your Interpretation

State your angle in one or two sentences. Under it, arrange the individual points you will make in the order you want to discuss them. Under each point list the evidence you intend to use.

Drafting Your Paper

Think about your angle on the story, about maintaining the impersonal voice of interpretation, and about developing and organizing your points.

How Can I Maintain My Focus?

Because no interpretation can deal with everything in a story, interpretations always have an **angle**, *a concentration of attention on some part or parts of the story rather than others*. They develop by pointing to things said and done that support the angle expressed as a thesis about meaning.

Think, then, of the story as a source of evidence to back up your understanding of what it means, and organize your paper around what you have to say, *not around the unfolding of the story itself.*

Concentrate on stating your viewpoint clearly and supporting it by showing how details in the story back it up.

How Should I Sound to My Readers?

Here is a passage excerpted from the conclusion of the paper written by student Deniz Bennetts.

> By keeping Armand's racial heritage a secret from him, they hoped to guarantee him a happy and uncomplicated life; but, in reality, they were acquiescing to the social judgment of the time that saw the black race as cursed. In their view, God arranged things perfectly so that Armand, like his mother, was born light enough to pass for white.
>
> But they did him no favor by allowing him to grow up as a white slave owner whose own mixed race is revealed in the baby born to Désirée. Before reading this letter, Armand had blamed God for not arranging things for him: "He thought Almighty God had dealt cruelly and unjustly with him; and felt, somehow that he was paying Him back in kind when he stabbed . . . into his wife's soul" by coldly casting her away (paragraph 38). With this insight into Armand's thoughts, the narrator shows that Armand is so arrogant as to seek revenge even against God. Armand is a foolish man whose racial intolerance comes back at him to destroy his own life.

How does Bennetts' voice sound? It sounds informed about the story, confidently pulling together two parts of the story to make a strong indictment of Armand. Here, near the end of his paper, Bennetts pulled from an earlier part of the story to make his point about Armand's errors and arrogance. The voice aims to convince, to make the best possible case for Bennetts' interpretation of the story.

How Can I Select My Evidence?

Sometimes an interpreter discovers a point emerging from details in the story; sometimes the point comes first and you look for details in the story that confirm it. Either way, the important thing is to take out of the story everything that supports a point you want to make and then decide how much of it to actually use.

Under each point, arrange the evidence you find. Ask this question: **What single piece of evidence supports my point most clearly and strongly?** Perhaps it is a single scene, a conversational exchange between the characters, something the narrator says, or the thoughts a character reveals only to us, the readers. Ask yourself, if I use this piece of evidence, do I need anything else? Cite other evidence only when it shows something your best piece of evidence does not confirm or when you think the point you are making is so crucial to your interpretation that it needs proof from several places in the text.

Remember this, above all, in handling the evidence you cite: *It cannot speak for itself. Cite and explain, relating it to your angle, commenting on its details*. What you have to say about a piece of evidence is just as important as the evidence itself.

How Can I Organize My Points?

Just as no one can talk about everything in a story, so also *you can only develop your angle with individual points.* If, for instance, your angle is interpreting a single character, what traits can you distinguish? Organize your essay around those traits. If your angle

The story is a source of evidence to back up your understanding of what it means.

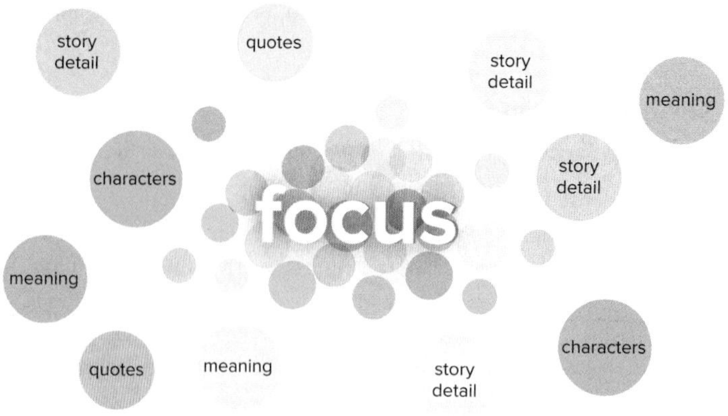

is a theme or idea, such as the futility of Armand's seeking love while living as a racist, you might organize as Bennetts did, around the conflicts within Armand that come together to destroy his marriage and family.

Revising Your Draft

The questions in Art of Questioning: Revision Checklist for Interpreting Short Stories below can help guide revision of your draft.

ART OF QUESTIONING Revision Checklist for Interpreting Short Stories

1. Look at your introduction. Is the focus of your interpretation clear? Do you give your reader some indication of the points you will make?
2. Look at the body of the paper. Does each point have a paragraph or paragraphs devoted to it? Are the transitions from one point to the next easy for the reader to recognize?
3. Look at your evidence for each point. Is there a good mix of quotation and paraphrase or summary? Do you explain how you are interpreting the evidence enough for the reader to follow your thinking?
4. Do any of your points seem "thin," underdeveloped? Return to the story and your notes about it to find additional evidence to develop your point.
5. Look at your conclusion. Does it make the implications of your entire interpretation clear?

Student Deniz Bennetts wrote an interpretation of "Désirée's Baby." As the following excerpts from his first draft show, he made significant changes for the final version.

Excerpt 1: The Importance of Topic Sentences

In his rough draft, Deniz opened some paragraphs with descriptions of the plot of the story, as here. The opening sentence sets up more explanation of what happens in the story. Putting too much plot summary into a paper is a common problem with first drafts. In the draft, these were paragraphs 5 and 6.

First Draft

Désirée has gone from being happy, "desired," and loved to being treated with suspicion and even hatred. She pens a letter to her mother, begging for answers: "My mother, they tell me I am not white. . . . I cannot be so unhappy, and live" (paragraph 28). At Armand's request, she leaves with their child, wandering away across an empty field. As she departs, some light reaches Désirée's hair through the trees that once cast only shadow: "the sun's rays brought a golden gleam from its brown meshes" (paragraph 43). But just as the details of Desiree's origins are obscured, so too is her fate. She descends into the bayou, where she "disappeared among the reeds and willows . . . and she did not come back again" (paragraph 44).

The central conflict of "Désirée's Baby" lies in the character of Désirée's husband, Armand. In contrast with the darkness and shadow surrounding Désirée and her child, Chopin equates Armand's character with explosive and fiery imagery. When he first sees Désirée, he falls in love "as if struck by a pistol shot" with passion "like a prairie fire" (paragraph 4). The violence of these images points to Armand's extreme and destructive passions and foreshadows the fallout to come.

This opening sentence describes the story and sets up a plot summary. Topic sentences should make claims that need to be supported with evidence.

This paragraph ends without making a strong analytical point. There is nothing to lead into the topic sentence of the next paragraph, creating a problem with coherence. There is no connection between this paragraph and the one that follows.

These are key words, so the paragraph needs to be more clear about how Armand's character shows conflicts and how they relate to the meaning of the story.

This paragraph does open with a good, strong topic sentence. However, it should come earlier in the paper. Deniz decided to move it closer to the introduction and develop the idea of conflict better.

This excerpt from the revision shows the thesis at the end of paragraph 1 and all of paragraph 2.

Revised Draft

A central theme in the story is the futility of Armand's desire to maintain control of his powerful and aristocratic position in his parish in the Old South.

The central conflict of "Désirée's Baby" lies in the character of Armand. He is emotionally volatile but also has a need to control others strictly. We learn that he is a harsh master to his slaves: "Young [Armand] Aubigny's rule was a strict one . . . and under it his negroes had forgotten how to be gay, as they had been during [his father's] easy-going and indulgent lifetime" (paragraph 6). When he falls in love with Désirée, his feelings are described in images of nature dangerously out of control: "The passion that awoke in him that day, when he saw her at the gate, swept along like an avalanche, or like a prairie fire, or like anything that drives headlong over all obstacles" (paragraph 4). In other words, he is determined to marry her, in spite of her having no family name or history. Her lack of a history may even be an asset from Armand's point of view. These are things he can provide for her.

In the revision, the sentence about Armand's conflict follows the thesis sentence, which is an interpretation of the story's theme.

This sentence follows up on the conflict, explaining what it is.

These sentences offer support from the text, showing his conflicting character traits: controlling and passionate.

Excerpt 2: Handling Conclusions

In his rough draft, Deniz relied too much on the plot of the story rather than making a strong point in support of his thesis. The paragraph begins with a strong topic sentence about hope and love, but turns too quickly to the actual conclusion in the story itself.

First Draft

Not everything in Chopin's story is obscured in shadow and darkness, or destroyed in fire. In the story's conclusion Chopin communicates a powerful message: the most crucial force against hate and intolerance is love. Despite Désirée's unknown origins, Madame Valmondé loves her without question or hesitation. Likewise, Désirée's love for her own child blinds her to the fact of the color of his skin—a fact for which her husband, and society as a whole, judge her harshly. But, in the end, Chopin brings the truth of Armand's conflict to a clearer light. As Armand throws the last remnants into the fire, he discovers an old letter written by his mother to his father. In it, his own racial heritage is expressed:

> "[N]ight and day, I thank the good God for having so arranged our lives that our dear Armand will never know that his mother, who adores him, belongs to the race that is cursed with the brand of slavery" (paragraph 48).

Armand must live with the error of his beliefs, and without the love of the family he has destroyed.

Revised Draft

As they see it, God arranged things perfectly so that Armand, like his mother, was born light enough to pass for white.

But [Armand's parents] did him no favor by allowing him to grow up as a white slave owner whose own mixed race is revealed in the baby born to Désirée. Before reading this letter, Armand had blamed God for *not* arranging things for him: "He thought Almighty God had dealt cruelly and unjustly with him; and felt, somehow that he was paying Him back in kind when he stabbed . . . into his wife's soul" when he coldly cast her away (paragraph 38). Armand is a flawed man whose desire for power and status destroys his own chance for happiness. He is also a victim of social attitudes about race in the days of slavery. But the setting of the story should not allow us to think that assumptions about race and superiority are safely in the past. We see evidence in the news every day about people who are presumed guilty and treated as less than equal merely on the basis of skin color. The ending of the story leaves the reader wondering what Armand thinks about the error of his beliefs and the loss of his wife and son. We do not know if he learns a lesson, but this tragedy offers a lesson for readers.

> This sentence wraps up the paragraph with the quotation from the letter, and comments on it.

> The topic sentence of the conclusion sums up the mistake of placing too much importance on racial purity.

> The conclusion puts the letter from his mother into the context of Armand's earlier arrogant attitude about Désirée's possible mixed race.

> The conclusion makes a larger point about the relevance of the story in today's world.

Editing Your Revised Draft

Integrating quotations smoothly usually requires taking more of the original text than just a few words. In his draft, Bennetts used two phrases from different sentences in the story and awkwardly joined them with a prepositional phrase.

Original Version

The story equates Armand's character with explosive and fiery imagery. When he first falls in love with Désirée, Armand is "as if struck by a pistol shot" with passion "like a prairie fire" (paragraph 4).

The edited version takes the entire sentence that Chopin used to describe Armand's feelings:

Edited Version

When he falls in love with Désirée, his feelings are described in images of nature dangerously out of control: "The passion that awoke in him that day, when he saw her at the gate, swept along like an avalanche, or like a prairie fire, or like anything that drives headlong over all obstacles" (paragraph 4).

There is no rule against taking complete sentences from a text, provided that they are well-chosen and relevant to the point you are making.

Editing usually means making improvements to the style of the writing, often to avoid repetitions and wordiness. Watch for sentences containing strings of prepositional phrases. These make writing sound choppy. Also watch for empty phrases with abstract nouns like "fact." Reading out loud will help you find places to edit.

Original Version

Désirée's love <u>for her child</u> blinds her <u>to the fact of the color of his skin</u>.

Edited Version

Desiree's love for her child blinds her to the color of his skin.

The resulting conciseness could allow Bennetts to add greater specificity to the sentence, such as "to the changing color of his skin."

REVISED STUDENT EXAMPLE

Bennetts 1

Deniz Bennetts

English 101

Professor Channell

September 30, 2018

The Futility of Control in "Désirée's Baby"

In her story "Désirée's Baby," Kate Chopin shows the tragic effects of racial prejudice 1 on what might have been a happy young family. Racial purity was a value widely shared in the pre-Civil War South, the setting for Chopin's story. Armand, the husband, is an aristocratic slave owner who marries Désirée, once an orphan of

Opening summarizes the story in a few sentences and states the main point of the interpretation to come.

Bennetts 2

"obscure origin," who was adopted as a foundling by another wealthy family, the Valmondés. Their marriage and the birth of a baby boy make the couple happier than they have ever been. However, their eventual realization that the child is of mixed race leads to immediate conflict and tragic consequences. Although the husband at first seems to love his wife with a fiery passion, his love is not strong enough to overcome his fear that Désirée and her baby will tarnish the racial purity of his proud family name. A central theme in the story is the futility of Armand's desire to maintain control of his powerful and aristocratic position in his parish in the Old South.

2 The central conflict of "Désirée's Baby" lies in the character of Armand. He is emotionally volatile but also has a need to control others strictly. We learn that he is a harsh master to his slaves: "Young [Armand] Aubigny's rule was a strict one . . . and under it his negroes had forgotten how to be gay, as they had been during [his father's] easy-going and indulgent lifetime" (paragraph 6). When he falls in love with Désirée, his feelings are described in images of nature dangerously out of control: "The passion that awoke in him that day, when he saw her at the gate, swept along like an avalanche, or like a prairie fire, or like anything that drives headlong over all obstacles" (paragraph 4). In other words, he is determined to marry her, in spite of her having no family name or history.

> Material quoted from the story is evidence confirming that Armand is "emotionally volatile" and controlling. Most quotations function as evidence.

> In a short story, use paragraph numbers to refer readers to passages cited; in longer stories, such as novels, use page numbers.

> Note transition: "having no family name or history" links with "invested in his white aristocratic heritage."

3 Armand is very invested in his white aristocratic heritage. He is proud that he can offer Désirée his name, which is "one of the oldest and proudest in Louisiana" (paragraph 5) and that he can buy his wife a corbeille (wedding and baby clothes) of silk from Paris. These gifts are ways in which he asserts his power. The birth of the baby boy solidifies Armand's position in his family and the community. Désirée tells her mother, "Oh, Armand is the proudest father in the parish, I believe, chiefly because it is a boy to bear his name" (paragraph 16). But even in their earliest and happiest times together, Armand holds a dangerous power over his wife, who loves him desperately. "When he frowned, she trembled, but loved him. When he smiled, she asked no greater blessing of God" (paragraph 17). We see that she is afraid of her husband and knows that her happiness is dependent on his changing moods. She tells Madame Valmondé, "[O]h mamma, I'm so happy, it frightens me."

> Provide brief parenthetical definitions of words your readers may not know.

Bennetts 3

In spite of the imbalance of power in their marriage, all seems well until a problem with the baby becomes apparent. Visiting, Madame Valmondé seems shocked at its appearance. "This is not the baby!" she abruptly exclaims (paragraph 9). She can see what her daughter, a young mother filled with joy, cannot—that the child is of mixed race. Eventually, even Désirée realizes that the baby has similar skin color to the quadroon boy (a term that means one-quarter black) who is fanning the child one afternoon. As Désirée comes to this realization, feelings of shock come over her and she cries out, "Ah!" She has a physical reaction as her "blood turned like ice in her veins, and a clammy moisture gathered upon her face" (paragraph 19). As she gazes at the baby, "her face [becomes] the picture of fright" (paragraph 21). She realizes that Armand cannot tolerate having his family name tainted by a wife and child with the blood of the slave class. 4

Désirée can see that Armand's passion for her is completely over. He is back in control of himself and calmly begins separating himself from his family. He does not confront Désirée with anger, but instead withdraws, averts his eyes from her, and avoids being at home with her and the baby. Désirée observes "a strange, awful change in her husband's manner," and in his eyes "the old love-light seemed to have gone out" (paragraph 18). The narrator explains that Armand "no longer loved her, because of the unconscious injury she had brought upon his home and name" (paragraph 38). His presumption that Désirée is not all white proves to be the obstacle that stops the headlong rush of his passion. As she reaches out to him, "he coldly but gently loosened her fingers from about his arm and thrust [her] hand away from him" (paragraph 24). His imperious nature reasserts itself and we learn that he resumes his cruel treatment of his slaves. 5

His rejection of Désirée suggests that all along, Armand was deluding himself about his love for her. It was never unconditional love, for he put the condition of racial purity on it. The story does show examples of real love and communicates a powerful message: the most crucial force against hate and intolerance is love. Désirée's love for her child blinds her to the color of his skin. She pays attention 6

A key paragraph that states the main point of interpretation, explains it, and confirms it with details from the story.

Bennetts 4

only to his healthy, loud crying, his growing fingernails and chubby legs. And despite Désirée's unknown origins, Madame Valmondé loves her without question or hesitation, and she wants Désirée and the baby to return to Valmondé after Armand casts them out.

The story also has a message about the limits of human control. Armand thinks that he can control his life, but the story's surprising twist at the end shows that belief is another delusion. Armand wants to erase all reminders of his relationship with Désirée, so he orders his servants to make a giant bonfire in the yard behind the house. He seats himself regally "in a wide hallway that commanded a view of the spectacle; and it was he who dealt out to a half dozen negroes the material which kept this fire ablaze" (paragraph 46). It is an image of a man in complete control of a scene of destruction. Into the fire went the baby's "priceless layette" and graceful willow cradle, Désirée's gowns of silk, velvet, satin, and lace, the entire wedding corbeille. He burns Désirée's letters to him, written during their courtship. Fire is a way of purging and sanitizing, and Armand wants to be free of this blemish on his life. But ironically, it is this attempt at control that reveals the futility of attempting control over life. 7

Another key interpretive point: stated, explained, and furnished with evidence.

In the back of a drawer with letters intended to fuel the fire, Armand finds an old one written by his mother to his father when they lived in France. She was "thanking God for the blessing of her husband's love": " 'But above all,' she wrote, 'night and day, I thank the good God for having so arranged our lives that our dear Armand will never know that his mother, who adores him, belongs to the race that is cursed with the brand of slavery.'" (paragraph 49). Apparently, the father loved the mixed-race mother unconditionally, and both loved their child. By keeping Armand's racial heritage a secret from him, they hoped to guarantee him a happy and uncomplicated life; but, in reality, they were acquiescing to the social judgment of the time that saw the black race as cursed. In their view, God arranged things perfectly so that Armand, like his mother, was born light enough to pass for white. 8

Bennetts 5

But they did him no favor by allowing him to grow up as a white slave owner whose own mixed race is revealed in the baby born to Désirée. Before reading this letter, Armand had blamed God for *not* arranging things for him: "He thought Almighty God had dealt cruelly and unjustly with him; and felt, somehow that he was paying Him back in kind when he stabbed . . . into his wife's soul" by coldly casting her away (paragraph 38). With this insight into Armand's thoughts, the narrator shows that Armand is so arrogant as to seek revenge even against God. Armand is a foolish man whose racial intolerance comes back at him to destroy his own life. We could argue that he is a victim of social attitudes about race in the days of slavery. But the setting of the story should not allow us to think that assumptions about race and superiority are safely in the past. We see evidence in the news every day about people who are presumed guilty and treated as less than equal merely on the basis of skin color. The ending of the story leaves the reader wondering what Armand thinks about the error of his beliefs and the loss of his wife and son. We do not know if he learns a lesson, but his tragedy offers a lesson for readers. 9

Concludes powerfully by connecting the racism of the past to the racism of the present.

READING **25.2**

Désirée's Baby

KATE CHOPIN

Kate Chopin, who lived from 1850 to 1904, wrote many stories and two novels, the best known of these is The Awakening. *All of her works are set in Louisiana, where she resided for most of her adult life. She wrote "Désirée's Baby" in 1892, but the story takes place much earlier, in the Old South, prior to the Civil War. It was first published in* Vogue *magazine in January 1893. As with many of her works, this story has feminist and anti-slavery themes.*

As the day was pleasant, Madame Valmondé drove over to L'Abri to see Désirée and the baby. 1

It made her laugh to think of Désirée with a baby. Why, it seemed but yesterday that Désirée was little more than a baby herself; when Monsieur in riding through the gateway of Valmondé had found her lying asleep in the shadow of the big stone pillar. 2

The little one awoke in his arms and began to cry for "Dada." That was as much as she could do or say. Some people thought she might have strayed there of her own accord, for she was of the toddling age. The prevailing belief was that she had been purposely left by a party of Texans, whose canvas-covered wagon, late in the day, had crossed the ferry that Coton Maïs kept, just below the plantation. In time Madame Valmondé abandoned every speculation but the one that Désirée had been sent to her by a beneficent Providence to be the child of her affection, seeing that she was without child of the flesh. For the girl grew to be beautiful and gentle, affectionate and sincere,— the idol of Valmondé. 3

It was no wonder, when she stood one day against the stone pillar in whose shadow she had lain asleep, eighteen years before, that Armand Aubigny riding by and seeing her there, had fallen in love with her. That was the way all the Aubignys fell in love, as if struck by a pistol shot. The wonder was that he had not loved her before; for he had known her since his father brought him home from Paris, a boy of eight, after his mother died there. The passion that awoke in him that day, when he saw her at the gate, swept along like an avalanche, or like a prairie fire, or like anything that drives headlong over all obstacles. 4

Monsieur Valmondé grew practical and wanted things well considered: that is, the girl's obscure origin. Armand looked into her eyes and did not care. He was reminded that she was nameless. What did it matter about a name when he could give her one of the oldest and proudest in Louisiana? He ordered the corbeille from Paris, and contained himself with what patience he could until it arrived; then they were married. 5

Madame Valmondé had not seen Désirée and the baby for four weeks. When she reached L'Abri she shuddered at the first sight of it, as she always did. It was a sad looking place, which for many years had not known the gentle presence of a mistress, old Monsieur Aubigny having married and buried his wife in France, and she having loved her own land too well ever to leave it. The roof came down steep and black like a cowl, reaching out beyond the wide galleries that encircled the yellow stuccoed house. Big, solemn oaks grew close to it, and their thick-leaved, far-reaching branches shadowed it like a pall. Young Aubigny's rule was a strict one, too, and under it his negroes had forgotten how to be gay, as they had been during the old master's easy-going and indulgent lifetime. 6

The young mother was recovering slowly, and lay full length, in her soft white muslins and laces, up on a couch. The baby was beside her, upon her arm, where he had fallen asleep, at her breast. The yellow nurse woman sat beside a window fanning herself. 7

Madame Valmondé bent her portly figure over Désirée and kissed her, holding her an instant tenderly in her arms. Then she turned to the child. 8

"This is not the baby!" she exclaimed, in startled tones. French was the language spoken at Valmondé in those days. 9

"I knew you would be astonished," laughed Désirée, "at the way he has grown. The little cochon de lait! Look at his legs, mamma, and his hands and finger-nails,—real finger nails. Zandrine had to cut them this morning Isn't it true, Zandrine?" 10

The woman bowed her turbaned head majestically, "Mais si, Madame." 11

"And the way he cries," went on Désirée, "is deafening. Armand heard him the other day as far away as La Blanche's cabin." 12

Madame Valmondé had never removed her eyes from the child. She lifted it and walked with it over to the window that was lightest. She scanned the baby narrowly, then looked as searchingly at Zandrine, whose face was turned to gaze across the fields. 13

"Yes, the child has grown, has changed;" said Madame Valmondé, slowly, as she replaced it beside its mother. "What does Armand say?" 14

Désirée's face became suffused with a glow that was happiness itself. 15

"Oh, Armand is the proudest father in the parish, I believe, chiefly because it is a boy, to bear his name; though he says not,—that he would have loved a girl as well. But I know it isn't true I know he says that to please me. And mamma," she added, drawing Madame Valmondé's head down to her, and speaking in a whisper, "he hasn't punished one of them—not one of them—since baby is born. Even Négrillon, who pretended to have burnt his leg that he might rest from work—he only laughed, and said Négrillon was a great scamp. Oh, mamma, I'm so happy; it frightens me." 16

What Désirée said was true. Marriage, and later the birth of his son had softened Armand Aubigny's imperious and exacting nature greatly. This was what made the gentle Désirée so happy, for she loved him desperately. When he frowned she trembled, but loved him. When he smiled, she asked no greater blessing of God. But Armand's dark, handsome face had not often been disfigured by frowns since the day he fell in love with her. 17

When the baby was about three months old, Désirée awoke one day to the conviction that there was something in the air menacing her peace. It was at first too subtle to grasp. It had only been a disquieting suggestion; an air of mystery among the blacks; unexpected visits from far-off neighbors who could hardly account for their coming. Then a strange, an awful change in her husband's manner, which she dared not ask him to explain. When he spoke to her, it was with averted eyes, from which the old love-light seemed to have gone out. He absented himself from home; and when there, avoided her presence and that of her child, without excuse. And the very spirit of Satan seemed suddenly to take hold of him in his dealings with the slaves. Désirée was miserable enough to die. 18

She sat in her room, one hot afternoon, in her peignoir, listlessly drawing through her fingers the strands of her long, silky brown hair that hung about her shoulders. The baby, half naked, lay asleep upon her own great mahogany bed, that was like a sumptuous throne, with its satin-lined half-canopy. One of La Blanche's little quadroon boys—half naked too—stood fanning the child slowly with a fan of peacock feathers. Désirée's eyes had been fixed absently and sadly upon the baby, while she was striving to penetrate the threatening mist that she felt closing about her. She looked from her child to the boy who stood beside him, and back again; over and over. "Ah!" It was a cry that she could not help; which she was not conscious of having uttered. The blood turned like ice in her veins, and a clammy moisture gathered upon her face. 19

She tried to speak to the little quadroon boy; but no sound would come, at first. When he heard his name uttered, he looked up, and his mistress was pointing to the door. He laid aside the great, soft fan, and obediently stole away, over the polished floor, on his bare tiptoes. 20

21 She stayed motionless, with gaze riveted upon her child, and her face the picture of fright. Presently her husband entered the room, and without noticing her, went to a table and began to search among some papers which covered it.

22 "Armand," she called to him, in a voice which must have stabbed him, if he was human. But he did not notice. "Armand," she said again. Then she rose and tottered towards him. "Armand," she panted once more, clutching his arm, "look at our child. What does it mean? tell me."

23 He coldly but gently loosened her fingers from about his arm and thrust the hand away from him. "Tell me what it means!" she cried despairingly.

24 "It means," he answered lightly, "that the child is not white; it means that you are not white."

25 A quick conception of all that this accusation meant for her nerved her with unwonted courage to deny it. "It is a lie; it is not true, I am white! Look at my hair, it is brown; and my eyes are gray, Armand, you know they are gray. And my skin is fair," seizing his wrist. "Look at my hand; whiter than yours, Armand," she laughed hysterically.

26 "As white as La Blanche's," he returned cruelly; and went away leaving her alone with their child.

27 When she could hold a pen in her hand, she sent a despairing letter to Madame Valmondé.

28 "My mother, they tell me I am not white. Armand has told me I am not white. For God's sake tell them it is not true. You must know it is not true. I shall die. I must die. I cannot be so unhappy, and live."

29 The answer that came was as brief:

30 "My own Désirée: Come home to Valmondé; back to your mother who loves you. Come with your child."

31 When the letter reached Désirée she went with it to her husband's study, and laid it open upon the desk before which he sat. She was like a stone image: silent, white, motionless after she placed it there.

32 In silence he ran his cold eyes over the written words. He said nothing. "Shall I go, Armand?" she asked in tones sharp with agonized suspense.

33 "Yes, go."

34 "Do you want me to go?"

35 "Yes, I want you to go."

36 He thought Almighty God had dealt cruelly and unjustly with him; and felt, somehow, that he was paying Him back in kind when he stabbed thus into his wife's soul. Moreover he no longer loved her, because of the unconscious injury she had brought upon his home and his name.

37 She turned away like one stunned by a blow, and walked slowly towards the door, hoping he would call her back.

38 "Good-by, Armand," she moaned.

39 He did not answer her. That was his last blow at fate.

40 Désirée went in search of her child. Zandrine was pacing the somber gallery with it.

41 She took the little one from the nurse's arms with no word of explanation, and descending the steps, walked away, under the live-oak branches.

42 It was an October afternoon; the sun was just sinking. Out in the still fields the negroes were picking cotton.

43 Désirée had not changed the thin white garment nor the slippers which she wore. Her hair was uncovered and the sun's rays brought a golden gleam from its brown meshes. She did not take the broad, beaten road which led to the far-off plantation of Valmondé. She walked across a deserted field, where the stubble bruised her tender feet, so delicately shod, and tore her thin gown to shreds.

44 She disappeared among the reeds and willows that grew thick along the banks of the deep, sluggish bayou; and she did not come back again.

45 Some weeks later there was a curious scene enacted at L'Abri. In the centre of the smoothly swept back yard was a great bonfire. Armand Aubigny sat in the wide hallway that commanded a view of the spectacle; and it was he who dealt out to a half dozen negroes the material which kept this fire ablaze.

46 A graceful cradle of willow, with all its dainty furbishings, was laid upon the pyre, which had already been fed with the richness of a priceless layette. Then there were silk gowns, and velvet and satin ones added to these; laces, too, and embroideries; bonnets and gloves; for the corbeille had been of rare quality.

47 The last thing to go was a tiny bundle of letters; innocent little scribblings that Désirée had sent to him during the days of their espousal. There was the remnant of one back in the drawer from which he took them. But it was not Désirée's; it was part of an old letter from his mother to his father. He read it. She was thanking God for the blessing of her husband's love:—

48 "But, above all," she wrote, "night and day, I thank the good God for having so arranged our lives that our dear Armand will never know that his mother, who adores him, belongs to the race that is cursed with the brand of slavery."

CREDITS

pages 480: N. Scott Momaday, *The Man Made of Words* (New York: St. Martin's, 1997), 1–3.

page 495: Courtesy of Deniz Bennets

CHAPTER 26

Writing an Editorial or Opinion Column

ENGAGING QUESTIONS

In this chapter, you will engage with the following questions:

- What are editorials and how do they differ from opinion columns?
- What are the purposes of editorials?
- How do writers choose appropriate topics for editorials?
- How do writers apply the steps of the writing process to editorial assignments?

PERHAPS THE MOST COMMON GENRE FOR CASE-MAKING IS THE EDITORIAL, in which writers argue for their solutions to problems; for their views on current issues; for the policies they favor at local, state, national, and international levels; and even for which candidate they favor in an upcoming election. Editorials play a significant role in shaping public opinion and therefore matter in the democratic process of our nation. A similar genre is the opinion column, in which regular or guest columnists argue for their position on some current topic or issue.

What Is an Editorial?

An **editorial** is a *short persuasive article in a newspaper, magazine, or news show that expresses the opinion of the editor or editorial board, usually about a current or debatable issue.* Similar in length and style to an editorial, an **op-ed piece** is *an opinion written by someone from outside the organization.* Called "op-ed" because these pieces were originally published on the page "opposite the editorial page," such writing tries to convince the general reading audience that a particular point of view is valid; it may also try to persuade readers to accept this point of view as the best. Op-eds and editorials are about 250–800 words, and because they are often one article among many that a reader could turn to, the genre attempts to attract and keep reader attention. The point is usually clearly stated within the first few sentences, and the argument needs to be short but adequately supported with logic and evidence.

THE ART OF QUESTIONING Anatomy of an Editorial

Ask and answer the following five questions:

1. Clear statement of point: **What do I want my readers to believe or do?** The claim (what you are advocating) usually appears within the first few sentences.

2. Background information: **What do my readers need to know?** Any information readers need to understand the argument must be provided. You cannot assume readers know what you know.
3. Logic and evidence: **How can I convince my readers?** Opinions have impact only when readers see them as logical and based on solid evidence. That is, you need to appeal to reason.
4. Appeals to emotions: **How can I move my readers?** In addition to making a good case, editorials appeal to the reader's values, such as love of country or sympathy for people treated unfairly.
5. Consideration of other viewpoints: **How should I handle competing points of view?** Other viewpoints should be treated respectfully even as you show why your opinion is better or best.

Why Write an Editorial?

People write editorials and op-eds because they want to make their opinions on current events known as part of their civic life within a community. They write about, for example, green space rezoning in their neighborhood or an issue connected with their business or professional life, such as the impact of taxation on the economy. As a student, you might be asked to write an editorial as an assignment in many courses, such as history, political science, or cultural studies. You could use what you have learned from any course or combination of courses to advocate prison reform, for instance. Writing editorials helps develop important skills, including

- Conveying an opinion persuasively
- Providing evidence and logical analysis
- Expressing ideas concisely and clearly
- Responding to current issues and debates

The following is an opinion column written by a university professor in Australia about the current conflict between news and fake news.

EXAMPLE **Editorial**

Dr. Anderson is a professor at Macquarie University in Australia. This op-ed piece appeared in 2017 in The Lighthouse, *a university publication that features the writings of scholars who dedicate their lives to finding the truth about controversial questions.*

The question posed, Who can we trust for our news? *has this answer: No one completely. Some news sources are certainly more professional than others, but we must all develop a critical sense capable of thinking through the news we encounter.*

Opinion Dressed Up as Fact: Who Can We Trust for Our News?

NICOLE ANDERSON

Blind trust has never been and never will be enough. 1

Fake news. Alternative facts. Fake massacres. 2

When Kellyanne Conway, a key advisor to US President Donald Trump, talked about the Bowling Green Massacre she claimed terrorists mounted in New York, the "non-fake" facts tell us it never happened. 3

Newspaper opinion columns usually open with a reference to recent events readers would be familiar with.

Conway later recanted her version of the non-events to CNN but also said she thought the Trump administration was besieged by media bias and said: "I think there are some reports everywhere, in print, on TV, in radio, in conversation that are not well-researched and that are sometimes based on falsehoods." 4

One way of dodging the impact of truths you don't like is to claim that the news coverage is not trustworthy.

Getting the facts wrong

I asked my colleague Professor Catharine Lumby, a senior researcher in our department who worked as a print and television journalist for two decades, what she made of Conway's claims about mainstream media reporting. 5

Anderson supports her argument with the opinion of a professional colleague.

She responded: "There is no doubt that the mainstream media often gets their facts wrong. More importantly, all journalists are human—they bring their own opinions to stories however hard they try to eliminate bias." 6

What she is saying, in a nutshell, is that there has never been something we might call objective news. Yet it's also true that we are now living in a world where the internet and social media have made it far more likely that conspiracy theories and genuine untruths spread rapidly and distort democracy. 7

Now everyone's a content producer

The rise of social media has democratized our conversations and the ability of anyone with access to the internet to produce and share their own opinions and media content. Yet there are also potential risks, in particular the risk that all opinions are treated as fact. 8

A key distinction: opinion vs. fact. Facts are statements we must concede are true, regardless of how we feel about them. They are not matters of opinion, which should designate honest, rational differences in outlook or viewpoint. We can differ, for example, on immigration policy for good reasons, but we must grant that border walls cannot deter illegal immigrants that come on a visa and just stay—a fact about immigration that all well-informed people must acknowledge.

More than ever, we are living in a world where opinion and facts are often treated as equivalent. Hence the term, "alternative facts." 9

Anderson is again referring to events in the news. On January 22, 2017, Kelleyanne Conway first used this term in a press conference.

In the academic sphere we are trained rigorously to make a distinction in the sciences and the humanities between opinion and argument, or our own opinions and what we find factually in our research. Naturally it rankles when our expertise is dismissed. Just ask climate change experts how they feel when decades of their research is wiped away by politicians who treat climate change as an inconvenient fact. 10

Anderson appeals to her readers, who are in the academic sphere. *The Lighthouse* is a college paper.

So where does that leave expert researchers? How do we respond to "alternative facts"? 11

Teachers and researchers push back

This section indicates what action expert researchers must take—namely, "push back against the tide of personal opinion dressed as fact."

In my view it makes our job as teachers and researchers all the more important. By promoting our research in the public domain and by educating the next generation to think critically and evaluate the information they receive, we are able to push back against the tide of personal opinion dressed as fact. 12

A large part of that is ensuring that all our students are given the skills to think in a discerning way about the deluge of information they will encounter outside the university walls.

It also gives academics an urgent call to action to communicate their research as widely as possible and to engage in public debates. Now is not the time to sit back. We need to speak out and disseminate what we know. 13

This is a common name for journalists and the news media in general, referring to their power in a country's political system.

The doom and gloom we read about when it comes to traditional media jobs—the allegations of "fake news", the jeremiads about young people no longer caring about the Fourth Estate, the failing business models of traditional media—are all depressing. 14

Yet, at Macquarie we are highly engaged in producing bright young, ethically engaged graduates who are going to be part of the generation who turn that tide. I am confident the tide will turn. 15

Questions for Discussion

After reviewing The Art of Questioning: Anatomy of an Editorial (pages 504–05) and the marginal annotations to the reading, discuss "Opinion Dressed Up as Fact" in class. How did the author attempt to catch your attention? How does she make her central point clear, and in what ways does she defend it with logic and evidence? What values does she appeal to?

What Can I Write About?

Editorials and op-ed pieces can be written about any subject that people are thinking, talking, and writing about: current events, controversial debates, and cultural events. Because editorials appear in particular publications, people write them for the community the publication serves: an interest group (for example, parents with young children), a neighborhood, a college campus, a city, or a nation.

You need to find a topic that you care about, that you want to express your opinion on, and that you want to convince others in your community to consider. The following questions should help you find an appropriate topic:

- **What current controversial issues are you passionate about?** Controversies and debates taking place in a community appear in the editorials and op-ed pages of newspapers and magazines. Reading them may help you find a topic that interests you.
- **What events are happening around me?** Current events are often the subject of editorials and opinions because people want to weigh in on important decisions that affect them. Perhaps your college is considering restructuring course requirements for graduation or a student group is bringing a controversial speaker to campus. Good editorials can respond to situations that are happening right now and give you a chance to help shape those events.

- **What have you read recently in magazines or newspapers (print or online) that you disagree with?** Sometimes op-ed pieces will respond to something that appeared previously in the publication. The op-ed pages give readers a space to state their own opinions on the subject. When you find yourself talking back to an article, you may have found the topic you should write about.

Regardless of the topic you choose, focus your discussion. Often the best way to get to your point is to think about your relationship to the issue. For example, if your topic is animal rights, think about local problems you have seen that relate to animal rights and experiences you have had, for example, working at an animal shelter.

How Do I Prepare to Write an Editorial?

Consider the task requirements, voice and style, and development and organization.

Task Requirements

Since editorials and op-ed pieces appear in particular publications, think about who you are writing to by where you would send your piece. A piece defending video games as socially interactive rather than isolating might go to your local newspaper or an online gaming magazine. In either case, writing for the publication's audience would be crucial. The more general reader of the newspaper would not know as much about video games as someone who reads an online gaming magazine. In other words, you could not persuade both audiences with the same article.

The same principle applies to editorials written for a class. Whom do you want to reach? Whose opinions do you want to influence most? These questions will help you decide how much background information you should supply, how much and what kind of evidence you need, and what values you can appeal to most effectively.

Voice and Style

Editorials and opinion pieces necessarily reveal your character and personality. You have choices, however, in how you will sound to your reader. Will emotion or calm rationality be best? Do you need to convey sadness or anger? Is your personal involvement in the issue relevant, and therefore does it need to be mentioned and perhaps explained? How you answer these questions matters because readers do respond to how attractive and trustworthy they sense a writer is. In the example of an editorial presented earlier (pages 505–07), Nicole Anderson presents herself as a professor and member of the Macquarie University community.

Development and Organization

The editorial is, by convention, short. You must generate a high-impact argument in no more than about 750 words. Unlike a research paper on the same topic, an editorial must focus on persuasion over depth and breadth of coverage, boiling down what you have to say to a central point, a few reasons justifying it, and only the best pieces of evidence you have.

Most editorials follow a simple organizational pattern: Introduce the argument, provide necessary background information, and lay out the evidence and logic to support the claim point by point. Therefore, in preparing to write, the following questions are crucial: Do you have data or information to justify the claims you make? If you are analyzing a problem and proposing a solution, what can you cite that supports your analysis and confirms that your solution can really work? The argument is the heart of the editorial; pay special attention to offering the best reasons you have and selecting the evidence that backs each reason most strongly.

What Are the Steps in Writing an Editorial?

An editorial is not simply your opinion; *it is a demonstration of why this opinion is a good one to hold.* The goal is to find the best way to convince your audience. Therefore, your editorial needs to be shaped thoughtfully.

1. **Draft your editorial.** The draft is the place to get all of your ideas and arguments on the table. You might even find that it is helpful to freewrite the argument section to make sure that you have identified all of your potential points. You might decide later to cut out some of them to develop better the ones that remain, but give them all free expression in your first draft.
2. **Revise your editorial.** The revision stage is critical to sharpening your argument, especially to making your case using the best strategies. Read over your editorial and ask yourself these questions:
   - Have you clearly stated your argument or point early? You do not have space for a long windup. Get to the point quickly.
   - Have you provided enough information to describe the situation and give crucial background information? Use your sense of your audience to judge which facts you feel certain they already know and which facts need to be introduced or reinforced.
   - Does each point in your argument follow a logical order? Are there some that seem out of place or too weak and need to be cut? Are there some that need more development? Examine your argument for flow: Does it lead from point to point logically and support its points with enough facts?
   - Examine your argument for coherence: Do you have the right tone of voice for your topic? Is the tone consistent throughout? Do you sound trustworthy and believable? Shifting voices, exaggerated or rude tones, and rants will confuse or put off your readers. How you say something is as important as what you say.
3. **Edit your editorial.** When you edit, make sure that you eliminate wordiness, unnecessary points, and excessive discussion. Pay special attention to the implications of the words you select. It makes a difference, for instance, whether you call an immigrant “illegal” or “undocumented.”
4. **Proofread your editorial.** Proofread carefully for misspellings and grammatical errors so that mistakes do not detract from your argument.

BEST PRACTICES Maintaining Editorial Integrity

1. Although any writing will be better when you keep in mind the rhetorical situation, the power of an editorial or op-ed depends especially on your purpose, your audience, and how you portray your relationship to the issue and audience. You need to be aware of what you want to achieve: Are you offering an opinion that has not been aired on the subject but needs to be considered? The best choice among many possibilities? The reasons for taking a particular action? Being clear about your goal matters and makes it easier to reach. Similarly, you need to understand for whom you are writing and how you need to portray yourself to get them to listen. Do you want your audience to see you as one of them? Or is it more important that they see you as a trustworthy observer? Correctly judging what your audience needs and wants is the key to being effective.
2. Often statistics and information are necessary for making an argument. Short quotations from something someone else has said or written are also common. In academic essays, we cite these sources of information in the text in parentheses or footnotes and include a list of works cited or bibliography at the end. Editorials do not contain such features, but you still need to be careful to attribute any quotations and ideas you use to their sources and say where you got your data.

   This reference can be accomplished most easily by introducing the quotations or data with a signal phrase, such as "In a recent report to Congress, the economist George Soros said. . . ." You can also refer your readers to a website, an article, or a book by including a URL for a website or the publication year for a book in parentheses at the end of the sentence.

See Chapter 18 for more discussion of signal phrases.

CHAPTER 27

Writing a Proposal

ENGAGING QUESTIONS

In this chapter, you will engage with the following questions:

- What are the elements that make up a proposal?
- What skills does proposal writing develop?
- How do writers identify topics for proposals?
- How do writers apply the steps of the writing process to proposal writing?

PROPOSALS ARE A MAJOR GENRE IN BUSINESS AND PROFESSIONAL SETTINGS of all kinds, and they take many forms: a request for funding, a project outline, a plan for a dissertation, and so on. Often proposals are elaborate and formal, written by teams of writers, and the results are evaluated by government agencies, corporations, educational institutions, and the like. This chapter deals with the basics of proposal writing at a level appropriate for first-year college writing courses.

What Is a Proposal?

A **proposal** is an *argument that attempts to persuade its audience to see a problem or opportunity in a particular way and convince them to take a particular action proposed.* Proposals must be persuasive, so ideas must be presented clearly, with an audience's needs in mind and in a way that draws the audience's support.

THE ART OF QUESTIONING Anatomy of a Proposal

Ask and answer the following questions:

1. Identification of the problem: **What problem am I trying to solve?** A proposal must establish a significant problem that needs to be solved or at least addressed in some way.
2. Detailed and clear outline of the solution: **What exactly am I proposing?** Your description of the problem must imply and connect logically to the solution you propose. In other words, the persuasive power of a proposal depends on your readers seeing the problem as you do and recognizing that the solution follows from your presentation of the problem.

3. Evidence to support the proposed solution: **How can I show that my solution will work?** A proposal must be supported by data and expert opinion in addition to being logically compelling.
4. Consideration of alternative actions or contrary arguments: **How can I establish that only my solution will address the problem adequately?** Especially when other solutions have been or will be proposed, it is important to show why yours has advantages over the competition. Perhaps, for example, you can establish that your solution is cheaper or easier to implement.
5. Conclusion: **How can I motivate my readers to act or support the action I have proposed?** Often the conclusion of a proposal includes a call to action that delineates precisely what you are asking your audience to do and encourages them to do it.

Why Write a Proposal?

Proposals are the means for taking effective action on any problem, question, or issue that requires people to cooperate. If you want to enlist the support of others to make life better, proposals are the way to do it.

From a marriage proposal to a business proposal to a grant application to a call by neighbors for greater green space, *people try to persuade others to see a situation the way they do and take the action they propose.* A consulting firm's proposal to evaluate the supply chain efficiency of a retail company and a scientist's proposal asking for research funding for a new DNA sequencing study differ in details, and both differ from a letter to a congressperson arguing for public libraries to stay open later. Yet they all have a similar logic and function. Each must identify the problem or need and make a convincing argument for taking the advised action.

See Chapter 28, pages 518–23, for specific information on writing a research proposal.

Students are often asked to write a research proposal in which they must convince their instructor that what they plan to write about for an upcoming research project is worthwhile. As examples of other proposals, students in a business course write proposals for solving child labor problems; students in political science propose solutions to problems with campaign funding; students in a writing course write letters to newspaper editors proposing solutions to campus or community problems, large and small. Writing a proposal helps develop important skills:

- Identifying a problem and the best solution.
- Clearly articulating how a solution will work.
- Making a convincing argument using appropriate evidence.
- Considering your audience and shaping your tone and argument for that audience.

The following is a proposal from an organization concerned with fair pricing in private colleges and universities.

PROMOTING COLLEGE AFFORDABILITY

National Association of Independent Colleges and Universities (NAICU)

The National Association of Independent Colleges and Universities (NAICU) is a federal advocacy organization whose goals include ensuring that all Americans have access to federal student aid programs, seeking appropriate regulation of private colleges and universities, and promoting tax policies that help families pay for college while also helping private colleges fulfill their missions.

This proposal relates to all three goals in urging Congress to temporarily suspend antitrust laws as they apply to private colleges and universities. In theory, such relief would allow the institutions to control costs and means of paying for college more efficiently.

PROPOSAL

1 Congress should provide private, nonprofit colleges temporary relief from anti-trust restrictions for the purpose of promoting affordability. The exemption would be limited to a 5-year period of time, and would be extended only if it served affordability purposes.

Antitrust law applies only to private schools, not to public schools, such as state-run universities. The proposal is for temporary relief because costs would have to be significantly reduced to justify suspension of the law. In short, if costs are reduced appreciably, then suspension could continue; if not, antitrust law would again apply.

RATIONALE

2 For more than 20 years, anti-trust restrictions have prevented private, nonprofit colleges from engaging in full discussions of new business models. These restrictions severely limit the sector's ability to explore issues thoroughly, and develop innovative solutions in areas such as financial aid, price, net price, discount rates, and myriad related topics. For many reasons, these restrictions must be eased:

Antitrust law was developed to prevent any single enterprise from dominating an entire industry. So, if one company, for instance, controlled all oil production and sales, they would have a monopoly and could set prices to increase profits at the expense of consumers. Antitrust law preserves competition. However, it also can prevent nonprofit enterprises, such as private colleges, from cooperating fully to accomplish worthy goals, such as making college more affordable.

Need for Creative Solutions:

3 Private, nonprofit colleges are deeply aware of the growing college pricing crisis, and related strains on both families and institutions: more students from low-income families are attending college; middle-income families are disappearing from the economic landscape; state support for all sectors of higher education has decreased; half of full-time students are borrowing; and the effects of the 2008 economic downturn continue to reverberate for many families and institutions.

Reasons for taking extraordinary measures to cope with college costs.

Efficiency:

4 For the past decade, private, nonprofit colleges have continuously identified and implemented efficiencies in delivering a quality education. A growing number have entered into consortia arrangements with other institutions. These partnerships have allowed institutions to maximize their joint purchasing power—and decrease overhead—in such areas as insurance, technology, energy, back-office functions, and cross-institutional academic offerings and calendars. These campus-by-campus efforts, however, are not enough to ensure affordability and access to the diverse options available in higher education across an entire sector.

Shows that cooperation has already worked to a limited extent, making the greater cooperation that could result from suspending antitrust law appealing.

Maintaining a Competitive Higher Education Marketplace:

5 Based on the discussion and promotion of free public college, it is conceivable that federal or state governments could set a price of $0 for the public sector—while still not allowing colleges in the nonprofit sector (that compete directly with state colleges) the ability to discuss their own pricing structures. Public

colleges are not restricted by anti-trust rules. Such an exemption would allow private, nonprofit colleges to develop new business models through mutual collaboration and understanding, while maintaining and enhancing the advantages of a competitive higher education market place. In turn, students and families would be able to better understand price earlier in the college selection process, giving them a better understanding of the cost of the college they want to attend.

Suspending anti-trust law would help private, nonprofit schools compete better with public ones, in theory reducing the price of college for everyone.

Questions for Discussion

In class, discuss "Promoting College Affordability." To find points for discussion, use The Art of Questioning: Anatomy of a Proposal (page 511) and the marginal annotations to the reading. What is the problem the proposal would address? How do the authors lead us to understand why the problem exists? How do they justify taking action? What impact do they claim for the proposal if it is implemented? Do you find the reasoning persuasive? Why or why not? ■

What Can I Write About?

Good topics for proposals are all around you:

- **In campus problems,** such as parking, dorm issues, and class scheduling.
- **In local community problems,** such as zoning, public transportation, and caring for the homeless.
- **In state-level problems,** such as public school financing, supervision of mental health facilities, and issues connected with legalized gambling.
- **In national-level problems,** such as the war in Afghanistan, the national debt, and financial aid for college students.

Finding problems is relatively easy; finding one that interests you and about which you know something already, either from reading or experience or both, is usually more challenging. The key question is: **Big or small, what problems bother me and seem to have solutions I can advocate with some degree of passion and commitment?**

Here is some good advice: You probably should not take on a very large problem like world poverty. If you are assigned or select a complicated problem, such as child labor in developing countries, a proposal for what a single company could do will probably work better than a sweeping solution for the entire problem. Large-scale problems usually require complex, multifaceted solutions that you will probably not be able to write about in a short paper. Also, focusing on one small aspect of a big problem often proves successful in addressing the big problem because local solutions can be implemented on a larger scale.

If discovering your problem proves to be a problem itself, consider the following:

- **Recent News** What's happening in your town, your state, the country, or the world and is making the headlines can offer many problems that you might propose solutions to. Glancing through print or online newspapers can call your attention to problems that you did not know existed.
- **Situations around Campus or Town** What problems are you aware of that people have perhaps not yet taken enough notice of?
- **Your Own Interests** Perhaps you are interested in animal welfare, environmental causes, child welfare, or other causes. The subjects that you are already involved in are good places to begin.

As you prepare your solution, you need to think about the following:

- **Contributing Factors** Sometimes the solution to a problem does not focus on the problem itself but on changing the factors contributing to the problem. For example, a proposed solution for childhood obesity might focus not on arguing for more exercise but on why children are not exercising more. Perhaps recess has been cut from their school, or perhaps there are no playgrounds within walking distance. The solution requires understanding the problem in more depth.
- **Previously Proposed or Attempted Solutions** Investigate what efforts have already been made to solve the problem you are addressing. This research can help you identify what has and has not worked. It will also offer support for your own proposal.
- **Controversies Surrounding Your Topic** If the solutions for your problem are hotly debated, be sure to consider all sides carefully, including why the topic is so controversial and how your solution might appeal to all sides.

How Do I Prepare to Write a Proposal?

Consider the task requirements, voice and style, development and organization, and visual appeal.

Task Requirements

Regardless of how passionate you are about your subject, the best proposals come from rational, practical, open-minded investigation. Take time to consider the whole problem carefully, in all of its dimensions, and with a willingness to rethink your preconceptions, biases, or assumptions. Often the key to a good solution is seeing the problem in a fresh "outside the box" way we hear so much about.

Voice and Style

The voice and style you choose in a proposal depends on your topic, your relation to it, and your readers. Perhaps you are indignant about the use of animals in product safety testing. If you want to propose the use of alternative forms of testing, implying that readers' current choices are cruel and insensitive will not prove persuasive. Instead, give readers better choices and more information for helping to be part of the solution.

Development and Organization

Each section of the proposal has a function:

1. **Introduction.** In addition to getting the audience's attention, the introduction to a proposal needs to set up the problem and identify the solution that you are attempting to convince your audience to adopt. Readers want information up front, and you want to get your proposal into their heads as soon as possible.
2. **Body.** The organization of the main section of the proposal will vary depending upon the problem and especially the solution. However, in this section you must define the problem, including the scope or urgency of the situation, and identify for your audience why this is a situation in which they need to act. You must describe your proposed solution. In this section, you might consider other options in order to emphasize that yours is the best choice. Finally, if your readers are likely to have objections to your proposal, respond to them after presenting your solution.
3. **Conclusion.** The conclusion should offer more than a recap of the problem and solution. You might have a call to action or examine the consequences of inaction, or make a final appeal for your solution. Make your conclusion memorable and persuasive rather than repetitive and boring.

Visual Appeal

Visuals such as photographs, maps, tables, or graphs can add to the persuasive impact of your proposal. Remember that to make visuals effective, you must refer to them in writing and comment on them, not just insert them in your paper.

What Are the Steps in Writing a Proposal?

Proposals require extensive thought and, typically, research. A plan or outline helps most writers stay on track with the first draft.

1. **Draft your proposal.** Decide what information you may need to gather in order to describe your problem and its solution in specific terms. See Chapter 16, Finding Sources, pages 358–71, for more help with this stage of the process. When you sit down to draft your proposal, focus on the logic of how you present the information you have gathered. Logic drives the proposal from point to point and has much to do with its power to persuade.
2. **Revise your proposal.** Read over the proposal with these questions in mind:
   - Is my problem defined early and clearly? Do I provide a sense of why this is a situation that requires action?
   - Is my solution clear and easy to comprehend? Does each piece of the solution have support that makes it convincing? Did I remember to defend the solution

against possible objections? As you read, play the role of your readers, imagining what additional information they might need or additional support for your key points.

- Is the tone of the proposal consistent and appropriate for the audience I envision? If I were a member of that audience, are there any moments that would offend or bore me and make me stop reading?
- Does my conclusion continue to uphold the proposed solution in a way my readers will likely remember?
- Have I used transitions to show how the parts of my proposal relate to each other? Where could I do a better job of signaling connections between ideas to the reader?

3. **Edit your proposal.** Work through the prose, eliminating wordiness, making ideas as clear as possible, and fine-tuning the voice and style to match the aim and audience of your proposal.
4. **Proofread your proposal.** For a proposal to be convincing, it must have authority. Errors of grammar and spelling will undermine this authority, so eliminate as many as you can.

CREDIT

page 513: Courtesy of National Association of Independent Colleges and Universities (NAICU).

CHAPTER 28

Writing a Research Proposal

ENGAGING QUESTIONS

In this chapter, you will engage with the following questions:

- What elements are included in a research proposal?
- What are the purposes of research proposals?
- How do writers identify appropriate topics for research proposals?
- How do writers apply the steps of the writing process to research proposals?

AS PART OF PLANNING A RESEARCH PROJECT, WRITERS ARE OFTEN REQUIRED TO PRESENT A PROPOSAL. For professors, graduate students, and other researchers, the research proposal can be part of a request for funding or for approval so a project can go forward. For undergraduates, the research proposal demonstrates that the project poses a worthwhile question and that sources are available for pursuing the answer.

What Is a Research Proposal?

See Chapter 38, Writing a Prospectus, for further discussion.

Similar to a prospectus, a research proposal demonstrates to your instructor or manager that you have done the preliminary work for a research project. Research proposals adhere to the following arrangement of parts.

THE ART OF QUESTIONING Anatomy of a Research Proposal

Ask and answer the following questions:

1. Overview of the project: **What question will my research answer?** You need to explain the focus and purpose of the research and tell why the question needs answering. Who will care about the answer to your question? Will the finished project be primarily informative, exploratory, or argumentative?
2. Review of the literature: **What research has already been done on this question?** Show that you have acquainted yourself with what has already been written on your topic. You need to describe the major

See Chapter 8, pages 161–91, for help with comparing sources' viewpoints.

contributors—who thinks what and why—and indicate how your sources agree and disagree. The literature review section ends by showing how your research relates to previous research or to a question not yet adequately answered.

3. Methods: **How will I conduct my research?** In the sciences, research involves actual experiments or surveys, so the methods section is a detailed plan for conducting the research and measuring the results. In the humanities, this section describes the primary and secondary sources containing information and opinions about your topic. It also explains your research strategy, such as databases you will search and what search terms you will use.
4. Working bibliography: **What sources have I already found on my topic?** To show that you have a foundation for your project, list the potentially relevant sources that you have found so far, using whatever documentation style your instructor requires.

See Chapter 15, pages 342–57, for guidance on kinds of sources.

See Chapter 16, pages 358–71, for guidance on databases and search terms.

Why Write a Research Proposal?

Research proposals are part of a longer class assignment. One goal is to ensure projects have gotten off to a timely start. Beyond keeping up with your work, a research proposal helps you move beyond selecting a topic to formulating the question your research will answer. Writing a research proposal encourages you to take stock of where you are after preliminary research and to map out the next steps.

See Chapter 20, pages 407–32, for help with MLA documentation and Chapter 21 pages 433–56, for APA. If your instructor wants an annotated bibliography, see Chapter 29, pages 524–27, for guidance.

What Can I Write About?

Writing the research proposal will direct your attention to the following questions:

- Significance: **Is my research question worthwhile?** Is the question genuinely open to debate? Does the answer matter to me and my readers? How could having an answer matter in changing how people think or behave?
- Knowledge of the conversation: **Who are the major people writing on this topic?** Do these authors refer to each other? About what do they agree and disagree? How do their angles (points of view) differ, and which angles are most relevant to my question and point of view?
- Feasibility of my research plan: **Can I find the answer to my question?** That is, does information exist that can help answer my question, or are there ways to do field research to generate my own information? Can I gather the materials I need in time to complete the assignment?

See Chapter 16, pages 358–71, for guidance in conducting field research.

The following proposal was written in a first-year course for an informative paper. The finished paper appears on pages 128–34.

EXAMPLE Research Proposal

1

Amie Hazama
English 1302
May 4, 2015

Research Proposal for a Paper, "Civility in the Workplace"

Clearly states the research question.

Why this question is worth asking and answering.

Who would be an audience for my project?

Overview of the Project: Within the large topic of incivility in American society, I will look at the question "What are the actual costs of incivility in the workplace?" Incivility makes for a stressful workplace, and this is becoming common knowledge. However, people do not know enough about the costs in terms of lost productivity and time. My preliminary research shows that rudeness, insensitivity, and hostility cost money. I want to make bosses and managers aware of the size of the problem and the benefits of improving the level of civility in the workplace. Students in the workforce or about to enter it should also know how important civility is.

Students were to narrow the assigned topic of incivility in daily life.

What is the aim or genre that the project will take?

The student has surveyed major works on the topic of civility published in the last ten years.

Review of the literature: I have discovered that incivility has gotten a lot of attention in the last ten years. P. M. Forni of Johns Hopkins (2002) wrote a best-selling book called *Choosing Civility: The Twenty-Five Rules of Considerate Conduct.* This book does not focus on the workplace, but many of the "rules" are relevant, such as the importance of listening and of giving praise when it is deserved.

Shows how this book is relevant to the research question.

In that same year, another book was published that focused just on incivility at work, *Rude Awakenings: Overcoming the Civility Crisis in the Workplace,* by a civility consultant, Giovinella Gonthier. Unlike Forni, Gonthier puts incivility into a historical context, showing what developments since the 1960's have contributed to people's increasing lack of polite behavior. Like Forni, Gonthier devotes most of her book to "rules" or advice about behavior. Most important to my research, however, is her chapter on "The Business Imperatives of Civility." Here, she reports on research into how incivility affects workers' performance.

Shows how this work takes a different angle from Forni's.

Shows another difference.

How this source is similar to Forni.

Two other academic researchers, Christine M. Pearson and Christine L. Porath (2009), published *The Cost of Bad Behavior: How Incivility Is Damaging Your Business and What to Do About It.* The authors previewed their research in an article published in *Academy of Management Executives* in 2005. They based the book on interviews with over 9,000 workers who were victims, witnesses, or perpetrators of "bad behavior" at work. They argue that workplaces can be transformed into more civil places if managers realize the costs and take steps to change the climate, not just the behavior of a few really bad offenders. Their view is similar to Forni's, because they believe that people need to pay attention to the little ways people are discourteous without even realizing it.

Shows the breadth of this research.

Shows how this source differs in angle from Forni.

2

Explains the direction of the research for this project. Shows the need for current data and where it might be found.

In my research, I intend to use some of the older sources to lay out some definitions and examples but then move to Pearson and Porath and others in order to document the cost to business and how training can help solve the problem.

Methods: I will rely on secondary sources, that is, the work of experts like Pearson and Porath, who have done interviews and surveys. I will look at their book and their 2005 article. They are the most prominent writers right now on this topic, so I will search the library databases to find other articles written by them.

Identifies a starting point and how those sources will lead to further sources with the same angle.

3

References

Forni, P.M. (2002). *Choosing civility: The twenty-five rules of considerate conduct.* St. Martin's Press.

Gallup study: Feeling good matters in the workplace. (2006, January 12). *Gallup Management Journal.* http://gmj.gallup.com/content/20770/Gallup-Study-Feeling-Good-Matters-in-the.aspx

Gonthier, G. (2002). *Rude awakenings: Overcoming the civility crisis in the workplace.* Dearborn Trade Publishing.

Hauser, S. (2011, January 16). The degeneration of decorum: Stress caused by rude behavior in the workplace might be costing the U. S. economy billions of dollars a year. *Workforce Management,* 16–18. http://www.workforce.com/articles/the-degeneration-of-decorum

Pearson, C., & Porath, C. (2009). *The cost of bad behavior: How incivility is damaging your business and what to do about it.* Penguin Portfolio.

Pearson, C., & Porath, C. (2005, February 1). On the nature, consequences and remedies of workplace incivility: No time for "nice"? Think again. *Academy of Management Executive, 19*(1), 7–18. https://doi.org/10.5465/ame.2005.15841946

Ramsey, R. (2008, December). The case for civility in the workplace. *Supervision, 69*(12), 3–6.

This student paper adheres to the APA style. See chapter 21 for specific guidance on applying APA guidelines to an assignment.

How Do I Prepare to Write a Research Proposal?

Task Requirements

In preparation for writing your research proposal, be aware of the specific requirements of the kind of proposal you will be writing. Different fields of study and programs have formats you should follow. Check your instructor's guidelines.

Gather together all of the results of preliminary research: copies of sources, notes on sources, your research journal or notes, and a working bibliography if you have one.

Voice and Style

The tone of your research proposal should be consistent with the purpose of the project itself, but a relatively formal tone is appropriate. You want to sound knowledgeable and confident, in control of the research and the project it supports; the formal tone helps to communicate the right impression.

Development and Organization

A basic outline might include overview, literature review, methods, and bibliography, but be sure to discuss *the significance of the project or the purpose of the study* in the overview or a separate section. Your reader must understand the contribution your project is making. Of course, add whatever sections you need to satisfy special requirements in a particular field or for an individual instructor's assignment.

What Are the Steps in Writing a Research Proposal?

You will be moving back and forth between your notes and your proposal as you work your way through each section. Focus on the information that needs to be included in each section while you write your draft; you can then go back during your revision and work on style and language.

1. **Draft your research proposal.** Before drafting, make an outline that includes the major sections your proposal needs to contain. Then, for each section, jot down the major points you want to include. For example, in your overview, you might describe the topic, tell what you hope to accomplish with your research, and explain what question you hope to answer. In your review of the literature section, jot down the authors and texts you will discuss in the order you think they should be presented. This may not be the order in which you read them. Present them instead to show how they relate to one another and how you see their relevance and significance to the question you want to pursue.
2. **Revise your research proposal.** After drafting, consider all of the following questions:
   - Have I introduced my research proposal in a way that would engage a reader's attention by, for example, giving some context that would show why the topic and question are interesting and relevant to my readers? If your readers are

classmates, have you shown how your research question relates to ideas the class has been studying?

- Do I develop and connect all of the points within each section? Is it clear that I have not only collected the relevant sources but also understand how the ideas all fit together? Remember: *Communicating your understanding of the sources is more important than summarizing what they say.* See the Hazama example (pages 520–21) for a good model.
- Is my research plan made clear in the methods section? Were you specific about search terms and databases that you plan to use? Have you identified good sources that will serve as leads to other possible good sources? Be sure to consult Chapter 15, Planning a Research Project, pages 342–57, and Chapter 16, Finding Sources, pages 358–71, to get further ideas if you are having trouble with methods.

3. **Edit your research proposal.** Read through the proposal trying to identify places where the ideas are overly complicated or where you have said too much about a source. You do not need to summarize entire sources to compare how they relate to key issues and points, so look for unnecessary details that might be getting in the way.
4. **Proofread your research proposal.** A research proposal full of errors and awkward sentences does not inspire confidence in the instructor or manager reviewing your proposal. Edit to eliminate grammatical and spelling errors. Make sure your bibliography entries conform exactly to the documentation style required for the assignment.

CREDIT

page 520: Courtesy of Amie Hazama

CHAPTER 29

Writing an Annotated Bibliography

ENGAGING QUESTIONS

In this chapter, you will engage with the following questions:

- What is a bibliography and what does it mean to annotate one?
- What are the purposes of annotated bibliographies?
- What are the elements of an annotated bibliography?
- What forms can an annotated bibliography take?
- How can plagiarism become a problem in annotated bibliographies?

ANNOTATED BIBLIOGRAPHIES SERVE MANY PURPOSES, AND THEIR CONTENTS CAN VARY from a one-sentence description of a source to a fully developed paragraph with an evaluation of the source and its possible uses.

What Is an Annotated Bibliography?

A **bibliography** is *an organized list of sources (books, articles, websites, maps, and so on) on a particular topic.* The citations in a bibliography conform to standard documentation formats, such as a works cited list in Modern Language Association style or a reference list in American Psychological Association style. Whatever style is used, it is important that all the citations conform to the same style of documentation.

To **annotate** a bibliography means to *add a note to each of the citations,* just as annotating a reading means to add notes to the margins. In the case of an annotated bibliography, the note follows the bibliographic information. It is customary to start a new line and indent annotations to set them off from the citation. The content of the annotations will depend on the writer's purpose in creating the bibliography.

Why Do Writers Create Annotated Bibliographies?

There are many reasons for creating an annotated bibliography.

- Scholars create them as research tools for other scholars. These published annotated bibliographies are good places to start a research project since they provide a list of possible sources and a description of the contents of each. An annotated bibliography can be a complete stand-alone book, an article in a scholarly journal, or a list of suggestions for further reading at the end of a book or article. For advice on finding these resources for research, see Chapter 16, Finding Sources, pages 358–71.

- Writers create them as annotated works cited or annotated reference lists so that readers of their papers can see what research went into the paper and use the list to pursue their own interest in the topic. Instructors may require such lists as part of a research project to ensure that students have read sources well enough to give a brief summary of each.
- Students in a class working on the same project create annotated bibliographies collaboratively in a wiki or discussion board to share the results of their research as they gather and evaluate sources.
- Researchers create annotated bibliographies as they find their sources. Known as working bibliographies, they are informal writing that the writer does just for himself or herself to keep track of the bibliographic information and record notes about the content and usefulness of a source as well as about how sources compare. This kind of annotated bibliography would be useful as a step before planning a paper or before writing a **literature review,** *an overview of previous research,* often required for science papers.

What Should an Annotation Include?

Depending on your purpose and audience, an annotation might include one or more of the following items:

- Description of what the source contains or covers, possibly including how it is organized.
- Summary of the contents of the source–its angle or argument.
- Information about the author of the source and his or her credentials.
- Genre or type of writing of the source, such as news article, editorial, scholarly book, and so on.
- Description of the audience the author was addressing.
- Description of the bias or agenda of the source.
- Suggestions about how the source, or portions of the source, is relevant to research on a particular topic.
- An evaluation of the quality of the source, possibly comparing it to other similar sources.
- A mention of any special features contained in the source such as illustrations, indexes, and bibliographies.
- Comments about the author's voice or style of writing and how it contributes to the quality and overall purpose of the source.

What Do Annotated Bibliography Entries Look Like?

Annotations can be single sentences or much longer, as the following examples from a professional scholar's bibliography illustrate.

Scholarly Annotated Bibliography

Note the range of works on just one novel, *The Awakening* by Kate Chopin, compiled by Neal Wyatt, a former graduate student at Virginia Commonwealth University. The entries are succinct summaries.

Abel, Elizabeth, et al., editors. *The Voyage In: Fictions of Female Development.* UP of New England, 1983.
A collection of essays on novels dealing with female development.

> Tells more about the genre, what kind of book it is.

> Shows the context in which *The Awakening* will be discussed.

Anastasopoulou, Maria. "Rites of Passage in Kate Chopin's *The Awakening.*" *Southern Literary Journal*, vol. 23, no. 2, 1991, pp. 19-30.
Maintains that *The Awakening* follows the structure of a rite of passage but that Edna fails in that passage due to two flaws.

> Describes the argument of the source, an article in a scholarly journal.

Batten, Wayne. "Illusion and Archetype: The Curious Story of Edna Pontellier." *Southern Literary Journal*, vol. 28, no. 1, 1985, pp. 73-88.
Interprets *The Awakening* as a series of illusions that Edna fails to incorporate into a workable and realistic life.

> Again, this describes the argument of the article in a single sentence.

Culley, Margaret, editor. *The Awakening. Kate Chopin. Norton Critical Edition.* Norton, 1976.
An authoritative text and collection of both contemporary and modern critical views of *The Awakening.*

> Assesses the quality of the source.

> Describes the genre and content.

Class Annotated Bibliographies

Class annotated bibliographies have the purpose of helping other students decide whether and how to use a source for a project assigned to the class. The three examples below, all part of a shared or "common" bibliography for a class project, show detailed annotations.

Booth, Wayne C. "For the Love of It: Spending, Wasting, and Redeeming Time." *The Essential Wayne Booth,* Edited by Walter Jost. U of Chicago, 2006, pp. 301–312.
This essay is actually a speech given to high school and college students. It was originally published in 1999 and is reprinted here in a collection of essays, all by Wayne C. Booth (1921–2005), who was the George M. Pullman Distinguished Professor Emeritus at the University of Chicago. Booth was a professor of English and Rhetoric with many publications in that field, but his interests were widespread, and the topic of this essay is the value of pursuing hobbies—or as he puts it "amateuring." Being an amateur means doing something just for the love of it. In his case, it was taking up the cello at age forty, an experience he describes here. If you can get past the somewhat preachy tone of the essay, it has some inspiring ideas and examples in it. This would be a good source for people writing on the rewards of investing mental effort in leisure activities. The book containing this essay is on reserve in Fondren Library.

> Tells what genre the source is.

> Tells the audience for the source.

> Tells when the source was first published.

> Tells who the author is.

> Summarizes the content and angle of the source.

> Tells how the source might be useful for others writing with this angle.

> Gives additional helpful information about accessing the source.

Glier, Ray. "Putting Civility and Sportsmanship Back in Game, if Not in the Stands." *The New York Times,* 22 Feb. 2008, pD4(L).

This news article is about how civility among sports fans has gone down and describes several events, in the NBA and college basketball, where incidents have occurred that highlight this ugly trend. It also talks about what has been done to curb the bad behavior. Ray Glier is a freelance writer who has written for *The New York Times, MSNBC, The Miami Herald,* and other papers.

- Gives the genre.
- Summarizes the contents of the article.
- Tells credentials of the writer.

Twenge, Jean. *Generation Me: Why Today's Young Americans Are More Confident, Assertive, Entitled—and More Miserable Than Ever Before.* Free Press, 2006.

This book is by a San Diego State U. psychology professor who has made a name for herself by arguing that people are becoming increasingly narcissistic. The chapter most relevant to our topic is the first one, titled "You Don't Need Their Approval: The Decline of Social Rules." Another relevant chapter is "Sex: Generation Prude Meets Generation Crude." As you can tell from these titles, Twenge writes with a reader-friendly style.

- Gives the genre.
- Gives author's credentials.
- Gives the author's angle or agenda.
- Directs readers to the chapters most relevant to the assigned project.
- Comments on the style and accessibility of the writing.

How Can I Support Academic Honesty When Writing Annotations?

You will find many sources that contain abstracts. The abstract may be in the database along with the citation, and it may also be at the opening of the text itself. While it might seem efficient to copy and paste the abstract into your annotated bibliography, doing so constitutes plagiarism. An annotated bibliography *must be your own writing and must reflect your own understanding of the source.* (For more on plagiarism, see Chapter 19, Using Sources Responsibly, pages 401–06.)

CHAPTER 30

Writing Instructions

ENGAGING QUESTIONS

In this chapter, you will engage with the following questions:

- What forms can instructions take?
- What are the purposes of instructions?
- How do writers identify appropriate topics for instructions?
- What steps do writers follow when writing instructions?

ALL INFORMATIVE WRITING AMOUNTS TO THE WRITER HAVING INFORMATION THE READER NEEDS OR WANTS and therefore imparting that information as clearly and efficiently as possible. Drafting instructions for doing something is one of the more common genres of informative writing, yet we all complain about how confusing instructions can be. Why is that? The problem is *reader awareness.* To write instructions well, we have to give our readers exactly what they need to know, no more and no less. That is, *we have to put ourselves in the position of our readers,* always a challenge, telling them precisely what to do, leaving out no steps and not assuming they know what we know.

What Are Instructions?

Instructions *explain the process that a person should follow to perform a particular task.* They take readers step-by-step through the procedure. Because instructions tell or narrate how to do something, they are sometimes called directive or instructional process narratives.

THE ART OF QUESTIONING Anatomy of Instructions

Ask and answer the following four questions:

1. Identifying the task: **What do I want my readers to be able to do?** Sometimes the goal is simple and self-evident—for example, an instruction sheet for assembling a toy. Sometimes instructions are part of a larger piece of writing or several pieces of writing, such as instructions for filling out a college application in a packet of materials universities send to high school students. Whatever the case may be, you need to leave no room for uncertainty: Your readers must know what the instructions are for and where they begin and end.

2. Step-by-step presentation: **What must my readers do first, second, and so on?** Do an analysis, a breakdown of the task, into discrete and well-ordered steps. For example, if your instructions require tools to assemble something, begin by specifying the tools required, such as a screwdriver, wrench, and so on.
3. Explanations: **What must my readers understand the reason or reasons for?** Readers may be tempted to take a shortcut or to do something different from what you have told them to do. If a particular step *must* be done in one way to get an acceptable result, say so, and above all, *be sure to warn your readers about anything they might do or not do that could be dangerous.* For example, use red type in bold to underscore the danger.
4. Definition of terms: **What words do I need to define?** If you use a word that may not be familiar to your readers, explain it the first time you use it. For example, if you tell them to fold egg whites into a batter, you cannot assume that inexperienced cooks will know what "fold" means exactly—and the soufflé will not come out as it should.

Why Write Instructions?

We write instructions anytime we need to explain to someone else how to do something. How many times have you e-mailed directions to a friend to explain how to get to your home? Or maybe you have had to explain over the phone to your parents how to load a new program onto their computer. We use instructions often in our personal lives, but we also must sometimes provide them in coursework. In a lab report, for example, you have to include the step-by-step instructions for your experiment so that others can duplicate it. On the job you might find that you have to provide instructions to colleagues for various tasks, from how to submit an invoice to how to exit the building in an emergency.

EXAMPLE Instructions

How to Do the Heimlich Maneuver

The Heimlich Maneuver® for CHOKING ADULTS

A choking victim can't speak or breathe and needs your help immediately. Follow these steps to help a choking victim:

- From behind, wrap your arms around the victim's waist.
- Make a fist and place the thumb side of your fist against the victim's upper abdomen, below the rib cage and above the navel.

- Grasp your fist with your other hand and press into their upper abdomen with a quick upward thrust. Do not squeeze the rib cage; confine the force of the thrust to your hands.
- Repeat until object is expelled.

Unconscious Victim, or When Rescuer Can't Reach around Victim
Place the victim on back. Facing the victim, kneel astride the victim's hips. With one of your hands on top of the other, place the heel of your bottom hand on the upper abdomen below the rib cage and above the navel. Use your body weight to press into the victim's upper abdomen with a quick upward thrust. Repeat until object is expelled. If the victim has not recovered, proceed with CPR. The victim should see a physician immediately after rescue.

Don't slap the victim's back. (This could make matters worse.)

The Heimlich Maneuver for CHOKING INFANTS
A choking victim can't speak or breathe and needs your help immediately. Follow these steps to help a choking infant:

- Lay the child down, face up, on a firm surface and kneel or stand at the victim's feet, or hold infant on your lap facing away from you.
- Place the middle and index fingers of both your hands below his rib cage and above his navel.
- Press into the victim's upper abdomen with a quick upward thrust; do not squeeze the rib cage. Be very gentle.
- Repeat until object is expelled.

If the victim has not recovered, proceed with CPR. The victim should see a physician immediately after rescue.

Don't slap the victim's back. (This could make matters worse.)

The Heimlich Maneuver for CHOKING (ONESELF)
When you choke, you can't speak or breathe and you need help immediately. Follow these steps to save yourself from choking:

- Make a fist and place the thumb side of your fist against your upper abdomen, below the rib cage and above the navel.
- Grasp your fist with your other hand and press into your upper abdomen with a quick upward thrust.
- Repeat until object is expelled.

Alternatively, you can lean over a fixed horizontal object (table edge, chair, railing) and press your upper abdomen against the edge to produce a quick upward thrust. Repeat until object is expelled.

See a physician immediately after rescue.

Collaborative Activity

Using The Art of Questioning: Anatomy of Instructions (pages 000–000), discuss "How to Do the Heimlich Maneuver" in class. Are the instructions simple enough to be used effectively by someone with no experience? Can you think of ways to improve the instructions without going into too much detail or making the instructions much longer or too complicated? Would photos or drawings make the instructions clearer and easier to follow? ■

What Can I Write About?

Most of the time, the need for instructions is self-evident, such as providing directions to a location or the recipe for your dad's chili. Good topics for instructions come from meeting practical needs like these and from hobbies, sports, outdoor activities, and what you know well from work experience. For example, if you are an experienced camper, you can provide instructions for setting up a campsite for a readership of first-time campers.

However, sometimes instructions can be part of a larger piece of writing. For example, if you are writing a paper on babysitting and trying to persuade your audience that it is fun and rewarding, you can make the point better if you provide instructions for entertaining eight-year-olds. Therefore, consider topics that include instructions but are not limited to giving instructions, such as guidance for do-it-yourself home improvements, advice to new students for coping with dorm life, and tips for how to approach getting involved with a civic activity, such as volunteering for Habitat for Humanity.

You also could write a personal narrative that describes how you dealt with losing someone close to you or some other experience almost everyone has had or will have. Because part of your goal is sharing your experience so that others might benefit from it, you could include instructions on dealing with grief, or buying a new car, or balancing college studies with work, or getting out of excessive credit card debt. Of course, these instructions would be quite different from directions for your cat sitter, but they are still instructions, a description of a process. Anytime you are describing steps to follow, you will write them better when you think about the best ways to write instructions.

How Do I Prepare to Write Instructions?

Consider what the task requires, voice and style, development and organization, and visual appeal.

Task Requirements

Try to write your instructions while performing the task itself, making notes about each step and any details important to doing that step properly. If it is not possible to perform the task with pencil and paper handy, try visualizing the process, walking yourself through each of the actions or steps.

Voice and Style

The voice and style of instructions will depend largely on the task described and the purpose of explaining these steps. Many instructions will simply be informative, like a recipe, and thus concise and straightforward.

Sometimes you need a different tone to achieve a different effect. When you want to make a process sound fun, such as describing how to use an online database, the drier the instructions are, the drier the experience will sound. Instead, you need humor or attention to the value of learning new things. Think, then, about how you want the process to sound to your readers and incorporate the appropriate tone in your directions.

Development and Organization

Instructions need to be organized explicitly in a chronological, step-by-step fashion, imagining that someone is reading along and following the steps one point at a time. Although it is wise to read instructions completely first and then go back and follow them, the reality is that people do not always take this step; you should be sure that your instructions could be successfully followed one step at a time, without an understanding of the whole process.

Often telling people what to do is not enough–they also need to know exactly how and why. In these cases you need to add explanations. In directions for making pancakes, for instance, explain that the ingredients should be stirred gently and some small lumps of flour should remain. This is the *how* of it. You might go on to explain that mixing the ingredients too thoroughly increases gluten development in the batter, which makes the pancakes tough rather than light and fluffy. This is the *why* of it.

Visual Appeal

Photographs, maps, drawings, and other visuals are usually essential for instructions. Think about how much easier it is to depict someone holding a baseball bat correctly as opposed to describing it with words. Give your readers an image and then call attention to what you want them to notice about it. Pull image and prose together to get the best results.

What Are the Steps in Writing Instructions?

Imagine that you are cooking dinner. The recipe you're following tells you to "add just enough water" and then "cook until done." But what is enough water, and exactly how can you tell if the dish is done? These instructions would not be helpful. The challenge of writing instructions is not to leave out steps or important details. Describe the process, therefore, *from the perspective of someone who has never done it before.*

1. **Draft your instructions.** Write out step-by-step what a person would do to perform the task you are explaining. Make sure to explain confusing steps or add information about what not to do.

2. **Revise your instructions.** As you revise, try to imagine yourself following these instructions as a person who has never performed the action before, and ask yourself the following questions:
   - **Are there any steps left out?** If you performed each step *exactly* as described, would you succeed?
   - **Are there any words that need to be defined in order to understand these instructions?** If you must use a technical term or a word that many people will not know, give a definition in parentheses or provide a graphic with the word joined to an image of the thing it refers to.
   - **Are there any directions that seem confusing?** Rewrite them to explain more clearly or to add more detail. Directions for changing the oil in a car, for instance, should specify how tightly the new filter should be attached. Otherwise the filter could leak or be damaged if it is tightened too much.
3. **Edit your instructions.** Instructions need to be complete enough to explain each step clearly, but unnecessary details can also confuse. Look for ways to simplify the process you are describing, and cut anything in the description that your readers have no need to know to get a good outcome. For example, instructions for when and how to water your lawn cannot take into account every possible climate variation or restriction on water use in times of drought. Deal with the common situations and trust readers to use common sense in dealing with the rest.
4. **Proofread your instructions.** The wrong word, a missing comma, or a misspelled word can change the meaning of a sentence and therefore make your instructions hard to follow. Proofread your instructions for errors.

BEST PRACTICES Writing Instructions

1. When you write instructions, you are giving your readers the ability to perform a task. Therefore, be sure to warn your readers about anything hazardous in your instructions—or even anything that might get them in trouble. For example, telling a child how to drop mints into a two-liter bottle of soda in order to create a geyser is advisable only when you are there to help clean up the mess!
2. Bear in mind that what you have learned in this chapter also applies to writing **process narratives,** *explanations of how something is done.* In an environmental science class you might describe how a factory recycles plastic bottles. In a business paper, you might describe how collateralized debt obligations (CDOs) contributed to the financial crisis in 2008. Writing a description of how something works or how something is done differs very little from writing instructions: Depict how the process works, step-by-step, explaining important concepts and describing key ideas.

CREDIT

page 529: Courtesy of Deaconess Heimlich Institute

CHAPTER 31

Writing and Giving Oral Presentations

ENGAGING QUESTIONS

In this chapter, you will engage with the following questions:

- What are the characteristics of oral presentations?
- What roles do audience and context play in the preparation of oral presentations?
- What are some guidelines for rehearsing oral presentations?
- How do writers revise oral presentations?
- What aspects of delivery should presenters keep in mind?
- What is the relationship between practice and public speaking anxiety?

> Some years ago in Hartford, we all went to church one sweltering night to hear the annual report of Mr. Hawley, a city missionary who went around finding people who needed help. . . . Well, Hawley worked me up to a great pitch. I could hardly wait for him to get through. I had $400 in my pocket. I wanted to give that and borrow more to give. You could see greenbacks in every eye. But instead of passing the plate then, he kept on talking and talking, and as he talked it grew hotter and hotter, and we grew sleepier and sleepier. My enthusiasm went down, down, down, down—$100 at a clip—until finally, when the plate did come around, I stole ten cents out of it. It all goes to show how a little thing like this can lead to crime.
>
> —Mark Twain

With his flair for telling a funny story with a point, Mark Twain addresses the importance of being responsive to situation in oral presentations. **Situation** designates *the concrete conditions in which you are speaking,* including the time of day or night, what your audience expects and needs from you, how much time you have, what you want your audience to walk away knowing or prepared to do, and so on.

In short, situation calls the shots. Above all else, understand your situation and respond to it appropriately.

What Are Oral Presentations?

Speeches, including oral presentations, are usually based on writing. Sometimes we speak from a text, more or less reading it word for word. More often we speak from notes that remind us of our main points, making up specific wording as we go along.

The dependence of speaking on writing, however, must not lead us to confuse the two. *Readers are not the same thing as listeners.* As writers, we are not in the same place at the same time as our readers; in speaking, we always are. Our audience both hears and sees us, and that makes the speaking situation entirely different from the writing situation.

CONCEPT CLOSE-UP The Characteristics of Oral Presentations

- **Simplicity.** Readers can reread; audiences cannot. Readers can stop and ponder what is on a page, look up a word, and even ask someone else for help. In speeches, the words go by once, and the audience must "get it" immediately or not at all. For this reason, as a speaker you need to be more simple and direct than you are as a writer.
- **Redundancy.** Again, readers can reread; audiences cannot. Audiences need more repetition than readers do. "Tell them what you are going to say; tell them; then tell them what you told them"—this old formula applies to all speaking situations. Remember: What counts is what your audience remembers when your speech is over. They will remember best what they hear more than once.
- **Explicit organization.** Writing has many ways to signal organization visually, such as subheadings and paragraphing. As a speaker you have to indicate your organization aurally: "My first point is. . . ." When you finish that first point, summarize it, and then state your second point and how it connects to the first one.

STUDENT EXAMPLE **Oral Presentation**

The following talk was given by a student at Whitman College in Walla Walla, Washington. It deals with date rape drugs and how to detect their presence in drinks. As you read, note how well the speaker connects her topic with the audience's situation in the opening and how successfully she combines solid information with persuasive, practical advice in the body of the speech.

Jaclyn Jenkins

Date Rape Coasters

1 In the next thirty days, as we scramble to write papers, attend classes, and survive tournaments, 6,000 men and women will fight to survive violent assault. Today, as we compete in or judge various events, 200 men and

Introduction emphasizes the seriousness of the problem.

women will compete with assailants for their lives. And this hour, as we listen to each other, 8 men and women will pray for someone to hear and save them. The sad thing about these statistics is that they're probably not even true. Not true, because the number is probably far greater than we can, or even want to, imagine. These statistics represent the number of people assaulted with the aid of date rape drugs, which, in 2000, the U.S. Department of Justice found were responsible for the fastest-growing drug-facilitated sexual assault crime in America. In my speech today, I'll give you the straight dope about date rape drugs, and then slip you information about the newest devices being developed to combat them. Finally, we'll wake up to the implications of these technologies.

Good use of word choice.

First, the straight dope about date rape drugs. At CNN.com, the section on date rape drugs is headed: "Drugs and rape: an old problem with a new face." That new face can be found in over 36 drugs, with more being developed every day. The three most infamous, however, are flunitrazepam, also called Rohypnol, "roofes" or "roaches"; Ketamine, also known as "K," "Vitamin K," or "Special K"; and gamma-hydroxybutyrate, which has a host of names, including GHB, "Easy Lay," "Georgia Home Boy," "G," or "Liquid E." All these drugs are ideal for sexual predators because they render their victims defenseless. The drugs themselves are colorless and odorless, either in powder, pill, or liquid form, which makes them easy to add to someone's drink. Moreover, all of them leave the system quickly, within 72 hours, taking the evidence of the crime away faster, in many cases, than the victim can report it. 2

Basic, easy-to-follow information about the drugs. Note especially their characteristics, which help to explain why sexual predators use them.

Calls attention to little known fact—men as victims.

And not all the victims are women. The Department of Justice found that one in every ten victims is a man. A federal task force recently estimated that college drinking leads to 70,000 sexual assaults annually. The problem with any of these statistics is, of course, that rape is the silencing predator, especially for men, who are less likely to report their rapists. For both men and women, law enforcement agents estimate that fewer than 30% of rapes are reported, perhaps as few as 10%. However, whether the statistic is 70,000 or 700,000, it is staggering and demands action. 3

Acknowledges doubts about data, but puts them in perspective, so that the doubts matter less.

4 That being said, sit back and relax as I slip you information on the latest date rape drug technologies. One product, the Guardian Angel test kit, is available off the Internet. Creators Charlyne Cutler and Alissa Garcia of Las Vegas developed strips which, when dipped in drinks, can detect GHB in 10 to 15 seconds. While $5.00 is a small price to pay for peace of mind, there are even more affordable options to assure drinking safety. A less expensive option is the Drink Safe Coaster. The concept of the coaster was developed by Francisco Guerra, after a friend told him about her own experience with date rape. He and a partner, Brian Glover, developed the small cardboard squares, which were named as one of the best inventions of 2002 in *Time Magazine.* The coasters, about the size of a credit card, have two areas on which drinks can be tested. According to the drink safe website at www.drinksafetech.com, "the test takes only seconds to perform, and is as easy as placing a couple of drops from the drink in question onto the active test spots using a swizzle stick or even one's finger." Should the spots turn blue, the drink has been tampered with. Perhaps one of the most advantageous aspects to this solution is its price. The coasters are available on the Internet for only 40 cents apiece. The company also offers companies or organizations the opportunity to personalize the coasters. Groups such as the Santa Clara YWCA have personalized the coasters before handing them out. According to the BBC Online, a new date rape drug-detecting device is in the works in the UK because of the rising number of date rape cases there. It is a swizzle stick that is left in a drink, which changes color if the drink is drugged at any point in time. The goal is to make the sticks cheaply enough to serve with all drinks.

Easy access, low cost encourage the audience to use the coasters.

5 There are, of course, problems with the date rape drug-detecting technologies. As small as the products are, they are generating a disproportionate amount of controversy. The first issue is whether the devices really work. Guardian Angel's effectiveness is limited to one drug, GHB, and the Drink Safe Coasters are only effective for two, GHB and Ketamine. With the large number of drugs already on the market, and those being developed, DEA spokeswoman Rogen Waite says, "In cases where there are scientific advances, the bad guys get around it faster than the good guys can develop them." Besides the limitation that coasters detect

Anticipates key point that ends the speech.

relatively few drugs, they also can detect them only in certain drinks. For instance, the coasters can only detect GHB in apple, grape, orange, or cranberry juice when the concentration of the drug is high, higher than is usually used by predators. Finally, the most dangerous aspect of the date rape coasters and strips is the possibility that they create a false sense of security. Even if these new technologies work, someone can always put something in a drink after it's tested. The danger of these new devices is that they could cause people to forget that there is no substitute for old-fashioned vigilance.

Perhaps the greatest benefit to the Drink Safe Coasters and like products is increased awareness. Their creation and the accompanying controversy brought attention to the very real problem of date rape drugs. 6

There are now new versions of the date rape coaster. Marea Stamper, from the University of Louisville's Women's Center, helped design a less high-tech drink coaster. It is solely a warning for potential victims of date rape drugs, as well as predators. The coasters are bright pink (so that they show up in black lights). On the front they read: "Drink Safe, Watch Your Drink . . . because right now somebody may be watching it for you." On the backside they say: "Date rape drugs can be anywhere! Throw away any drink that tastes salty or 'funny' quickly. Never leave your drink unattended. Don't take a drink from a punchbowl. Never accept any drink from a stranger. 80% of all sexual assaults involve one or both of the parties being intoxicated. If you suspect that you or a friend has been drugged, don't wait!" It then lists several numbers that can be called. 7

Conclusion emphasizes precautions available to all and more effective than the high-tech devices.

Whether using a date rape coaster or not, it's important to remember the suggestions listed on Stamper's coaster. In addition, go out with a friend. Keep an eye on each other! Also, know where your drink is coming from. Be careful about taking drinks from people you don't know. Should any of these precautions fail, pay attention to what you're drinking! Intense flavors often mask GHB. . . . Also, pay attention to how you feel. If you get drunk extremely fast or feel sick, your drink might have been tampered with. If any of these things happen to you, be sure to report it to the authorities. 8

How Do I Prepare an Oral Presentation?

In composing an oral presentation, consider all of your senses. The following advice encourages attention to not only the audience and purpose of your presentation but also the *sound* of your message and the *physical* act of speaking in front of a group.

Before You Begin

Before you make notes or compose the text of your oral presentation, consider the following:

- **Who is my audience?** You cannot know too much about the group you will address: Age, gender, politics, background knowledge, view of your topic and you–all matter more than anything else. *Know your audience, and adapt everything in your speech to their interests, values, and concerns.*
- **What is the size of my audience?** You can give an informal talk to an audience of about twenty-five to forty people or less. Talks tend to become speeches, and speeches tend to become more formal, as the audience size increases. *Know how many people you will be talking to.*
- **What does my audience expect from me?** Different occasions call for different kinds of talks or speeches. Sometimes your job is to entertain; sometimes to inform; sometimes to persuade; sometimes to reflect on an issue, question, or problem–or some combination of these. *Know what your audience wants and deliver the goods.*
- **Where and when will I speak?** Whenever you can, visit the place where you will speak in advance. When this is not possible, be sure to get a thorough and reliable account of the place from the person who has invited you to speak. It will help you

Using visual supplements such as PowerPoint slides during your speech can add interest to your presentation.

Caiaimage/Martin Barraud/Getty Images

envision what you will face when you give the speech and help you design your supporting visual materials appropriately. The time of day also matters. An audience at ten o'clock in the morning is not the same as an audience getting tired and hungry by five o'clock in the afternoon. An audience that has already listened to a speaker or two before your turn comes is not the same as one there to hear only you. *Know place and time and plan accordingly.*

- **Should I use visual or other multimedia supplements?** Speakers often neglect the advantages of visual, audio, and other multimedia supplements to speech: slides, PowerPoint, video clips, or just paper handouts. Such supplements are not always needed or always appropriate, but use them when they are functional and suited to the occasion.

Once you have answers to these questions, you are ready to prepare the notes or text you will use for the content of your talk or speech.

How Do I Rehearse an Oral Presentation?

"The basics" take in what you must think about in preparing to do any oral presentation; the guidance on practicing out loud will help you develop confidence, especially if you have little previous experience with public speaking.

Practicing: The Basics

Focus on the following considerations when you practice your oral presentation:

- **Voice Level** You have to be heard. If your normal speaking voice is soft and low, you will need to raise it a decibel or two so that people sitting in the back row of the room can hear you without strain. For large groups in big rooms, you will have to become comfortable using a microphone.
- **Voice Modulation and Speed** If you speak in a monotone, the audience will think you are bored or boring and tune you out. If you get nervous and talk too fast, your audience may miss key points and you may run out of things to say well before your time is up.
- **Strict Adherence to Time Limit** If you have twenty minutes for a speech, it is all right to finish a little sooner–in eighteen or nineteen minutes–but it is *never* all right to go well over–twenty-five or thirty minutes. Remember also that even well-trained listeners cannot maintain concentration for longer than about forty-five minutes. Try to keep any speech shorter than that.

Practicing your speech, including presentation of and commentary on all visual supplements, is important to the success of your actual speech delivery.

Hero Images/Getty Images

Practicing Out Loud

This point cannot be emphasized too much: *There is no substitute for practicing your speech out loud, including presentation of and commentary on all visual supplements.* Why?

- Only through actual delivery can you know how long the speech will take.
- Only by practicing it beforehand can you become thoroughly familiar with and confident about what you are going to say.
- Only by speaking it can you decide what to do with your voice, movement, and gestures.

Practice alone in an empty room, perhaps in front of a mirror; practice with people present–anyone willing to listen to a rehearsal and give you feedback. Practice your speech not just once but at least two or three times, stopping after each go-through to make notes to yourself ("Slow down here." "Repeat this point." "Pause here to let the audience take this graphic in.")

When you rehearse, envision the place and audience as best you can. If you do, facing the real audience will be far less daunting.

How Do I Revise an Oral Presentation?

Just as writing requires revision after drafts, speeches need large- and small-scale adjustments after rehearsals. Common changes include

- **Dropping your least important point or points** because you don't have time for it or them.
- **Adding a point or points,** or developing one or several points more, because you are well short of the time allotted.
- **Altering paragraphs or sections of the speech** because your practice audience had trouble following them.
- **Making your opening or conclusion more effective,** especially gaining rapport in the introduction and getting the gist across in the conclusion.
- **Modifying multimedia support,** such as taking away or adding graphics, simplifying PowerPoint screens, using a shorter video clip, or substituting a more striking photo for one with less impact.

If you make major changes in your speech text or notes, rehearse the speech again.

How Do I Deliver an Oral Presentation?

If you have prepared and rehearsed adequately, in the actual delivery of the speech you can and should have only a few things in mind. Here are the key points:

- **Eye contact matters.** One of the challenges of delivering a speech from a prepared text is to read it without losing eye contact entirely. You must know it well enough to look up often without losing your place. Allocate eye contact to all parts of your audience, varying your point of focus from time to time: Look sometimes in the middle, sometimes to your left and right–even up, if there is a balcony.
- **Posture and dress matters.** No one takes a slouching speaker seriously. Match your dress to the occasion and to what your audience will be wearing. It is usually better

Dress nicely and stand up straight when it's time to deliver your speech. You want to project the best, most professional image possible.

Directphoto Collection/ Alamy

to err by dressing more formally than is required, not less. However, you should also feel comfortable in whatever you wear.

- **Movement and gesture matter.** Sometimes you will have a fixed microphone attached to a lectern. When that is part of the situation, you cannot leave the microphone, so movement will be restricted. Otherwise, some movement is good, especially when matched to a change of pace or focus in the speech. Gesture, like movement and even eye contact, can help to capture or keep the audience's attention. It also helps emphasize key points.
- **Respect Murphy's Law.** No speaker can anticipate everything that might go wrong, and some things that do cannot be helped, such as a general power failure that leaves everyone in the dark. However, if your talk depends on a slide show, and thus on a projector and laptop, double-check that both machines are working beforehand, verify that you will have an Internet connection before the day of the speech, and have a spare bulb in your pocket and a laptop cord. *Know the most likely things that can go wrong and decide in advance how to handle them.*

What Are Some Key Points to Remember?

In many jobs, speaking well is at least as important as writing well. The higher your position, the more likely you will need to talk with and address people–coworkers, customers, potential clients–almost every working day. So if you are uneasy about the idea of giving talks or leading meetings, do not fall into a common trap (which too many people do): avoiding speaking situations as much as possible. Do the opposite, and welcome opportunities to practice public speaking. You can only become more comfortable and better at it by doing it.

Remember that competence is usually all you need. Few people are genuinely brilliant public speakers, and those who are have special talent and the right personality for it. The rest of us just need to be good enough to handle work and community demands for speaking competently.

We strongly recommend taking a course or courses in public speaking. Such courses used to be required of all undergraduates, but too often now they are not. Take them anyway, even if they're not required. You will be glad you did.

CREDIT

page 535: Courtesy of Jaclyn Jenkins

CHAPTER 32

Designing Documents and Using Graphics

ENGAGING QUESTIONS

In this chapter, you will engage with the following questions:

- How can design contribute to a document's appeal?
- What are the elements that make up a document's design?
- How do writers apply the elements of design?
- How do writers use graphics?
- What are some common types of documents that writers model?

OUR WORLD IS INCREASINGLY DOMINATED BY INFORMAL WRITTEN COMMUNICATION, especially text messages and e-mails, addressed mainly to friends or acquaintances. In these genres, the appearance of the text has little importance. Likewise papers written for classes seldom require much attention to visual impact. Consequently, unless you have technical or business writing experience, you have probably never thought much about how to make document design and graphics work for you.

This chapter is about **visual appeal,** otherwise known as *document design and graphics.* Its purpose is to raise your awareness of how important visual appeal is in modern communication and to encourage you to begin using that awareness in creating papers for college assignments.

What Are Document Design and Graphics?

Document design refers to *the appearance of any paper, printed text, or online site or text.* Sometimes called page layout, document design involves decisions about the use of margins and white space, typeface style and size, and line spacing to achieve maximum reader appeal.

Graphics include *photographs, diagrams, tables, charts, and graphs (bar, line, and pie).* Referred to as visuals or art in print publication, graphics supplement writing, the blocks of prose in a text.

ACTIVITY 32.1 ***Collaborative Activity***

Evaluating Document Design and Graphics

Raise your awareness of document design and graphics by examining the features of this book. Look at the covers (both outside and inside) and at a few of the pages. Consider the use of margins and white space, headings, color, and typeface style and size. Also look at the visuals, such as boxes, cartoons, and photographs.

In class discussion, focus on the impression the book makes when you pick it up and when you first leaf through the pages. What features do you like best? What features do you like least? Why? ■

Why Consider Document Design and Graphics?

The key variables for all writing are audience, purpose, and type of text (genre or kind of writing) you are doing. How you understand these variables *in each case* determines your strategy: what you say and do not say, how you order what you say, how relatively formal or informal you are, and so on. You will use the same document design features over and over—in almost every business letter you write, for instance—but your strategy will never be exactly the same in any two cases.

Not recognizing the importance of strategy is one of the main reasons for ineffective writing. For example, sending e-mails to your professors with misspellings and grammatical errors is bad strategy. Before you compose any message, even a simple e-mail requesting an assignment you missed in class, consider who will read it and the impression they will have of you from reading it. *Strategy matters.*

How Does Document Design Work?

Document design includes decisions about typeface style and size, margins, line spacing, headings, the use of lists, kinds of emphasis, and color.

Typeface Style

Computer software programs offer dozens of typeface styles, but only a few are commonly used in college and business writing. These include

Times New Roman

Arial

Century Schoolbook

Verdana

Times New Roman and Calibri are the most common typefaces. Computer software often comes with these typefaces preset for word processing.

Does typeface choice matter? Compare these lines of type:

Every good boy does fine. (Times New Roman)

Every good boy does fine. (Century Schoolbook)

Every good boy does fine. (Verdana)

The most obvious difference is the amount of space the different typefaces take to say the same thing. Choice of typeface can shorten or lengthen a paper appreciably. But that is not the only difference. The first two typefaces have a more conservative, traditional look; the last, with its block letters, has a more contemporary look.

Font Size

Each typeface has fonts in different point sizes. Each **point** designates *1/72 of an inch.* Here are the point sizes you are likely to use frequently in any typeface:

This is 10-point type.

This is 12-point type.

This is 14-point type.

This is 18-point type.

Use 12-point type for all college papers and business documents. Ten-point type is useful for the labels and captions in graphics. Fourteen-point type is sometimes used for major headings to set them off for emphasis from the 12-point size used for everything else. Finally, 18-point type is common in PowerPoint presentations because its larger size makes it easier for audience members to read. Even larger sizes may be necessary for big rooms, such as auditoriums.

Margins and White Space

For most college papers you have few choices in margins. The norm is a 1-inch margin at the top, bottom, and on both sides. Use a "ragged" right margin (the typed lines differ a little in where they end) and a "justified" left margin (the lines all begin in the same place, except for paragraph indentations and indented block quotes). (See Figure 32.1.)

Business communication favors the block paragraph–that is, use *no indentations, but rather line skips between paragraphs.* See our example of a business letter later in this chapter.

When margins leave little white space on the edges of a page, the look is crowded and uninviting. When you leave relatively more white space, the look is open and accessible. The message of margins is subliminal–readers react to them without being aware of how they are reacting and why.

Line Spacing

Line spacing conventions are simple and admit few exceptions. College papers are double-spaced to allow room for your instructor's comments. Texts submitted for publication are also double-spaced to allow room for editorial notes. Otherwise, single-spacing is the norm.

Headings

Of all document design features, college students need headings most but use them least. Why use headings?

FIGURE **32.1**

Spacing Conventions for Paragraphs

College Papers

For most college papers you have few choices in margins. The norm is a 1-inch margin at the top, bottom, and on both sides. Use a "ragged" right margin (the typed lines differ a little in where they end) and a "justified" left margin (the lines all begin in the same place, except for paragraph indentations and indented block quotes).

Business communication favors the **block paragraph**—that is, use *no indentations but line skips between paragraphs.*

Business Communication, Block Paragraph

For most college papers you have few choices in margins. The norm is a 1-inch margin at the top, bottom, and on both sides. Use a "ragged" right margin (the typed lines differ a little in where they end) and a "justified" left margin (the lines all begin in the same place, except for paragraph indentations and indented block quotes).

Business communication favors the **block paragraph**—that is, use *no indentations but line skips between paragraphs.*

- They help you organize content so you are writing about one major division of your topic at a time.
- They help your readers see how the content is organized, making your text easier to follow.
- They eliminate the need to make up transitions between major parts of a paper. The heading is the transition.
- It is easier for you and your reader to look back—that is, to find material in a heading without having to skim through the entire paper.

For these and other reasons, you will find major headings in almost all print and online texts. Even short texts often use them.

Below is an example of a well-designed document, an important announcement of a new grading policy distributed by e-mail to a university faculty. As you read it, notice its layout, especially the use of headings. How do the headings make a complicated message easier to understand and remember?

At its October 20, 2005, meeting, the Faculty Senate, having received a favorable recommendation from the Academic Affairs Committee, voted to approve the creation and Autumn Quarter implementation of two new grades: "X" and "WX."

Definition of "X" and "WX" Grades, Effective Autumn Quarter 2005

- "X" (nonattendance):
  Instructors will record an "X" on the final grade roster for students who never attended any classes and did not submit any assigned work.

  The "X" will appear on the transcript and will carry zero (0.00) quality points, thus computed into the GPA like the grades of "F" and "UW."
- "WX" (official withdrawal, nonattending):

  Instructors will record a "WX" for those students who officially withdrew from the class (as denoted on the grade roster by either EW or W) but who never attended any classes and did not submit any assigned work.

  The "WX" may be entered to overwrite a "W" appearing on the grade roster. An assignment of "WX" has no impact on the student's GPA. A "W" will appear on the student's online grade report and on the transcript. The "WX" recognizes the student's official withdrawal from the class and only records the fact of nonparticipation. The need to record nonparticipation is defined in "Rationale" below.

Participation and Nonparticipation Grades

With the introduction of the "X" and "WX" grades to denote nonparticipation, by definition all other grades can only be awarded to students who had participated in the class in some way.

Instructors will record a "UW" (unofficial withdrawal) only for students who cease to attend a class following some participation. Previously, instructors utilized the "UW" both for those students who had never attended classes and for those who had attended and participated initially but had ceased to attend at some point during the term.[1]

Note these common features of major headings:

- They work like *titles for a section of the text.*
- They are commonly emphasized visually by *bolding.*
- They separate *approximately equal amounts of material.*

Lists

There are two types of lists: *bulleted* and *numbered.* Use the numbered list when there is a sequence requiring a one, two, three (and so on) order. Use bulleted

1. Raymond V. Lesikar, Marie E. Flatley, and Kathryn Rentz, *Business Communication: Making Connections in a Digital World*, 11th ed. (New York: McGraw-Hill, 2008). 92.

lists when the sequence of the items does not matter. Lists aid organization, help readers anticipate and follow the structure of papers and individual major headings, and stand out for easy reference because they are indented and either bulleted or numbered.

Emphasis

You can emphasize a word, phrase, or sentence by using **bold,** *italics,* or underlining. In memos and business letters, often the key bit of information is emphasized by one or a combination of these emphatic features. Because people read hastily, often just skimming the content, **emphasis** *draws the eye to what they must get from the message.*

Of course, if used too much, emphasis loses its power. Use it sparingly.

Color

Advances in technology have led to the widespread use of color in writing, especially in graphics, as you will see shortly. As with all design features, use color to accomplish something and not for its own sake. If a black-and-white photo conveys the information as well as or better than one in color, use it rather than the color version.

For college and business writing, printout copies should always result in sharp, black print on clean, white paper. *Reserve color for graphics when it enhances communication.*

How Do Graphics Work?

Much of what we know about the world comes through images rather than printed words. Consider using graphics because people connect to the world primarily through vision. When your readers see the information you want them to have, that experience has an impact that words arranged in sentences alone cannot convey.

Graphics also

- Condense much information in a small space
- Make that information stand out for readers
- Present the information memorably

Look at Figure 32.2, a graphic depicting how technology helps scientists gather information about the oceans.

Imagine how many words it would take to describe what the drawing depicts. *Visuals condense a great deal of information into a small space.*

Even if you could get all the information into words, readers would still have trouble envisioning the three devices and how they complement each other. *Visuals enable readers to take in the information better and faster.*

Now imagine you have read the entire article in which the graphic appears. What will you remember? You will remember best what you have seen depicted in graphics. Furthermore, because graphics stand out in printed texts, if you want to refresh your mind, it is easy to find the relevant graphic and give it another look.

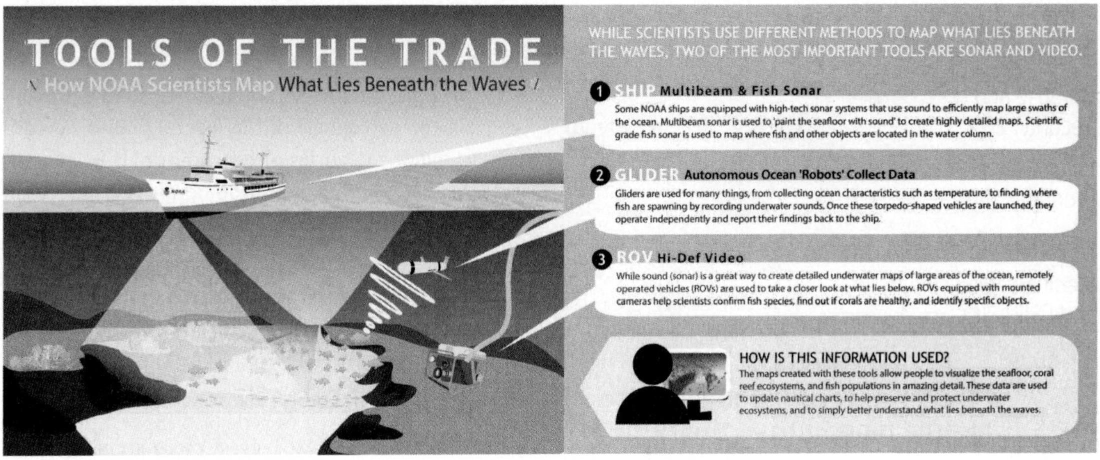

FIGURE **32.2**

This figure is a good example of how visuals condense a great deal of information into a small space.

National Oceanic and Atmospheric Association

Most graphics fall into one of the following types:

- Tables and charts
- Graphs (including bar, line, and pie)
- Photographs
- Drawings (including maps and cartoons)

Let's take a brief look at what each does best.

Tables and Charts

Both tables and charts arrange data in columns and rows for easy access and interpretation (see Figure 32.3). They are designed to be read left to right and top to bottom. The purpose of both is to eliminate the need for boring lists of information in your main text. You can simply refer readers to the numbered figure, reserving your prose for explanation and commentary.

Components of Physical Fitness	
Cardiorespiratory fitness	The ability to perform large-muscle, whole-body exercise at moderate-to-vigorous.
Musculoskeletal fitness	The integrated function of muscle strength, muscle endurance, and muscle power to enable performance of work.
Flexibility	The range of motion available at a joint or group of joints
Balance	The ability to maintain equilibrium while moving or while stationary.
Speed	The ability to move the body quickly.

FIGURE **32.3**

Table

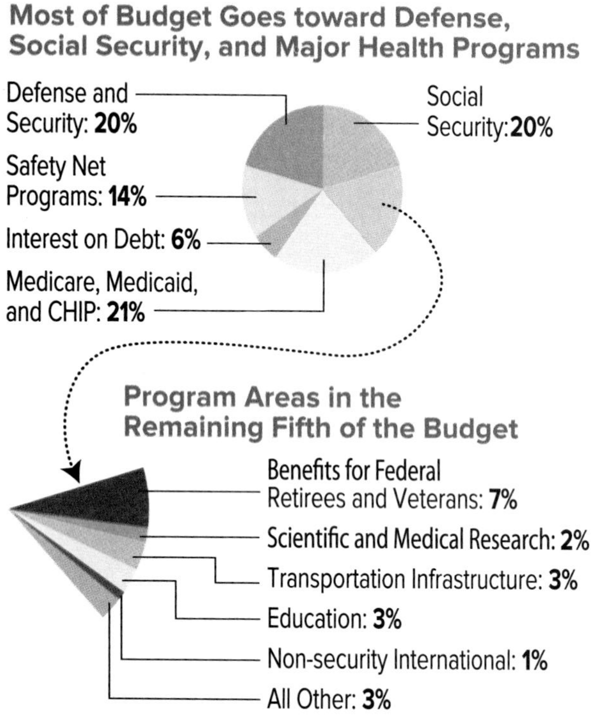

FIGURE **32.4**

Pie Graph

Note: Percentages may not total 100 due to rounding.

Source: 2010 figures from Office of Management and Budget, 2011.

Graphs

Graphs are typically *tables transformed into visuals.* For example, we could create a table presenting the percentage of the federal budget devoted to major categories of expenditure. If we present the same information in a pie graph, as in Figure 32.4, readers can see relationships better. The bigger pieces of the pie show where most of their tax dollars go, and they can compare, for example, the slice for defense with the slice for Medicare and Medicaid.

Note that the largest slice should begin at about the twelve o'clock position, and, reading clockwise, the next biggest piece should go second, the next to that third, and so on. Distinguish each slice with a different color. Be sure to label each slice with the actual percentage.

Use bar graphs, as in Figure 32.5, for *showing comparisons at a single point in time.*

Use line graphs *to depict trends over time.* The graph in Figure 32.6, for example, depicts the decrease in wages and salaries for jobs in manufacturing over twenty years and includes projections for an additional ten years.

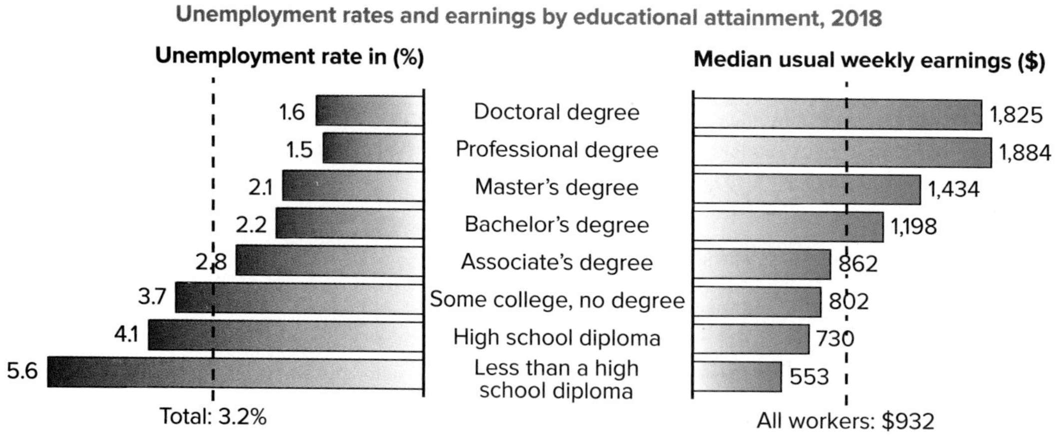

FIGURE **32.5**

Bar Graph

Note: Data are for persons age 25 and over. Earnings are for full-time wage and salary workers.

Source: Bureau of Labor Statistics, Current Population Survey.

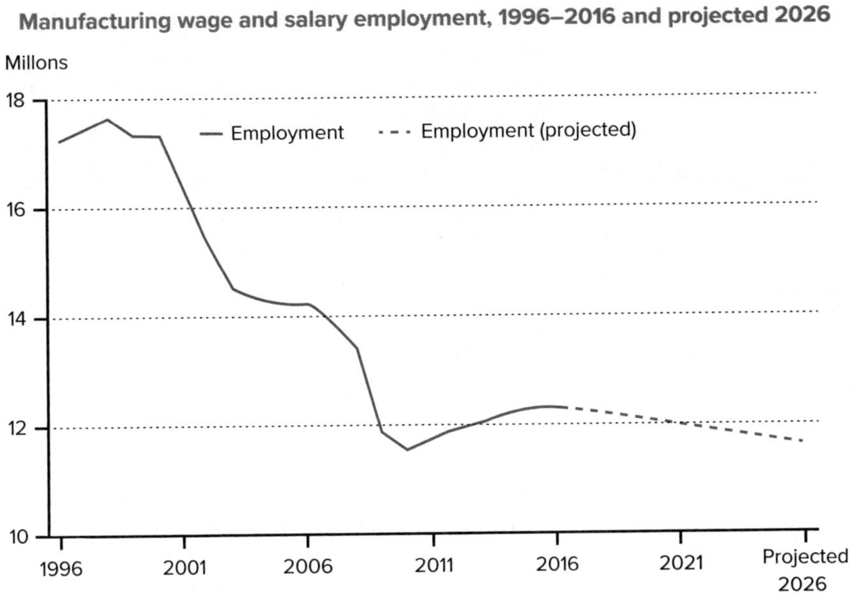

FIGURE **32.6**

Line Graph

Source: U.S. Bureau of Labor Statistics

Photographs

Photographs have many uses, but for graphic purposes they *represent people, objects, and scenes realistically and concretely.* For instance, Fredrik Sandström, in an online article designed to inform readers about nautical terms, defines "a full-rigged ship" as "a vessel that has at least three masts, all of them fully square rigged."[2] Without the image shown in Figure 32.7, or a similar photograph, most readers would not fully understand what he means.

FIGURE **32.7**

Photographs show what something looks like, such as a ship, making understanding more complete.

Deb Perry/Getty Images

2. Fredrik Sandström, "Full-Rigged Ship," *Sailing Ships*, Oktett.net, 2000.

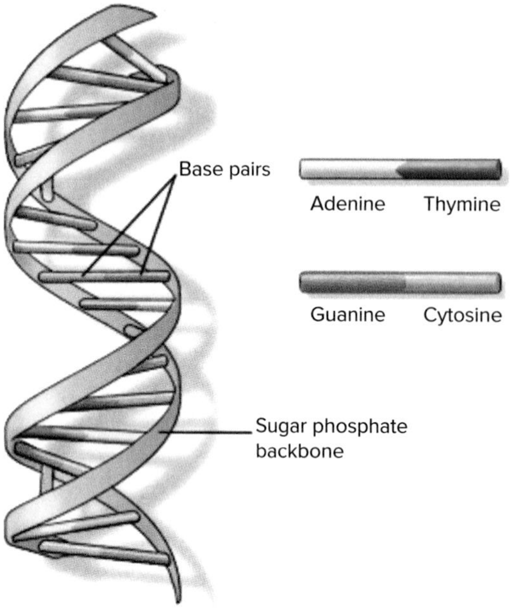

FIGURE **32.8**

Drawing

Source: U.S. National Library of Medicine

Photographs are also used for more complex purposes—for example, in ads, news stories, histories, and biographies. We get a better sense of Abraham Lincoln's life and times when pictures of him, his family, his home, and so on are included in a written account about him.

Photographs can do much more than inform: They can be highly dramatic and powerfully emotional in ways that only the most talented writers can achieve with words alone.

Drawings

The art of photography is now so sophisticated that we tend to forget the power of a drawing. The great virtue of drawings is that they can show you how something is put together and/or depict internal structures. (See Figure 32.8.) You can eliminate irrelevant details that photos would include of the same object or process by simply omitting them from your drawing. For many scientific and technical purposes especially, drawings are more common than photographs.

The Features of Graphs

Look at the bar graph in Figure 32.5 with its features distinguished by various colors.

The blue text is the graph's title, which tells your reader what a graph depicts. Graphs should have simple, descriptive titles.

The blue text is the figure number. Number your figures in the order in which they appear in your paper and refer to them in the text by number.

Note the vertical and horizontal axes used in both bar and line graphs. They designate the variables you are putting together (in this case, degree level, unemployment rate, and median earnings).

Note the source line at the bottom left side of the graph. It designates the source of the graphic or the information you used in creating the graphic. In college papers, *supply a source line for any graphic except one you created from information you also gathered.*

Some Other Graphic Types

Three other commonly used graphic types are maps, flowcharts, and organizational charts (see Figures 32.9 to 32.11). Their respective functions are to depict the distribution of something in geographical space; to depict a process; and to depict the structure of a company or organization.

Some Considerations When Using Graphics

Consult Best Practices: Guidelines for Using Visuals below for what matters most whenever you use graphics in a paper or document.

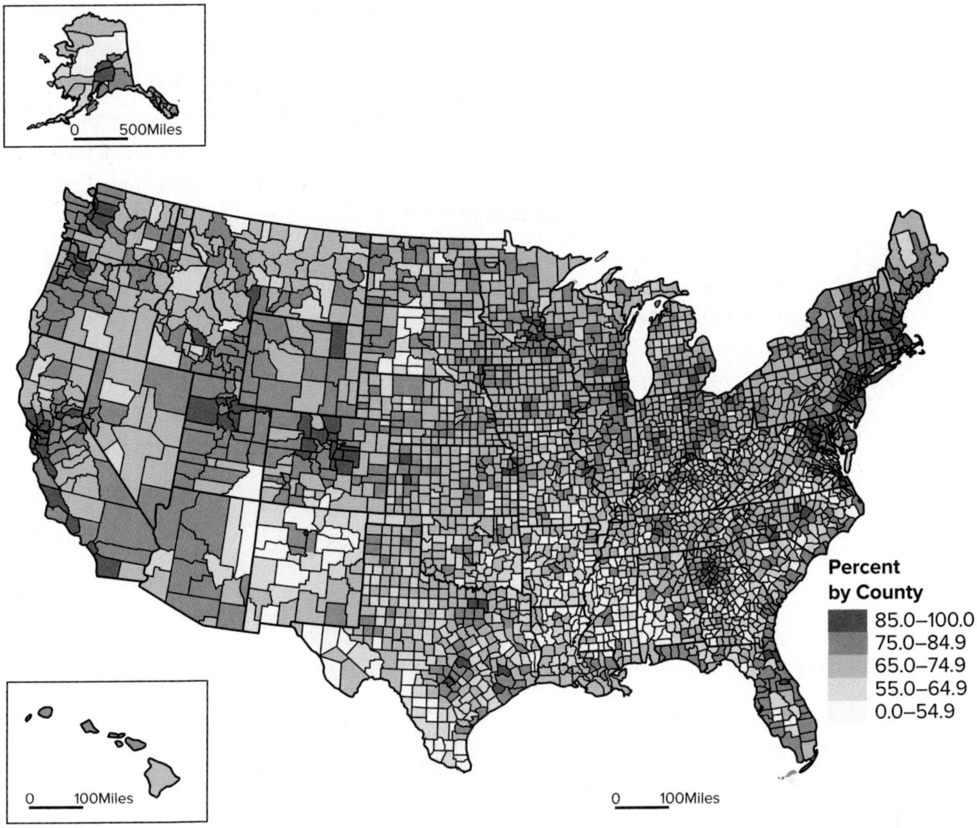

FIGURE **32.9**

Map

The percentage of households with subscriptions to broadband service, 2013–2017.

BEST PRACTICES Guidelines for Using Visuals

Graphics include tables to display data economically; graphs to depict data for comparisons, proportions, or trends; photographs to convey realism and drama; and drawings to depict structures. Be sure to observe the following principles in borrowing them from sources or creating them yourself:

- Every graphic must have *a definite function.* In college and business writing, graphics are not decorative.
- Choose the kind of visual best suited to conveying the information or the point you are trying to make with the information.
- Design graphics so that they are easy to interpret. Keep them simple, make them large enough to be read without strain, and use clear and legible print for labeling and captions. *Remember: Graphics should be easier to understand than the text they supplement.*

- Graphics can be created by hand or by using one of the software programs available for graphic design. The programs are powerful tools, but *use their power to realize function.* For instance, avoid 3-D graphs except when the illusion of three dimensions helps to convey the information.
- Place graphics as close as possible to the text they explain and illustrate—on the same page of a paper printed on one side is best, no farther away than the facing page for documents printed on both sides.
- Refer your reader to all graphics in your text. *Readers need both the graphic and some text discussion of it for full understanding.* Use the text discussion to help your reader interpret the information depicted in the graph and to comment on its implications.
- Graphics may be borrowed intact from a source or modified in some way (enlarged, for instance) for your own purposes. Of course, when you borrow, you must acknowledge the source, just as you must cite the source for information you found in creating a graphic of your own. If you publish a paper that uses borrowed graphics, you must obtain written permission from your source.

Thought and effort must go into designing graphics. Experiment with design ideas. Expect to revise them just as you revise your writing.

What Are the Common Model Documents?

The following pages offer examples of common document types:

Memos (Example 1)
Letters (Example 2)
E-mails (Example 3)

Use these examples as models in two ways. First, these documents have *strong conventions,* that is, customary forms everybody expects to see, such as the "Dear Mr. Forbes:" opener of a business letter. Our marginal annotations for each document type call your attention to these standard forms. Follow them with any of the document types you create.

Second, study the models for their use of document design features discussed in this chapter: typeface style and size, margins, line spacing, headings, lists, emphasis, and color. The model provides a version of "the look" you should be after for each document type.

Job-related correspondence–that is, résumés and letters of application–are so important that we gave them their own chapter, Chapter 39. However, in the next section we will take a look at models for other types of business documents, such as those you will be expected to prepare once you have landed a job.

Business Documents

Business communication is a special arena for writing. The examples and advice we offer here are enough for many purposes, but you should take a course in business and

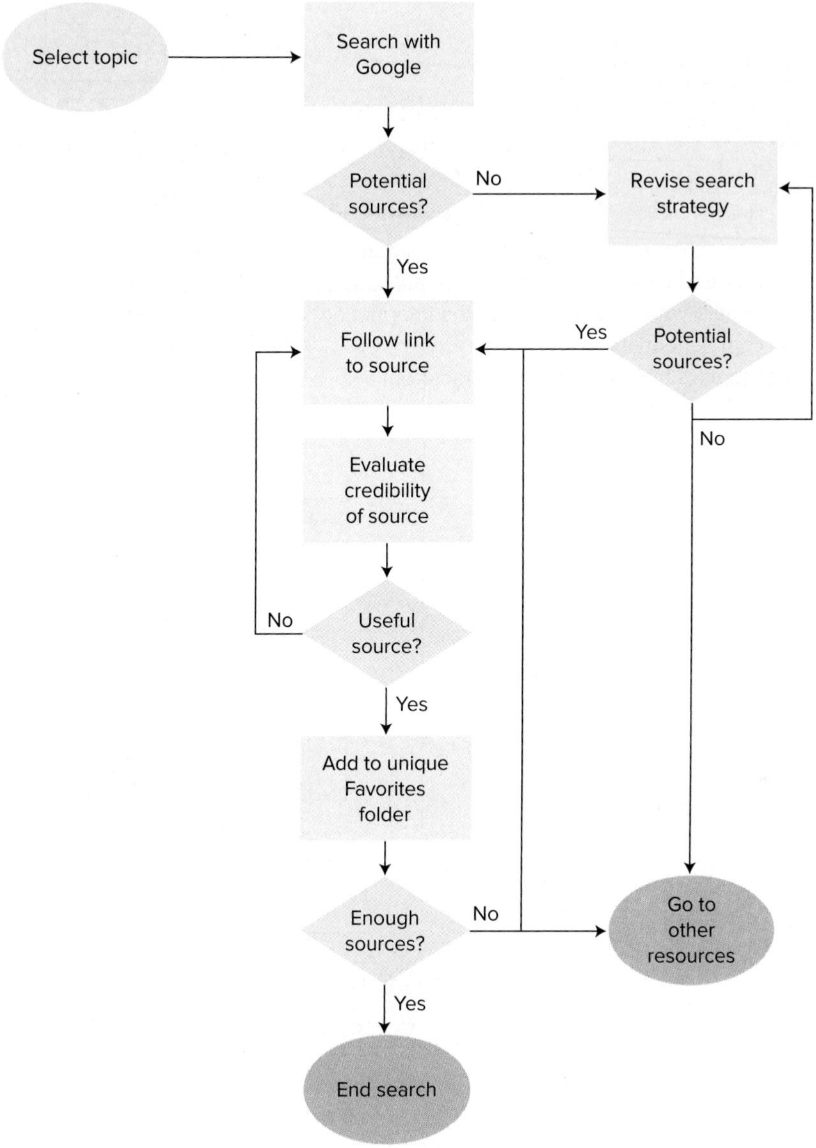

FIGURE **32.10**

Flowchart

Steps for doing a search on Google.

technical communication and keep your book for future reference. Some of our model documents come from *Business Communication: Making Connections in a Digital World,* 11th Edition (McGraw-Hill, 2008). We recommend it.

Business communication is intensely image-conscious. Any document you prepare represents both you and your company. It will have concrete outcomes, such as people deciding whether to do business with you. That is why so much care and effort go into business communication.

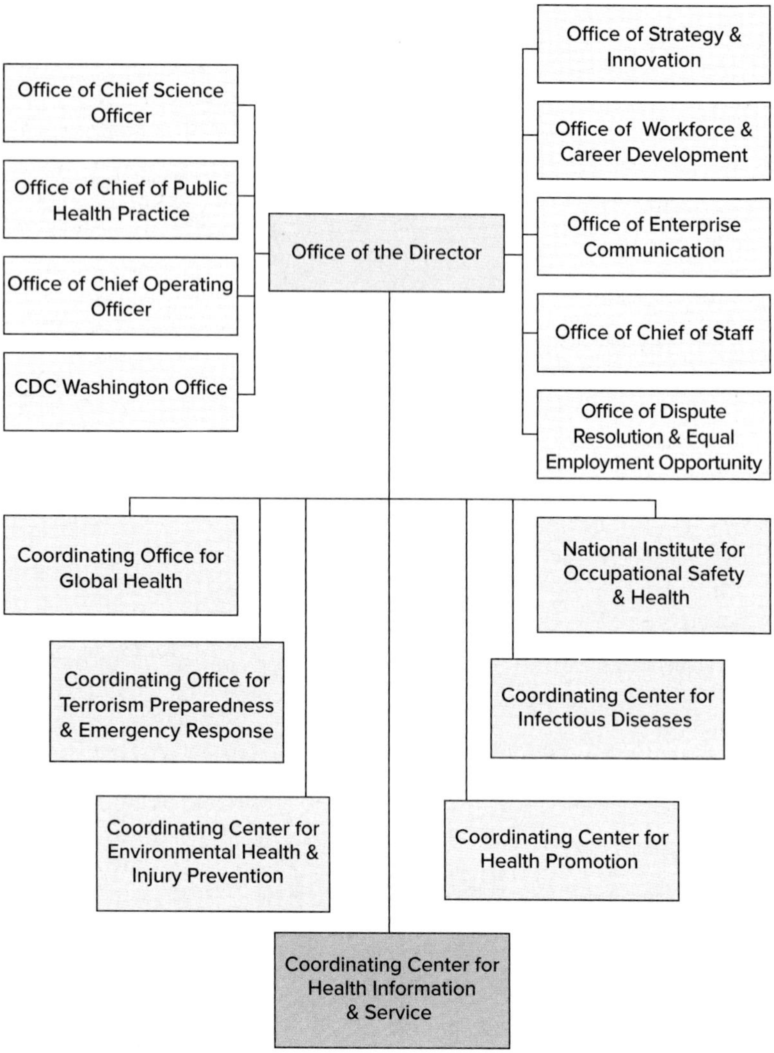

FIGURE **32.11**

Organizational Chart

Organizational structure of the Centers for Disease Control, Atlanta, Georgia.

Source: Office of Enterprise Communication

Memos (Memoranda)

Memos are used to communicate within a company or organization. Most are now transmitted electronically but retain the format of the standard memo form for paper distribution. Memos should be as brief as possible, and headings and bold type should be used to call your reader's attention to the crucial "must see, must remember" information. A memo that looks like a college paper–big blocks of prose–may not be read at all.

The following example is a memo of proposal stating plans for a project, which is common in business communication.

EXAMPLE 1 Memorandum

September 12, 2018

From: Denise Gomez

To: Christian Carrere, Jessica Wikstrom, and Adrian Dizer

Cc: Mary Jackman

Re: Research Proposal

I. Introduction

Many oil and gas resources are found in remote areas with difficult operating environments like Ukraine. In addition to its potential in producing petroleum and natural gas, Ukraine has the seventh-largest amount of coal resources in the world, which has been virtually untapped due to underinvestment. However since the 1986 Chernobyl accident, which resulted in the nuclear contamination of one-tenth of Ukraine's land area, Ukraine's environmental policies have become very strict. To assure ExxonMobil is fully informed of Ukraine's environmental agenda and issues, I will research its environmental policies, the country's physical terrain, and existing technology compatible with the environmental and economic needs of the country. By understanding the potential impact UKRMobil will have on Ukraine's physical surroundings, ExxonMobil can anticipate the best strategy to conduct business that protects the environment. I will lead the environmental research team in the Eastern European office to make sure that UKRMobil stays true to its commitment to the environment.

II. Scope

The scope of my research and contribution to this collaborative project will be limited to environmental policy as it applies to UKRMobil. I will examine the feasibility of conducting business in Ukraine with strict environmental regulations. I will also focus on the issue of using new technology in drilling and coal extraction to reduce the company's environmental impact.

III. Methods

I will conduct research, review articles, and study geological surveys regarding Ukraine's current environmental situation.

Letters

Business letters are used for communication outside a company or by individuals to communicate with businesses. There are many types of business letters, and many have their own common strategies, such as ways to soften the blow of bad news and ways to make a complaint letter be taken seriously rather than tossed in a wastebasket.

EXAMPLE 2 Business Letter

March 16, 2019

Ernie English

1234 Writing Lab Lane

Write City, IN 12345

Dear Mr. English:

The first paragraph of a typical business letter is used to state the main point of the letter. Begin with a friendly opening; then quickly transition into the purpose of your letter. Use a couple of sentences to explain the purpose, but do not go into detail until the next paragraph.

Beginning with the second paragraph, state the supporting details to justify your purpose. These may take the form of background information, statistics, or firsthand accounts. A few short paragraphs within the body of the letter should be enough to support your reasoning.

Finally, in the closing paragraph, briefly restate your purpose and why it is important. If the purpose of your letter is employment-related, consider ending your letter with your contact information. However, if the purpose is informational, think about closing with gratitude for the reader's time.

Sincerely,

Lucy Letter

123 Winner's Road

New Employee Town, PA 54321

E-Mail

E-mail has so many advantages that it has become by far the most common form of business communication. Messages are relatively fast to write, are inexpensive to distribute, get to the recipient immediately, and can be read and responded to when convenient.

But e-mail has a downside. Many people get hundreds of messages each day and thus race through them quickly, deleting as many as possible without reading them. Those that do get read often are not read carefully, which explains why misunderstanding is so common. Composing e-mail messages hastily also contributes to miscommunication.

Do not let the informality of e-mail seduce you into careless writing. Consider first whether an e-mail is the best choice for a particular purpose. If you choose e-mail, keep the message short, and use bulleted or numbered lists for important information to help your recipient compose a response.

Check the whole message thoughtfully before you hit "Send." Did you address the message to everyone who should get it and to no one who should not? Did you copy it to all parties that might also need to be in the loop? Did you attach the enclosure that you meant to attach?

Finally, remember that an e-mail can be easily accessed by people other than your recipient and that your recipient can forward it to others at will. It could even wind up in a court of law, where e-mails are increasingly used as evidence. Be careful about what you say, especially when you are not communicating with trusted friends or close associates.

EXAMPLE 3 **Business E-Mail**

Subject: A plan to increase profits

Ms. Collins,

You have probably heard in the trade about the services I provide to restaurant management. I am now pleased to be able to offer these services to you.

From 28 years of experience, I have learned the details of restaurant management. I know what food costs should be. I know how to find other cost problems, be they the buying end or the selling end. I know how to design menu offerings for the most profitability. I have studied kitchen operations and organization. And I know how the service must be conducted for best results.

From all this knowledge, I have perfected a simple system for analyzing a restaurant and finding its weaknesses. This I do primarily from guest checks, invoices, and a few other records. As explained on my website, my system finds the trouble spots. It shows exactly where to correct all problems.

I can provide you with the benefits of my system for only $1,500—$700 now and $800 when you receive my final report on your operations. If you will fill out and return by email the information requested below, I will show you how to make more money.

Larry Kopel, Consultant

Websites

Websites permit a wide variety of expressive devices as long as they remain functional and professional. Many corporate and personal sites are designed by professional web designers and use the full resources of computers, including graphics programs, sound, and animation. However, many companies and individuals make use of software for hosting and building websites. Services such as Squarespace offer a variety of templates for designing websites and allow users to enhance functionality using drag-and-drop tools. Even those who lack a background in coding and web design can create a functional and professional website.

What Matters Most in Document Design and Using Graphics?

We have introduced you to the basics of document design, graphics, and business documents. What is most important?

- Pay attention to visual appeal in all your reading. You can learn a great deal from what other people do.
- Take the time to prepare each of your college papers for the professor reading it. Follow his or her guidelines for submitting the paper. Use headings when appropriate. Submit a copy with dark, black ink on clean, white bond paper.
- When a paper assignment permits graphic use, experiment with the graphic types discussed in this chapter. They communicate information efficiently and memorably. You will use graphics extensively in writing after college.

- In professional and business contexts, be sensitive to the level of formality expected. The model documents in this chapter observe an appropriate level of formality and are excellent models for your own writing.

CREDITS

page 547: Reprinted by permission of Douglas Burgess, University of Cincinnati. **page 559:** Raymond V. Lesikar, Marie E. Flatley, and Kathryn Rentz. *Business Communication: Making Connections in a Digital World.* 11th ed. McGraw-Hill, 2008. 224.

INDEX

Page numbers printed in purple refer to content available in SmartBook for Engaging Questions, part of Connect Composition.